KU-406-964

Oxford School Thesaurus

Chief Editor: Andrew Delahunty

OXFORD
UNIVERSITY PRESS

Great Clarendon Street, Oxford OX2 6DP

Oxford University Press is a department of the University of Oxford. It furthers the University's objective of excellence in research, scholarship, and education by publishing worldwide in

Oxford New York

Auckland Cape Town Dar es Salaam Hong Kong Karachi Kuala Lumpur Madrid Melbourne Mexico City Nairobi New Delhi Shanghai Taipei Toronto

With offices in

Argentina Austria Brazil Chile Czech Republic France Greece Guatemala Hungary Italy Japan Poland Portugal Singapore South Korea Switzerland Thailand Turkey Ukraine Vietnam

Oxford is a registered trade mark of Oxford University Press in the UK and in certain other countries

• First published 2005 • Second edition 2007 • Third edition 2012 • This edition 2016

British Library Cataloguing in Publication Data

Data available

ISBN-13: 978-0-19-274351-0

10 9 8 7 6 5 4 3

Printed in China by Leo Paper Products Ltd.

Paper used in the production of this book is a natural, recyclable product made from wood grown in sustainable forests. The manufacturing process conforms to the environmental regulations of the country of origin.

Contents

Preface

The *Oxford School Thesaurus* has been specially written for students aged 10 and above. It is particularly useful for students who are about to start secondary school and who need an up-to-date, student-friendly reference tool that they can consult at home or at school.

This thesaurus is easy to use and understand. The vocabulary has been carefully selected and covers school curriculum topics ranging from English Language and Science and Technology to Sports and Music in order to support students in their writing assignments and homework.

The *Oxford School Thesaurus* gives all the information that students need for exam success in a simple and accessible format.
Use of the thesaurus will help students develop the best English language skills and equip them with excellent writing and speaking skills for years to come.

The *Oxford School Thesaurus* can also be used very effectively in conjunction with the *Oxford School Dictionary*, which offers further support with reading, writing and vocabulary building.

The publisher and editors are indebted to all the advisors, consultants and teachers who were involved in planning and compiling this thesaurus.

Introduction – how a thesaurus can help you

A thesaurus gives you alternatives – often more interesting and colourful ones – to the words you already know and use; these are known as **synonyms**. In some cases it also gives you the opposites of words, which are known as **antonyms**. Using a thesaurus regularly will extend your vocabulary and help you to be more accurate and imaginative in the way that you express yourself.

➤ When you are preparing for a presentation, writing and redrafting, a thesaurus can be very useful in helping you to avoid such things as overused words or words that are too general to have any impact. For example, *nice* is a perfectly acceptable word in conversation, but a thesaurus will allow you to replace it with more interesting words like *pleasant*, *agreeable*, *enjoyable*, *likeable* or *friendly*.

➤ When you are writing or giving a presentation at school, you need to think about such things as whether your language should be formal or colloquial. A word that is 'right' for one audience might not be for another. An important role for a thesaurus is to provide you with more choices of words for different situations. For example, *kill* is a word for general use, whereas *slay* is mostly found in stories and dramas; *little* is a much more affectionate and intimate word than its more neutral **synonym** *small* (compare a *small child* and a *little child*).

The difference between a dictionary and a thesaurus

Dictionaries and thesauruses help you in different ways with using language. A dictionary tells you mostly about what words mean whereas a thesaurus helps you to find alternative words to the ones you know and so helps you to put more words into use. When you are writing you might want to look up a word in a dictionary to check its exact meaning or spelling, but you use a thesaurus when you want to find a better, more interesting or more exact way of expressing your ideas.

Finding a better word

When you are writing a first draft, you quite often put down the first appropriate word that comes to mind. Using a thesaurus might help you to come up with one that makes a different impact on the reader. In the sentences below, they all mean the same thing but one is more formal, one less formal, and one uses a metaphor. Which sentence is the best for you will depend on the purpose of your writing.

- *The new school uniform rules made me **lose my temper**.*
- *The new school uniform rules made me **freak out**.*
- *The new school uniform rules made me **see red**.*

Finding a more interesting word

There are nearly always different ways of expressing the same idea. In your writing you will often need to think of different ways of saying the same thing. For example, suppose you are writing a letter of complaint about *non-stop noise*. You can say *non-stop* the first time, but a thesaurus will help you describe the noise as *continuous*, *constant*, *endless*, *unending* or *ceaseless*.

Special panels

Special panels give extra help or more information for certain words.

➤ The **OVERUSED WORD** panels offer more interesting alternatives for common words like *bad*, *good*, *happy* and *sad*.

➤ The **WORD WEBS** list words which are related to a particular topic, such as *football*, *music* and *space*. Some **WORD WEBS** list words which belong to a particular category, such as *collective noun*, *dog* or *phobia*.

➤ Some thesaurus entries feature **WRITING TIPS**, which give help for descriptive writing. For example, at the entry for *weather* there is a panel on describing the weather and at *colour* on describing colours.

Young Writer's Toolkit

This thesaurus contains a section called the **Young Writer's Toolkit**, where you will find useful tips on how to improve your writing skills.

➤ It covers key skills such as using sentences and paragraphs effectively and choosing the right language for formal and informal writing.

➤ It also offers advice on how to avoid some common mistakes in punctuation and spelling, and on how to make your writing more interesting by being creative with language.

WORD WEB

- accommodation
- aircraft
- amphibian
- animal
- anniversary
- armed services
- art
- artist
- athletics
- bee
- bell
- bicycle
- bird
- blue
- boat
- body
- bone
- book
- bridge
- brown
- building
- camel
- car
- castle
- cat
- chess
- clock
- clothes
- coin
- collective noun
- communication
- computer
- cook
- cricket
- criminal
- crustacean
- cutlery
- dance
- dinosaur
- dog
- drama
- earthquake
- electricity
- eye
- fabric
- family
- film
- finger
- fish
- flower
- foot
- football
- frog
- fruit
- fuel
- furniture
- gem
- green
- hat
- herb
- horse
- ice
- illness
- injury
- insect
- jewellery
- light
- mammal
- mathematics
- meal
- measure
- meat
- medicine
- metal
- moon
- music
- musician
- nut
- occupation
- ocean
- paper
- pattern
- phobia
- pink
- planet
- plant
- poetry
- politics
- pottery
- prehistoric
- punctuation
- purple
- red
- religion
- reptile
- restaurant
- rock
- rodent
- room
- royalty
- ruler
- science
- sea
- shape
- shellfish
- shoes
- shop
- snake
- song
- space
- spice
- sport
- swim
- temperature
- tennis
- textiles
- time
- tooth
- tree
- vegetable
- vehicle
- volcano
- weapon
- writer
- yellow
- zodiac

OVERUSED WORDS

- all right
- bad
- beautiful
- big
- bit
- eat
- funny
- good
- happy
- hard
- hit
- like
- little
- look
- lovely
- move
- nice
- old
- sad
- say
- small
- strong
- walk

WRITING TIPS

- animal
- bird
- body
- building
- clothes
- colour
- crime
- face
- fantasy
- hair
- historical
- horror
- landscape
- light
- science fiction
- smell
- sound
- sport
- spy
- taste
- texture
- weather

How to use this thesaurus

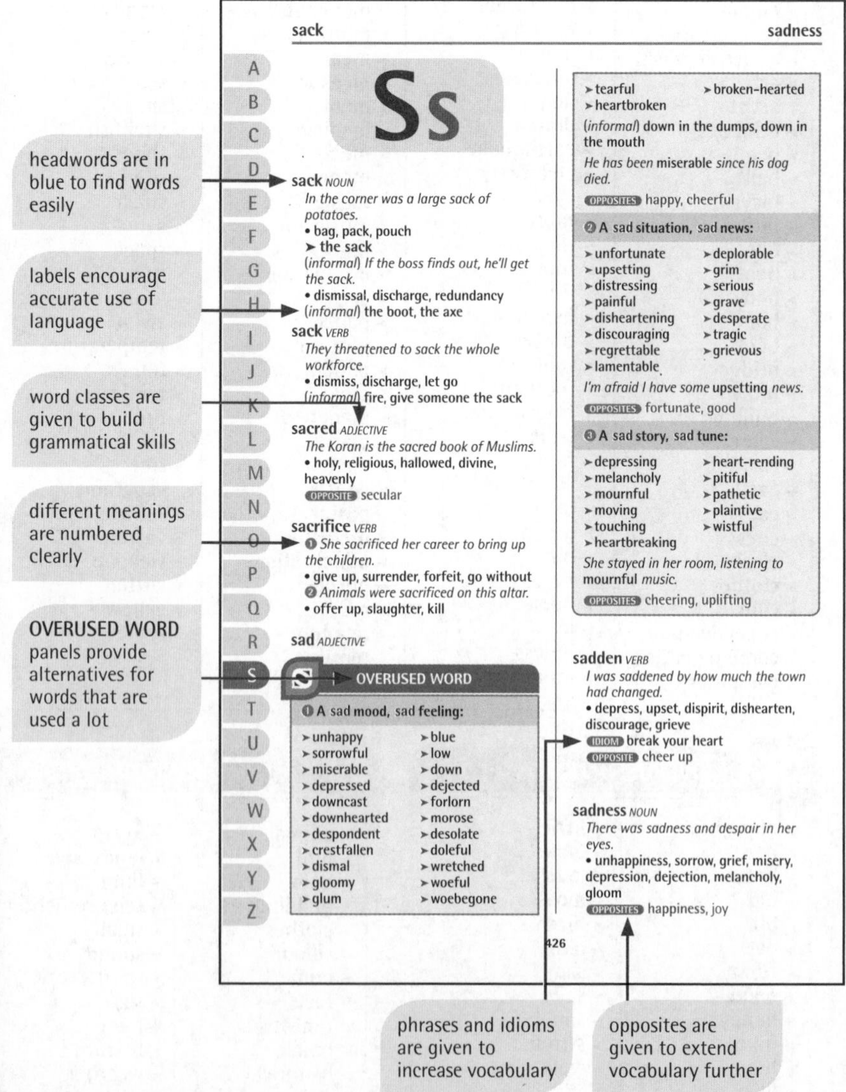
headwords are in blue to find words easily
labels encourage accurate use of language
word classes are given to build grammatical skills
different meanings are numbered clearly
OVERUSED WORD panels provide alternatives for words that are used a lot
phrases and idioms are given to increase vocabulary
opposites are given to extend vocabulary further

sack — sadness

A B C D E F G H I J K L M N O P Q R S T U V W X Y Z

Ss

sack *NOUN*
In the corner was a large sack of potatoes.
• bag, pack, pouch
➤ **the sack**
(*informal*) *If the boss finds out, he'll get the sack.*
• dismissal, discharge, redundancy
(*informal*) the boot, the axe

sack *VERB*
They threatened to sack the whole workforce.
• dismiss, discharge, let go
(*informal*) fire, give someone the sack

sacred *ADJECTIVE*
The Koran is the sacred book of Muslims.
• holy, religious, hallowed, divine, heavenly
OPPOSITE secular

sacrifice *VERB*
❶ *She sacrificed her career to bring up the children.*
• give up, surrender, forfeit, go without
❷ *Animals were sacrificed on this altar.*
• offer up, slaughter, kill

sad *ADJECTIVE*

OVERUSED WORD

❶ **A sad mood, sad feeling:**
➤unhappy ➤sorrowful ➤miserable ➤depressed ➤downcast ➤downhearted ➤despondent ➤crestfallen ➤dismal ➤gloomy ➤glum ➤blue ➤low ➤down ➤dejected ➤forlorn ➤morose ➤desolate ➤doleful ➤wretched ➤woeful ➤woebegone ➤tearful ➤heartbroken ➤broken-hearted
(*informal*) down in the dumps, down in the mouth
He has been miserable *since his dog died.*
OPPOSITES happy, cheerful

❷ **A sad situation, sad news:**
➤unfortunate ➤upsetting ➤distressing ➤painful ➤disheartening ➤discouraging ➤regrettable ➤lamentable ➤deplorable ➤grim ➤serious ➤grave ➤desperate ➤tragic ➤grievous
I'm afraid I have some upsetting *news.*
OPPOSITES fortunate, good

❸ **A sad story, sad tune:**
➤depressing ➤melancholy ➤mournful ➤moving ➤touching ➤heartbreaking ➤heart-rending ➤pitiful ➤pathetic ➤plaintive ➤wistful
She stayed in her room, listening to mournful *music.*
OPPOSITES cheering, uplifting

sadden *VERB*
I was saddened by how much the town had changed.
• depress, upset, dispirit, dishearten, discourage, grieve
IDIOM break your heart
OPPOSITE cheer up

sadness *NOUN*
There was sadness and despair in her eyes.
• unhappiness, sorrow, grief, misery, depression, dejection, melancholy, gloom
OPPOSITES happiness, joy

426

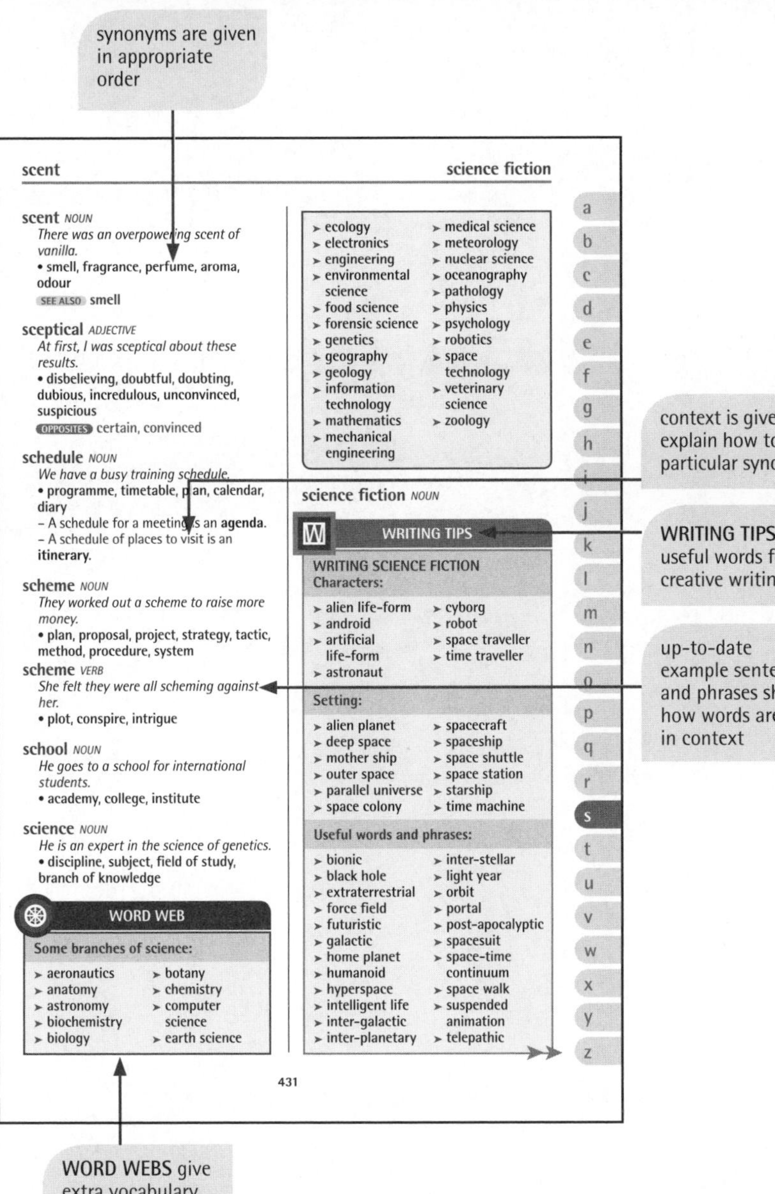

scent — science fiction

scent *NOUN*
There was an overpowering scent of vanilla.
• **smell, fragrance, perfume, aroma, odour**
SEE ALSO smell

sceptical *ADJECTIVE*
At first, I was sceptical about these results.
• **disbelieving, doubtful, doubting, dubious, incredulous, unconvinced, suspicious**
OPPOSITES certain, convinced

schedule *NOUN*
We have a busy training schedule.
• **programme, timetable, plan, calendar, diary**
– A schedule for a meeting is an **agenda**.
– A schedule of places to visit is an **itinerary**.

scheme *NOUN*
They worked out a scheme to raise more money.
• **plan, proposal, project, strategy, tactic, method, procedure, system**

scheme *VERB*
She felt they were all scheming against her.
• **plot, conspire, intrigue**

school *NOUN*
He goes to a school for international students.
• **academy, college, institute**

science *NOUN*
He is an expert in the science of genetics.
• **discipline, subject, field of study, branch of knowledge**

WORD WEB

Some branches of science:

- aeronautics
- anatomy
- astronomy
- biochemistry
- biology
- botany
- chemistry
- computer science
- earth science
- ecology
- electronics
- engineering
- environmental science
- food science
- forensic science
- genetics
- geography
- geology
- information technology
- mathematics
- mechanical engineering
- medical science
- meteorology
- nuclear science
- oceanography
- pathology
- physics
- psychology
- robotics
- space technology
- veterinary science
- zoology

science fiction *NOUN*

WRITING TIPS

WRITING SCIENCE FICTION

Characters:

- alien life-form
- android
- artificial life-form
- astronaut
- cyborg
- robot
- space traveller
- time traveller

Setting:

- alien planet
- deep space
- mother ship
- outer space
- parallel universe
- space colony
- spacecraft
- spaceship
- space shuttle
- space station
- starship
- time machine

Useful words and phrases:

- bionic
- black hole
- extraterrestrial
- force field
- futuristic
- galactic
- home planet
- humanoid
- hyperspace
- intelligent life
- inter-galactic
- inter-planetary
- inter-stellar
- light year
- orbit
- portal
- post-apocalyptic
- spacesuit
- space-time continuum
- space walk
- suspended animation
- telepathic

431

a b c d e f g h i j k l m n o p q r s t u v w x y z

synonyms are given in appropriate order
context is given to explain how to use particular synonyms
WRITING TIPS give useful words for creative writing
up-to-date example sentences and phrases show how words are used in context
WORD WEBS give extra vocabulary around topic words

aback *ADVERB*
➤ **taken aback**
He was clearly taken aback by my question.
• **surprised, astonished, startled, shocked, disconcerted, dumbfounded**

abandon *VERB*
❶ *He abandoned his family and went off to Australia.*
• **desert, leave, leave behind, strand**
(*informal*) **dump, ditch**
(*old use*) **forsake**
IDIOM **turn your back on**
❷ *The search for the missing climbers was abandoned after two days.*
• **give up, scrap, drop, cancel, abort, discard, renounce**

abbreviate *VERB*
Saint is often abbreviated to St.
• **shorten, reduce, abridge, contract**

abdomen *NOUN*
see **stomach**

abduct *VERB*
He claims he was abducted by aliens.
• **kidnap, seize, capture, carry off**
(*informal*) **snatch**

ability *NOUN*
❶ *Tiredness affects your ability to concentrate.*
• **capability, capacity, power, facility, means**
❷ *She is a player of exceptional ability.*
• **talent, skill, aptitude, competence, expertise, proficiency**

able *ADJECTIVE*
Penguins are very able swimmers.
• **competent, capable, accomplished, expert, skilful, proficient, talented, gifted**
OPPOSITE incompetent

➤ **able to**
Will you be able to play on Saturday?
• **capable of, in a position to, up to, fit to, allowed to, permitted to**
OPPOSITE unable to

abnormal *ADJECTIVE*
It is abnormal weather for this time of year.
• **unusual, uncommon, atypical, extraordinary, exceptional, peculiar, odd, strange, weird, bizarre, unnatural, freak**
OPPOSITES normal, typical

abolish *VERB*
Slavery was abolished in Britain in 1807.
• **get rid of, do away with, put an end to, eliminate, eradicate, stamp out**
OPPOSITE create

about *PREPOSITION*
❶ *The tour takes about an hour.*
• **approximately, roughly, close to, around, in the region of**
❷ *He was reading a book about the solar system.*
• **regarding, relating to, on the subject of, on**
➤ **be about something**
The film is about a teenage spy.
• **concern, deal with, involve, relate to**

about *ADVERB*
❶ *Rats were scurrying about in the attic.*
• **around, here and there, in all directions**
❷ *There were not many people about.*
• **near, nearby, around, hereabouts**

above *PREPOSITION*
❶ *There was a window above the door.*
• **over, higher than**
❷ *The temperature was just above freezing.*
• **more than, larger than, over**

abroad *ADVERB*
We spent a year abroad.
• **overseas, in a foreign country**

abrupt *ADJECTIVE*
❶ *The riders came to an abrupt halt.*
• **sudden, hurried, hasty, quick, rapid,**

A B C D E F G H I J K L M N O P Q R S T U V W X Y Z

unexpected
OPPOSITE gradual
❷ *I was put off by his abrupt manner.*
• **curt, blunt, rude, brusque, terse, short, brisk, sharp, impolite, uncivil**
OPPOSITE polite

absence *NOUN*
❶ *No one noticed his absence.*
• **non-attendance, being away, leave**
OPPOSITE presence
❷ *Outside there was a complete absence of birdsong.*
• **lack, want, non-existence, deficit, shortage, dearth**
OPPOSITE presence

absent *ADJECTIVE*
She was absent from school yesterday.
• **away, missing**
– To be absent from school without a good reason is to **play truant**.
– Someone who is absent is an **absentee**.
OPPOSITE present

absent-minded *ADJECTIVE*
I'm sure Dad is getting more absent-minded.
• **forgetful, inattentive, distracted, scatterbrained**
IDIOM with a memory like a sieve

absolute *ADJECTIVE*
There was a look of absolute terror on her face.
• **complete, total, utter, outright, pure, sheer**

absolutely *ADVERB*
The stench was absolutely disgusting.
• **completely, totally, utterly, thoroughly, wholly, entirely, quite**

absorb *VERB*
Let the rice absorb all the water.
• **soak up, suck up, take in, draw in, mop up**

absorbed *ADJECTIVE*
➤ **be absorbed in**
I was so absorbed in my book that I forgot the time.
• **be engrossed in, be interested in, be preoccupied with, be immersed in, concentrate on, focus on**

absorbing *ADJECTIVE*
It is an absorbing book.
• **interesting, fascinating, intriguing, gripping, enthralling, engrossing, captivating, riveting, spellbinding**

abstain *VERB*
➤ **abstain from**
I'm abstaining from junk food for a month.
• **go without, give up, forgo, refrain from, avoid, reject, renounce, deny yourself, desist from**
OPPOSITE indulge in

abstract *ADJECTIVE*
Beauty and truth are abstract ideas.
• **theoretical, intellectual, philosophical**
OPPOSITE concrete

absurd *ADJECTIVE*
That's an absurd idea!
• **ridiculous, ludicrous, nonsensical, senseless, irrational, illogical, preposterous, stupid, foolish, silly, laughable**
(*informal*) **daft**
OPPOSITES sensible, reasonable

abundance *NOUN*
There was an abundance of food and drink.
• **plenty, profusion, plethora**
OPPOSITES scarcity, lack, shortage

abundant *ADJECTIVE*
The birds have an abundant supply of food.
• **ample, plentiful, generous, profuse, lavish, liberal**
OPPOSITES meagre, scarce

abuse *VERB*
❶ *The dog had been abused by its owner.*
• **mistreat, maltreat, ill-treat, hurt, injure, beat**
❷ *He was booked for abusing the referee.*
• **insult, be rude to, swear at**
IDIOM call someone names

abuse *NOUN*
❶ *They campaigned against the abuse of animals.*
• **mistreatment, maltreatment, ill-treatment, harm, injury**
❷ *A spectator was yelling abuse at the referee.*
• **insults, name-calling, swear words, expletives**

abusive *ADJECTIVE*
He was thrown out for using abusive language.
• **insulting, rude, offensive, derogatory, hurtful, impolite, slanderous, libellous**
OPPOSITE polite

abysmal *ADJECTIVE*
The service in the restaurant was abysmal.
• **poor, very bad, awful, appalling, dreadful, disgraceful, terrible, worthless, woeful**
(*informal*) **rotten, dire**

abyss *NOUN*
I felt as if I were falling into an abyss.
• **chasm, pit, void, gulf, crater, rift, fissure**

academy *NOUN*
He attended an academy of music and drama.
• **college, school, university, institute, conservatory, conservatoire**

accelerate *VERB*
The bus accelerated to its top speed.
• **go faster, speed up, pick up speed**
OPPOSITES decelerate, slow down

accent *NOUN*
❶ *She speaks with a slight Welsh accent.*
• **pronunciation, intonation, tone**
❷ *The accent is on the first syllable.*
• **beat, stress, emphasis, rhythm, pulse**

accept *VERB*
❶ *Will you accept my apology?*
• **take, receive, welcome**
OPPOSITES reject, refuse
❷ *Do you accept responsibility for the damage?*
• **admit, acknowledge, recognize, face up to**
❸ *He accepted my decision as final.*
• **go along with, abide by, defer to, put up with, resign yourself to**

acceptable *ADJECTIVE*
She said my handwriting was not acceptable.
• **satisfactory, adequate, good enough, sufficient, suitable, tolerable, passable**
OPPOSITE unacceptable

access *NOUN*
The access to the house is through the garden.
• **entrance, entry, way in, approach**

access *VERB*
Can I access my email on this computer?
• **get at, obtain, reach, make use of**

accident *NOUN*
❶ *He was injured in a climbing accident.*
• **misfortune, mishap, disaster, calamity, catastrophe**
– Someone who is always having accidents is **accident-prone**.
❷ *A motorway accident is causing traffic delays.*
• **crash, collision, smash**
– An accident involving a lot of vehicles is a **pile-up**.
– A railway accident may involve a **derailment**.
➤ **by accident**
I found the letter by accident.
• **by chance, accidentally, coincidentally, unintentionally**

accidental *ADJECTIVE*
❶ *The damage to the window was accidental.*
• **unintentional, unintended, unwitting, incidental**
❷ *We made an accidental discovery.*
• **unexpected, unforeseen, unplanned, chance, fortuitous**
OPPOSITES deliberate, intentional

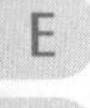

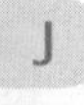

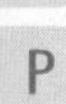

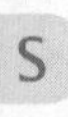

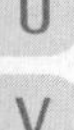

acclaim *VERB*
Her latest film has been acclaimed by the critics.
• **praise, applaud, commend, cheer, welcome**

accommodate *VERB*
❶ *The tent can accommodate two people.*
• **house, shelter, lodge, put up, take in, hold, sleep, have room for**
❷ *The staff tried to accommodate our needs.*
• **serve, assist, help, cater for, oblige, supply, satisfy**

accommodation *NOUN*
The price includes food and accommodation.
• **housing, lodging, living quarters, residence, dwelling, shelter, home**
IDIOM **a roof over your head**

WORD WEB

Some types of accommodation:

➤ apartment	➤ hostel
➤ barracks	➤ hotel
➤ bed and breakfast	➤ house
➤ bedsit	➤ inn
➤ boarding house	➤ motel
➤ chalet	➤ (*informal*) pad
➤ (*informal*) digs	➤ studio
➤ flat	➤ timeshare
➤ guest house	➤ villa
➤ hall of residence	➤ youth hostel

SEE ALSO **building**

accompany *VERB*
❶ *I'll accompany you to the door.*
• **escort, go with, show, conduct, usher, attend**
IDIOM **keep someone company**
❷ *You can have a free drink to accompany your meal.*
• **go along with, complement, partner**

accomplish *VERB*
The team had accomplished their mission.
• **achieve, fulfil, complete, finish, succeed in, realize, attain, carry out, perform**

accomplishment *NOUN*
Reaching the Moon was a remarkable accomplishment.
• **achievement, feat, success, effort, exploit**

account *NOUN*
❶ *She wrote a vivid account of her childhood in Russia.*
• **report, record, description, history, narrative, story, chronicle, log** (*informal*) **write-up**
❷ *Your opinion is of no account to me.*
• **importance, significance, consequence, interest, value**
➤ **on account of**
He gave up work on account of ill health.
• **because of, owing to, due to**

account *VERB*
➤ **account for**
How do you account for the missing money?
• **explain, give reasons for, justify, make excuses for**

accumulate *VERB*
❶ *He had accumulated a fortune by the age of twenty.*
• **collect, gather, amass, assemble, heap up, pile up, hoard**
OPPOSITES **disperse, lose**
❷ *Dust had accumulated on the mantelpiece.*
• **build up, grow, increase, multiply, accrue**
OPPOSITE **decrease**

accuracy *NOUN*
Can we trust the accuracy of these figures?
• **correctness, precision, exactness, validity, reliability**

accurate *ADJECTIVE*

❶ *Make sure you take accurate measurements of the room.*

• **exact, precise, correct, careful, meticulous**

OPPOSITES inexact, rough

❷ *Is this an accurate account of what happened?*

• **faithful, true, reliable, truthful, factual, authentic**

OPPOSITES inaccurate, false

accusation *NOUN*

There were several false accusations of witchcraft.

• **allegation, charge, indictment, claim**

accuse *VERB*

➤ **accuse of**

Two contestants were accused of cheating.

• **charge with, blame for, condemn for, denounce for**

OPPOSITE defend

accustomed *ADJECTIVE*

➤ **accustomed to**

He was clearly not accustomed to being laughed at.

• **used to, familiar with**

OPPOSITE unaccustomed to

ache *NOUN*

The ache in my tooth was getting worse.

• **pain, soreness, throbbing, discomfort, pang, twinge**

ache *VERB*

Our legs ached from the long walk.

• **hurt, be painful, be sore, throb, pound, smart**

achieve *VERB*

❶ *She achieved her ambition to run a marathon.*

• **accomplish, attain, succeed in, carry out, fulfil**

❷ *He achieved the highest score in the test.*

• **acquire, win, gain, earn, get, score**

achievement *NOUN*

Winning the title was a fantastic achievement.

• **accomplishment, attainment, success, feat, triumph**

acknowledge *VERB*

❶ *Do you acknowledge that there is a problem?*

• **admit, accept, concede, grant, allow, recognize**

OPPOSITE deny

❷ *She didn't even acknowledge my email.*

• **answer, reply to, respond to**

OPPOSITE ignore

acquaintance *NOUN*

He was an old acquaintance of mine.

• **associate, contact, colleague**

acquainted *ADJECTIVE*

➤ **acquainted with**

I'm not acquainted with the area myself.

• **familiar with, aware of, knowledgeable about**

OPPOSITE ignorant of

acquire *VERB*

Her family acquired the land years ago.

• **get, get hold of, obtain, come by, gain, secure**

IDIOM **get your hands on**

OPPOSITE lose

across *PREPOSITION*

They live in the house across the road.

• **on the other side of, over**

act *NOUN*

❶ *It was an act of great courage.*

• **action, deed, feat, exploit, operation, gesture**

❷ *His friendliness was just an act.*

• **pretence, show, pose, charade, masquerade**

❸ *They opened the show with a song-and-dance act.*

• **performance, sketch, turn, routine, number**

A B C D E F G H I J K L M N O P Q R S T U V W X Y Z

act *VERB*
❶ *She had only a second in which to act.*
• **do something, take action, make a move**
❷ *Just try to act normally.*
• **behave, conduct yourself, react**
❸ *The beaver's tail acts as a rudder.*
• **function, operate, serve, work**
❹ *Have you acted in a musical before?*
• **perform, play, appear**

action *NOUN*
❶ *The rocks have been worn smooth by the action of the waves.*
• **operation, working, effect, mechanism**
❷ *The driver's action prevented an accident.*
• **deed, act, effort, exploit, feat, undertaking, measure, step**
❸ *The film was packed with action.*
• **drama, excitement, activity, liveliness**
❹ *He was killed in action in the First World War.*
• **battle, fighting, combat**

activate *VERB*
Press any key to activate the screen.
• **switch on, turn on, start, trigger, set off**
OPPOSITES deactivate, switch off

active *ADJECTIVE*
❶ *She is very active for her age.*
• **energetic, lively, busy, vigorous, dynamic**
IDIOM (*informal*) **on the go**
OPPOSITE inactive
❷ *He is an active member of the drama group.*
• **hard-working, dedicated, tireless, industrious**
❸ *Is this email account still active?*
• **functioning, working, operational, in operation, live**
IDIOM **up and running**
OPPOSITES inactive, dormant

activity *NOUN*
❶ *The streets were full of activity.*
• **action, life, liveliness, excitement, movement, animation**
IDIOM **hustle and bustle**
❷ *She enjoys activities such as hillwalking and horse riding.*
• **hobby, interest, pastime, pursuit, recreation, occupation, task**

actor, actress *NOUN*
A number of well-known actors trained at this drama school.
• **performer, player**
– The main actor in a play or film is the **lead** or **star**.
– The other actors are the **supporting actors**.
– All the actors in a play or film are the **cast** or the **company**.

actual *ADJECTIVE*
This photograph shows the actual size.
• **real, true, genuine, authentic**
OPPOSITES imaginary, supposed

actually *ADVERB*
Just tell me what actually happened.
• **really, truly, definitely, in fact, in reality, for real**
IDIOM **as a matter of fact**

acute *ADJECTIVE*
❶ *She felt an acute pain in her leg.*
• **intense, strong, piercing, agonizing, searing**
OPPOSITES mild, slight
❷ *There is an acute shortage of food.*
• **severe, serious, urgent, critical**
❸ *Dogs have an acute sense of smell.*
• **keen, sharp, perceptive**
OPPOSITE dull

adapt *VERB*
❶ *The play has been adapted for television.*
• **modify, adjust, change, alter, convert, customize**
❷ *They adapted quickly to their new surroundings.*
• **become accustomed, adjust, acclimatize**

add *VERB*
She has added an extra line in the last verse of the poem.
• **attach, join on, append, tack on, insert**

➤ **add to**
The sound effects add to the atmosphere.
• increase, enhance, intensify, heighten, deepen
➤ **add up**
❶ *Can you add up these figures for me?*
• count up, find the sum of
(*informal*) tot up
❷ (*informal*) *His story just doesn't add up.*
• be convincing, make sense
➤ **add up to**
The angles in a triangle add up to 180°.
• total, amount to, come to, run to, make

addition *NOUN*
The waiter said there was an addition to the menu.
• add-on, supplement, adjunct, extra, appendage
➤ **in addition**
In addition, I would like to say thanks.
• also, as well, too, moreover, furthermore
➤ **in addition to**
In addition to fiction, she also wrote poetry.
• as well as, besides, apart from, on top of, over and above

additional *ADJECTIVE*
You should bring an additional change of clothes.
• extra, further, added, supplementary, spare

address *NOUN*
❶ *Is this your usual address?*
• home, residence, dwelling
❷ *In 1863 Lincoln gave his famous address at Gettysburg.*
• speech, lecture, talk, presentation, sermon

address *VERB*
She stood up to address the crowd.
• speak to, talk to, make a speech to, lecture to

adequate *ADJECTIVE*
❶ *The room was barely adequate for one person.*
• enough, sufficient
❷ *The work must be of an adequate standard.*
• satisfactory, acceptable, tolerable, passable, competent
OPPOSITE inadequate

adjacent *ADJECTIVE*
I waited in an adjacent room.
• adjoining, connecting, neighbouring, next-door
➤ **adjacent to**
The playing fields are adjacent to the school.
• next to, next door to, beside, alongside, bordering

adjust *VERB*
You may need to adjust the height of your seat.
• modify, alter, change, customize, rearrange, regulate, tune, set
(*informal*) tweak
➤ **adjust to**
It took a moment for her eyes to adjust to the dark.
• adapt to, get used to, get accustomed to, become acclimatized to, come to terms with

adjustment *NOUN*
We had to make some minor adjustments to the script.
• change, alteration, modification, amendment, edit
(*informal*) tweak

administer *VERB*
❶ *The island is administered by its own council.*
• manage, run, regulate, govern, direct, preside over, control, supervise, command, oversee
❷ *She is learning how to administer first aid.*
• dispense, distribute, give out, hand out, issue, provide, supply, dole out, deal out

A B C D E F G H I J K L M N O P Q R S T U V W X Y Z

admirable *ADJECTIVE*
Your plan is admirable, but will it work?
• **commendable, praiseworthy, laudable, creditable, exemplary, worthy, honourable, deserving, pleasing**
OPPOSITE deplorable

admiration *NOUN*
I'm full of admiration for her music.
• **respect, appreciation, approval, high regard, esteem**
OPPOSITES contempt, scorn

admire *VERB*
❶ *I admire your honesty.*
• **respect, think highly of, look up to, have a high opinion of, hold in high regard, applaud, approve of, esteem**
OPPOSITE despise
❷ *We stopped to admire the view.*
• **enjoy, appreciate, be delighted by**

admirer *NOUN*
He is a great admirer of Steven Spielberg.
• **fan, devotee, enthusiast, follower, supporter**

admission *NOUN*
❶ *It was an admission of guilt.*
• **confession, declaration, acknowledgement, acceptance**
OPPOSITE denial
❷ *Admission to the show is by ticket only.*
• **entrance, entry, access, admittance**

admit *VERB*
❶ *He was admitted to hospital last night.*
• **take in, receive, accept, allow in, let in**
OPPOSITE exclude
❷ *I admit that I was wrong.*
• **acknowledge, confess, concede, accept, grant, own up**
OPPOSITE deny

admittance *NOUN*
There is no admittance to the park after dark.
• **entry, entrance, admission, access**

adopt *VERB*
❶ *We have adopted a stray kitten.*
• **foster, take in**
❷ *They had to adopt new methods of working.*
• **take on, take up, choose, follow, accept, embrace, assume**

adorable *ADJECTIVE*
What an adorable kitten!
• **lovable, delightful, charming, appealing, enchanting**
(*informal*) **cute**

adore *VERB*
❶ *She adored both her grandchildren.*
• **love, be devoted to, dote on, cherish, treasure, worship**
IDIOM **think the world of**
❷ (*informal*) *I simply adore chocolate ice cream.*
• **love, like, enjoy**
OPPOSITES hate, detest

adult *ADJECTIVE*
He found himself face to face with an adult gorilla.
• **grown-up, mature, full-size, fully grown**
OPPOSITES young, immature

advance *NOUN*
❶ *You can't stop the advance of science.*
• **progress, development, growth, evolution**
❷ *The programme discusses some of the latest advances in medicine.*
• **improvement, breakthrough, step forward**
➤ **in advance**
We knew about the test in advance.
• **beforehand, ahead of time**

advance *VERB*
❶ *The army advanced towards the capital.*
• **move forward, go forward, proceed, press on, make progress, gain ground, make headway**
OPPOSITE retreat

❷ *Computer animation has advanced rapidly.*
• **progress, develop, grow, improve, evolve**

advantage *NOUN*
One of the advantages of living in the country is the fresh air.
• **benefit, strong point, asset, blessing, plus, bonus, boon**
OPPOSITES disadvantage, drawback, downside

advent *NOUN*
These calculations were made before the advent of computers.
• **arrival, appearance, emergence, invention**

adventure *NOUN*
❶ *She's been telling me about her adventures on holiday.*
• **exploit, venture, escapade**
❷ *He travelled the world in search of adventure.*
• **excitement, thrills, action**

adventurous *ADJECTIVE*
❶ *She's more adventurous than her brother.*
• **bold, daring, enterprising, intrepid**
❷ *He has led an adventurous life.*
• **exciting, eventful, challenging, risky**
OPPOSITE unadventurous

advertise *VERB*
He designed a poster to advertise the concert.
• **publicize, promote, announce, make known**
(*informal*) **plug**

advertisement *NOUN*
We put an advertisement in the local paper.
• **announcement, notice, promotion, commercial**
(*informal*) **ad, advert, plug**

advice *NOUN*
The website offers advice on coping with exam nerves.
• **guidance, help, directions, recommendations, suggestions, tips, hints, pointers**

advise *VERB*
❶ *He advised her to go to the police.*
• **recommend, counsel, encourage, urge**
❷ *The doctor advised a period of rest.*
• **suggest, prescribe, urge, advocate**

aeroplane *NOUN*
see **aircraft**

affair *NOUN*
Dinner time was a gloomy affair.
• **event, incident, happening, occasion, occurrence, episode**
➤ **affairs**
I don't discuss my private affairs on the phone.
• **business, matters, concerns, questions, subjects, topics, activities**

affect *VERB*
❶ *The area was badly affected by the drought.*
• **influence, have an effect on, have an impact on, change, modify, alter**
❷ *Her story affected me deeply.*
• **move, touch, make an impression on, disturb, upset, concern, trouble, distress**

affection *NOUN*
They clearly have feelings of affection for one another.
• **fondness, liking, love, friendship, friendliness, attachment, devotion, warmth**
OPPOSITE dislike

affectionate *ADJECTIVE*
She gave him an affectionate kiss.
• **loving, tender, caring, fond, friendly, warm**
OPPOSITES unfriendly, cold

affirm *VERB*
The police affirmed that they had a suspect.
• **declare, confirm, assert, state, pronounce**
OPPOSITE deny

a b c d e f g h i j k l m n o p q r s t u v w x y z

affirmative *ADJECTIVE*
He was hoping for an affirmative answer.
• **positive**
OPPOSITE negative

affluent *ADJECTIVE*
This is an affluent neighbourhood.
• **prosperous, wealthy, rich, well off, well-to-do**
(*informal*) **flush, well-heeled**
OPPOSITES poor, impoverished

afford *VERB*
❶ *I can't afford a new phone.*
• **have enough money for, pay for, run to**
❷ *How much time can you afford?*
• **spare, allow**

afraid *ADJECTIVE*
❶ *She was too afraid to move.*
• **frightened, scared, terrified, petrified, alarmed, fearful, intimidated, cowardly**
IDIOMS **frightened out of your wits, scared to death, scared stiff**
❷ *Don't be afraid to ask.*
• **hesitant, reluctant, unwilling, shy**
➤ **be afraid of**
I used to be afraid of the dark.
• **be frightened of, be scared of, fear, dread**

afterwards *ADVERB*
Shortly afterwards, the phone rang.
• **later, later on, subsequently, in due course, thereafter**

again *ADVERB*
Can I see you again next week?
• **another time, once more, once again, over again, afresh**

against *PREPOSITION*
❶ *A bike was leaning against the wall.*
• **touching, up against, in contact with**
❷ *We started a campaign against bullying.*
• **in opposition to, opposed to, hostile to, averse to**

age *NOUN*
The book is set in the age of the Vikings.
• **period, time, era, epoch, days**

age *VERB*
❶ *Dogs age faster than humans.*
• **become older, grow old**
❷ *The cheese is left to age for six months.*
• **mature, mellow, ripen**

agency *NOUN*
My brother works for a travel agency.
• **office, business, department, service, bureau**

agenda *NOUN*
What's on the agenda for today?
• **programme, plan, schedule, timetable**

agent *NOUN*
❶ *When she became a writer she needed an agent.*
• **representative, spokesperson, negotiator, intermediary, mediator**
❷ *The main character is a CIA agent.*
• **spy, secret agent, operative**
For tips on writing spy fiction see **spy**.

aggression *NOUN*
The attack was an act of mindless aggression.
• **hostility, violence, aggressiveness, confrontation, militancy, belligerence**

aggressive *ADJECTIVE*
Why are you in such an aggressive mood?
• **hostile, violent, confrontational, antagonistic, argumentative, quarrelsome, bullying, warlike, belligerent**
OPPOSITES friendly, peaceful, peaceable

agile *ADJECTIVE*
She is as agile as a mountain goat.
• **nimble, graceful, sure-footed, sprightly, acrobatic, supple, lithe**
OPPOSITES clumsy, stiff

agitated *ADJECTIVE*
As time passed, I grew more and more agitated.
• **upset, nervous, anxious, flustered, unsettled, edgy, restless, disturbed, ruffled**
OPPOSITES calm, cool

agonizing *ADJECTIVE*
It was an agonizing decision.
• painful, excruciating, torturous, harrowing, distressing

agony *NOUN*
The creature writhed in agony.
• pain, suffering, torture, torment, anguish, distress

agree *VERB*
❶ *I'm glad that we agree.*
• concur, think the same, be unanimous
IDIOM see eye to eye
OPPOSITE disagree
❷ *I agree that you are right.*
• accept, acknowledge, admit, grant, allow, assent
OPPOSITE deny
❸ *I agreed to pay my share.*
• consent, promise, be willing, undertake, acquiesce
OPPOSITE refuse
❹ *The two stories don't agree.*
• match, correspond, tally
(*informal*) square
➤ **agree on**
Can we agree on a price?
• decide, fix, settle, choose, establish
➤ **agree with**
❶ *I don't agree with this decision.*
• support, advocate, defend, back
❷ *Spicy food doesn't agree with me.*
• suit

agreement *NOUN*
❶ *Everyone nodded their heads in agreement.*
• accord, consensus, assent, consent, unanimity, harmony
OPPOSITE disagreement
❷ *Eventually the two sides reached an agreement.*
• settlement, deal, bargain, pact, treaty, contract, understanding
– An agreement to end fighting is an **armistice** or **truce**.

ahead *ADVERB*
❶ *A messenger was sent ahead with the news.*
• in advance, in front, before
❷ *Keep looking straight ahead.*
• forwards, to the front

aid *NOUN*
❶ *She walks with the aid of a stick.*
• help, support, assistance, backing, cooperation
❷ *The government is increasing aid for the victims of the earthquake.*
• relief, support, funding, subsidy, donations, contributions

aid *VERB*
They were accused of aiding him in his escape.
• help, assist, support, back, collaborate with, cooperate with
IDIOM lend a hand to

aim *NOUN*
What is the aim of the experiment?
• objective, purpose, object, goal, intention, end, target, ambition, wish, dream, hope

aim *VERB*
❶ *He aimed his gun at her.*
• point, direct, train, line up, focus, take aim
❷ *The book is aimed at teenagers.*
• target, direct, design, tailor, pitch
❸ *She aims to go to drama school.*
• intend, mean, plan, propose, want, wish, seek

air *NOUN*
❶ *We shouldn't pollute the air we breathe.*
• atmosphere
– The word **aerial** means 'in or from the air', as in **aerial photograph**.
❷ *Open the window and let some air in.*
• fresh air, ventilation, draught, breeze
❸ *The words are set to a traditional air.*
• song, tune, melody
❹ *The castle had an air of menace about it.*
• appearance, look, atmosphere, aura, impression, mood, tone, feeling

air *VERB*
❶ *He opened the window to air the room.*
• ventilate, freshen, refresh

❷ *This is an opportunity to air your views.*
• **express, voice, make known, make public, articulate, declare, state**

aircraft *NOUN*

WORD WEB

Some types of aircraft:

➤ aeroplane (*North American* airplane)
➤ airliner
➤ air ambulance
➤ airship
➤ biplane
➤ bomber
➤ delta wing
➤ fighter
➤ glider
➤ hang-glider
➤ helicopter
➤ hot-air balloon
➤ jet
➤ jumbo jet
➤ microlight
➤ monoplane
➤ seaplane
➤ spy plane
➤ (*historical*) Zeppelin

Parts of an aircraft:

➤ cabin
➤ cargo hold
➤ cockpit
➤ engine
➤ fin
➤ flap
➤ flight deck
➤ fuselage
➤ joystick
➤ passenger cabin
➤ propeller
➤ rotor
➤ rudder
➤ tail
➤ tailplane
➤ undercarriage
➤ wing

- The flying of aircraft is **aviation**.
- A person who flies aircraft is a **pilot** or **aviator**.
- The pilot of a hot-air balloon is a **balloonist**.
- The study of aircraft and aviation is **aeronautics**.

airy *ADJECTIVE*
The room I was given was light and airy.
• **well-ventilated, fresh, breezy, cool**
OPPOSITES airless, stuffy

aisle *NOUN*
I had a seat next to the aisle.
• **passageway, passage, gangway, lane**

alarm *NOUN*
❶ *Something set off the burglar alarm.*
• **signal, warning, alert, siren**
❷ *Her eyes widened in alarm.*
• **fear, fright, panic, anxiety, apprehension, distress, terror**

alarm *VERB*
The sudden noise alarmed the horses.
• **frighten, scare, panic, agitate, upset, distress, unnerve, startle, shock**
OPPOSITE reassure

alarming *ADJECTIVE*
We have just received some alarming news.
• **frightening, terrifying, shocking, startling, disturbing**
(*informal*) **scary**
OPPOSITE reassuring

alert *NOUN*
➤ **be on the alert**
Police are warning residents to be on the alert.
• **be vigilant, be on your guard, be on the lookout**
IDIOMS **stay on your toes, keep your eyes peeled**

alert *ADJECTIVE*
Security guards need to be alert at all times.
• **vigilant, watchful, attentive, observant, wide awake, on the alert, on the lookout**
IDIOM (*informal*) **on the ball**
OPPOSITE inattentive

alert *VERB*
We alerted them to the danger.
• **warn, notify, inform, make aware, forewarn**
(*informal*) **tip off**

alien *NOUN*
I wrote a story about aliens who invade the Earth.
• **extraterrestrial, alien life form**
For tips on writing science fiction see **science fiction**.

alien *ADJECTIVE*
❶ *The dry desert landscape looked*

alien to us.
• **foreign, strange, unfamiliar, exotic**
OPPOSITES native, familiar
❷ *Scientists are searching for alien life.*
• **extraterrestrial**

alight *ADJECTIVE*
One of the sparks set the grass alight.
• **burning, on fire, in flames, blazing, ablaze**

align *VERB*
Align the text with the left-hand margin.
• **line up, even up, straighten up**

alike *ADJECTIVE*
The twins look exactly alike.
• **similar, the same, identical, indistinguishable, uniform**
OPPOSITES dissimilar, different

alive *ADJECTIVE*
Do you think that cactus is still alive?
• **living, live, existing, in existence, surviving, flourishing**
OPPOSITE dead
➤ **alive to**
She has always been alive to new ideas.
• **receptive to, open to, alert to, aware of, conscious of**
OPPOSITE unaware of

allege *VERB*
He alleged that I had cheated.
• **claim, assert, contend, maintain, accuse, charge**

allegiance *NOUN*
They pledged an oath of allegiance to the king.
• **loyalty, faithfulness, obedience, fidelity, devotion**
OPPOSITES disloyalty, treachery

alley *NOUN*
He disappeared around a corner into an alley.
• **passage, passageway, lane, backstreet**

alliance *NOUN*
The two countries formed an alliance.
• **partnership, association, union, confederation, league**
– An alliance between political parties is a **coalition**.

allocate *VERB*
A sum of money has been allocated to each project.
• **allot, assign, set aside, reserve, earmark**

allow *VERB*
❶ *Do you allow calculators in the exam?*
• **permit, let, authorize, approve of, consent to, agree to, give permission for, put up with, stand, tolerate**
OPPOSITE forbid
❷ *We've allowed three hours for the journey.*
• **allocate, set aside, assign, allot, designate, earmark**

alloy *NOUN*
Brass is an alloy of copper and zinc.
• **blend, combination, composite, compound, amalgam, fusion, mixture**

all right *ADJECTIVE*

OVERUSED WORD

❶ **Saying that something is all right:**

➤ satisfactory ➤ acceptable ➤ adequate ➤ reasonable ➤ passable ➤ tolerable ➤ not bad

(*informal*) OK or okay

The food on the plane was tolerable.

OPPOSITES unsatisfactory, unacceptable, below standard

❷ **Being all right to do something:**

➤ permissible ➤ permitted ➤ acceptable ➤ allowed

Taking photographs here is not permitted.

❸ **Feeling, looking all right:**

➤ well ➤ unhurt ➤ unharmed ➤ uninjured

A B C D E F G H I J K L M N O P Q R S T U V W X Y Z

> in good health > fine
> safe
IDIOM in one piece
The stunt man was **uninjured**, *apart from a few bruises.*

ally *NOUN*
The two countries work together as allies.
• **friend, partner**
OPPOSITE **enemy**

almost *ADVERB*
I've almost finished my homework.
• **nearly, practically, just about, virtually, all but, well-nigh, as good as, not quite**

alone *ADVERB*
Did you go to the party alone?
• **on your own, by yourself, unaccompanied**

alone *ADJECTIVE*
She had no friends and felt very alone.
• **lonely, friendless, isolated, solitary, lonesome**

also *ADVERB*
We need some bread and also some butter.
• **in addition, besides, too, additionally, furthermore, further, moreover, to boot**

alter *VERB*
We had to alter our plans for the weekend.
• **change, adjust, adapt, modify, amend, revise, redo, work, transform, vary**

alternate *ADJECTIVE*
The club meets on alternate Tuesdays.
• **every other, every second**

alternative *ADJECTIVE*
Do you have an alternative plan?
• **different, other, second, substitute, standby, reserve, backup, fallback**

alternative *NOUN*
I had no alternative but to pay the fine.
• **choice, option, substitute, replacement**

altogether *ADVERB*
❶ *I have six cousins altogether.*
• **in all, in total, all told**
❷ *I'm not altogether convinced.*
• **completely, entirely, absolutely, quite, totally, utterly, wholly, fully, perfectly, thoroughly, one hundred per cent**

always *ADVERB*
❶ *The planets are always in motion.*
• **continually, continuously, constantly, endlessly, all the time, day and night, unceasingly, perpetually, eternally, for ever**
❷ *My bus is always late.*
• **consistently, invariably, persistently, regularly, repeatedly, habitually, unfailingly, without fail, every time**

amateur *NOUN*
All the players in the team are amateurs.
• **non-professional**
OPPOSITE **professional**

amaze *VERB*
It amazes me that anyone could be so stupid.
• **astonish, astound, surprise, stun, stagger, dumbfound, startle, shock**
(*informal*) **flabbergast, bowl over**
IDIOM (*informal*) **knock for six**

amazed *ADJECTIVE*
I was amazed by the number of people in the audience.
• **astonished, astounded, stunned, surprised, dumbfounded, speechless, staggered, thunderstruck, at a loss for words**
(*informal*) **flabbergasted**

amazing *ADJECTIVE*
98 per cent is an amazing score!
• **astonishing, astounding, staggering, stunning, extraordinary, remarkable, incredible, unbelievable, breathtaking, awesome, phenomenal, sensational, stupendous, tremendous, wonderful**
(*informal*) **mind-boggling, jaw-dropping**
(*literary*) **wondrous**

ambition *NOUN*
❶ *At that age, he was full of ambition.*
• drive, determination, enthusiasm, enterprise, initiative, motivation
❷ *Her ambition is to go to art college.*
• goal, aim, dream, desire, intention, objective, target, wish, hope, aspiration

ambitious *ADJECTIVE*
❶ *She is a very ambitious young woman.*
• enterprising, determined, motivated, purposeful, committed, keen
(*informal*) go-ahead, go-getting
OPPOSITES unambitious, laid-back
❷ *I think your plan is too ambitious.*
• demanding, challenging, formidable, difficult, grand, large-scale
OPPOSITES modest, low-key

ambush *VERB*
Highwaymen used to ambush wealthy travellers.
• waylay, pounce on, surprise

amend *VERB*
I amended the last paragraph to make it clearer.
• revise, change, alter, adjust, modify, adapt, edit, rewrite, reword

amends *PLURAL NOUN*
➤ **make amends for**
He's trying to make amends for what he did.
• make up for, atone for

among *PREPOSITION*
We spotted a deer among the trees.
• amid, in the middle of, surrounded by, in, between

amount *NOUN*
❶ *A computer can store a huge amount of information.*
• quantity, measure, supply, volume, mass, bulk
❷ *He wrote out a cheque for the full amount.*
• sum, total, lot, quantity, number

amount *VERB*
➤ **amount to**
The bill amounted to 40 euros.
• add up to, come to, run to, total, equal, make

amphibian *NOUN*

WORD WEB

Some animals which are amphibians:

➤ bullfrog
➤ frog
➤ natterjack toad
➤ newt
➤ salamander
➤ toad
➤ tree frog

ample *ADJECTIVE*
❶ *There is ample space for parking.*
• enough, sufficient, adequate, plenty of, lots of, more than enough
(*informal*) loads of
OPPOSITES insufficient, inadequate
❷ *We had an ample supply of water.*
• plentiful, abundant, copious, profuse, generous, lavish, liberal
OPPOSITES meagre, scanty

amuse *VERB*
❶ *I think this story will amuse you.*
• make you laugh, entertain, please, divert, cheer up
(*informal*) tickle
OPPOSITE bore
❷ *We were left to amuse ourselves.*
• entertain, occupy, busy, engage

amusement *NOUN*
❶ *Our favourite amusement was catching tadpoles.*
• pastime, activity, recreation, entertainment, diversion, game, hobby, interest, sport
❷ *a source of much amusement*
• mirth, merriment, hilarity, laughter, glee
❸ *He built the boat for his own amusement.*
• entertainment, pleasure, enjoyment, fun, delight

amusing *ADJECTIVE*
It is an amusing story about a pig who can talk.
• **funny, humorous, comical, witty, hilarious, diverting, entertaining, droll**
OPPOSITES solemn, serious

analyse *VERB*
We then analysed the results of the experiment.
• **examine, study, inspect, investigate, scrutinize, evaluate, interpret**

analysis *NOUN*
Here is an analysis of the data.
• **examination, study, inspection, investigation, scrutiny, evaluation, interpretation**

ancestor *NOUN*
His ancestors came from Russia.
• **forebear, forefather, predecessor, antecedent**
OPPOSITE descendant

ancestry *NOUN*
Sofia was proud of her Polish ancestry.
• **descent, origins, heredity, heritage, lineage, extraction, roots, blood**

ancient *ADJECTIVE*
❶ *In ancient times, our ancestors were hunters.*
• **early, prehistoric, primitive, olden**
OPPOSITE modern
❷ *Honey is an ancient remedy for wounds.*
• **old, age-old, archaic, time-honoured**
OPPOSITES new, recent
❸ *That old computer game looks ancient now.*
• **antiquated, old-fashioned, dated, archaic**
OPPOSITES contemporary, up to date

anecdote *NOUN*
They swapped anecdotes about their childhood.
• **story, tale, narrative, reminiscence**
(*informal*) **yarn**

angelic *ADJECTIVE*
She has an angelic smile.
• **innocent, virtuous, pure, saintly, cherubic**
OPPOSITES devilish, demonic

anger *NOUN*
She was filled with anger.
• **rage, fury, rancour, indignation, vexation, outrage**
(*literary*) **ire, wrath**
– An outburst of anger is a **tantrum** or a **fit of temper**.

anger *VERB*
I was angered by his reply.
• **enrage, infuriate, incense, inflame, madden, outrage, annoy, vex, irk, exasperate, antagonize, provoke**
IDIOMS **make your blood boil, make you see red**
OPPOSITE pacify

angle *NOUN*
❶ *A cupboard is built into the angle between the two walls.*
• **corner, point, nook**
❷ *She wore a beret set at a slight angle.*
• **slope, slant, tilt, gradient**
❸ *Let's look at the problem from a different angle.*
• **perspective, point of view, viewpoint, standpoint, view, outlook, aspect, approach, slant, tack**

angry *ADJECTIVE*
He was angry at his parents for lying to him.
• **cross, furious, irate, enraged, infuriated, incensed, outraged, annoyed, exasperated, in a temper, fuming, indignant, raging, seething**
(*informal*) **mad, livid**
IDIOMS **up in arms, foaming at the mouth, seeing red**
OPPOSITE calm
➤ **get angry**
She turns purple when she gets angry.
• **lose your temper, fly into a rage, go berserk**
IDIOMS (*informal*) **blow a fuse, blow your top, flip your lid, fly off the handle,**

hit the roof, lose your rag, go off the deep end

anguish *NOUN*
He let out a cry of anguish.
• **agony, pain, distress, torment, suffering, misery, woe, sorrow, heartache**

animal *NOUN*
Wild animals roam freely in the safari park.
• **creature, beast**
– A word for wild animals in general is **wildlife**.
– The animals of a particular place or time are its **fauna**.

WORD WEB

Types of animal:

- amphibian
- arachnid
- bird
- fish
- insect
- mammal
- marsupial
- mollusc
- reptile
- rodent

- Animals with a backbone are **vertebrates** and those without a backbone are **invertebrates**.
- Animals that eat meat are **carnivores** and those that eat plants are **herbivores**.
- Animals that eat both meat and plants are **omnivores**.
- Animals that are kept by people are **domestic animals** and those kept on a farm are **livestock**.
- Animals that sleep most of the winter are **hibernating animals**.
- Animals that are active at night are **nocturnal animals**.
- The scientific study of animals is **zoology**.
- The study of plants and animals is **natural history** and a person who studies them is a **naturalist**.
- The medical treatment of animals is **veterinary medicine**.

SEE ALSO **amphibian, bird, cat, dog, fish, horse, insect, reptile, rodent**
For groups of animals see **collective noun**.

WRITING TIPS

DESCRIBING ANIMALS
Body parts:

- antler
- coat
- fang
- fin
- fleece
- flipper
- fluke
- foreleg
- forelimbs
- fur
- hide
- hind leg
- hoof
- horn
- mane
- muzzle
- paw
- pelt
- snout
- tail
- tentacle
- trotter
- trunk
- tusk
- whisker

Skin or coat:

- camouflaged
- coarse
- drab
- furry
- glossy
- hairy
- leathery
- matted
- mottled
- patchy
- piebald
- prickly
- scaly
- shaggy
- shiny
- silky
- sleek
- slimy
- smooth
- spiky
- spotted
- striped
- wiry
- woolly

Movement:

- bound
- canter
- crouch
- dart
- gallop
- gambol
- leap
- lumber
- nuzzle
- pad
- paw
- pounce
- range
- roam
- scuttle
- skip
- skulk
- slink
- slither
- spring

a b c d e f g h i j k l m n o p q r s t u v w x y z

A B C D E F G H I J K L M N O P Q R S T U V W X Y Z

- ➤ stalk
- ➤ stamp
- ➤ stampede
- ➤ trot

Sounds:

- ➤ bark
- ➤ bay
- ➤ bellow
- ➤ bleat
- ➤ bray
- ➤ buzz
- ➤ cluck
- ➤ croak
- ➤ gabble
- ➤ growl
- ➤ grunt
- ➤ hiss
- ➤ howl
- ➤ jabber
- ➤ low
- ➤ mew
- ➤ neigh
- ➤ pipe
- ➤ purr
- ➤ roar
- ➤ snap
- ➤ snarl
- ➤ snort
- ➤ snuffle
- ➤ squeak
- ➤ trumpet
- ➤ whimper
- ➤ whine
- ➤ whinny
- ➤ yap
- ➤ yelp
- ➤ yowl

animated *ADJECTIVE*
We had an animated discussion about our favourite films.
• **lively, spirited, energetic, enthusiastic, vibrant, vivacious, exuberant, perky**
OPPOSITES lifeless, lethargic

annihilate *VERB*
They threatened to annihilate the whole population of the planet.
• **destroy, wipe out, eradicate, obliterate**

anniversary *NOUN*

WORD WEB

Special anniversaries:

- ➤ centenary (100 years)
- ➤ bicentenary (200 years)
- ➤ tercentenary (300 years)
- ➤ quatercentenary (400 years)
- ➤ quincentenary (500 years)
- ➤ millenary (1000 years)

Wedding anniversaries:

- ➤ silver wedding (25 years)
- ➤ ruby wedding (40 years)
- ➤ golden wedding (50 years)
- ➤ diamond wedding (60 years)

announce *VERB*
I will now announce the winner of the competition.
• **make known, make public, declare, state, report, present, proclaim, give out, broadcast, release**

announcement *NOUN*
Ladies and gentlemen, I'd like to make an announcement.
• **statement, declaration, pronouncement, proclamation, bulletin**

annoy *VERB*
❶ *The comments had clearly annoyed her.*
• **irritate, displease, exasperate, anger, antagonize, upset, vex, irk, nettle**
(*informal*) **rile, aggravate**
OPPOSITES **please, gratify**
❷ *Please don't annoy me while I'm working.*
• **pester, bother, trouble, harass, badger, nag, plague**
(*informal*) **bug, hassle**

annoyance *NOUN*
❶ *Much to my annoyance, the DVD was scratched.*
• **irritation, exasperation, indignation, anger, vexation, displeasure**
❷ *Junk mail is a constant annoyance.*
• **nuisance, bother, trouble, worry**

annoyed *ADJECTIVE*
He sounded quite annoyed on the phone.
• **irritated, exasperated, vexed, irked, nettled**
(*informal*) **riled, aggravated, put out**

annoying *ADJECTIVE*
My brother has a lot of annoying habits.
• **irritating, exasperating, maddening, provoking, tiresome, trying, vexing, irksome, troublesome, bothersome**

anonymous *ADJECTIVE*
❶ *It was an anonymous donation.*
• **unnamed, nameless, unidentified, unknown**
❷ *I received an anonymous letter today.*
• **unsigned**

answer *NOUN*
❶ *Did you get an answer to your letter?*
• **reply, response, acknowledgement, reaction**
– A quick or angry answer is a **retort**.
❷ *The answers to the quiz are on the next page.*
• **solution, explanation**
OPPOSITE question

answer *VERB*
❶ *You haven't answered my question.*
• **reply to, respond to, react to, acknowledge, give an answer to**
❷ *'I don't know,' she answered.*
• **reply, respond, return**
– To answer quickly or angrily is to **retort**.

anthology *NOUN*
I'm reading an anthology of ghost stories.
• **collection, compilation, selection, compendium, miscellany**

anticipate *VERB*
❶ *No one anticipated that the harvest would fail.*
• **expect, predict, foresee, foretell, bargain on**
❷ *We are eagerly anticipating their arrival.*
• **look forward to, await, long for**

anticlimax *NOUN*
After all the hype, the match was an anticlimax.
• **let-down, disappointment**
(*informal*) **washout**

antiquated *ADJECTIVE*
He still uses an antiquated typewriter.
• **out of date, outdated, outmoded, old-fashioned, ancient, obsolete**
OPPOSITES modern, up to date

antique *ADJECTIVE*
The palace is full of antique furniture.
• **old, vintage, antiquarian**
OPPOSITES modern, contemporary

antisocial *ADJECTIVE*
❶ *Neighbours complained about his antisocial behaviour.*
• **objectionable, offensive, disruptive, disorderly, discourteous**
❷ *I'm feeling a bit antisocial today.*
• **unsociable, unfriendly**
OPPOSITES sociable, gregarious

anxiety *NOUN*
We waited for news with a growing sense of anxiety.
• **apprehension, concern, worry, fear, dread, nervousness, nerves, unease, disquiet**
(*informal*) **the jitters**
OPPOSITES calmness, confidence

anxious *ADJECTIVE*
❶ *We are all anxious about what will happen next.*
• **nervous, worried, apprehensive, concerned, uneasy, fearful, edgy, fraught, tense, troubled**
(*informal*) **uptight, jittery**
OPPOSITES calm, confident
❷ *I'm anxious to do my best.*
• **eager, keen, enthusiastic, willing, impatient, itching**

apart *ADVERB*
➤ **apart from**
No one knows, apart from us.
• **except for, aside from, besides, other than, excepting, with the exception of**

apartment *NOUN*
He lives in an apartment in the centre of town.
• **flat, suite, rooms**

apologetic *ADJECTIVE*
An apologetic email arrived the next day.
• **sorry, repentant, remorseful, regretful, penitent, contrite**
OPPOSITE unrepentant

apologize *VERB*
She apologized for her mistake.
• **say you are sorry, repent, be penitent**

appal *VERB*
We were appalled by the number of casualties.
• **horrify, shock, dismay, distress, outrage, scandalize, revolt, disgust, sicken**

appalling *ADJECTIVE*
❶ *Some of the children live in appalling conditions.*
• **shocking, horrifying, horrific, dreadful, horrendous, atrocious, horrible, terrible, distressing, sickening, revolting**
❷ (*informal*) *My handwriting is appalling.*
• **very bad, awful, terrible, deplorable, disgraceful**
(*informal*) **abysmal**

apparatus *NOUN*
This apparatus is for breathing underwater.
• **equipment, tackle**
(*informal*) **gear**

apparent *ADJECTIVE*
❶ *She quit her job for no apparent reason.*
• **obvious, evident, clear, noticeable, detectable, perceptible, recognizable, conspicuous, visible**
OPPOSITE **unclear**
❷ *I could not understand his apparent lack of interest.*
• **seeming, outward, ostensible**

apparently *ADVERB*
Apparently you did not receive my email.
• **evidently, seemingly, ostensibly**

appeal *VERB*
Police are appealing for information.
• **ask, request, call, entreat, plead, beg, implore**
➤ **appeal to**
That kind of film doesn't appeal to me.
• **attract, interest, please, fascinate, tempt, draw in**

appeal *NOUN*
❶ *We have launched an appeal for donations to the charity.*
• **request, call, cry, entreaty**
– An appeal signed by a lot of people is a **petition**.
❷ *Baby animals always have great appeal.*
• **attraction, interest, fascination, allure, charm, attractiveness**

appear *VERB*
❶ *Cracks started to appear on the surface.*
• **become visible, come into view, emerge, develop, occur, show up, surface, arise, crop up, spring up**
❷ *Our visitors didn't appear until midnight.*
• **arrive, come, turn up**
(*informal*) **show up**
❸ *At first, the room appeared to be empty.*
• **seem, look**
❹ *She appears in two new films this week.*
• **act, perform, take part, feature**

appearance *NOUN*
❶ *Her sudden appearance in the doorway startled me.*
• **approach, arrival, entrance, entry**
❷ *I apologize for my rather scruffy appearance.*
• **look, air, aspect, bearing**
❸ *He gave every appearance of enjoying himself.*
• **impression, air, semblance, show**

appetite *NOUN*
❶ *I've lost my appetite.*
• **hunger**
❷ *She had a great appetite for adventure.*
• **desire, eagerness, enthusiasm, passion, keenness, wish, urge, taste, thirst, longing, yearning, craving, lust, zest**

appetizing *ADJECTIVE*
The appetizing smell of baking filled the house.
• **delicious, tasty, tempting, mouth-watering**

applaud *VERB*
❶ *The spectators applauded loudly.*
• **clap, cheer**
OPPOSITE boo
❷ *I applaud your honesty.*
• **praise, commend, admire, welcome**
OPPOSITES condemn, criticize

applause *NOUN*
The audience burst into applause.
• **clapping, cheering, ovation**

appliance *NOUN*
The shop sells and repairs kitchen appliances.
• **device, machine, gadget, instrument, apparatus, contraption**
(*informal*) **gizmo**

application *NOUN*
❶ *Thank you for your application for a refund.*
• **request, claim, appeal, petition**
❷ *The job needs patience and application.*
• **effort, hard work, diligence, commitment, dedication, perseverance, persistence, devotion**

apply *VERB*
❶ *She applied lipstick to her mouth.*
• **put on, lay on, spread**
❷ *You will need to apply all your skill and concentration.*
• **use, employ, exercise, utilize**
❸ *I applied for a place on the course.*
• **make an application for, ask for, request, bid, petition**
➤ **apply to**
Answer all the questions that apply to you.
• **be relevant to, relate to, refer to, concern, affect, cover**

appoint *VERB*
We have appointed a new team captain.
• **choose, select, elect, vote for, decide on, settle on**

appointment *NOUN*
❶ *I have an appointment to see the doctor.*
• **arrangement, engagement, date**
❷ *The team are waiting for the appointment of a new coach.*
• **nomination, naming, selection, choice, choosing, election**
❸ *My uncle has got a new appointment at the university.*
• **job, post, position, situation, office**

appreciate *VERB*
❶ *He appreciates good music.*
• **enjoy, like, love, admire, respect, esteem**
OPPOSITES disparage, disdain
❷ *I appreciate your help with this.*
• **value, be grateful for, be glad of**
❸ *I appreciate that this is a difficult time.*
• **recognize, realize, understand, comprehend, be aware**
❹ *Antique jewellery will appreciate in value.*
• **grow, increase, go up, mount, rise**
OPPOSITES depreciate, decrease

appreciation *NOUN*
❶ *She had a keen appreciation of poetry.*
• **enjoyment, love, admiration**
OPPOSITES disparagement, disdain (for)
❷ *Please accept this small token of our appreciation.*
• **gratitude, thanks**
❸ *They had no appreciation of the danger.*
• **recognition, acknowledgement, realization, awareness**

appreciative *ADJECTIVE*
They were an appreciative audience.
• **admiring, enthusiastic, approving, complimentary**

apprehend *VERB*
Police have apprehended a third suspect.
• **arrest, capture, detain, seize**
OPPOSITE release

apprehension *NOUN*
His mouth was dry with apprehension.
• **anxiety, worry, concern, unease, disquiet, nervousness, trepidation**

A B C D E F G H I J K L M N O P Q R S T U V W X Y Z

apprehensive *ADJECTIVE*
She gave an apprehensive glance over her shoulder.
• **anxious, worried, nervous, tense, agitated, edgy, uneasy, unsettled, troubled, frightened, fearful**
OPPOSITES **calm, untroubled**

apprentice *NOUN*
His first job was as a plumber's apprentice.
• **trainee, learner, novice, probationer**
(*informal*) **rookie**

approach *VERB*
❶ *She approached the door on tiptoe.*
• **move towards, draw near to, come near to, near, advance on, close in on, gain on**
❷ *They approached me with an offer to join the squad.*
• **speak to, talk to, go to, contact, sound out**
❸ *What is the best way to approach this problem?*
• **tackle, undertake, set about, go about, embark on, address**

approach *NOUN*
❶ *We could hear the approach of footsteps.*
• **arrival, advance, coming**
❷ *They made an approach to the bank for a loan.*
• **application, appeal, proposal, submission, request**
❸ *He brought a fresh approach to filmmaking.*
• **attitude, manner, style, method, system, way**
❹ *Two soldiers guarded the approach to the bridge.*
• **access, entry, entrance, way in**

approachable *ADJECTIVE*
The staff are always very approachable.
• **friendly, pleasant, agreeable, welcoming, sympathetic**
OPPOSITES **unapproachable, aloof**

appropriate *ADJECTIVE*
Jeans are not appropriate for a formal party.
• **suitable, proper, fitting, apt, right, well-judged, relevant, pertinent**
OPPOSITE **inappropriate**

approval *NOUN*
❶ *The head gave her approval to our plan.*
• **agreement, consent, support, acceptance, assent, permission, authorization, go-ahead, blessing**
OPPOSITE **refusal**
❷ *He looked at them with approval.*
• **appreciation, admiration, praise, high regard, acclaim, respect, support, liking**
OPPOSITE **disapproval**

approve *VERB*
A majority voted to approve the plan.
• **agree to, consent to, authorize, allow, accept, pass, permit, support, back**
IDIOMS **give the green light to, give the thumbs-up to**
OPPOSITES **refuse, give the thumbs-down to**
➤ **approve of**
Her family did not approve of the marriage.
• **agree with, be in favour of, favour, welcome, support, endorse, like, think well of, take kindly to, admire, commend, applaud**
OPPOSITE **condemn**

approximate *ADJECTIVE*
All the measurements are approximate.
• **estimated, rough, broad, loose, inexact**
(*informal*) **ballpark**
OPPOSITE **exact**

approximately *ADVERB*
The film finishes at approximately five o'clock.
• **roughly, about, around, round about, close to, nearly, more or less**
OPPOSITE **precisely**

apt *ADJECTIVE*
❶ *He is apt to forget things.*
• **inclined, likely, liable, prone, given**

❷ *Each chapter begins with an apt quotation.*
• **appropriate, suitable, proper, fitting, right, well-judged, relevant, pertinent** (*informal*) **spot on**
OPPOSITE inappropriate

aptitude *NOUN*
She has a remarkable aptitude for music.
• **talent, gift, ability, skill, flair, expertise, bent**

arbitrary *ADJECTIVE*
It was an apparently arbitrary decision.
• **illogical, irrational, random, subjective, capricious**
OPPOSITE rational

arc *NOUN*
I could see the arc of a rainbow.
• **arch, bow, curve, crescent**

arch *NOUN*
They waited under the arch of the bridge.
• **curve, arc, bow, crescent**

arch *VERB*
The cat arched its back and hissed.
• **curve, bend, bow, hunch**

archive *NOUN*
The library contains the family archives.
• **records, annals, history**

arduous *ADJECTIVE*
It was an arduous climb to the summit.
• **tough, difficult, hard, laborious, strenuous, taxing, demanding, challenging, gruelling, punishing**

area *NOUN*
❶ *From the plane we saw a vast area of desert.*
• **expanse, stretch, tract, space**
– A small area is a **patch**.
– An area of water or ice is a **sheet**.
❷ *They live in an inner-city area.*
• **district, locality, neighbourhood, region, zone, vicinity**
❸ *This is a fascinating area of study.*
• **field, sphere, province, domain**

arena *NOUN*
A new indoor sports arena will open next year.
• **stadium, amphitheatre, ground, park**

argue *VERB*
❶ *Those two are always arguing about something.*
• **quarrel, disagree, fight, have an argument, squabble, wrangle, bicker**
IDIOMS **cross swords, lock horns**
– To argue about the price of something is to **haggle**.
OPPOSITE agree
❷ *I argued that it was my turn to use the computer.*
• **claim, assert, maintain, contend, reason, allege**

argument *NOUN*
❶ *There was an argument over who should pay for the meal.*
• **disagreement, quarrel, dispute, row, clash, fight, squabble, altercation**
❷ *There are strong arguments both for and against this decision.*
• **reasoning, justification, evidence, case**

arid *ADJECTIVE*
It is an arid landscape.
• **dry, barren, parched, waterless, lifeless, infertile, sterile, unproductive**
OPPOSITES fertile, lush

arise *VERB*
❶ *Let me know if any problems arise.*
• **occur, emerge, develop, ensue, appear, come about, come up, crop up, happen, come to light, surface**
❷ (*old use*) *Arise, Sir Francis.*
• **stand up, get up**

aristocrat *NOUN*
The house belongs to a Spanish aristocrat.
• **noble, nobleman or noblewoman, peer**
OPPOSITE commoner

aristocratic *ADJECTIVE*
She comes from an aristocratic family.
• **noble, titled, upper-class, blue-blooded**

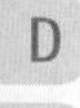
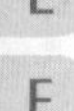

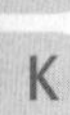
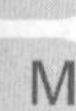
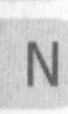

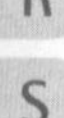

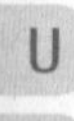

arm *VERB*
The men were armed with heavy sticks.
• **equip, supply, provide, furnish, fit out**

armed services *PLURAL NOUN*

WORD WEB

The main armed services:

➤ air force
➤ army
➤ navy

- Men and women in the services are **troops.**
- A new serviceman or servicewoman is a **recruit.**
- A young person training to be in the armed services is a **cadet.**

Various groups in the armed services:

➤ battalion
➤ brigade
➤ company
➤ corps
➤ fleet
➤ garrison
➤ legion
➤ patrol
➤ platoon
➤ regiment
➤ squad
➤ squadron

Servicemen and servicewomen:

➤ aircraftman
➤ aircraftwoman
➤ commando
➤ marine
➤ paratrooper
➤ sailor
➤ soldier

SEE ALSO **soldier**

armour *NOUN*
The illustration shows a knight in armour.
• **chain-mail**
– An outfit of armour is a **suit of armour.**
– Something fitted with armour is **armoured** or **armour-plated.**

arms *PLURAL NOUN*
The two armies laid down their arms and made peace.
• **weapons, weaponry, guns, firearms, armaments, fire-power**
– A store of arms is an **armoury** or **arsenal.**

army *NOUN*
❶ *He served with the army in France.*
• **armed force, military, militia, troops, infantry**
– A country's army, navy and air force are its **armed services.**
❷ *An army of servants was working in the kitchen.*
• **mass, horde, mob, swarm, throng**

aroma *NOUN*
The aroma of fresh coffee filled the room.
• **smell, scent, odour, fragrance, perfume**

around *PREPOSITION*
❶ *She wore a silver necklace around her neck.*
• **about, round, encircling, surrounding**
❷ *There were around a hundred people in the audience.*
• **about, approximately, roughly, more or less**

arouse *VERB*
I had to get into the house without arousing suspicion.
• **cause, generate, lead to, evoke, produce, provoke, set off, excite, stimulate, incite, stir up, whip up**
OPPOSITES calm, quell

arrange *VERB*
❶ *The books are arranged in alphabetical order.*
• **sort, order, organize, set out, lay out, display, group, categorize, classify, collate**
❷ *We're arranging a surprise party for Mum.*
• **plan, organize, prepare, set up, fix up, see to**

arrangement *NOUN*
❶ *I don't like the arrangement of the furniture.*
• **layout, positioning, organization, grouping, display, design**
❷ *I said I'd deal with the arrangements for our holiday.*
• **plan, preparation, planning**
❸ *We have an arrangement to share*

the costs.
• **agreement, deal, bargain, contract**

array *NOUN*
There was an array of dials on the control panel.
• **range, display, line-up, arrangement**

arrest *VERB*
❶ *A man has been arrested for murder.*
• **seize, capture, apprehend, detain, take prisoner, take into custody**
(*informal*) **nick**
❷ *Doctors are trying to arrest the spread of the disease.*
• **stop, halt, check, curb, block, prevent, obstruct**

arrival *NOUN*
We awaited the arrival of our guests.
• **coming, appearance, entrance, approach**

arrive *VERB*
When is the train due to arrive?
• **come, appear, turn up, get in**
(*informal*) **show up**
➤ **arrive at**
❶ *We arrived at our hotel before noon.*
• **get to, reach**
❷ *Have you arrived at a decision?*
• **make, reach, settle on, decide on**

arrogant *ADJECTIVE*
His arrogant manner annoys me.
• **boastful, conceited, proud, haughty, self-important, pompous, superior, bumptious**
(*informal*) **big-headed, cocky**
IDIOMS **full of yourself,** (*informal*) **too big for your boots**
OPPOSITE modest

arrow *NOUN*
She shot an arrow into the middle of the target.
– The spine of an arrow is the **shaft**.
– The point of an arrow is the **arrowhead**.
– Arrows are shot using a **bow**.
– A holder for several arrows is a **quiver**.
– The sport of shooting arrows at a target is **archery**.
– Someone who practises archery is an **archer**.

art *NOUN*
❶ *She took a course in art and design.*
• **visual arts, fine art**
❷ *The art of writing letters is disappearing.*
• **skill, craft, technique, talent, knack, trick**

WORD WEB

Terms used in art, craft and design:

➤ **2D**
➤ **3D**
➤ **abstract**
➤ **applied art**
➤ **artist**
➤ **artwork**
➤ **ceramics**
➤ **collage**
➤ **composition**
➤ **crafts**
➤ **craftsperson**
➤ **design**
➤ **designer**
➤ **drawing**
➤ **fine art**
➤ **form**
➤ **graphic design**
➤ **illustration**
➤ **image**
➤ **installation**
➤ **jewellery**
➤ **landscape**
➤ **life form**
➤ **materials**
➤ **media**
➤ **modelling**
➤ **montage**
➤ **painter**
➤ **painting**
➤ **pattern**
➤ **plastic arts**
➤ **portrait**
➤ **pottery**
➤ **printmaking**
➤ **process**
➤ **modern**
➤ **sculptor**
➤ **sculpture**
➤ **shape**
➤ **technique**
➤ **textile art**
➤ **textiles**
➤ **texture**
➤ **visual arts**

article *NOUN*
❶ *On the table were various articles for sale.*
• **item, object, thing**
❷ *I wrote an article for the school magazine.*
• **essay, report, piece, feature**

articulate *ADJECTIVE*
He is certainly an articulate speaker.
• **fluent, eloquent, lucid**
OPPOSITE inarticulate

A B C D E F G H I J K L M N O P Q R S T U V W X Y Z

artificial *ADJECTIVE*
❶ *On the shelf was a vase of artificial flowers.*
• **man-made, synthetic, imitation, unreal, unnatural, manufactured, fake, false**
OPPOSITES **real, natural**
❷ *She gave us an artificial smile.*
• **pretended, sham, affected, assumed, simulated**
(*informal*) **put on**
OPPOSITES **genuine, natural**

artist *NOUN*

WORD WEB

Some artists and craftspeople:

- ➤ animator
- ➤ blacksmith
- ➤ carpenter
- ➤ cartoonist
- ➤ designer
- ➤ draughtsman
- ➤ draughtswoman
- ➤ embroiderer
- ➤ engraver
- ➤ goldsmith
- ➤ graphic designer
- ➤ illustrator
- ➤ knitter
- ➤ mason
- ➤ painter
- ➤ photographer
- ➤ potter
- ➤ printer
- ➤ quilter
- ➤ sculptor
- ➤ silversmith
- ➤ weaver

artistic *ADJECTIVE*
The room was decorated in an artistic style.
• **creative, imaginative, aesthetic, attractive, tasteful**
(*informal*) **arty**

ascend *VERB*
❶ *He slowly ascended the staircase.*
• **climb, go up, mount, move up, scale**
❷ *A kite ascended into the air.*
• **fly up, rise, soar, lift off, take off**
OPPOSITE **descend**

ascent *NOUN*
❶ *Next year they will attempt the ascent of Everest.*
• **climbing, mounting, scaling**
❷ *The trail follows a steep ascent.*
• **slope, gradient, incline, rise**
OPPOSITES **descent, drop**

ashamed *ADJECTIVE*
He felt ashamed of what he had done.
• **sorry, remorseful, regretful, repentant, shamefaced, embarrassed, contrite, mortified, penitent**
(*informal*) **red-faced**
OPPOSITES **unashamed, unrepentant**

ask *VERB*
❶ *She asked us to be quiet.*
• **request, entreat, appeal to, beg, implore**
❷ *I asked him where he came from.*
• **enquire, demand, query, question**
❸ *Who are you asking to the party?*
• **invite**
(*formal*) **request the pleasure of your company**
➤ ask for
❶ *I asked for their advice.*
• **request, appeal for, call for, seek, solicit**
❷ *They were asking for trouble!*
• **encourage, attract, cause, provoke, stir up**

asleep *ADJECTIVE*
My brother is still fast asleep.
• **sleeping, dozing, having a nap, napping**
(*informal*) **snoozing**
(*formal*) **slumbering**
IDIOMS (*informal*) **dead to the world,** (*humorous*) **in the land of Nod**
– An animal asleep for the winter is **hibernating**.
OPPOSITE **awake**
➤ fall asleep
I fell asleep on the couch.
• **go to sleep, doze, drop off, nod off**
– To fall asleep quickly is to **go out like a light**.

aspect *NOUN*
❶ *The writer covers most aspects of life on a submarine.*
• **part, feature, element, angle, detail, side, facet**

❷ *The ruined tower had a grim aspect.*
• appearance, look, manner, air, expression, face, countenance
❸ *The front room has a southern aspect.*
• outlook, view, prospect

aspire *VERB*
➤ **aspire to**
He aspires to be Olympic champion.
• aim for, hope for, dream of, long for, desire, seek
IDIOMS set your heart on, set your sights on

assault *NOUN*
She was the victim of a serious assault.
• attack, mugging

assault *VERB*
He was charged with assaulting a police officer.
• attack, strike, hit, beat up, mug

assemble *VERB*
❶ *A crowd assembled to watch the rescue.*
• gather, come together, congregate, convene, converge, meet, rally
OPPOSITE disperse
❷ *We assembled our luggage in the hall.*
• collect, gather, bring together, put together, round up, marshal, muster
❸ *The machine is now ready to be assembled.*
• construct, build, put together, fit together

assembly *NOUN*
❶ *There was a large assembly of people in the market square.*
• gathering, meeting, convention, congregation, crowd
(*informal*) get-together
– An assembly to show support for something, often out of doors, is a **rally**.
– An assembly to discuss political matters is a **council** or **parliament**.
❷ *The bookcase is now ready for assembly.*
• construction, building, fabrication, manufacture

assent *NOUN*
She has already given us her assent.
• agreement, approval, consent, go-ahead, permission
OPPOSITE refusal

assert *VERB*
❶ *The prisoner asserts that he is innocent.*
• state, claim, contend, declare, argue, maintain, proclaim, insist
❷ *Mary asserted her claim to the English throne.*
• insist on, stand up for, uphold, defend

assertive *ADJECTIVE*
You should try to be more assertive.
• confident, self-confident, bold, forceful, insistent, commanding

assess *VERB*
People came out of their houses to assess the damage.
• evaluate, determine, judge, rate, appraise, measure, gauge, estimate, calculate, work out, value, weigh up
(*informal*) size up

assessment *NOUN*
What is your assessment of the situation?
• judgement, estimation, rating, appraisal, valuation

asset *NOUN*
She has proved a real asset to the team.
• advantage, benefit, blessing, help, strength, good point
OPPOSITE liability

assign *VERB*
❶ *I was assigned the job of guarding the door.*
• allocate, allot, give, consign, hand over, delegate, charge with, entrust with
❷ *An experienced detective was assigned to the case.*
• appoint, nominate

A B C D E F G H I J K L M N O P Q R S T U V W X Y Z

assignment *NOUN*
I have a homework assignment to finish.
• **task, project, exercise, piece of work, job, mission, undertaking**

assist *VERB*
Your job is to assist the crew with their duties.
• **help, aid, support, back up, cooperate with, collaborate with**
IDIOM **lend a hand to**
OPPOSITE **hinder**

assistance *NOUN*
Can I be of any assistance?
• **help, aid, support, backing, cooperation, collaboration, reinforcement**
IDIOM **a helping hand**

assistant *NOUN*
The team leader has three assistants.
• **helper, aide, partner, colleague, associate, supporter**

associate *VERB*
➤ **associate with**
❶ *Black cats are often associated with witchcraft.*
• **connect with, identify with, link with, relate to**
❷ *He used to associate with members of the band.*
• **be friends with, go about with, mix with**

association *NOUN*
❶ *We have started a junior tennis association.*
• **club, society, organization, group, league, fellowship, partnership, union, alliance**
– A political association is a **party**.
❷ *Our association goes back a long way.*
• **relationship, partnership, friendship, relation, connection, link, bond**

assorted *ADJECTIVE*
There are assorted flavours of ice cream on the menu.
• **various, different, mixed, diverse, miscellaneous, several, sundry**

assortment *NOUN*
There is an assortment of sandwiches to choose from.
• **variety, selection, mixture, array, choice, collection, medley, miscellany**

assume *VERB*
❶ *I assume that you agree with me.*
• **presume, suppose, take for granted, believe, fancy, think, understand, gather**
❷ *This is my fault and I assume full responsibility for it.*
• **accept, take on, undertake, shoulder, bear**
❸ *He assumed an air of wide-eyed innocence.*
• **adopt, put on, feign, affect**

assumed *ADJECTIVE*
She writes under an an assumed name.
• **false, fake, fictitious, bogus, invented, made-up**

assumption *NOUN*
The assumption is that prices will stay the same.
• **belief, presumption, supposition, theory, hypothesis**

assurance *NOUN*
❶ *You have my assurance that I will be there.*
• **promise, guarantee, pledge, vow**
❷ *She had an air of calm assurance.*
• **confidence, self-confidence, self-assurance, self-possession**

assure *VERB*
❶ *He assured us that he was telling the truth.*
• **promise, reassure, give your word to, vow to**
❷ *We worked hard to assure the success of the mission.*
• **ensure, make certain of, secure, guarantee**

assured *ADJECTIVE*
Her voice was calm and assured.
• **confident, self-confident, self-assured, poised, composed**
(*informal*) **unflappable**

astonish *VERB*
They were astonished at the size of the crater.
• amaze, astound, surprise, stagger, shock, dumbfound, startle, stun, take aback, take by surprise
(*informal*) flabbergast
IDIOMS leave you speechless, take your breath away, bowl you over,
(*informal*) knock you for six

astonishing *ADJECTIVE*
It was an astonishing result.
• amazing, astounding, staggering, stunning, remarkable, surprising, extraordinary, incredible, breathtaking, phenomenal, sensational, stupendous, tremendous, dazzling
(*informal*) mind-boggling

astound *VERB*
see **astonish**

astounding *ADJECTIVE*
see **astonishing**

astrology *NOUN*
see **zodiac**

astronomy *NOUN*
For terms used in astronomy see **space**.

astute *ADJECTIVE*
He made some very astute comments.
• shrewd, sharp, acute, smart, clever, canny

ate
past tense see **eat**

athletic *ADJECTIVE*
He is tall with an athletic build.
• muscular, fit, strong, sturdy, powerful, strapping, well-built, brawny, burly
(*informal*) sporty
OPPOSITES puny, weedy

athletics *PLURAL NOUN*

WORD WEB

Some athletic events:

- cross-country
- decathlon
- discus
- heptathlon
- high jump
- hurdles
- javelin
- long jump
- marathon
- pentathlon
- pole vault
- relay
- shot put
- sprint
- steeplechase
- triathlon
- triple jump

For tips on writing about sport see **sport**.

atmosphere *NOUN*
❶ *The atmosphere on Mars is unbreathable.*
• air, sky
❷ *There was a relaxed atmosphere at the end of term.*
• feeling, feel, mood, spirit, air, ambience, aura
(*informal*) vibe

atrocious *ADJECTIVE*
❶ *He committed a series of atrocious murders.*
• wicked, brutal, barbaric, cruel, vicious, savage, monstrous, inhuman, vile, fiendish, horrifying, abominable, terrible, dreadful
❷ *The weather has been atrocious.*
• very bad, terrible, dreadful, awful

attach *VERB*
❶ *Attach this label to the parcel.*
• fasten, fix, join, tie, bind, secure, connect, link, couple, stick, affix, add, append
OPPOSITE detach
❷ *She attaches great importance to punctuality.*
• ascribe, assign, give

A B C D E F G H I J K L M N O P Q R S T U V W X Y Z

attached *ADJECTIVE*

➤ **attached to**

Some people get very attached to their pets.

• **fond of, close to, devoted to, keen on, loyal to, affectionate towards, friendly towards**

attack *NOUN*

❶ *The enemy attack took them by surprise.*

• **assault, strike, charge, raid, ambush, invasion, onslaught, offensive**

– An attack from the air is an **air raid** or **blitz** and a continuous attack with guns or missiles is a **bombardment**.

❷ *She was upset by this attack on her character.*

• **criticism, censure, condemnation, outburst, tirade**

❸ *I had an attack of coughing.*

• **bout, fit, spasm, episode**
(*informal*) **turn**

attack *VERB*

❶ *They were attacked by a mob armed with sticks.*

• **assault, set on, beat up, mug, charge, pounce on, assail, raid, storm, bombard**

– To attack someone from a hidden place is to **ambush** them.

– If an animal attacks you, it might **savage** you.

❷ *A number of articles attacked the author's reputation.*

• **criticize, censure, denounce, condemn**
(*informal*) **knock**

OPPOSITE defend

attacker *NOUN*

He managed to escape his attacker.

• **assailant, mugger, raider, invader**

OPPOSITE defender

attain *VERB*

This is the highest speed ever attained on the sea.

• **achieve, obtain, reach, get, accomplish, gain, secure**

attempt *VERB*

She will attempt to beat the world record.

• **try, endeavour, strive, seek, aim, venture, make an effort, have a go at**
(*informal*) **have a shot at, have a bash at**

attempt *NOUN*

This is my first attempt at writing a novel.

• **try, effort, go**
(*informal*) **shot, bash**

attend *VERB*

Over a hundred people attended the rally.

• **be present at, go to, appear at, take part in, turn up at**
(*informal*) **show up at**

➤ **attend to**

❶ *Excuse me, I have some business to attend to.*

• **deal with, see to, take care of, look after**

❷ *A nurse attended to the injured.*

• **take care of, care for, look after, help, tend, mind, treat**

❸ *Please attend to what I say.*

• **listen to, pay attention to, follow, heed, mark, mind, note**

attendance *NOUN*

❶ *Attendance at these classes is not compulsory.*

• **presence, appearance, participation**

OPPOSITE non-attendance

❷ *The attendance was low because of the rain.*

• **audience, turnout, gate, crowd**

attendant *NOUN*

She was the personal attendant of Queen Victoria.

• **assistant, aide, companion, escort, retainer, servant**

attention *NOUN*

❶ *Please give this task your full attention.*

• **concentration, consideration, study, focus, observation, scrutiny, thought, awareness**

– To **pay heed to something** or **take**

heed of it is to pay careful attention to something.
❷ *The survivors needed urgent medical attention.*
• **treatment, care**

attentive *ADJECTIVE*
Thank you for being such an attentive audience.
• **alert, paying attention, observant, watchful, aware, vigilant, on the alert, on the lookout**

attic *NOUN*
We have a lot of boxes stored in the attic.
• **loft, garret**

attitude *NOUN*
She now has a more positive attitude to life.
• **outlook, approach, stance, position, view, manner, disposition, frame of mind**

attract *VERB*
The show continues to attract a wide audience.
• **interest, appeal to, captivate, charm, entice, lure, draw in, pull in**
OPPOSITES repel, put off

attraction *NOUN*
❶ *I can't see the attraction of living in the countryside.*
• **appeal, desirability, charm, allure, pull**
OPPOSITE repulsion
❷ *The Eiffel Tower is one of Paris's main tourist attractions.*
• **place of interest, sight, draw**

attractive *ADJECTIVE*
❶ *She is an attractive young woman.*
• **beautiful, pretty, good-looking, handsome, gorgeous, glamorous, striking, fetching, fascinating, captivating, enchanting, arresting**
OPPOSITES unattractive, ugly, repulsive
❷ *It was an attractive offer.*
• **appealing, interesting, agreeable, desirable, pleasing, tempting, inviting**
OPPOSITES unattractive, uninviting

attribute *VERB*
The quote is sometimes attributed to Shakespeare.
• **ascribe, assign, credit**

attribute *NOUN*
He has all the attributes of a top striker.
• **quality, characteristic, trait, property, feature, element, aspect, mark, hallmark**

audible *ADJECTIVE*
Her voice was barely audible.
• **perceptible, detectable, discernible, distinct**
OPPOSITE inaudible

audience *NOUN*
Some members of the audience cheered.
• **crowd, spectators**
– The audience for a TV programme is the **viewers**.
– The audience for a radio programme is the **listeners**.

authentic *ADJECTIVE*
❶ *This is an authentic Roman coin.*
• **genuine, real, actual**
OPPOSITES imitation, fake
❷ *His diary is an authentic account of life at sea.*
• **accurate, truthful, reliable, true, honest, dependable, factual**
OPPOSITES false, inaccurate

author *NOUN*
My copy of the book is signed by the author.
• **writer, novelist, poet, playwright**

authority *NOUN*
❶ *I need your authority to read these files.*
• **permission, authorization, consent, approval, clearance**
❷ *They dared to challenge the authority of the king.*
• **power, command, control, domination, rule, charge**
❸ *She is a leading authority on handwriting.*
• **expert, specialist, pundit, connoisseur**

authorize *VERB*
Has this payment been authorized?
• **approve, agree to, consent to, sanction, clear, allow**

automatic *ADJECTIVE*
❶ *We took our car through the automatic car wash.*
• **automated, mechanical, programmed, computerized**
❷ *His reaction was automatic.*
• **instinctive, involuntary, impulsive, spontaneous, reflex, unconscious, unthinking**

auxiliary *ADJECTIVE*
Fortunately we have an auxiliary power supply.
• **supplementary, secondary, reserve, back-up**
OPPOSITE primary

available *ADJECTIVE*
❶ *Is the Internet available in the library?*
• **accessible, obtainable, at hand, within reach**
OPPOSITES unavailable, inaccessible
❷ *There are no more seats available.*
• **unoccupied, unsold, free**
(*informal*) **up for grabs**
OPPOSITES unavailable, taken

average *ADJECTIVE*
It was just an average day at school.
• **ordinary, normal, typical, standard, usual, regular, everyday, commonplace**
OPPOSITES unusual, extraordinary

averse *ADJECTIVE*
➤ **averse to**
I'm not averse to the idea.
• **against, opposed to, hostile to**
OPPOSITES keen on, for

aversion *NOUN*
➤ **aversion to**
She had an aversion to water and soap.
• **dislike of, distaste for, antipathy to, hostility to**
OPPOSITE liking for

avert *VERB*
❶ *He averted his eyes from the glare.*
• **turn away, turn aside**
❷ *We must take steps to avert a disaster.*
• **prevent, avoid, ward off, stave off, pre-empt, forestall**

avid *ADJECTIVE*
My sister is an avid reader.
• **keen, eager, enthusiastic, passionate, ardent, fervent**

avoid *VERB*
❶ *I swerved to avoid the lamp post.*
• **get out of the way of, keep clear of, steer clear of, dodge, fend off**
❷ *We narrowly avoided defeat.*
• **prevent, preclude, avert, pre-empt, forestall**
❸ *I've been avoiding getting down to work all day.*
• **get out of, evade, dodge, shirk**

await *VERB*
We are awaiting further instructions.
• **wait for, look out for, expect, look forward to, anticipate**

awake *VERB*
Our guests awoke early.
• **wake up, wake, awaken, rise, stir**

awake *ADJECTIVE*
She lay awake all night worrying.
• **wide awake, sleepless, restless, conscious, astir**
– Not being able to sleep is to be suffering from **insomnia**.
OPPOSITE asleep

awaken *VERB*
❶ *I was awakened by birds singing.*
• **wake up, waken, wake, rouse**
❷ *The song awakened memories of her youth.*
• **arouse, stir up, stimulate, evoke, kindle, revive**

award *VERB*
They awarded her the Nobel Peace Prize.
• **give, grant, accord, bestow on, confer on, present to**

award *NOUN*
He won the award for best singer.
• **prize, trophy, medal**

aware *ADJECTIVE*
➤ **aware of**
Were you aware of the danger?
• **acquainted with, conscious of, familiar with, informed about**
OPPOSITE ignorant of

awe *NOUN*
The audience listened in awe.
• **wonder, amazement, admiration, reverence**

awesome *ADJECTIVE*
The mountains were an awesome sight.
• **awe-inspiring, amazing, breathtaking, spectacular, stunning, staggering, formidable**

awful *ADJECTIVE*
❶ *The weather was awful last weekend.*
• **very bad, dreadful, terrible, dire, appalling, abysmal**
(*informal*) **rubbish, lousy**
❷ *The whole country was shocked by this awful crime.*
• **horrifying, shocking, appalling, atrocious, abominable**
❸ *What an awful thing to say!*
• **unpleasant, disagreeable, nasty, horrid, detestable**
❹ *I feel awful about forgetting your birthday.*
• **sorry, ashamed, embarrassed, guilty, remorseful**

awkward *ADJECTIVE*
❶ *The box isn't heavy, but it's awkward to carry.*
• **difficult, cumbersome, unmanageable, unwieldy**
(*informal*) **fiddly**
OPPOSITES easy, handy
❷ *You've arrived at an awkward time.*
• **inconvenient, inappropriate, inopportune, difficult**
OPPOSITES convenient, opportune
❸ *There was then an awkward silence.*
• **uncomfortable, embarrassing, uneasy, tense**
OPPOSITES comfortable, relaxed
❹ *I often feel awkward in a group of people.*
• **embarrassed, uncomfortable, uneasy, out of place**
OPPOSITES comfortable, at ease
❺ *Why are you being so awkward?*
• **uncooperative, unhelpful, unreasonable, stubborn, obstinate**
OPPOSITE cooperative
❻ *He runs in an awkward way.*
• **clumsy, graceless, unskilful, ungainly, inept, blundering**
OPPOSITES graceful, skilful, dexterous

axe *NOUN*
He has an axe for splitting wood.
• **hatchet, cleaver, chopper**

axe *VERB*
The company is going to axe thousands of jobs.
• **terminate, discontinue, abolish, cancel, get rid of, cut, drop, scrap**

A B C D E F G H I J K L M N O P Q R S T U V W X Y Z

Bb

babble *VERB*
What was that man babbling about?
• **chatter, prattle, gabble, jabber, burble**
(*informal*) **witter**

baby *NOUN*
The woman was holding a baby.
• **infant, child, newborn**
(*poetic*) **babe**
– A baby just learning to walk is a **toddler**.
– The time when someone is a baby is their **babyhood**.

babyish *ADJECTIVE*
She is too old for such babyish toys.
• **childish, immature, infantile**
OPPOSITES grown-up, mature

back *NOUN*
❶ *We always sit at the back of the bus.*
• **rear, end, tail end**
– The back end of an animal is its **hindquarters, rear** or **rump**.
– The back of a ship is the **stern**.
OPPOSITES front, head
❷ *I wrote a shopping list on the back of an envelope.*
• **reverse, underside**
OPPOSITES front, face

back *ADJECTIVE*
The back door of the house was unlocked.
• **rear, rearmost**
– The back legs of an animal are its **hind** legs.
OPPOSITE front

back *VERB*
❶ *I began backing towards the door.*
• **go backwards, reverse, retreat, step back, draw back**
OPPOSITE advance
❷ *The government is backing the city's bid to host the Games.*
• **support, endorse, favour, advocate, sponsor**
IDIOMS **give your blessing to, throw your weight behind**
OPPOSITE oppose
❸ *Which horse did you back?*
• **bet on, put money on**
➤ **back down**
We've come too far to back down now.
• **give in, surrender, concede defeat**
➤ **back off**
The men backed off at the sight of the dog.
• **retreat, withdraw, retire, recoil, give way**
➤ **back out of**
They now want to back out of the deal.
• **withdraw from, pull out of, drop out of**
➤ **back up**
❶ *I'll back you up if you need help.*
• **support, stand by, second**
❷ *The new evidence backs up his story.*
• **confirm, substantiate, corroborate, bear out**

backfire *VERB*
His plan backfired spectacularly.
• **fail, go wrong, go awry**
IDIOM **blow up in your face**

background *NOUN*
❶ *You can see a steeple in the background.*
• **backdrop, setting, distance**
OPPOSITE foreground
❷ *The first chapter deals with the background to the war.*
• **circumstances surrounding, lead-up to, history of**
❸ *There are people from many different backgrounds living here.*
• **family circumstances, environment, upbringing, tradition, culture, class**

backing *NOUN*
The new manager has the backing of the players.
• **support, endorsement, approval, blessing**

backward *ADJECTIVE*

❶ *She walked off without a backward glance.*
• **towards the rear, rearward**
OPPOSITE forward

❷ *It is an economically backward country.*
• **underdeveloped, undeveloped**
OPPOSITES advanced, progressive

bad *ADJECTIVE*

OVERUSED WORD

❶ **Bad in quality, bad at doing something:**

➤ **poor** ➤ **inferior** ➤ **unsatisfactory** ➤ **substandard** ➤ **second-rate** ➤ **inadequate** ➤ **weak** ➤ **incompetent** ➤ **imperfect** ➤ **awful** ➤ **hopeless** ➤ **terrible** ➤ **dreadful** ➤ **useless** ➤ **worthless** ➤ **abysmal** ➤ **woeful** ➤ **pathetic** ➤ **shoddy** ➤ **slipshod**

(*informal*) **rubbish, lousy, duff**

The film was spoilt by the **incompetent** *acting.*

OPPOSITES excellent, fine

❷ **A bad experience, bad news:**

➤ **unpleasant** ➤ **unwelcome** ➤ **disagreeable** ➤ **upsetting** ➤ **horrific** ➤ **horrendous** ➤ **disastrous** ➤ **horrible** ➤ **awful** ➤ **terrible** ➤ **dreadful** ➤ **appalling** ➤ **shocking** ➤ **hideous** ➤ **ghastly** ➤ **frightful** ➤ **abominable**

– Another word for a bad experience is an **ordeal**.

Some patients experienced **unwelcome** *side effects.*

OPPOSITES good, excellent

❸ **A bad accident, bad illness:**

➤ **severe** ➤ **serious** ➤ **grave** ➤ **profound** ➤ **critical** ➤ **acute**

She sometimes suffers from **severe** *headaches.*

OPPOSITES minor, slight

❹ **A bad habit, something that is bad for you:**

➤ **harmful** ➤ **damaging** ➤ **detrimental** ➤ **dangerous** ➤ **hazardous** ➤ **injurious**

The sun's rays are **damaging** *to your eyes.*

❺ **A bad smell, bad taste:**

➤ **disgusting** ➤ **revolting** ➤ **repulsive** ➤ **sickening** ➤ **nauseating** ➤ **repugnant** ➤ **foul** ➤ **loathsome** ➤ **offensive** ➤ **vile**

A **nauseating** *smell invaded our nostrils.*

OPPOSITES pleasant, appetizing

❻ **Bad timing, a bad moment:**

➤ **inconvenient** ➤ **unsuitable** ➤ **unfortunate** ➤ **inappropriate** ➤ **inopportune**

Is this an **inconvenient** *time to call?*

OPPOSITES convenient, opportune

❼ **Bad weather, a bad reception:**

➤ **harsh** ➤ **hostile** ➤ **unfavourable** ➤ **adverse** ➤ **miserable**

(*formal*) **inclement**

The **adverse** *weather is forecast to continue.*

OPPOSITES fine, favourable

❽ **A bad person, bad deed:**

➤ **wicked** ➤ **evil** ➤ **malevolent** ➤ **malicious** ➤ **villainous** ➤ **cruel** ➤ **vicious** ➤ **corrupt** ➤ **sinful** ➤ **nefarious** ➤ **monstrous** ➤ **diabolical** ➤ **immoral** ➤ **detestable**

- **hateful**
- **nasty**
- **mean**

– A bad person is a **scoundrel**, **rogue** or **rascal**. A bad character in a story or film is a **villain** or (*informal*) **baddy**.

He plays a **monstrous** *villain in the film.*

OPPOSITES good, virtuous

9 A bad mood, bad temper:

- **angry**
- **foul**
- **ill-humoured**

She arrived in a **foul** *temper.*

OPPOSITE good-humoured

10 Bad behaviour:

- **disobedient**
- **undisciplined**
- **naughty**
- **wayward**
- **mischievous**
- **disgraceful**
- **unruly**
- **deplorable**

A player has been suspended for **unruly** *conduct.*

OPPOSITES exemplary, angelic

11 Feeling bad about something:

- **guilty**
- **remorseful**
- **ashamed**
- **repentant**
- **sorry**

Claudius feels **guilty** *about murdering King Hamlet.*

OPPOSITES unashamed, unrepentant

12 Food going bad:

- **mouldy**
- **sour**
- **rotten**
- **spoiled**
- **off**
- **rancid**
- **decayed**
- **putrid**

Eat the bananas before they go **mouldy**.

OPPOSITE fresh

13 Not bad:

- **acceptable**
- **passable**
- **adequate**
- **tolerable**
- **reasonable**
- **all right**

The prices are **reasonable** *if you book early.*

badly *ADVERB*

1 *The wall was badly painted.*
• **not well, poorly, unsatisfactorily, inadequately, incorrectly, shoddily**
OPPOSITES well, properly

2 *These animals have been badly treated.*
• **ill, unkindly, harshly, cruelly, unfairly**
OPPOSITES well, humanely, fairly

3 *A rescue worker has been badly injured.*
• **seriously, severely, gravely, critically**
OPPOSITE slightly

4 *She badly wanted to win.*
• **very much, desperately**

bad-tempered *ADJECTIVE*

She is always bad-tempered when she gets up.
• **cross, grumpy, grouchy, irritable, moody, quarrelsome, fractious, ill-tempered, short-tempered, cantankerous, crotchety, curmudgeonly, snappy, testy, tetchy, sullen, peevish**
OPPOSITES good-humoured, affable

baffle *VERB*

The instructions baffled me completely.
• **puzzle, confuse, perplex, bewilder, mystify, stump**
(*informal*) **flummox, fox, flabbergast, bamboozle**

bag *NOUN*

I put my wet clothes in a plastic bag.
• **sack, carrier, holdall, satchel, handbag, shoulder bag**
– A bag you carry on your back is a **backpack** or **rucksack**.

baggage *NOUN*

We loaded our baggage onto a trolley.
• **luggage, bags, cases, suitcases, belongings, things**
(*informal*) **gear, stuff**

baggy *ADJECTIVE*
He was wearing a pair of baggy jeans.
• **loose, loose-fitting, roomy**

bait *NOUN*
Some people fell for the bait and answered the email.
• **lure, enticement, trap, decoy, inducement**

bake *VERB*
The hot sun was baking the earth.
• **scorch, burn, parch, sear**

balance *NOUN*
She lost her balance and fell to the ground.
• **stability, equilibrium, footing**

balance *VERB*
The waiter arrived, balancing a tray on each hand.
• **steady, keep balanced, stabilize, poise**

bald *ADJECTIVE*
Uncle Ted has a bald patch on the top of his head.
• **bare, hairless**
OPPOSITE hairy

ball *NOUN*
Wind the string into a ball.
• **sphere, globe, orb**
– A small ball of something is a **pellet** or **globule**.

ballot *NOUN*
The club held a secret ballot to choose a new president.
• **vote, poll, election, referendum**

ban *VERB*
❶ *Mobile phones are banned in school.*
• **forbid, prohibit, bar, veto, proscribe, exclude, outlaw, banish**
OPPOSITES allow, permit
❷ *The sprinter has been banned from international competition.*
• **exclude, bar, banish, outlaw, expel**
OPPOSITE admit

banal *ADJECTIVE*
a disappointingly banal ending
• **unoriginal, commonplace, predictable, hackneyed, trite, unimaginative, uninspiring**

band *NOUN*
❶ *The captain wears a red arm band.*
• **strip, stripe, ring, line, belt, hoop**
❷ *They were captured by a band of outlaws.*
• **gang, group, company, party, body, troop, crew, mob, team, set**
(*informal*) **bunch**
❸ *A jazz band was playing in the town square.*
• **group, ensemble, orchestra**

bandage *NOUN*
You need a bandage round that knee.
• **dressing, plaster, gauze, lint**

bandit *NOUN*
Bandits used to live in these mountains.
• **robber, brigand, thief, outlaw, desperado, highwayman, pirate**

bang *NOUN*
❶ *Suddenly there was a loud bang.*
• **blast, boom, crash, crack, thud, thump, pop, explosion, report**
❷ *He got a bang on the head from the low ceiling.*
• **bump, knock, blow, hit, bash, thump, punch, smack, crack**
(*informal*) **whack, wallop, clout**

bang *VERB*
She banged her fist on the table.
• **hit, strike, beat, bash, thump, knock, hammer, pound, rap, slam**
(*informal*) **whack, wallop**

banish *VERB*
❶ *He was banished from the kingdom forever.*
• **exile, expel, deport, send away, eject**
❷ *She struggled to banish these fears.*
• **dispel, remove, dismiss, allay, drive away**

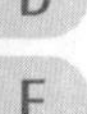

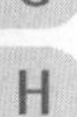

bank *NOUN*

❶ *The temple was built on the banks of the River Nile.*
• **edge, side, shore, embankment, margin, verge, brink**
❷ *We ran down the steep grassy bank.*
• **slope, mound, ridge, rise, knoll**
❸ *Below the screen was a bank of dials and switches.*
• **array, row, line, series**

banner *NOUN*

❶ *The turrets were decorated with colourful banners.*
• **flag, standard, streamer, pennant**
❷ *Demonstrators marched past, carrying banners.*
• **placard, sign, notice, poster**

banquet *NOUN*

There was a state banquet in their honour.
• **dinner, feast**
(*informal*) **spread**

bar *NOUN*

❶ *There were bars across the window.*
• **rod, rail, spar, strut, beam, pole**
❷ *I bought a bar of chocolate.*
• **block, slab, wedge, tablet, cake**
– A bar of gold or silver is an **ingot**.

bar *VERB*

❶ *The door had been barred on the inside.*
• **bolt, fasten, secure, barricade**
❷ *A fallen tree barred the way ahead.*
• **block, hinder, impede, obstruct, stop, check**
❸ *She has been barred from entering the country.*
• **ban, prohibit, forbid, exclude, keep out**

barbaric *ADJECTIVE*

the barbaric treatment of slaves
• **cruel, brutal, inhuman, inhumane, barbarous, savage, brutish**

bare *ADJECTIVE*

❶ *I put suncream on my bare arms and legs.*
• **naked, nude, exposed, uncovered, unclothed, undressed**
OPPOSITES **clothed, covered**
❷ *We looked out on a bare landscape.*
• **barren, bleak, desolate, treeless, leafless**
OPPOSITES **fertile, lush**
❸ *The room was bare except for a single bed.*
• **empty, clear, unfurnished, undecorated**
OPPOSITE **furnished**
❹ *Here are the bare facts of the case.*
• **plain, simple, unembellished, bald, stark**
❺ *Only pack the bare essentials.*
• **basic, minimum**

barely *ADVERB*

We barely had time to get changed.
• **hardly, scarcely, only just**

bargain *NOUN*

❶ *I'll make a bargain with you.*
• **deal, agreement, arrangement, promise, contract, pact**
❷ *We went looking for bargains in the sales.*
• **good buy, special offer**
(*informal*) **snip, steal**

bargain *VERB*

I am not going to bargain with you.
• **haggle, do a deal, negotiate**
➤ **bargain on**
I hadn't bargained on sleeping in a tent.
• **expect, anticipate, envisage, foresee, count on, reckon on, allow for**

barge *VERB*

➤ **barge into**
❶ *People were running around and barging into each other.*
• **bump into, collide with, veer into**
❷ *Don't just barge into my room without knocking.*
• **push into, rush into, storm into**

bark *VERB*

Dogs barked from behind the fence.
• **woof, yap, yelp, growl**

barrage *NOUN*
❶ *a tidal barrage*
• **dam, weir, barrier**
❷ *a heavy artillery barrage*
• **bombardment, volley, gunfire**
❸ *facing a barrage of questions*
• **mass, stream, flood, torrent, deluge, onslaught, avalanche**

barrel *NOUN*
He hid in an empty beer barrel.
• **cask, drum, tub, keg, butt**

barren *ADJECTIVE*
The surface of the planet was a barren landscape.
• **arid, dry, bare, infertile, sterile, unproductive, unfruitful**
OPPOSITES fertile, lush

barricade *NOUN*
They built a barricade of sandbags.
• **barrier, blockade, obstacle, obstruction**

barrier *NOUN*
❶ *Spectators must stay behind the barrier.*
• **fence, railing, barricade, blockade**
– A barrier across a road is a **roadblock**.
❷ *Lack of confidence can be a barrier to success.*
• **obstacle, obstruction, bar, hindrance, impediment, hurdle, stumbling block**

base *NOUN*
❶ *We stood at the base of the pyramid.*
• **bottom, foot, foundation, support, stand**
– A base under a statue is a **pedestal** or **plinth**.
❷ *The decimal system has 10 as its base.*
• **basis, foundation, root, starting point**
❸ *The lifeboat crew returned to base safely.*
• **headquarters, camp, station, post, depot**

base *VERB*
❶ *She based the story on an event in her own childhood.*
• **found, build, construct, establish, ground**
❷ *The company is based in Wales.*
• **locate, site, situate, position**

basement *NOUN*
Steps led down to the basement.
• **cellar, vault**
– A room underneath a church is a **crypt**.
– An underground cell in a castle is a **dungeon**.

bashful *ADJECTIVE*
He was too bashful to ask for a dance.
• **shy, reserved, timid, diffident**

basic *ADJECTIVE*
❶ *The basic ingredients of bread are flour, yeast and water.*
• **fundamental, essential, main, primary, principal, chief, key, central, crucial**
OPPOSITES secondary, extra
❷ *The campsite has very basic facilities.*
• **plain, simple, minimal, rudimentary, elementary, limited, unsophisticated**
OPPOSITES elaborate, advanced

basically *ADVERB*
Basically, I think you're right.
• **fundamentally, essentially, in essence, at heart, at bottom**

basics *PLURAL NOUN*
That week I learnt the basics of fishing.
• **fundamentals, essentials, first principles, foundations, groundwork**
IDIOM **nuts and bolts**

basin *NOUN*
Fill a basin with soapy water.
• **sink, bowl, dish**

basis *NOUN*
What is the basis of your argument?
• **base, foundation, grounds**

basket *NOUN*
She was carrying a basket of fruit.
– A basket of food is a **hamper**.
– A basket on a bicycle is a **pannier**.
– A small basket of fruit is a **punnet**.

A B C D E F G H I J K L M N O P Q R S T U V W X Y Z

bass *ADJECTIVE*
He sang in a loud, bass voice.
• **low, deep**
OPPOSITES **high-pitched, high**

bat *NOUN*
a heavy, wooden bat
• **club, stick**

batch *NOUN*
She made a fresh batch of pancakes for us.
• **group, quantity, set, lot, bunch, bundle**

bathe *VERB*
❶ *It was too cold to bathe in the sea.*
• **swim, go swimming, take a dip**
– To walk about in shallow water is to **paddle**.
❷ *You should bathe the wound carefully.*
• **clean, wash, rinse, cleanse**

batter *VERB*
Huge waves battered the rocks.
• **beat, pound, thump, pummel, buffet**

battle *NOUN*
❶ *The battle took place a few miles north of the city.*
• **fight, conflict, action, engagement, hostilities, skirmish, armed struggle**
– A place where a battle takes place is a **battlefield, battleground** or **field of battle**.
❷ *The legal battle lasted several years.*
• **argument, dispute, struggle, clash, conflict**

bawl *VERB*
❶ *I heard someone bawl out my name.*
• **shout, cry, yell, roar, bellow, bark** (*informal*) **holler**
❷ *A baby was bawling in the next room.*
• **cry, wail, howl, sob**

bay *NOUN*
The ship was anchored in a sheltered bay.
• **cove, inlet, gulf, sound**

be *VERB*
❶ *I'll be at home all morning.*
• **stay, continue, remain**
❷ *The concert will be in March.*
• **take place, happen, come about, occur**
❸ *She wants to be a famous writer.*
• **become, develop into**

beach *NOUN*
In front of the hotel is a sandy beach.
• **sands, seashore, seaside, shore, strand**

bead *NOUN*
He stopped to wipe beads of sweat from his brow.
• **drop, droplet, drip, blob, pearl**

beam *NOUN*
❶ *Wooden beams ran across the ceiling.*
• **bar, timber, plank, post, joist, rafter, boom, spar, strut, support**
❷ *A beam of sunlight entered the cave.*
• **ray, shaft, stream, streak, gleam**
❸ *A huge beam spread across her face.*
• **smile, grin**

beam *VERB*
❶ *In the photo, we are all beaming at the camera.*
• **smile, grin**
❷ *The satellite will beam a signal back to Earth.*
• **transmit, send out, broadcast, emit**

bear *VERB*
❶ *The rope won't bear my weight.*
• **support, hold, take, sustain**
❷ *A messenger arrived, bearing news.*
• **carry, bring, convey, transport, take, transfer**
❸ *The gravestone bears an old inscription.*
• **display, show, exhibit, carry, have**
❹ *I can't bear all this noise.*
• **endure, tolerate, put up with, stand, withstand, cope with, abide, stomach**
❺ *Queen Victoria bore nine children.*
• **give birth to, have, produce**
❻ *Several trees in the garden bear fruit.*
• **produce, yield, give, supply**

➤ **bear out**
This bears out everything I said.
• **confirm, support, substantiate, corroborate, back up**
➤ **bear with**
Please bear with me a little longer.
• **be patient with, put up with, tolerate**

bearable *ADJECTIVE*
The pain was only just bearable.
• **tolerable, endurable, acceptable**
OPPOSITE unbearable

bearings *PLURAL NOUN*
We lost our bearings in the fog.
• **sense of direction, orientation, position, whereabouts**

beast *NOUN*
They could hear the roars of wild beasts.
• **animal, creature, brute**

beat *VERB*
1 *The man was beating a dog with a stick.*
• **hit, strike, thrash, thump, batter, whip, lash, flog, lay into, rain blows on**
(*informal*) **whack, wallop**
2 *Spain beat Germany in the final.*
• **defeat, conquer, win against, vanquish, get the better of, overcome, overwhelm, rout, trounce, thrash**
(*informal*) **hammer, lick**
3 *Beat the eggs, milk and sugar together.*
• **whisk, whip, blend, mix, stir**
4 *Her heart was beating with excitement.*
• **pound, thump, palpitate**
➤ **beat someone up**
They threatened to beat us up.
• **assault, attack**
(*informal*) **rough up**

beat *NOUN*
1 *Can you feel the beat of your heart?*
• **pulse, throb, palpitation, pounding, thumping**
2 *The music has a strong beat.*
• **rhythm, accent, stress**

beautiful *ADJECTIVE*

OVERUSED WORD

1 **A beautiful person:**

➤ **attractive**	➤ **elegant**
➤ **good-looking**	➤ **enchanting**
➤ **pretty**	➤ **dazzling**
➤ **gorgeous**	➤ **stunning**
➤ **glamorous**	➤ **magnificent**
➤ **radiant**	➤ **resplendent**

(*Scottish*) **bonny**

The queen looked **radiant** *in a red silk gown.*

– A man who is pleasing to look at is **good-looking** or **handsome.**

OPPOSITES ugly, unattractive

2 **A beautiful day, beautiful weather:**

➤ **fine**	➤ **sunny**
➤ **excellent**	➤ **superb**
➤ **glorious**	➤ **splendid**
➤ **marvellous**	➤ **wonderful**

We are hoping for **fine** *weather tomorrow.*

OPPOSITES dull, gloomy, drab

3 **A beautiful sight, beautiful view:**

➤ **picturesque**	➤ **splendid**
➤ **scenic**	➤ **glorious**
➤ **charming**	➤ **magnificent**
➤ **delightful**	➤ **spectacular**

I chose a postcard with a **scenic** *view of the Alps.*

4 **A beautiful sound, beautiful voice:**

➤ **harmonious**	➤ **melodious**
➤ **mellifluous**	➤ **sweet-sounding**

The nightingale has a **sweet-sounding** *song.*

OPPOSITES grating, harsh

beauty *NOUN*
The film star was famous for her beauty.
• **attractiveness, prettiness, loveliness,**

A B C D E F G H I J K L M N O P Q R S T U V W X Y Z

charm, allure, magnificence, radiance, splendour
OPPOSITE ugliness

because *CONJUNCTION*
I came here because I was invited.
• since, as, seeing that, in view of the fact that
➤ **because of**
Play was stopped because of bad light.
• as a result of, on account of, thanks to, owing to, due to, by virtue of

beckon *VERB*
The old man beckoned me to come forward.
• gesture, signal, motion, wave, gesticulate

become *VERB*
❶ *Women's football is becoming more popular.*
• begin to be, turn, get
❷ *Eventually, the tadpoles will become frogs.*
• grow into, change into, develop into, turn into
❸ *Short hair really becomes you.*
• suit, flatter, look good on
➤ **become of**
Whatever became of your plan to go abroad?
• happen to, come of

bed *NOUN*
❶ *The room has a double bed.*
• bunk, mattress
– A bed for a baby is a **cot**, **cradle** or **crib**.
– A bed on a ship or train is a **berth**.
❷ *We planted daffodils in the flower bed.*
• plot, patch, border
❸ *These creatures feed on the bed of the ocean.*
• bottom, floor
OPPOSITE surface
➤ **go to bed**
Is it time to go to bed yet?
• retire, turn in
IDIOM (*informal*) hit the sack

bedraggled *ADJECTIVE*
We carried the wet and bedraggled kitten into the house.
• dishevelled, disordered, untidy, unkempt, scruffy
OPPOSITES smart, spruce

bee *NOUN*

WORD WEB

Some types of bee:

➤ bumblebee
➤ drone
➤ honeybee
➤ queen
➤ worker

- A young bee after it hatches is a **larva**.
- A group of bees is a **swarm** or a **colony**.
- A place where bees live is a **hive**.
- A person who keeps bees is an **apiarist**.

before *ADVERB*
❶ *Those people were before us in the queue.*
• in front of, ahead of, in advance of
OPPOSITES after, behind
❷ *Please switch off the lights before you leave.*
• prior to, previous to, earlier than, preparatory to
OPPOSITE after
❸ *Have you seen this film before?*
• previously, in the past, earlier, sooner
OPPOSITE later

beg *VERB*
❶ *The prisoners begged for mercy.*
• ask, plead, call
❷ *They begged her not to leave.*
• implore, plead with, entreat, beseech, appeal to

begin *VERB*
❶ *The builders began work yesterday.*
• start, commence, embark on, set about
OPPOSITES end, finish, conclude
❷ *When did the trouble begin?*
• appear, arise, emerge, originate, start,

commence, spring up
OPPOSITES end, stop, cease

beginner *NOUN*
This swimming class is for beginners.
• **learner, starter, novice**
(*informal*) **rookie**
– A beginner in a trade or a job is an **apprentice** or **trainee**.
– A beginner in the police or armed services is a **cadet** or **recruit**.

beginning *NOUN*
❶ *I missed the beginning of the film.*
• **start, opening, commencement, introduction, preamble**
– A piece of writing at the beginning of a book is an **introduction, preface** or **prologue**.
– A piece of music at the beginning of a musical or opera is a **prelude** or **overture**.
OPPOSITES end, conclusion
❷ *The programme is about the beginning of life on Earth.*
• **starting point, origin, inception, genesis, onset, establishment, foundation, emergence, birth, launch, dawn**

behave *VERB*
❶ *Our neighbour is behaving very oddly.*
• **act, conduct yourself, react, perform**
❷ *My little brother promised to behave.*
• **be good, be on your best behaviour, behave yourself**
OPPOSITE misbehave

behaviour *NOUN*
I apologize for my behaviour yesterday.
• **conduct, manners, actions, performance**

being *NOUN*
They looked like beings from another planet.
• **creature, individual, person, entity**

belch *VERB*
The chimney belched clouds of black smoke.
• **discharge, emit, give out, send out, gush, spew**

belief *NOUN*
❶ *She is a woman of strong religious beliefs.*
• **faith, principle, creed, doctrine**
❷ *It is my belief is that he stole the money.*
• **opinion, view, conviction, feeling, notion, theory**

believable *ADJECTIVE*
Few of the characters in the book are believable.
• **credible, plausible**
OPPOSITES unbelievable, implausible

believe *VERB*
❶ *I don't believe anything he says.*
• **accept, have faith in, have confidence in, rely on, trust**
OPPOSITES disbelieve, doubt
❷ *I believe you know my parents.*
• **think, understand, assume, presume, gather**
(*informal*) **reckon**

bell *NOUN*
I can hear the bell.
• **chime, alarm, carillon, knell, peal**

WORD WEB

Words for how a bell sounds:

➤ **chime**	➤ **peal**
➤ **clang**	➤ **ring**
➤ **jangle**	➤ **tinkle**
➤ **jingle**	➤ **toll**

bellow *VERB*
He started to bellow out orders.
• **shout, roar, bawl, yell, bark, boom, thunder**

belong *VERB*
❶ *This ring belonged to my grandmother.*
• **be owned by, be the property of, be in the hands of**
❷ *Do you belong to a sports club?*
• **be a member of, be in, be associated with**

❸ *I never felt that I really belonged in my old school.*
• **fit in, be suited to, feel welcome, be at home**

belongings *PLURAL NOUN*
Put any personal belongings in a locker.
• **possessions, property, goods, things, effects, bits and pieces**
(*informal*) **gear, stuff**

beloved *ADJECTIVE*
She finally returned to her beloved homeland.
• **much loved, adored, dear, darling, cherished, treasured, precious**
OPPOSITE hated

below *PREPOSITION*
❶ *Fish were swimming just below the surface.*
• **under, underneath, beneath**
OPPOSITE above
❷ *The temperature never fell below 20 degrees.*
• **less than, lower than**
OPPOSITES above, over

belt *NOUN*
❶ *He wore a black leather belt.*
• **girdle, sash, strap, band**
– A broad sash worn round the waist is a **cummerbund**.
❷ *We drove through a belt of thick fog.*
• **band, strip, line, stretch, zone, area**

bench *NOUN*
We sat on a bench in the park.
• **seat, form**
(*North American*) **bleacher**
– A long seat in a church is a **pew**.

bend *VERB*
❶ *The fire had bent the railings out of shape.*
• **curve, curl, coil, loop, hook, twist, crook, angle, flex, arch, warp**
– Things which bend easily are **flexible** or **pliable**.
OPPOSITE straighten
❷ *I bent down to tie my shoelaces.*
• **stoop, bow, crouch, lean over**
❸ *Just ahead the road bends to the right.*
• **turn, swing, veer, wind**

bend *NOUN*
We came to a sharp bend in the road.
• **curve, turn, angle, corner, twist, kink**

beneath *PREPOSITION*
She was sitting beneath a cherry tree.
• **under, underneath, below, at the foot of**
OPPOSITES above, on top of

beneficial *ADJECTIVE*
Eating fruit is beneficial to health.
• **favourable, advantageous, helpful, useful, valuable, salutary**
OPPOSITES harmful, detrimental

benefit *NOUN*
She always talks about the benefits of regular exercise.
• **advantage, reward, gain, good point, blessing, boon**
(*informal*) **perk**
OPPOSITES disadvantage, drawback

benefit *VERB*
The rainy weather will benefit gardeners.
• **be good for, be of service to, help, aid, assist, serve, profit**
OPPOSITES hinder, harm

benevolent *ADJECTIVE*
She greeted everyone with a benevolent smile.
• **kind, kindly, friendly, warm-hearted, kind-hearted, good-natured, sympathetic, charitable, caring, benign**
OPPOSITES malevolent, unkind

benign *ADJECTIVE*
❶ *There was a benign expression on her face.*
• **kindly, friendly, kind-hearted, good-natured, genial, sympathetic, well-disposed, benevolent**
OPPOSITES unfriendly, hostile
❷ *The island has a benign climate.*
• **mild, temperate, balmy, favourable**
OPPOSITE hostile

bent *ADJECTIVE*
❶ *After the crash, the car was a mass of bent metal.*
• **curved, twisted, coiled, looped, buckled, crooked, warped, misshapen, out of shape, deformed, contorted**
OPPOSITE straight
❷ *The old man had a bent back and walked with a stick.*
• **crooked, hunched, curved, arched, bowed**
OPPOSITE straight
➤ **bent on**
Are you still bent on going?
• **intent on, determined on, set on**

bent *NOUN*
She has a definite artistic bent.
• **talent, gift, flair, aptitude, inclination**

berserk *ADJECTIVE*
➤ **go berserk**
The crowd went berserk when the band appeared.
• **go mad, go crazy, go wild**
IDIOMS (*informal*) **go off your head, go bananas, freak out**

beside *PREPOSITION*
They sat beside each other on the bus.
• **next to, alongside, abreast of, adjacent to, next door to, close to, near, by**
➤ **beside the point**
The fact that I'm a girl is beside the point.
• **irrelevant, unimportant, neither here nor there**

besides *PREPOSITION*
No one knows the password, besides you and me.
• **as well as, in addition to, apart from, other than, aside from**

besides *ADVERB*
Besides, it's too late to phone now.
• **also, in addition, furthermore, moreover**

besiege *VERB*
❶ *The Greeks besieged the city of Troy for ten years.*
• **blockade, lay siege to**
❷ *Fans besieged the singer after the concert.*
• **surround, mob, harass, plague**

best *ADJECTIVE*
❶ *She is our best player.*
• **finest, foremost, greatest, leading, top, premier, supreme, pre-eminent, outstanding, unequalled, unrivalled, second to none**
(*informal*) **star, top-drawer**
OPPOSITE worst
❷ *I did what I thought was best.*
• **most suitable, most appropriate, most advisable**

best *ADVERB*
Which song did you like best?
• **most, the most**
OPPOSITE least

bestow *VERB*
➤ **bestow on**
The ring is said to bestow power on the wearer.
• **confer on, give to, grant to, present with**

bet *NOUN*
I had a bet that they would win.
• **wager, gamble, stake**
(*informal*) **flutter**

bet *VERB*
❶ *Do you ever bet on the lottery?*
• **wager, gamble, stake**
(*informal*) **have a flutter**
❷ (*informal*) *I bet I'm right.*
• **feel sure, be certain, be convinced, expect, predict**

betray *VERB*
❶ *He was betrayed by one of his own men.*
• **be disloyal to, be unfaithful to, inform on, conspire against, double-cross**
IDIOMS **stab someone in the back, sell someone down the river**
– Someone who betrays you is a **traitor**.
– To betray your country is to commit **treason**.
❷ *Her face betrayed no emotion.*
• **reveal, show, indicate, disclose, divulge, expose, tell**

A B C D E F G H I J K L M N O P Q R S T U V W X Y Z

better *ADJECTIVE*

❶ *This computer is much better than my old one.*
• superior, finer, preferable
IDIOM a cut above
OPPOSITES worse, inferior
❷ *I hope you feel better soon.*
• recovered, cured, healed, well, fitter, stronger
OPPOSITE worse

between *PREPOSITION*

❶ *There is a path between the house and the garden.*
• connecting, joining, linking
❷ *We divided the food between us.*
• among, amongst

beware *VERB*

Beware! There are thieves about.
• be careful, watch out, look out, take care, be on your guard
➤ **beware of**
Beware of the bull.
• watch out for, avoid, mind, heed, keep clear of

bewilder *VERB*

We were bewildered by the directions on the map.
• puzzle, confuse, perplex, mystify, baffle, bemuse
(*informal*) flummox, fox, flabbergast

beyond *PREPOSITION*

The village lies just beyond those hills.
• past, after, behind, the other side of, further away than
OPPOSITES in front of, before

bias *NOUN*

Does the author show signs of bias?
• prejudice, partiality, one-sidedness, favouritism, discrimination, unfairness, imbalance
OPPOSITE impartiality

biased *ADJECTIVE*

The referee was clearly biased.
• prejudiced, partial, one-sided, partisan, discriminatory, bigoted, unbalanced
OPPOSITE impartial

bicycle *NOUN*

There is a rack outside for parking bicycles.
• push bike
(*informal*) bike
– A person who rides a bicycle is a **cyclist**.

WORD WEB

Types of bicycle:

➤ BMX bike
➤ mountain bike
➤ racing bicycle
➤ reclining or recumbent bicycle
➤ road bicycle
➤ tandem
➤ trailer bike
➤ touring bicycle
➤ track bicycle
➤ (*historical*) penny-farthing

- A cycle with one wheel is a **unicycle**.
- A cycle with three wheels is a **tricycle** or (*informal*) **trike**.
- A cycle without pedals is a **scooter**.
- An arena for track cycling is a **velodrome**.

bid *NOUN*

❶ *The painting attracted bids of thousands of dollars.*
• offer, tender, proposal
❷ *His bid to beat the world record failed.*
• attempt, effort, try, go, endeavour

bid *VERB*

Someone bid $2 million for the painting.
• offer, tender, propose, put up

big *ADJECTIVE*

OVERUSED WORD

❶ **Big in size, scale:**

➤ large
➤ huge
➤ great
➤ massive
➤ immense
➤ enormous
➤ gigantic
➤ giant
➤ colossal
➤ mammoth
➤ monstrous
➤ monumental
➤ titanic

(*informal*) whopping, mega

(*literary*) gargantuan

Our class made a giant *model of a human ear.*

OPPOSITES small, little, tiny

❷ Big in area, distance:

- vast
- immense
- expansive
- considerable
- sweeping

Some day spaceships will be able to travel vast *distances.*

❸ Big inside:

- spacious
- roomy
- capacious
- extensive
- sizeable
- palatial
- cavernous

Inside, the car is surprisingly roomy.

OPPOSITES cramped, confined, poky

❹ Big and heavy, awkward:

- bulky
- cumbersome
- weighty
- hefty

What could be inside that bulky *envelope?*

❺ Big and strong, tall:

- well built
- hulking
- hefty
- strapping
- burly
- beefy
- brawny
- sturdy
- mighty
- towering
- mountainous
- giant

His strapping *physique is perfect for an action hero.*

❻ A big part, big portion:

- ample
- considerable
- substantial
- sizeable
- generous
- lavish
- bumper

Each character gets an ample *share of the treasure.*

OPPOSITES meagre, paltry

❼ A big decision, big moment:

- important
- serious
- grave
- weighty
- significant
- key
- momentous
- historic
- far-reaching
- crucial
- vital
- major

This year's final promises to be a momentous *occasion.*

OPPOSITES insignificant, minor

bill *NOUN*

❶ *Please send us the bill by email.*
• account, invoice, statement, charges
❷ *The first act on the bill was a comedian.*
• programme, line-up

billow *VERB*

❶ *Smoke was billowing from the chimney.*
• pour, swirl, spiral, roll
❷ *The huge sail billowed in the wind.*
• swell, fill out, puff out, bulge, balloon

bind *VERB*

❶ *We bound the sticks together with some rope.*
• tie, fasten, secure, join, clamp, lash
❷ *The leaves can be used to bind wounds.*
• bandage, wrap, strap up
OPPOSITES untie, unwrap
❸ *They were bound by ties of friendship.*
• unite, connect, join, attach
OPPOSITE separate

bird *NOUN*

WORD WEB

Some common british birds:

- blackbird
- blue tit
- bullfinch
- bunting
- chaffinch
- crow
- cuckoo
- dove
- finch
- great tit
- greenfinch
- jackdaw
- jay
- linnet

- magpie
- martin
- nightingale
- pigeon
- raven
- robin
- rook
- skylark
- sparrow
- starling
- swallow
- swift
- thrush
- wagtail
- woodpecker
- wren

Birds of prey:

- buzzard
- eagle
- falcon
- hawk
- kestrel
- kite
- merlin
- osprey
- owl
- sparrowhawk
- vulture

Farm and game birds:

- chicken
- duck
- goose
- grouse
- guinea fowl
- partridge
- pheasant
- quail
- turkey

- Birds kept by farmers are called **poultry**.

Sea-birds and water birds:

- albatross
- auk
- bittern
- coot
- cormorant
- crane
- curlew
- duck
- gannet
- goose
- guillemot
- gull
- heron
- kingfisher
- kittiwake
- lapwing
- mallard
- moorhen
- oystercatcher
- peewit
- pelican
- penguin
- puffin
- seagull
- snipe
- stork
- swan
- teal

Birds from other countries:

- bird of paradise
- budgerigar
- canary
- cockatoo
- flamingo
- humming bird
- ibis
- kookaburra
- macaw
- mynah bird
- parakeet
- parrot
- peacock or peafowl
- toucan

Birds which cannot fly:

- emu
- kiwi
- ostrich
- penguin

- A female bird is a **hen** and a male bird is a **cock**.
- A young bird is a **chick**, **fledgling** or **nestling** and a family of chicks is a **brood**.
- A group of birds is a **colony** or **flock** and a group of flying birds is a **flight** or **skein**.
- The scientific study of birds is **ornithology**.
- A person who observes birds in their natural habitat is a **birdwatcher**.

WRITING TIPS

DESCRIBING BIRDS
Body parts:

- beak
- bill
- breast
- claw
- comb
- crest
- crop
- feathers
- plumage
- tail
- talon
- wattle
- wing

Plumage:

- bedraggled
- downy
- drab
- feathery
- fluffy
- ruffled
- speckled
- spotted

Movement:

- circle
- dart
- flap
- flit
- flutter
- fly
- glide
- perch
- soar
- swoop
- waddle
- wheel

Sounds:

- caw
- chirp

- ➤ cluck
- ➤ coo
- ➤ gabble
- ➤ honk
- ➤ hoot
- ➤ quack
- ➤ screech
- ➤ squawk
- ➤ trill
- ➤ twitter
- ➤ warble

bit *NOUN*

OVERUSED WORD

❶ A bit of a whole:

- ➤ piece
- ➤ part
- ➤ section
- ➤ portion
- ➤ fraction
- ➤ share
- ➤ segment
- ➤ slice

The first **section** *of the film is shot in black and white.*

❷ A large, heavy bit:

- ➤ chunk
- ➤ lump
- ➤ hunk
- ➤ wedge
- ➤ slab
- ➤ brick

Saturn's rings are made of **lumps** *of ice and rock.*

❸ A small bit:

- ➤ fragment
- ➤ scrap
- ➤ shaving
- ➤ shred
- ➤ sliver
- ➤ snippet
- ➤ chip
- ➤ speck
- ➤ spot
- ➤ particle
- ➤ atom
- ➤ mite
- ➤ jot
- ➤ modicum
- ➤ pinch
- ➤ touch
- ➤ dab
- ➤ daub
- ➤ trace
- ➤ hint
- ➤ suggestion

(*informal*) **smidgen, tad**

The map was drawn on a **scrap** *of old paper.*

❹ A bit of food:

- ➤ morsel
- ➤ crumb
- ➤ bite
- ➤ nibble
- ➤ taste
- ➤ mouthful
- ➤ soupçon

We ate every last **morsel** *of breakfast.*

❺ A bit of liquid:

- ➤ drop
- ➤ dash
- ➤ dribble
- ➤ drizzle
- ➤ dollop
- ➤ blob
- ➤ splash

(*informal*) **swig**

Add a **dash** *of lemon juice to the sauce.*

❻ A bit:

- ➤ slightly
- ➤ rather
- ➤ fairly
- ➤ somewhat
- ➤ quite
- ➤ vaguely
- ➤ faintly
- ➤ a little
- ➤ a shade

I found the whole evening **slightly** *dull.*

❼ To bits:

- ➤ to pieces

(*informal*) **to smithereens**

The raft will surely be pounded **to pieces.**

bite *VERB*

❶ *I bit a chunk out of my apple.*
• **munch, nibble, chew, crunch, gnaw**
(*informal*) **chomp**
❷ *I've been bitten all over by midges.*
• **nip, pinch, sting, pierce, wound, snap at**
– A fierce animal **mauls** or **savages** its prey.

bite *NOUN*

❶ *Can I have a bite of your sandwich?*
• **mouthful, nibble, taste, morsel**
❷ *She was covered in mosquito bites.*
• **nip, sting, wound**

biting *ADJECTIVE*

❶ *There was a biting wind outside.*
• **freezing, bitter, piercing, raw, wintry, icy**
(*informal*) **perishing**
❷ *He faced biting criticism.*
• **sharp, critical, scathing, cutting, savage, caustic**

A B C D E F G H I J K L M N O P Q R S T U V W X Y Z

bitter *ADJECTIVE*
❶ *The medicine has a bitter taste.*
• **sour, sharp, acid, acrid, tart**
OPPOSITE sweet
❷ *I still feel bitter about what happened.*
• **resentful, embittered, disgruntled, aggrieved**
OPPOSITE contented
❸ *The decision was a bitter disappointment.*
• **upsetting, hurtful, distressing, cruel**
OPPOSITES mild, slight
❹ *A bitter wind was blowing in from the sea.*
• **freezing, biting, piercing, raw, wintry, icy**
(*informal*) **perishing**

bizarre *ADJECTIVE*
It was a bizarre coincidence.
• **strange, odd, peculiar, weird, uncanny, extraordinary, outlandish**
(*informal*) **freaky**

black *ADJECTIVE*
❶ *The horse had a shiny black coat.*
• **jet-black, pitch-black, ebony, inky, raven, charcoal, sooty**
For tips on describing colours see **colour**.
❷ *He arrived in a black mood.*
• **bad-tempered, ill-humoured, angry, foul**
OPPOSITES bright, cheerful

blame *VERB*
Nobody blames you for what happened.
• **hold responsible, accuse, condemn, reproach, scold**
➤ **to blame**
Who do you think was most to blame?
• **responsible, culpable, guilty, at fault, in the wrong**

blame *NOUN*
They were cleared of all blame for the accident.
• **responsibility, culpability, guilt, fault**

bland *ADJECTIVE*
❶ *The cheese has a bland flavour.*
• **mild, weak, insipid, flavourless, tasteless**
OPPOSITES strong, pungent
❷ *He has a bland style of writing.*
• **dull, uninteresting, unexciting, lacklustre, monotonous, boring**
(*informal*) **wishy-washy**
OPPOSITES exciting, thrilling

blank *ADJECTIVE*
❶ *On the desk was a blank sheet of paper.*
• **empty, bare, clean, plain, unmarked, unused**
❷ *The assistant at the counter gave me a blank look.*
• **expressionless, vacant, stony, impassive, deadpan**

blank *NOUN*
Fill in the blanks to complete the sentence.
• **space, break, gap**

blanket *NOUN*
❶ *The baby was wrapped in a woollen blanket.*
• **cover, sheet, quilt, rug, throw**
❷ *A blanket of snow covered the ground.*
• **covering, layer, film, sheet, carpet, mantle**

blast *NOUN*
❶ *A blast of cold air came through the door.*
• **gust, rush, draught, burst**
❷ *The referee gave a long blast on his whistle.*
• **blare, honk, toot, peep**
❸ *Several people were injured in the blast.*
• **explosion, detonation, shock**

blast *VERB*
❶ *Dynamite was used to blast through the rock.*
• **explode, blow up, burst**
❷ *Music was blasting out of the speakers.*
• **blare, boom**

blatant *ADJECTIVE*
It was a blatant lie.
• **obvious, flagrant, glaring, shameless, barefaced, brazen, unabashed**

blaze *NOUN*
❶ *Firefighters fought the blaze for hours.*
• **fire, flames, inferno**
❷ *She was dazzled by the sudden blaze of light.*
• **glare, burst, flare, flash**

blaze *VERB*
❶ *Soon the campfire was blazing.*
• **burn, flare up, be alight, be in flames**
❷ *Lights blazed from the top floor.*
• **shine, beam, flare, flash, gleam**

bleach *VERB*
In the old days, linen was bleached in the sun.
• **turn white, whiten, blanch, make pale**

bleak *ADJECTIVE*
❶ *Ahead was a bleak mountainside.*
• **bare, barren, desolate, empty, exposed, stark**
❷ *The future looks bleak for the club.*
• **gloomy, hopeless, depressing, dismal, grim, miserable**
OPPOSITES bright, promising

blemish *NOUN*
This peach has a slight blemish on the skin.
• **flaw, defect, imperfection, mark, spot, stain**

blend *VERB*
❶ *Blend the ingredients together.*
• **mix, combine, stir, whisk**
❷ *The colours blend well with each other.*
• **go together, match, fit, be compatible, harmonize, coordinate**
OPPOSITE clash

blend *NOUN*
The book is a blend of action, history and horror.
• **mixture, mix, combination, compound, amalgam, fusion**

blessing *NOUN*
❶ *The author has given the film her blessing.*
• **approval, backing, support, consent, permission**
OPPOSITE disapproval
❷ *Having an open fire is a blessing in the winter.*
• **benefit, advantage, asset, plus, bonus, boon, godsend**
OPPOSITES curse, evil

blew
past tense see **blow**

blight *NOUN*
That tower block is a blight on the landscape.
• **curse, affliction, nuisance, menace, plague**
OPPOSITES blessing, boon

blight *VERB*
Knee injuries have blighted his career.
• **afflict, plague, menace, curse, ruin, spoil, mar**

blind *ADJECTIVE*
Polar bear cubs are born blind.
• **sightless, unsighted, unseeing, visually impaired**
OPPOSITES sighted, seeing
➤ **blind to**
They remained blind to the danger around them.
• **ignorant of, unaware of, oblivious to, indifferent to, heedless of**
OPPOSITES aware of, mindful of

bliss *NOUN*
The poem is about the sheer bliss of being in love.
• **joy, delight, pleasure, happiness, heaven, ecstasy**
OPPOSITE misery

blissful *ADJECTIVE*
We have enjoyed a blissful week of sunshine.
• **joyful, delightful, pleasurable, heavenly, ecstatic**
OPPOSITE miserable

blob *NOUN*
There was a blob of glue on the table.
• **drop, lump, spot, dollop, daub, globule**

block *NOUN*
❶ *A block of ice fell from the glacier.*
• **chunk, hunk, lump, piece, wedge, slab, brick**

❷ *There must be a block in the drainpipe.*
• **blockage, jam, obstacle, obstruction, impediment**

block *VERB*
❶ *A mass of leaves had blocked the drain.*
• **clog, choke, jam, plug, stop up, congest**
(*informal*) **bung up**
OPPOSITE **clear**
❷ *The new building will block our view.*
• **obstruct, interfere with, hamper, hinder, impede**

blockage *NOUN*
The main pipe has a blockage.
• **block, jam, obstruction, congestion**

blond or **blonde** *ADJECTIVE*
She was wearing a blonde wig.
• **fair-haired, fair, golden, flaxen**
OPPOSITE **dark**

blood *NOUN*
Do you have any Spanish blood?
• **ancestry, family, lineage, roots, descent, parentage**

bloodshed *NOUN*
In ancient times, this was a scene of bloodshed.
• **killing, massacre, slaughter, butchery, carnage**

bloodthirsty *ADJECTIVE*
Outside we could hear the bloodthirsty cries of an angry mob.
• **murderous, vicious, barbaric, savage, brutal**

bloody *ADJECTIVE*
❶ *He handed back the bloody handkerchief.*
• **bloodstained, blood-soaked, gory**
❷ *It was the bloodiest battle of the war.*
• **gory, bloodthirsty, brutal, barbaric, savage, murderous**

bloom *NOUN*
The pear tree was covered in white blooms.
• **flower, blossom, bud**

bloom *VERB*
❶ *The daffodils bloomed early this year.*
• **blossom, flower, open**
OPPOSITES **fade, wither**
❷ *New ideas began to bloom.*
• **develop, grow, flourish, thrive, burgeon**

blossom *NOUN*
I love to see the cherry blossom in spring.
• **blooms, buds, flowers**

blossom *VERB*
❶ *The seeds we've sown will blossom next year.*
• **bloom, flower, open**
OPPOSITES **fade, wither**
❷ *She has blossomed into a fine young actress.*
• **develop, grow, mature, progress, evolve**

blot *NOUN*
The page was covered with ink blots.
• **spot, blotch, mark, blob, splodge, smudge, smear, stain**

blot *VERB*
➤ **blot out**
A huge dark cloud blotted out the sun.
• **block out, hide, mask, conceal, obscure, obliterate**

blotch *NOUN*
There were damp blotches on the walls.
• **patch, blot, spot, mark, blob, splodge, splash, stain**

blow *VERB*
❶ *The wind was blowing from the east.*
• **blast, gust, bluster, puff, fan**
❷ *Leaves were blowing across the road.*
• **drift, flutter, waft, float, glide, whirl, swirl**
❸ *The wind nearly blew my hat off.*
• **sweep, force, drive, carry, toss**
❹ *Cars blew their horns.*
• **sound, play, blast, honk, hoot**
➤ **blow out**
I blew out all the candles on the cake.
• **extinguish, put out, snuff**
➤ **blow something up**
❶ *I need to blow up the tyres on my bike.*
• **inflate, pump up, swell, fill out, expand**

❷ *A small group of soldiers were sent to blow up the bridge.*
• **blast, bomb, destroy**
❸ *Do you think you could blow up this photograph?*
• **enlarge, magnify**

blow *NOUN*
❶ *He received a painful blow on the head.*
• **knock, bang, bash, hit, punch, clout, slap, smack, swipe, thump**
(*informal*) **wallop, whack**
❷ *Losing the match was a terrible blow.*
• **shock, upset, setback, disappointment, catastrophe, misfortune, disaster, calamity**

blue *ADJECTIVE & NOUN*

WORD WEB

Some shades of blue:

➤ aquamarine
➤ azure
➤ baby blue
➤ cobalt
➤ cyan
➤ indigo
➤ lapis
➤ navy
➤ sapphire
➤ sky blue
➤ turquoise
➤ ultramarine

For tips on describing colours see **colour**.

bluff *VERB*
He tried to bluff his way through the interview.
• **deceive, trick, fake, fool, hoodwink**
(*informal*) **con, kid**

blunder *NOUN*
I spotted a few blunders in the spelling.
• **mistake, error, fault, slip, slip-up, gaffe, faux pas**
(*informal*) **howler**

blunder *VERB*
❶ *The goalkeeper blundered again and let in a second goal.*
• **make a mistake, err, miscalculate, slip up**
❷ *I could hear someone blundering about in the dark.*
• **stumble, stagger, founder, lurch**

blunt *ADJECTIVE*
❶ *I had to use a blunt pencil.*
• **dull, worn, unsharpened**
OPPOSITES sharp, pointed
❷ *Her reply to my question was very blunt.*
• **abrupt, frank, candid, plain-spoken, direct, brusque, curt**

blur *VERB*
The steam had blurred her glasses.
• **cloud, fog, obscure, dim, smudge**
OPPOSITES sharpen, focus

blurred *ADJECTIVE*
The old photo was blurred at the edges.
• **indistinct, hazy, fuzzy, unclear, vague, out of focus**
OPPOSITES sharp, clear

blush *VERB*
He felt his face start to blush.
• **flush, redden, go red, colour, burn**

blustery *ADJECTIVE*
It was a blustery day in autumn.
• **gusty, windy, blowy, stormy, squally, wild**
OPPOSITES calm, still

board *NOUN*
❶ *The table top was made from a wooden board.*
• **plank, panel, beam, timber**
❷ *The board of directors meet every month.*
• **committee, panel, council**

board *VERB*
Passengers may now board the aircraft.
• **get on, go on board, enter, embark**

boast *VERB*
❶ *My father never boasted about his success.*
• **brag, show off, crow, gloat, swagger**
IDIOM **blow your own trumpet**
❷ *The film boasts an impressive cast.*
• **feature, possess, have, enjoy**

boastful *ADJECTIVE*
I tried not to sound too boastful.
• **arrogant, big-headed, conceited, vain, bumptious**

(*informal*) cocky, big-mouted, full of oneself, swanky
OPPOSITES modest, humble

boat *NOUN*
Several fishing boats were moored in the harbour.
• ship, craft, vessel

WORD WEB

Some types of boat or ship:

- barge
- canoe
- catamaran
- cruise liner
- dhow
- dinghy
- dugout
- ferry
- freighter
- gondola
- hovercraft
- hydrofoil
- junk
- kayak
- launch
- lifeboat
- motor boat
- oil tanker
- punt
- raft
- rowing boat
- schooner
- skiff
- speedboat
- steamship
- tanker
- trawler
- tug
- yacht

Military boats or ships:

- aircraft carrier
- battleship
- destroyer
- frigate
- gunboat
- minesweeper
- submarine
- warship

Some boats used in the past:

- brigantine
- clipper
- coracle
- cutter
- galleon
- galley
- man-of-war
- paddle steamer
- schooner
- trireme
- windjammer

Parts of a boat or ship:

- boom
- bridge
- bulwark
- cabin
- crow's nest
- deck
- engine room
- fo'c'sle or forecastle
- funnel
- galley
- helm
- hull
- keel
- mast
- poop
- porthole
- propeller
- quarterdeck
- rigging
- rudder
- sail
- tiller

- The front part of a boat is the **bow** or **prow** and the back part is the **stern.**
- The left-hand side of a boat when you are facing forward is called **port** and the right-hand side is called **starboard.**

bob *VERB*
Little boats bobbed up and down in the water.
• bounce, toss, dance, wobble, jiggle

body *NOUN*

WORD WEB

Outer parts of the human body:

- abdomen
- ankle
- arm
- armpit
- breast
- buttocks
- calf
- cheek
- chest
- chin
- ear
- elbow
- eye
- finger
- foot
- forehead
- genitals
- groin
- hand
- head
- heel
- hip
- instep
- jaw
- knee
- kneecap
- knuckle
- leg
- lip
- mouth
- navel
- neck
- nipple
- nose
- pores
- shin
- shoulder
- skin
- stomach
- temple
- thigh
- throat
- waist
- wrist

Inner parts of the human body:

- arteries
- bladder
- bowels
- brain
- eardrum
- glands

- gullet
- gums
- guts
- heart
- intestines
- kidneys
- larynx
- liver
- lungs
- muscles
- nerves
- ovaries
- pancreas
- prostate
- sinews
- stomach
- tendons
- tongue
- tonsils
- tooth
- uterus
- veins
- windpipe
- womb

- The study of the human body is **anatomy**.
- The main part of your body except your head, arms and legs is your **trunk** or **torso**.
- The shape of your body is your **build**, **figure** or **physique**.
- The dead body of a person is a **corpse** and the dead body of an animal is a **carcass**.

W WRITING TIPS

DESCRIBING PEOPLE'S BODIES

Big or strong:

- athletic
- beefy
- brawny
- bulky
- burly
- hefty
- hulking
- muscular
- sinewy
- statuesque
- tall
- wiry

Overweight:

- chubby
- corpulent
- dumpy
- fat
- flabby
- heavyset
- obese
- plump
- podgy
- portly
- rotund
- round
- stocky
- stout
- tubby
- well-rounded

Small or thin:

- bony
- diminutive
- gangling or gangly
- gaunt
- lanky
- lean
- petite
- puny
- scraggy
- scrawny
- short
- skeletal
- skinny
- slender
- slight
- spindly
- squat
- svelte
- thin
- trim
- weedy
- willowy

bog *NOUN*

We felt out boots sinking into the bog.

• **swamp, marsh, mire, quagmire, wetland, fen**

bogus *ADJECTIVE*

The man had given a bogus address.

• **fake, false, spurious, fraudulent, counterfeit, sham**
(*informal*) **phoney**

OPPOSITES genuine, authentic

boil *VERB*

Let the water boil before you add the pasta.

• **bubble, simmer, seethe, steam**

boisterous *ADJECTIVE*

A group of boisterous children were playing on the beach.

• **lively, high-spirited, noisy, rowdy, unruly, wild, exuberant, uproarious, riotous**

OPPOSITES restrained, calm

bold *ADJECTIVE*

❶ *It was a bold move to attack with such a small army.*

• **brave, courageous, daring, heroic, adventurous, audacious, fearless, dauntless, valiant, intrepid, plucky, daredevil**

OPPOSITES timid, cowardly

❷ *The picture is painted in bold colours.*

• **striking, strong, vivid, bright, eye-catching, prominent, showy, loud, gaudy, garish**

OPPOSITES pale, subtle

A B C D E F G H I J K L M N O P Q R S T U V W X Y Z

bolt *NOUN*

The fence panels were held together with metal bolts.

• **pin, bar, peg, rivet**

bolt *VERB*

❶ *Did you remember to bolt the door?*

• **fasten, bar, latch, lock, secure**

❷ *He saw us coming and bolted out of the shop.*

• **run away, dash away, flee, fly, rush off, dart off, escape**

❸ *I just had time to bolt down a sandwich.*

• **gobble, gulp, guzzle, wolf down** (*informal*) **scoff**

bombard *VERB*

❶ *Enemy ships bombarded the harbour.*

• **shell, pound, bomb, blast, blitz**

❷ *When she finished speaking she was bombarded with questions.*

• **overwhelm, besiege, inundate, swamp, flood, snow under**

bond *NOUN*

❶ *There is a special bond between our countries.*

• **relationship, association, connection, tie, link**

❷ *The prisoner tried to escape from his bonds.*

• **rope, restraint, chain, fetter, shackle**

bone *NOUN*

WORD WEB

Some bones in the human body:

- backbone or spine
- collarbone
- cranium or skull
- pelvis
- ribs
- shoulder blade
- vertebrae

- The bones of your body are your **skeleton**.

bonus *NOUN*

❶ *Every member of staff received a Christmas bonus.*

• **handout, supplement, reward, gratuity, tip**

❷ *The climate here is certainly a bonus.*

• **advantage, benefit, strong point, plus, blessing**

OPPOSITES disadvantage, downside

bony *ADJECTIVE*

He stretched out his long bony arms.

• **skinny, lean, skeletal, emaciated, gaunt**

book *NOUN*

WORD WEB

Parts of a book:

- binding
- cover
- jacket
- spine
- contents
- design
- layout
- illustrations
- typeface
- title page
- preface
- introduction
- chapter
- epilogue
- appendix
- prelims
- appendices
- index
- end pages
- blurb

Some types of book:

- album
- annual
- anthology
- atlas
- audiobook
- diary
- dictionary
- directory
- e-book
- encyclopedia
- graphic novel
- fiction
- guidebook
- manual
- novel
- non-fiction
- picture book
- reading book
- reference book
- story book
- textbook
- thesaurus

- A book with hard covers is a **hardback**.
- A book with soft covers is a **paperback**.
- A book which is typed or handwritten but not printed is a **manuscript**.
- A thin book in paper covers is a **booklet**, **leaflet** or **pamphlet**.
- A book which is part of a set is a **volume**.
- A large, heavy book is a **tome**.

book *VERB*

❶ *Have you booked a seat on the train?*
• **order, reserve**

❷ *I've booked the disco for the party.*
• **arrange, engage, organize, lay on, line up**

➤ **book in**
You need to book in at the front desk.
• **register, check in, enrol**

boom *VERB*

❶ *A voice boomed along the corridor.*
• **roar, bellow, shout, blast, thunder, resound, reverberate**

❷ *Business was booming in the restaurant.*
• **flourish, thrive, prosper, do well, expand, progress**

boom *NOUN*

❶ *A loud boom shook the building.*
• **blast, roar, rumble, thunder, reverberation, resonance**

❷ *There has been a recent boom in teenage fiction.*
• **growth, increase, escalation, expansion, upsurge**
OPPOSITE slump

boost *VERB*

Being in the drama group has really boosted his confidence.
• **increase, enhance, improve, strengthen, bolster, help, encourage, raise, uplift**
OPPOSITES lower, dampen

boost *NOUN*

❶ *We have recently had a boost in sales.*
• **increase, growth, rise, upsurge, upturn**

❷ *Winning that game gave my confidence a great boost.*
• **lift, uplift, encouragement, spur**

boot *NOUN*

He wore a pair of leather boots.
For tips on describing clothes see **clothes**.

boot *VERB*

The goalkeeper booted the ball to midfield.
• **kick, strike, drive, punt**

booth *NOUN*

Is there a photo booth in the station?
• **cubicle, kiosk, stall, stand, compartment**

border *NOUN*

❶ *The town is on the border between France and Germany.*
• **boundary, frontier**

❷ *The tablecloth is white with a blue border.*
• **edge, margin, perimeter, rim, fringe, verge**

border *VERB*

Their orchard was bordered by a stone wall.
• **surround, enclose, encircle, edge, fringe, bound**

bore *VERB*

❶ *Computer games like this bore me now.*
• **weary, tire, pall on**
IDIOM **send you to sleep**
OPPOSITE thrill

❷ *The thieves bored a hole through the wall.*
• **drill, pierce, perforate, puncture, burrow, tunnel, sink**

bore *NOUN*

Filling in forms is such a bore.
• **bother, nuisance, pest, trial**
(*informal*) **drag, hassle**
OPPOSITE thrill

bored *ADJECTIVE*

I sat at home feeling bored.
• **weary, uninterested, uninspired**
(*informal*) **fed up**

boring *ADJECTIVE*

The film was so boring I fell asleep.
• **dull, dreary, tedious, unexciting, uninteresting, dry, monotonous, uninspiring, insipid, unimaginative, uneventful, humdrum, tiresome**
OPPOSITES interesting, exciting

borrow *VERB*

Can I borrow some money?
• **get on loan, have use of**

A B C D E F G H I J K L M N O P Q R S T U V W X Y Z

(*informal*) scrounge, cadge
OPPOSITE lend

boss *NOUN*
He was the boss of a film studio.
• head, chief, manager, leader, director, chair, president

bossy *ADJECTIVE*
The new receptionist is a bit bossy.
• domineering, bullying, overbearing, officious, imperious, pushy

bother *VERB*
❶ *Would it bother you if I played some music?*
• disturb, trouble, inconvenience, annoy, irritate, pester, vex, exasperate
(*informal*) bug, hassle
❷ *I can see that something is bothering you.*
• worry, trouble, concern, perturb
IDIOM prey on your mind
❸ *Don't bother to phone tonight.*
• make an effort, take trouble, concern yourself, care, mind

bother *NOUN*
❶ *It's such a bother to remember the password.*
• nuisance, annoyance, irritation, inconvenience, pest, trouble, difficulty, problem
(*informal*) hassle, drag
❷ *I went to a lot of bother to get your present.*
• trouble, fuss, effort, care

bottle *NOUN*
Bring a bottle of water with you.
• flask, flagon, jar, pitcher
– A bottle for serving water or wine is a **carafe** or **decanter**.
– A small bottle for perfume or medicine is a **phial**.

bottle *VERB*
➤ **bottle something up**
It's not good to keep your feelings bottled up.
• hold in, cover up, conceal, suppress
OPPOSITES show, express

bottom *NOUN*
❶ *We camped at the bottom of the mountain.*
• foot, base, foundation
OPPOSITES top, peak
❷ *The divers found a wreck at the bottom of the sea.*
• bed, floor
OPPOSITE surface
❸ *We have a shed at the bottom of the garden.*
• end, far end, extremity
❹ *A wasp stung me on the bottom.*
• buttocks, rear, rump, seat
(*informal*) behind, backside, bum

bottom *ADJECTIVE*
I keep my paints on the bottom shelf.
• lowest, last, bottommost
OPPOSITES top, highest

bough *NOUN*
The robin perched on the bough of a tree.
• branch, limb

bought
past tense see **buy**

bounce *VERB*
❶ *The ball bounced twice before it reached the net.*
• rebound, ricochet
❷ *The children were bouncing on their beds.*
• jump, spring, leap, bound, bob, prance

bound *VERB*
❶ *She came bounding down the stairs.*
• leap, bounce, jump, spring, vault, skip, hop, prance
❷ *Their land is bounded by the river.*
• border, edge, hem in, enclose, surround, encircle

bound *NOUN*
A kangaroo can cover 10 metres in a single bound.
• leap, jump, spring, vault, skip, hop

bound *ADJECTIVE*
➤ **bound for**
The ship was bound for the West Indies.
• going to, heading for, making for, travelling towards, off to

bound *ADJECTIVE*
❶ *It's bound to rain at the weekend.*
• **certain, sure, destined, fated**
❷ *I felt bound to invite them to the party.*
• **obliged, duty-bound, committed, compelled, forced, required**

boundary *NOUN*
Some animals use scent to mark the boundary of their territory.
• **border, frontier, edge, end, limit, perimeter, dividing line**

bouquet *NOUN*
She was holding a bouquet of flowers.
• **bunch, posy, sprig, spray**

bout *NOUN*
❶ *She's recovering from a bout of flu.*
• **attack, fit, dose, spasm**
❷ *He challenged me to a fencing bout.*
• **contest, match, round, fight, encounter**

bow *VERB*
❶ *The man bowed his head.*
• **lower, bend, incline, duck**
❷ *In the end they had to bow to pressure.*
• **give in, submit, yield, succumb, surrender**

bow *NOUN*
❶ *She greeted me with a slight bow of her head.*
• **nod, bend, lowering, dip, duck, stoop**
❷ *We stood at the bow of the ship.*
• **front, prow, nose, head**

bowl *NOUN*
There was a bowl of fresh fruit on the table.
• **basin, dish, pot, vessel**
– A large bowl for serving soup is a **tureen**.

bowl *VERB*
He ran up to bowl the last ball of the match.
• **throw, pitch, fling, hurl, toss**

box *NOUN*
In the corner was a box full of junk.
• **case, chest, carton, packet, crate, trunk, casket**

boy *NOUN*
He was a boy of ten or eleven.
• **lad, youngster, youth**
(*informal*) kid

brag *VERB*
My brother was still bragging about the goal he scored.
• **boast, gloat, crow, show off**
IDIOM **blow your own trumpet**
– A person who is always bragging is a **braggart**.

brain *NOUN*
I racked my brain, trying to remember.
• **mind, reason, sense, wit, intellect, intelligence, brainpower**
IDIOM (*humorous*) **grey matter**

brainy (*informal*) *ADJECTIVE*
She is the brainy one in the family.
• **clever, intelligent, bright, smart**

branch *NOUN*
❶ *A robin perched on a branch of the tree.*
• **bough, limb, arm**
❷ *I've joined the local branch of the Kennel Club.*
• **section, division, department, wing**

branch *VERB*
Follow the road until it branches into two.
• **divide, fork, split**

brand *NOUN*
Which brand of ice cream do you like?
• **make, kind, sort, type, variety, label**
– The sign of a particular brand of goods is a **trademark**.

brandish *VERB*
The men leapt out of the boat, brandishing their swords.
• **flourish, wield, wave, flaunt**

A B C D E F G H I J K L M N O P Q R S T U V W X Y Z

brave *ADJECTIVE*
They put up a brave fight.
• **courageous, heroic, valiant, bold, fearless, daring, gallant, intrepid, plucky**
OPPOSITE cowardly

bravery *NOUN*
She was awarded a medal for bravery.
• **courage, heroism, valour, fearlessness, daring, nerve, gallantry, grit, pluck**
(*informal*) **guts, bottle**
OPPOSITE cowardice

brawl *NOUN*
We could hear a brawl on the street outside.
• **fight, quarrel, skirmish, scuffle, tussle**
(*informal*) **scrap**

brawny *ADJECTIVE*
The guard stepped forward, a big, brawny man.
• **muscular, athletic, well built, strapping, burly, beefy, hulking**
OPPOSITES puny, scrawny

breach *NOUN*
❶ *Handling the ball is a breach of the rules.*
• **breaking, violation, infringement, offence (against)**
❷ *The storm caused a breach in the sea wall.*
• **break, rupture, split, crack, opening, fracture, fissure**

breach *VERB*
They finally breached the castle walls.
• **break through, burst, rupture**

break *VERB*
❶ *Break the chocolate bar into small pieces.*
• **divide, split, snap, crack**
❷ *The vase fell off the shelf and broke.*
• **smash, shatter, burst, fracture, crack, split, splinter, snap, chip**
(*informal*) **bust**
❸ *The flash on my camera has broken again.*
• **stop working, go wrong, malfunction, fail, crash, break down**
(*informal*) **pack in, conk out**
❹ *If you do that you will be breaking the law.*
• **disobey, contravene, violate, breach, infringe, flout**
❺ *In the final, she broke the world record.*
• **beat, better, exceed, surpass, top, outdo**

➤ **break down**
❶ *Our car broke down on the motorway.*
• **stop working, go wrong, malfunction, fail**
(*informal*) **pack in, conk out**
❷ *The peace talks have broken down.*
• **fail, fall through, collapse, founder**

➤ **break in**
❶ *Thieves broke in during the night.*
• **force your way in**
❷ *Excuse me for breaking into your conversation.*
• **interrupt, cut in, butt in**
(*informal*) **chip in**

➤ **break off**
Let's break off for lunch.
• **have a rest, pause, stop**

➤ **break out**
A flu epidemic broke out last winter.
• **begin, spread, start**

➤ **break out of**
Two prisoners managed to break out of the jail.
• **escape from, break loose from, abscond from**

➤ **break up**
❶ *After the speeches, the crowd began to break up.*
• **disperse, scatter, disband**
❷ *The couple broke up after only two years.*
• **separate, split up**

break *NOUN*
❶ *Can you see any breaks in the chain?*
• **breach, crack, hole, gap, opening, split, rift, rupture, fracture, fissure**
❷ *Let's take a break for lunch.*
• **interval, pause, rest, lull, time-out**
(*informal*) **breather**
❸ *The prisoners made a break for freedom.*
• **escape, dash, bid**

breakable *ADJECTIVE*
Does the parcel contain anything breakable?
• **fragile, delicate, brittle, frail**
OPPOSITE unbreakable

breakdown *NOUN*
❶ *There has been a breakdown in the peace talks.*
• **failure, collapse**
❷ *Can you give me a breakdown of the figures?*
• **analysis**

break-in *NOUN*
There was a break-in at the local bank.
• **burglary, robbery, theft, raid**

breakthrough *NOUN*
Scientists believe this is a major breakthrough in cancer research.
• **advance, leap forward, discovery, development, revolution, progress, innovation**
OPPOSITE setback

breast *NOUN*
The painting shows a baby at its mother's breast.
• **bosom, bust, chest**

breath *NOUN*
❶ *Take a deep breath.*
• **inhalation**
OPPOSITE exhalation
❷ *There wasn't a breath of wind in the air.*
• **breeze, puff, waft, whiff, whisper, sigh**

breathe *VERB*
❶ *The doctor asked me to breathe in and out.*
- To breathe in is to **inhale** and to breathe out is to **exhale**.
- The formal word for breathing is **respiration**.
- To breathe heavily is to **pant** or **puff**.
- To breathe with difficulty is to **gasp** or **wheeze**.
❷ *Don't breathe a word of this to anyone.*
• **speak, say, relate, pass on**

breathless *ADJECTIVE*
I was breathless after running for the bus.
• **out of breath, gasping, panting, puffing, wheezing**

breathtaking *ADJECTIVE*
The view from the summit is breathtaking.
• **spectacular, stunning, staggering, astonishing, amazing, overwhelming, awe-inspiring, awesome**

breed *VERB*
❶ *Salmon swim upstream to breed every year.*
• **reproduce, have young, procreate, multiply, spawn**
❷ *I was born and bred in the city.*
• **bring up, rear, raise, nurture**
❸ *Bad hygiene breeds disease.*
• **cause, produce, generate, encourage, promote, cultivate, induce**

breed *NOUN*
What breed of dog is that?
• **variety, type, kind, sort, class, strain**

breeze *NOUN*
A cool breeze was coming in from the sea.
• **wind, breath of air, gust, draught**

breezy *ADJECTIVE*
❶ *It was a bright and breezy morning.*
• **windy, blowy, blustery, gusty, fresh, brisk**
❷ *He had a breezy manner.*
• **cheerful, cheery, carefree, jaunty** (*informal*) **upbeat**

brew *VERB*
❶ *I'm just going to brew some tea.*
• **make, prepare, infuse**
- When you brew beer it **ferments**.
❷ *It looks like a storm is brewing.*
• **develop, form, loom, build up, gather, threaten**

brew *NOUN*
The witches concocted an evil-smelling brew.
• **mixture, mix, concoction, blend, cocktail**

bridge *NOUN*

WORD WEB

Some types of bridge:

- ➤ cantilever bridge
- ➤ flyover
- ➤ footbridge
- ➤ pontoon bridge
- ➤ rope bridge
- ➤ suspension bridge
- ➤ swing bridge

- A bridge to carry water is an **aqueduct** and a long bridge carrying a road or railway is a **viaduct**.

brief *ADJECTIVE*

❶ *We paid a brief visit to our cousins on the way home.*
• **short, quick, hasty, fleeting, flying, short-lived, temporary, cursory**
❷ *She gave us a brief account of what happened.*
• **concise, succinct, short, abbreviated, condensed, compact, potted, pithy**
OPPOSITES long, lengthy

bright *ADJECTIVE*

❶ *We saw the bright lights of the town in the distance.*
• **shining, brilliant, blazing, dazzling, glaring, gleaming**
OPPOSITES dim, weak
❷ *The day was cold, but bright.*
• **sunny, fine, fair, clear, cloudless**
OPPOSITES dull, cloudy, overcast
❸ *Her shoes were a bright shade of pink.*
• **strong, intense, vivid, vibrant, bold, lurid, garish**
– Colours that glow in the dark are **luminous** colours.
OPPOSITES dull, faded, muted
❹ *She was a bright student.*
• **clever, intelligent, sharp, quick-witted, smart**
(*informal*) **brainy**
OPPOSITES stupid, dull-witted
❺ *He gave me a bright smile.*
• **cheerful, happy, lively, merry, jolly, radiant**
OPPOSITES sad, gloomy

brighten *VERB*

Her eyes brightened and she began to smile.
• **light up, lighten, become bright**
➤ **brighten something up**
A new coat of paint will brighten up the place.
• **cheer up, perk up, light up, enliven**

brilliant *ADJECTIVE*

❶ *The fireworks burned with a brilliant light.*
• **bright, blazing, dazzling, glaring, gleaming, glittering, glorious, shining, splendid, vivid**
OPPOSITES dim, dull
❷ *Brunel was a brilliant engineer.*
• **clever, exceptional, outstanding, gifted, talented**
OPPOSITES incompetent, talentless
❸ (*informal*) *I saw a brilliant film last week.*
• **excellent, marvellous, outstanding, wonderful, superb**
(*informal*) **fantastic, fabulous**

brim *NOUN*

My glass was full to the brim.
• **rim, edge, brink, lip**

bring *VERB*

❶ *Did you remember to bring the sandwiches?*
• **carry, bear, deliver, transport, fetch**
❷ *You can bring a friend to the party.*
• **invite, escort, accompany, conduct, lead, guide**
❸ *This road will bring you to the centre of town.*
• **lead, take, conduct**
❹ *The drought brought famine and disease.*
• **cause, produce, lead to, result in, give rise to, generate**
➤ **bring something about**
They are campaigning to bring about a change in the law.
• **cause, effect, achieve, create, engineer**
➤ **bring something off**
The author manages to bring off a surprise ending.
• **accomplish, carry out, pull off, achieve**

➤ **bring someone up**
It is a story about a boy who is brought up by wolves.
• **rear, raise, care for, foster, look after, nurture**
➤ **bring something up**
Why did you have to bring up the subject of money?
• **mention, raise, introduce, broach, air**

brink *NOUN*
❶ *They stood on the brink of a deep crater.*
• **edge, lip, rim, verge, brim**
❷ *We were on the brink of a great discovery.*
• **verge, threshold, point**

brisk *ADJECTIVE*
❶ *The runners set off at a brisk pace.*
• **quick, fast, rapid, swift, energetic, invigorating, vigorous, refreshing**
OPPOSITES slow, leisurely
❷ *A brisk, business-like voice answered the phone.*
• **curt, abrupt, blunt, short, terse, brusque**
❸ *The shops do a brisk trade in the summer.*
• **busy, lively, bustling, hectic**
OPPOSITES quiet, slack, slow

bristle *NOUN*
Shrimps have fine bristles on their legs.
• **hair, whisker, spine, pickle, barb, quill**
– Short hairs that grow on a person's chin are **stubble**.

bristle *VERB*
❶ *She bristled at the idea of being left behind.*
• **take offence, bridle, take umbrage**
❷ *The room bristled with computer screens.*
• **be full of, be packed with, abound in, overflow with**

brittle *ADJECTIVE*
The bones of the skeleton were dry and brittle.
• **breakable, fragile, crisp, crumbly**
OPPOSITE flexible

broach *VERB*
He seemed unwilling to broach the subject.
• **mention, bring up, raise, introduce, air**

broad *ADJECTIVE*
❶ *Above the hills was a broad expanse of blue sky.*
• **wide, extensive, vast, open, large, spacious, expansive, sweeping**
OPPOSITE narrow
❷ *Give me a broad outline of the plot.*
• **general, rough, vague, loose, indefinite, imprecise**
OPPOSITES specific, detailed
❸ *She spoke with a broad Australian accent.*
• **strong, distinct, marked, obvious**
OPPOSITE slight

broadcast *VERB*
The concert will be broadcast live on TV.
• **transmit, relay, beam, air, screen, show, televise**

broaden *VERB*
❶ *You need to broaden your interests.*
• **expand, increase, enlarge, extend, develop, diversify**
❷ *The river broadens as it nears the ocean.*
• **widen, expand, open out, spread out, stretch out**

brochure *NOUN*
We've been looking at holiday brochures.
• **leaflet, pamphlet, booklet, catalogue**
– A brochure advertising a school or university is a **prospectus**.

broke
past tense see **break**

broken *ADJECTIVE*
❶ *I started to pick up the pieces of the broken vase.*
• **smashed, shattered, cracked, splintered, in pieces, in bits** (*informal*) **in smithereens**
OPPOSITES intact, whole

A B C D E F G H I J K L M N O P Q R S T U V W X Y Z

❷ *Which of these computers is broken?*
• **faulty, defective, malfunctioning, damaged, out of order**
OPPOSITE working
❸ *I had a night of broken sleep.*
• **disturbed, interrupted, fitful, restless**
❹ *From that day on, he was broken in spirit.*
• **crushed, defeated, beaten, shattered**

brood *VERB*
Are you still brooding over what I said?
• **worry, fret, mope, dwell on, agonize over**

brother *NOUN*
I have an elder brother.
– A formal name for a brother or sister is a **sibling.**
For other members of a family see **family.**

brought
past tense see **bring**

brown *ADJECTIVE & NOUN*

WORD WEB

Some shades of brown:

➤ beige
➤ bronze
➤ buff
➤ caramel
➤ chestnut
➤ chocolate
➤ coffee
➤ dun
➤ fawn
➤ hazel
➤ khaki
➤ mahogany
➤ russet
➤ sandy
➤ sepia
➤ tan
➤ tawny

For tips on describing colours see **colour.**

browse *VERB*
I was just browsing through a magazine.
• **look through, leaf through, scan, skim, peruse**

bruise *NOUN*
He had a bruise on his leg.
• **swelling, bump, contusion**

bruise *VERB*
I fell and bruised my knee.
• **mark, discolour, hurt, injure**

brush *VERB*
❶ *Wait while I brush my hair.*
• **groom, comb, tidy, smooth**
❷ *I'll just brush my teeth.*
• **scrub, clean, polish**
❸ *He brushed a few crumbs off the table.*
• **sweep, flick**
❹ *Something soft brushed against my cheek.*
• **touch, stroke, graze, scrape, sweep**
➤ **brush aside**
My question was just brushed aside.
• **dismiss, disregard, shrug off, make light of**
➤ **brush up**
I have two weeks to brush up my French.
• **revise, improve, go over, refresh your memory of**
(*informal*) **mug up on, swot up on**

brutal *ADJECTIVE*
He committed a series of brutal murders.
• **savage, vicious, violent, cruel, barbaric, ferocious, bloodthirsty, inhuman, merciless, pitiless, ruthless, callous, sadistic**
OPPOSITES gentle, humane

bubble *NOUN*
The water was full of soap bubbles.
• **lather, suds, foam, froth**
– The bubbles in a fizzy drink are called **effervescence.**

bubble *VERB*
Heat the water until it starts to bubble.
• **boil, seethe, gurgle, froth, foam**

bubbly *ADJECTIVE*
❶ *I like bubbly drinks.*
• **fizzy, sparkling, effervescent, carbonated, gassy**
❷ *She has a bright and bubbly personality.*
• **cheerful, lively, vivacious, bouncy, high-spirited, spirited, animated**

bucket *NOUN*
He was carrying a bucket of water.
• **pail, can**

buckle *NOUN*
He wore a belt with a large silver buckle.
• **clasp, fastener, fastening, clip, catch**

buckle *VERB*
❶ *Please buckle your seat belts.*
• **fasten, secure, clasp, clip, do up, hook up**
❷ *The bridge buckled under our weight.*
• **bend, warp, twist, crumple, cave in, collapse**

bud *NOUN*
Buds are appearing on the apple trees.
• **shoot, sprout**

budding *ADJECTIVE*
She is a budding actress.
• **aspiring, promising, potential, would-be, up-and-coming, rising**

budge *VERB*
The window was stuck and wouldn't budge.
• **move, shift, give way, stir**

budget *NOUN*
I have a budget of £50 to spend on clothes.
• **allowance, allocation, funds, resources**

budget *VERB*
How much have you budgeted for the holidays?
• **allocate, set aside, allow, allot, earmark**

buffet *VERB*
The coast was buffeted by strong winds all day.
• **batter, pound, beat, lash, pummel**

bug *NOUN*
❶ *I spent the morning collecting bugs from the garden.*
• **insect, minibeast**
(*informal*) **creepy-crawly**
❷ *There are still a few bugs in the computer program.*
• **fault, error, defect, flaw**
(*informal*) **glitch, gremlin**
❸ (*informal*) *I can't get rid of this stomach bug.*
• **infection, virus, disease, germ, illness**
❹ *Someone had planted a bug in the room.*
• **hidden microphone, wire, tap**
For words to do with writing spy fiction see **spy**.

bug *VERB*
❶ *Our conversations were being bugged.*
• **tap, record, monitor, intercept, listen in to**
❷ (*informal*) *Please stop bugging me with questions.*
• **bother, annoy, pester, trouble, harass**

build *VERB*
❶ *Dad is going to build a shed in the garden.*
• **construct, erect, put together, put up, set up, assemble**
❷ *Traffic has been building steadily.*
• **increase, accumulate, grow, build up**

➤ **build up**
Tension was building up in the crowd.
• **increase, intensify, grow, rise, mount, escalate**

➤ **build something up**
❶ *You need to build up your strength.*
• **increase, improve, strengthen, develop, boost**
❷ *He has built up a reputation for getting results.*
• **establish, develop, create, amass, accumulate, assemble, collect, put together**

build *NOUN*
She was a woman of slender build.
• **body, form, frame, figure, physique**

A B C D E F G H I J K L M N O P Q R S T U V W X Y Z

building *NOUN*

It is one of the tallest buildings in New York.

• **construction, structure, dwelling**

– A person who designs buildings is an **architect** and the process of designing buildings is **architecture**.

WORD WEB

Some types of building:

➤ apartment block
➤ bungalow
➤ cabin
➤ castle
➤ cinema
➤ cottage
➤ factory
➤ fort
➤ hut
➤ lighthouse
➤ mansion
➤ mill
➤ observatory
➤ palace
➤ school
➤ shed
➤ shop
➤ skyscraper
➤ stadium
➤ tenement
➤ terrace
➤ theatre
➤ tower
➤ tower block
➤ townhouse
➤ villa
➤ warehouse

For religious buildings see **religion**.

WRITING TIPS

DESCRIBING BUILDINGS

Parts of a building:

➤ arch
➤ balcony
➤ balustrade
➤ bay window
➤ bow window
➤ buttress
➤ chimney
➤ colonnade
➤ column
➤ courtyard
➤ cupola
➤ dome
➤ dormer window
➤ drainpipe
➤ eaves
➤ foundations
➤ gable
➤ gutter
➤ masonry
➤ parapet
➤ pediment
➤ pillar
➤ pipes
➤ porch
➤ quadrangle
➤ roof
➤ shutter
➤ spire
➤ storey
➤ terrace
➤ tower
➤ turret
➤ vault
➤ veranda
➤ wall
➤ window
➤ windowsill
➤ wing

Parts you might find inside a building:

➤ attic
➤ basement
➤ ceiling
➤ cellar
➤ conservatory
➤ corridor
➤ crypt
➤ dungeon
➤ foyer
➤ gallery
➤ garret
➤ lobby
➤ mezzanine
➤ room (*old use* chamber)
➤ staircase
➤ stairwell

Adjectives:

➤ airy
➤ compact
➤ cramped
➤ crumbling
➤ forbidding
➤ grand
➤ imposing
➤ ramshackle
➤ rickety
➤ ruined
➤ run-down
➤ solid
➤ spacious
➤ sprawling
➤ squalid
➤ stark
➤ stately
➤ towering
➤ tumbledown

bulge *NOUN*

Asian elephants have two bulges on their foreheads.

• **bump, hump, lump, swelling, protuberance**

bulge *VERB*

His eyes bulged with excitement.

• **stick out, swell, protrude, balloon, curve outwards**

bulk *NOUN*

❶ *The sheer bulk of a blue whale is staggering.*

• **size, dimensions, magnitude, mass, largeness**

❷ *We did the bulk of the work ourselves.*

• **main part, most part, majority**

IDIOM **the lion's share**

OPPOSITE **minority**

bulky *ADJECTIVE*

The parcel is too bulky to post.

• **unwieldy, cumbersome, awkward,**

unmanageable, hefty
OPPOSITE compact

bulletin *NOUN*
❶ *We listened to the news bulletin.*
• **report, announcement, broadcast**
❷ *The society publishes a quarterly bulletin.*
• **newsletter, review, magazine, gazette**

bully *VERB*
Some of the other children used to bully him.
• **persecute, intimidate, torment, terrorize**
(*informal*) **push around**

bump *VERB*
❶ *He bumped his head on the low ceiling.*
• **hit, strike, knock, bang**
❷ *My bicycle was bumping up and down over the cobbles.*
• **bounce, shake, jerk, jolt**
➤ **bump into**
❶ *I nearly bumped into a lamp post.*
• **collide with, bang into, run into, crash into**
❷ *We bumped into some friends in town.*
• **meet, come across, run into**

bump *NOUN*
❶ *We felt a bump as the plane landed.*
• **thud, thump, bang, blow, knock**
❷ *How did you get that bump on your head?*
• **lump, swelling, bulge, protuberance**

bumpy *ADJECTIVE*
❶ *The car jolted up and down on the bumpy road.*
• **rough, uneven, irregular, lumpy**
OPPOSITES smooth, even
❷ *We had a bumpy ride in the back of a truck.*
• **bouncy, jerky, jolting, jarring, lurching, choppy**

bunch *NOUN*
❶ *He handed me a bunch of keys.*
• **bundle, collection, set, cluster, clump**
❷ *She picked a bunch of flowers.*
• **bouquet, posy, spray**
❸ (*informal*) *They're a friendly bunch of people.*
• **group, set, circle, band, gang, crowd**

bundle *NOUN*
I found a bundle of old newspapers.
• **bunch, batch, pile, stack, collection, pack, bale**

bundle *VERB*
❶ *I quickly bundled up the papers that were on the desk.*
• **pack, tie, fasten, bind, wrap, roll**
❷ *They bundled him into the back of a taxi.*
• **shove, push, jostle, thrust, manhandle**

burden *NOUN*
❶ *Each mule was carrying a heavy burden.*
• **load, weight, cargo**
❷ *We should share the burden of all the work that needs doing.*
• **responsibility, obligation, duty, pressure, stress, trouble, worry**

burden *VERB*
❶ *She staggered in, burdened with shopping.*
• **load, weigh down, encumber, lumber**
❷ *I won't burden you with my problems.*
• **bother, worry, trouble, distress, afflict, oppress**
(*informal*) **saddle**

burglar *NOUN*
The burglars got in through the window.
• **robber, thief, housebreaker**

burglary *NOUN*
There have been reports of burglaries in the area.
• **robbery, theft, break-in, stealing**

burly *ADJECTIVE*
Two burly security guards appeared.
• **well built, strapping, sturdy, muscular, beefy**

a b c d e f g h i j k l m n o p q r s t u v w x y z

A B C D E F G H I J K L M N O P Q R S T U V W X Y Z

burn *VERB*

❶ *Forest fires are burning out of control.*
• **be alight, be on fire, blaze, flame, flare**
– To burn without flames is to **glow** or **smoulder.**
❷ *He burnt the letters in the fire.*
• **set fire to, incinerate, reduce to ashes**
– To start something burning is to **ignite, kindle** or **light** it.
– To burn a dead body is to **cremate** it.
❸ *The match had burnt a hole in the carpet.*
• **scorch, singe, sear, char, blacken**
– To burn yourself with hot liquid is to **scald** yourself.
– To burn a mark on an animal is to **brand** it.

burning *ADJECTIVE*

He has a burning ambition to become an actor.
• **strong, intense, extreme, acute, eager, fervent, passionate**

burrow *NOUN*

The field was full of rabbit burrows.
• **hole, tunnel**
– A piece of ground with many burrows is a **warren.**
– A fox's burrow is called an **earth.**
– A badger's burrow is called an **earth** or a **set.**

burrow *VERB*

Rabbits had burrowed under the fence.
• **tunnel, dig, excavate, mine, bore**

burst *VERB*

❶ *People started bursting the balloons.*
• **break, rupture, split, tear, pop**
(*informal*) **bust**
❷ *The dam burst under the weight of water.*
• **break apart, split apart, fall to pieces, give way, rupture, explode**
❸ *A man suddenly burst into the room.*
• **charge, barge, rush, dash, hurtle, plunge**

burst *NOUN*

There was a short burst of gunfire.
• **outbreak, outburst, rush, wave, explosion**

bury *VERB*

❶ *They were buried in an unmarked grave.*
• **inter, entomb**
OPPOSITES disinter, exhume, unearth
❷ *The letter was buried under a pile of papers.*
• **cover, conceal, hide, secrete**

bush *NOUN*

The ball was caught up in a bush.
• **shrub, thicket, undergrowth**

bushy *ADJECTIVE*

He has bushy eyebrows.
• **thick, dense, hairy, shaggy, bristly**

business *NOUN*

❶ *What kind of business are you in?*
• **trade, trading, commerce, industry, work, occupation**
❷ *She wants to run her own business.*
• **company, firm, organization, enterprise**
❸ *The whole business was a mystery to me.*
• **matter, issue, affair, point, concern, question**

bustle *VERB*

The square was full of people bustling about.
• **rush, dash, hurry, scurry, scuttle**
(*informal*) **buzz**

busy *ADJECTIVE*

❶ *I've been busy all afternoon.*
• **occupied, engaged, employed, working, hard-pressed**
(*informal*) **hard at it**
IDIOMS **up to your eyes, run off your feet**
OPPOSITE idle
❷ *We've got a busy day ahead of us.*
• **hectic, active, full, eventful, frantic**
OPPOSITES quiet, restful
❸ *The town is always busy on Saturdays.*
• **crowded, bustling, lively, teeming**
OPPOSITES quiet, peaceful

but *CONJUNCTION*

It was morning but it was still dark.
• **however, nevertheless**

but *PREPOSITION*
No one spoke but me.
• **except, except for, other than**

butt *VERB*
The ship had to butt its way through the ice.
• **ram, shove, push, thrust, bump, knock**
➤ **butt in**
Please don't butt in when I'm talking.
• **interrupt, cut in, break in**
(*informal*) **chip in**
IDIOM (*informal*) **put your oar in**

buy *VERB*
Where did you buy your trainers?
• **purchase, pay for, obtain, acquire**
OPPOSITE **sell**

buzz *NOUN*
❶ *The buzz of conversation suddenly stopped.*
• **hum, drone**
❷ (*informal*) *I always get a buzz from going to the cinema.*
• **thrill, excitement, tingle**
(*informal*) **kick**

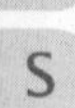

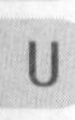

Cc

cabin *NOUN*

1 *He lived in a log cabin in the woods.*
• **hut, shack, shed, lodge, chalet, shelter**
2 *The crew assembled in the captain's cabin.*
• **berth, compartment, quarters**

cable *NOUN*

1 *The tent was held down with strong cables.*
• **rope, cord, line, chain**
2 *Don't trip over the computer cable.*
• **flex, lead, wire, cord**

cadet *NOUN*

She is a cadet in the police force.
• **recruit, trainee**

cafe *NOUN*

We had lunch at a local cafe.
• **snack bar, cafeteria, coffee shop, tea-room, bistro, brasserie**

cage *NOUN*

I put the hamster back into its cage.
• **enclosure, pen, pound, hutch**
– A large cage or enclosure for birds is an **aviary**.
– A cage or enclosure for poultry is a **coop**.

cake *NOUN*

1 *Would you like a piece of birthday cake?*
• **sponge, flan, gateau, pastry**
2 *I unwrapped a fresh cake of soap.*
• **bar, block, tablet, slab**

caked *ADJECTIVE*

My boots were caked with mud.
• **coated, covered, plastered, encrusted**

calamity *NOUN*

The earthquake was a national calamity.
• **disaster, catastrophe, tragedy, misfortune, mishap, blow**

calculate *VERB*

1 *I calculated that it would take an hour to walk home.*
• **compute, work out, reckon, add up, count up, tally, total**
(*informal*) **tot up**
– To calculate something roughly is to **estimate**.
2 *Her remarks were clearly calculated to hurt me.*
• **intend, mean, design**

call *VERB*

1 *'Stop that infernal noise!' I called.*
• **cry out, shout, yell, exclaim**
(*informal*) **holler**
2 *I'll call you tonight.*
• **phone, ring, telephone, give someone a call**
(*informal*) **give someone a ring**
3 *The website is called 'News4U'.*
• **name, dub, title, entitle, term**
4 *She called us all for a meeting.*
• **summon, send for, order**
5 *The doctor called to see if I was feeling better.*
• **visit, pay a visit, drop in, drop by**

➤ **call for**

1 *This calls for a celebration.*
• **require, need, necessitate, justify, warrant, be grounds for**
2 *They are calling for a ban on fireworks.*
• **request, demand, appeal for, ask for, seek**

➤ **call something off**

The race was called off at the last minute.
• **cancel, abandon, scrap**
(*informal*) **scrub**

call *NOUN*

1 *We heard a call for help from the upstairs window.*
• **cry, shout, yell, exclamation**
2 *I'll give you a call at the weekend.*
• **phone call**
(*informal*) **ring, buzz, bell**
3 *I need to pay a quick call on grandma.*
• **visit, stop**
4 *There has been a call for action on climate change.*
• **demand, request, appeal, plea**

❺ *There's no call for that kind of language.*
• **need, necessity, reason, justification**

callous *ADJECTIVE*
It was a callous and mindless attack.
• **cold-hearted, hard-hearted, heartless, unfeeling, insensitive, unsympathetic**
OPPOSITES compassionate, kind

calm *ADJECTIVE*
❶ *Please try to stay calm.*
• **composed, cool, level-headed, relaxed, serene, sedate, unruffled, unflustered, unperturbed, unemotional, unexcitable**
OPPOSITES anxious, nervous
❷ *It was a calm sunny day.*
• **still, quiet, peaceful, tranquil, windless**
OPPOSITES stormy, windy
❸ *The sea was calm that morning.*
• **smooth, still, flat, motionless, tranquil**
OPPOSITES rough, choppy

came
past tense see **come**

camel *NOUN*

WORD WEB
- A **dromedary** camel has one hump and a **Bactrian** camel has two humps.

camouflage *VERB*
We used branches to camouflage our tent.
• **disguise, mask, screen, cover up, conceal**

camp *NOUN*
We could see a camp in the field below us.
• **campsite, camping ground, base**
– A military camp is an **encampment**.

campaign *NOUN*
❶ *He planned each military campaign with great care.*
• **operation, offensive, action, war**
❷ *She joined the campaign to end child poverty.*
• **movement, crusade, drive, fight, effort, struggle**

campaign *VERB*
They are campaigning to save the rainforests.
• **fight, battle, push, lobby, agitate**

cancel *VERB*
❶ *We had to cancel the race because of the weather.*
• **call off, abandon, scrap, drop** (*informal*) **scrub, ditch, axe**
– To cancel something after it has already begun is to **abort** it.
– To put something off until later is to **postpone** it.
❷ *They agreed to cancel the debt.*
• **revoke, annul, rescind, erase, retract, withdraw**

candid *ADJECTIVE*
Thank you for that candid answer.
• **frank, direct, open, honest, straightforward, forthright** (*informal*) **upfront**
OPPOSITE guarded

candidate *NOUN*
They interviewed four candidates for the job.
• **applicant, contender, entrant**

canopy *NOUN*
The trees formed a canopy overhead.
• **covering, awning, shade**

cap *NOUN*
Who left the cap off the toothpaste?
• **lid, top, cover, stopper**

cap *VERB*
The mountains were capped with snow.
• **top, crown, cover, tip**

capable *ADJECTIVE*
She is a very capable student.
• **competent, able, accomplished, proficient, skilful, talented, gifted**
OPPOSITE incompetent

A B C D E F G H I J K L M N O P Q R S T U V W X Y Z

➤ **be capable of**
Do you think he is capable of murder?
• **be able to do, be equal to, be up to**
OPPOSITE **be incapable of**

capacity *NOUN*
❶ *What is the capacity of this glass?*
• **size, volume, space, extent, room**
❷ *He has a great capacity for making friends.*
• **ability, capability, power, potential, aptitude, competence, skill**
❸ *She spoke in her capacity as team captain.*
• **position, function, role, office**

cape *NOUN*
❶ *She wore a black cape.*
• **cloak, shawl, wrap, robe**
(*old use*) **mantle**
❷ *Gibraltar is situated on a narrow cape.*
• **headland, promontory, point, head**

capital *NOUN*
❶ *Kingston is the capital of Jamaica.*
• **capital city**
❷ *In three years he had enough capital to start his own business.*
• **funds, money, finance, cash, assets, means, resources**

capsize *VERB*
The boat struck a rock and capsized.
• **overturn, tip over, turn over, keel over**
IDIOM **turn turtle**

capsule *NOUN*
❶ *The medicine is taken in the form of capsules.*
• **pill, tablet, lozenge, pastille**
❷ *The space capsule was designed to carry astronauts.*
• **module, craft, pod**

captain *NOUN*
❶ *The ship's captain made an announcement.*
• **commander, commanding officer, master**
(*informal*) **skipper**
❷ *She has been the team captain for two years.*
• **leader, head, chief**
(*informal*) **skipper**

caption *NOUN*
Write a caption for the picture.
• **title, heading, legend, description**

captive *NOUN*
The gunmen agreed to release their captives.
• **prisoner, convict, detainee**
– A person who is held captive until a demand is met is a **hostage**.

captive *ADJECTIVE*
They were held captive for ten days.
• **imprisoned, captured, in captivity, arrested, detained, jailed**
IDIOM **behind bars**
OPPOSITES **free, released**

captivity *NOUN*
He was held in captivity for three years.
• **imprisonment, confinement, detention, incarceration**
OPPOSITE **freedom**

capture *VERB*
❶ *He was captured boarding a ship for France.*
• **catch, arrest, apprehend, seize, take prisoner**
(*informal*) **nab**
❷ *Rome was captured in 410.*
• **occupy, seize, take, conquer**

car *NOUN*
Our car is parked round the corner.
• **motor car, motor, vehicle**
(*North American*) **automobile**
– An informal name for an old, noisy car is a **banger**.

WORD WEB

Some types of car:

➤ convertible
➤ coupé
➤ electric car
➤ estate
➤ four-wheel drive or four-by-four
➤ hatchback

➤ limousine (*informal* limo)	➤ racing car
➤ MPV (multi-purpose vehicle)	➤ saloon
➤ people carrier	➤ sports car
	➤ SUV (sports utility vehicle)

- Very early cars are **veteran** or **vintage** cars.

Parts of a car:

➤ accelerator	➤ gear lever
➤ bonnet	➤ handbrake
➤ brake	➤ headlamps
➤ boot (*North American* trunk)	➤ ignition
➤ bumper (*North American* fender)	➤ lights
➤ chassis	➤ mirrors
➤ choke	➤ mudguards
➤ clutch	➤ roof
➤ doors	➤ steering wheel
➤ engine	➤ tyres
➤ exhaust pipe	➤ undercarriage
➤ fuel tank	➤ wheels
➤ gearbox	➤ windscreen
	➤ windscreen wipers
	➤ wings

SEE ALSO **vehicle**

carcass *NOUN*
The lions fed on the carcass of an antelope.
• **dead body, corpse, remains** (*formal*) **cadaver**

care *NOUN*
❶ *I took great care with my handwriting.*
• **attention, concentration, thoroughness, thought, meticulousness**
OPPOSITE carelessness
❷ *Please choose your words with care.*
• **caution, discretion, thought, consideration, regard, sensitivity**
OPPOSITE disregard
❸ *We left our cat in the care of a neighbour.*
• **charge, keeping, protection, safe keeping, supervision**
❹ *The old woman's face was full of care.*
• **worry, anxiety, trouble, concern, burden, responsibility, sorrow, stress**

➤ **take care**
Please take care crossing the road.
• **be careful, be on your guard, look out, watch out**
➤ **take care of**
Who will take care of my plants?
• **care for, look after, mind, watch over, attend to, tend**

care *VERB*
I don't care which film we see.
• **mind, bother, be interested, be bothered, be worried**
➤ **care about**
He really cares about the environment.
• **be concerned about, be interested in, be worried about, be bothered about**
➤ **care for**
❶ *The veterinary hospital cares for sick animals.*
• **look after, take care of, attend to, tend, nurse**
❷ *They obviously care for each other.*
• **love, be fond of, cherish, adore, hold dear, dote on**
IDIOM **think the world of**
❸ *I don't really care for broccoli.*
• **like, be fond of, be keen on, be partial to**

career *NOUN*
He had a long career as a teacher.
• **job, occupation, profession, trade, business, employment, calling**

carefree *ADJECTIVE*
He looked happy and carefree.
• **unworried, untroubled, easy-going, light-hearted, relaxed** (*informal*) **laid-back**
OPPOSITE anxious

careful *ADJECTIVE*
❶ *We kept a careful watch on the bonfire.*
• **attentive, cautious, watchful, alert, wary, vigilant**
OPPOSITES careless, inattentive
❷ *You must be more careful with your spelling.*
• **diligent, conscientious, thoughtful, meticulous, painstaking, thorough, precise**

OPPOSITES careless, negligent

➤ **be careful**
Please be careful with those scissors.
• **take care, be on your guard, look out, watch out**

careless *ADJECTIVE*

❶ *This is a careless piece of work.*
• **messy, untidy, thoughtless, inaccurate, slapdash, shoddy, scrappy, sloppy, slovenly, slipshod**
OPPOSITES careful, thoughtful
❷ *I was careless and cut my finger.*
• **inattentive, thoughtless, absent-minded, heedless, irresponsible, negligent, reckless**
OPPOSITES careful, attentive

caress *VERB*

The woman gently caressed her baby.
• **stroke, touch, fondle, pet**

cargo *NOUN*

The plane was carrying cargo rather than passengers.
• **goods, freight, merchandise**

carnival *NOUN*

The town was holding its annual carnival.
• **festival, fair, fête, gala, parade, procession, pageant**

carpenter *NOUN*

Next door was a carpenter's workshop.
• **woodworker, joiner, cabinetmaker**

carriage *NOUN*

a horse-drawn carriage
• **cab, hansom cab, stagecoach, coach, trap, wagon**

carry *VERB*

❶ *I'll help you carry the shopping to the car.*
• **take, transfer, convey, move, bring, fetch, lift**
(*informal*) **cart, lug**
❷ *These ships carry both passengers and freight.*
• **transport, convey, handle, ferry, ship**
❸ *Most of these cables carry electricity.*
• **transmit, conduct, relay, convey, send**
❹ *The road bridge has to carry a lot of traffic.*
• **bear, support, hold up**
❺ *Her voice carried to the back of the hall.*
• **be audible, be heard, reach, travel**
❻ *The vote was carried by a huge majority.*
• **approve, accept, pass, endorse, ratify**

➤ **carry on**
We carried on in spite of the rain.
• **continue, go on, persevere, persist, keep on**
(*informal*) **stick with it, stick at it**

➤ **carry something out**
Did you carry out my instructions?
• **perform, execute, accomplish, achieve, complete, finish**

cart *NOUN*

The fruit was taken to the barns in carts.
• **barrow, wheelbarrow, handcart, trolley**

carton *NOUN*

I bought a carton of ice cream.
• **box, pack, packet, package, case, container**

cartoon *NOUN*

❶ *The kids were watching a Bugs Bunny cartoon.*
• **animation, animated film**
❷ *Batman first appeared in a cartoon.*
• **cartoon strip, comic strip, comic, graphic novel**
❸ *On the cover was a cartoon of the Prime Minister.*
• **caricature**

carve *VERB*

❶ *The statue was carved out of marble.*
• **sculpt, chisel, hew, shape, fashion**
❷ *She had carved her initials on the tree.*
• **engrave, incise, score, cut**
❸ *Mum started to carve the chicken.*
• **cut up, slice**

cascade *NOUN*

Cascades of water tumbled down the rock face.
• **torrent, waterfall, fall**

case *NOUN*
❶ *Put your cases on the trolley.*
• **suitcase, bag, trunk, holdall, baggage, luggage**
❷ *The camera comes with its own case.*
• **box, container, holder, covering, casing, canister, carton, casket**
❸ *It was a clear case of mistaken identity.*
• **instance, example, occurrence, illustration**
❹ *The film is based on a famous murder case.*
• **inquiry, investigation**
❺ *She put forward a good case for equality.*
• **argument, line of reasoning, thesis**

cash *NOUN*
❶ *Can I pay by cash?*
• **currency, change, coins, notes**
❷ *They have plenty of cash in the bank.*
• **money, finance, funds**

cast *VERB*
❶ *He cast a coin into the fountain.*
• **throw, toss, pitch, fling, sling, lob**
❷ *The light from the candle cast her shadow on the wall.*
• **emit, send out, give off, shed**
❸ *I cast a glance backwards.*
• **direct, send, shoot**
❹ *The statue is cast in bronze.*
• **form, mould, shape, fashion**

castle *NOUN*
These are the remains of a twelfth-century castle.
• **fortress, fort, fortification, citadel, chateau, stronghold**

WORD WEB

Parts of a castle:

➤ bailey
➤ barbican
➤ battlements
➤ buttress
➤ courtyard
➤ donjon
➤ drawbridge
➤ dungeon
➤ gate
➤ gateway
➤ keep
➤ magazine
➤ moat
➤ motte
➤ parapet
➤ portcullis
➤ postern
➤ rampart
➤ tower
➤ turret
➤ wall
➤ watchtower

casual *ADJECTIVE*
❶ *It was just a casual remark.*
• **unthinking, off-hand, unconsidered, impromptu, throwaway, chance**
(*informal*) **off-the-cuff**
OPPOSITES considered, thoughtful
❷ *The restaurant had a casual atmosphere.*
• **easy-going, informal, relaxed**
(*informal*) **laid-back, chilled-out, chilled**
OPPOSITE formal
❸ *He has a casual approach to life.*
• **relaxed, nonchalant, carefree, easy-going, slack**
(*informal*) **laid-back**
❹ *She had changed into casual clothes.*
• **informal, everyday, leisure**
OPPOSITE formal

casualty *NOUN*
There are reports of heavy casualties.
• **victim, sufferer, death, injury, loss, fatality**

cat *NOUN*
Our cat has very long whiskers.
• (*informal*) **puss, pussy cat, kitty, moggy**

WORD WEB

Some breeds of domestic cat:

➤ Abyssinian
➤ Burmese
➤ chinchilla
➤ Manx
➤ Persian
➤ Siamese

- A male cat is a **tom** or **tomcat**.
- A young cat is a **kitten**.
- A cat with streaks in its fur is a **tabby**.
- A cat with mottled brown fur is a **tortoiseshell**.
- A word meaning 'to do with cats' is **feline**.

A B C D E F G H I J K L M N O P Q R S T U V W X Y Z

For tips on describing animals see **animal**.

Wild animals of the cat family:

- ➤ bobcat
- ➤ cheetah
- ➤ cougar
- ➤ jaguar
- ➤ leopard
- ➤ lion
- ➤ lynx
- ➤ mountain lion
- ➤ ocelot
- ➤ panther
- ➤ puma
- ➤ tiger
- ➤ wild cat

catalogue *NOUN*

❶ *I checked the library catalogue.*
• **list, listing, index, register, directory, inventory, archive**
❷ *Look in our Christmas catalogue.*
• **brochure, pamphlet, leaflet**

catastrophe *NOUN*

The floods were a catastrophe for the area.
• **disaster, calamity, tragedy, cataclysm, debacle**

catch *VERB*

❶ *I leapt up to catch the ball.*
• **seize, grab, grasp, grip, clutch, snatch, receive, intercept, get**
OPPOSITES drop, miss
❷ *They didn't catch many fish that day.*
• **hook, net, trap**
❸ *The police have caught the culprits.*
• **capture, apprehend, arrest, seize, take prisoner**
(*informal*) **nab, collar**
OPPOSITE release
❹ *I think I've caught a cold.*
• **contract, pick up, get, develop, be taken ill with**
(*informal*) **go down with, come down with**
❺ *I caught my brother listening at the door.*
• **discover, surprise, find out**
❻ *You must hurry if you want to catch the bus.*
• **be in time for, get on, get**
❼ *I caught my foot in the stirrup.*
• **get stuck, snag, jam, wedge, lodge**
➤ catch on
❶ *E-books soon caught on.*
• **become popular, do well, succeed, thrive, flourish**
(*informal*) **take off**
❷ *It took me a while to catch on.*
• **understand, comprehend**
(*informal*) **cotton on, latch on**

catch *NOUN*

❶ *The fishermen returned with a large catch of salmon.*
• **haul, yield, net**
❷ *It looks like a good offer, but there must be a catch.*
• **disadvantage, drawback, snag, hitch, problem, trap, trick**
❸ *All the windows are fitted with safety catches.*
• **fastening, latch, lock, bolt, clasp**

catching *ADJECTIVE*

Chickenpox is catching.
• **infectious, contagious, communicable**
OPPOSITE non-infectious

catchy *ADJECTIVE*

It's a very catchy tune.
• **memorable, unforgettable, appealing**

category *NOUN*

He won first prize in the under-16s category.
• **class, group, grouping, section, division, set, grade, rank**

cater *VERB*

➤ cater for
❶ *The hotel can cater for a hundred wedding guests.*
• **cook for, provide food for, feed, serve**
❷ *The school caters for children of all abilities.*
• **provide for, serve, accommodate, meet the needs of**

cattle *PLURAL NOUN*

Cattle were grazing in the meadow.
• **cows, herd, livestock**
– Male cattle are **bulls, steers** or **oxen**.
– Young male cattle are **calves** or **bullocks**.
– Young female cattle are **calves** or **heifers**.

– A word meaning 'to do with cattle' is **bovine**.

caught
past tense see **catch**

cause *NOUN*
❶ *The cause of the accident is a mystery.*
• **source, root, origin, starting point**
❷ *There is no cause for alarm.*
• **reason, grounds, need, justification, call**
❸ *They are raising money for a good cause.*
• **purpose, object, aim, objective**

cause *VERB*
A single spark caused the fire.
• **bring about, give rise to, lead to, result in, create, generate, engender, produce, prompt, induce, provoke, trigger**

caution *NOUN*
❶ *Drivers were advised to proceed with caution.*
• **care, attention, alertness, watchfulness, wariness, vigilance, discretion, prudence**
❷ *He received a caution from the police.*
• **warning, reprimand, admonishment, rebuke**
(*informal*) **telling-off**

cautious *ADJECTIVE*
My grandad is a cautious driver.
• **careful, attentive, alert, watchful, wary, vigilant, prudent**
OPPOSITES careless, reckless

cave *NOUN*
There are caves at the foot of the cliffs.
• **cavern, pothole, chamber**
– A man-made cave with decorative walls is a **grotto**.
– The entrance to a cave is the **mouth**.
– The hobby of exploring caves is **caving** or **potholing**.

cave *VERB*
➤ **cave in**
❶ *The whole roof had caved in.*
• **collapse, fall in**
❷ *She finally caved in and agreed that he could go.*
• **give in, yield, surrender**

cavity *NOUN*
There is a hidden cavity in the wall.
• **hole, hollow, space, chamber, pocket, gap**

cease *VERB*
❶ *The fighting ceased at midnight.*
• **come to an end, end, finish, stop, halt, conclude**
OPPOSITES begin, resume, continue
❷ *The firm ceased trading last year.*
• **bring to an end, stop, discontinue, terminate, suspend, wind up**

celebrate *VERB*
❶ *Let's celebrate!*
• **enjoy yourself, have fun, have a good time**
(*informal*) **party**
❷ *The couple celebrate their silver wedding anniversary last week.*
• **commemorate, observe, mark, keep, honour**

celebrated *ADJECTIVE*
She is now a celebrated author.
• **famous, well-known, acclaimed, renowned, eminent, notable, prominent, esteemed**
OPPOSITES little-known, obscure

celebration *NOUN*
❶ *We had a big celebration for his birthday.*
• **party, function, festivity, festival, jamboree**
❷ *Her triumph was a cause for celebration.*
• **festivities, merrymaking, enjoying yourself, partying**

celebrity *NOUN*
❶ *He never really enjoyed his celebrity.*
• **fame, renown, stardom, popularity, prominence**
❷ *The award is usually presented by a TV celebrity.*
• **famous person, personality, VIP, star, superstar, idol, big name**
(*informal*) **celeb**

cellar *NOUN*
We keep our bikes in the cellar.
• **basement, vault**
– A room underneath a church is a **crypt**.

cemetery *NOUN*
Some famous people are buried in the local cemetery.
• **graveyard, burial ground, churchyard**
– A place where dead people are cremated is a **crematorium**.

central *ADJECTIVE*
❶ *We were looking at a map of central Europe.*
• **middle, core, inner, innermost, interior**
OPPOSITE outer
❷ *The film's central character is a fifteen-year-old girl.*
• **main, chief, principal, major, primary, foremost, key, core, essential, vital, fundamental**
OPPOSITES minor, lesser

centre *NOUN*
The burial chamber is in the centre of the pyramid.
• **middle, heart, core, hub**
– The edible part in the centre of a nut is the **kernel**.
– The central part of an atom or cell is the **nucleus**.
– The centre of a storm or hurricane is the **eye**.
OPPOSITES edge, periphery

ceremony *NOUN*
❶ *We watched the opening ceremony of the Olympic Games.*
• **rite, ritual, formalities, service, observance**
– A ceremony to celebrate something new is an **inauguration** or **opening**.
– A ceremony to remember a dead person or a past event is a **commemoration**.
– A ceremony where someone is given a special honour is an **investiture**.
❷ *The presentation was made with a great deal of ceremony.*
• **formality, pomp, pageantry, spectacle**

certain *ADJECTIVE*
❶ *I'm certain we'll get tickets.*
• **confident, convinced, positive, sure, determined**
OPPOSITE uncertain
❷ *We have certain proof that the painting is a forgery.*
• **definite, clear, convincing, absolute, unquestionable, reliable, trustworthy, undeniable, infallible, genuine, valid**
OPPOSITE unreliable
❸ *They were facing certain disaster.*
• **inevitable, unavoidable**
OPPOSITE possible
❹ *It is certain to be a success.*
• **bound, sure**
➤ **for certain**
I'll give you the money tomorrow for certain.
• **certainly, definitely, for sure, without doubt**
➤ **make certain**
Please make certain that you switch off the lights.
• **make sure, ensure**

certainly *ADVERB*
I'd certainly like to meet her.
• **definitely, undoubtedly, unquestionably, assuredly, without a doubt**

certainty *NOUN*
❶ *We may never know the answer with certainty.*
• **confidence, conviction, assurance, sureness**
OPPOSITE doubt
❷ *They are a certainty to win the title.*
• **inevitability, foregone conclusion** (*informal*) **sure thing, dead cert**
OPPOSITE possibility

certificate *NOUN*
At the end of the course, you will receive a certificate.
• **diploma, document, licence, guarantee**

chain *NOUN*
❶ *The police formed a chain to keep the crowd back.*
• **line, row, cordon**

❷ *It was an unfortunate chain of events.*
• **series, sequence, succession, string**

chain *VERB*
He chained his bike up outside.
• **secure, fasten, tie, hitch, tether, shackle, fetter**

chair *NOUN*
see **seat**

challenge *NOUN*
❶ *The role will be the biggest challenge of his acting career.*
• **test, trial**
❷ *Do you accept my challenge?*
• **dare**

challenge *VERB*
❶ *I challenge you not to eat chips for a week.*
• **dare, defy**
IDIOM **throw down the gauntlet to**
❷ *This job doesn't really challenge me.*
• **test, stretch, tax, make demands on**
❸ *We will have to challenge the decision.*
• **question, dispute, call into question**

challenging *ADJECTIVE*
She has a challenging new job.
• **demanding, testing, taxing, exacting**
OPPOSITE **undemanding**

champion *NOUN*
❶ *She is the current Paralympic champion.*
• **title-holder, prizewinner, victor, winner, conqueror**
(*informal*) **champ**
❷ *Martin Luther King was a champion of civil rights.*
• **supporter, advocate, defender, proponent, promoter, upholder, backer, patron**

champion *VERB*
The charity champions the rights of children.
• **advocate, support, promote, uphold, defend, back, espouse, stand up for**

championship *NOUN*
Sixteen schools took part in the hockey championship.
• **competition, contest, tournament**

chance *NOUN*
❶ *There's a chance of rain later.*
• **possibility, prospect, likelihood, probability, danger, threat, risk**
OPPOSITE **certainty**
❷ *Give me a chance to answer.*
• **opportunity, time, occasion, opening, turn**
❸ *Are you prepared to take a chance?*
• **gamble, risk**
(*informal*) **punt**
IDIOM **leap in the dark**
➤ **by chance**
We found the place purely by chance.
• **by accident, accidentally, unintentionally, fortuitously, by coincidence**
OPPOSITE **intentionally**

change *VERB*
❶ *We will have to change all our plans.*
• **alter, modify, rearrange, reorganize, adjust, adapt, amend, revise, transform, vary**
OPPOSITES **preserve, retain**
❷ *The town has changed a lot since Victorian times.*
• **alter, become different, develop, evolve, move on, metamorphose**
❸ *Could I change this shirt for a larger size?*
• **exchange, replace, switch, substitute**
(*informal*) **swap**
➤ **change into**
Tadpoles change into frogs.
• **become, turn into, metamorphose into, be transformed into**

change *NOUN*
❶ *There has been a last-minute change of plan.*
• **alteration, modification, variation, revision, amendment, adjustment, adaptation, metamorphosis**
❷ *Have you brought a change of clothes?*
• **exchange, replacement, switch, substitution**
(*informal*) **swap**

changeable *ADJECTIVE*
The weather has been changeable today.
• **variable, unsettled, unpredictable,**

unreliable, inconsistent, erratic, unstable
– If your loyalty is changeable you are **fickle**.
OPPOSITE steady

channel *NOUN*
❶ *The rainwater runs along this channel.*
• **duct, conduit, gutter, drain, ditch, trough, sluice**
❷ *How many TV channels do you get?*
• **station**

chaos *NOUN*
After the earthquake, the city was in chaos.
• **disorder, confusion, mayhem, turmoil, tumult, pandemonium, disorganization, anarchy, lawlessness, bedlam, muddle, a shambles**
OPPOSITES order, orderliness

chaotic *ADJECTIVE*
At first the music seemed to be a chaotic jumble of sounds.
• **disorderly, disorganized, confused, muddled, topsy-turvy, in turmoil, anarchic, unruly, riotous**
(*informal*) **shambolic**
OPPOSITES orderly, organized

chapter *NOUN*
❶ *I read the opening chapter last night.*
• **section, part, division**
❷ *This was to be a new chapter in my life.*
• **period, phase, stage, era**

character *NOUN*
❶ *She was a woman with a strong character.*
• **personality, temperament, nature, disposition, mentality, make-up, manner, spirit, identity**
❷ *He's a bit of an odd character.*
• **person, individual, figure, personality, creature**
❸ *Who is your favourite character in the play?*
• **part, role**
❹ *The sign was written in Chinese characters.*
• **letter, figure, symbol, hieroglyph**

characteristic *NOUN*
The building has some interesting characteristics.
• **feature, attribute, trait, property, quality, peculiarity, idiosyncrasy, quirk**

characteristic *ADJECTIVE*
Windmills are a characteristic feature of this area.
• **typical, distinctive, recognizable, representative, particular, special, peculiar, idiosyncratic, singular**

charge *NOUN*
❶ *The admission charge is six euros.*
• **price, payment, fee, rate, tariff, levy**
– The charge made for a ride on public transport is the **fare**.
– A charge made to join a club is a **fee** or **subscription**.
– A charge made for certain things by the government is a **duty** or **tax**.
– A charge made to use a private road, bridge or tunnel is a **toll**.
❷ *He is facing three charges of burglary.*
• **accusation, allegation, indictment**
❸ *The infantry suffered heavy casualties in the charge.*
• **attack, assault, offensive, onslaught, drive, push**
❹ *We are leaving the house in your charge.*
• **care, keeping, protection, custody, trust**
➤ **be in charge of**
She was now in charge of the expedition.
• **manage, supervise, oversee, direct, lead, command, run**
(*informal*) **head up**

charge *VERB*
❶ *How much do you charge for lessons?*
• **ask for, make someone pay, invoice**
❷ *The men have been charged with attempted robbery.*
• **accuse (of), indict**
❸ *The bull put its head down and charged.*
• **attack, storm, rush, drive, stampede, go headlong**

charitable *ADJECTIVE*
Let's be charitable and assume she just made a mistake.
• **generous, magnanimous, considerate, compassionate, unselfish, benevolent, humanitarian, philanthropic**

charity *NOUN*
Show some charity towards those in need.
• **compassion, generosity, kindness, benevolence, consideration, caring, goodwill**
OPPOSITE selfishness

charm *NOUN*
❶ *He was a man of great charm.*
• **appeal, attractiveness, allure, charisma**
❷ *The sorcerer recited a magic charm.*
• **spell, incantation**
❸ *She carried special coin as a lucky charm.*
• **talisman, mascot, amulet, trinket**

charm *VERB*
She charmed the audience with her humour and wit.
• **delight, please, captivate, enchant, entrance, fascinate, beguile, bewitch, win over**

charming *ADJECTIVE*
We drove through some charming scenery.
• **delightful, endearing, appealing, likeable, pleasing, attractive, captivating**

chart *NOUN*
❶ *This chart shows the average monthly rainfall.*
• **diagram, graph, table**
❷ *The captain consulted a chart of the Pacific.*
• **map**

charter *VERB*
We can charter an aircraft over the mountains.
• **hire, lease, rent**

chase *VERB*
My dog likes chasing rabbits.
• **pursue, run after, follow, track, trail, hunt**

chasm *NOUN*
Below the bridge was a deep chasm.
• **opening, gulf, fissure, rift, ravine, crevasse, canyon, gorge, pit, abyss**

chat *NOUN*
Do you have time for a quick chat?
• **talk, conversation, gossip**
(*informal*) **natter, chinwag**

chat *VERB*
They spend hours chatting on the phone.
• **talk, converse, gossip**
(*informal*) **natter, have a chinwag**

chatter *VERB*
❶ *They chattered away happily for a while.*
• **prattle, babble, chat**
(*informal*) **natter, rabbit on**
❷ *My teeth were chattering with the cold.*
• **rattle, jangle**

chatter *NOUN*
I don't engage in idle chatter.
• **prattle, babble**
(*informal*) **chit-chat, nattering**

chatty *ADJECTIVE*
She seemed to be in a chatty mood.
• **talkative, communicative, garrulous**
OPPOSITES uncommunicative, taciturn

cheap *ADJECTIVE*
❶ *We got a cheap flight to Paris.*
• **inexpensive, low-priced, low-cost, affordable, reasonable, economical, budget, bargain, cut-price, discount**
❷ *These tyres are made from cheap rubber.*
• **inferior, poor-quality, second-rate, substandard, shoddy, trashy**
(*informal*) **rubbishy, cheapo, tacky**
OPPOSITES superior, good-quality

cheat *VERB*
The bank is accused of cheating its customers.
• **deceive, defraud, trick, swindle, dupe, double-cross, hoodwink**
(*informal*) **con, diddle, fleece, rip off, sucker**

cheat *NOUN*
Are you calling me a cheat?
• **cheater, deceiver, swindler, fraudster, fraud, charlatan**

check *VERB*
❶ *Remember to check your spelling.*
• **examine, inspect, look over, scrutinize**
IDIOM (*informal*) **give the once-over**
❷ *I'll just check that the door is locked.*
• **make sure, confirm, verify**
❸ *Firebreaks are used to check the spread of forest fires.*
• **halt, stop, arrest, block, obstruct, curb, hold back, hamper, hinder, slow, slow down**

check *NOUN*
❶ *I need to run some checks on my computer.*
• **test, examination, inspection, check-up, study, scrutiny, perusal**
❷ *Parliament acts as a check on the power of the sovereign.*
• **control, curb, limitation, restraint, restriction, constraint**

cheeky *ADJECTIVE*
My little sister has a cheeky answer for everything!
• **impudent, impertinent, insolent, disrespectful, rude, irreverent, flippant**
OPPOSITE **respectful**

cheer *NOUN*
There was a loud cheer from the crowd.
• **applause, ovation, hurray, hurrah, whoop**

cheer *VERB*
❶ *We'll be there to cheer when you win.*
• **applaud, clap, shout, yell**
OPPOSITES **jeer, boo**
❷ *The good news cheered them a good deal.*
• **comfort, console, gladden, delight, please, encourage, uplift**
OPPOSITE **sadden**

➤ **cheer up**
Everyone had cheered up by the afternoon.
• **brighten up, perk up, rally, revive, take heart, bounce back**
(*informal*) **buck up**

➤ **cheer someone up**
What can I do to cheer you up?
• **raise your spirits, brighten, hearten, gladden, uplift, buoy up, perk up**
(*informal*) **buck up**
OPPOSITES **sadden, depress**

cheerful *ADJECTIVE*
❶ *We set out in a cheerful mood.*
• **happy, good-humoured, light-hearted, cheery, merry, jolly, joyful, bright, sunny, chirpy, perky, lively, animated, elated, buoyant, jovial, gleeful**
(*informal*) **upbeat**
IDIOM **full of beans**
OPPOSITES **sad, gloomy**
❷ *It was a sunny and cheerful room.*
• **pleasant, agreeable, attractive, bright, welcoming, friendly**
OPPOSITES **dark, dismal**

chemist *NOUN*
I bought some skin cream from the chemist.
• **pharmacist**
(*old use*) **apothecary, alchemist**
– A chemist's shop is a **dispensary** or **pharmacy**.

chequered *ADJECTIVE*
The tablecloth had a chequered pattern.
• **check, criss-cross**
– Scottish cloth with a chequered pattern is **tartan**.

cherish *VERB*
❶ *I shall cherish this gift all my life.*
• **treasure, prize, value, hold dear, care for, keep safe**
❷ *We have lost a dear and cherished friend.*
• **love, adore, dote on, be devoted to, revere**
IDIOM **think the world of**

chess *NOUN*

WORD WEB

Names of chess pieces:

- bishop
- castle or rook
- king
- knight
- pawn
- queen

Other terms used in chess:

- castling
- check
- checkmate
- chessboard
- endgame
- gambit
- grandmaster
- mate
- move
- opening
- queening
- sacrifice
- stalemate
- tournament

chest *NOUN*
❶ *The bullet hit him in the chest.*
• **breast, torso, ribcage, front**
❷ *I found a chest full of old clothes.*
• **box, crate, case, trunk, casket, coffer**

chew *VERB*
He is always chewing a piece of gum.
• **munch, gnaw, chomp**

chicken *NOUN*
A few chickens scratched around in the yard.
– A female chicken is a **hen**.
– A male chicken is a **rooster**.
– A young chicken is a **chick**.
– A group of chickens is a **brood**.
– A farm which keeps chickens is a **poultry farm**.

chief *NOUN*
❶ *Sitting Bull was chief of the Lakota.*
• **leader, ruler, commander, captain, chieftain, master**
❷ *He is the chief of NASA.*
• **head, chief executive, director, president, governor, principal, CEO**
(*informal*) **boss**

chief *ADJECTIVE*
❶ *The chief ingredients are butter and icing sugar.*
• **main, principal, primary, prime, major, foremost, key, central, basic, essential, vital, fundamental, predominant, prominent**
OPPOSITES minor, secondary
❷ *She became the chief editor of the magazine.*
• **head, senior, top, leading, principal, supreme, highest**
OPPOSITE subordinate

chiefly *ADVERB*
Kangaroos are found chiefly in Australia.
• **mainly, mostly, primarily, principally, predominantly, generally, usually, typically, in the main, on the whole**

child *NOUN*
❶ *The book festival is aimed especially at children.*
• **boy or girl, infant, juvenile, youngster, youth, lad or lass**
(*informal*) **kid, tot, nipper**
❷ *How many children do you have?*
• **son or daughter, descendant, offspring**
– A child whose parents are dead is an **orphan**.
– A child looked after by a guardian is a **ward**.

childhood *NOUN*
He spent much of his childhood by the sea.
• **boyhood or girlhood, youth, early life, infancy**
– The time when someone is a baby is their **babyhood**.
– The time when someone is a teenager is their **adolescence** or **teens**.
OPPOSITE adulthood

childish *ADJECTIVE*
Don't be so childish!
• **immature, babyish, juvenile, infantile, puerile**
OPPOSITE mature

chill *NOUN*
We felt a distinct chill in the air.
• **coldness, chilliness, coolness, nip**

A B C D E F G H I J K L M N O P Q R S T U V W X Y Z

chill *VERB*
❶ *Chill the pudding before serving it.*
• **cool, refrigerate, freeze**
OPPOSITES **warm, heat**
❷ *The look in his eyes chilled me to my core.*
• **frighten, scare, terrify, petrify**
IDIOMS **make your blood run cold, give you goosebumps**
➤ **chill out**
(*informal*) *We've been chilling out in front of the TV.*
• **relax, unwind, take it easy**
(*informal*) **chill**
IDIOM **put your feet up**

chilly *ADJECTIVE*
❶ *It was a chilly evening.*
• **cold, cool, frosty, icy, crisp, fresh, raw, wintry**
(*informal*) **nippy**
OPPOSITE **warm**
❷ *They gave us a very chilly reception.*
• **unfriendly, unwelcoming, cold, cool, frosty**
OPPOSITES **friendly, warm**

chime *VERB*
The hall clock chimes every hour.
• **ring, sound, strike, peal, toll**

chimney *NOUN*
I could see smoke coming from the chimney.
– A chimney on a ship or steam engine is a **funnel**.
– A pipe to take away smoke and fumes is a **flue**.

china *NOUN*
There were pieces of broken china on the floor.
• **crockery, dishes, plates, tableware, cups and saucers, porcelain**

chink *NOUN*
❶ *I looked through a small chink in the wall.*
• **gap, space, crack, crevice, hole, opening, aperture, fissure, split, slit, rift, cleft**
❷ *There was a chink of coins as the money changed hands.*
• **clink, jingle, jangle, tinkle**

chip *NOUN*
❶ *There were chips of broken glass on the pavement.*
• **bit, piece, fragment, scrap, sliver, splinter, flake, shaving**
❷ *This teapot has a chip on the lid.*
• **crack, nick, notch, flaw**

chip *VERB*
Someone has chipped my favourite mug.
• **crack, nick, notch**

choice *NOUN*
❶ *I'm afraid you have no choice.*
• **alternative, option**
❷ *There is now a wide choice of TV channels.*
• **range, selection, variety, assortment, array**
❸ *She wouldn't be my choice as team captain.*
• **selection, preference, choosing, pick**

choice *ADJECTIVE*
We use only choice ingredients.
• **superior, first-class, first-rate, top-quality, best, finest, prime, premier, select, prize**
(*informal*) **top-notch**
OPPOSITES **inferior, second-rate**

choke *VERB*
❶ *The fumes were nearly choking them.*
• **suffocate, smother, stifle, asphyxiate, throttle**
❷ *She was choking on a fish bone.*
• **gag, cough, retch**
❸ *The drain is choked with leaves.*
• **block, clog, obstruct, congest, bung up, stop up**

choose *VERB*
❶ *It has not been easy to choose this year's winner.*
• **select, decide on, pick out, opt for, plump for, settle on, vote for, elect**
❷ *I would never choose to live there.*
• **decide, determine, prefer, resolve**

chop *VERB*
He was outside, chopping wood for the fire.
• **cut, split, hew, hack, slash, cleave**
– To chop down a tree is to **fell** it.
➤ **chop something off**
We chopped off the lower branches.
• **cut off, lop off, sever, shear**
– To chop off an arm or a leg is to **amputate** it.
➤ **chop something up**
Help me chop up some vegetables.
• **cut up, cube, dice, mince**

chronicle *NOUN*
At the front is a chronicle of her early life.
• **story, history, narrative, account, record, journal, annals, saga**

chubby *ADJECTIVE*
He was a chubby little baby.
• **plump, tubby, podgy, round, dumpy**

chuck (*informal*) *VERB*
Just chuck your bag on the floor.
• **throw, fling, sling, toss, hurl, pitch, cast**
(*informal*) **bung, dump**

chuckle *VERB*
He was chuckling as he left the room.
• **laugh, giggle, snigger, chortle, titter**

chunk *NOUN*
I bit a chunk out of my apple.
• **piece, portion, lump, block, hunk, slab, wedge**
(*informal*) **wodge**

church *NOUN*
I could see the spire of an old parish church.
• **chapel, cathedral, minster, abbey**
For other religious buildings see **religion.**

churn *VERB*
Vast crowds had churned the field into a sea of mud.
• **agitate, disturb, stir up**

circle *NOUN*
❶ *We arranged the chairs in a circle.*
• **ring, round, hoop, loop, band, circlet**
– A flat, solid circle is a **disc**.
– A three-dimensional round shape is a **sphere**.
– An egg shape is an **oval** or **ellipse**.
– The distance round a circle is the **circumference**.
– The distance across a circle is the **diameter**.
– The distance from the centre to the circumference is the **radius**.
– A circular movement is a **revolution** or **rotation**.
– A circular trip round the world is a **circumnavigation**.
– A circular trip of a satellite round a planet is an **orbit**.
❷ *She has a wide circle of friends.*
• **group, set, crowd**
(*informal*) **gang, bunch**

circle *VERB*
❶ *Vultures were circling overhead.*
• **go round, wheel, revolve, rotate, whirl, spiral**
❷ *Satellites circle the earth.*
• **go round, orbit, circumnavigate, revolve round**

circuit *NOUN*
We have to complete two circuits of the race track.
• **lap, round, circle, revolution, orbit**

circular *ADJECTIVE*
Most of Saturn's rings are circular.
• **round, ring-shaped, disc-shaped**

circulate *VERB*
❶ *Blood circulates in the body.*
• **pass round, go round, move round**
❷ *I asked friends to circulate our newsletter.*
• **distribute, send round, broadcast, communicate, publicize, disseminate**

A B C D E F G H I J K L M N O P Q R S T U V W X Y Z

circumference *NOUN*
There is a path around the circumference of the lake.
• **perimeter, edge, rim, border, boundary**

circumstances *PLURAL NOUN*
The police pieced together the circumstances surrounding the murder.
• **situation, conditions, background, context, state of affairs, factors, particulars, details**

citizen *NOUN*
❶ *The citizens of New York are proud of their city.*
• **resident, inhabitant, city-dweller, townsman or townswoman**
(*formal*) **denizen**
❷ *She is an Australian citizen.*
• **national, passport holder, subject**

city *NOUN*
Nairobi is a city in Kenya.
– The chief city of a country or region is the **metropolis**.
– An area of houses outside the central part of a city is the **suburbs**.
– Words meaning 'to do with a city' are **urban, civic** and **metropolitan**.
SEE ALSO **town**

civil *ADJECTIVE*
❶ *Please try to be civil.*
• **polite, courteous, well-behaved, well-mannered**
OPPOSITES **uncivil, rude**
❷ *He is good at recognizing civil aircraft.*
• **civilian, non-military**
OPPOSITE **military**

civilization *NOUN*
We are studying the civilization of ancient Egypt.
• **culture, society, way of life**

civilized *ADJECTIVE*
Try to behave in a civilized manner.
• **polite, courteous, well-behaved, well-mannered, civil, sophisticated, cultured, polished, refined**
OPPOSITES **uncivilized, rude**

claim *VERB*
❶ *You can claim a refund at the office.*
• **ask for, apply for, request, demand**
❷ *He claims that he can speak Russian.*
• **declare, assert, allege, maintain, contend, argue, insist**

clamber *VERB*
It was dangerous clambering over the rocks.
• **climb, scramble, crawl, move awkwardly**

clammy *ADJECTIVE*
The walls of the dungeon were cold and clammy.
• **damp, moist, dank, slimy, sticky**

clamp *VERB*
The rack is clamped onto the car roof.
• **fasten, attach, fix, secure, screw, bolt**

clap *VERB*
❶ *The audience clapped loudly at the end of the concert.*
• **applaud, cheer, give a round of applause**
IDIOMS **give a big hand (to), put your hands together (for)**
❷ *Suddenly, a hand clapped me on the shoulder.*
• **slap, hit, pat, smack**

clarify *VERB*
Can you clarify the situation for me?
• **explain, make clear, elucidate, illuminate**
IDIOMS **throw light on, spell out**
OPPOSITE **confuse**

clarity *NOUN*
She explained everything with great clarity.
• **clearness, coherence, lucidity, transparency, precision**
OPPOSITE **confusion**

clash *VERB*
❶ *We heard the sound of cymbals clashing.*
• **crash, resound**

❷ *Demonstrators clashed with the police.*
• argue, fight, contend, squabble
IDIOMS come to blows, lock horns
❸ *The film clashes with the football highlights.*
• coincide, happen at the same time, conflict
❹ *Do these colours clash?*
• conflict, jar, be incompatible
IDIOM be at odds
OPPOSITES harmonize, go together

clash *NOUN*
❶ *The clash of cymbals made me jump.*
• crash, bang, ringing
❷ *There was a clash between rival supporters.*
• fight, confrontation, argument, conflict, scuffle
(*informal*) scrap

clasp *VERB*
❶ *The little boy clasped his mother's hand.*
• grasp, grip, hold, squeeze, clutch
❷ *She clasped him in her arms.*
• embrace, hug, hold, cling to

clasp *NOUN*
The cloak was held in place by a gold clasp.
• clip, pin, fastener, brooch, buckle

class *NOUN*
❶ *There are 24 children in our class.*
• form, set, stream
– The other pupils in your class are your **classmates**.
❷ *There are many different classes of plants.*
• category, group, classification, division, grade, set, sort, type, kind, species
❸ *He appeals to people from all classes of society.*
• level, rank, status, stratum

class *VERB*
Our books are classed according to size.
• classify, categorize, group, rank, grade, designate

classic *ADJECTIVE*
❶ *That was a classic tennis final this year.*
• outstanding, exceptional, excellent, first-class, first-rate, fine, great, admirable, masterly
(*informal*) top-notch
OPPOSITES ordinary, second-rate
❷ *It was a classic case of overconfidence.*
• typical, representative, characteristic, perfect, textbook, model, archetypal, quintessential
OPPOSITE atypical

classify *VERB*
All living things can be classified into species.
• categorize, class, group, grade, rank, sort, order, bracket

claw *NOUN*
❶ *Lions have very sharp claws.*
• talon, nail
❷ *The crab had something in one of its claws.*
• pincer

claw *VERB*
We could hear the bear clawing at the door.
• scratch, scrape, tear, rip

clean *ADJECTIVE*
❶ *He found a clean pair of socks.*
• washed, cleaned, laundered, scrubbed, swept, tidy, immaculate, spotless, unstained, unsullied, hygienic, sanitary
OPPOSITE dirty
❷ *You need to keep the wound clean.*
• sterile, sterilized, disinfected, uninfected
OPPOSITES infected, septic
❸ *I love the clean air of the mountains.*
• pure, clear, fresh, unpolluted, uncontaminated
OPPOSITES polluted, contaminated
❹ *I started the story on a clean page.*
• blank, unused, unmarked, empty, bare, fresh, new, pristine
OPPOSITES used, marked

5 *The referee said he wanted a clean fight.*
• **fair, honest, honourable, sporting, sportsmanlike**
OPPOSITES unfair, dirty

clean *VERB*
1 *We cleaned the house from top to bottom.*
• **wash, wipe, mop, swab, sponge, scour, scrub, dust, sweep, vacuum, shampoo, swill**
– To clean clothes is to **launder** them.
OPPOSITES dirty, mess up
2 *The nurse cleaned the wound with antiseptic.*
• **cleanse, bathe, disinfect, sterilize, sanitize**
OPPOSITES infect, contaminate

clear *ADJECTIVE*
1 *We saw fish swimming in the clear pool.*
• **clean, pure, transparent, translucent**
OPPOSITES opaque, muddy
2 *It was a beautiful clear day.*
• **bright, sunny, cloudless, unclouded**
– A clear night is a **moonlit** or **starlit** night.
OPPOSITES cloudy, overcast
3 *The address on the envelope is not clear.*
• **legible, recognizable, visible**
OPPOSITE illegible
4 *Your camera takes very clear pictures.*
• **sharp, well defined, focused**
OPPOSITE blurred
5 *He spoke in a clear voice.*
• **distinct, audible**
OPPOSITES indistinct, muffled
6 *I gave you clear instructions.*
• **understandable, intelligible, comprehensible, lucid, coherent, plain, explicit, straightforward, unambiguous**
OPPOSITES ambiguous, confusing
7 *It was a clear case of mistaken identity.*
• **definite, unambiguous, indisputable, unmistakable, evident, obvious, patent, manifest, noticeable, distinct, conspicuous, perceptible, pronounced, glaring**
OPPOSITE imperceptible
8 *Is the road clear ahead?*
• **open, unobstructed, passable, empty, free**
OPPOSITES blocked, obstructed
9 *My conscience is clear.*
• **innocent, untroubled, blameless**
OPPOSITE guilty

clear *VERB*
1 *I cleared the weeds from the path.*
• **get rid of, remove, eliminate, strip**
2 *The plumber came to clear the blocked drain.*
• **unblock, unclog, unstop, open up**
– To clear a channel is to **dredge** it.
3 *If the alarm goes, clear the building by the nearest exit.*
• **evacuate, empty**
4 *The fog cleared slowly.*
• **disappear, go away, vanish, evaporate, disperse, dissipate, shift, lift, melt away, fade**
5 *He was cleared of all the charges against him.*
• **acquit, free, absolve, exonerate** (*informal*) **let off**
6 *All the runners cleared the first hurdle.*
• **go over, get over, jump over, pass over, vault**

➤ **clear up**
1 *The weather should clear up by the afternoon.*
• **become clear, brighten, brighten up**
2 *The symptoms often clear up by themselves.*
• **heal, get better, recover, mend**

➤ **clear something up**
1 *I'll clear up the mess later.*
• **clean up, tidy up, put right, put straight, put in order**
2 *Thank you for clearing up that little mystery.*
• **explain, answer, solve, resolve**
IDIOM get to the bottom of

clearly *ADVERB*
1 *Speak slowly and clearly.*
• **distinctly, plainly, intelligibly, audibly, legibly**
2 *Clearly, we need to talk.*
• **obviously, evidently, plainly, patently,**

undoubtedly, unquestionably, without question

clench *VERB*
❶ *He clenched his teeth in anger.*
• close tightly, squeeze together, grit, clamp
❷ *She clenched the coin tightly in her hand.*
• grip, clasp, grasp, hold

clergyman or **clergywoman** *NOUN*
see **religion**

clever *ADJECTIVE*
❶ *He was an exceptionally clever student.*
• intelligent, bright, smart, quick-witted, astute, able, capable, competent, gifted, talented
(*informal*) brainy
OPPOSITE unintelligent
❷ *They came up with a clever scheme to make money.*
• ingenious, crafty, cunning, canny, shrewd, smart, artful, wily
OPPOSITE stupid
❸ *She has always been clever with her hands.*
• skilful, dexterous, adroit, nimble, deft, adept, handy
OPPOSITES unskilful, clumsy

client *NOUN*
The firm has a number of overseas clients.
• customer, user, consumer, buyer, shopper

cliff *NOUN*
The village is perched on the top of a cliff.
• crag, rock face, precipice, ridge, bluff, escarpment, scar

climate *NOUN*
She has studied the effects of pollution on our climate.
• weather conditions, weather patterns
SEE ALSO **weather**

climax *NOUN*
The climax of the film is a stunning car chase.
• high point, highlight, height, culmination, peak, pinnacle
OPPOSITE anticlimax

climb *VERB*
❶ *It took us several hours to climb the mountain.*
• ascend, go up, scale, mount, clamber up
OPPOSITE descend
❷ *We watched the balloons climb into the sky.*
• rise, soar, ascend, mount, rocket
❸ *The road climbs steeply up to the village.*
• go uphill, rise, slope, incline
➤ **climb down**
❶ *I carefully climbed down from the roof.*
• descend, go down, get down
❷ *You'll never get him to climb down.*
• back down, give in, surrender, admit defeat
IDIOMS eat your words, do a U-turn

climb *NOUN*
It's a steep climb to the cave entrance.
• ascent, rise, slope, gradient, incline

clinch *VERB*
A late goal clinched the victory for the home team.
• secure, seal, settle, decide, confirm, conclude, finalize, close
(*informal*) sew up

cling *VERB*
❶ *She clung to the rope with all her strength.*
• clasp, clutch, grasp, hold on
❷ *Ivy clings to the wall.*
• stick, adhere, fasten on

clip *NOUN*
❶ *She undid the clip and opened the case.*
• fastener, clasp, catch, hook
❷ *They showed a clip from his latest film.*
• extract, excerpt, snippet, trailer

clip *VERB*
❶ *The two sheets were clipped together.*
• **pin, staple, fasten, attach**
❷ *Dad was clipping the hedge in the back garden.*
• **cut, trim, prune, crop**
❸ *The back wheel just clipped the kerb.*
• **hit, strike, scrape, nudge**

cloak *NOUN*
She wrapped her cloak tightly around herself.
• **cape, coat, wrap**
(*old use*) **mantle**

clock *NOUN*

WORD WEB

Instruments used to measure time:

- ➤ **atomic clock**
- ➤ **chronograph**
- ➤ **cuckoo clock**
- ➤ **digital clock**
- ➤ **hourglass**
- ➤ **pocket watch**
- ➤ **quartz clock**
- ➤ **stopwatch**
- ➤ **sundial**
- ➤ **water clock**
- ➤ **wristwatch**

- The study of clocks and timekeeping is **horology**.
- A person who makes clocks or watches is a **clockmaker** or **watchmaker**.

clog *VERB*
Dead leaves are clogging the drain.
• **block, choke, congest, obstruct, bung up, stop up, jam, plug**

close *ADJECTIVE*
❶ *Our house is close to the shops.*
• **near, nearby, not far (from)**
– To be actually by the side of something is to be **adjacent** to it.
OPPOSITES **far, distant**
❷ *She is one of my closest friends.*
• **intimate, dear, devoted, firm, faithful, inseparable, bosom, close-knit**
OPPOSITES **distant, casual**
❸ *The police made a close examination of the stolen car.*
• **careful, detailed, thorough, painstaking, minute, meticulous, rigorous**
OPPOSITES **casual, cursory**
❹ *He bears a close resemblance to the prime minister.*
• **strong, firm, distinct, marked, noticeable, unmistakable**
OPPOSITES **slight, passing**
❺ *It was a very close race.*
• **equal, even, level, well-matched**
IDIOM **neck and neck**
OPPOSITE **one-sided**
❻ *The air is very close in this room.*
• **humid, muggy, stuffy, clammy, heavy, airless, stifling, sticky, sultry**
OPPOSITES **fresh, airy**

close *VERB*
❶ *Don't forget to close the lid.*
• **shut, fasten, seal, secure**
❷ *The road is now closed to traffic.*
• **block, seal off, barricade, obstruct**
❸ *They closed the concert with my favourite song.*
• **finish, end, conclude, stop, terminate, complete**
(*informal*) **wind up**

close *NOUN*
What was the score at the close of play?
• **finish, end, stop, conclusion, termination, completion**

clot *VERB*
Blood will clot when exposed to the air.
• **coagulate, solidify, thicken, congeal**

cloth *NOUN*
❶ *The curtains were made of striped cotton cloth.*
• **fabric, material, textile**
For types of cloth see **fabric**.
❷ *Use a cloth to wipe the windows.*
• **rag, duster, flannel, wipe**

clothe *VERB*
➤ **be clothed in**
He was clothed in green from head to toe.
• **be dressed in, be wearing, be clad in, be decked in, be fitted out in**

clothes *PLURAL NOUN*
What clothes are you taking on holiday?
• **clothing, garments, outfits, dress, attire, garb, finery**
(*informal*) **gear, get-up, togs**
– A set of clothes to wear is a **costume, outfit** or **suit**.
– An official set of clothes worn for school or work is a **uniform**.
– A collection of clothes or costumes is a **wardrobe**.

WORD WEB

Some items of clothing:

- anorak
- apron
- ball gown
- bandanna
- bikini
- blazer
- blouse
- bow tie
- boxer shorts (*informal* boxers)
- bra
- briefs
- cagoule
- camisole
- cape
- cardigan
- cloak
- coat
- cowl
- cravat
- cummerbund
- dinner jacket (*North American* tuxedo)
- dress
- dressing gown
- dungarees
- gloves
- gown
- Hawaiian shirt
- headscarf
- hoody
- jacket
- jeans
- jersey
- jodhpurs
- jumper
- kaftan
- kilt
- knickerbockers
- knickers
- leggings
- leotard
- mackintosh (*informal* mac)
- mini skirt
- mittens
- nightdress (*informal* nightie)
- overalls
- overcoat
- petticoat
- pinafore
- plus-fours
- polo shirt
- pullover
- pyjamas
- raincoat
- robe
- rugby shirt
- sari
- sarong
- scarf
- shawl
- shirt
- shorts
- shrug
- skirt
- slip
- socks
- stockings
- stole
- suit
- sweater
- sweatshirt
- swimsuit
- tails
- tank top
- three-piece suit
- tie
- tights
- top
- tracksuit
- trousers (*North American* pants)
- trunks
- T-shirt
- tunic
- twinset
- underpants
- underwear (*informal* undies)
- veil
- vest
- waistcoat
- wetsuit
- wrap

SEE ALSO **hat**

For clothes worn in the past see **historical**.

WRITING TIPS

DESCRIBING CLOTHES
Parts and accessories:

- belt
- bodice
- braces (*North American* suspenders)
- braid
- buckle
- buttons
- collar
- cuff
- flounce
- frill
- fringe
- hem
- hood
- lapel
- leg
- lining
- pintucks
- pocket
- ruffle
- seam
- sleeve
- trim
- turn-ups
- waist
- waistband
- zip

Adjectives:

- baggy
- casual
- chic
- creased
- crumpled
- dapper
- designer
- dingy
- drab
- elegant
- fashionable
- frayed
- frilly
- frumpy
- grubby
- ill-fitting
- in good or bad repair

- ➤ patched
- ➤ printed
- ➤ ragged
- ➤ scruffy
- ➤ shabby
- ➤ slovenly
- ➤ sporty
- ➤ stylish
- ➤ tailored
- ➤ tattered
- ➤ tatty
- ➤ threadbare
- ➤ unfashionable
- ➤ waterproof
- ➤ windproof
- ➤ worn

- Someone who wears smart clothes is **well dressed** or **well groomed**.

cloud *NOUN*
A cloud of steam billowed from the kettle.
• **billow, puff, haze, mist**

cloud *VERB*
Don't let anger cloud your judgement.
• **obscure, confuse, muddle**

cloudy *ADJECTIVE*
❶ *It was a cold and cloudy day.*
• **overcast, dull, grey, dark, dismal, gloomy, sunless, leaden**
OPPOSITES cloudless, clear
❷ *The pond water was cloudy.*
• **muddy, murky, milky, dirty**
OPPOSITES clear, transparent

club *NOUN*
❶ *He brandished a wooden club.*
• **stick, bat, baton, truncheon, cudgel**
❷ *She belonged to a book club.*
• **group, society, association, organization, circle, union**

club *VERB*
The victim was clubbed over the head with a blunt instrument.
• **hit, strike, beat, batter, bludgeon** (*informal*) **clout, clobber**

clue *NOUN*
❶ *Can you give me a clue?*
• **hint, suggestion, indication, pointer, tip, idea**
❷ *The police are still looking for clues.*
• **piece of evidence, lead**

clump *NOUN*
The owl flew into a clump of trees.
• **group, thicket, cluster, mass**
– A clump of grass or hair is a **tuft**.

clumsy *ADJECTIVE*
❶ *My fingers were clumsy with the cold.*
• **awkward, graceless, ungainly, inelegant, lumbering**
OPPOSITE graceful
❷ *He apologized for his clumsy handling of the situation.*
• **unskilful, inept, incompetent**
OPPOSITE skilful

cluster *NOUN*
There was a cluster of buildings at the top of the hill.
• **bunch, group, clump, mass, knot, collection, gathering, crowd**

cluster *VERB*
We all clustered around the computer screen.
• **crowd, huddle, gather, collect, group**

clutch *VERB*
In her hand, she clutched a handkerchief.
• **grip, grasp, clasp, cling to, hang on to, hold on to**

clutches *PLURAL NOUN*
At last he was free from their clutches.
• **grasp, power, control**

clutter *NOUN*
It's difficult to work with all this clutter around.
• **mess, muddle, disorder, untidiness, junk, litter, rubbish**

coach *NOUN*
❶ *We will travel there by coach.*
• **bus**
❷ *The football team has a new coach.*
• **trainer, instructor, teacher, tutor**

coach *VERB*
He was coached by a former champion.
• **train, teach, instruct, drill**

coarse *ADJECTIVE*
❶ *All he had on his bed was a coarse woollen blanket.*
• **rough, harsh, scratchy, bristly, hairy**
OPPOSITES soft, fine
❷ *We were shocked by their coarse table manners.*
• **rude, impolite, uncouth, improper, crude, vulgar**
OPPOSITES polite, refined

coast *NOUN*
We walked along the coast for three miles.
• **shore, coastline, shoreline, seaside, seashore**

coast *VERB*
I coasted downhill on my bike.
• **cruise, freewheel, glide**

coat *NOUN*
❶ *Put on a coat if you go out.*
• **overcoat, jacket**
❷ *The fox had a reddish-brown coat.*
• **hair, fur, hide, pelt, skin**
– A sheep's coat is a **fleece**.
❸ *The front door needs a new coat of paint.*
• **layer, coating, covering, film, skin**

coat *VERB*
I bought a packet of raisins coated with chocolate.
• **cover, spread, smear, plaster, daub, glaze**

coax *VERB*
A woman was trying to coax a kitten out of a tree.
• **persuade, cajole, wheedle, tempt, entice**

code *NOUN*
❶ *The message was written in a secret code.*
• **cipher**
– To put a message in code is to **encode** or **encrypt** it.
– To understand a message in code is to **decode**, **decipher** or (*informal*) **crack** it.
❷ *There is a strict code of conduct for using the pool.*
• **rules, regulations, laws**

coil *NOUN*
He passed me a coil of rope.
• **spiral, twist, curl, twirl, screw, corkscrew, whirl, whorl, roll, scroll**
– A coil of wool or thread is a **skein**.

coil *VERB*
The snake coiled itself round a branch.
• **curl, loop, wind, wrap, roll, twist, twirl, twine, spiral**

coin *NOUN*
Do you have a pound coin?
• **piece, bit**

WORD WEB

Some coins used in the past:

- denarius
- doubloon
- ducat
- farthing
- florin
- groat
- guinea
- halfpenny
- shilling
- sixpence
- sovereign

– A series of coins used for currency is **coinage**.
– The making of coins for currency is **minting**.
– The study of coins is **numismatics** and a person who studies or collects coins is a **numismatist**.

coin *VERB*
The word 'robot' was coined by a Czech writer.
• **invent, make up, think up, dream up, conceive, create, devise**

coincide *VERB*
❶ *This year, half-term coincides with my birthday.*
• **co-occur, fall together, happen together, clash**
❷ *Our opinions rarely coincide.*
• **agree, correspond, tally, accord, be in accord, be compatible, match up**

coincidence *NOUN*
By a strange coincidence, we have the same birthday.
• **chance, accident, luck, fortune, fluke, happenstance**

cold *ADJECTIVE*
❶ *We can expect a spell of cold weather.*
• **chilly, chill, frosty, freezing, icy, raw, arctic, bitter, cool, crisp, snowy, wintry**
(*informal*) **perishing, nippy**
OPPOSITES hot, warm
❷ *I was feeling cold.*
• **chilled, chilly, frozen, freezing, shivering, shivery**
– Someone with an abnormally low body temperature is suffering from **hypothermia**.
❸ *She gave me a cold stare.*
• **unfriendly, unkind, unfeeling, distant, cool, indifferent, stony, uncaring, unemotional, unsympathetic**
OPPOSITES warm, friendly

collaborate *VERB*
❶ *Several zoos collaborated on the rhino project.*
• **work together, cooperate, join forces, pool resources**
❷ *They were accused of collaborating with the enemy.*
• **cooperate, collude, consort, fraternize**

collapse *VERB*
❶ *Many buildings collapsed in the earthquake.*
• **fall down, fall in, cave in, give way, crumple, buckle, disintegrate, tumble down**
❷ *Some of the runners collapsed in the heat.*
• **faint, pass out, black out, fall over, keel over**

colleague *NOUN*
He said he would discuss the case with his colleagues.
• **co-worker, workmate, teammate, partner, associate, collaborator**

collect *VERB*
❶ *My brother and I were collecting shells on the beach.*
• **gather, accumulate, amass, hoard, pile up, store up, stockpile**
❷ *We are collecting money for charity.*
• **raise, take in**
❸ *I need to collect a parcel from the post office.*
• **fetch, pick up, get, call for**
OPPOSITES drop off, hand in
❹ *A crowd collected at the stage door.*
• **assemble, gather, come together, congregate, convene, converge, muster**
OPPOSITES scatter, disperse

collection *NOUN*
She has a wonderful collection of old photographs.
• **hoard, store, stock, pile, accumulation, set, assortment, array**
– A collection of books is a **library**.
– A collection of stories or poems is an **anthology**.

collective *ADJECTIVE*
It was a collective decision.
• **common, shared, joint, group, mutual, communal, combined**

collective noun *NOUN*

WORD WEB

- an **army** or a **colony** of ants
- a **flock** of birds
- a **herd** of cattle
- a **brood** of chicks
- a **pod** of dolphins
- a **herd** of elephants
- a **shoal** of fish
- a **gaggle** or **skein** of geese
- a **band** of gorillas
- a **swarm** of insects
- a **troop** of kangaroos
- a **pride** of lions
- a **troop** of monkeys

- a **colony** of penguins
- a **litter** of piglets or kittens or puppies
- a **pack** of rats
- a **flock** of sheep
- a **school** of whales
- a **pack** of wolves

college *NOUN*
He studied at a music college.
• **academy, school, university, institute**

collide *VERB*
➤ **collide with**
The car collided head-on with the van.
• **crash into, smash into, bump into, run into, hit, strike**

collision *NOUN*
He had to brake hard to avoid a collision with the car in front.
• **crash, accident, smash, bump, knock**
– A collision involving a lot of vehicles is a **pile-up**.

colloquial *ADJECTIVE*
Her books are written in a colloquial style.
• **informal, conversational, casual, everyday, idiomatic, vernacular**
OPPOSITE formal

colony *NOUN*
Australia and New Zealand were once British colonies.
• **territory, dependency, protectorate, settlement**

colossal *ADJECTIVE*
A colossal statue towered above us.
• **huge, enormous, gigantic, immense, massive, giant, mammoth, monumental, towering, vast**
OPPOSITES small, tiny

colour *NOUN*
These T-shirts are available in a range of colours.
• **hue, shade, tint, tone, tinge**

WRITING TIPS

DESCRIBING COLOURS
Light colours:

➤ delicate
➤ faded
➤ muted
➤ neutral
➤ pale
➤ pastel
➤ soft
➤ subtle
➤ washed-out

Dark or strong colours:

➤ bold
➤ bright
➤ deep
➤ fiery
➤ flaming
➤ fluorescent
➤ garish
➤ gaudy
➤ intense
➤ iridescent
➤ (*informal*) jazzy
➤ loud
➤ luminous
➤ lurid
➤ neon
➤ radiant
➤ vibrant
➤ vivid
➤ (*informal*) zingy

- The colours red, blue and yellow are known as **primary colours**.
- A colour made by mixing two primary colours is a **secondary colour**.
- The pattern of colours seen in a rainbow is called a **spectrum**.

colour *VERB*
❶ *She decided to colour her hair green.*
• **tint, dye, stain, tinge, paint**
❷ *The experience coloured his whole childhood.*
• **affect, influence, have an impact on, skew**

colourful *ADJECTIVE*
❶ *The poster has a very colourful design.*
• **multicoloured, vibrant, vivid, bright, showy, garish, gaudy**
(*informal*) **jazzy**
OPPOSITE colourless
❷ *She gave a colourful account of her trip.*
• **vivid, lively, interesting, exciting, striking, rich, picturesque**
OPPOSITE dull

colourless *ADJECTIVE*

❶ *The flask contained a colourless liquid.*
• **uncoloured, clear, transparent, neutral**
– Something which has lost its colour is **bleached** or **faded**.
❷ *All the characters in the book are colourless.*
• **dull, boring, uninteresting, unexciting, drab, dreary, lacklustre**
OPPOSITES colourful, interesting

column *NOUN*

❶ *The roof of the temple was supported by stone columns.*
• **pillar, post, support, upright, shaft, pile**
❷ *She writes a column in the local newspaper.*
• **article, piece, report, feature**
❸ *The troops marched in three columns.*
• **line, file, procession, row, convoy**

comb *VERB*

❶ *I'm just combing my hair.*
• **groom, brush, tidy, arrange, untangle**
❷ *The police combed the crime scene for evidence.*
• **search, scour, sweep, ransack, rummage through**

combat *NOUN*

In the square is a memorial for soldiers killed in combat.
• **battle, war, warfare, fighting, action, hostilities**

combat *VERB*

There is a new campaign to combat crime in the city.
• **fight, oppose, counter, resist, stand up to, tackle, battle against, grapple with**

combination *NOUN*

He succeeded through a combination of talent and hard work.
• **mixture, mix, union, fusion, blend, merger, amalgamation, synthesis**

combine *VERB*

❶ *Combine all the ingredients in a saucepan.*
• **mix, blend, fuse, bind, merge, marry, integrate, amalgamate**
OPPOSITES separate, divide
❷ *Three schools combined to stage the event.*
• **unite, join forces, get together**

come *VERB*

❶ *My parents will be coming tomorrow.*
• **arrive, appear, visit, turn up** (*informal*) **show up**
OPPOSITES leave, go
❷ *Summer is coming at last.*
• **advance, draw near**
❸ *How did you come to write the novel?*
• **happen, chance**

➤ **come about**
How did the accident come about?
• **happen, occur, take place, arise, result**

➤ **come across**
I came across an old friend of mine.
• **find, discover, chance upon, meet, bump into**

➤ **come from**
Where does your family come from?
• **originate from, hail from, be from**

➤ **come round or to**
How long did it take to come round after the operation?
• **become conscious, revive, wake up**

➤ **come to**
❶ *We came to the end of the road.*
• **reach, get to, arrive at**
❷ *The hotel bill came to a hundred euros.*
• **add up to, amount to, total**

comfort *NOUN*

❶ *He tried to offer a few words of comfort.*
• **consolation, support, encouragement, sympathy, condolence**
❷ *They had enough money to live in comfort.*
• **ease, contentment, well-being, prosperity, luxury, affluence**
OPPOSITES hardship, discomfort

comfort *VERB*

She went upstairs to comfort the baby.
• **console, soothe, calm, reassure, cheer up, hearten**
OPPOSITES distress, upset

comfortable *ADJECTIVE*
❶ *It is a very comfortable sofa.*
• **cosy, snug, relaxing, soft, roomy, padded, plush**
(*informal*) **comfy**
OPPOSITE uncomfortable
❷ *Wear comfortable clothes for travelling.*
• **casual, informal, loose-fitting**
OPPOSITES restrictive, tight-fitting
❸ *Our cat leads a comfortable life.*
• **contented, pleasant, agreeable, well-off, prosperous, luxurious, affluent**
OPPOSITE hard

comic *ADJECTIVE*
The act opens with a comic scene.
• **humorous, funny, amusing, comical, light-hearted**
OPPOSITES serious, tragic

comical *ADJECTIVE*
Her impersonation of the queen is quite comical.
• **funny, amusing, humorous, hilarious, witty, droll**
– To be comical in a cheeky way is to be **facetious**.
– To be comical in a silly way is to be **absurd, farcical, ludicrous** or **ridiculous**.
– To be comical in a hurtful way is to be **sarcastic**.

command *NOUN*
❶ *The general gave the command to attack.*
• **order, instruction, direction, commandment, edict**
❷ *Who has command of the ship?*
• **control, charge, authority, dominion, jurisdiction, leadership, management, supervision, power**
❸ *The job requires a good command of German.*
• **knowledge, mastery, grasp, understanding, comprehension, ability (in)**

command *VERB*
❶ *The officer commanded his troops to fire.*
• **order, instruct, direct, tell, bid**
❷ *Nelson commanded the British fleet.*
• **be in charge of, control, direct, govern, head, lead, manage, supervise, oversee**
(*informal*) **head up**

commander *NOUN*
He was the commander of the Roman fleet.
• **leader, head, chief, officer-in-charge, commanding officer**

commemorate *VERB*
A plaque on the wall commemorates the battle.
• **celebrate, remember, mark, observe, pay tribute to, be a memorial to, honour, salute**

commence *VERB*
Let the battle commence.
• **begin, start, get going, get under way**
(*informal*) **kick off**
IDIOM **get off the ground**

commend *VERB*
My photo was commended in the under-18 category.
• **praise, compliment, congratulate, applaud**
OPPOSITE criticize

comment *NOUN*
❶ *He was always making sarcastic comments.*
• **remark, statement, observation, opinion, pronouncement, mention**
– A hostile comment is a **criticism**.
❷ *She wrote a few comments in the margin.*
• **note, annotation, footnote, gloss, reference**

comment *VERB*
➤ **comment on**
Several people commented on my dress.
• **remark on, mention, make mention of, notice, discuss, talk about**

commentary *NOUN*
We were listening to the match commentary.
• **narration, description, report, voice-over, review**

A B C D E F G H I J K L M N O P Q R S T U V W X Y Z

commerce *NOUN*
The port became a centre of commerce.
• **business, trade, trading, dealing**

commit *VERB*
❶ *It is still a mystery who committed the murder.*
• **carry out, do, perform, execute, accomplish, perpetrate**
(*informal*) **pull off**
❷ *She committed a lot of time and energy to the project.*
• **devote, allocate, dedicate, make available, assign, consign, pledge**

commitment *NOUN*
❶ *No one can doubt her total commitment to her sport.*
• **dedication, devotion, allegiance, loyalty, passion**
❷ *I have made a commitment to finish the job by next week.*
• **promise, pledge, vow, undertaking, resolution**

committee *NOUN*
The club is run by a committee of volunteers.
• **board, panel, council, body**

common *ADJECTIVE*
❶ *Colds are a common complaint in winter.*
• **commonplace, everyday, frequent, normal, ordinary, familiar, well known, regular, widespread**
OPPOSITE rare
❷ *'Good morning' is a common way to greet people.*
• **typical, usual, regular, standard, routine, customary, conventional, habitual, popular**
OPPOSITE uncommon
❸ *Humans and apes share a common ancestor.*
• **shared, mutual, joint, communal, collective**

commonplace *ADJECTIVE*
It is a city where cycling is commonplace.
• **common, everyday, regular, routine, normal, ordinary, frequent, familiar, usual**
OPPOSITES rare, unusual

commotion *NOUN*
Someone was causing a commotion in the street.
• **disturbance, row, uproar, racket, rumpus, fuss, stir, unrest, disorder, furore, fracas, hullabaloo, brouhaha, pandemonium, bedlam**

communal *ADJECTIVE*
There is a communal kitchen at the end of the corridor.
• **shared, joint, public, common, collective**
OPPOSITES private, individual

communicate *VERB*
❶ *Someone has to communicate the bad news to her.*
• **convey, relay, transmit, relate, pass on, report, tell, impart, express**
❷ *We usually communicate by email.*
• **contact each other, correspond, be in touch, liaise**
❸ *Malaria is communicated by mosquitoes.*
• **transmit, transfer, pass on, spread**

communication *NOUN*
❶ *Dolphins use sound for communication.*
• **communicating, contact, dialogue, conversation**
❷ *I have received an urgent communication.*
• **message, dispatch, statement, announcement, letter, report**

WORD WEB

Some forms of communication:

- advertising
- blog
- body language
- Braille
- broadcast
- bulletin board
- chat
- email
- fax
- instant messaging
- junk mail
- letter
- mailshot

- ➤ memo or memorandum
- ➤ mobile phone
- ➤ Morse code
- ➤ newspaper
- ➤ podcast
- ➤ postcard
- ➤ radio
- ➤ satellite
- ➤ semaphore
- ➤ sign language or signing
- ➤ smartphone
- ➤ social networking
- ➤ telegram
- ➤ telepathy
- ➤ telephone
- ➤ television
- ➤ texting
- ➤ video conference
- ➤ videophone
- ➤ webcast
- ➤ website
- ➤ wiki

communicative *ADJECTIVE*
I'm not feeling very communicative today.
• talkative, expressive, vocal, chatty, forthcoming
OPPOSITES uncommunicative, taciturn

community *NOUN*
He grew up in a small farming community.
• society, population, people, residents, inhabitants, neighbourhood, district, region, locality

compact *ADJECTIVE*
❶ *The camera is light and compact.*
• small, portable, handy, neat, petite
OPPOSITE bulky
❷ *The fabric has a compact weave.*
• dense, tight, close, firm, solid, compressed
OPPOSITE loose

companion *NOUN*
He turned to speak to his companions.
• friend, associate, partner, comrade
(*informal*) mate, pal, buddy, chum

company *NOUN*
❶ *She works for a computer company.*
• firm, business, corporation, organization, establishment, enterprise, agency, office
❷ *He missed the company of his friends.*
• fellowship, companionship, society, friendship

compare *VERB*
We have been comparing the two sets of figures.
• contrast, juxtapose, set side by side, weigh up
➤ compare with something
It doesn't compare with the original version.
• be as good as, rival, emulate, equal, match up to, come close to, be on a par with

comparison *NOUN*
❶ *We put the signatures side by side for comparison.*
• comparing, contrast, juxtaposition
❷ *There's no comparison between their team and ours.*
• resemblance, similarity, likeness, correspondence

compartment *NOUN*
The money was hidden in a secret compartment.
• section, division, pocket, space, cubicle

compassion *NOUN*
He feels compassion for these victims of war.
• sympathy, empathy, fellow feeling, concern, consideration, understanding, kindness, charity
OPPOSITE indifference

compatible *ADJECTIVE*
The couple were never really compatible.
• well-suited, well matched, like-minded
IDIOMS on the same wavelength, in tune
OPPOSITE incompatible

compel *VERB*
Villagers were compelled to leave their homes.
• force, make, press, push
(*informal*) lean on

compelling *ADJECTIVE*
❶ *She has written a compelling story of love and revenge.*
• captivating, enthralling, absorbing, gripping, riveting, spellbinding, mesmerizing

A B C D E F G H I J K L M N O P Q R S T U V W X Y Z

❷ *It is a compelling argument.*
• **convincing, persuasive, powerful, strong, irresistible**

compensate *VERB*
They promised to compensate him for his loss of earnings.
• **recompense, repay, reimburse, remunerate**
➤ **compensate for**
This victory compensates for our earlier defeats.
• **make up for, offset, counteract, balance out, cancel out**

compensation *NOUN*
She put in a claim for compensation.
• **recompense, repayment, reimbursement, remuneration, damages**

compete *VERB*
Eight schools will be competing in the hockey tournament.
• **participate, take part, enter, play, go in (for)**
➤ **compete against**
We are competing against a strong team this week.
• **oppose, play against, contend with, vie with, challenge**
IDIOM **go head to head with**

competent *ADJECTIVE*
You have to be a competent swimmer to join the club.
• **able, capable, skilful, skilled, accomplished, proficient, expert**
OPPOSITE incompetent

competition *NOUN*
❶ *He won first prize in a poetry competition.*
• **contest, quiz, championship, tournament, match, game, trial, race**
❷ *There was fierce competition for the job.*
• **rivalry, competitiveness**
❸ *I stood on the starting line, eyeing up the competition.*
• **opposition, rivals, opponents, other side**

competitor *NOUN*
❶ *The competitors lined up for the start of the race.*
• **contestant, contender, participant, player, entrant**
❷ *Who are your main competitors?*
• **rival, opponent, challenger**

compile *VERB*
She has compiled a collection of children's poems.
• **assemble, put together, make up, compose, organize, gather, collect, collate, edit**

complacent *ADJECTIVE*
We've done well so far but we mustn't become complacent.
• **self-satisfied, smug, overconfident**

complain *VERB*
My brother spent most of the weekend complaining.
• **protest, grumble, grouse, carp, bleat, whine, make a fuss**
(*informal*) **gripe, moan, whinge**
➤ **complain about something**
The neighbours complained about the noise.
• **protest about, object to, criticize, find fault with**
OPPOSITE praise

complaint *NOUN*
❶ *They received hundreds of complaints about the programme.*
• **criticism, objection, protest, grievance, grouse, grumble**
(*informal*) **gripe, whinge**
❷ *I had a nasty stomach complaint.*
• **disease, illness, ailment, sickness, disorder, infection, condition, problem, upset**

complement *NOUN*
❶ *The music is a perfect complement to the film.*
• **accompaniment, accessory, supplement, companion, partner**
OPPOSITES contrast, foil

❷ *We had our full complement of players for the match.*
• quota, contingent, amount, allowance, capacity

complement *VERB*
That shade of green complements your eyes.
• accompany, go with, suit, set off, enhance
OPPOSITES contrast with, clash with

complete *ADJECTIVE*
❶ *I have collected the complete set of cards.*
• whole, entire, full, intact
OPPOSITES incomplete, partial
❷ *The new building is not yet complete.*
• finished, completed, ended, concluded
OPPOSITE unfinished
❸ *My audition was a complete disaster.*
• total, absolute, thorough, utter, pure, sheer, downright, unqualified, unmitigated, out-and-out

complete *VERB*
❶ *She has another year to complete her training.*
• finish, end, conclude, finalize
(*informal*) wind up, wrap up
❷ *I only need one more card to complete the set.*
• finish off, round off, top off, crown, cap

completely *ADVERB*
I'm not completely convinced.
• totally, wholly, entirely, thoroughly, utterly, fully, absolutely

complex *ADJECTIVE*
Defusing a bomb is a complex task.
• complicated, intricate, difficult, elaborate, detailed, involved
(*informal*) fiddly
OPPOSITES simple, straightforward

complexion *NOUN*
The girl had red hair and a pale complexion.
• skin, skin tone, colour, colouring

complicated *ADJECTIVE*
❶ *It is a complicated task.*
• complex, intricate, difficult
(*informal*) fiddly
OPPOSITES simple, straightforward
❷ *The film has a very complicated plot.*
• involved, elaborate, convoluted

compliment *NOUN*
She blushed at the unexpected compliment.
• commendation, tribute, accolade
IDIOM pat on the back
OPPOSITES criticism, insult
➤ **compliments**
I'm not used to receiving compliments about my cooking.
• praise, acclaim, admiration, appreciation, congratulations

complimentary *ADJECTIVE*
❶ *The comments were all complimentary.*
• appreciative, approving, admiring, positive, favourable, flattering, congratulatory
OPPOSITES critical, insulting, negative
❷ *We were given complimentary tickets for the film.*
• free, gratis, courtesy
IDIOM on the house

component *NOUN*
The factory makes components for computers.
• part, piece, bit, element, ingredient, constituent, module

compose *VERB*
Beethoven composed nine symphonies.
• create, devise, write, pen, produce, make up, think up, invent

➤ **be composed of**
Water is composed of hydrogen and oxygen.
• be made of, consist of, comprise

composition *NOUN*
❶ *Is the song your own composition?*
• creation, work, piece, study
(*formal*) opus

A B C D E F G H I J K L M N O P Q R S T U V W X Y Z

❷ *Scientists have studied the composition of the soil.*
• make-up, structure, formation, constitution

compound *NOUN*
Steel is a compound of iron and carbon.
• amalgam, alloy, mixture, mix, blend

comprehend *VERB*
The crowd couldn't comprehend what was happening.
• understand, make sense of, grasp, appreciate, perceive, follow, fathom, take in
(*informal*) figure out, get

comprehension *NOUN*
She spoke in a dialect that was beyond my comprehension.
• understanding, knowledge, awareness, conception, grasp, mastery
OPPOSITE ignorance

comprehensive *ADJECTIVE*
She gave us a comprehensive account of her travels.
• complete, full, thorough, detailed, extensive, exhaustive, inclusive, all-inclusive, all-embracing, wide-ranging, encyclopedic, sweeping, wholesale
(*informal*) blow-by-blow
OPPOSITES selective, partial

compress *VERB*
I tried to compress all my clothes into one bag.
• press, squeeze, squash, crush, jam, flatten

comprise *VERB*
The team comprised athletes from several countries.
• be composed of, consist of, be made up of, include, contain

compromise *VERB*
Neither side was willing to compromise.
• come to an understanding, make a deal, make concessions
IDIOMS meet each other halfway, find a happy medium

compulsive *ADJECTIVE*
❶ *Suddenly, I felt a compulsive urge to laugh.*
• irresistible, uncontrollable, compelling, overwhelming, overpowering
❷ *She is a compulsive liar.*
• obsessive, habitual, chronic, incurable, persistent

compulsory *ADJECTIVE*
The wearing of seat belts is compulsory.
• obligatory, mandatory, required, necessary
OPPOSITE optional

computer *NOUN*

WORD WEB

Some types of computer:

- desktop
- handheld
- laptop
- mainframe
- netbook
- notebook
- palmtop
- PC
- server
- tablet

Parts of a computer system:

- CD-ROM drive
- DVD drive
- hard disk
- hub
- keyboard
- memory stick
- microchip
- microprocessor
- modem
- monitor
- motherboard
- mouse
- processor
- router
- screen
- terminal
- touchpad
- USB port
- webcam

Other terms used in computing:

- back-up
- bit
- broadband
- browser
- bug
- byte
- cursor
- data
- database
- digital
- download
- email
- firewall
- gigabyte
- hacker
- hardware
- ICT
- input
- interface
- Internet (*informal* Net)
- malware

> ➤ megabyte
> ➤ memory
> ➤ menu
> ➤ network
> ➤ offline
> ➤ online
> ➤ operating system
> ➤ peripheral
> ➤ printout
> ➤ program
> ➤ reboot
> ➤ software
> ➤ spam
> ➤ spreadsheet
> ➤ start-up
> ➤ surfing
> ➤ upload
> ➤ virus
> ➤ Web
> ➤ wi-fi
> ➤ window
> ➤ wireless
> ➤ word processor

concave *ADJECTIVE*
a concave lens
• **diverging**
OPPOSITES convex, converging

conceal *VERB*
❶ *The prisoners concealed the entrance to the tunnel.*
• **hide, cover up, screen, disguise, mask, camouflage**
OPPOSITES uncover, reveal
❷ *He managed to conceal the truth for years.*
• **keep quiet about, keep secret, hush up, suppress**
IDIOM **keep a lid on**
OPPOSITES disclose, confess

conceited *ADJECTIVE*
What a conceited man you are!
• **arrogant, proud, vain, self-satisfied, self-important, boastful**
(*informal*) **big-headed, cocky**
IDIOMS **full of yourself,** (*informal*) **too big for your boots**
OPPOSITES modest, self-effacing

conceive *VERB*
❶ *Who conceived this silly plan?*
• **think up, originate, devise, invent, formulate, design, develop**
(*informal*) **dream up**
❷ *I can't conceive what it must have been like for them.*
• **imagine, envisage, see, visualize, grasp**

concentrate *VERB*
❶ *Be quiet! I'm trying to concentrate.*
• **think hard, focus, pay attention**
❷ *This term, we are concentrating on the First World War.*
• **focus, centre**
❸ *The shops are concentrated in the centre of town.*
• **collect, gather, cluster, mass, converge**

concept *NOUN*
I find the concept of time travel fascinating.
• **idea, thought, notion, theory**

concern *VERB*
❶ *This conversation doesn't concern you, so go away.*
• **affect, involve, be relevant to, apply to, be important to, matter to, relate to**
❷ *The melting of the ice caps concerns me deeply.*
• **worry, trouble, disturb, distress, upset, bother**
❸ *The story concerns a group of rabbits.*
• **be about, deal with, relate to, pertain to**

concern *NOUN*
❶ *People are too wrapped up in their own concerns.*
• **affair, business, responsibility, interest**
❷ *A new virus is causing concern among beekeepers.*
• **anxiety, worry, apprehension, unease, disquiet, fear**
❸ *She's the head of a large banking concern.*
• **company, business, firm, enterprise, establishment, corporation**

concerned *ADJECTIVE*
❶ *Many scientists are concerned about global warming.*
• **worried, anxious, troubled, upset, distressed, bothered**
❷ *We will be emailing all those concerned.*
• **involved, affected, interested, implicated**

concerning *PREPOSITION*
The head spoke to me concerning my future.
• **about, regarding, relating to, with**

reference to, referring to, relevant to, with regard to, in connection with

concert *NOUN*
Tonight there's a concert of jazz music at the town hall.
• recital, performance, show

concise *ADJECTIVE*
His diary entry gives a concise account of what happened.
• brief, short, condensed, succinct, abridged, abbreviated, compact, pithy
– A concise account of something is a **précis** or **summary**.
OPPOSITES lengthy, expanded

conclude *VERB*
❶ *This concludes our tour of the library.*
• bring to an end, complete, close, finish, terminate, round off, wind up
(*informal*) wrap up
❷ *The festival concluded with some fireworks.*
• come to an end, finish, close, terminate, culminate, draw to a close
❸ *The jury concluded that she was guilty.*
• decide, judge, deduce, infer, gather

conclusion *NOUN*
❶ *The conclusion of the book was disappointing.*
• end, ending, close, finale, finish, completion, culmination
❷ *It took the jury some time to reach a conclusion.*
• decision, judgement, opinion, verdict, deduction

concrete *ADJECTIVE*
The police did not have much concrete evidence.
• real, actual, definite, conclusive, firm, solid, substantial, physical, material, tangible
OPPOSITE abstract

condemn *VERB*
❶ *The manager condemned the behaviour of the players.*
• criticize, censure, denounce, deplore, disapprove of
OPPOSITES praise, condone
❷ *The two men were condemned to death.*
• sentence, punish

condense *VERB*
Try to condense the story into a hundred words.
• shorten, abridge, reduce, compress, abbreviate, summarize, edit
OPPOSITE expand

condescending *ADJECTIVE*
She has a very condescending manner.
• superior, patronizing, disdainful, snobbish
(*informal*) snooty, stuck-up

condition *NOUN*
❶ *Is the guitar in good condition?*
• state, order, repair, shape, form, fitness
❷ *These people are living in overcrowded conditions.*
• circumstances, environment, situation
❸ *There are strict conditions for using this information.*
• requirement, obligation, term, proviso
➤ **on condition that**
You can come on condition that you keep quiet.
• provided, providing that, on the understanding that, only if

condone *VERB*
We do not condone this sort of behaviour.
• accept, allow, disregard, let pass, pardon, excuse, tolerate
IDIOM turn a blind eye to
OPPOSITE condemn

conduct *VERB*
❶ *She conducted a series of important experiments.*
• organize, administer, run, carry out, coordinate, manage, preside over, direct, control, supervise, handle
❷ *A guide conducted us round the site.*
• guide, lead, escort, accompany, usher, take

➤ **conduct yourself**
They conducted themselves with dignity.
• behave, act, acquit yourself

conduct *NOUN*
The referee sent him off for violent conduct.
• behaviour, manners, actions, deeds

confer *VERB*
❶ *You are allowed to confer with your teammates.*
• consult, have a discussion, converse, deliberate, talk things over
❷ *Thank you for conferring this honour upon me.*
• bestow (on), award (to), grant (to), present (to)

conference *NOUN*
He was invited to give a speech at a scientific conference.
• meeting, congress, convention, forum, summit, discussion

confess *VERB*
❶ *She confessed that she had stolen the money.*
• admit, own up, acknowledge, reveal, divulge
(*informal*) come clean
OPPOSITE deny
❷ *I confess I don't know the answer.*
• acknowledge, admit, concede, grant, allow

confide *VERB*
He was afraid to confide the secret to anyone.
• reveal, disclose, tell, divulge, confess

confidence *NOUN*
❶ *The team had lost all confidence in the manager.*
• trust, faith, belief
❷ *We can face the future with confidence.*
• hope, optimism, faith
❸ *I wish I had her confidence.*
• self-assurance, self-confidence, assertiveness, boldness, conviction

confident *ADJECTIVE*
❶ *I am confident that we will win.*
• certain, sure, positive, hopeful, optimistic, convinced, satisfied, in no doubt
OPPOSITE doubtful
❷ *She is more confident than her sister.*
• self-assured, self-confident, bold, fearless, assertive

confidential *ADJECTIVE*
The details of the plan are confidential.
• private, secret, classified, restricted
(*informal*) hush-hush
OPPOSITE public

confine *VERB*
❶ *They confined their discussion to the weather.*
• limit, restrict, keep
❷ *Our chickens are not confined indoors.*
• enclose, shut in, coop up, incarcerate

confirm *VERB*
❶ *His guilty expression confirmed my suspicions.*
• prove, substantiate, corroborate, justify, verify, vindicate, bear out, back up
OPPOSITE disprove
❷ *Please phone to confirm your booking.*
• verify, make official
OPPOSITE cancel

confiscate *VERB*
One of the teachers confiscated my phone.
• take possession of, seize, impound

conflict *NOUN*
❶ *There's a lot of conflict in their family.*
• disagreement, quarrelling, hostility, friction, antagonism, opposition, discord, strife, unrest
❷ *Both countries wanted to avoid a military conflict.*
• war, warfare, combat, fighting, engagement, hostilities

conflict *VERB*
➤ **conflict with**
Her statement conflicts with the evidence.
• **disagree with, differ from, contradict, contrast with, clash with, be at odds with**

conflicting *ADJECTIVE*
My brother and I have conflicting tastes in music.
• **contrasting, incompatible, contradictory, opposite, contrary, irreconcilable**

conform *VERB*
➤ **conform to or with**
The building does not conform with safety regulations.
• **comply with, follow, keep to, obey, observe, abide by, fit in with, submit to**
OPPOSITES disobey, flout

confront *VERB*
❶ *I decided to confront her and demand an apology.*
• **challenge, stand up to, face up to, take on, tackle**
❷ *He was confronted with a very difficult decision.*
• **face, stand in your way, threaten**

confuse *VERB*
❶ *I was confused by her message.*
• **puzzle, bewilder, mystify, baffle, perplex, bemuse**
(*informal*) **flummox, fox**
❷ *You must be confusing me with someone else.*
• **mix up, muddle**

confusing *ADJECTIVE*
These instructions are confusing.
• **puzzling, perplexing, baffling, bewildering, unclear, misleading, ambiguous**
OPPOSITES clear, unambiguous

confusion *NOUN*
❶ *There was a look of confusion on his face.*
• **bewilderment, perplexity, bafflement, puzzlement**
OPPOSITES certainty, clarity
❷ *It was a scene of utter confusion.*
• **chaos, disorder, disarray, mayhem, pandemonium, bedlam**
OPPOSITES order, calm

congested *ADJECTIVE*
The roads are congested during the rush hour.
• **blocked, jammed, choked, clogged, obstructed, crowded**
(*informal*) **snarled up, jam-packed, gridlocked**
OPPOSITE clear

congratulate *VERB*
We congratulated the winners.
• **praise, applaud, compliment, pay tribute to, salute**
IDIOMS **pat someone on the back, take your hat off to**
OPPOSITE criticize

congregate *VERB*
The guests congregated in the hall.
• **gather, assemble, collect, convene, come together, muster, cluster**
OPPOSITE disperse

connect *VERB*
❶ *Have you connected the printer to the computer?*
• **join, attach, fasten, link, couple, fix together, tie together**
OPPOSITE separate
❷ *Police believe the two murders could be connected.*
• **associate, link, relate, couple, bracket together**

connection *NOUN*
There is a connection between the Moon and the tides.
• **relationship, link, association, interconnection, bond, tie**

conquer *VERB*
❶ *The Romans used people they had conquered as slaves.*
• **defeat, beat, vanquish, subjugate, overcome, overwhelm, crush**
❷ *Alexander the Great conquered Egypt*

in 332 BC.
• seize, capture, take, win, occupy, possess
❸ *She's trying to conquer her fear of flying.*
• overcome, suppress, master, control, curb, get the better of

conquest *NOUN*
Next week's programme is about the Mongol conquest of China.
• capture, seizure, invasion, occupation, possession, takeover

conscientious *ADJECTIVE*
She is a conscientious student.
• hard-working, diligent, industrious, careful, attentive, meticulous, painstaking, thorough, dedicated, dutiful, responsible
OPPOSITES careless, irresponsible

conscious *ADJECTIVE*
❶ *The patient was conscious throughout the operation.*
• awake, alert, aware
OPPOSITES unconscious, unaware
❷ *We are making a conscious effort to save energy.*
• deliberate, intentional, planned, calculated, premeditated
OPPOSITES accidental, unintentional

consecutive *ADJECTIVE*
It rained for three consecutive days.
• successive, succeeding, running, straight, in a row, in succession
IDIOM (*informal*) on the trot
You can say *three days straight* or *three straight days* but only *three days running*.

consent *NOUN*
You can only go on the trip if your parents give their consent.
• agreement, assent, permission, authorization, approval, acceptance
(*informal*) go-ahead

consent *VERB*
➤ **consent to**
The head has consented to our request.
• agree to, grant, allow, approve of, authorize, go along with
IDIOM give the green light to
OPPOSITE refuse

consequence *NOUN*
❶ *He drove too fast, with tragic consequences.*
• result, effect, outcome, upshot, repercussion
OPPOSITE cause
❷ *Her wealth was of no consequence to him.*
• importance, significance, concern, account, value

conservation *NOUN*
Our group supports the conservation of wildlife.
• preservation, protection, maintenance, upkeep
OPPOSITE destruction

conservative *ADJECTIVE*
❶ *My dad has a very conservative taste in music.*
• old-fashioned, conventional, unadventurous, traditional, restrained
OPPOSITES progressive, up-to-date
❷ *At a conservative estimate, the work will take six months.*
• cautious, moderate, modest, reasonable
OPPOSITE extreme

conserve *VERB*
You can conserve electricity by switching off lights.
• save, preserve, be sparing with, safeguard, look after, protect, sustain
OPPOSITE waste

consider *VERB*
❶ *She paused to consider all the options.*
• think about, examine, contemplate, ponder on, reflect on, study, evaluate, meditate on, weigh up, mull over
(*informal*) size up
❷ *His first novel is considered to be his best.*
• reckon, judge, deem, regard as, rate

considerable *ADJECTIVE*
1000 dollars is a considerable sum of money.
• large, sizeable, substantial, significant
OPPOSITE negligible

considerate *ADJECTIVE*
How considerate of you to offer me a lift.
• thoughtful, kind, helpful, obliging, unselfish, neighbourly
OPPOSITE selfish

consist *VERB*
➤ **consist of**
A comet consists largely of ice and dust.
• be made up of, be composed of, comprise, contain, include, involve

consistency *NOUN*
The mixture had the consistency of porridge.
• texture, thickness, density

consistent *ADJECTIVE*
The greenhouse is kept at a consistent temperature.
• steady, constant, regular, stable, even, unchanging, uniform
OPPOSITES variable, fluctuating
➤ **be consistent with**
The injuries are consistent with a crocodile attack.
• be compatible with, be in keeping with, be in line with
OPPOSITE be inconsistent with

consolation *NOUN*
A late goal provided some consolation for the losers.
• comfort, solace, sympathy, commiseration, support

console *VERB*
I tried everything I could to console her.
• comfort, sympathize with, commiserate with, support, soothe, cheer up

conspicuous *ADJECTIVE*
The clock tower is a conspicuous landmark.
• noticeable, prominent, obvious, clear, unmistakable, eye-catching, visible, evident, apparent, glaring
OPPOSITE inconspicuous

conspiracy *NOUN*
They were involved in a conspiracy to overthrow the government.
• plot, intrigue, scheme, ploy, plan

constant *ADJECTIVE*
❶ *We have to put up with the constant noise of traffic outside.*
• continual, continuous, non-stop, ceaseless, incessant, persistent, perpetual, interminable, endless, unending, never-ending, everlasting, permanent
OPPOSITE intermittent
❷ *The wheel should turn at a constant speed.*
• steady, consistent, regular, stable, even, unchanging, uniform
OPPOSITE variable
❸ *She proved to be a constant friend.*
• faithful, loyal, devoted, dependable, reliable, firm, true, trustworthy
OPPOSITE unreliable

constitute *VERB*
❶ *Eleven players constitute a hockey team.*
• make up, compose, comprise, form
❷ *The oil spill constitutes a danger to wildlife.*
• amount to, represent, be equivalent to, be tantamount to

construct *VERB*
When was the bridge constructed?
• build, erect, assemble, put together, put up, set up
OPPOSITE demolish

construction *NOUN*
❶ *He was put in charge of the construction of the emperor's palace.*
• building, erecting, erection, assembly, setting-up
❷ *The bridge is a temporary construction.*
• structure, edifice, building

consult *VERB*
❶ *You should consult a doctor first.*
• seek advice from, speak to, ask, talk things over with
❷ *If you don't know how to spell a word, consult your dictionary.*
• refer to, check, look something up in

consume *VERB*
❶ *An adult penguin consumes up to 500g of fish a day.*
• eat, devour, swallow
❷ *Refrigerators consume a vast amount of energy.*
• use up, go through, spend, exhaust, deplete
❸ *The building was consumed by fire.*
• destroy, devastate, lay waste, gut, raze
➤ **be consumed with**
The king was consumed with jealousy.
• be filled with, be overwhelmed by, be gripped by

contact *VERB*
I'll contact you when I have some news.
• get in touch with, communicate with, notify, speak to, talk to, correspond with, write to, call, phone, ring

contact *NOUN*
❶ *Rugby is a sport which involves physical contact.*
• touch, touching, handling
❷ *Have you had any contact with him lately?*
• communication, correspondence, connection, dealings

contagious *ADJECTIVE*
Measles is a very contagious disease.
• infectious, communicable
(*informal*) catching
OPPOSITE non-infectious

contain *VERB*
❶ *The box contains various odds and ends.*
• have inside, hold, accommodate
❷ *This book contains a great deal of information.*
• include, incorporate, comprise, consist of
❸ *I tried hard to contain my impatience.*
• restrain, hold back, suppress, control, curb, rein in, bottle up

container *NOUN*
Put the leftover sauce in a container.
• receptacle, vessel, holder, repository, box, case, canister, carton, pot, tub, tin

contaminate *VERB*
The drinking water may have become contaminated.
• pollute, poison, defile, taint, soil
OPPOSITE purify

contemplate *VERB*
❶ *She contemplated herself in the mirror.*
• look at, view, regard, observe, gaze at, stare at, survey, study
❷ *I am contemplating what to do next.*
• think about, consider, ponder, reflect on, meditate on, weigh up, mull over

contemporary *ADJECTIVE*
The gallery is putting on an exhibition of contemporary art.
• modern, current, recent, present-day, the latest, up-to-date, fashionable

contempt *NOUN*
She gave a snort of contempt.
• scorn, disdain, derision, disrespect
OPPOSITES admiration, respect

contemptuous *ADJECTIVE*
He gave me a contemptuous look.
• scornful, disdainful, derisive, disrespectful
OPPOSITES admiring, respectful

contend *VERB*
❶ *The witness contends that he heard a noise.*
• assert, declare, claim, maintain, argue, insist
❷ *Four teams are contending for a place in the final.*
• compete, vie, battle, strive, struggle
➤ **contend with**
We had to contend with bad weather

A B C D E F G H I J K L M N O P Q R S T U V W X Y Z

and midges!
• **cope with, deal with, put up with, grapple with, face, confront, take on**

content *ADJECTIVE*
I was content to sit and wait.
• **happy, contented, satisfied, pleased, willing**
OPPOSITE unwilling

contented *ADJECTIVE*
She sank into the armchair with a contented sigh.
• **happy, pleased, content, satisfied, fulfilled, serene, peaceful, relaxed, comfortable, tranquil, untroubled**
OPPOSITE discontented

contents *PLURAL NOUN*
Try to guess the contents of the mystery parcel.
• **constituents, components, ingredients, elements**

contest *NOUN*
The final was an exciting contest.
• **competition, challenge, tournament, match, game, encounter, bout, fight, battle, struggle, tussle**

contest *VERB*
❶ *Six parties will be contesting the election.*
• **compete for, fight for, contend for, vie for**
❷ *No one contested the referee's decision.*
• **challenge, disagree with, object to, dispute, oppose, call into question**

contestant *NOUN*
She was once a contestant on a TV quiz show.
• **competitor, participant, contender, player, entrant**

continual *ADJECTIVE*
It was a day of continual interruptions.
• **recurrent, repeated, constant, frequent, perpetual**
OPPOSITE occasional
The words *continual* and *continuous* are not synonyms. *Continual noises* happen repeatedly, whereas a *continuous noise* never stops.

continue *VERB*
❶ *We continued our search until it got dark.*
• **keep up, prolong, sustain, persevere with, pursue**
(*informal*) **stick at**
❷ *This rain can't continue for long.*
• **carry on, last, persist, endure, extend, keep on, go on, linger, drag on**
❸ *We'll continue the lesson after lunch.*
• **resume, carry on with, proceed with, return to, pick up**

continuous *ADJECTIVE*
She has continuous pain in her ankle.
• **persistent, uninterrupted, unbroken, never-ending, non-stop, incessant, unceasing**
– An illness which continues for a long time is a **chronic** illness.
OPPOSITE intermittent
SEE ALSO **continual**

contract *NOUN*
The actress has signed a contract for a new film.
• **agreement, deal, compact, bargain, undertaking**
– A contract between two countries is an **alliance** or **treaty**.
– A contract to end a dispute about money is a **settlement**.

contract *VERB*
❶ *Metal contracts when it gets colder.*
• **shrink, constrict, tighten, draw in, reduce, lessen**
OPPOSITE expand
❷ *The crew contracted a mysterious disease.*
• **catch, pick up, get, develop**
(*informal*) **go down with, come down with**

contradict *VERB*
❶ *No one dared to contradict the boss.*
• **challenge, disagree with, speak against, oppose**

❷ *The two stories contradict each other.*
• go against, be at odds with, counter, dispute

contraption *NOUN*
The room was full of weird contraptions.
• machine, device, gadget, invention, apparatus, contrivance, mechanism
(*informal*) gizmo

contrary *ADJECTIVE*
❶ *She had always been a contrary child.*
• awkward, difficult, stubborn, disobedient, obstinate, uncooperative, unhelpful, wilful, perverse
OPPOSITE cooperative
❷ *Other people may take a contrary view.*
• opposite, opposing, conflicting, contradictory, different
OPPOSITE similar
➤ **contrary to**
Contrary to popular belief, snakes are not slimy.
• in opposition to, at odds with, differing from

contrast *NOUN*
There is a sharp contrast between the two paintings.
• difference, distinction, dissimilarity, disparity, variance
OPPOSITE similarity

contrast *VERB*
❶ *We were asked to contrast two of our favourite poems.*
• compare, juxtapose, distinguish between, differentiate
❷ *The title of the book contrasts with its theme.*
• differ (from), conflict, be at variance, be at odds, clash, disagree
OPPOSITES match, suit

contribute *VERB*
Many people contributed blankets and clothing.
• donate, give, provide, supply, grant
(*informal*) chip in
➤ **contribute to**
The good weather contributed to the success of the occasion.
• add to, enhance, help, play a part in

contrive *VERB*
➤ **contrive to**
She contrived to get away without anyone seeing her.
• manage to, find a way to, succeed in

control *VERB*
❶ *The government controls the country's affairs.*
• be in control of, be in charge of, run, direct, command, manage, lead, guide, govern, administer, regulate, rule, superintend, supervise
❷ *Please try to control your temper.*
• restrain, contain, hold back, check, curb

control *NOUN*
❶ *Spain once had control over a rich empire.*
• authority, power, command, rule, government, management, direction, leadership, dominance
❷ *The government imposed tighter controls on the import of live animals.*
• restriction, limit, restraint, regulation, curb, check

controversial *ADJECTIVE*
It was a controversial decision by the umpire.
• debatable, questionable, arguable, contentious

controversy *NOUN*
There is much controversy about the election results.
• disagreement, dispute, debate, argument, quarrelling, contention, storm
(*informal*) row

convalescence *VERB*
She needed a month's convalescence after the operation.
• recovery, recuperation, rehabilitation

a b c d e f g h i j k l m n o p q r s t u v w x y z

A B C D E F G H I J K L M N O P Q R S T U V W X Y Z

convenient *ADJECTIVE*
❶ *I'll call back at a more convenient time.*
• **suitable, appropriate, fitting, favourable, opportune, timely**
OPPOSITE inconvenient
❷ *A bike is often more convenient than a car in towns.*
• **practical, useful, helpful, handy, labour-saving**

convention *NOUN*
❶ *We have many social conventions, such as shaking hands.*
• **custom, tradition, practice, norm**
❷ *He attended a convention of leading scientists.*
• **conference, congress, meeting, forum**

conventional *ADJECTIVE*
This is the conventional way of cooking a turkey.
• **customary, traditional, usual, accepted, common, normal, ordinary, everyday, routine, standard, regular, habitual, orthodox**
OPPOSITES unconventional, unorthodox

converge *VERB*
The two rivers converge at this point.
• **come together, join, meet, merge, combine, coincide**
OPPOSITE divide

conversation *NOUN*
My mum overheard our conversation.
• **discussion, talk, chat, gossip**
– Conversation in a play, film or novel is **dialogue**.

convert *VERB*
❶ *They converted their attic into a bedroom.*
• **adapt, turn, change, alter, transform, modify**
❷ *My sister converted me into becoming a vegetarian.*
• **win over, reform, persuade**

convex *ADJECTIVE*
a convex lens
• **converging**
OPPOSITES concave, diverging

convey *VERB*
❶ *The craft was designed to convey astronauts to the Moon.*
• **transport, carry, bring, deliver, take, fetch, bear, transfer**
– To convey something by sea is to **ferry** or **ship** it.
❷ *The tone of his voice conveyed his disgust.*
• **communicate, indicate, impart, signify, relay, pass on, carry, tell, relate, mean**

convict *VERB*
Three of the men were convicted of fraud.
• **find guilty, condemn, sentence**
OPPOSITE acquit

convict *NOUN*
Police are looking for two escaped convicts.
• **prisoner, inmate, criminal, offender**

convince *VERB*
How can I convince you that I am not lying?
• **persuade, assure, satisfy, prove to, win over**

convincing *ADJECTIVE*
❶ *I tried to think of a convincing excuse.*
• **believable, credible, plausible, likely**
❷ *He saved his most convincing argument until the end.*
• **persuasive, powerful, strong, compelling, telling, conclusive**

cook *VERB*
Who's going to cook lunch?
• **prepare, make**
(*informal*) **rustle up**
– The art or skill of cooking is **cookery**.
– To cook food for guests or customers is to **cater** for them.

WORD WEB

Some ways to cook food:

➤ bake
➤ barbecue
➤ boil
➤ braise
➤ brew
➤ broil
➤ casserole
➤ chargrill

➤ deep-fry	➤ scramble
➤ fry	➤ sear
➤ grill	➤ simmer
➤ microwave	➤ steam
➤ poach	➤ stew
➤ roast	➤ stir-fry
➤ sauté	➤ toast

Other ways to prepare food:

➤ baste	➤ marinade
➤ blend	➤ mince
➤ chop	➤ mix
➤ dice	➤ peel
➤ grate	➤ purée
➤ grind	➤ sieve
➤ infuse	➤ sift
➤ knead	➤ stir
➤ liquidize	➤ whisk

Equipment used in cooking:

➤ baking tin	➤ mincer
➤ blender	➤ oven
➤ casserole	➤ roasting tin
➤ chopping board	➤ rolling pin
➤ colander	➤ saucepan
➤ food mixer	➤ sieve
➤ food processor	➤ skewer
➤ frying pan	➤ spatula
➤ grill	➤ tandoor
➤ ladle	➤ whisk
➤ liquidizer	➤ wok
➤ microwave	

Measurements used in cooking:

➤ cup or cupful	➤ spoonful
➤ dessertspoon	➤ teaspoon
➤ pinch	➤ tablespoon

cook *NOUN*

He trained as a ship's cook.

- The chief cook in a restaurant or hotel is the **chef**.

- A person who cooks food as a business is a **caterer**.

cool *ADJECTIVE*

1 *There was a cool breeze outside.*
• **chilly, coldish, fresh, bracing**
(*informal*) **nippy**
OPPOSITE **warm**

2 *I'd like a cool glass of lemonade.*
• **chilled, iced, refreshing**

3 *She remained cool when everyone else panicked.*
• **calm, composed, collected, level-headed, relaxed, at ease, unflustered, unruffled, unflappable**
(*informal*) **laid-back**

4 *We got a cool reception.*
• **unfriendly, unwelcoming, distant, remote, aloof, frosty, chilly**
(*informal*) **stand-offish**
OPPOSITE **warm**

5 *There was a cool response to my idea.*
• **unenthusiastic, half-hearted, indifferent, lukewarm, tepid**
OPPOSITE **enthusiastic**

6 (*informal*) *Your new shoes are really cool!*
• **impressive, fashionable, chic, smart**
(*informal*) **trendy**

cool *VERB*

Cool the mixture in the fridge overnight.
• **chill, refrigerate, freeze**
OPPOSITES **warm, heat up**

cooperate *VERB*

➤ **cooperate with**
Local people refused to cooperate with the authorities.
• **work with, collaborate with, aid, assist, support, be of service to**
IDIOM (*informal*) **play ball with**

cooperation *NOUN*

The game was developed with the cooperation of NASA.
• **collaboration, assistance, participation, teamwork**

cooperative *ADJECTIVE*

I found him surprisingly cooperative.
• **supportive, helpful, obliging, accommodating, willing**
OPPOSITE **uncooperative**

cope *VERB*

Shall I help you or can you cope on your own?
• **manage, carry on, get by, make do, survive**

➤ **cope with**
I can't cope with all this homework!
• **deal with, handle, manage, tackle, face**
IDIOM **get to grips with**

copy *NOUN*
That isn't the original painting–it's a copy.
• **replica, reproduction, duplicate, imitation, likeness**
– A copy made to deceive someone is a **fake**, **forgery** or **counterfeit**.
– A living organism which is identical to another is a **clone**.

copy *VERB*
❶ *I copied the message into my notebook.*
• **duplicate, reproduce, replicate**
– To copy something in order to deceive is to **fake, forge** or **counterfeit** it.
❷ *Lots of bands tried to copy the Beatles.*
• **imitate, mimic, impersonate, emulate**

cord *NOUN*
He pulled the cord to open his parachute.
• **string, rope, cable, thread, twine, flex**

core *NOUN*
❶ *It is extremely hot at the Earth's core.*
• **centre, interior, middle, heart, nucleus**
❷ *This is the core of the problem.*
• **essence, heart, basis, nub, crux** (*informal*) **nitty-gritty**

corn *NOUN*
The farmer was growing corn in the field.
• **grain, cereal, cereal crop, wheat**

corner *NOUN*
❶ *I'll meet you at the corner of the road.*
• **turn, turning, bend, curve, junction, intersection**
– The place where two lines meet is an **angle**.
❷ *I sat in a quiet corner and read her letter.*
• **alcove, recess, nook**

corny *ADJECTIVE*
What a corny joke!
• **overused, clichéd, stale, banal, trite, hackneyed, feeble**

corpse *NOUN*
Police found the corpse under the floorboards.
• **dead body, body, remains, carcass** (*formal*) **cadaver**

correct *ADJECTIVE*
❶ *Your answers are all correct.*
• **right, accurate, true, exact, precise, faultless, perfect**
❷ *What is the correct way to address this letter?*
• **proper, right, acceptable, accepted, regular, appropriate, suitable**

correct *VERB*
❶ *She quickly corrected a couple of spelling mistakes.*
• **rectify, amend, put right, remedy, repair, fix, sort**
❷ *Most of the teachers were busy correcting exam papers.*
• **mark**

correspond *VERB*
➤ **correspond to**
Each symbol corresponds to a sound.
• **equate to, relate to, be equivalent to, match**
➤ **correspond with**
❶ *The paint doesn't correspond with the colour on the tin.*
• **agree with, match, be similar to, be consistent with, tally with**
❷ *I correspond regularly with a friend in Paris.*
• **write to, communicate with, send letters to**

corrode *VERB*
This acid will corrode metal.
• **eat away, erode, rot, rust**

corrupt *ADJECTIVE*
Corrupt officials had accepted millions of pounds in bribes.
• **dishonest, criminal, unethical, unscrupulous, untrustworthy**

(*informal*) **bent, crooked**
OPPOSITES honest, ethical

cost *NOUN*
❶ *The bill shows the total cost.*
• **price, charge, payment, fee, amount, figure, tariff, fare, toll, levy, outlay, expense, expenditure, spend**
(*humorous*) **damage**
❷ *The cost in human lives was too great.*
• **loss, sacrifice, toll, penalty, damage**

cost *VERB*
How much did your camera cost?
• **sell for, go for, come to, amount to**
(*informal*) **set you back**

costly *ADJECTIVE*
Buying new furniture may prove too costly.
• **dear, expensive, high-cost**
(*informal*) **pricey**
OPPOSITE cheap

costume *NOUN*
The guards wear the Greek national costume.
• **outfit, dress, clothing, suit, attire, garment, garb**
(*informal*) **get-up**
– A costume you dress up in for a party is **fancy dress**.
– An official set of clothes worn for school or work is a **uniform**.

cosy *ADJECTIVE*
They lived in a cosy little house.
• **snug, comfortable, warm**
(*informal*) **comfy**
OPPOSITE uncomfortable

couch *NOUN*
The cat sat next to me on the couch.
• **settee, sofa**

council *NOUN*
They are both members of the school council.
• **committee, board, panel**

counsel *VERB*
His advisors counselled him to surrender.
• **advise, guide, direct, recommend, urge, warn, caution**

count *VERB*
❶ *I am counting the days until the end of term.*
• **add up, calculate, compute, estimate, reckon, figure out, work out, total**
❷ *It's playing well that counts, not winning.*
• **matter, be important, be significant, carry weight**
❸ *I would count it an honour to be asked.*
• **regard, consider, judge, deem, rate**
➤ **count on**
You can count on my support.
• **depend on, rely on, trust, bank on, be sure of**

countless *ADJECTIVE*
He has appeared in countless TV programmes.
• **innumerable, numerous, numberless, untold**
OPPOSITE finite

country *NOUN*
❶ *England and Wales are separate countries.*
• **nation, state, land, territory**
– A country ruled by a king or queen is a **kingdom, monarchy** or **realm**.
– A country governed by leaders elected by the people is a **democracy**.
– A democratic country with a president is a **republic**.
❷ *They bought a house in the country.*
• **countryside, provinces, outdoors**
(*informal*) **the sticks**
– A word meaning 'to do with the country' is **rural** and its opposite is **urban**.
OPPOSITES town, city
❸ *You drive through lovely open country.*
• **terrain, countryside, territory, landscape, environment, scenery, surroundings**

coupon *NOUN*
You can exchange this coupon for a free sandwich.
• **voucher, token, ticket**

courage *NOUN*
He showed great courage and determination.
• **bravery, valour, fearlessness, boldness, daring, audacity, heroism, gallantry, nerve, pluck, grit**
(*informal*) **guts**
OPPOSITE **cowardice**

courageous *ADJECTIVE*
It was a courageous decision.
• **brave, valiant, fearless, bold, daring, audacious, heroic, gallant, intrepid, plucky**
OPPOSITE **cowardly**

course *NOUN*
❶ *The spacecraft could drift off its course.*
• **route, path, track, way, trajectory, bearing, direction**
❷ *The best course is to wait and watch.*
• **plan of action, procedure, approach, strategy**
❸ *Some changes have been made to the geography course.*
• **syllabus, programme, curriculum**
➤ **of course**
Of course you can come to my party.
• **naturally, certainly, definitely, undoubtedly, needless to say, it goes without saying**

courteous *ADJECTIVE*
I received a courteous reply to my letter.
• **polite, respectful, well-mannered, civil, gracious, considerate**
OPPOSITES **rude, impolite**

cover *VERB*
❶ *Cover the chicken with foil.*
• **envelop, enclose, protect, overlay**
❷ *A rug covered the hole in the carpet.*
• **conceal, obscure, disguise, hide, mask, blot out**
❸ *Wear goggles to cover your eyes.*
• **shield, screen, protect, shade, veil**
❹ *My new shoes were covered with mud.*
• **cake, coat, plaster, encrust**
❺ *The book covers all aspects of photography.*
• **deal with, include, incorporate, take in, embrace**
❻ *The cyclists will cover 150 km over two days.*
• **progress, travel**

cover *NOUN*
❶ *Leave the cover of the jar loose.*
• **lid, top, cap**
❷ *The cover of the book was torn.*
• **wrapper, binding, jacket, envelope**
❸ *On the bare hillside, there was no cover from the storm.*
• **shelter, protection, shield, refuge, sanctuary**

covering *NOUN*
There was a light covering of snow on the hills.
• **coating, coat, layer, blanket, carpet, film, veneer, skin, sheet, veil, shroud**

cowardly *ADJECTIVE*
They made a cowardly retreat.
• **faint-hearted, spineless, lily-livered, craven, timid, fearful**
(*informal*) **gutless, yellow, chicken**
OPPOSITES **brave, courageous**

cower *VERB*
A tiny creature was cowering in the corner.
• **cringe, shrink, crouch, flinch, quail**

crack *NOUN*
❶ *There's a crack in this cup.*
• **break, chip, fracture, flaw, chink, split**
❷ *She peered through a crack in the rock.*
• **gap, space, opening, crevice, fissure, rift, cleft, cranny**
❸ *I heard the crack of a pistol shot.*
• **bang, explosion, report, pop**
❹ *In the scuffle I got a crack on the head.*
• **blow, knock, hit, bash, bang, thump, smack**
(*informal*) **whack, wallop, clout**

crack *VERB*

❶ *I dropped the vase and cracked it.*
• **break, fracture, chip, split, rupture, shatter, splinter**
❷ *He was beginning to crack under the strain.*
• **break down, lose control**
(*informal*) **lose it**
IDIOM **go to pieces**
❸ (*informal*) *The code proved difficult to crack.*
• **decipher, decode, interpret, solve, break**

craft *NOUN*

❶ *I'd like to learn the craft of weaving.*
• **art, skill, technique, expertise, handicraft**
– A person who is skilled in a particular craft is a **craftsman** or **craftswoman.**
For terms used in art, craft and design see **art**.
❷ *All sorts of craft were in the harbour.*
• **vessels, boats, ships**

crafty *ADJECTIVE*

We came up with a crafty plan.
• **cunning, shrewd, canny, artful, devious, sly, tricky, wily, scheming**

cram *VERB*

❶ *I managed to cram all my clothes into one bag.*
• **stuff, pack, squeeze, squash, force, jam, thrust, push, shove, compress, crush**
❷ *We all crammed into the back of the car.*
• **crowd, push, pile, squeeze, squash**
❸ *My sister is cramming for an exam.*
• **revise, study**
(*informal*) **swot**

cramped *ADJECTIVE*

The seating on the plane was cramped.
• **confined, restricted, tight, narrow, uncomfortable, crowded**
(*informal*) **poky**
OPPOSITE **roomy**

crash *NOUN*

❶ *There was a loud crash from the kitchen.*
• **bang, clash, clatter, racket**
– A crash of thunder is a **peal**.
For tips on describing sound see **sound**.
❷ *We saw a nasty crash on the motorway.*
• **collision, accident, smash, bump**
– A crash involving a lot of vehicles is a **pile-up.**
– A train crash may involve a **derailment**.

crash *VERB*

❶ *Their car crashed into the back of a lorry.*
• **bump, smash, collide, knock, plough**
❷ *The satellite may crash to Earth soon.*
• **fall, drop, plunge, plummet, dive, tumble**

crate *NOUN*

We packed all our belongings into crates.
• **box, case, chest, packing case, container**

crater *NOUN*

The surface of the Moon is full of craters.
• **pit, hollow, hole, dip, depression, bowl, basin, cavity**

craving *NOUN*

I often have a craving for chocolate.
• **desire, longing, yearning, hankering, hunger, appetite, thirst**

crawl *VERB*

I watched a caterpillar crawling along a leaf.
• **creep, edge, inch, slither, wriggle**

craze *NOUN*

These shoes are the latest craze in footwear.
• **fad, trend, vogue, fashion, obsession, mania, rage**
(*informal*) **thing**

crazy *ADJECTIVE*

❶ *It's enough to drive you crazy!*
• **mad, insane, demented, deranged, unbalanced, hysterical, frantic, frenzied, wild, berserk**

a b c d e f g h i j k l m n o p q r s t u v w x y z

(*informal*) **nuts, bonkers, loopy, crackers**
IDIOMS (*informal*) **off your head, round the bend, round the twist**
OPPOSITE **sane**
❷ *Everyone told me it was a crazy idea.*
• **absurd, ridiculous, ludicrous, idiotic, senseless, silly, stupid, foolhardy, preposterous, hare-brained, half-baked**
(*informal*) **crackpot, cockeyed, wacky, zany, daft, barmy**
OPPOSITE **sensible**
❸ (*informal*) *She is crazy about football.*
• **fanatical, enthusiastic, passionate, fervent, wild**
(*informal*) **mad, nuts**

creamy *ADJECTIVE*
That ice cream is really creamy.
• **rich, smooth, thick, velvety**

crease *NOUN*
Can you iron the creases out of this shirt?
• **wrinkle, crinkle, pucker, fold, furrow, line, ridge, groove**
– A crease made deliberately in a garment is a **pleat**.

crease *VERB*
Try not to crease the paper.
• **wrinkle, crinkle, crumple, crush, pucker, scrunch up**

create *VERB*
❶ *You have created a beautiful work of art there.*
• **make, produce, generate, originate, fashion, build, construct, compose, devise, design**
OPPOSITE **destroy**
❷ *We have created a website for our chess club.*
• **establish, set up, start up, launch, institute, initiate, found**
OPPOSITE **abolish**
❸ *The bad weather created huge problems for us.*
• **cause, bring about, lead to, produce, give rise to, prompt**

creation *NOUN*
❶ *The TV series is about the creation of life on earth.*
• **beginning, origin, birth, generation, initiation**
❷ *They raised money for the creation of a sports centre.*
• **establishment, foundation, institution, setting up, construction**
❸ *This pasta sauce is my own creation.*
• **work, invention, concoction, concept**
(*informal*) **brainchild**

creative *ADJECTIVE*
He is a writer with a very creative mind.
• **imaginative, inventive, innovative, original, experimental, artistic, inspired**
OPPOSITE **unimaginative**

creator *NOUN*
Walt Disney was the creator of Mickey Mouse.
• **inventor, maker, originator, producer, designer, deviser, author, architect**

creature *NOUN*
A hideous creature emerged from the swamp.
• **animal, beast, being, brute**
For mythological creatures see **fantasy**.

credible *ADJECTIVE*
Did you find the plot credible?
• **believable, plausible, conceivable, likely, possible, probable, reasonable, persuasive, convincing**
OPPOSITES **incredible, implausible**

credit *NOUN*
She is finally getting the credit she deserves.
• **recognition, honour, praise, distinction, fame, glory, reputation**
OPPOSITE **dishonour**

credit *VERB*
❶ *It's hard to credit that they are brother and sister.*
• **believe, accept, have faith in, give credence to, trust**
(*informal*) **swallow, buy**
OPPOSITE **doubt**

❷ *Edison is credited with inventing the light bulb.*
• recognize, attribute, identify

creed NOUN
Pupils of all races and creeds attend the school.
• faith, religion, belief, ideology, principle

creep VERB
❶ *The snail crept halfway out of its shell.*
• crawl, edge, inch, slither, wriggle
❷ *I crept out of bed without waking the others.*
• tiptoe, sneak, slip, slink, steal

creepy (*informal*) ADJECTIVE
The graveyard was creepy at night.
• frightening, eerie, ghostly, sinister, uncanny, unearthly, weird
(*informal*) spooky, scary

crest NOUN
❶ *The bird had a large red crest on its head.*
• comb, crown, plume, tuft
❷ *There was a wonderful view from the crest of the hill.*
• summit, top, peak, crown, ridge, head, brow
❸ *On the wall was a carving of the family crest.*
• emblem, insignia, coat of arms, regalia, badge

crevice NOUN
Moss was growing in the crevices in the rock.
• crack, split, gap, fissure, rift, cleft, chink, cranny
– A deep crack in a glacier is a **crevasse**.

crew NOUN
❶ *None of the passengers or crew were injured.*
• company, corps, squad, hands
❷ *A film crew was setting up outside.*
• team, unit, party, band, gang

cricket NOUN

WORD WEB

Terms used in cricket:

- bails
- batsman
- batting average
- boundary
- bowler
- century
- crease
- cricketer
- declaration
- dismissal
- duck
- fielder
- googly
- innings
- LBW
- leg spin
- maiden over
- not out
- over
- run
- six
- spin bowler
- stump
- test match
- umpire
- wicket
- wicketkeeper

crime NOUN
❶ *Blackmail is a serious crime.*
• offence, misdemeanour, felony
❷ *Police have announced a crackdown on petty crime.*
• lawbreaking, wrongdoing, criminality, illegality

WRITING TIPS

WRITING CRIME FICTION
Characters:

- criminologist
- detective
- forensic scientist
- master criminal
- murderer
- pathologist
- police officer
- private detective
- private eye
- sleuth
- toxicologist

Useful words and phrases:

- accessory
- accomplice
- alibi
- bloodstain
- case history
- circumstantial evidence
- clue
- confession
- corroborate
- crime scene
- cross-examine
- CSI
- deduction
- DNA sample
- dusting for fingerprints
- evidence

- examination
- expert witness
- false identity
- fingerprint analysis
- forensics
- forgery
- homicide
- hunch
- hypothesis
- incriminate
- in custody
- inquiry
- investigation
- lead
- line of enquiry
- manhunt
- morgue
- motive
- perpetrator
- post-mortem
- prime suspect
- profiling
- proof
- reconstruction
- questioning
- sequence of events
- statement
- suspect
- testimony
- (*informal*) tip-off
- whodunnit
- witness
- victim

criminal *NOUN*
These men are dangerous criminals.
• **lawbreaker, offender, felon, wrongdoer** (*informal*) **crook**
– A criminal who has been sent to prison is a **convict**.

WORD WEB

Some types of criminal:

- assassin
- bandit
- blackmailer
- burglar
- cat burglar
- (*informal*) con man
- cybercriminal
- forger
- gangster
- hacker
- highwayman
- hijacker
- identity thief
- kidnapper
- money launderer
- mugger
- murderer
- outlaw
- pickpocket
- pirate
- poacher
- robber
- shoplifter
- smuggler
- terrorist
- thief
- thug
- vandal

criminal *ADJECTIVE*
Police have uncovered a criminal network.
• **illegal, unlawful, corrupt, dishonest** (*informal*) **crooked**
OPPOSITES **lawful, honest, above board**

cringe *VERB*
The eerie sound made him cringe in fear.
• **shrink, flinch, wince, cower**

cripple *VERB*
❶ *The fall may have crippled the horse.*
• **disable, handicap, maim, lame**
❷ *The country was nearly crippled by war and famine.*
• **ruin, destroy, crush, wreck, damage, weaken, paralyse, incapacitate**

crisis *NOUN*
The country was facing a financial crisis.
• **emergency, calamity, catastrophe, disaster, predicament, meltdown**

crisp *ADJECTIVE*
❶ *These sweets have a crisp coating of chocolate.*
• **crunchy, crispy, brittle, hard**
OPPOSITES **soft, soggy**
❷ *It was a crisp winter morning.*
• **fresh, brisk, bracing, refreshing, invigorating**

critic *NOUN*
❶ *She is the newspaper's film critic.*
• **reviewer, commentator, columnist, analyst, pundit, expert**
❷ *He is a major critic of government policy.*
• **opponent, attacker, detractor**

critical *ADJECTIVE*
❶ *Why do you always have to be so critical?*
• **negative, disapproving, derogatory, uncomplimentary, unfavourable, scathing, disparaging, censorious**
OPPOSITES **complimentary, positive**
❷ *Fortunately, he ducked his head at the critical moment.*
• **crucial, important, vital, essential, pivotal, key, paramount, decisive**
OPPOSITE **unimportant**
❸ *The patient is in a critical condition.*
• **serious, grave, dangerous, precarious**

criticism *NOUN*
❶ *The team has received a lot of criticism recently.*
• **condemnation, censure, fault-finding, disparagement, disapproval, reproach**
(*informal*) **flak**
OPPOSITE praise
❷ *He wrote many works of literary criticism.*
• **analysis, evaluation, assessment, appraisal, commentary**

criticize *VERB*
The film has been criticized for its poor script.
• **condemn, find fault with, censure, attack, denigrate, disparage, reproach, berate**
(*informal*) **knock, pan, slam, slate**
OPPOSITE praise

crockery *NOUN*
The top shelf was full of crockery.
• **china, dishes, plates**

crooked *ADJECTIVE*
❶ *She put a crooked finger to her lips.*
• **bent, twisted, warped, contorted, misshapen, deformed, gnarled**
OPPOSITE straight
❷ (*informal*) *Several crooked lawyers made money from the case.*
• **criminal, dishonest, corrupt**
OPPOSITE honest

crop *NOUN*
We had a good crop of apples this year.
• **harvest, yield, produce**

crop *VERB*
I need to crop the edges of the picture.
• **cut, trim, clip, snip, shear, shave, chop**
➤ **crop up**
Several problems have cropped up.
• **arise, occur, appear, emerge, surface, come up, turn up, pop up**
IDIOM **come to light**

cross *VERB*
❶ *Cross the road at the traffic lights.*
• **go across, travel across, pass over, traverse, span**
– To cross a river or stream is to **ford** it.
❷ *The two sets of footprints cross here.*
• **intersect, meet, join, connect**
– To form a pattern of crossing lines is to **criss-cross**.
➤ **cross out**
My name had been crossed out on the list.
• **delete, score out, strike out, cancel**

cross *ADJECTIVE*
The coach will be cross if we miss training.
• **angry, annoyed, irate, upset, vexed, irked, bad-tempered, ill-tempered, irritable, grumpy, testy, surly, snappy**
OPPOSITE pleased

crossroads *NOUN*
Turn left at the crossroads.
• **intersection, junction**
– A junction of two motorways is an **interchange**.

crouch *VERB*
I waited outside, crouching behind a bush.
• **squat, stoop, duck, bend, bob down, hunch, cower**

crowd *NOUN*
❶ *A crowd formed outside the gates.*
• **gathering, assembly, throng, multitude, horde, swarm, mob, mass, crush, rabble**
❷ *The show attracted a huge crowd.*
• **audience, spectators, gate, attendance**

crowd *VERB*
❶ *People crowded outside to watch the fireworks.*
• **gather, collect, cluster, assemble, congregate, mass, flock, throng, muster**
❷ *Hundreds of people crowded into the hall.*
• **push, pile, squeeze, pack, cram, crush, jam, bundle, herd**

crowded *ADJECTIVE*
The shops are always crowded at the weekend.
• **full, packed, busy, teeming, swarming, overflowing, jammed, congested**
(*informal*) **chock-a-block, jam-packed**
OPPOSITES empty, deserted

A B C D E F G H I J K L M N O P Q R S T U V W X Y Z

crown *NOUN*
The Queen wore a crown of solid gold.
• **coronet, circlet, diadem, tiara**

crown *VERB*
❶ *Queen Victoria was crowned in 1837.*
– A ceremony at which a monarch is crowned is a **coronation**.
❷ *The mountain peaks were crowned with snow.*
• **top, cap, tip, surmount**
❸ *They crowned a remarkable season with yet another win.*
• **round off, cap, complete**

crucial *ADJECTIVE*
Copernicus made a crucial discovery about the universe.
• **important, critical, decisive, vital, pivotal, key, momentous, all-important**
OPPOSITE unimportant

crude *ADJECTIVE*
❶ *The refinery processes crude oil.*
• **raw, natural, unprocessed, unrefined, untreated**
OPPOSITES refined, treated
❷ *It was a crude carving of a horse.*
• **rough, clumsy, makeshift, primitive, rudimentary, rough and ready**
OPPOSITES skilful, sophisticated
❸ *He tells a lot of crude jokes.*
• **rude, obscene, indecent, dirty, smutty, vulgar, coarse, lewd**
OPPOSITE clean

cruel *ADJECTIVE*
❶ *I detest people who are cruel to animals.*
• **brutal, savage, inhumane, barbaric, barbarous, heartless, ruthless, merciless, callous**
OPPOSITES compassionate, humane
❷ *This was a cruel blow to all our hopes.*
• **severe, harsh, bitter, painful, agonizing**

cruelty *NOUN*
He has campaigned against cruelty to animals.
• **brutality, inhumanity, heartlessness, ruthlessness, barbarity, savagery**
OPPOSITES compassion, humanity

crumb *NOUN*
There were only a few cake crumbs on the plate.
• **bit, fragment, scrap, morsel, particle**

crumble *VERB*
❶ *The castle walls were beginning to crumble.*
• **disintegrate, break up, fall apart, fall to pieces, collapse, decay, decompose**
❷ *Crumble the dried leaves between your fingers.*
• **crush, grind, pulverize**

crumpled *ADJECTIVE*
Your shirt is crumpled.
• **creased, wrinkled, crinkled, rumpled, crushed**

crunch *VERB*
❶ *The dog was crunching on a bone.*
• **chew, munch, chomp, grind**
❷ *I could hear footsteps crunching through the snow.*
• **crush, grind, pound, smash**

crush *VERB*
❶ *I crushed my jumper into my school bag.*
• **squash, squeeze, mangle, pound, press, bruise, crunch, scrunch**
– To crush something into a soft mess is to **mash** or **pulp** it.
– To crush something into a powder is to **grind** or **pulverize** it.
– To crush something out of shape is to **crumple** or **smash** it.
❷ *The army soon crushed the rebellion.*
• **defeat, conquer, vanquish, overcome, overwhelm, quash, trounce, rout**

crush *NOUN*
There was a crush of people at the front gates.
• **crowd, throng, mob, press, jam, congestion**

crust *NOUN*
The liquid rock cooled to form a crust.
• **skin, shell, coating, film, exterior**
– A crust that forms over a cut or graze is a **scab**.

crustacean *NOUN*

WORD WEB

Some animals which are crustaceans:

- barnacle
- crab
- crayfish
- langoustine
- lobster
- prawn
- sea slater
- shrimp
- woodlouse

cry *NOUN*
Someone let out a cry of pain.
• **call, shout, yell, roar, howl, exclamation, bellow, scream, screech, shriek, yelp**

cry *VERB*
❶ *She looked like she was going to cry.*
• **weep, sob, shed tears, wail, whimper, snivel**
(*informal*) **blubber**
– When someone starts to cry, their eyes **well up with tears.**
❷ *We heard someone crying for help.*
• **call, shout, yell, exclaim, roar, bawl, bellow, scream, screech, shriek**
(*informal*) **holler**

cuddle *VERB*
My little brother cuddles a teddy bear in bed.
• **hug, clasp, embrace, caress, fondle, nestle against, snuggle against**

cue *NOUN*
When I nod, that is your cue to speak.
• **signal, sign, prompt, reminder**

culminate *VERB*
➤ **culminate in**
The film culminates in a tense shoot-out.
• **finish with, conclude with, close with, build up to, lead up to**

culprit *NOUN*
Police are still searching for the culprits.
• **offender, wrongdoer, criminal, felon**

cultivate *VERB*
❶ *Farmers have cultivated this land for centuries.*
• **farm, work, till, plough, grow crops on**
❷ *We need to cultivate good training habits.*
• **develop, encourage, promote, further, foster, nurture**

cultural *ADJECTIVE*
The city has a rich cultural life.
• **artistic, intellectual, aesthetic, creative**

culture *NOUN*
❶ *She is a woman of culture.*
• **refinement, taste, sophistication**
❷ *He is an expert on the culture of ancient Greece.*
• **civilization, society, traditions, customs, heritage**

cunning *ADJECTIVE*
❶ *He was as cunning a criminal as you'll ever meet.*
• **crafty, devious, artful, scheming, sly, tricky, wily, sneaky**
❷ *I came up with a cunning plan.*
• **clever, shrewd, ingenious, inventive, creative, inspired, brilliant**

cup *NOUN*
He handed me a cup and saucer.
– A tall cup with straight sides is a **mug**.
– A tall cup without a handle is a **beaker** or **tumbler**.
– A decorative drinking cup is a **goblet** or **chalice**.

cupboard *NOUN*
There are some spare pillows in the cupboard.
• **cabinet, dresser, sideboard**
– A cupboard for food is a **larder**.

curb *VERB*
I tried hard to curb my anger.
• **control, restrain, hold back, suppress, contain, check, limit, restrict, rein in, keep in check**
IDIOM **keep a lid on**

A B C D E F G H I J K L M N O P Q R S T U V W X Y Z

cure *VERB*

❶ *A good night's rest will cure your headache.*

• **heal, ease, improve, make better, relieve**

OPPOSITE aggravate

❷ *He finally cured the rattling noise in his car.*

• **remedy, put right, sort, solve, repair, mend, fix, put an end to, eliminate**

cure *NOUN*

Scientists continue to search for a cure for cancer.

• **remedy, treatment, antidote, therapy, medicine, medication**

– A cure for all kinds of diseases or troubles is a **panacea**.

curiosity *NOUN*

Babies are full of curiosity about the world.

• **inquisitiveness, interest**

– Uncomplimentary words are **nosiness, prying** and **snooping**.

curious *ADJECTIVE*

❶ *We were all curious about the visitors.*

• **intrigued, interested (in), agog, inquisitive**

– An uncomplimentary word is **nosy**.

OPPOSITES uninterested (in), indifferent (to)

❷ *What is that curious smell?*

• **odd, strange, peculiar, abnormal, unusual, extraordinary, funny, mysterious, puzzling, weird, bizarre**

curl *NOUN*

❶ *Her hair was a mass of golden curls.*

• **wave, ringlet, lock**

❷ *A curl of smoke rose up from the fire.*

• **coil, twist, scroll, spiral, swirl**

curl *VERB*

❶ *The snake curled itself around a branch.*

• **wind, twist, loop, coil, wrap, twine**

❷ *Smoke curled upwards from the chimney.*

• **coil, spiral, twirl, swirl, furl, snake, writhe, ripple**

curly *ADJECTIVE*

The boy had curly black hair.

• **wavy, curled, curling, frizzy, crinkly, ringleted**

OPPOSITE straight

current *ADJECTIVE*

❶ *The shop sells all the current teenage fashions.*

• **modern, contemporary, present-day, up to date, topical, prevailing, prevalent**

OPPOSITES past, old-fashioned

❷ *Have you got a current passport?*

• **valid, usable, up to date**

OPPOSITE out of date

❸ *Who is the current prime minister?*

• **present, existing, incumbent, reigning**

OPPOSITES past, former

current *NOUN*

The raft was drifting along with the current.

• **flow, tide, stream**

– A current of air is a **draught**.

curse *NOUN*

❶ *According to legend, there is a curse on the family.*

• **jinx, hex**

❷ *I could hear him muttering curses.*

• **swear word, oath, expletive, profanity**

cursed *ADJECTIVE*

It seemed to me that our voyage was cursed.

• **doomed, damned, jinxed, ill-fated, ill-starred**

curt *ADJECTIVE*

I received a very curt reply.

• **abrupt, terse, blunt, brusque, short**

curve *NOUN*

He looked out on the gentle curve of the bay.

• **bend, turn, loop, arch, arc, bow, bulge**

– A curve in the shape of a new moon is a **crescent**.

– A curve on a road surface is a **camber**.

curve *VERB*
The road ahead curves round to the right.
• **bend, turn, wind, loop, curl, arc, arch, swerve, veer, snake, meander**

curved *ADJECTIVE*
The wall was painted with a pattern of curved lines.
• **curving, curvy, bent, looped, arched, bowed, bulging, winding, meandering, serpentine, undulating**
– A surface curved like the inside of a circle is **concave** and one curved like the outside of a circle is **convex**.

cushion *VERB*
The mat will cushion your fall.
• **soften, reduce the effect of, lessen, alleviate, absorb, deaden, dampen, muffle**

custody *NOUN*
➤ **in custody**
Two men are being held in custody.
• **in jail, in prison**
(*informal*) **inside**
IDIOMS **under lock and key, behind bars**

custom *NOUN*
❶ *When did the custom of giving presents at Christmas begin?*
• **tradition, practice, convention, habit, routine, observance, ritual**
❷ *We need to attract more custom.*
• **customers, buyers, clients, trade, business**

customary *ADJECTIVE*
It is customary to leave the waiter a tip.
• **traditional, conventional, usual, normal, common, typical, expected, habitual, routine, regular, everyday, ordinary, prevailing, prevalent**
OPPOSITE unusual

customer *NOUN*
There was a queue of angry customers.
• **buyer, shopper, client, purchaser, consumer**

cut *VERB*
❶ *Cut the vegetables into chunks.*
• **chop, slice, carve, split, slit, sever, cleave**
– To cut food into cubes is to **dice** it.
– To cut something up to examine it is to **dissect** it.
– To cut down a tree is to **fell** it.
❷ *A name had been cut into the stone.*
• **carve, score, incise, engrave, notch, chisel, chip**
❸ *You've had your hair cut!*
• **trim, clip, crop, snip, shave**
– To cut grass is to **mow** it.
– To cut twigs off a growing plant is to **prune** it.
– To cut wool off a sheep is to **shear** it.
– To cut corn is to **harvest** or **reap** it.
❹ *He fell and cut his knee.*
• **gash, slash, wound, lacerate, scratch, graze, nick**
❺ *I had to cut my essay to make it fit the page.*
• **shorten, condense, edit, abbreviate, abridge**
❻ *We are cutting our prices by 10%.*
• **lower, reduce, decrease, drop, slash**
– If you cut something by half, you **halve** it.
➤ **cut something off**
❶ *Help me cut off the lower branches.*
• **chop off, lop, sever**
– To cut off a limb is to **amputate** it.
❷ *They threatened to cut off the electricity.*
• **discontinue, disconnect, shut off, suspend**

cut *NOUN*
❶ *Make a small cut in the fabric.*
• **slash, slit, incision, snip, nick, gash**
❷ *I got a nasty cut on my forehead.*
• **gash, wound, injury, scratch, graze, laceration**
❸ *There has been a cut in the price of fuel.*
• **fall, reduction, decrease, lowering, drop**

A B C D E F G H I J K L M N O P Q R S T U V W X Y Z

cutlery *NOUN*

WORD WEB

Some items of cutlery:

- ➤ bread knife
- ➤ butter knife
- ➤ carving knife
- ➤ cheese knife
- ➤ chopsticks
- ➤ dessert spoon
- ➤ fish knife
- ➤ fork
- ➤ knife
- ➤ ladle
- ➤ spoon
- ➤ steak knife
- ➤ tablespoon
- ➤ teaspoon

cutting *ADJECTIVE*

He made a cutting remark about my tie.
• **hurtful, wounding, scathing, biting, caustic, barbed**

cycle *NOUN*

This ancient myth is about the cycle of the seasons.
• **round, circle, rotation, succession, sequence, pattern**

Dd

dab *NOUN*
a little dab of glue
• **spot, drop, bit, blob, daub, dollop**

dab *VERB*
She dabbed her eyes with a handkerchief.
• **pat, touch, press, wipe, daub**

daily *ADJECTIVE*
a daily exercise routine
• **everyday, day-to-day, regular**

daily *ADVERB*
The rooms are cleaned daily.
• **every day, each day, once a day**

dainty *ADJECTIVE*
a dainty little ribbon
• **delicate, neat, charming, elegant, fine, exquisite, bijou**
(*informal*) **cute, dinky**
OPPOSITE **clumsy**

dam *NOUN*
a dam built by beavers
• **barrage, barrier, embankment, dyke, weir**

damage *NOUN*
The floods caused a lot of damage.
• **harm, destruction, devastation, injury, ruin**

damage *VERB*
Many paintings were damaged in the fire.
• **harm, spoil, mar, break, impair, weaken, disfigure, deface, mutilate, scar**
– To damage something beyond repair is to **destroy**, **ruin** or **wreck** it.
– To damage something deliberately is to **sabotage** or **vandalize** it.

damp *ADJECTIVE*
❶ *These clothes are still damp.*
• **moist, dank, soggy, clammy**
OPPOSITE **dry**
❷ *It was a cold and damp morning.*
• **drizzly, foggy, misty, rainy, wet**
– Weather which is both damp and warm is **humid** or **muggy**.

dampen *VERB*
❶ *Dampen the cloth with a little water.*
• **moisten, wet**
❷ *Nothing could dampen my enthusiasm.*
• **lessen, decrease, diminish, reduce, stifle, suppress**

dance *VERB*
I could have danced for joy.
• **caper, cavort, skip, prance, gambol, leap, hop, whirl, twirl, gyrate, pirouette**

dance *NOUN*

WORD WEB

Some kinds of dance or dancing:

- ballet
- ballroom dancing
- barn dance
- belly dancing
- bolero
- breakdancing
- cancan
- disco
- flamenco
- folk dance
- Highland dancing
- hornpipe
- jazz dance
- jig
- jive dancing
- limbo dancing
- line dancing
- mazurka
- morris dance
- quadrille
- reel
- rumba
- samba
- Scottish country dancing
- square dance
- step dancing
- street dance
- tap dancing
- tarantella

Some ballroom dances:

- foxtrot
- minuet
- polka
- quickstep
- tango
- waltz

- A person who writes the steps for a dance is a **choreographer**.

danger *NOUN*
❶ *Is the crew in any danger?*
• **peril, jeopardy, menace, threat, trouble, crisis**
OPPOSITE **safety**

❷ *The article explains the dangers of sunbathing.*
• **risk, hazard, problem, pitfall, trap**
❸ *There is a danger that the volcano may erupt.*
• **chance, possibility, risk**

dangerous *ADJECTIVE*
❶ *Finding and removing landmines is dangerous work.*
• **hazardous, perilous, risky, unsafe, precarious, treacherous**
(*informal*) **hairy, dicey**
❷ *She was arrested for dangerous driving.*
• **careless, reckless**
❸ *It is a highly dangerous chemical.*
• **harmful, destructive, poisonous, deadly, toxic**
OPPOSITES harmless, safe

dangle *VERB*
There was a bunch of keys dangling from the chain.
• **hang, swing, sway, wave, droop, flap, trail**

dare *VERB*
❶ *Who dares to enter the Mummy's Tomb?*
• **have the courage, be brave enough, have the nerve, venture**
❷ *My friends dared me to ring the doorbell.*
• **challenge, defy, provoke, goad**

daring *ADJECTIVE*
He began to plan a daring escape.
• **bold, brave, courageous, audacious, fearless, valiant, intrepid, plucky**
(*informal*) **gutsy**
– A daring person is a **daredevil**.
OPPOSITES timid, cowardly

dark *ADJECTIVE*
❶ *It was a dark winter night.*
• **black, murky, dim, gloomy, dingy, inky, shadowy**
OPPOSITE bright
❷ *He wore a dark blue coat.*
OPPOSITES pale, light
❸ *She has long dark hair.*
• **black, brunette, raven, ebony**
(*literary*) **sable**
OPPOSITE fair
❹ *It was a dark period of my life.*
• **bleak, unhappy, miserable, grim, gloomy, dismal, negative**
OPPOSITE happy
❺ *This peaceful island holds a dark secret.*
• **mysterious, sinister, ominous, disturbing**

dark *NOUN*
❶ *I can't see you in the dark.*
• **darkness, blackout, gloom**
OPPOSITES light, brightness
❷ *No one was allowed out after dark.*
• **nightfall, night-time**
OPPOSITES daytime, daybreak

darken *VERB*
Suddenly, the sky darkened.
• **grow dark, become overcast, blacken, cloud over**
OPPOSITES brighten, lighten

dart *VERB*
A rabbit darted out of the bushes.
• **run, dash, race, sprint, speed, rush, tear, pelt, scurry, scamper**

dash *VERB*
❶ *We dashed home as soon as we could.*
• **hurry, run, rush, race, hasten, speed, sprint, tear, fly, zoom**
❷ *She dashed her cup against the wall.*
• **throw, hurl, fling, toss, smash**
(*informal*) **sling, chuck**
❸ *Injury dashed his hopes of winning a medal.*
• **destroy, wreck, ruin, shatter, scotch**
(*informal*) **scupper**
IDIOM **put paid to**

dash *NOUN*
❶ *We made a dash for shelter.*
• **run, rush, race, sprint, bolt, charge**
❷ *Add a dash of milk.*
• **drop, splash, spot, swig, dribble, drizzle**

data *NOUN*
I entered all the data into the computer.
• **information, details, facts, figures, statistics**

date *NOUN*
When is your lunch date?
• **meeting, appointment, engagement**

date *VERB*
❶ *Some films never seem to date.*
• **age, become dated, show its age**
❷ (*informal*) *Is she dating someone just now?*
• **go out with, see, be involved with**

dated *ADJECTIVE*
The special effects look dated now.
• **old-fashioned, outdated, outmoded, antiquated, behind the times**
(*informal*) **old hat**
IDIOM **out of the ark**
OPPOSITES **modern, cutting-edge**

daunting *ADJECTIVE*
An audition can be a daunting prospect.
• **formidable, challenging, forbidding, unnerving, discouraging, off-putting**

dawdle *VERB*
Don't dawdle—we haven't got all day!
• **linger, dally, drag your feet, delay, lag behind, straggle**
(*informal*) **dilly-dally**
OPPOSITE **hurry**

dawn *NOUN*
❶ *We were woken at dawn by birdsong.*
• **daybreak, sunrise, first light**
OPPOSITES **dusk, sunset**
❷ *It was the dawn of a new era.*
• **beginning, start, birth, origin, genesis, onset, rise**

dawn *VERB*
A new era in medicine is dawning.
• **begin, start, emerge, arise, develop, unfold**
OPPOSITE **end**
➤ **dawn on someone**
The truth was beginning to dawn on me.
• **become clear to, occur to, register with, strike, hit**

day *NOUN*
❶ *Badgers sleep during the day.*
• **daytime, daylight**
OPPOSITES **night, night-time**
❷ *Things were different in my grandfather's day.*
• **age, era, time, period, epoch**

daze *VERB*
She was dazed by the news.
• **stun, shock, stupefy, stagger, bewilder, perplex, take aback**

dazzle *VERB*
❶ *My eyes were dazzled by the light.*
• **blind, daze**
❷ *She dazzled the audience with her performance.*
• **amaze, astonish, stun, impress, overwhelm, awe**
(*informal*) **bowl over, blow away, knock out**

dead *ADJECTIVE*
❶ *Both her parents were dead.*
• **deceased, departed, lifeless**
– You can describe a person who is recently dead as **the late**. *a tribute to the late actor*
– A dead body is a **corpse**.
– The dead body of an animal is a **carcass**.
OPPOSITES **alive, living**
❷ *The town centre is dead at this time of night.*
• **quiet, dull, boring, lifeless, sleepy, flat, slow**
OPPOSITES **lively, animated**
❸ *Suddenly the phone went dead.*
• **not working, broken, inoperative, defective, worn out**
– A battery which is dead is **flat**.
❹ *Latin is a dead language.*
• **extinct, obsolete, defunct, disused**
OPPOSITE **living**

deaden *VERB*
❶ *The doctor gave me an injection to deaden the pain.*
• **anaesthetize, lessen, reduce, suppress**
OPPOSITE **increase**

A B C D E F G H I J K L M N O P Q R S T U V W X Y Z

❷ *Double glazing deadens the noise of traffic.*
• **dampen, muffle, quieten**
OPPOSITE amplify

deadly *ADJECTIVE*
❶ *the deadly sting of a scorpion*
• **lethal, fatal, mortal, life-threatening**
OPPOSITE harmless
❷ *A deadly hush descended on the room.*
• **complete, total, absolute, utter**

deafening *ADJECTIVE*
There was a deafening roar from the crowd.
• **loud, blaring, booming, thunderous, ear-splitting, penetrating**

deal *VERB*
❶ *Who is going to deal the cards?*
• **give out, distribute, share out, hand out, pass round, dispense**
❷ *He deals in scrap metal.*
• **do business, trade**
➤ **deal with something**
❶ *I'll deal with the washing-up.*
• **cope with, sort out, attend to, see to, handle, manage, look after, take charge of, take in hand**
❷ *This chapter deals with whales and dolphins.*
• **be concerned with, cover, discuss, explore, examine**

deal *NOUN*
This year she signed a deal with a record company.
• **agreement, contract, bargain, settlement, arrangement**
➤ **a good deal or a great deal**
It is a good deal colder than last year.
• **a lot, considerably, markedly, substantially**

dear *ADJECTIVE*
❶ *She is a very dear friend of mine.*
• **close, loved, beloved, valued, cherished, treasured**
OPPOSITE distant
❷ *Their shoes are far too dear for me.*
• **expensive, costly, high-priced, exorbitant**
(*informal*) **pricey**
OPPOSITE cheap

death *NOUN*
❶ *He vowed to avenge the death of his friend.*
• **dying, end, passing, decease**
– A death caused by an accident or war is a **fatality**.
❷ *The news meant the death of all their dreams.*
• **end, extinction, destruction**

debate *NOUN*
We had a debate about animal rights.
• **discussion, argument, dispute**
– Something which people argue about a lot is a **controversy**.

debate *VERB*
❶ *We debated whether it is right to kill animals for food.*
• **discuss, argue about, talk through, thrash out**
❷ *I was debating whether to go or not.*
• **consider, ponder, deliberate, weigh up, reflect on, mull over**

debris *NOUN*
Debris from the shipwreck was scattered over a large area.
• **remains, wreckage, fragments, flotsam and jetsam**

decay *VERB*
❶ *Dead leaves fall to the ground and decay.*
• **decompose, rot, disintegrate, putrefy, spoil, perish**
❷ *Ancient Greek civilization eventually decayed.*
• **decline, deteriorate, degenerate**
IDIOM go downhill

deceit *NOUN*
I saw through his lies and deceit.
• **deception, trickery, dishonesty, fraud, duplicity, double-dealing, pretence, bluff, cheating, deceitfulness, lying**
OPPOSITE honesty

deceitful *ADJECTIVE*
Foxes are often portrayed as deceitful in stories.
• dishonest, underhand, insincere, duplicitous, untruthful, false, cheating, hypocritical, lying, treacherous, two-faced, sneaky
OPPOSITE honest

deceive *VERB*
She had been deceiving all of us for years.
• fool, trick, delude, dupe, hoodwink, cheat, double-cross, mislead, swindle (*informal*) con, take in
IDIOMS pull the wool over your eyes, take you for a ride

decent *ADJECTIVE*
❶ *I did the decent thing and owned up.*
• honourable, honest, proper
❷ *Mum didn't think my dress was decent.*
• proper, appropriate, respectable, modest, seemly
OPPOSITES indecent, improper
❸ *I haven't had a decent night's sleep for ages.*
• satisfactory, adequate, sufficient, reasonable, tolerable, acceptable, fair
OPPOSITE inadequate

deception *NOUN*
see **deceit**

deceptive *ADJECTIVE*
The blurb on the back of the book is deceptive.
• misleading, unreliable, false

decide *VERB*
❶ *Have you decided what to wear yet?*
• choose, make a decision, make up your mind, opt, elect, resolve
❷ *The umpire decided that the ball was in play.*
• conclude, judge, rule, adjudicate
❸ *There will be a play-off to decide the medals.*
• determine, settle

decision *NOUN*
We are waiting for the judges' decision.
• judgement, verdict, ruling, conclusion, findings

decisive *ADJECTIVE*
❶ *The knife was a decisive piece of evidence.*
• conclusive, deciding, irrefutable, critical, key
❷ *A referee needs to be decisive.*
• firm, forceful, strong-minded, resolute
OPPOSITES indecisive, hesitant

declare *VERB*
❶ *She declared her intention to retire next year.*
• announce, make known, state, express, reveal, voice, proclaim
❷ *He declared that he was innocent.*
• assert, affirm, profess, state, maintain, contend, insist

decline *VERB*
❶ *She declined his offer of help.*
• refuse, reject, rebuff, turn down, say no to, pass up
OPPOSITE accept
❷ *The band's popularity declined rapidly.*
• decrease, diminish, lessen, dwindle, wane, shrink, subside, tail off
OPPOSITE increase

decline *NOUN*
❶ *There has been a sharp decline in sales.*
• fall, drop, lowering, decrease, reduction, downturn, slump
❷ *The region fell into a decline after the mines closed.*
• descent, slide, fall, degeneration

decode *VERB*
see **code**

decorate *VERB*
❶ *We decorated the tree with tinsel.*
• adorn, ornament, beautify, prettify, deck, festoon, garnish
❷ *Here are some ideas for decorating your bedroom.*
• refurbish, renovate, paint, wallpaper (*informal*) do up, make over

a b c d e f g h i j k l m n o p q r s t u v w x y z

❸ *Several firefighters were decorated for bravery.*
• **award a medal to, honour, reward**

decoration *NOUN*
❶ *We've been putting up the Christmas decorations.*
• **ornament, bauble, garland, trinket, knick-knack**
❷ *Look at the rich decoration inside the dome.*
• **ornamentation, embellishment, adornment, furnishing**
❸ *a decoration for bravery*
• **medal, award**

decorative *ADJECTIVE*
The book had a decorative design on the cover.
• **ornamental, elaborate, fancy, ornate, colourful, attractive, pretty**
OPPOSITES plain, functional

decrease *VERB*
❶ *Our enthusiasm decreased as the day went on.*
• **decline, diminish, lessen, weaken, dwindle, flag, wane, shrink, subside, tail off**
OPPOSITE increase
❷ *The jet decreased its speed.*
• **reduce, cut, lower, lessen, minimize** (*informal*) **slash**

decrease *NOUN*
There has been a decrease in the use of plastic bags.
• **decline, drop, fall, cut, reduction, downturn**
OPPOSITE increase

decree *VERB*
The king decreed that the day would be a holiday.
• **order, command, declare, pronounce, proclaim, ordain**

dedicate *VERB*
She dedicated her whole life to helping others.
• **commit, devote, set aside, sacrifice**

dedicated *ADJECTIVE*
The band have hundreds of dedicated fans.
• **committed, devoted, keen, enthusiastic, faithful, staunch, firm**

dedication *NOUN*
It requires years of dedication to master kung fu.
• **commitment, devotion, application, resolve, effort**

deduce *VERB*
From her name I deduced that she was Russian.
• **conclude, work out, infer, reason, gather**

deduct *VERB*
Points are deducted for each incorrect answer.
• **subtract, take away, take off, knock off, debit**
OPPOSITE add

deed *NOUN*
There are many stories of his heroic deeds.
• **act, action, feat, exploit, effort, achievement**

deep *ADJECTIVE*
❶ *Loch Ness is deep, dark and murky.*
– A very deep pit or lake may be described as **bottomless**.
OPPOSITE shallow
❷ *a deep feeling of unease*
• **intense, strong, extreme, profound, deep-seated**
OPPOSITE slight
❸ *The letter expressed his deep regret.*
• **wholehearted, earnest, genuine, sincere, heartfelt**
OPPOSITE superficial
❹ *She fell into a deep sleep.*
• **heavy, sound, profound**
OPPOSITE light
❺ *A deep voice answered the phone.*
• **low, low-pitched, bass, resonant**
OPPOSITE high

➤ **deep in**
They were deep in conversation.
• **absorbed in, immersed in, preoccupied by, lost in**

deer *NOUN*
a herd of red deer
– A male deer is a **buck, hart, roebuck** or **stag.**
– A female deer is a **doe** or **hind.**
– A young deer is a **fawn.**
– Deer's flesh used as food is **venison.**

defeat *VERB*
Hannibal defeated the Roman army at Cannae.
• **beat, conquer, vanquish, triumph over, get the better of, overcome, overpower, crush, rout, trounce**
(*informal*) **lick**

defeat *NOUN*
It's our first defeat of the season.
• **conquest, loss, rout, trouncing**
(*informal*) **drubbing**
OPPOSITE **victory**

defect *NOUN*
He will need surgery to correct a heart defect.
• **fault, flaw, imperfection, deformity, shortcoming, failure, weakness**
– A defect in a computer program is a **bug.**

defective *ADJECTIVE*
The disease is caused by a defective gene.
• **faulty, flawed, imperfect, unsound, malfunctioning, damaged, out of order**
OPPOSITES **perfect, intact**

defence *NOUN*
❶ *The castle was built as a defence against enemy attack.*
• **protection, barricade, fortification, shield, guard, safeguard**
❷ *He stood up to speak in defence of his friend.*
• **support, justification, vindication, excuse, explanation, argument, case**

defend *VERB*
❶ *We will defend ourselves against enemy attack.*
• **protect, guard, fortify, shield, secure, safeguard, keep safe**
OPPOSITE **attack**
❷ *He gave a speech defending his actions.*
• **justify, vindicate, support, back, stand up for, make a case for**
OPPOSITE **accuse**

defensive *ADJECTIVE*
The Roman army took up a defensive position.
• **protective, defending**
OPPOSITES **offensive, attacking**

defer *VERB*
We deferred our departure until the weekend.
• **delay, put off, put back, postpone**

defiant *ADJECTIVE*
The prisoner gave a defiant answer.
• **rebellious, uncooperative, obstinate, mutinous, insubordinate**
OPPOSITES **cooperative, compliant**

deficiency *NOUN*
a vitamin deficiency
• **lack, shortage, want, inadequacy, insufficiency**
OPPOSITE **sufficiency**

deficient *ADJECTIVE*
Their diet is deficient in vitamins.
• **lacking (in), short (of), wanting, inadequate, insufficient, unsatisfactory**
OPPOSITE **sufficient**

define *VERB*
How would you define this word?
• **explain, give the meaning of, interpret, clarify**

definite *ADJECTIVE*
❶ *Have you made a definite decision?*
• **certain, sure, fixed, settled, decided**
OPPOSITES **uncertain, undecided**
❷ *She is showing definite signs of improvement.*
• **clear, distinct, noticeable, obvious,**

marked, positive, pronounced, unmistakable
OPPOSITES indistinct, vague

definitely *ADVERB*
That is definitely the paw print of a bear.
• **certainly, for certain, surely, unquestionably, undoubtedly, absolutely, positively, without doubt, without fail**

definition *NOUN*
❶ *Give a definition of the following words.*
• **explanation, interpretation, meaning, sense**
❷ *The face in the photograph lacks definition.*
• **clarity, focus, sharpness, resolution**

deflect *VERB*
He deflected the blow with his shield.
• **divert, turn aside, parry, avert, fend off, ward off, stave off**

deft *ADJECTIVE*
With a few deft strokes she painted a fish.
• **skilful, agile, nimble, dexterous, expert, proficient, adept**
(*informal*) **nifty**
OPPOSITE clumsy

defy *VERB*
❶ *They continued to defy the law.*
• **disobey, resist, flout, violate, contravene, breach, challenge**
OPPOSITE obey
❷ *I defy you to come up with a better idea.*
• **challenge, dare**
❸ *The door defied all efforts to open it.*
• **resist, withstand, defeat, prevent, frustrate**

degrading *ADJECTIVE*
His parents thought that any kind of manual labour was degrading.
• **shameful, humiliating, demeaning, undignified**

degree *NOUN*
Playing the oboe requires a high degree of skill.
• **level, standard, grade, measure, extent, amount**

dejected *ADJECTIVE*
I felt dejected after we lost the game.
• **depressed, dispirited, disheartened, downhearted, downcast, despondent, disconsolate, crestfallen, miserable, forlorn**
IDIOMS (*informal*) **down in the mouth, down in the dumps**
OPPOSITES cheerful, upbeat
SEE ALSO **sad**

delay *VERB*
❶ *My bus was delayed again this morning.*
• **detain, hold up, keep waiting, make late, hinder, slow down**
❷ *They had to delay the start of the race.*
• **postpone, put off, defer, hold over**
❸ *We cannot delay any longer.*
• **hesitate, hold back, dawdle, shilly-shally, stall, linger, loiter**
(*informal*) **dilly-dally**
IDIOM **drag your feet**

delay *NOUN*
There has been an unexpected delay.
• **hold-up, wait, stoppage, postponement**

delete *VERB*
I deleted your email by mistake.
• **remove, erase, cancel, cross out, strike out, cut**
OPPOSITES add, insert

deliberate *ADJECTIVE*
❶ *It was a deliberate attempt to sink the ship.*
• **intentional, planned, calculated, conscious, premeditated**
OPPOSITES accidental, unintentional
❷ *She walked slowly, taking small, deliberate steps.*
• **careful, steady, cautious, unhurried, measured**
OPPOSITES hasty, careless

deliberately *VERB*
Are you ignoring me deliberately?
• **on purpose, intentionally, knowingly**
OPPOSITES accidentally, unintentionally

delicate *ADJECTIVE*
❶ *The blouse has delicate embroidery on the cuffs.*
• **fine, dainty, intricate, exquisite**
OPPOSITES coarse, crude
❷ *He carefully picked up one of the delicate glass ornaments.*
• **fragile, frail, flimsy**
OPPOSITE sturdy
❸ *Her scarf was a delicate shade of lilac.*
• **subtle, soft, muted, pale, light**
OPPOSITES garish, lurid
❹ *The child was born with a delicate constitution.*
• **frail, weak, feeble, sickly, unhealthy, tender**
OPPOSITES strong, hardy, robust
❺ *I admired his delicate handling of the situation.*
• **tactful, sensitive, careful, considerate, discreet, diplomatic**
OPPOSITE insensitive
❻ *This is rather a delicate issue.*
• **awkward, embarrassing, tricky, ticklish**
❼ *Listen to her delicate playing of the piano concerto.*
• **sensitive, gentle, light, soft**
OPPOSITE clumsy

delicious *ADJECTIVE*
This soup is delicious.
• **tasty, appetizing, mouth-watering, delectable, flavoursome**
(*informal*) **scrumptious, yummy, moreish**
OPPOSITE unappetizing
For tips on describing taste see **taste**.

delight *VERB*
The magic of this book never fails to delight me.
• **please, charm, amuse, divert, entertain, enchant, entrance, fascinate, captivate, thrill**
OPPOSITE dismay

➤ **delight in**
He delights in playing tricks on people.
• **enjoy, get pleasure from, relish, savour, lap up, revel in**

delight *NOUN*
Her eyes lit up with delight.
• **happiness, joy, pleasure, enjoyment, bliss, ecstasy**
OPPOSITE displeasure

delighted *ADJECTIVE*
My friend was delighted with her present.
• **pleased, happy, glad, joyful, thrilled, ecstatic, overjoyed, elated, exultant**

delightful *ADJECTIVE*
What a delightful surprise!
• **lovely, pleasant, pleasing, enjoyable, appealing, attractive, charming**

delirious *ADJECTIVE*
He was raving in his sleep, as if delirious.
• **feverish, frenzied, frantic, deranged, mad, crazy, wild, beside yourself**
OPPOSITE calm

deliver *VERB*
❶ *The postman delivered a parcel this morning.*
• **convey, carry, transport, hand over, present, supply, distribute, dispatch, ship**
❷ *She stood up to deliver her speech.*
• **give, make, read out, pronounce, utter, broadcast**
❸ *He raised his sword to deliver the final blow.*
• **strike, deal, administer, inflict, give**
(*informal*) **land**

delude *VERB*
You're deluding yourself if you think that.
• **deceive, fool, trick, mislead, hoax, bluff**
(*informal*) **con**

delusion *NOUN*
People were under the delusion that the Earth was flat.
• **misconception, misapprehension, false impression, fantasy, self-deception**

A B C D E F G H I J K L M N O P Q R S T U V W X Y Z

demand *VERB*
❶ *I demanded a refund for my ticket.*
• **insist on, claim, call for, seek, request**
❷ *'What do you want?' a voice demanded.*
• **ask, enquire**
❸ *Archery demands skill and concentration.*
• **require, need, call for, involve, entail**

demand *NOUN*
❶ *King John agreed to the demands of his barons.*
• **request, requirement, call, claim**
❷ *There was a great demand for tickets.*
• **desire, call, need, appetite, market**

demanding *ADJECTIVE*
❶ *Nursing is a demanding profession.*
• **difficult, challenging, exhausting, hard, tough, testing, taxing, onerous, arduous**
OPPOSITE **easy**
❷ *Toddlers can be very demanding.*
• **difficult, trying, tiresome, insistent**

demolish *VERB*
❶ *The building was demolished in the 1960s.*
• **knock down, pull down, tear down, flatten, level, destroy, bulldoze**
OPPOSITES **build, construct**
❷ *She demolished his argument in one sentence.*
• **destroy, pull apart, tear to pieces, ruin, wreck, overturn**

demonstrate *VERB*
❶ *These results demonstrate that our theory is correct.*
• **prove, indicate, verify, establish, confirm**
❷ *The crew demonstrated how to use a life jacket.*
• **show, exhibit, illustrate, exemplify**
❸ *Campaigners were demonstrating in the street.*
• **protest, march, parade**

demonstration *NOUN*
❶ *I watched a demonstration of the new software.*
• **show, display, presentation**
❷ *Thousands joined the demonstration against world poverty.*
• **protest, rally, march, parade** (*informal*) **demo**

demote *VERB*
After this defeat, the head of the army was demoted.
• **downgrade, put down, relegate**
OPPOSITE **promote**

den *NOUN*
❶ *the winter den of a polar bear*
• **lair, burrow, hole**
❷ *This room is my private den.*
• **hideout, shelter, hiding place**

denote *VERB*
What does this symbol denote?
• **indicate, signify, stand for, mean, express, symbolize, represent**

denounce *VERB*
They denounced him as a spy.
• **attack, condemn, censure, criticize, disparage, condemn, accuse, expose**

dense *ADJECTIVE*
❶ *a blanket of dense fog*
• **thick, heavy**
❷ *a rainforest with dense undergrowth*
• **compact, thick, impenetrable, solid, packed, crowded**
❸ (*informal*) *I'm being rather dense today!*
• **stupid, slow, foolish, simple-minded** (*informal*) **dim, thick**

dent *NOUN*
There was a large dent in the car door.
• **indentation, depression, hollow, dip, dimple**

dent *VERB*
A football hit the door and dented it.
• **make a dent in, knock in, push in**

dentist *NOUN*
a check-up at the dentist
– A dentist who specializes in straightening teeth is an **orthodontist**.
– A dental assistant who helps you look after your teeth is a **hygienist**.

deny *VERB*
❶ *The boy denied that he had stolen the money.*
• repudiate, contradict, refute, dispute, challenge, contest
OPPOSITES admit, confirm
❷ *He denied our request for an interview.*
• refuse, reject, rebuff, decline, dismiss, turn down
OPPOSITES accept, agree to, allow

depart *VERB*
Our guests departed after breakfast.
• leave, set off, get going, set out, go away, exit, withdraw
IDIOM make tracks
OPPOSITES arrive, get in

department *NOUN*
Mr Lloyd works in the sales department.
• section, branch, division, sector, unit, office, agency

departure *NOUN*
The weather delayed our departure.
• leaving, leave-taking, going, exit, withdrawal
OPPOSITES arrival, entrance

depend *VERB*
➤ **depend on someone**
You can depend on me.
• rely on, count on, bank on, trust
➤ **depend on something**
Good health depends on many different things.
• be decided by, be determined by, be dependent on, rest on, hinge on

dependable *ADJECTIVE*
Are these friends of yours dependable?
• reliable, trustworthy, loyal, faithful, trusty, honest, sound, steady
OPPOSITE unreliable

dependent *ADJECTIVE*
➤ **dependent on**
Our plans are dependent on the weather.
• determined by, decided by, subject to, controlled by, reliant on

depict *VERB*
❶ *The painting depicts a village in winter.*
• portray, illustrate, picture, represent, reproduce, paint, draw, sketch
❷ *The film depicts the horror of war.*
• describe, present, show, outline, detail, relate, set forth

deplorable *ADJECTIVE*
Their rudeness was deplorable.
• disgraceful, shameful, scandalous, shocking, unforgivable, lamentable, reprehensible, inexcusable
OPPOSITE admirable

deplore *VERB*
We all deplore cruelty to animals.
• condemn, denounce, disapprove of, frown on
(*formal*) abhor

depose *VERB*
The last Roman emperor was deposed in 476 AD.
• overthrow, dethrone, unseat, topple, oust

deposit *NOUN*
❶ *Today we paid the deposit on a new computer.*
• down payment, first instalment, prepayment
❷ *The country has large deposits of oil and natural gas.*
• layer, seam, vein, stratum, sediment

deposit *VERB*
❶ *She deposited a pile of papers on the desk.*
• put down, set down, place, rest, drop
(*informal*) dump, plonk
❷ *The flood water deposited layers of mud.*
• leave behind, cast up, wash up

depress *VERB*
The long, dark nights were depressing me.
• sadden, dispirit, dishearten, demoralize, get you down, weigh down on you
OPPOSITE cheer

depressed *ADJECTIVE*
The argument left me feeling depressed.
• **downhearted, dispirited, disheartened, unhappy, sad, miserable, gloomy, glum, melancholy, morose, despondent, dejected, desolate, downcast, low, down, blue**
IDIOMS (*informal*) **down in the dumps, down in the mouth**
OPPOSITE cheerful

depressing *ADJECTIVE*
I found the ending of the book depressing.
• **disheartening, dispiriting, gloomy, sad, dismal, dreary, sombre, bleak, cheerless**
OPPOSITE cheerful

depression *NOUN*
❶ *She sank into a state of depression.*
• **despair, sadness, gloom, unhappiness, low spirits, melancholy, misery, dejection, despondency**
OPPOSITE cheerfulness
❷ *the Great Depression of the 1930s*
• **recession, slump, downturn**
OPPOSITE boom
❸ *The rain had collected in several depressions in the ground.*
• **hollow, indentation, dent, dip, pit, cavity, crater, basin, bowl**

deprive *VERB*
➤ **to deprive someone of something**
The prisoners were deprived of food.
• **deny, refuse, strip of, rob**
OPPOSITE provide with

deprived *ADJECTIVE*
The charity tries to help deprived families.
• **poor, needy, underprivileged, disadvantaged, destitute**
OPPOSITES wealthy, privileged

depth *NOUN*
➤ **in depth**
Let's examine the poem in depth.
• **in detail, thoroughly, comprehensively**
OPPOSITE superficially

deputy *NOUN*
The Sheriff's Office has two deputies.
• **second-in-command, assistant, aide, stand-in, substitute, reserve**
The prefix vice- can also be used to mean a deputy, for example a *vice-captain* or a *vice-president*.

derelict *ADJECTIVE*
They plan to pull down those derelict buildings.
• **dilapidated, run-down, neglected, disused, deserted, abandoned, ramshackle**

derision *NOUN*
His idea was greeted with shouts of derision.
• **scorn, ridicule, mockery, disdain, taunts, jeers**

derive *VERB*
❶ *Bill derives a lot of pleasure from his garden.*
• **get, gain, obtain, receive**
❷ *She derives many of her plots from news stories.*
• **borrow, draw, pick up, acquire, take, extract**
(*informal*) **lift**

derogatory *ADJECTIVE*
His email was full of derogatory remarks.
• **critical, uncomplimentary, insulting, disparaging, scornful, pejorative, negative**
OPPOSITES complimentary, positive

descend *VERB*
❶ *She descended the stairs slowly.*
• **go down, come down, climb down, move down**
– To descend through the air is to **drop** or **fall**.
– To descend through water is to **sink**.
OPPOSITES ascend, climb
❷ *The road descends gradually into the valley.*
• **drop, fall, slope, slant, incline, dip, sink**
OPPOSITES ascend, climb

➤ **be descended from**
Humans are descended from apes.
• **come from, originate from, be related to, spring from, stem from**

descendant *NOUN*
the descendants of Queen Victoria
• **successor, heir**
OPPOSITE ancestor

descent *NOUN*
❶ *The path makes a steep descent into the valley.*
• **drop, fall, dip, incline, gradient, slide**
OPPOSITE ascent
❷ *a family of Polish descent*
• **ancestry, lineage, origin, extraction, roots, stock, blood**

describe *VERB*
❶ *Can you describe what you saw?*
• **report, recount, relate, tell about, narrate, outline**
❷ *Friends described him as a modest man.*
• **portray, characterize, represent, present, depict, label**

description *NOUN*
❶ *An eyewitness was able to give a detailed description of what happened.*
• **report, account, narrative, story**
❷ *Write a description of your favourite character.*
• **portrait, portrayal, characterization, representation, sketch**
❸ *We sell antiques of every description.*
• **kind, type, sort, variety**

descriptive *ADJECTIVE*
The author writes in a very descriptive style.
• **expressive, colourful, detailed, graphic, vivid**

desert *NOUN*
The surface of Mars is a cold and dry desert.
• **wasteland, wilderness, wastes**

desert *VERB*
He deserted his friends when they needed him most.
• **abandon, leave**
(*informal*) **walk out on, ditch**
(*old use*) **forsake**
IDIOMS **leave high and dry, leave in the lurch**
– To leave someone in a place from which they cannot escape is to **maroon** or **strand** them.

deserted *ADJECTIVE*
By midnight, the streets were deserted.
• **empty, unoccupied, uninhabited, vacant, desolate, abandoned**
OPPOSITES crowded, inhabited

deserve *VERB*
You deserve a break after all your hard work.
• **be entitled to, be worthy of, have earned, merit, warrant**

design *NOUN*
❶ *This is the winning design for the new art gallery.*
• **plan, drawing, outline, blueprint, sketch**
– A first version of something, from which others are made, is a **prototype**.
❷ *Do you like the design of this wallpaper?*
• **style, pattern, motif, arrangement, composition, layout**

design *VERB*
❶ *Ada Lovelace designed the first computer language.*
• **create, develop, invent, devise, conceive, think up**
❷ *The course is designed for beginners.*
• **intend, plan, devise, aim (at), mean**

desirable *ADJECTIVE*
❶ *The house has many desirable features.*
• **appealing, attractive, sought-after, tempting**
(*informal*) **must-have**
OPPOSITE unappealing
❷ *It is desirable to phone in advance.*
• **advisable, sensible, prudent, wise,**

recommended, preferable
OPPOSITE unwise

desire *NOUN*
She had a burning desire to visit China.
• wish, want, longing, yearning, craving, ambition, aspiration, fancy, hankering, yen, urge, hunger, itch

desire *VERB*
I will grant you whatever your heart desires.
• wish for, long for, want, aspire to, crave, fancy, hanker after, yearn for, pine for, have a yen for, hunger for
IDIOM set your heart on

desolate *ADJECTIVE*
❶ *He felt desolate and utterly alone.*
• depressed, dejected, miserable, sad, melancholy, hopeless, wretched, forlorn
OPPOSITE cheerful
❷ *It was a desolate landscape.*
• bleak, barren, stark, bare, deserted, uninhabited, inhospitable, godforsaken, dismal, cheerless
OPPOSITE pleasant

despair *NOUN*
He threw his hands up in despair.
• desperation, anguish, wretchedness, hopelessness, misery, despondency, unhappiness, gloom
OPPOSITE hope

despair *VERB*
There are many reasons not to despair.
• lose hope, be discouraged, be despondent, lose heart
OPPOSITE hope

despatch *NOUN & VERB*
see **dispatch**

desperate *ADJECTIVE*
❶ *The crew were in a desperate situation.*
• difficult, critical, grave, serious, severe, drastic, dire, urgent, extreme
❷ *We were desperate for news.*
• anxious, frantic, eager, impatient, longing, itching
❸ *a band of desperate outlaws*
• dangerous, reckless, rash, impetuous

despicable *ADJECTIVE*
They were known for despicable acts of cruelty.
• disgraceful, hateful, shameful, contemptible, loathsome, vile

despise *VERB*
I despise people who cheat.
• hate, loathe, deplore, disdain, feel contempt for, have a low opinion of, look down on, scorn, sneer at
(*formal*) abhor
OPPOSITES admire, respect

despite *PREPOSITION*
We went for a walk despite the rain.
• in spite of, regardless of, notwithstanding
OPPOSITE because of

dessert *NOUN*
There is plum crumble for dessert.
• pudding, sweet
(*informal*) afters

destination *NOUN*
The train arrived at its destination five minutes early.
• terminus, stop, objective
IDIOM journey's end

destined *ADJECTIVE*
❶ *They felt they were destined to win.*
• fated, doomed, preordained, intended, meant, certain
❷ *The ship was destined for Australia.*
• bound, headed, intended, directed

destiny *NOUN*
She felt that it was her destiny to be a great singer.
• fate, fortune, future, doom, lot

destroy *VERB*
❶ *An avalanche destroyed the village.*
• demolish, devastate, crush, smash, shatter, flatten, level, knock down, sweep away
❷ *The injury has destroyed her chances of a medal.*
• ruin, wreck, spoil, sabotage, thwart, undo

destruction *NOUN*
❶ *The hurricane caused widespread destruction.*
• **devastation, damage, demolition, ruin, wreckage, havoc**
OPPOSITE creation
❷ *The species is threatened by the destruction of its habitat.*
• **eradication, obliteration, elimination, annihilation, extermination, extinction**
OPPOSITES preservation, conservation

destructive *ADJECTIVE*
Tornadoes have a great destructive power.
• **damaging, devastating, catastrophic, disastrous, harmful, injurious, ruinous, violent**

detach *VERB*
The camera lens can be detached for cleaning.
• **remove, separate, disconnect, take off, split off, release, undo, unfasten, part**
– To detach a trailer from a vehicle is to **unhitch** it.
– To detach railway carriages is to **uncouple** them.
OPPOSITE attach

detail *NOUN*
Her account was accurate in every detail.
• **fact, particular, feature, characteristic, aspect, respect, element, item, point, specific**

detailed *ADJECTIVE*
The novel gives a detailed description of Victorian London.
• **precise, exact, specific, full, thorough, elaborate, comprehensive, exhaustive, minute**
OPPOSITES rough, vague

detain *VERB*
❶ *I'll try not to detain you for long.*
• **delay, hold up, keep, keep waiting**
❷ *Police have detained two suspects.*
• **hold, arrest, apprehend, imprison, confine, take into custody**
OPPOSITE release

detect *VERB*
❶ *I could detect a note of fear in her voice.*
• **perceive, discern, be aware of, notice, spot, recognize, make out, catch**
❷ *They have detected evidence of snow on Mars.*
• **discover, find, uncover, unearth, reveal, identify, track down**

detective *NOUN*
Hercule Poirot is a fictional detective.
• **investigator, sleuth**
(*informal*) **private eye**
For tips on writing crime fiction see **crime**.

deter *VERB*
How can we deter slugs from eating our vegetables?
• **discourage, dissuade, prevent, stop, avert, put off, scare off**
OPPOSITE encourage

deteriorate *VERB*
Her sight has begun to deteriorate.
• **worsen, decline, fail, degenerate, get worse**
IDIOM **go downhill**
OPPOSITES improve, get better

determination *NOUN*
All of the players showed great determination.
• **resolve, commitment, will-power, courage, dedication, drive, grit, perseverance, persistence, spirit**
(*informal*) **guts**

determine *VERB*
❶ *I determined to follow their advice.*
• **resolve, decide, make up your mind**
❷ *Your genes determine your body size.*
• **dictate, decide, control, regulate, govern**
❸ *Can you determine the height of the mountain?*
• **calculate, compute, establish, ascertain, work out, figure out**

determined *ADJECTIVE*
❶ *My grandmother was a very determined woman.*
• **resolute, decisive, purposeful, strong-minded, persistent, tenacious, adamant**
OPPOSITES weak-minded, irresolute
❷ *She was determined to finish the race.*
• **resolved, committed, dogged**
OPPOSITES feeble, half-hearted

detest *VERB*
I detest the smell of boiled cabbage.
• **dislike, hate, loathe, despise**
(*informal*) **can't bear, can't stand**
(*formal*) **abhor**
OPPOSITES love, adore

detour *NOUN*
We wasted time by taking a detour.
• **diversion, indirect route, roundabout route**

detrimental *ADJECTIVE*
Too much water can be detrimental to plants.
• **damaging, harmful, destructive, adverse**
OPPOSITE beneficial

devastate *VERB*
❶ *The tsunami devastated the island.*
• **destroy, wreck, ruin, demolish, flatten, level, lay waste**
❷ *We were devastated by the news.*
• **shock, stun, daze, overwhelm, shatter**

develop *VERB*
❶ *The zoo is developing its education programme.*
• **expand, extend, enlarge, build up, enhance, improve, broaden, diversify**
❷ *Their fan base has developed over the years.*
• **grow, spread, expand, flourish, build up**
❸ *The symptoms developed quickly.*
• **emerge, arise, break out, grow, spread**
❹ *Her piano playing has developed this year.*
• **improve, progress, evolve, get better, advance, refine, mature**
❺ *They soon developed bad habits.*
• **get, acquire, pick up, cultivate**

development *NOUN*
❶ *We are pleased with the development of our website.*
• **growth, evolution, expansion, improvement, progress, spread**
❷ *Have there been any further developments?*
• **event, happening, occurrence, incident, change**

deviate *VERB*
We were forced to deviate from our original plan.
• **diverge, differ, vary, depart, digress, stray**

device *NOUN*
The TV comes with a remote control device.
• **tool, implement, instrument, appliance, apparatus, gadget, contraption**
(*informal*) **gizmo**

devious *ADJECTIVE*
❶ *He got rich by devious means.*
• **deceitful, underhand, dishonest, furtive, scheming, cunning, sly, sneaky, treacherous, wily**
❷ *The bus took a devious route.*
• **indirect, roundabout, winding, meandering, circuitous**
OPPOSITE direct

devise *VERB*
Between them they devised a plan to escape.
• **conceive, form, invent, contrive, formulate, make up, come up with, plan, prepare, map out, think out, think up**

devote *VERB*
She devotes her spare time to the garden.
• **dedicate, allocate, set aside, allot, assign, commit**

devoted *ADJECTIVE*
The band has many devoted fans.
• loyal, faithful, dedicated, committed, staunch, steadfast

devotion *NOUN*
It is the story of a dog's devotion to his master.
• loyalty, fidelity, commitment, dedication, attachment, fondness, allegiance

devour *VERB*
He devoured a whole plateful of sandwiches.
• eat, consume, gobble up, bolt down, gulp down, swallow
(*informal*) guzzle, scoff, wolf down
SEE ALSO **eat**

devout *ADJECTIVE*
a devout Catholic
• dutiful, committed, loyal, pious, sincere, reverent

diagnose *VERB*
No one could diagnose the cause of her illness.
• identify, determine, detect, recognize, name, pinpoint

diagram *NOUN*
This is a diagram of the digestive system.
• chart, plan, sketch, drawing, representation, outline

dialogue *NOUN*
The play consists of a series of dialogues.
• conversation, talk, discussion, exchange, debate, chat

diary *NOUN*
She kept a diary from the age of nine.
• journal, chronicle, record, memoir
– A diary describing a voyage or mission is a **log** or **logbook**.
– A diary published on a website is a **blog**.

dictate *VERB*
➤ **dictate to someone**
You have no right to dictate to me!
• order about, give orders to, command, bully
(*informal*) boss about, push around
IDIOM **lord it over**

dictator *NOUN*
Hitler became a ruthless dictator.
• autocrat, absolute ruler, tyrant, despot

die *VERB*
❶ *She died in 2002 at the age of 94.*
• expire, perish, pass away, pass on
(*informal*) snuff it, croak
IDIOM **give up the ghost**
IDIOMS (*informal*) **kick the bucket, pop your clogs**
– To die of hunger is to **starve**.
❷ *My computer has died on me again.*
• fail, crash, break down, malfunction
(*informal*) pack up, conk out
➤ **die down**
The wind should die down soon.
• lessen, decrease, decline, subside, abate, ease off, let up, peter out, wane, ebb
➤ **die out**
When did the dinosaurs die out?
• become extinct, cease to exist, disappear, vanish

diet *NOUN*
You should include plenty of fruit and vegetables in your diet.
• food, nourishment, nutrition
– A diet which does not include meat is a **vegetarian** diet.
– A diet which does not include any animal products is a **vegan** diet.
SEE ALSO **food**

differ *VERB*
The statements differ on a number of points.
• disagree, conflict, clash, contradict each other
IDIOM **be at odds**
OPPOSITE **agree**
➤ **differ from**
How do the poems differ from each other?
• be different from, contrast with, vary from, run counter to
OPPOSITE **resemble**

a b c d e f g h i j k l m n o p q r s t u v w x y z

A B C D E F G H I J K L M N O P Q R S T U V W X Y Z

difference *NOUN*
❶ *Can you see any difference between these two colours?*
• contrast, distinction, dissimilarity, disparity, variation, divergence
OPPOSITE similarity
❷ *This money will make a difference to their lives.*
• change, alteration, modification, improvement
❸ *We've had our differences in the past.*
• disagreement, argument, quarrel, dispute

different *ADJECTIVE*
❶ *The twins have very different personalities.*
• dissimilar, unlike, differing, contrasting, varying, disparate
IDIOMS like chalk and cheese, poles apart
OPPOSITES identical, similar
❷ *Every person's handwriting is different.*
• distinct, distinctive, distinguishable, individual, unique, special
❸ *Birds have beaks of different shapes and sizes.*
• various, assorted, several, diverse, numerous
❹ *Your hair looks different today.*
• changed, altered, unfamiliar
❺ *Let's do something different this weekend.*
• unusual, original, fresh, new, novel, out of the ordinary

difficult *ADJECTIVE*
❶ *This is a really difficult crossword puzzle.*
• hard, complicated, complex, involved, intricate, baffling, perplexing, puzzling, tricky
(*informal*) thorny, knotty
OPPOSITE simple
❷ *It is a difficult climb to the top of the hill.*
• challenging, arduous, demanding, taxing, exhausting, formidable, gruelling, laborious, strenuous, tough
OPPOSITE easy
❸ *Mum says I was a difficult child.*
• troublesome, awkward, demanding, uncooperative, obstinate, stubborn, trying, tiresome
OPPOSITES cooperative, accommodating

difficulty *NOUN*
❶ *One of the climbers got into real difficulty.*
• trouble, adversity, hardship, distress, problems, challenges
(*informal*) hassle
❷ *We ran into one difficulty after another.*
• problem, complication, hitch, obstacle, snag, stumbling block

dig *VERB*
❶ *We spent the afternoon digging the garden.*
• cultivate, fork over, turn over
❷ *Rabbits dig holes in the ground.*
• burrow, excavate, tunnel, bore, gouge out, hollow out, scoop out
❸ *I felt someone dig me in the ribs.*
• poke, prod, jab, stab
➤ **dig up**
Can you dig up some more information?
• discover, uncover, find, reveal, expose, turn up

dignified *ADJECTIVE*
He rose to his feet in a calm and dignified manner.
• stately, distinguished, grand, noble, majestic, august, imposing, formal, solemn, sedate
OPPOSITE undignified

dignity *NOUN*
❶ *The joke spoilt the dignity of the occasion.*
• formality, seriousness, solemnity, propriety, decorum
❷ *She faced her death with great dignity.*
• calmness, poise, self-control

dilemma *NOUN*
I now faced the dilemma of whether to stay or go.
• quandary, predicament
IDIOM catch-22

diligent *ADJECTIVE*
❶ *She is a diligent student.*
• hard-working, conscientious, industrious
❷ *Police made a diligent search of the crime scene.*
• careful, attentive, painstaking, meticulous, rigorous, thorough

dilute *VERB*
Dilute the juice before serving.
• thin, water down, weaken
OPPOSITE concentrate

dim *ADJECTIVE*
❶ *the dim light of a single candle*
• faint, muted, subdued
OPPOSITE bright
❷ *a long, dim corridor*
• dark, dull, dingy, murky, gloomy, badly lit
OPPOSITE bright
❸ *I have only a dim memory of the plot.*
• vague, indistinct, faint, blurred, fuzzy, hazy, sketchy
OPPOSITE clear

dimension *NOUN*
First we need to measure the dimensions of the room.
• measurements, size, extent, capacity
SEE ALSO **measurement**

diminish *VERB*
❶ *The bad news did not diminish her enthusiasm.*
• lessen, reduce, decrease, minimize, curtail
❷ *Our water supply was diminishing rapidly.*
• become less, decrease, decline, subside, dwindle, wane
OPPOSITE increase

din *NOUN*
I can't hear above that din!
• noise, racket, row, clatter, commotion, uproar, hullabaloo, hubbub, cacophony

dine *VERB*
We will be dining at eight o'clock.
• eat, have dinner, have lunch

dingy *ADJECTIVE*
How can we brighten up this dingy room?
• dull, drab, dreary, dowdy, colourless, dismal, gloomy, murky
OPPOSITE bright

dinosaur *NOUN*

WORD WEB

Some types of dinosaur:

- apatosaurus
- archaeopteryx
- brachiosaurus
- diplodocus
- gallimimus
- iguanodon
- megalosaurus
- pterodactylus
- stegosaurus
- triceratops
- tyranno-saurus rex
- velociraptor

- The study of dinosaurs and other fossils is **palaeontology**.

SEE ALSO **prehistoric**

dip *VERB*
❶ *I dipped my hand in the water.*
• immerse, lower, submerge, plunge, dunk
❷ *The road dips down into the valley.*
• descend, go down, slope down, drop down, fall away, sink

dip *NOUN*
❶ *There's a dip in the road ahead.*
• slope, slide, decline, hollow, depression
❷ *It was hot so we took a dip in the sea.*
• swim, bathe, paddle

dire *ADJECTIVE*
❶ *They warned us of dire consequences.*
• dreadful, terrible, awful, appalling, severe, grave

❷ *The ground is in dire need of rain.*
• **urgent, desperate, drastic, extreme, pressing**

direct *ADJECTIVE*
❶ *Which is the most direct route?*
• **straight, short, quick**
OPPOSITES indirect, roundabout
❷ *Please give me a direct answer.*
• **straightforward, frank, honest, sincere, blunt, plain, candid, unambiguous, unequivocal**
OPPOSITE evasive
❸ *She is a shy girl but her sister is the direct opposite.*
• **exact, complete**

direct *VERB*
❶ *Can you direct me to the station?*
• **guide, point, show the way, give directions to**
❷ *The advert is directed at young people.*
• **aim, target, point**
❸ *Dr Knox will direct the experiment.*
• **manage, run, be in charge of, control, administer, govern, superintend, supervise, take charge of**
– To direct an orchestra is to **conduct** it.
❹ *Officers directed the crowd to move back.*
• **instruct, command, order, tell**

direction *NOUN*
Which direction did they go in?
• **way, route, course, path, bearing**
➤ **directions**
Follow the directions on the packet.
• **instructions, guidance, guidelines**

director *NOUN*
She is the director of the town's new art gallery.
• **manager, head, chief, chief executive, leader, president**
(*informal*) **boss**

dirt *NOUN*
❶ *The floor was covered in dirt.*
• **filth, grime, mess, muck, mud, dust**
❷ *Chickens were scratching about in the dirt.*
• **earth, soil, clay, ground**

dirty *ADJECTIVE*
❶ *There's a pile of dirty washing to do.*
• **unclean, unwashed, soiled, stained, grimy, grubby, filthy, messy, mucky, muddy, squalid**
(*informal*) **manky, grotty**
OPPOSITE clean
❷ *It's dangerous to drink dirty water.*
• **impure, polluted, foul, contaminated**
OPPOSITE pure
❸ *That was a dirty trick!*
• **unfair, dishonest, underhand, mean, unsporting**
OPPOSITE honest
❹ *He was telling dirty jokes.*
• **rude, obscene, indecent, coarse, crude, smutty, filthy**
OPPOSITE decent

disability *NOUN*
The Paralympics are open to athletes with disabilities.
• **handicap, incapacity, impairment, infirmity**

disabled *ADJECTIVE*
He has been disabled since the accident.
• **handicapped, incapacitated**
– An animal which is injured and cannot walk is **lame**.
– A person who cannot move part of their body is **paralysed**.
OPPOSITE able-bodied

disadvantage *NOUN*
Being short is a disadvantage for basketball players.
• **drawback, handicap, hindrance, inconvenience, downside, snag, catch**
OPPOSITES advantage, plus

disagree *VERB*
We often disagree about music.
• **argue, differ, clash, quarrel, be of a different opinion**
IDIOMS **be at odds, be at loggerheads**
OPPOSITE agree
➤ **disagree with**
❶ *He disagrees with everything I say.*
• **argue with, contradict, oppose, object to, dispute, contest, challenge, take issue with**

❷ *Onions disagree with me.*
• **make you ill, upset your stomach, have a bad effect on you**

disagreeable *ADJECTIVE*
What a disagreeable man!
• **unpleasant, nasty, horrible, offensive, revolting, repellent, repulsive, obnoxious**
OPPOSITE pleasant

disagreement *NOUN*
There was some disagreement over the bill.
• **argument, dispute, difference of opinion, conflict, discord, quarrel, row, clash, squabble**
OPPOSITE agreement

disappear *VERB*
❶ *The scar has nearly disappeared.*
• **vanish, fade away, melt away, clear**
OPPOSITE appear
❷ *It is a way of life that has almost disappeared.*
• **die out, cease to exist, come to an end, vanish, pass away**
OPPOSITES emerge, arise

disappoint *VERB*
The announcement will disappoint some fans.
• **let down, fail, dissatisfy, displease, dismay, upset, sadden**
OPPOSITES please, satisfy

disappointed *ADJECTIVE*
I was disappointed with my score.
• **displeased, unhappy, upset, unsatisfied, saddened, downhearted, disheartened, discouraged, let down**
(*informal*) **gutted**
OPPOSITES pleased, satisfied

disapprove *VERB*
➤ **disapprove of**
Her family disapproved of her marriage.
• **object to, take exception to, dislike, deplore, condemn, criticize, denounce, frown on**
IDIOM take a dim view of
OPPOSITE approve of

disaster *NOUN*
❶ *The country was rocked by a series of disasters.*
• **catastrophe, calamity, tragedy, misfortune, blow**
– Events such as earthquakes, hurricanes and floods are called **natural disasters**.
❷ *The show was a complete disaster.*
• **failure, fiasco, shambles**
(*informal*) **flop, wash-out**

disastrous *ADJECTIVE*
This mistake had disastrous results.
• **catastrophic, devastating, calamitous, destructive, dire, dreadful, terrible, ruinous**

disbelief *NOUN*
We stared at the TV screen in disbelief.
• **incredulity, doubt, distrust, mistrust, scepticism**

disc *NOUN*
the disc of the full moon
see **circle**

discard *VERB*
It's time to discard some of these old clothes.
• **get rid of, throw away, throw out, reject, cast off, dispose of, dump, scrap, toss out**
(*informal*) **ditch, bin**

discharge *VERB*
❶ *He was found not guilty and discharged.*
• **free, release, let go, liberate**
❷ *The chimneys were discharging thick smoke.*
• **emit, expel, eject, give out, give off, produce**

disciple *NOUN*
Confucius had many disciples.
• **follower, supporter, adherent, admirer, devotee**
– In Christianity, the disciples of Jesus are called the **apostles**.

A B C D E F G H I J K L M N O P Q R S T U V W X Y Z

discipline *NOUN*
❶ *Discipline is important in the army.*
• control, order, good behaviour, obedience
❷ *Genetics is a relatively new discipline.*
• field, subject, area of study, speciality

disclose *VERB*
Someone has been disclosing top-secret information.
• reveal, divulge, make known, pass on, tell, impart, make public
OPPOSITE conceal

discomfort *NOUN*
❶ *Is your tooth still giving you discomfort?*
• pain, soreness, aching
❷ *I could sense her discomfort at my question.*
• uneasiness, unease, embarrassment, awkwardness, distress

disconnect *VERB*
First you need to disconnect the computer cable.
• detach, unplug, unhook, cut off, disable

discontented *ADJECTIVE*
She was feeling discontented with life.
• dissatisfied, disgruntled, displeased, unhappy, miserable
(*informal*) fed up
OPPOSITES contented, satisfied

discount *NOUN*
They are offering a discount of 20 per cent.
• reduction, deduction, cut, concession, markdown

discount *VERB*
We cannot discount that possibility.
• ignore, dismiss, disregard, pay no attention to, overlook
OPPOSITE acknowledge

discourage *VERB*
❶ *Don't let her words discourage you.*
• dishearten, demoralize, depress, unnerve
OPPOSITE encourage
❷ *The burglar alarm will discourage thieves.*
• deter, dissuade, prevent, restrain, hinder
(*informal*) put you off

discover *VERB*
❶ *I discovered some old games in the attic.*
• find, come across, spot, stumble across, track down, uncover, unearth
❷ *We discovered the truth years later.*
• find out, learn, realize, recognize, ascertain, work out

discovery *NOUN*
This drug was an important discovery in the history of medicine.
• find, breakthrough, innovation

discreet *ADJECTIVE*
I made a few discreet enquiries.
• tactful, sensitive, delicate, careful, cautious, diplomatic
OPPOSITE tactless

discretion *NOUN*
❶ *You can count on my discretion.*
• tact, sensitivity, delicacy, diplomacy
OPPOSITE tactlessness
❷ *Marks are awarded at the discretion of the judges.*
• option, choice, preference, inclination, will

discriminate *VERB*
It's sometimes hard to discriminate between fact and fiction.
• distinguish, differentiate, tell the difference, tell apart, draw a distinction
➤ **discriminate against**
It's wrong to discriminate against people because of their age.
• be biased against, be prejudiced against, treat unfairly, victimize

discrimination *NOUN*
❶ *The school has a policy against any form of discrimination.*
• prejudice, bias, intolerance, bigotry, unfairness, favouritism
– Discrimination against people because of their sex is **sexism**.

– Discrimination against people because of their race is **racism**.
❷ *She shows discrimination in her choice of music.*
• **good taste, good judgement**

discuss *VERB*
❶ *I discussed the idea with my friends.*
• **talk about, confer about, debate**
❷ *This topic is discussed in the next chapter.*
• **examine, explore, deal with, analyse, consider, tackle**

discussion *NOUN*
We had a lively discussion about Internet safety.
• **conversation, talk, dialogue, exchange of views**
– A formal discussion is a **conference** or **debate**.

disease *NOUN*
He was suffering from a serious disease.
• **illness, sickness, ailment, disorder, complaint, affliction, condition** (*informal*) **bug**
– An outbreak of disease that spreads quickly is an **epidemic**.
SEE ALSO **illness**

diseased *ADJECTIVE*
Gardeners throw away diseased plants.
• **unhealthy, sickly, ailing, infected**
OPPOSITE healthy

disgrace *NOUN*
❶ *He never got over the disgrace of being caught cheating.*
• **humiliation, shame, dishonour, scandal, ignominy, disrepute**
IDIOM **loss of face**
❷ *The litter on the streets is a disgrace.*
• **outrage, scandal**

disgraceful *ADJECTIVE*
We were shocked by her disgraceful behaviour.
• **shameful, shocking, appalling, outrageous, scandalous, reprehensible**
OPPOSITES honourable, admirable

disguise *VERB*
❶ *She disguised herself as a boy.*
• **dress up, be in disguise, pretend to be, pose as**
❷ *I tried to disguise my feelings.*
• **conceal, hide, cover up, camouflage, mask**
OPPOSITES reveal, expose

disguise *NOUN*
I wore a wig as a disguise.
• **costume, camouflage, mask**

disgust *NOUN*
She wrinkled her nose in disgust at the smell.
• **revulsion, repugnance, repulsion, abhorrence, distaste, dislike, loathing, detestation**
OPPOSITES delight, liking

disgust *VERB*
The sight of blood disgusts me.
• **repel, revolt, repulse, sicken, appal, offend, distress, horrify**
IDIOM **turn your stomach**
OPPOSITES delight, please

disgusting *ADJECTIVE*
What a disgusting smell!
• **repulsive, revolting, horrible, nasty, loathsome, repellent, repugnant, offensive, sickening, nauseating, stomach-turning** (*informal*) **yucky, icky, gross**
OPPOSITES delightful, pleasing

dish *NOUN*
❶ *He tipped the pasta into a dish.*
• **bowl, basin, plate, platter**
– A dish to serve soup from is a **tureen**.
❷ *What's your favourite dish?*
• **food, recipe, meal, course**

dish *VERB*
➤ **dish out**
Mr Elliot began dishing out sheets of paper.
• **distribute, hand out, dole out, dispense, allocate**

dishevelled *ADJECTIVE*
He arrived looking flushed and dishevelled.
• **messy, untidy, scruffy, unkempt,**

A B C D E F G H I J K L M N O P Q R S T U V W X Y Z

bedraggled, slovenly, ruffled
OPPOSITES neat, tidy

dishonest *ADJECTIVE*
❶ *They were taken in by a dishonest salesman.*
• **deceitful, corrupt, untrustworthy, immoral, disreputable, cheating, lying, swindling, thieving**
(informal) **bent, crooked, dodgy, shady**
❷ *The website makes some dishonest claims.*
• **false, fraudulent, misleading, untruthful**
OPPOSITE honest

dishonesty *NOUN*
She accused him of dishonesty.
• **deceit, cheating, lying, insincerity, fraud, corruption**
(informal) **crookedness**
OPPOSITE honesty

disinfect *VERB*
The nurse disinfected my wound.
• **cleanse, sterilize**
– *To disinfect an infected place is to* **decontaminate** *it.*
– *To disinfect a room with fumes is to* **fumigate** *it.*
OPPOSITE infect

disintegrate *VERB*
The fuel tank exploded and the spacecraft started to disintegrate.
• **break up, fall apart, break into pieces, crumble, decay, decompose**

disinterested *ADJECTIVE*
Referees have to remain disinterested.
• **impartial, neutral, unbiased, unprejudiced, detached, fair**
OPPOSITE biased
The word uninterested is not a synonym of disinterested. A disinterested referee is unbiased, but an uninterested referee is bored.

dislike *NOUN*
She had already taken a dislike to him.
• **hatred, loathing, detestation, antipathy, distaste, disgust, disapproval, revulsion**
OPPOSITE liking

dislike *VERB*
I dislike people who lie to me.
• **hate, loathe, detest, disapprove of, object to, take exception to**
OPPOSITE like

dislodge *VERB*
The wind dislodged some tiles on the roof.
• **displace, move, shift, disturb**

disloyal *ADJECTIVE*
They were accused of being disloyal to the king.
• **unfaithful, treacherous, faithless, false, unreliable, untrustworthy**
OPPOSITES loyal, faithful

dismal *ADJECTIVE*
❶ *She led him into a dismal little room.*
• **dull, drab, dreary, mournful, dingy, colourless, cheerless, gloomy, murky**
OPPOSITES bright, cheerful
❷ (*informal*) *It was a dismal performance by our team.*
• **dreadful, awful, terrible, feeble, useless, hopeless**
(*informal*) **pathetic**

dismantle *VERB*
We were busy dismantling the bunk beds.
• **take apart, take down, break up**
– To dismantle a group of tents is to **strike camp.**
OPPOSITES assemble, put together

dismay *NOUN*
We watched the news reports with dismay.
• **distress, alarm, shock, concern, anxiety, consternation**

dismayed *ADJECTIVE*
We were dismayed by the recent news.
• **distressed, disturbed, discouraged, disconcerted, depressed, taken aback, shocked, alarmed**
OPPOSITES pleased, encouraged

dismiss *VERB*
❶ *Mrs Owen dismissed her class.*
• **send away, discharge, free, let go, release**

❷ *The firm dismissed ten workers.*
• **sack, give the sack to, discharge, let go, give notice to, make redundant**
(*informal*) **fire**
❸ *I dismissed the idea as nonsense.*
• **discard, drop, reject, banish, set aside, brush aside, wave aside, put out of your mind**

disobedient *ADJECTIVE*
She said she had never known such a disobedient child.
• **badly behaved, naughty, insubordinate, undisciplined, uncontrollable, unmanageable, unruly, troublesome, defiant, disruptive, rebellious, mutinous**
OPPOSITE **obedient**

disobey *VERB*
❶ *He was too frightened to disobey her.*
• **be disobedient to, defy, rebel against**
– To refuse to obey orders from a commanding officer is to **mutiny**.
OPPOSITE **obey**
❷ *You will be penalized if you disobey the rules.*
• **break, disregard, ignore, violate, infringe, flout**

disorder *NOUN*
❶ *She stared at the disorder of her desk.*
• **untidiness, mess, muddle, chaos, confusion, clutter, jumble**
OPPOSITE **order**
❷ *The meeting broke up in disorder.*
• **disturbance, uproar, commotion, quarrelling, rioting, brawling, fighting, lawlessness, anarchy**
❸ *The patient was suffering from an eating disorder.*
• **disease, condition, complaint, affliction, illness, ailment, sickness**

disorderly *ADJECTIVE*
❶ *Books were arranged on the shelves in a disorderly fashion.*
• **untidy, disorganized, chaotic, messy, in disarray**
(*informal*) **higgledy-piggledy**
OPPOSITE **orderly**
❷ *The class were behaving in a disorderly manner.*
• **disobedient, unruly, uncontrollable, undisciplined, ungovernable, unmanageable**

dispatch *VERB*
The parcel has already been dispatched.
• **post, send, transmit, forward**

dispatch *NOUN*
A messenger brought a dispatch from headquarters.
• **message, communication, report, letter, bulletin**

dispense *VERB*
❶ *Waiters were there to dispense drinks.*
• **distribute, hand out, dole out, pass round, supply, provide**
❷ *He was like a feudal lord dispensing justice.*
• **administer, issue, deliver, deal out, mete out**
➤ **dispense with**
We are dispensing with fees altogether.
• **get rid of, dispose of, do without, forego, waive, drop, omit**
IDIOM (*informal*) **give something a miss**

disperse *VERB*
❶ *Dandelion seeds are dispersed by the wind.*
• **scatter, spread, distribute, disseminate**
❷ *The crowd dispersed quickly after the match.*
• **break up, scatter, disband, separate, split up, go in different directions**
OPPOSITE **gather**
❸ *The morning fog soon dispersed.*
• **dissipate, dissolve, melt away, vanish, clear, lift**

displace *VERB*
❶ *The gales displaced some roof tiles.*
• **dislodge, put out of place, shift**
OPPOSITE **replace**
❷ *Last year she displaced him as captain.*
• **replace, take the place of, succeed, supersede, supplant**

A B C D E F G H I J K L M N O P Q R S T U V W X Y Z

display *VERB*
❶ *The students' work was displayed in the foyer.*
• exhibit, present, show, set out, put on show, show off, parade, showcase
– To display something boastfully is to **flaunt** it.
❷ *They displayed great courage.*
• show, demonstrate, reveal, show evidence of

display *NOUN*
We set out a display of our recent art work.
• exhibition, show, presentation, demonstration, parade, spectacle, showcase

displease *VERB*
I must have done something to displease her.
• annoy, irritate, upset, put out, anger, irk, exasperate, vex

dispose *VERB*
➤ **dispose of something**
Please dispose of all your rubbish.
• get rid of, discard, throw away, throw out, jettison, scrap
(*informal*) dump
➤ **be disposed to do something**
No one seems disposed to help us.
• be willing to, be inclined to, be ready to, be likely to

disposition *NOUN*
Our dog has a very friendly disposition.
• temperament, nature, character, make-up, personality, mentality

disprove *VERB*
There is no evidence to disprove her story.
• refute, rebut, prove false, demolish, debunk
IDIOM shoot full of holes
OPPOSITE prove

dispute *VERB*
Some disputed her claim to the throne.
• disagree with, object to, challenge, contest, call into question, take issue with

dispute *NOUN*
There was a dispute over who should pay.
• argument, disagreement, debate, controversy, difference of opinion, quarrel, row, squabble, clash

disregard *VERB*
I disregarded the doctor's advice.
• ignore, pay no attention to, take no notice of, discount, reject, brush aside, shrug off
IDIOM turn a blind eye to
OPPOSITE heed

disrespectful *ADJECTIVE*
It's disrespectful to walk on someone's grave.
• rude, bad-mannered, insulting, impolite, insolent, cheeky
OPPOSITE respectful

disrupt *VERB*
The roadworks are disrupting bus services.
• interrupt, disturb, upset, unsettle, interfere with, play havoc with, throw into confusion

dissatisfied *ADJECTIVE*
I felt dissatisfied with my score.
• displeased, discontented, disappointed, disgruntled, unhappy, frustrated
OPPOSITES satisfied, contented

dissolve *VERB*
Stir the mixture until the sugar dissolves.
• disperse, disintegrate, melt

dissuade *VERB*
➤ **dissuade someone from**
I tried to dissuade her from leaving.
• discourage from, persuade not to, talk out of, deter from, warn against
OPPOSITES persuade to, encourage to

distance *NOUN*
What is the distance from the Earth to the Sun?
• measurement, space, extent, reach, mileage
– The distance across something is the **breadth** or **width**.

– The distance along something is the **length.**
– The distance between two points is a **gap** or **interval.**
SEE ALSO **measurement**

distant *ADJECTIVE*
❶ *She was always travelling to distant countries.*
• **faraway, far-off, remote, out-of-the-way**
OPPOSITES nearby, close
❷ *His distant manner puts me off.*
• **unfriendly, unapproachable, formal, reserved, withdrawn, cool, haughty, aloof**
OPPOSITES friendly, warm

distinct *ADJECTIVE*
❶ *I can see a distinct improvement.*
• **definite, evident, noticeable, obvious, perceptible**
OPPOSITE imperceptible
❷ *The image is quite distinct.*
• **clear, well defined, distinguishable, recognizable, sharp, unmistakable, visible, plain to see**
OPPOSITE indistinct
❸ *The country is divided into three distinct regions.*
• **separate, discrete, different, individual**

distinction *NOUN*
❶ *What is the distinction between reptiles and amphibians?*
• **difference, contrast, distinctiveness, differentiation**
❷ *He had the distinction of being the youngest ever captain of the team.*
• **honour, glory, merit, credit, prestige**

distinctive *ADJECTIVE*
She has a very distinctive laugh.
• **characteristic, recognizable, unmistakable, particular, special, peculiar, unique**

distinguish *VERB*
❶ *It was impossible to distinguish one twin from the other.*
• **tell apart, tell, differentiate, tell the difference between, discriminate between**
❷ *I was too far away to distinguish what they were saying.*
• **make out, identify, recognize, tell, determine, discern, perceive**

distinguished *ADJECTIVE*
❶ *The school has a distinguished academic record.*
• **excellent, first-rate, outstanding, exceptional**
OPPOSITE ordinary
❷ *He is a distinguished Hollywood actor.*
• **famous, celebrated, well-known, eminent, notable, prominent, renowned, acclaimed**
OPPOSITES unknown, obscure

distort *VERB*
❶ *The crash distorted the front wheel.*
• **bend, buckle, twist, warp, contort, deform, put out of shape**
❷ *The newspaper distorted the facts of the story.*
• **misrepresent, twist, slant, garble**

distract *VERB*
Don't distract the bus driver.
• **divert the attention of, disturb, put off, sidetrack**

distress *NOUN*
She let out a cry of distress.
• **suffering, torment, anguish, pain, misery, dismay, anxiety, grief, sadness, sorrow, wretchedness**

distress *VERB*
I could see that my words distressed him.
• **upset, disturb, trouble, worry, dismay, perturb, alarm, agitate, torment, pain**
OPPOSITE comfort

distribute *VERB*
❶ *They spent the day distributing leaflets.*
• **give out, hand round, circulate, dispense, issue, deal out, share out, dole out, dish out**
❷ *Distribute the seeds evenly.*
• **scatter, spread, disperse**

district *NOUN*
a mountainous district of Nepal
• **area, region, territory, locality, vicinity, neighbourhood, quarter, sector, zone**

distrust *VERB*
I distrusted him from the moment I met him.
• **doubt, mistrust, be suspicious of, be wary of, question, suspect, be sceptical about, have misgivings about**
OPPOSITE trust

disturb *VERB*
1 *Please don't let me disturb you.*
• **interrupt, intrude on, disrupt, bother, pester, trouble, distract**
2 *Some of the pictures may disturb you.*
• **distress, trouble, upset, unsettle, worry, perturb**
3 *Someone had disturbed the papers on my desk.*
• **rearrange, move around, mix up, muddle up, mess up**

disused *ADJECTIVE*
They turned the disused railway line into a cycle track.
• **abandoned, unused, neglected, obsolete, closed down**

ditch *NOUN*
He slipped and fell into a muddy ditch.
• **trench, channel, drain, gutter, gully**

dither *VERB*
I'm still dithering over what to do.
• **hesitate, waver, be in two minds, vacillate**
(*informal*) **shilly-shally**

dive *VERB*
1 *A group of penguins dived into the water.*
• **plunge, jump, leap**
– A dive in which you land flat on your front is a **bellyflop.**
2 *The eagle dived towards its prey.*
• **swoop, plummet, plunge, drop, fall, pitch, nosedive**

diverse *ADJECTIVE*
People from many diverse cultures live in the area.
• **varied, mixed, assorted, miscellaneous, various, different, differing, varying**

diversion *NOUN*
1 *The police had set up a traffic diversion.*
• **detour, alternative route, deviation**
2 *There were lots of diversions on offer at the theme park.*
• **entertainment, amusement, recreation**

divert *VERB*
1 *Our plane was diverted to another airport.*
• **redirect, re-route, switch**
2 *She diverted herself by browsing the Internet.*
• **entertain, amuse, occupy, interest, distract, keep happy**

divide *VERB*
1 *We divided the class into two teams.*
• **separate, split, split up, break up, part, partition**
OPPOSITE combine
2 *We divided the chocolate between us.*
• **distribute, share out, ration, give out, deal out, dish out, dispense**
3 *The river divides into several channels.*
• **diverge, branch off, fork, split, part**
OPPOSITE converge

divine *ADJECTIVE*
1 *The temple is used for divine worship.*
• **religious, sacred, holy, spiritual**
2 *The Greeks believed divine beings lived on Mount Olympus.*
• **godly, godlike, immortal, heavenly**
3 (*informal*) *These muffins taste divine!*
• **excellent, wonderful, superb**

division *NOUN*
1 *The map shows the division of Europe after the war.*
• **dividing, splitting, break-up, separation, partition, dividing up, carving up**

❷ *There were deep divisions within the government.*
• **disunity, disagreement, discord, conflict, split, feud**
❸ *She has a job in the sales division.*
• **branch, department, section, arm, unit**

divulge *VERB*
He refused to divulge any more details.
• **disclose, make known, reveal, tell, impart, pass on, give away**

dizzy *ADJECTIVE*
When she looked down she felt dizzy.
• **light-headed, giddy, dazed, faint, reeling, unsteady, wobbly**
(*informal*) **woozy**

do *VERB*
❶ *She didn't know what to do.*
• **act, behave, conduct yourself**
❷ *I have a lot of work to do this morning.*
• **attend to, cope with, deal with, handle, look after, perform, undertake**
❸ *It took half an hour to do the washing-up.*
• **accomplish, achieve, carry out, complete, execute, finish**
❹ *I need to do all of these sums.*
• **answer, puzzle out, solve, work out**
❺ *Sunbathing can do damage to your skin.*
• **bring about, cause, produce, result in**
❻ *If you don't have milk, water will do.*
• **be acceptable, be enough, be satisfactory, be sufficient, serve**
➤ **do away with**
I wish our school would do away with homework.
• **get rid of, abolish, eliminate, end, put an end to**
(*informal*) **scrap**
➤ **do something up**
❶ *He bent down to do up his shoelaces.*
• **fasten, tie, lace**
❷ *We're doing up the spare room.*
• **redecorate, make over, refurbish, renovate, restore**

docile *ADJECTIVE*
Our dog is quite docile.
• **tame, gentle, meek, obedient, manageable, submissive**
OPPOSITE **fierce**

dock *NOUN*
The ferry was pulling in to the dock.
• **harbour, quay, jetty, wharf, landing stage, dockyard, pier, port, marina**

dock *VERB*
❶ *The ferry docks at 8 a.m.*
• **moor, berth, tie up, anchor**
❷ *I am going to dock ten points from your final score.*
• **deduct, take away, subtract, remove, cut**

doctor *NOUN*
She needs to see a doctor.
• **physician, general practitioner, GP, consultant**
(*informal*) **doc, medic**
SEE ALSO **medicine**

document *NOUN*
He found a box containing old documents.
• **paper, record, file, certificate, deed, report**

dodge *VERB*
❶ *I just managed to dodge the snowball.*
• **avoid, evade, sidestep**
❷ *She tried to dodge the question.*
• **avoid, evade, sidestep, duck**
❸ *He dodged in and out of the line of cars.*
• **dart, dive, slip, duck, wriggle**

dog *NOUN*
Our dog has a very shaggy coat.
• **hound**
(informal) **mutt, pooch**
– *An uncomplimentary word for a dog is* **cur**.

WORD WEB

Some breeds of dog:

➤ Afghan hound ➤ Alsatian

a b c d e f g h i j k l m n o p q r s t u v w x y z

➤ basset hound
➤ beagle
➤ bloodhound
➤ boxer
➤ bulldog
➤ bull terrier
➤ cairn terrier
➤ chihuahua
➤ cocker spaniel
➤ collie
➤ corgi
➤ dachshund
➤ Dalmatian
➤ Dobermann
➤ fox terrier
➤ golden retriever
➤ Great Dane
➤ greyhound
➤ husky
➤ Irish setter
➤ Labrador
➤ mastiff
➤ Pekinese or Pekingese
➤ Pomeranian
➤ pointer
➤ poodle
➤ pug
➤ retriever
➤ Rottweiler
➤ St Bernard
➤ Schnauzer
➤ setter
➤ sheepdog
➤ spaniel
➤ terrier
➤ Weimaraner
➤ West Highland terrier
➤ whippet
➤ wolfhound
➤ Yorkshire terrier (*informal* Yorkie)

- A female dog is a **bitch**.
- A young dog is a **pup, puppy** or **whelp**.
- A dog of pure breed with known ancestors has a **pedigree**.
- A dog of mixed breeds is a **mongrel**.
- A word meaning 'to do with dogs' is **canine**.

For tips on describing animals see **animal**.

dole *VERB*
➤ dole out
She started doling out cartons of fruit juice.
• **give out, distribute, dispense, hand out, dish out, deal out**

domestic *ADJECTIVE*
❶ *At weekends I do various domestic chores.*
• **household, family**
❷ *Cats and dogs are domestic animals.*
• **domesticated, tame, pet**
OPPOSITE wild

dominant *ADJECTIVE*
❶ *Arabic is the dominant language of the Middle East.*
• **leading, main, primary, chief, major, foremost, principal, powerful, important, influential**
OPPOSITE minor
❷ *The castle is a dominant feature of the landscape.*
• **conspicuous, prominent, obvious, large, imposing, eye-catching**
OPPOSITE insignificant

dominate *VERB*
❶ *Their team dominated the first half.*
• **control, direct, monopolize, govern, take control of, take over**
❷ *The mountain dominates the whole landscape.*
• **tower over, loom over, overlook, command, dwarf**

donate *VERB*
She donates a lot of money to charity.
• **give, contribute, grant, present**

donation *NOUN*
We rely on donations from the public.
• **contribution, gift, grant, offering**

done *ADJECTIVE*
❶ *My thank-you letters are all done now.*
• **finished, complete, over**
❷ *The cake will be brown on top when it's done.*
• **cooked, ready**

donor *NOUN*
The money was a gift of an anonymous donor.
• **benefactor, contributor, sponsor, patron, backer**

doomed *ADJECTIVE*
The mission was doomed from the start.
• **ill-fated, ill-starred, fated, cursed, jinxed, damned**

door *NOUN*
She walked out through the door.
• **entrance, exit, doorway, portal**
– A door in a floor or ceiling is a **hatch** or **trapdoor**.
– The plank or stone underneath a door is the **threshold**.

– The beam or stone above a door is the **lintel**.

dose *NOUN*
a dose of medicine
• **measure, dosage, portion**

dot *NOUN*
There were dots of paint on the carpet.
• **spot, speck, fleck, point, mark, speckle**
➤ **on the dot**
(*informal*) *The bus leaves at nine on the dot.*
• **exactly, precisely, on time**

dot *VERB*
The hillside was dotted with sheep.
• **spot, fleck, mark, spatter, scatter, sprinkle, pepper**

dote *VERB*
➤ **dote on someone**
She dotes on her grandchildren.
• **adore, be devoted to, love dearly, worship, idolize, cherish, treasure**

double *ADJECTIVE*
You enter the room through a double set of doors.
• **dual, twofold, paired, twin, matching, duplicate**

double *NOUN*
Anna is the double of her sister.
• **twin, duplicate, lookalike**
IDIOMS **spitting image, dead ringer**
– A living organism created as an exact copy of another one is a **clone**.

doubt *NOUN*
❶ *Have you any doubt about his story?*
• **distrust, suspicion, mistrust, hesitation, reservation, scepticism, wariness, misgivings**
OPPOSITE confidence
❷ *There is no doubt that you will pass your exam.*
• **question, uncertainty, ambiguity, controversy, confusion**
OPPOSITE certainty

doubt *VERB*
There is no reason to doubt his story.
• **distrust, feel uncertain about, feel unsure about, question, disbelieve, mistrust, suspect, be sceptical about, be suspicious of, be wary of, have misgivings about**
OPPOSITE trust

doubtful *ADJECTIVE*
❶ *I was doubtful about the idea at first.*
• **unsure, uncertain, unconvinced, hesitant, distrustful, sceptical, suspicious, wary**
IDIOM **in two minds**
OPPOSITE certain
❷ *Our plans for the weekend are looking doubtful.*
• **unlikely, improbable, in doubt**
❸ *It was a doubtful decision by the referee.*
• **questionable, debatable, arguable, open to question**
(*informal*) **iffy**

downfall *NOUN*
His enemies began to plot his downfall.
• **ruin, fall, collapse, overthrow, failure, undoing**

downward *ADJECTIVE*
We took the downward path into the valley.
• **downhill, descending**
OPPOSITE upward

doze *VERB*
He began to doze by the fire.
• **rest, sleep, nap, nod off**
(*informal*) **drop off, have a snooze**
IDIOM (*informal*) **have forty winks**

drab *ADJECTIVE*
The room was painted in drab colours.
• **dull, dingy, dreary, cheerless, colourless, dismal, gloomy, sombre**
OPPOSITES bright, cheerful

draft *NOUN*
I wrote a first draft of my story.
• **outline, plan, sketch, rough version**

draft *VERB*
I began to draft my first chapter.
• **outline, plan, prepare, sketch, work out**

A B C D E F G H I J K L M N O P Q R S T U V W X Y Z

drag *VERB*

He came in, dragging a suitcase behind him.
• pull, tow, haul, draw, tug, trail, heave, lug
OPPOSITE push

dragon *NOUN*

For creatures found in fantasy fiction see **fantasy**.

drain *NOUN*

Surplus water runs away along a drain.
• ditch, channel, drainpipe, gutter, pipe, sewer

drain *VERB*

❶ *If they drain the marsh, lots of water birds will die.*
• dry out, empty out, remove water from
❷ *You need to drain oil from the engine.*
• draw off, empty, extract, siphon off, bleed
❸ *The water slowly drained away.*
• flow, stream, trickle, seep, leak, ooze
❹ *The tough climb drained my energy.*
• use up, consume, exhaust, deplete, expend, sap
❺ *I waited till everyone had drained their glass.*
• drink up, empty, swallow, quaff (*informal*) knock back, swig

drama *NOUN*

❶ *a television drama*
• play, dramatization
❷ *She is studying drama at college.*
• acting, the theatre, the stage, stagecraft
❸ *We were witnessing the drama of a real robbery.*
• action, excitement, suspense, spectacle

WORD WEB

Some types of drama:

- ballet
- comedy
- comic sketch
- dance theatre
- improvisation
- melodrama
- mime
- musical
- music theatre
- mystery play
- one-act play
- opera
- pantomime (*informal* panto)
- review
- situation comedy (*informal* sitcom)
- soap opera (*informal* soap)
- tragedy

Parts of a play:

- act
- scene
- prologue
- intermission
- finale
- script or playscript
- dialogue
- monologue
- soliloquy

Parts of a theatre:

- apron
- auditorium
- balcony or circle
- box office
- curtain
- dressing room
- foyer
- front of house
- green room
- orchestra pit
- proscenium
- stage
- stalls
- wings

People involved in drama:

- actor (*formal* thespian)
- actress
- audience
- cast
- director
- dramatis personae
- dramatist or playwright
- producer
- prompter
- set designer
- stagehand
- stage manager
- voice coach

Other terms relating to drama:

- acting
- amphitheatre
- aside
- audition
- backdrop
- backstage
- blocking
- casting
- characters
- chorus
- cue
- downstage
- dress rehearsal
- ensemble
- entrance
- exit
- lines
- off-stage
- on-stage
- premiere
- props
- protagonist
- read-through
- rehearsal
- scenery
- set design

> ➤ stage directions
> ➤ stage set
> ➤ tableau
> ➤ theatre in the round
> ➤ upstage

dramatic *ADJECTIVE*
❶ *She is a member of the local dramatic society.*
• **theatrical, stage**
❷ *The ending of the film is very dramatic.*
• **exciting, thrilling, action-packed, sensational, spectacular, eventful, gripping, riveting**
❸ *The next day saw a dramatic change in the weather.*
• **noticeable, considerable, substantial, remarkable, marked, extreme**

drank
past tense see **drink**

drastic *ADJECTIVE*
It was time to take drastic action.
• **desperate, extreme, radical, harsh, severe, serious, far-reaching**
OPPOSITE moderate

draught *NOUN*
I could feel a cold draught from the window.
• **breeze, current of air, gust, puff**

draw *VERB*
❶ *My brother is good at drawing animals.*
• **sketch, trace, doodle, outline, illustrate, depict, portray**
❷ *She drew her chair up to the table.*
• **pull, drag, haul, tow, tug, lug, heave**
❸ *The train drew slowly into the station.*
• **move, progress, proceed, roll, inch, cruise, glide**
❹ *The samurai warrior drew his sword.*
• **pull out, take out, withdraw, unsheathe**
❺ *The fair drew large crowds.*
• **attract, bring in, pull in**
❻ *The two teams drew 1-1.*
• **finish equal, tie**
❼ *Where did you draw your information from?*
• **take, extract, derive**

➤ **draw near**
A shadowy figure drew near us.
• **approach, advance, come near**
➤ **draw something up**
The lawyers will draw up a new contract.
• **compose, write out, formulate, prepare, draft, devise, design**

draw *NOUN*
❶ *The game ended in a draw.*
• **tie, dead heat**
❷ *I won a television in the prize draw.*
• **lottery, raffle**

drawback *NOUN*
The only real drawback is the cost.
• **disadvantage, downside, difficulty, handicap, obstacle, inconvenience, hindrance, snag, catch**
IDIOM **fly in the ointment**
OPPOSITES advantage, plus

drawing *NOUN*
There was a drawing of a bowl of fruit on the wall.
• **sketch, illustration, picture, design, study, cartoon, doodle, scribble**

dread *NOUN*
The thought of entering the cave filled me with dread.
• **fear, terror, trepidation, alarm, apprehension, anxiety**

dread *VERB*
She was dreading the exam results.
• **fear, be afraid of, worry about, be anxious about**
OPPOSITE look forward to

dreadful *ADJECTIVE*
❶ *There has been a dreadful accident at sea.*
• **terrible, appalling, horrendous, horrible, distressing, shocking, upsetting, tragic, grim**
❷ *I thought the acting was dreadful.*
• **bad, awful, terrible, abysmal, atrocious, abominable, dire** (*informal*) **rotten, rubbish, lousy**
OPPOSITES good, excellent

dream *NOUN*
❶ *I was woken by a bad dream.*
– A bad dream is a **nightmare**.
– A dreamlike experience you have while awake is a **daydream**, **fantasy** or **reverie**.
– Something you see in a dream or daydream is a **vision**.
– The dreamlike state when you are hypnotized is a **trance**.
– Something you think you see that is not real is a **hallucination** or an **illusion**.
❷ *Her dream is to be on the stage.*
• **ambition, hope, wish, desire, longing, yearning, aspiration, goal**

dream *VERB*
I dreamed I was lost in a maze.
• **imagine, fancy, fantasize, daydream**
➤ **dream of**
I've always dreamt of being an astronomer.
• **wish to, hope to, aspire to, long to, yearn to, hanker after**

dreary *ADJECTIVE*
❶ *The coach driver had a very dreary voice.*
• **dull, boring, tedious, flat, monotonous, unexciting, uninteresting**
OPPOSITE lively
❷ *When will this dreary weather end?*
• **dull, dismal, depressing, gloomy, cheerless, murky, overcast**
OPPOSITES bright, sunny

drench *VERB*
The rain drenched me to the skin.
• **soak, saturate, wet through, steep, douse, drown**

dress *NOUN*
❶ *She wore a beautiful red dress.*
• **frock, gown, robe**
❷ *The invitation said to wear casual dress.*
• **clothes, clothing, attire, outfit, costume, garments, wear**
SEE ALSO **clothes**

dress *VERB*
❶ *I woke and dressed quickly.*
• **get dressed, put clothes on**
OPPOSITE undress
❷ *She was dressed in a smart suit.*
• **clothe, attire, deck out, garb**
❸ *A nurse dressed my wound.*
• **bandage, bind, wrap, put a dressing on**

dressing *NOUN*
The nurse put a dressing on the wound.
• **bandage, plaster**

drew
past tense see **draw**

dribble *VERB*
❶ *The baby was dribbling down its chin.*
• **drool, slobber**
❷ *Water dribbled out of the tap.*
• **drip, trickle, drizzle, leak, ooze, seep**

drift *VERB*
❶ *The boat began to drift downstream.*
• **float, be carried, be borne, glide, waft**
❷ *People started to drift out of the hall.*
• **wander, stray, meander**

drift *NOUN*
❶ *The car was stuck in a snow drift.*
• **bank, heap, mound, pile, ridge**
❷ *I'm afraid I don't get your drift.*
• **meaning, point, gist, sense**

drill *NOUN*
❶ *There was a fire drill at school today.*
• **practice, training**
❷ *You all know the drill by now.*
• **procedure, routine, system**

drill *VERB*
It took a long time to drill through the wall.
• **bore, penetrate, pierce, puncture**

drink *VERB*
I drank the potion in one go.
• **swallow, gulp, quaff, drain, sip, slurp**
(*informal*) **swig, glug, knock back, down**

drink *NOUN*
❶ *They sell a selection of soft drinks.*
• **beverage**
❷ *He took a long drink from his flask.*
• **swallow, draught, gulp, sip**
(*informal*) **swig, slug, glug**

❸ *We listened to a talk on the dangers of drink.*
• **alcohol, liquor, spirits**
(*informal*) **booze**

drip *VERB*
Water was dripping from the ceiling.
• **drop, dribble, splash, trickle, leak**

drip *NOUN*
He found a bucket to catch the drips of water.
• **drop, dribble, spot, splash, trickle**

drive *VERB*
❶ *Can you drive a tractor?*
• **control, operate, handle, manage, steer, work**
❷ *She offered to drive us to the station.*
• **run, give someone a lift, take, transport, convey, ferry**
❸ *The engine is driven by wind power.*
• **power, propel, move, push**
❹ *The dogs drove the sheep into the field.*
• **direct, guide, herd**
❺ *Hunger drove them to steal.*
• **compel, lead, force, oblige, prompt, spur**
❻ *He drove a nail into the wall.*
• **push, thrust, plunge, sink, ram, hammer**
➤ **drive someone out**
Many people were driven out of their homes.
• **eject, throw out, expel, evict**
– To drive people out of their country is to **banish** or **exile** them.

drive *NOUN*
❶ *We went for a drive in the country.*
• **ride, trip, journey, outing, excursion, jaunt**
(*informal*) **spin**
❷ *She definitely has the drive to succeed.*
• **ambition, determination, commitment, motivation, keenness, energy, zeal**

driver *NOUN*
Many drivers go too fast.
• **motorist**
– A person who drives someone's car as a job is a **chauffeur**.

droop *VERB*
The roses have begun to droop.
• **wilt, sag, hang down, bend, flop, slump**

drop *NOUN*
❶ *Large drops of rain began to fall.*
• **drip, droplet, spot, bead, blob, globule**
❷ *Add a drop or two of milk.*
• **dash, dribble, splash, trickle, spot**
❸ *Experts predict a drop in the price of oil.*
• **decrease, reduction, cut, fall, slump**
❹ *There's a drop of two metres on the other side of the wall.*
• **descent, drop, plunge**

drop *VERB*
❶ *Suddenly a hawk dropped out of the sky.*
• **descend, dive, swoop, dip, plunge, plummet**
❷ *I dropped to the ground exhausted.*
• **collapse, fall, sink, subside, slump, tumble**
❸ *Harry dropped the ball and ran.*
• **let fall, let go of, release, lose your grip on**
❹ *Temperatures have dropped sharply.*
• **decrease, decline, reduce, fall, dip, slump**
❺ *Let's drop the idea altogether.*
• **abandon, discard, reject, give up, scrap, dispense with**
(*informal*) **ditch, dump**
❻ *He's been dropped from the team.*
• **omit, eliminate, exclude, leave out**
➤ **drop in**
Do drop in on your way home.
• **visit, call, pay a call**
➤ **drop off**
I felt myself starting to drop off.
• **fall asleep, doze off, drift off**
(*informal*) **nod off**
➤ **drop out**
Three contestants have now dropped out.
• **withdraw, back out, pull out**
(*informal*) **quit**

A B C D E F G H I J K L M N O P Q R S T U V W X Y Z

drove
past tense see **drive**

drown *VERB*
The music from upstairs drowned our conversation.
• **overwhelm, overpower, drown out**

drowsy *ADJECTIVE*
By midnight, I was starting to feel drowsy.
• **sleepy, tired, weary**

drug *NOUN*
a new drug for cancer
• **medicine, remedy, treatment**
– A drug which relieves pain is an **analgesic** or a **painkiller**.
– A drug which calms you down is a **sedative** or **tranquillizer**.
– Drugs which make you more active are **stimulants**.

drum *NOUN*
For musical instruments see **music**.

dry *ADJECTIVE*
❶ *Nothing will grow in this dry soil.*
• **arid, parched, waterless, moistureless, dehydrated, desiccated, barren, shrivelled**
OPPOSITES wet, moist
❷ *He gave rather a dry speech.*
• **dull, boring, uninteresting, dreary, tedious, unimaginative, uninspiring**
OPPOSITES interesting, lively
❸ *She has a dry sense of humour.*
• **ironic, wry, subtle**

dry *VERB*
❶ *If it's sunny, I'll hang the clothes out to dry.*
• **get dry, dry out**
❷ *The earth had been dried by the desert sun.*
• **parch, scorch, dehydrate, desiccate, shrivel, wither**

dual *ADJECTIVE*
This building has a dual purpose.
• **double, twofold, twin, combined**

dubious *ADJECTIVE*
❶ *I'm a bit dubious about the idea.*
• **doubtful, uncertain, unsure, hesitant, sceptical, suspicious**
OPPOSITES certain, sure
❷ *The firm has a dubious reputation.*
• **unreliable, untrustworthy, questionable, suspect**
(*informal*) **shady, dodgy**

duck *NOUN*
a yellow-billed duck
– A male duck is a **drake**.
– A young duck is a **duckling**.

duck *VERB*
❶ *I ducked to avoid the snowball.*
• **bend down, bob down, crouch, stoop**
❷ *They threatened to duck me in the pool.*
• **dip, immerse, plunge, submerge**
❸ *Stop trying to duck the question.*
• **avoid, evade, dodge, shirk, sidestep**

due *ADJECTIVE*
❶ *The train is due in five minutes.*
• **expected, anticipated, scheduled for**
❷ *Your subscription is now due.*
• **owed, owing, payable, outstanding, unpaid**
❸ *We should treat animals with due respect.*
• **proper, suitable, appropriate, fitting, adequate, sufficient, deserved**

dug
past tense see **dig**

dull *ADJECTIVE*
❶ *The walls were a dull shade of green.*
• **drab, dingy, dreary, sombre, muted, subdued**
OPPOSITE bright
❷ *It was a dull morning.*
• **cloudy, overcast, grey, sunless, murky, dreary**
OPPOSITE clear
❸ *The film was so dull that I fell asleep.*
• **uninteresting, boring, tedious, unexciting, unimaginative, monotonous, flat, lacklustre, lifeless, uneventful**
OPPOSITE interesting

❹ *I heard a dull thud from upstairs.*
• **indistinct, muffled, muted**
OPPOSITES distinct, sharp
❺ *He's rather a dull student.*
• **stupid, slow, unintelligent, unimaginative, obtuse**
(*informal*) **dim, dense**
OPPOSITES clever, bright

dumb *ADJECTIVE*
❶ *We were all struck dumb with amazement.*
• **silent, mute, speechless, tongue-tied**
IDIOM **at a loss for words**
❷ (*informal*) *What a dumb question!*
• **stupid, silly, unintelligent, brainless, idiotic**
(*informal*) **daft**

dumbfounded *ADJECTIVE*
I was dumbfounded when I heard the news.
• **amazed, astonished, astounded, stunned, staggered, thunderstruck, speechless, struck dumb**
(*informal*) **flabbergasted**
(*British informal*) **gobsmacked**

dump *NOUN*
❶ *a rubbish dump*
• **tip, dumping ground, scrapheap**
❷ (*informal*) *This place is a bit of a dump.*
• **tip, hovel, pigsty, mess**
(*informal*) **hole**

dump *VERB*
❶ *An old mattress had been dumped at the side of the road.*
• **get rid of, throw away, throw out, discard, dispose of, scrap**
❷ *Just dump your things in the bedroom.*
• **put down, set down, place, drop, deposit, throw down**
(*informal*) **plonk, bung**

duplicate *NOUN*
This is an exact duplicate of the letter.
• **copy, reproduction, replica**
– An exact copy of a document is a **facsimile**.
– A person who looks exactly like you is your **double** or **twin**.
– A living organism which is a duplicate of another one is a **clone**.

durable *ADJECTIVE*
Denim is a very durable material.
• **hard-wearing, lasting, strong, tough, robust**
OPPOSITE flimsy

duration *NOUN*
We'll be away for the duration of the holidays.
• **length, period, extent, span**

dusk *NOUN*
Bats begin to emerge at dusk.
• **twilight, nightfall, sunset, sundown, close of day**
(*poetic*) **gloaming**
OPPOSITE dawn

dust *NOUN*
The furniture was covered in dust.
• **dirt, grime, particles, powder, grit**

dust *VERB*
❶ *I dusted the bookshelves.*
• **wipe, clean, brush, sweep**
❷ *Now dust the top of the cake with icing sugar.*
• **sprinkle, sift, powder**

dusty *ADJECTIVE*
In the attic were piles of dusty old books.
• **dirty, grimy, grubby**
OPPOSITE clean

dutiful *ADJECTIVE*
She had always been a dutiful daughter.
• **faithful, loyal, obedient, devoted, conscientious, reliable, responsible, trustworthy**
OPPOSITES irresponsible, lazy

duty *NOUN*
❶ *It's our duty to help those in need.*
• **responsibility, obligation, mission**
❷ *Here is a list of your daily duties on board the boat.*
• **job, task, assignment, chore**
❸ *The government is increasing the duty on petrol.*
• **tax, charge**

dwell *VERB*
➤ **dwell on**
Try not to dwell on the past.
• **keep thinking about, worry about, brood over**

dwelling *NOUN*
see **house**

dwindle *VERB*
Our supplies are dwindling fast.
• **diminish, decrease, decline, lessen, shrink, subside, wane**
OPPOSITE increase

dye *VERB*
My sister has dyed her hair red.
• **colour, tint, stain**

dynamic *ADJECTIVE*
The team has a dynamic new captain.
• **energetic, lively, spirited, enthusiastic, vigorous, forceful, active**
OPPOSITES apathetic, laid-back

Ee

eager *ADJECTIVE*
Vicky is always eager to help.
• **keen, enthusiastic, anxious, impatient, desperate, willing**
(*informal*) **itching**
OPPOSITE unenthusiastic

early *ADJECTIVE*
❶ *The bus was early today.*
• **ahead of time, ahead of schedule**
OPPOSITE late
❷ *the early attempts at manned flight*
• **first, initial, preliminary, advance**
OPPOSITES recent, latest
❸ *an example of early cave painting*
• **old, primitive, ancient**
OPPOSITES modern, later

earn *VERB*
❶ *How much do you earn each week?*
• **be paid, receive, get, make, bring in**
OPPOSITE lose
❷ *She trained hard and earned her success.*
• **deserve, merit, warrant, justify, be worthy of**

earnest *ADJECTIVE*
He's a terribly earnest young man.
• **serious, sincere, solemn, thoughtful, grave, sober**
OPPOSITES casual, flippant

earth *NOUN*
❶ *Four-fifths of the Earth's surface is covered by water.*
• **world, globe, planet**
❷ *an area of hard, parched earth*
• **ground, land, soil, dirt, clay**
– Rich, fertile earth is **loam**.
– The top layer of fertile earth is **topsoil**.
– Rich earth consisting of decayed plants is **humus**.

earthquake *NOUN*

WORD WEB

- When there is an earthquake, you feel a **shock** or **tremor**.
- A word meaning 'to do with earthquakes' is **seismic**.
- The scientific study of earthquakes is **seismology**.

ease *NOUN*
❶ *She can swim ten lengths of the pool with ease.*
• **effortlessness, no trouble, no difficulty, simplicity**
OPPOSITE difficulty
❷ *Wealthy Romans led lives of ease.*
• **comfort, contentment, leisure, relaxation, rest, tranquillity**
OPPOSITE stress

ease *VERB*
❶ *The doctor gave her some pills to ease the pain.*
• **relieve, lessen, reduce, soothe, alleviate, moderate**
OPPOSITE aggravate
❷ *My headache slowly began to ease.*
• **decrease, lessen, abate, subside, let up, die down, slacken**
OPPOSITES increase, intensify
❸ *We eased the piano into position.*
• **edge, guide, manoeuvre, inch, slide, slip**

easily *ADVERB*
The rules of the game are easily understood.
• **without difficulty, with ease, effortlessly, comfortably, readily**
OPPOSITE with difficulty

east *NOUN, ADJECTIVE & ADVERB*
Queensland is in the east of Australia.
– The parts of a country or continent in the east are the **eastern** parts.
– To travel towards the east is to travel **eastward** or **eastwards**.
– A wind from the east is an **easterly** wind.

A B C D E F G H I J K L M N O P Q R S T U V W X Y Z

– In the past, the countries of east Asia were called **oriental** countries.

easy *ADJECTIVE*

❶ *Tonight's homework is really easy.*
• **undemanding, effortless, light**
(*informal*) **a cinch, a doddle**
IDIOMS **a piece of cake, plain sailing**
❷ *The instructions were easy to understand.*
• **simple, straightforward, uncomplicated, clear, plain, elementary**
❸ *Our cat has an easy life.*
• **carefree, comfortable, peaceful, relaxed, leisurely, restful, tranquil, untroubled**
OPPOSITES difficult, hard

eat *VERB*

❶ *Seals eat their own weight in fish every day.*
• **consume, devour, swallow, feed on, dine on**
(*informal*) **put away**
❷ *Let's eat out tonight.*
• **have a meal, have dinner, dine, feed**
The synonyms feed and feed on are used mainly about animals: *Bats typically feed around dusk and dawn..*
➤ **eat away at or eat into**
Salt water had eaten away at the timbers.
• **corrode, erode, wear away, decay, rot**

OVERUSED WORD

❶ **To eat quickly, greedily:**

➤ bolt down ➤ gobble
➤ demolish ➤ gulp
(*informal*) guzzle, scoff, wolf down
Todd and his friends **demolished** *a whole pizza each.*

❷ **To eat noisily:**

➤ chomp ➤ gnaw
➤ crunch ➤ munch
➤ gnash ➤ slurp
The contestants were dared to **munch** *live insects.*

❸ **To eat large amounts:**

➤ feast ➤ gorge
IDIOM eat like a horse
The guests **gorged** *themselves on roasted meats.*

❹ **To eat too much:**

➤ overeat
(*informal*) stuff yourself, make a pig of yourself
Uncle Amos had **overeaten** *and had to lie down.*

❺ **To eat small amounts:**

➤ nibble ➤ pick away at
➤ peck ➤ snack on
➤ pick at ➤ taste
Nicole **nibbled** *nervously on a cracker.*

❻ **To eat something completely:**

➤ eat up ➤ gobble up
(*informal*) polish off
I **ate up** *every last crumb on my plate.*

❼ **To eat with pleasure:**

➤ relish ➤ savour
(*informal*) tuck into, get stuck into
The cheese is best eaten slowly to **savour** *the taste.*
SEE ALSO bite, chew

ebb *VERB*

❶ *The fishermen waited for the tide to ebb.*
• **recede, go out, retreat, flow back**
❷ *She felt her strength began to ebb.*
• **decline, weaken, lessen, diminish, dwindle, fade, wane**

eccentric *ADJECTIVE*

He had an eccentric style of dress.
• **odd, peculiar, strange, weird, bizarre, abnormal, unusual, curious, unconventional, unorthodox, outlandish, quirky, zany**

(*informal*) way-out, dotty
OPPOSITES conventional, orthodox

echo *VERB*
❶ *The sound echoed across the valley.*
• resound, reverberate, ring
❷ *Her words echoed my own feelings.*
• repeat, reproduce, restate, imitate, mimic, parrot

ecological *ADJECTIVE*
an ecological campaigner
• environmental, green, conservation, eco-
SEE ALSO **environment**

economic *ADJECTIVE*
❶ *a global economic crisis*
• financial, fiscal, monetary, budgetary
❷ *The theatre is no longer economic to run.*
• profitable, lucrative, fruitful, productive
OPPOSITE unprofitable

economical *ADJECTIVE*
❶ *You need to be economical with your money.*
• careful, prudent, thrifty, frugal
– If you are economical with money in a selfish way, you are **mean**, **miserly** or **parsimonious**.
OPPOSITES wasteful, profligate
❷ *This car is economical to run.*
• cheap, inexpensive, low-cost, reasonable
OPPOSITES expensive, costly

ecstatic *ADJECTIVE*
I was ecstatic when I was told that I had won.
• elated, delighted, overjoyed, gleeful, joyful, blissful, rapturous, euphoric, exultant
IDIOMS (*informal*) over the moon, tickled pink

edge *NOUN*
❶ *a house on the edge of a lake*
• border, margin, side, fringe, brink, verge, perimeter, boundary
❷ *The edge of this cup is chipped.*
• brim, rim, lip
❸ *Her voice had an edge to it.*
• sharpness, keenness, intensity, bite

edge *VERB*
❶ *He edged slowly away from the door.*
• creep, inch, work your way, sidle, steal, slink
❷ *Her bonnet was edged with black lace.*
• trim, hem

edgy *ADJECTIVE*
Sitting there all alone, I began to feel edgy.
• nervous, restless, anxious, agitated, excitable, tense, jumpy, fidgety
(*informal*) jittery, uptight
OPPOSITE calm

edible *ADJECTIVE*
Are these berries edible?
• safe to eat, fit to eat, non-poisonous
OPPOSITE poisonous
The words edible and eatable do not mean the same thing. An edible mushroom is safe to eat, whereas an eatable mushroom is in a good enough condition to be eaten.

edit *VERB*
The letters were edited before they were published.
• revise, correct, adapt, modify, rework, rewrite, rephrase

edition *NOUN*
a special Christmas edition of the magazine
• issue, number, version

educate *VERB*
The job of a school is to educate young people.
• teach, train, inform, instruct, tutor, school

educated *ADJECTIVE*
She is an educated woman.
• knowledgeable, learned, literate, well informed, well read, cultivated, cultured, intellectual, scholarly

education *NOUN*
a school for the education of local children
• schooling, teaching, training,

instruction, tuition, tutoring, coaching
– A programme of education is a **curriculum** or **syllabus**.

eerie *ADJECTIVE*
There was an eerie silence in the hall.
• **weird, uncanny, sinister, ghostly, unearthly, other-worldly**
(*informal*) **scary, spooky, creepy**

effect *NOUN*
❶ *the harmful effects of the sun's rays*
• **result, consequence, outcome, sequel, upshot**
❷ *The music had a strange effect on me.*
• **impact, influence**
❸ *The lighting gives an effect of warmth.*
• **feeling, impression, sense, illusion**

effective *ADJECTIVE*
❶ *an effective treatment for spots*
• **successful, powerful, potent**
OPPOSITES ineffective, weak
❷ *He presented an effective argument against hunting.*
• **convincing, persuasive, compelling, impressive, strong, powerful, telling**
OPPOSITE unconvincing

efficient *ADJECTIVE*
❶ *Hyenas are supremely efficient hunters.*
• **competent, capable, able, proficient, skilled, effective, productive**
❷ *an efficient method of transport*
• **economic, cost-effective, streamlined, organized, orderly**
OPPOSITE inefficient

effort *NOUN*
❶ *A lot of effort went into making the film.*
• **work, trouble, exertion, application, industry, labour, toil**
❷ *I made an effort to be friends with her.*
• **attempt, try, endeavour, go**
(*informal*) **shot, stab, bash**

eject *VERB*
❶ *Lava is ejected from volcanoes.*
• **discharge, emit, send out, vent, belch, spew out**
❷ *The protesters were ejected from the meeting.*
• **remove, expel, evict, banish, throw out, turn out**
(*informal*) **kick out**

elaborate *ADJECTIVE*
It is a clever story with an elaborate plot.
• **complicated, complex, detailed, intricate, involved, convoluted**
OPPOSITE simple

elated *ADJECTIVE*
We were elated when we won the match.
• **delighted, pleased, thrilled, joyful, ecstatic, gleeful, exultant, delirious**
IDIOMS (*informal*) **over the moon, tickled pink**

elbow *VERB*
He elbowed his way to the front of the queue.
• **push, shove, nudge, jostle**

elder *ADJECTIVE*
My elder brother is at college now.
• **older, big**
OPPOSITE younger

elderly *ADJECTIVE*
I helped an elderly lady onto the bus.
• **aged, ageing, old, senior**
OPPOSITE young

elect *VERB*
We elected a new team captain.
• **vote for, vote in, appoint, choose, pick, select**

election *NOUN*
We had an election to choose a new captain.
• **vote, ballot, poll**

electricity *NOUN*
The electricity went off in the middle of the thunderstorm.
• **power, power supply, current**
– Someone whose job is to fit and repair electrical equipment is an **electrician**.

WORD WEB

- A flow of electricity is called a **current**.
- An electrical **circuit** is a complete path that an electric current can flow around.
- The units used to measure electric current are called **amps** or **amperes**.
- **Volts** are a measure of the energy of a flow of electricity.
- **Watts** are a measure of electrical power.

elegant *ADJECTIVE*
She always wears elegant clothes.
• **graceful, stylish, fashionable, chic, smart, tasteful, sophisticated**
OPPOSITE inelegant

element *NOUN*
We discussed various elements of the play.
• **part, feature, aspect, factor, facet, component, ingredient, strand**
➤ **be in your element**
Owen is in his element on stage.
• **be at home, be comfortable, be happy, enjoy yourself**

elementary *ADJECTIVE*
a course in elementary maths
• **basic, simple, easy, fundamental, rudimentary, straightforward**
OPPOSITES advanced, complex

eligible *ADJECTIVE*
Children under twelve are not eligible to enter.
• **qualified, allowed, authorized, permitted, entitled**
OPPOSITE ineligible

eliminate *VERB*
a spray to eliminate bad odours
• **get rid of, put an end to, do away with, stamp out**
– To be eliminated from a competition is to be **knocked out**.

eloquent *ADJECTIVE*
The winning author gave an eloquent speech.
• **articulate, fluent, well expressed, expressive, powerful**

elude *VERB*
He eluded his pursuers with ease.
• **avoid, evade, escape from, get away from, dodge, shake off**

embark *VERB*
Passengers may embark at any port.
• **board, go aboard**
OPPOSITE disembark
➤ **embark on something**
They were about to embark on a dangerous mission.
• **begin, start, commence, undertake, set out on**

embarrass *VERB*
I didn't mean to embarrass you in front of your friends.
• **humiliate, shame, mortify, make you blush**

embarrassed *ADJECTIVE*
I feel embarrassed when I speak in public.
• **humiliated, ashamed, awkward, uncomfortable, bashful, mortified, self-conscious, red-faced**

embarrassing *ADJECTIVE*
The show was so bad it was embarrassing.
• **humiliating, mortifying, shameful** (*informal*) **cringe-making, toe-curling**

emblem *NOUN*
The dove is an emblem of peace.
• **symbol, sign, representation, image, mark, badge, crest**

embrace *VERB*
❶ *The old man got up and embraced his son.*
• **hug, clasp, cuddle, hold**
❷ *The exhibition embraces both modern and traditional art.*
• **include, incorporate, take in, cover**

A B C D E F G H I J K L M N O P Q R S T U V W X Y Z

❸ *She's always ready to embrace new ideas.*
• **welcome, accept, adopt, take up**
IDIOM **take on board**

emerge *VERB*
❶ *Zak emerged gingerly from his hiding place.*
• **appear, issue, come out, come into view**
❷ *Gradually more details began to emerge.*
• **become known, be revealed, come out, come to light, unfold**

emergency *NOUN*
Try to keep calm in an emergency.
• **crisis, disaster, catastrophe, calamity**

emigrate *VERB*
Thousands were forced to emigrate to America.
• **leave the country, move abroad, relocate, resettle**
OPPOSITE **immigrate**

eminent *ADJECTIVE*
a group of eminent scientists
• **renowned, celebrated, famous, great, well known, distinguished, notable, prominent, respected, acclaimed, esteemed, illustrious**
OPPOSITE **unknown**

emit *VERB*
❶ *The chimney was now emitting clouds of smoke.*
• **discharge, expel, belch, blow out, give off**
❷ *The satellite emits radio signals.*
• **transmit, broadcast, give out, send out**
OPPOSITE **receive**

emotion *NOUN*
His voice was full of emotion.
• **feeling, passion, sentiment, heart, fervour, strength of feeling**

emotional *ADJECTIVE*
❶ *He gave an emotional farewell speech.*
• **moving, touching, stirring, affecting, poignant**
❷ *She's a very emotional woman.*
• **passionate, intense, excitable, sensitive, temperamental**
OPPOSITES **unemotional, cold**

emphasis *NOUN*
❶ *This term we will give more emphasis to creative writing.*
• **importance, prominence, weight, attention, priority**
❷ *Put the emphasis on the first syllable.*
• **stress, accent, weight, beat**

emphasize *VERB*
Let me emphasize the need to stay calm.
• **highlight, stress, focus on, draw attention to, spotlight, underline**

employ *VERB*
❶ *The new centre will employ 100 workers.*
• **hire, recruit, engage, take on, sign up, appoint**
❷ *They employed a variety of methods to collect the information.*
• **use, utilize, make use of, apply**

employee *NOUN*
100 employees will work at the new centre.
• **worker, member of staff**
– All the employees of an organization are its **staff**, **personnel** or **workforce**.

employment *NOUN*
She is still looking for suitable employment.
• **work, a job, an occupation, a profession, a trade**
SEE ALSO **job**

empty *ADJECTIVE*
❶ *This bottle is empty.*
OPPOSITE **full**
❷ *The building has been empty for years.*
• **unoccupied, uninhabited, vacant, deserted**
OPPOSITE **occupied**
❸ *There's an empty space in the corner.*
• **free, clear, blank, bare, unused**
❹ *These warnings were not just empty threats.*
• **meaningless, idle, hollow, ineffectual**

empty *VERB*
❶ *Empty the dirty water from the sink.*
• **drain, pour out, tip out, remove, extract**
OPPOSITE **fill**
❷ *She emptied her handbag onto the table.*
• **unload, unpack**
❸ *The building emptied when the alarm went off.*
• **clear, evacuate, vacate**

enable *VERB*
❶ *The money will enable us to build a sports centre.*
• **allow, make it possible for**
❷ *A passport enables you to travel abroad.*
• **permit, allow, entitle, authorize, qualify**
OPPOSITE **prevent (from)**

enchanting *ADJECTIVE*
Sirens were said to lure sailors with their enchanting voices.
• **captivating, charming, delightful, attractive, appealing, engaging, bewitching, spellbinding**

enchantment *NOUN*
❶ *The island had an air of enchantment.*
• **magic, wonder, delight, pleasure**
❷ *a book of ancient enchantments*
• **spell, incantation**

enclose *VERB*
❶ *The garden was enclosed by a high wall.*
• **surround, encircle, bound, close in, fence in, shut in**
❷ *The documents were enclosed in a brown envelope.*
• **contain, insert, wrap, bind, sheathe**

enclosure *NOUN*
the new chimpanzee enclosure at the zoo
• **compound, pen, cage**
– An enclosure for chickens is a **coop** or **run**.
– An enclosure for horses is a **paddock**.
– An enclosure for sheep is a **fold**.

encounter *VERB*
❶ *He had never encountered a creature like this before.*
• **meet, come across, run into, come face to face with**
(*informal*) **bump into**
❷ *The space crew encountered some problems.*
• **experience, come upon, confront, be faced with**

encourage *VERB*
❶ *We went along to encourage our team.*
• **support, motivate, inspire, cheer, spur on, egg on**
❷ *She encouraged me to try the audition.*
• **persuade, urge, press, coax**
❸ *The scheme is designed to encourage new research.*
• **stimulate, promote, boost, further, strengthen, foster, nurture, cultivate**
OPPOSITE **discourage**

encouragement *NOUN*
My coach gave me a lot of encouragement.
• **support, inspiration, motivation, morale boosting, incitement, stimulation, urging, incentive, stimulus, reassurance**

encouraging *ADJECTIVE*
The results of the tests were encouraging.
• **hopeful, positive, promising, reassuring, optimistic, cheering, favourable**

end *NOUN*
❶ *There is a surprise twist at the end of the film.*
• **ending, finish, close, conclusion, culmination, termination, finale**
– A section added at the end of a letter is a **postscript**.
– A section added at the end of a story is an **epilogue**.
OPPOSITES **start, beginning**

a b c d e f g h i j k l m n o p q r s t u v w x y z

A B C D E F G H I J K L M N O P Q R S T U V W X Y Z

❷ *At last we had reached the end of our journey.*
• termination, destination
❸ *The fence marks the end of the garden.*
• boundary, limit, extremity, bottom
OPPOSITE top
❹ *We found ourselves at the end of the queue.*
• back, rear, tail
OPPOSITE head
❺ *What end did you have in mind?*
• aim, purpose, intention, objective, plan, outcome, result

end *VERB*
❶ *The concert ended with a firework display.*
• close, conclude, come to an end, finish, stop, cease, terminate, culminate
(*informal*) round off, wind up
❷ *Britain ended its slave trade in 1807.*
• abolish, do away with, get rid of, put an end to, discontinue, terminate, eliminate, cancel

endanger *VERB*
Bad driving endangers other people.
• put at risk, put in danger, jeopardize, threaten, imperil
OPPOSITES protect, safeguard

endeavour *VERB*
We will endeavour to respond within 24 hours.
• try, attempt, aim, seek, strive, make an effort

endeavour *NOUN*
Despite our best endeavours, things can go wrong.
• attempt, effort, try, bid

ending *NOUN*
The ending of the film was the best part.
• end, finish, close, conclusion, culmination, finale

endless *ADJECTIVE*
❶ *Teachers need endless patience.*
• unending, limitless, infinite, inexhaustible, unlimited
❷ *There's an endless procession of cars along the main road.*
• continual, continuous, constant, incessant, interminable, perpetual, unbroken, uninterrupted, everlasting, ceaseless

endurance *NOUN*
The climb was a test of our endurance.
• perseverance, persistence, determination, resolution, stamina, fortitude, staying power

endure *VERB*
❶ *Many mill workers endured harsh conditions.*
• bear, stand, suffer, cope with, experience, go through, put up with, tolerate, face, undergo
❷ *These traditions have endured for centuries.*
• survive, continue, last, persist, abide, carry on, live on, keep going

enemy *NOUN*
They used to be friends but now they are bitter enemies.
• opponent, antagonist, adversary, rival
(*literary*) foe
OPPOSITES friend, ally

energetic *ADJECTIVE*
❶ *My mum has always been an energetic person.*
• dynamic, active, animated, spirited, tireless, indefatigable
IDIOM full of beans
OPPOSITES inactive, lethargic
❷ *It is a very energetic dance.*
• lively, vigorous, brisk, fast, quick moving, strenuous
OPPOSITES slow-paced, sluggish

energy *NOUN*
❶ *The dancers had tremendous energy.*
• liveliness, vitality, spirit, vigour, life, drive, zest, verve, gusto, enthusiasm, dynamism
(*informal*) get-up-and-go, zip, oomph
OPPOSITE lethargy

❷ *Wind power is a renewable source of energy.*
• power, fuel

enforce *VERB*
The umpire's job is to enforce the rules.
• impose, apply, administer, carry out, implement, put into effect, insist on

engage *VERB*
❶ *The plot failed to engage my attention.*
• capture, catch, grab, gain, hold, arrest, grip, absorb, occupy
❷ *It was a mistake to engage in conversation with him.*
• take part, participate, partake, join
❸ *We engaged the enemy at dawn.*
• attack, encounter, clash with, do battle with, take on, fight
❹ *The store always engages extra staff for Christmas.*
• employ, hire, recruit, take on, appoint

engaged *ADJECTIVE*
❶ *I'll be engaged all afternoon.*
• busy, occupied, employed, immersed (in), preoccupied (with)
(*informal*) tied up
❷ *I tried phoning but the line was engaged.*
• busy, being used, unavailable
OPPOSITES free, available

engagement *NOUN*
a business engagement
• meeting, appointment, commitment, date

engine *NOUN*
a wind-powered engine
• motor, mechanism, turbine
– A railway engine is a **locomotive**.

engrave *VERB*
The following words were engraved on the tombstone.
• carve, cut, etch, inscribe

engrossed *ADJECTIVE*
He was still engrossed in his book.
• absorbed, busy, occupied, preoccupied, engaged, immersed

engulf *VERB*
The tsunami engulfed several villages.
• flood, swamp, drown, immerse, inundate, overwhelm, submerge, swallow up

enhance *VERB*
The award will enhance the author's reputation.
• improve, strengthen, boost, further, increase, heighten

enjoy *VERB*
I enjoyed the film very much.
• like, love, be fond of, be keen on, relish, revel in, delight in, take pleasure in
(*informal*) get a kick out of
OPPOSITES dislike, hate
➤ **enjoy yourself**
We all enjoyed ourselves at the party.
• have fun, have a good time, celebrate
(*informal*) have a ball

enjoyable *ADJECTIVE*
I hope you find the show enjoyable.
• pleasant, agreeable, entertaining, amusing, pleasing, delightful, pleasurable, satisfying
OPPOSITE unpleasant

enlarge *VERB*
The zoo is enlarging its lion enclosure.
• expand, extend, develop, make bigger, broaden, widen, elongate, stretch
– To make something seem larger is to **magnify** it.
OPPOSITE reduce

enormous *ADJECTIVE*
Enormous waves battered the ship.
• huge, gigantic, immense, colossal, massive, monstrous, monumental, mountainous, towering, tremendous, vast, mighty, mammoth
(*informal*) whopping, humongous
(*literary*) gargantuan
OPPOSITES small, tiny

enough *DETERMINER*
We have enough food for thirty guests.
• sufficient, adequate, ample

A B C D E F G H I J K L M N O P Q R S T U V W X Y Z

enquire *VERB*
➤ **enquire about**
I enquired about train times to York.
• **ask for, make enquiries about, request**

enquiry *NOUN*
Please send your enquiries by email.
• **question, query, request**

enrage *VERB*
I was enraged by their stupidity.
• **anger, infuriate, madden, incense, exasperate, provoke**
IDIOMS **make you see red, make your blood boil**
OPPOSITES **placate, pacify**

enrol *VERB*
She enrolled at the local art school.
• **join, sign up, register, put your name down, apply**

ensure *VERB*
Please ensure that you lock the door.
• **make certain, make sure, guarantee, see to it**

enter *VERB*
❶ *Silence fell as she entered the room.*
• **come in, walk in, go into**
IDIOM **set foot in**
OPPOSITE **leave**
❷ *The bullet entered his left shoulder.*
• **go into, penetrate, pierce, puncture**
❸ *Please enter your details on the form.*
• **insert, record, register, log, put down, set down, sign, write**
OPPOSITE **cancel**
❹ *Four teams are entering the competition.*
• **take part in, enrol in, sign up for, go in for, join in, participate in, compete in**
OPPOSITE **withdraw from**

enterprise *NOUN*
❶ *Deep-sea diving is still a hazardous enterprise.*
• **undertaking, activity, venture, task, business, exercise, project, scheme, mission**
❷ *All the contestants showed enterprise and enthusiasm.*
• **resourcefulness, initiative, drive, ambition, imagination**

enterprising *ADJECTIVE*
The website was created by an enterprising group of students.
• **resourceful, imaginative, creative, ambitious, entrepreneurial, intrepid, bold, adventurous, industrious**
(*informal*) **go-ahead**

entertain *VERB*
❶ *We entertained ourselves by telling ghost stories.*
• **amuse, divert, keep amused, interest, occupy**
OPPOSITE **bore**
❷ *You can entertain guests in the private dining room.*
• **receive, welcome, cater for, give hospitality to**
❸ *She would never entertain such a foolish idea.*
• **consider, contemplate, countenance, accept, hear of, think of**

entertainer *NOUN*
For musicians and other performing artists see **music, performance**.

entertainment *NOUN*
Gladiators fought for the entertainment of huge crowds.
• **amusement, recreation, diversion, enjoyment, fun**

enthusiasm *NOUN*
We ran onto the pitch full of enthusiasm.
• **keenness, commitment, drive, passion, fervour, zeal, zest, energy, vigour, gusto**
OPPOSITE **apathy**

enthusiast *NOUN*
My brother is a motor racing enthusiast.
• **fan, fanatic, devotee, lover, supporter, admirer, addict**
(*informal*) **freak, nut**

enthusiastic *ADJECTIVE*
❶ *She has been an enthusiastic supporter of the club for years.*
• **keen, passionate, avid, devoted, energetic, fervent, zealous**
OPPOSITE apathetic
❷ *The crowd burst into enthusiastic applause.*
• **eager, excited, lively, vigorous, exuberant, hearty**

entire *ADJECTIVE*
My brother spent the entire morning in bed.
• **whole, complete, total, full**

entirely *ADVERB*
I'm not entirely sure that I agree with you.
• **completely, absolutely, totally, wholly, utterly, fully, perfectly, quite**

entitle *VERB*
❶ *This coupon entitles you to a free ticket.*
• **permit, allow, enable, authorize, qualify**
❷ *The story is entitled 'The Return of Dracula'.*
• **name, title, call, designate**

entrance *NOUN*
❶ *Please pay at the main entrance.*
• **entry, way in, access, approach, door, gate, portal**
– The entrance to a cave is the **mouth**.
– An entrance hall is a **foyer** or **lobby**.
– When you go through the entrance to a building, you cross the **threshold**.
OPPOSITE exit
❷ *Entrance to the museum is free.*
• **admission, access, entry, admittance**
❸ *My aunt made a dramatic entrance.*
• **entry, arrival, appearance**

entrant *NOUN*
A prize will be awarded to the winning entrant.
• **contestant, competitor, contender, candidate, participant**

entry *NOUN*
❶ *A van was blocking the entry to the school.*
• **entrance, way in, access, approach, door, gate**
❷ *We were refused entry.*
• **admission, access, entrance, admittance**
❸ *Every evening I write an entry in my diary.*
• **item, note, memo, record, log**

envelop *VERB*
A thick mist enveloped the whole city.
• **cover, surround, hide, mask, conceal, cloak, shroud, veil**

envious *ADJECTIVE*
He was envious of his brother's success.
• **jealous, resentful, grudging**
IDIOM **green with envy (at)**

environment *NOUN*
The team study gorillas in their natural environment.
• **habitat, surroundings, setting, conditions, situation**
➤ **the environment**
the impact of humans on the environment
• **the natural world, nature, the earth, the world**

envy *NOUN*
He was consumed with envy and rage.
• **jealousy, resentment, bitterness**

envy *VERB*
She had never envied her sister's fame.
• **be jealous of, begrudge, grudge, resent**

episode *NOUN*
❶ *It was so embarrassing and I want to forget the whole episode.*
• **event, incident, occurrence, occasion, experience**
❷ *the first episode of the new series*
• **instalment, part, programme, show, section**

equal *ADJECTIVE*
❶ *Give everyone an equal amount.*
• **equivalent, identical, matching,**

A B C D E F G H I J K L M N O P Q R S T U V W X Y Z

corresponding, uniform, the same
❷ *The scores were equal at half-time.*
• even, level, tied, drawn
IDIOMS all square, level pegging, neck and neck
– To make the scores equal is to **equalize**.

equal *VERB*
❶ *Six plus five equals eleven.*
• be equal to, come to, add up to, total, amount to, make
❷ *Her time equals the Olympic record.*
• match, be level with, be the same as

equip *VERB*
Each classroom is equipped with a computer.
• provide, supply, furnish
– To equip soldiers with weapons is to **arm** them.

equipment *NOUN*
The shed is full of gardening equipment.
• apparatus, tools, implements, materials, machinery, gadgetry, hardware, paraphernalia, tackle, kit (*informal*) gear

equivalent *ADJECTIVE*
A metre is equivalent to a hundred centimetres.
• matching, the same as, identical, corresponding, parallel, similar

era *NOUN*
Shakespeare lived in the Elizabethan era.
• age, period, time, epoch

erase *VERB*
Someone had erased the message.
• delete, remove, rub out, wipe out, obliterate

erect *ADJECTIVE*
The dog sat up with its ears erect.
• upright, vertical, perpendicular, bristling, standing on end

erect *VERB*
The town hall was erected in 1890.
• build, construct, raise, put up, set up
– To erect a tent is to **pitch** it.
OPPOSITE demolish

erode *VERB*
Rainwater has eroded the soil.
• wear away, eat away, grind down

errand *NOUN*
I went on an errand to the corner shop.
• task, job, assignment, mission, trip, journey

erratic *ADJECTIVE*
The team's performance has been erratic this season.
• inconsistent, irregular, uneven, variable, changeable, fluctuating, unpredictable, unreliable, unstable
OPPOSITE consistent

error *NOUN*
❶ *a grammatical error*
• mistake, fault, lapse, blunder, slip, slip-up
❷ *I think there is an error in your argument.*
• flaw, inaccuracy, misunderstanding, inconsistency

erupt *VERB*
Ash continued to erupt from the volcano.
• be discharged, be emitted, pour out, issue, spout, gush, spurt, belch

escape *VERB*
❶ *They must have had help to escape from prison.*
• get away, run away, break free, break out, slip away, make a getaway
❷ *The driver narrowly escaped injury.*
• avoid, sidestep
IDIOM steer clear of
❸ *Oil was escaping from a crack in the hull.*
• leak, seep, ooze, drain, spill out, run out

escape *NOUN*
❶ *The prisoner's escape was filmed by security cameras.*
• getaway, breakout, flight
❷ *The explosion was caused by an escape of gas.*
• leak, leakage, spill, seepage, discharge

escort *NOUN*
The mayor always travels with a police escort.
• **bodyguard, guard, convoy, entourage, minder**

escort *VERB*
An usher will escort you to your seat.
• **accompany, conduct, take, lead, guide, usher**

especially *ADVERB*
I love shopping, especially for clothes.
• **above all, chiefly, particularly, primarily, most of all**

espionage *NOUN*
see **spy**

essential *ADJECTIVE*
Fruit and vegetables are an essential part of our diet.
• **important, necessary, crucial, basic, vital, fundamental, key, intrinsic, all-important, indispensable**
OPPOSITES **unimportant, trivial**

establish *VERB*
❶ *She plans to establish a new children's hospital.*
• **set up, start, create, found, initiate, institute, inaugurate, launch**
❷ *The police have not managed to establish his guilt.*
• **prove, demonstrate, determine, confirm, verify**

estate *NOUN*
❶ *a new housing estate*
• **area, development, scheme**
❷ *The castle is sited on a large estate.*
• **land, grounds, park**
❸ *The millionaire left his estate to charity.*
• **property, fortune, wealth, possessions**

estimate *NOUN*
an estimate of the age of the universe
• **assessment, calculation, evaluation, guess, judgement, opinion**
– An estimate of the value of something is a **valuation**.
– An estimate of what a job is going to cost is a **quotation** or **tender**.

estimate *VERB*
Scientists estimate that the Earth is 4.5 billion years old.
• **calculate, assess, work out, compute, count up, evaluate, judge, reckon**

eternal *ADJECTIVE*
❶ *The magic fountain was believed to give eternal life.*
• **everlasting, unending, never-ending, permanent, perpetual, infinite, undying**
OPPOSITES **transitory, transient**
❷ (*informal*) *I'm tired of her eternal complaining.*
• **constant, continual, continuous, never-ending, non-stop, perpetual, endless, persistent, incessant, unbroken, uninterrupted**
IDIOM **round the clock**
OPPOSITES **occasional, intermittent**

evacuate *VERB*
❶ *Hundreds of residents were evacuated.*
• **remove, send away, move out**
❷ *We were told to evacuate the building.*
• **leave, vacate, abandon, withdraw from, clear, empty, quit**

evade *VERB*
❶ *They managed to evade capture for six months.*
• **elude, avoid, escape, steer clear of, fend off**
❷ *Stop trying to evade my question!*
• **avoid, dodge, bypass, sidestep, skirt around, shirk**
(*informal*) **duck**
OPPOSITES **confront, tackle**

even *ADJECTIVE*
❶ *You need an even surface for ice-skating.*
• **level, flat, smooth, plane**
OPPOSITE **uneven**
❷ *The runners kept up an even pace.*
• **regular, steady, unvarying, constant, uniform**
OPPOSITE **irregular**

A B C D E F G H I J K L M N O P Q R S T U V W X Y Z

❸ *The scores were even at half time.*
• **equal, level, tied, drawn**
IDIOMS **all square, level pegging, neck and neck**
❹ *2, 4 and 6 are even numbers.*
OPPOSITE odd
❺ *She has a very even temperament.*
• **calm, cool, placid, unexcitable**
OPPOSITE excitable

even *VERB*
➤ **even something up**
We need another player to even up the numbers.
• **equalize, balance, match, level out, square up**

evening *NOUN*
By evening, the temperature had dropped.
• **dusk, nightfall, sunset, twilight** (*North American*) **sundown**

event *NOUN*
❶ *The biography gives the main events of her life.*
• **happening, incident, occurrence**
❷ *We are holding a couple of events to mark the bicentenary.*
• **function, occasion, ceremony, reception**
❸ *a major sporting event*
• **competition, contest, fixture, game, match, tournament**

eventful *ADJECTIVE*
It has been an eventful two weeks.
• **interesting, exciting, busy, action-packed, lively, hectic**
OPPOSITES uneventful, dull

eventual *ADJECTIVE*
Who was the eventual winner?
• **final, ultimate, overall, resulting, ensuing**

eventually *ADVERB*
The bus eventually arrived.
• **finally, in the end, at last, ultimately**

evergreen *ADJECTIVE*
Most pine trees are evergreen.
OPPOSITE deciduous
SEE ALSO **tree**

everlasting *ADJECTIVE*
Peter Pan has an everlasting childhood.
• **never-ending, unending, endless, ceaseless, eternal, infinite, perpetual, undying**
– Everlasting life is **immortality**.
OPPOSITES transitory, transient

everyday *ADJECTIVE*
Just wear your everyday clothes.
• **ordinary, normal, day-to-day, usual, regular, standard, customary, routine, commonplace, run-of-the-mill**

evict *VERB*
Thousands were evicted from their farms.
• **expel, eject, remove, throw out, turn out, put out**

evidence *NOUN*
This letter is evidence of his guilt.
• **proof, confirmation, verification**
– Evidence given in a law court is a **testimony**.
– To give evidence in court is to **testify**.

evident *ADJECTIVE*
It was evident that he didn't like her.
• **clear, obvious, apparent, plain, certain, unmistakable, undeniable, noticeable, conspicuous**

evidently *ADVERB*
The woman was evidently upset.
• **clearly, obviously, plainly, undoubtedly, unmistakably, patently**

evil *ADJECTIVE*
❶ *The charm was used to ward off evil spirits.*
• **malevolent, malign, sinister, fiendish, diabolical**
OPPOSITES good, benign
❷ *Who would do such an evil deed?*
• **wicked, immoral, cruel, sinful, villainous, malicious, foul, hateful, vile**
OPPOSITES good, virtuous

evil *NOUN*
❶ *The message of the film is that good triumphs over evil.*
• **wickedness, malevolence, badness, wrongdoing, sin, immorality, villainy, malice, the dark side**
OPPOSITE good
❷ *the twin evils of famine and drought*
• **disaster, misfortune, suffering, pain, affliction, curse, woe**

evolve *VERB*
Life evolved on Earth over millions of years.
• **develop, grow, progress, emerge, mature**

exact *ADJECTIVE*
❶ *I can't tell you the exact number of people who are coming.*
• **accurate, precise, correct, definite**
OPPOSITES inaccurate, rough
❷ *She gave us exact instructions.*
• **specific, clear, detailed, meticulous, strict**
OPPOSITE vague

exactly *ADVERB*
❶ *The room was exactly as I remembered it.*
• **precisely, strictly, in every respect, absolutely, just**
OPPOSITES roughly, more or less
❷ *The bus leaves at 9 a.m. exactly.*
• **specifically, precisely, strictly**
IDIOM **on the dot**
❸ *I copied down her words exactly.*
• **accurately, correctly, perfectly, faithfully, literally**
IDIOM **word for word**

exaggerate *VERB*
He tends to exaggerate his problems.
• **magnify, inflate, overstate, make too much of**
IDIOM **blow out of all proportion**
OPPOSITES minimize, understate

examination *NOUN*
❶ *We sit our examinations in June.*
• **test, assessment**
(*informal*) **exam**
❷ *I have an appointment for an eye examination.*
• **check-up, test**
– A medical examination of a dead person is a **post-mortem**.
❸ *The judge made a thorough examination of the evidence.*
• **investigation, inspection, scrutiny, study, analysis, survey, review, appraisal**

examine *VERB*
❶ *Detectives examined all the evidence.*
• **inspect, study, investigate, analyse, look closely at, pore over, scrutinize, probe, survey, review, weigh up, sift**
❷ *You will be examined on your chosen subject.*
• **question, interrogate, quiz**
– To examine someone rigorously is to **grill** them.

example *NOUN*
❶ *Give me an example of what you mean.*
• **instance, illustration, sample, specimen, case**
❷ *Her courage is an example to us all.*
• **model, ideal, standard, benchmark**

exasperate *VERB*
All these delays were beginning to exasperate us.
• **annoy, irritate, upset, frustrate, anger, infuriate, madden, vex**

exceed *VERB*
The amount we raised exceeded all our expectations.
• **surpass, better, outdo, go beyond, beat, top**

excel *VERB*
She's a good all-round athlete, but she excels at sprinting.
• **do best, stand out, shine**
IDIOM **be second to none**

excellent *ADJECTIVE*
What an excellent idea!
• **outstanding, exceptional, tremendous, marvellous, wonderful, superb, great, fine, superior, superlative, top-notch, first-class, first-rate**

A B C D E F G H I J K L M N O P Q R S T U V W X Y Z

(*informal*) **brilliant, fantastic, terrific, fabulous, sensational, super**
OPPOSITES bad, awful, second-rate
SEE ALSO **good**

except *PREPOSITION*
Everyone knew the answer except me.
• **apart from, aside from, other than, with the exception of, excluding, not counting, barring, bar, but**

exception *NOUN*
It is an exception to the usual spelling rule.
• **oddity, peculiarity, deviation, special case, anomaly**
➤ **take exception to something**
I took exception to what he said.
• **dislike, object to, complain about, disapprove of, take issue with**

exceptional *ADJECTIVE*
❶ *It is exceptional to have such cold weather in June.*
• **unusual, uncommon, abnormal, unexpected, unprecedented, unheard-of, surprising**
OPPOSITES normal, usual
❷ *He showed exceptional talent for art when he was young.*
• **extraordinary, outstanding, phenomenal, amazing, rare, special, uncommon, remarkable, prodigious**
OPPOSITE average

excerpt *NOUN*
He read an excerpt from his new novel.
• **extract, passage, quotation, section**
– An excerpt from a film is a **clip**.

excess *NOUN*
They have an excess of fat in their diet.
• **surplus, surfeit, glut**
➤ **in excess of**
speeds in excess of 60 mph
• **more than, greater than, over, beyond**

excessive *ADJECTIVE*
❶ *I find their prices excessive.*
• **too great, too high, outrageous, extortionate, exorbitant, extravagant, unreasonable**
IDIOM (*informal*) **over the top**
❷ *Police were accused of using excessive force.*
• **extreme, superfluous, unreasonable, disproportionate**

exchange *VERB*
The shop will exchange faulty goods.
• **change, replace, substitute, swap, switch, trade**
– To exchange goods for other goods without using money is to **barter**.

excite *VERB*
The prospect of seeing a whale excited him.
• **thrill, enthuse, exhilarate, elate, stimulate, enliven, rouse, electrify**
OPPOSITE calm

excited *ADJECTIVE*
I was too excited to sleep.
• **agitated, lively, enthusiastic, exuberant, thrilled, elated, eager, animated**
OPPOSITE calm

excitement *NOUN*
I could hardly bear the excitement.
• **suspense, tension, drama, thrill, eagerness, anticipation**
(*informal*) **buzz**

exciting *ADJECTIVE*
The last ten minutes of the match were the most exciting.
• **dramatic, eventful, thrilling, gripping, compelling, sensational, stirring, rousing, stimulating, electrifying, exhilarating**
OPPOSITES dull, boring

exclaim *VERB*
❶ *'Run for your lives!' he exclaimed.*
• **call, shout, cry out, yell**
SEE ALSO **say**

exclamation *NOUN*
He let out a sudden exclamation of pain.
• **cry, shout, yell**

exclude *VERB*
❶ *Adults are excluded from our club.*
• **ban, bar, reject, keep out, banish,**

prohibit
OPPOSITE admit (to)
❷ *She had to exclude dairy products from her diet.*
• **leave out, omit, rule out**
OPPOSITE include

excluding *PREPOSITION*
The zoo is open every day excluding Christmas.
• **except, except for, with the exception of, apart from, aside from, other than, barring, bar, but**

exclusive *ADJECTIVE*
❶ *They stayed at a very exclusive hotel.*
• **select, upmarket, high-class, elite** (*informal*) **posh, fancy, swish, classy**
OPPOSITE downmarket
❷ *The room is for your exclusive use.*
• **private, personal, individual, sole**
OPPOSITES shared, joint

excursion *NOUN*
We went on an excursion to the seaside.
• **trip, journey, outing, expedition, jaunt, day out**

excuse *VERB*
I can't excuse his behaviour.
• **forgive, overlook, disregard, pardon, condone, justify**
OPPOSITE condemn
➤ **be excused**
May I be excused swimming?
• **be exempt from, be let off, be relieved from**

excuse *NOUN*
I had a perfect excuse for being late.
• **reason, explanation, defence, justification, pretext**

execute *VERB*
❶ *The tsar and his family were executed in 1918.*
• **put to death**
– Someone who executes people is an **executioner**.
– To execute someone unofficially without a proper trial is to **lynch** them.
❷ *She executed a perfect dive.*
• **perform, carry out, implement, complete, accomplish, bring off**

exempt *ADJECTIVE*
➤ **exempt from**
Some students will be exempt from fees.
• **free from, not liable to, not subject to**
OPPOSITES subject to, liable to

exercise *NOUN*
❶ *Regular exercise helps to keep you fit.*
• **physical activity, working out, workouts, keep-fit, training**
❷ *Doing guitar exercises will improve your playing.*
• **drill, practice, lesson, task**

exercise *VERB*
❶ *If you exercise regularly, you will keep fit.*
• **do exercises, work out, train**
❷ *I sometimes exercise our neighbour's dog.*
• **take for a walk, take out, walk**
❸ *You need to exercise more patience.*
• **use, make use of, employ, practise, apply**

exert *VERB*
He exerted a huge influence on younger artists.
• **bring to bear, exercise, apply, use, employ**

exertion *NOUN*
He was tired from the exertion of climbing the hill.
• **effort, hard work, labour, toil**

exhale *VERB*
Please exhale slowly.
• **breathe out**
OPPOSITE inhale

exhaust *VERB*
❶ *Walking in the midday heat had exhausted me.*
• **tire, tire out, wear out, fatigue, weary, drain, take it out of you** (*informal*) **do you in**

❷ *Within three days they had exhausted their supply of food.*
• **use up, go through, consume, deplete, drain**

exhausted *ADJECTIVE*
The climb had left us all exhausted.
• **tired, weary, worn out, fatigued, breathless, gasping, panting**
(*informal*) **all in, done in, bushed, zonked**

exhausting *ADJECTIVE*
Digging the garden is exhausting work.
• **tiring, demanding, hard, laborious, strenuous, difficult, gruelling, wearisome**
OPPOSITE easy

exhaustion *NOUN*
He was overcome by sheer exhaustion.
• **tiredness, fatigue, weariness, weakness**

exhibit *VERB*
❶ *Her paintings are currently being exhibited in the local gallery.*
• **display, show, present, put on display**
❷ *The patient is exhibiting signs of anxiety.*
• **show, demonstrate, display, reveal**
OPPOSITE hide

exhibition *NOUN*
an exhibition of Japanese art
• **display, show**

exile *VERB*
Thousands were exiled from their own country.
• **banish, expel, deport, eject, drive out**

exile *NOUN*
❶ *The poet is returning to his country after years in exile.*
• **banishment, expulsion, deportation**
❷ *the return of political exiles*
• **refugee, deportee, displaced person**

exist *VERB*
❶ *Do you think that vampires really exist?*
• **be real, be found, occur**
❷ *Plants cannot exist without sunlight.*
• **live, stay alive, survive, subsist, keep going, last, continue, endure**

existence *NOUN*
❶ *Do you believe in the existence of life on other planets?*
• **occurrence, reality**
❷ *For several years he led a lonely existence.*
• **life, way of life, lifestyle**
➤ **in existence**
This is the oldest human skeleton in existence.
• **existing, surviving, remaining, living, alive**

existing *ADJECTIVE*
❶ *There are two existing species of elephants.*
• **surviving, living, remaining**
❷ *Next year the existing rules will be replaced by new ones.*
• **present, current**

exit *NOUN*
❶ *I'll wait for you by the exit.*
• **door, way out, doorway, gate, barrier**
OPPOSITE entrance
❷ *The robbers made a hurried exit.*
• **departure, escape, retreat, withdrawal, exodus**
OPPOSITES entrance, arrival

exit *VERB*
Please exit by the main door.
• **go out, leave, depart, withdraw**
OPPOSITE enter

exotic *ADJECTIVE*
❶ *The marketplace was filled with exotic sights and smells.*
• **unusual, unfamiliar, alien, exciting, romantic**
OPPOSITES familiar, commonplace
❷ *an exotic holiday destination*
• **faraway, far-off, far-flung, remote, distant**
OPPOSITE nearby

expand *VERB*
❶ *Wood expands when it gets wet.*
• **swell, enlarge, extend, stretch,**

lengthen, broaden, widen, thicken, fill out
OPPOSITE contract
❷ *Their business is expanding rapidly.*
• **increase, enlarge, grow, build up, develop, branch out**
OPPOSITES decrease, reduce

expanse *NOUN*
They crossed a vast expanse of desert.
• **area, stretch, tract**
– An expanse of water or ice is a **sheet**.

expect *VERB*
❶ *I expect you'd like something to eat.*
• **suppose, presume, imagine, assume** (*informal*) **guess, reckon**
❷ *They are expecting a lot of visitors to the exhibition.*
• **anticipate, envisage, predict, foresee, look forward to**
❸ *She expects me to do everything for her!*
• **require, want, count on, insist on, demand**

expedition *NOUN*
a scientific expedition to Antarctica
• **voyage, exploration, mission, quest**
– An expedition to worship at a holy place is a **pilgrimage**.
– An expedition to watch or hunt wild animals is a **safari**.

expel *VERB*
❶ *Whales expel air through their blowholes.*
• **send out, force out, eject**
❷ *The entire team was expelled from the tournament.*
• **dismiss, throw out, send away, ban, evict, deport, banish, exile**

expense *NOUN*
She was worried about the expense of staying in a hotel.
• **cost, price, charges, expenditure, outlay**

expensive *ADJECTIVE*
an expensive pair of trainers
• **dear, costly, high-priced, exorbitant, extortionate, overpriced** (*informal*) **pricey**
OPPOSITE cheap

experience *NOUN*
❶ *Have you had any experience of singing in a choir?*
• **practice, involvement, participation, knowledge, know-how, track record**
❷ *It was the most terrifying experience of my life.*
• **happening, event, occurrence, incident**
– An exciting experience is an **adventure**.
– An unpleasant experience is an **ordeal**.

experienced *ADJECTIVE*
He is an experienced stage actor.
• **skilled, qualified, expert, knowledgeable, trained, professional, seasoned, practised**
OPPOSITE inexperienced

experiment *NOUN*
We carried out a scientific experiment.
• **test, trial, examination, investigation, observation, research**

experiment *VERB*
➤ **experiment with**
I need to experiment with the camera's different settings.
• **try out, test out, trial, sample** (*informal*) **check out**

expert *NOUN*
She's an expert in web design.
• **specialist, authority, genius, ace, wizard, master, maestro** (*informal*) **whizz, dab hand**

expert *ADJECTIVE*
He's an expert cook.
• **skilful, skilled, capable, experienced, knowledgeable, professional, proficient, qualified, trained**
OPPOSITES amateur, unskilful

expertise *NOUN*
I don't have much expertise in tying knots.
• **skill, competence, knowledge, ability, know-how, proficiency, prowess**

expire *VERB*
❶ *Your library card has expired.*
• **run out, come to an end, become invalid, lapse**
❷ *I felt as if I was about to expire from the heat.*
• **die, pass away**

explain *VERB*
❶ *My teacher explained how to tune a guitar.*
• **make clear, describe, clarify**
IDIOMS **throw light on, spell out**
❷ *Your theory does not explain the footprints.*
• **account for, give reasons for, excuse, justify**

explanation *NOUN*
❶ *She gave a brief explanation of how her invention works.*
• **account, description, demonstration, clarification**
❷ *They found no explanation for the accident.*
• **reason, excuse, justification**

explode *VERB*
❶ *The firework exploded with a bang.*
• **blow up, go off, make an explosion, detonate, burst**
❷ *They exploded the dynamite in the tunnel.*
• **detonate, set off, let off**

exploit *NOUN*
The book records the exploits of a teenage spy.
• **adventure, deed, feat, act, escapade**

exploit *VERB*
❶ *They plan to exploit the area as a tourist attraction.*
• **make use of, make the most of, capitalize on, develop, profit by** (*informal*) **cash in on**
❷ *The company is accused of exploiting its workers.*
• **take advantage of, abuse, misuse, ill-treat**

explore *VERB*
❶ *The vehicle will explore the surface of Mars.*
• **travel through, survey, inspect, search, probe**
❷ *We must explore all the possibilities.*
• **examine, investigate, look into, research, analyse, scrutinize**

explorer *NOUN*
a team of undersea explorers
• **voyager, traveller, discoverer, researcher**

explosion *NOUN*
The explosion rattled the windows.
• **blast, bang, boom, detonation**
– An explosion of laughter is an **outburst**.
– The sound of a gun going off is a **report**.

export *VERB*
China exports many of its goods to the US.
• **sell abroad, send abroad, ship overseas**
OPPOSITE import

expose *VERB*
❶ *The creature snarled, exposing its fangs.*
• **uncover, reveal, lay bare**
❷ *The truth about his past was exposed in the newspaper.*
• **make known, publish, reveal, disclose**

express *VERB*
He's always quick to express his opinions.
• **voice, state, convey, communicate, air, put into words, put across, give vent to**

expression *NOUN*
❶ *An expression of horror flooded his face.*
• **look, face, appearance, countenance**
For facial expressions see **face**.
❷ *'Cheesed off' is a colloquial expression.*
• **phrase, saying, idiom, term**
– An expression that people use too much is a **cliché**.

❸ *She plays the piano with great expression.*
• **feeling, emotion, passion, intensity**

expressive *ADJECTIVE*

❶ *My sister gave me an expressive nudge.*
• **meaningful, significant, revealing, telling**
❷ *Try to be more expressive in your playing.*
• **passionate, emotional, moving, stirring**
OPPOSITES expressionless, flat

exquisite *ADJECTIVE*

Notice the exquisite stitching on the quilt.
• **beautiful, fine, delicate, intricate, dainty**

extend *VERB*

❶ *He sat back and extended his legs.*
• **stretch out, hold out, put out, reach out, stick out**
OPPOSITES pull back, withdraw
❷ *We extended our visit by a couple of days.*
• **lengthen, prolong, delay, draw out, spin out**
OPPOSITES shorten, cut
❸ *The company plans to extend its range of products.*
• **enlarge, expand, increase, build up, develop, enhance, add to, widen the scope of**
OPPOSITES reduce, cut back
❹ *We extended a warm welcome to the visitors.*
• **give, offer, proffer**
❺ *The road extends as far as the border.*
• **continue, carry on, reach, stretch**

extension *NOUN*

They are building an extension to the school.
• **addition, annex, add-on**

extensive *ADJECTIVE*

❶ *The rainforest covers an extensive area.*
• **large, great, substantial, considerable, vast, broad, wide, spread out**
OPPOSITE small
❷ *My brother has an extensive knowledge of the film business.*
• **wide, wide-ranging, comprehensive, thorough, broad**
OPPOSITE narrow

extent *NOUN*

❶ *The map shows the extent of the island.*
• **area, expanse, spread, breadth, length, dimensions, proportions, measurement**
❷ *No one guessed the full extent of the damage.*
• **amount, degree, level, size, scope, magnitude, range**

exterior *ADJECTIVE*

an exterior wall
• **outside, external, outer, outward, outermost**
OPPOSITE interior

exterior *NOUN*

The exterior of the house has been repainted.
• **outside, external surface**
OPPOSITE interior

exterminate *VERB*

They used poison to exterminate the rats.
• **destroy, kill, get rid of, annihilate, wipe out**

external *ADJECTIVE*

In external appearance, the house was shabby.
• **exterior, outside, outer, outward, outermost**
OPPOSITE internal

extinct *ADJECTIVE*

Dodos became extinct in the seventeenth century.
– An extinct species is one that has **died out**, **vanished** or been **wiped out**.
– An extinct volcano is an **inactive** volcano.

extinguish *VERB*
Extinguish all fires before leaving the campsite.
• **put out, quench, douse, smother, snuff out, stamp out**
OPPOSITE ignite

extra *ADJECTIVE*
❶ *There is an extra charge for taking your bike on the train.*
• **additional, further, added, supplementary, excess**
❷ *We brought extra clothes just in case.*
• **more, spare, surplus, reserve**

extract *VERB*
❶ *The dentist extracted my tooth.*
• **take out, remove, pull out, draw out, withdraw**
(*informal*) **whip out**
❷ *It was difficult to extract any names from him.*
• **obtain, wrest, draw, glean, derive, gather**

extract *NOUN*
There's an extract from her latest novel in the magazine.
• **excerpt, quotation, citation, passage, section**
– An extract from a newspaper is a **cutting**.
– An extract from a film is a **clip**.

extraordinary *ADJECTIVE*
an ordinary woman who led an extraordinary life
• **amazing, astonishing, astounding, remarkable, exceptional, incredible, outstanding, phenomenal, sensational, marvellous, miraculous, rare, special, unheard of, unusual**
OPPOSITE ordinary

extravagant *ADJECTIVE*
They planned a large and extravagant wedding.
• **lavish, expensive, showy, ostentatious, fancy**
(*informal*) **flashy**
– Someone who spends money in an extravagant way is a **spendthrift**.
OPPOSITES modest, low-key

extreme *ADJECTIVE*
❶ *Polar bears can withstand extreme cold.*
• **great, intense, severe, acute, exceptional, excessive, utmost, maximum**
OPPOSITE slight
❷ *an island in the extreme north of Canada*
• **farthest, furthest, remotest**
OPPOSITE near
❸ *He holds extreme views on religion.*
• **radical, immoderate, extremist, fanatical**
OPPOSITE moderate

extremely *ADVERB*
Crows are extremely intelligent birds.
• **very, exceptionally, especially, highly, extraordinarily, immensely, hugely, tremendously, supremely**
(*informal*) **awfully, terribly**

eye *NOUN*

WORD WEB

Parts of an eye:

- cornea
- eyeball
- eyebrow
- eyelash
- eyelid
- iris
- lens
- pupil
- retina

- Words meaning 'to do with eyes' are **ocular, optic** and **optical**.
- A person who tests your eyesight is an **optician**.

For tips on describing faces see **face**.

eye *VERB*
The two strangers eyed each other warily.
• **look at, regard, watch, observe, scrutinize, view, survey, gaze at, stare at, contemplate**

fable *NOUN*

the fable of the Tortoise and the Hare

• **legend, story, tale, parable**

SEE ALSO **fiction**

fabric *NOUN*

His jacket is made of windproof fabric.

• **cloth, material, textile**

WORD WEB

Some types of fabric:

- calico
- canvas
- cheesecloth
- chiffon
- chintz
- corduroy
- cotton
- crepe
- damask
- denim
- felt
- fleece
- flannel
- gabardine
- gingham
- hessian
- jersey
- linen
- (*trademark*) Lurex
- (*trademark*) Lycra
- moleskin
- muslin
- nylon
- organdie
- organza
- polyester
- rayon
- satin
- serge
- silk
- taffeta
- tulle
- tweed
- velour
- velvet
- velveteen
- vinyl
- wool

fabulous *ADJECTIVE*

1 (*informal*) *Thank you for a fabulous weekend!*

• **excellent, first-class, outstanding, wonderful, tremendous, marvellous, splendid, superb**

(*informal*) **fantastic, terrific, brilliant, smashing**

2 *Dragons are fabulous creatures.*

• **fictitious, imaginary, legendary, mythical**

face *NOUN*

1 *Donna's face flushed with anger.*

• **countenance, features, visage**

(*informal*) **mug**

(*formal*) **physiognomy**

– A side view of someone's face is their **profile.**

2 *Why are you making that funny face?*

• **expression, look, appearance**

3 *a clock face*

• **front, facade, cover**

OPPOSITE back

4 *the north face of the Eiger*

• **side, surface, plane**

WRITING TIPS

DESCRIBING FACES

Facial features:

- beauty spot
- bloom
- brow
- cheekbones
- complexion
- crow's feet
- dimple
- double chin
- ear lobes
- forehead
- freckles
- jawline
- jowl
- laugh-lines
- lower lip
- mole
- pimple
- scar
- spot
- temples
- upper lip
- wrinkles

Facial expressions:

- beam
- frown
- glare
- glower
- grimace
- grin
- leer
- pout
- scowl
- smile
- smirk
- sneer
- wince
- yawn

Adjectives:

- bloated
- chinless
- chiselled
- clean-shaven
- craggy
- drawn
- fine-boned
- florid
- flushed
- freckled
- gaunt
- haggard
- heart-shaped
- heavy
- lined
- livid
- olive
- pallid

- ➤ pasty
- ➤ pimply
- ➤ pinched
- ➤ pockmarked
- ➤ rosy
- ➤ ruddy
- ➤ sallow
- ➤ scarred
- ➤ spotless
- ➤ spotty
- ➤ sunburned
- ➤ tanned
- ➤ unshaven
- ➤ wan
- ➤ wasted
- ➤ weather-beaten
- ➤ weathered
- ➤ wizened
- ➤ wrinkled

Chin:

- ➤ jutting
- ➤ lantern
- ➤ pointed
- ➤ square
- ➤ stubbly
- ➤ weak

Ears:

- ➤ earringed
- ➤ flappy
- ➤ lobed
- ➤ pendulous
- ➤ pierced
- ➤ sticking-out (*informal* jug)

Eyebrows:

- ➤ arched
- ➤ beetling
- ➤ bushy
- ➤ knitted
- ➤ shaggy
- ➤ tufted
- ➤ unruly

Eyes:

- ➤ baggy
- ➤ beady
- ➤ bleary
- ➤ bloodshot
- ➤ bulging
- ➤ close-set
- ➤ cross-eyed
- ➤ deep-set
- ➤ downcast
- ➤ glassy
- ➤ heavy-lidded
- ➤ hollow
- ➤ hooded
- ➤ piercing
- ➤ protuberant
- ➤ puffy
- ➤ steely
- ➤ sunken
- ➤ swollen
- ➤ tearful
- ➤ twinkling
- ➤ watery

Lips:

- ➤ full
- ➤ pouting
- ➤ puckered
- ➤ pursed
- ➤ thin

Nose:

- ➤ aquiline
- ➤ beaked
- ➤ bulbous
- ➤ button
- ➤ classical
- ➤ crooked
- ➤ hooked
- ➤ Roman

SEE ALSO hair

face *VERB*

❶ *She turned to face me.*

• be opposite to, look towards

❷ *We had to face some tough questions.*

• stand up to, face up to, deal with, cope with, tackle, meet, encounter, confront

OPPOSITE avoid

facet *NOUN*

❶ *Each facet of the gem shone as it caught the light.*

• side, surface, plane, face

❷ *the many facets of Indian culture*

• aspect, feature, element, dimension, strand, component

fact *NOUN*

It is a fact that dodos are now extinct.

• reality, truth, certainty

OPPOSITE fiction

➤ **the facts**

Let us consider the facts of the case.

• details, particulars, information, data, evidence

➤ **in fact**

In fact, rhubarb is not a fruit.

• actually, as a matter of fact, in reality

factor *NOUN*

Many factors affect the climate.

• element, component, feature, aspect, dimension

factory *NOUN*

an old tyre factory

• works, plant, mill

factual *ADJECTIVE*

a factual account of life in China

• true, truthful, accurate, authentic, faithful, genuine, correct, exact

OPPOSITES fictitious, made-up

fad *NOUN*

the latest fad in computer games

• craze, trend, vogue, fashion

fade *VERB*

❶ *The colours will fade over time.*
• **become paler, become dim, bleach, blanch**
OPPOSITE brighten
❷ *Gradually the afternoon light began to fade.*
• **weaken, decline, diminish, dwindle, die away, wane, ebb**
OPPOSITE grow

fail *VERB*

❶ *Their first attempt to climb Everest failed.*
• **be unsuccessful, go wrong, fall through, founder, come unstuck, come to grief, miscarry**
(*informal*) **flop, bomb**
OPPOSITE succeed
❷ *The rocket engine failed before take-off.*
• **break down, stop working, cut out, malfunction**
(*informal*) **pack in, conk out**
❸ *By late afternoon, the light was failing.*
• **weaken, decline, diminish, dwindle, fade, deteriorate, peter out**
OPPOSITE improve
❹ *You failed to warn us of the danger.*
• **neglect, forget, omit**
OPPOSITE remember
❺ *My brother failed his driving test.*
• **be unsuccessful in**
(*informal*) **flunk**
OPPOSITE pass

fail *NOUN*

➤ **without fail**
Deliver this message without fail.
• **for certain, assuredly, without exception**

failing *NOUN*

Vanity is one of his failings.
• **fault, flaw, imperfection, weakness, defect**
OPPOSITES strength, strong point

failure *NOUN*

❶ *The storm caused a power failure.*
• **breakdown, fault, malfunction, crash, loss, collapse, stoppage**
❷ *Our first experiment was a failure.*
• **defeat, disappointment, disaster, fiasco**
(*informal*) **flop, wash-out**
OPPOSITE success

faint *ADJECTIVE*

❶ *a faint line*
• **indistinct, unclear, dim, vague, faded, blurred, hazy, pale, shadowy, misty**
OPPOSITES clear, distinct
❷ *a faint smell of burning*
• **delicate, slight**
OPPOSITE strong
❸ *a faint cry for help*
• **weak, feeble, muted, subdued, muffled, hushed, soft, low, distant**
OPPOSITE loud
❹ *Are you feeling faint?*
• **dizzy, giddy, light-headed, unsteady, weak, feeble**
(*informal*) **woozy**

faint *VERB*

I nearly fainted in the midday heat.
• **become unconscious, collapse, pass out, black out, keel over**
(*old use*) **swoon**

faintly *ADVERB*

❶ *Lights glimmered faintly in the distance.*
• **indistinctly, unclearly, dimly, hazily, weakly**
OPPOSITES clearly, distinctly
❷ *His face seemed faintly familiar.*
• **slightly, vaguely, somewhat, a little, a bit**

fair *ADJECTIVE*

❶ *a fair trial*
• **just, equitable, even-handed, impartial, unbiased, honest, honourable, fair-minded, unprejudiced, disinterested**
OPPOSITE unfair
❷ *a boy with fair hair*
• **blond, blonde, light, golden, yellow, flaxen**
OPPOSITE dark
❸ *The forecast is for fair weather.*
• **fine, dry, sunny, bright, clear, cloudless**
OPPOSITE inclement

❹ *We have a fair chance of winning.*
• **reasonable, moderate, average, acceptable, adequate, satisfactory, passable, respectable, tolerable**
OPPOSITE poor

fair *NOUN*
❶ *a village fair*
• **fête, gala, funfair, festival, carnival**
❷ *a book fair*
• **show, exhibition, display, market, bazaar**

fairly *ADVERB*
❶ *The competition will be judged fairly.*
• **justly, impartially, honestly, properly**
IDIOM **fair and square**
OPPOSITE unfairly
❷ *The stew is fairly spicy.*
• **quite, rather, somewhat, slightly, moderately**
❸ *I'm fairly certain he's lying.*
• **reasonably, up to a point, tolerably, passably, adequately**

fairy *NOUN*
Tinker Bell is a mischievous fairy.
• **pixie, elf, imp, brownie, sprite, leprechaun**
SEE ALSO **fantasy**

faith *NOUN*
❶ *I have complete faith in my teammates.*
• **trust, belief, confidence, conviction**
OPPOSITES doubt, mistrust
❷ *people of many faiths*
• **religion, belief, creed, doctrine**
SEE ALSO **religion**

faithful *ADJECTIVE*
❶ *a faithful friend*
• **loyal, constant, devoted, true, reliable, dependable, firm, staunch, steadfast, trusty**
OPPOSITE disloyal
❷ *a faithful copy of the original painting*
• **accurate, exact, precise, true**
OPPOSITE inaccurate

fake *NOUN*
❶ *It's not a real Leonardo: it's a fake.*
• **imitation, copy, forgery, replica, reproduction**
❷ *That fortune-teller was a fake.*
• **charlatan, fraud, impostor**

fake *ADJECTIVE*
❶ *a fake passport*
• **false, forged, counterfeit, bogus** (*informal*) **phoney, dud**
❷ *a fake diamond*
• **imitation, artificial, pretend, simulated, mock, sham**
OPPOSITES real, genuine, authentic

fake *VERB*
❶ *Someone managed to fake my signature.*
• **forge, copy, counterfeit, fabricate, falsify, imitate, reproduce**
❷ *I tried to fake interest in what she was saying.*
• **feign, pretend, put on, simulate, affect**

fall *VERB*
❶ *Thousands of meteorites fall to Earth each year.*
• **drop, descend, come down, plunge, plummet, nosedive**
❷ *The athlete fell and sprained her ankle.*
• **tumble, topple, trip, stumble**
❸ *The temperature fell to below freezing.*
• **go down, become lower, decrease, decline, lessen, diminish, dwindle**
❹ *Sea levels have fallen dramatically.*
• **go down, subside, recede, sink, ebb**
❺ *Edinburgh fell to the Jacobites without any fighting.*
• **give in, surrender, yield, capitulate**
❻ *a memorial to those who fell in the war*
• **die, be killed, perish** (*old use*) **be slain**
❼ *My birthday falls on a Saturday this year.*
• **happen, occur, take place**
➤ **fall apart**
The paper fell apart in my hands.
• **break up, go to pieces, disintegrate, shatter**
➤ **fall in**
The roof fell in during the storm.
• **collapse, cave in, give way**
➤ **fall out**
Those two are always falling out.
• **argue, disagree, quarrel, squabble,**

bicker, fight

➤ fall through

Our holiday plans have fallen through.

• **fail, come to nothing, collapse, founder**

fall *NOUN*

❶ *a fall from a great height*

• **tumble, topple, trip, plunge, dive, descent**

❷ *a sharp fall in temperature*

• **drop, lowering**

OPPOSITE rise

❸ *a fall in the number of pupils*

• **decrease, reduction, decline, slump**

OPPOSITE increase

❹ *a story about the fall of Troy*

• **downfall, defeat, overthrow, surrender**

false *ADJECTIVE*

❶ *We were given false information.*

• **wrong, incorrect, untrue, inaccurate, mistaken, erroneous, faulty, invalid, misleading, deceptive**

OPPOSITE correct

❷ *He was travelling under a false identity.*

• **fake, bogus, sham, counterfeit, forged**

OPPOSITES genuine, authentic

❸ *wearing false eyelashes*

• **artificial, imitation, synthetic, simulated, fake, mock, pretend**

OPPOSITES real, natural

❹ *a false friend*

• **unfaithful, disloyal, unreliable, untrustworthy, deceitful, dishonest, treacherous**

OPPOSITES faithful, loyal

falter *VERB*

❶ *The actor faltered slightly over his lines.*

• **hesitate, stumble, pause, waver, vacillate, stammer, stutter**

❷ *Her courage began to falter.*

• **weaken, diminish, flag, wane**

fame *NOUN*

His plays brought him international fame.

• **celebrity, stardom, renown, glory, reputation, name, standing, stature, prominence**

– Fame that you get for doing something bad is **notoriety**.

familiar *ADJECTIVE*

❶ *Bicycles are a familiar sight in Beijing.*

• **common, everyday, normal, ordinary, usual, regular, customary, frequent, mundane, routine**

OPPOSITE rare

❷ *Don't be too familiar with the customers.*

• **informal, friendly, intimate, relaxed, close**

OPPOSITES formal, unfriendly

➤ be familiar with

Are you familiar with the story of Frankenstein?

• **be acquainted with, be aware of, know**

familiarity *NOUN*

❶ *There was an air of familiarity between them.*

• **friendship, closeness, intimacy, friendliness**

❷ *I have some familiarity with her music.*

• **knowledge of, acquaintance with, experience of, understanding of**

family *NOUN*

Most of her family live in South Africa.

• **relations, relatives, kin, clan**

IDIOMS flesh and blood, kith and kin

WORD WEB

Members of a family:

- ➤ ancestor
- ➤ forebear
- ➤ forefather
- ➤ descendant (*literary* scion)
- ➤ father
- ➤ mother
- ➤ husband
- ➤ wife
- ➤ spouse
- ➤ parent
- ➤ child
- ➤ daughter
- ➤ son
- ➤ brother
- ➤ sister
- ➤ sibling
- ➤ aunt
- ➤ uncle
- ➤ nephew
- ➤ niece
- ➤ cousin
- ➤ second cousin
- ➤ grandparent
- ➤ great-grand-parent
- ➤ grandfather
- ➤ grandmother
- ➤ granddaughter
- ➤ grandson

➤ great-aunt
➤ great-uncle
➤ father-in-law
➤ mother-in-law
➤ daughter-in-law
➤ son-in-law
➤ brother-in-law
➤ sister-in-law
➤ stepfather
➤ stepmother
➤ stepchild
➤ stepdaughter
➤ stepson
➤ stepbrother
➤ stepsister
➤ half-brother
➤ half-sister
➤ foster-parent
➤ foster-child

- The study of family history and ancestors is **genealogy**. A **family tree** is a diagram which shows how people in a family are related.

SEE ALSO **father, mother**

famine *NOUN*
years of drought and famine
• **starvation, hunger**

famous *ADJECTIVE*
J K Rowling is a famous author.
• **well-known, celebrated, renowned, acclaimed, distinguished, revered, eminent, illustrious, noted, notable**
– A **notorious** person or place is famous for a bad reason. *a notorious accident blackspot.*
OPPOSITES unknown, obscure
The word infamous is not the opposite of famous. An infamous person has a bad reputation: *Blackbeard was an infamous pirate.*

fan *NOUN*
a football fan
• **enthusiast, admirer, devotee, follower, supporter**

fanatic *NOUN*
a fitness fanatic
• **enthusiast, addict, devotee**
(*informal*) **freak, nut**

fanatical *ADJECTIVE*
Josh is fanatical about football.
• **enthusiastic, passionate, obsessive, extreme, fervent, over-enthusiastic, rabid, zealous**
OPPOSITE moderate

fanciful *ADJECTIVE*
a fanciful tale set in ancient Japan
• **imaginary, fictitious, made-up, fantastic, fabulous, whimsical**
OPPOSITE realistic

fancy *VERB*
❶ (*informal*) *Which film do you fancy seeing?*
• **feel like, want, wish for, desire, prefer**
❷ *I fancied I heard a noise upstairs.*
• **imagine, think, believe, suppose**
(*informal*) **reckon**

fancy *ADJECTIVE*
The guitarist wore a fancy waistcoat.
• **elaborate, decorative, ornate, ornamented, showy**
(*informal*) **flashy, snazzy**
OPPOSITE plain

fancy *NOUN*
❶ *Painting is much more than a passing fancy for her.*
• **whim, urge, desire, caprice**
❷ *The author is given to strange flights of fancy.*
• **imagination, fantasy, dreaming, creativity**

fantastic *ADJECTIVE*
❶ *The rock had been carved into fantastic shapes.*
• **fanciful, extraordinary, strange, odd, weird, outlandish, incredible, imaginative, far-fetched**
OPPOSITE realistic
❷ (*informal*) *We had a fantastic time on holiday.*
• **excellent, outstanding, superb, splendid, wonderful, tremendous, marvellous**
(*informal*) **brilliant, fabulous, smashing**

fantasy *NOUN*
❶ *She has a fantasy about being a movie star.*
• **dream, daydream, delusion, wish, hope**
❷ *The book is a mixture of science fiction and fantasy.*
• **make-believe, invention, imagination, fancy**

WRITING TIPS

WRITING FANTASY FICTION

Characters:

- alchemist
- apprentice
- changeling
- druid
- enchanter
- enchantress
- magus
- seer
- shaman
- shape-shifter
- soothsayer
- sorcerer
- sorceress
- warlock
- witch
- witchfinder
- wizard

Creatures:

- banshee
- basilisk
- centaur
- chimera
- cyclops
- dragon
- dwarf
- elf
- fairy
- faun
- genie
- giant
- goblin
- gorgon
- gryphon
- harpie
- kelpie
- mermaid
- merman
- ogre
- phoenix
- selkie
- sphinx
- troll
- unicorn
- yeti

Setting:

- castle
- cave or cavern
- den
- dungeon
- empire
- enchanted forest
- fortress
- island
- kingdom
- labyrinth
- lair
- maze
- realm
- stronghold
- underworld

Useful words and phrases:

- amulet
- augury
- bewitch
- charm
- chronicle
- clairvoyance
- coven
- crucible
- curse
- dark arts
- divination
- elixir
- enchantment
- hex
- immortality
- incantation
- invisibility
- legend
- lore
- mace
- magic
- nemesis
- omen
- oracle
- portal
- potion
- prophecy
- quest
- riddle
- rune
- sorcery
- spell
- spirit guide
- spirit quest
- staff
- superhuman
- talisman
- vision
- wand
- witchcraft
- wizardry

far *ADJECTIVE*

❶ *They live in the far north of Canada.*
• **distant, faraway, far-off, far-flung, remote, outlying**
❷ *We rowed to the far side of the lake.*
• **opposite, other**
OPPOSITE near

➤ **by far**
They are by far the best team.
• **far and away, easily**
IDIOMS **by a long shot, by a mile**

far *ADVERB*

❶ *We were still far from sight of land.*
• **far away, a long way, at a distance** (*informal*) **miles**
❷ *The road is far more dangerous in winter.*
• **much, considerably, significantly, markedly, decidedly, greatly, a good deal**

fare *NOUN*

How much is the train fare?
• **charge, cost, price, fee, payment**

far-fetched *ADJECTIVE*

Her story sounds far-fetched to me.
• **unbelievable, unlikely, improbable, unconvincing, unrealistic, incredible, dubious, fanciful**
OPPOSITES likely, believable

farm *NOUN*

a sheep farm
• **farmstead, holding, ranch** (*Australia & New Zealand*) **station**

A B C D E F G H I J K L M N O P Q R S T U V W X Y Z

farm *VERB*
This land has been farmed for centuries.
• **cultivate, work, till, plough**

farming *NOUN*
organic methods of farming
• **agriculture, cultivation, husbandry**

fascinate *VERB*
Wells was fascinated by the idea of time travel.
• **interest (in), captivate, enthral, engross, absorb, attract, beguile, entrance, charm, enchant**
OPPOSITES bore, repel

fascinating *ADJECTIVE*
I found the programme fascinating.
• **interesting, absorbing, enthralling, captivating, engrossing, riveting, gripping, entertaining, intriguing, diverting, engaging, stimulating**
OPPOSITES boring, dull

fashion *NOUN*
❶ *She was behaving in a very odd fashion.*
• **manner, way, style**
❷ *This is the latest fashion in footwear.*
• **trend, vogue, craze, fad, style, look**

fashionable *ADJECTIVE*
a fashionable new hairstyle
• **stylish, chic, up-to-date, popular, elegant, smart**
(*informal*) **trendy, hip, in**
IDIOM **all the rage**
OPPOSITES unfashionable, out-of-date

fast *ADJECTIVE*
❶ *a fast lap around the track*
• **quick, rapid, speedy, swift, brisk, hurried, hasty, high-speed, headlong, breakneck**
(*informal*) **nippy**
OPPOSITES slow, unhurried
❷ *Be sure to make the rope fast.*
• **secure, fastened, firm, tight**
OPPOSITE loose

fast *ADVERB*
❶ *A boy was running very fast across the field.*
• **quickly, speedily, swiftly, rapidly, briskly**
(*informal*) **flat out**
IDIOMS **at full tilt, like a shot, like the wind**
❷ *The jeep was stuck fast in the mud.*
• **firmly, securely, tightly**
❸ *By now he was fast asleep.*
• **deeply, sound, completely**

fasten *VERB*
❶ *They fastened their ropes to the rock face.*
• **tie, fix, attach, connect, join, link, bind, hitch, tether, clamp, pin, clip, tack, stick**
OPPOSITES unfasten, untie
❷ *Please fasten your seat belts.*
• **secure, lock, bolt, make fast, seal**
OPPOSITES unfasten, release

fat *ADJECTIVE*
❶ *Eating too much sugary food will make you fat.*
• **overweight, obese, plump, chubby, podgy, dumpy, tubby, round, rotund, portly, stout, heavy, beefy, corpulent, flabby**
– Someone with a fat stomach is **pot-bellied.**
OPPOSITES thin, skinny
For tips on describing people's bodies see **body.**
❷ *a large fat envelope*
• **thick, bulky, chunky, weighty, substantial**
(*informal*) **stuffed**
OPPOSITE thin

fatal *ADJECTIVE*
❶ *a fatal wound*
• **deadly, lethal, mortal**
❷ *a fatal disease*
• **incurable, terminal**
❸ *a fatal error*
• **disastrous, catastrophic, dreadful, calamitous**

fate *NOUN*
❶ *I didn't know what fate had in store for me.*
• **fortune, destiny, providence, chance, luck, future, lot**
IDIOM **the lap of the gods**
❷ *Each of the crew met with a grisly fate.*
• **death, demise, end, doom**

father *NOUN*
❶ *My father grew up in South Africa.*
• (*informal*) **dad, daddy, pa, old man**
(*North American informal*) **pop**
– A word meaning 'to do with a father' is **paternal**.
For other members of a family see **family**.
❷ *Galileo is considered the father of astronomy.*
• **founder, originator, inventor, creator, architect**

fatigue *NOUN*
Some of the runners were overcome with fatigue.
• **exhaustion, tiredness, weariness, weakness**

fatty *ADJECTIVE*
Try to cut down on fatty foods.
• **fat, greasy, oily**
OPPOSITE lean

fault *NOUN*
❶ *a fault in the electrical wiring*
• **defect, flaw, malfunction, snag, problem, weakness**
(*informal*) **glitch, bug**
❷ *It's not my fault that you overslept.*
• **responsibility, liability**
➤ **at fault**
Both the drivers were at fault.
• **to blame, guilty, responsible, culpable**

faultless *ADJECTIVE*
a faultless performance
• **perfect, flawless, immaculate, impeccable**
OPPOSITES imperfect, flawed

faulty *ADJECTIVE*
a faulty DVD
• **broken, not working, malfunctioning, defective, out of order, unusable, damaged**
IDIOM (*informal*) **on the blink**
OPPOSITES working, in good order

favour *NOUN*
❶ *Would you do me a favour?*
• **good turn, good deed, kindness, service, courtesy**
❷ *The idea found favour with the public.*
• **approval, support, liking, goodwill**
➤ **be in favour of**
Hands up all those who are in favour of longer holidays.
• **approve of, support, be on the side of, be for, be pro**
OPPOSITES be against, disapprove of

favour *VERB*
I favour the second explanation.
• **approve of, support, back, advocate, choose, like, opt for, prefer**
(*informal*) **fancy, go for**
OPPOSITE oppose

favourable *ADJECTIVE*
❶ *The weather is favourable for flying.*
• **advantageous, beneficial, helpful, good, suitable, encouraging**
OPPOSITE unfavourable
❷ *The film received favourable reviews.*
• **positive, complimentary, good, glowing, approving, agreeable, enthusiastic, sympathetic**
(*informal*) **rave**
OPPOSITES critical, hostile, negative

favourite *ADJECTIVE*
What's your favourite book?
• **preferred, best-loved, favoured, treasured, dearest, special, top**

fear *NOUN*
❶ *He was shaking with fear.*
• **fright, terror, horror, alarm, panic, dread, anxiety, apprehension, trepidation**
OPPOSITE courage
SEE ALSO **afraid**
❷ *a fear of snakes and spiders*
• **phobia, dread**
For special types of fear see **phobia**.

A B C D E F G H I J K L M N O P Q R S T U V W X Y Z

fear *VERB*

❶ *As a child, I used to fear the dark.*
• **be frightened of, be afraid of, be scared of, dread**
❷ *I fear we may be too late.*
• **suspect, expect, anticipate**

fearful *ADJECTIVE*

❶ *She was fearful of being left behind.*
• **frightened, afraid, scared, terrified, petrified, nervous, apprehensive, anxious, timid, panicky**
❷ *We came across a fearful sight.*
• **frightening, terrifying, shocking, ghastly, dreadful, appalling, terrible, awful, frightful, fearsome, gruesome**

fearless *ADJECTIVE*

The fearless explorers entered the dark cave.
• **brave, courageous, daring, bold, heroic, valiant, intrepid, plucky, unafraid**
OPPOSITES cowardly, timid

fearsome *ADJECTIVE*

The dragon yawned, revealing a fearsome set of teeth.
• **frightening, fearful, horrifying, terrifying, dreadful, awesome**
(*informal*) **scary**

feasible *ADJECTIVE*

Is it feasible to fly there and back in a day?
• **possible, practicable, practical, achievable, realistic, workable, viable**
(*informal*) **doable**
OPPOSITES impractical, impossible

feast *NOUN*

❶ *a wedding feast*
• **banquet, dinner**
(*informal*) **spread**
❷ *the feast of Saint Valentine*
• **festival, holiday**

feast *VERB*

a band of hyenas feasting on their prey
• **gorge, feed, dine**

feat *NOUN*

The Channel Tunnel was an incredible feat of engineering.
• **act, action, deed, exploit, achievement, undertaking, performance**

feather *NOUN*

a goose feather
• **plume, quill**
– All the feathers on a bird are its **plumage**.
– Soft, fluffy feathers are **down**.

feature *NOUN*

❶ *The room has several unusual features.*
• **characteristic, attribute, property, aspect, quality, peculiarity, trait, facet, element, hallmark**
❷ *a feature in the school magazine*
• **article, report, story, item, piece, column**
➤ **features**
a tall, thin man with fine features
• **face, countenance, visage**
(*formal*) **physiognomy**
For tips on describing faces see **face**.

feature *VERB*

❶ *The film features some stunning special effects.*
• **present, show off, highlight, spotlight, showcase**
❷ *Holmes features in over fifty short stories.*
• **appear, participate, take part, figure, star**

fed up (*informal*) *ADJECTIVE*

She looked tired and fed up.
• **depressed, dispirited, dejected, unhappy, bored**
(*informal*) **cheesed off, hacked off**
➤ **be fed up with**
I'm fed up with doing all the work.
• **be tired of, be sick of, have had enough of**
(*informal*) **be sick and tired of**

fee *NOUN*

an annual membership fee
• **charge, cost, payment, price**

feeble *ADJECTIVE*
❶ *The king was growing old and feeble.*
• **weak, frail, infirm, poorly, sickly, puny, weedy**
OPPOSITES **strong, powerful**
❷ *I made a feeble attempt to catch the ball.*
• **weak, poor, ineffective, inadequate, unconvincing, lame, flimsy**

feed *VERB*
❶ *There's enough food to feed everyone.*
• **provide for, cater for, give food to, nourish, sustain**
❷ *Bats usually feed at night.*
• **eat, take food**
➤ **feed on**
Chameleons feed on a variety of insects.
• **eat, consume, devour, live on**

feel *VERB*
❶ *Feel how soft this material is.*
• **touch, stroke, caress, fondle, handle**
SEE ALSO **texture**
❷ *In the dark I felt my way along the landing.*
• **grope, fumble**
❸ *The animal won't feel any pain.*
• **experience, undergo, endure, suffer from**
❹ *I usually don't feel the cold.*
• **perceive, sense, notice, detect, be aware of, be conscious of**
❺ *I feel that I've met you before.*
• **think, believe, consider, maintain**
(*informal*) **reckon**
❻ *It feels warmer today.*
• **appear, seem, strike you as**
➤ **feel for**
I feel for the people who live there.
• **sympathize with, pity**
➤ **feel like**
Do you feel like something to eat?
• **fancy, want, desire, wish for**

feel *NOUN*
the feel of sand between your toes
• **feeling, sensation, touch, texture**

feeling *NOUN*
❶ *She had lost all feeling in her toes.*
• **sense of touch, sensation, sensitivity**
❷ *I didn't mean to hurt your feelings.*
• **emotion, passion, sentiment**
❸ *I had a feeling that something was wrong.*
• **suspicion, notion, inkling, idea, impression, intuition, hunch**
❹ *the strength of public feeling*
• **opinion, belief, view, attitude, mood**

fell
past tense see **fall**

fellow *NOUN*
an odd-looking fellow with a squint
• **man, person, character, individual**
(*informal*) **guy**
(*British informal*) **bloke, chap**

female *ADJECTIVE*
a female friend
OPPOSITE **male**
For female animals see **animal**.

feminine *ADJECTIVE*
a feminine style of dress
• **womanly, ladylike, girlish**
(*informal*) **girlie**
OPPOSITE **masculine**

fence *NOUN*
The garden was surrounded by a tall fence.
• **railing, barrier, paling, stockade**

fence *VERB*
a field fenced by hedgerows
• **enclose, surround, bound, encircle**

fend *VERB*
➤ **fend for yourself**
We were left to fend for ourselves.
• **look after yourself, take care of yourself, care for yourself**
➤ **fend off**
The small force managed to fend off the attack.
• **repel, resist, ward off, fight off, hold off, repulse**

ferment *NOUN*
All Europe was in a state of ferment.
• **turmoil, unrest, upheaval, agitation, excitement, commotion, turbulence, confusion, disorder, tumult**

A B C D E F G H I J K L M N O P Q R S T U V W X Y Z

ferocious *ADJECTIVE*
The gate was guarded by a ferocious dog.
• **fierce, fiercesome, savage, vicious, violent, wild, brutal**
OPPOSITES gentle, tame

fertile *ADJECTIVE*
The area has very fertile soil.
• **fruitful, productive, rich, lush**
OPPOSITES barren, sterile
a fertile imagination
• **inventive, creative, rich, prolific, teeming**

fertilize *VERB*
❶ *a good compost to fertilize the soil*
• **manure, feed, enrich**
❷ *How do frogs fertilize their eggs?*
• **inseminate, pollinate**

fervent *ADJECTIVE*
It was her fervent wish to return to Ireland.
• **eager, keen, avid, ardent, intense, wholehearted, heartfelt, passionate**
OPPOSITES indifferent, lukewarm

festival *NOUN*
❶ *The town holds a music festival every summer.*
• **celebration, carnival, fiesta, fête, gala, fair, jubilee, jamboree**
(*informal*) **fest**
❷ For religious festivals see **religion**.

festive *ADJECTIVE*
Chinese New Year is a festive occasion.
• **cheerful, happy, merry, jolly, cheery, joyful, joyous, jovial, light-hearted, celebratory**
OPPOSITES gloomy, sombre

fetch *VERB*
❶ *I went to fetch a torch.*
• **get, bring, collect, pick up, retrieve, obtain, carry, convey, transport**
❷ *We had better fetch the doctor.*
• **send for, call for, summon, go for, get, bring**
❸ *How much will the painting fetch?*
• **sell for, go for, make, raise, bring in, earn**

feud *NOUN*
a feud between two families
• **quarrel, dispute, conflict, hostility, enmity, rivalry, strife, antagonism**
– A feud that lasts a long time is a **vendetta**.

fever *NOUN*
❶ *a fever of 39 degrees Celsius*
• **temperature, delirium**
❷ *We were all in a fever of impatience.*
• **frenzy, ferment, excitement, agitation, mania, passion**

feverish *ADJECTIVE*
❶ *I stayed in bed all day, feeling feverish.*
• **hot, burning, flushed, delirious**
❷ *There was feverish activity in the kitchen.*
• **frenzied, frantic, excited, agitated, hectic, frenetic, busy, hurried, restless**

few *ADJECTIVE*
on a few occasions
• **not many, hardly any, a small number of, a handful of, one or two**
OPPOSITE many

fiasco *NOUN*
the fiasco of the cancelled concert
• **failure, disaster, catastrophe, mess, farce, debacle**
(*informal*) **shambles**
OPPOSITE success

fibre *NOUN*
❶ *Nylon is a synthetic fibre.*
• **thread, strand, hair, filament**
❷ *She is on a diet low in fibre.*
• **roughage**

fickle *ADJECTIVE*
the fickle support of the public
• **changeable, erratic, unreliable, unsteady, unpredictable, inconstant**
OPPOSITES constant, steady

fiction *NOUN*
❶ *'The Lord of the Rings' is a work of fiction.*
• **creative writing, storytelling**
OPPOSITE non-fiction

❷ *Most of the newspaper story was pure fiction.*
• **fantasy, invention, fabrication, lies**
IDIOMS **pack of lies, flight of fancy**
OPPOSITE fact

fictional *ADJECTIVE*
Middle-earth is a fictional realm.
• **imaginary, made-up, invented, fanciful**
OPPOSITES factual, real

fictitious *ADJECTIVE*
She was travelling under a fictitious name.
• **false, fake, fabricated, fraudulent, bogus, assumed, spurious, unreal**
OPPOSITES genuine, real
The words fictional and fictitious do not mean the same thing. A *fictional* character exists only in fiction, whereas a *fictitious* identity is created to deceive others.

fiddle *VERB*
❶ *He was fiddling with the DVD player.*
• **tinker, meddle, tamper, twiddle, play about, mess about**
❷ (*informal*) *They had been fiddling the accounts for years.*
• **falsify, alter, rig, doctor**
IDIOM (*informal*) **cook the books**

fiddly (*informal*) *ADJECTIVE*
Wiring a plug can be a fiddly job.
• **intricate, complicated, awkward, involved**
OPPOSITE simple

fidget *VERB*
Luke was fidgeting in his chair.
• **be restless, move about, wriggle, squirm**

fidgety *ADJECTIVE*
After waiting an hour, we began to get fidgety.
• **restless, unsettled, impatient, agitated, jumpy, nervy, twitchy, jittery, on edge**

field *NOUN*
❶ *Cattle were grazing in the field.*
• **meadow, pasture, paddock**
❷ *a football field*
• **ground, pitch, playing field**
❸ *advances in the field of medicine*
• **area, sphere, speciality, discipline, domain, province**

fiend *NOUN*
❶ *like a fiend from Hell*
• **demon, devil, evil spirit**
❷ (*informal*) *a fresh-air fiend*
• **enthusiast, fanatic, devotee**
(*informal*) **freak, nut**

fierce *ADJECTIVE*
❶ *a fierce attack by armed robbers*
• **vicious, ferocious, savage, brutal, violent, wild, cruel, merciless, ruthless, pitiless**
❷ *Competition between the two companies was fierce.*
• **strong, intense, keen, eager, aggressive, relentless, cut-throat**
❸ *the fierce heat of the desert sun*
• **intense, severe, blazing, raging**

fiery *ADJECTIVE*
❶ *the fiery heat of the midday sun*
• **burning, blazing, flaming, red-hot**
OPPOSITES cool, mild
❷ *the fiery taste of chilli pepper*
• **hot, spicy, peppery**
OPPOSITE mild
❸ *a fiery temper*
• **passionate, excitable, volatile, violent, raging, explosive**
OPPOSITES calm, mild

fight *NOUN*
❶ *the fight to capture the island*
• **battle, conflict, action, engagement, hostilities**
❷ *a fight in the street*
• **brawl, scuffle, skirmish, tussle, fracas, set-to**
(*informal*) **scrap, punch-up**
– A fight arranged between two people is a **duel**.
❸ *a heavyweight fight*
• **boxing match, contest, bout**
❹ *a fight with your girlfriend*
• **argument, quarrel, squabble, row, dispute**

A B C D E F G H I J K L M N O P Q R S T U V W X Y Z

5 *the fight to save the rainforest*
• **campaign, crusade, struggle, battle, effort**

fight VERB
1 *They were caught fighting in the playground.*
• **brawl, exchange blows, come to blows, scuffle, grapple, wrestle**
(*informal*) **scrap, have a punch-up**
2 *The boys were fighting over who should go first.*
• **argue, quarrel, squabble, row, bicker, wrangle**
3 *The two countries fought each other in the war.*
• **do battle with, wage war with, attack**
4 *Local people are fighting the decision to close the library.*
• **protest against, oppose, resist, challenge, contest, make a stand against, campaign against**

fighter NOUN
a guerrilla fighter
• **soldier, warrior, combatant**

fighting NOUN
soldiers killed during the fighting
• **combat, hostilities, war, battle, conflict**

figurative ADJECTIVE
the poet's use of figurative language
• **metaphorical, symbolic**
OPPOSITE literal

figure NOUN
1 *I'd better check these figures again.*
• **number, numeral, digit, integer**
2 *Can you put a figure on it?*
• **price, value, amount, sum, cost**
3 *See the figure on page 22.*
• **diagram, graph, illustration, drawing**
4 *Rose has a good figure.*
• **body, build, frame, shape, physique**
5 *an important figure in Irish history*
• **person, character, individual**
6 *a clay figure of a bison*
• **statue, carving, sculpture**

figure VERB
Wolves often figure in fairy tales.
• **appear, feature, be mentioned, be referred to, take part**

➤ **figure out**
I'm trying to figure out what it all means.
• **work out, make out, understand, comprehend, make sense of, see, grasp, fathom**
IDIOM **get to the bottom of**

file NOUN
1 *I keep my notes in a file.*
• **folder, binder, portfolio, wallet**
2 *The agency kept a secret file on her.*
• **dossier, report, record, archive**
3 *We followed her in single file.*
• **line, row, column, queue, string, chain, procession**

file VERB
1 *The cards are filed alphabetically.*
• **organize, arrange, categorize, classify, catalogue, store**
2 *We all filed out of the hall.*
• **walk in a line, march, troop, parade**
3 *She sat there filing her nails.*
• **smooth, grind down, rub down, rasp, hone**

fill VERB
1 *Dad filled the trolley with shopping.*
• **load, pack, stuff, cram, top up**
– To fill something with air is to **inflate** it.
OPPOSITE empty
2 *What can I use to fill this hole?*
• **close up, plug, seal, block up, stop up**
3 *The scent of roses filled the room.*
• **spread through, permeate, pervade, suffuse**
4 *Hundreds of protesters filled the streets.*
• **crowd, throng, cram, pack**
5 *That job has already been filled.*
• **take up, occupy**

filling NOUN
a sandwich filling
• **stuffing, insides, innards, contents, padding, wadding**

filling ADJECTIVE
That meal was very filling!
• **substantial, hearty, ample, heavy**

film NOUN
1 *the latest James Bond film*
• **movie, picture, video, DVD**

❷ *a career in film*
• cinema, movies
IDIOMS the big screen, the silver screen
❸ *a film of grease on the wall*
• coat, coating, layer, covering, sheet, skin

WORD WEB

Types of film:

- action picture
- animation
- (*informal*) biopic
- (*informal*) buddy movie
- (*informal*) chick flick
- costume drama
- disaster movie
- documentary
- epic
- feature film
- film noir
- horror film
- road movie
- (*informal*) romcom
- short
- silent film
- thriller
- (*informal*) weepie
- western

People involved in films:

- actor
- animator
- camera crew
- cast
- cinemato-grapher
- co-star
- director
- editor
- extras
- film crew
- film star
- film studio
- producer
- projectionist
- screenwriter
- sound engineer
- stunt artist
- voice coach

Other terms relating to film:

- 3-D
- adaptation
- CGI
- cinematography
- clip
- costumes
- credits
- cut
- dubbing
- editing
- fade-out
- film score
- flashback
- footage
- Hollywood
- IMAX
- leading role
- lighting
- montage
- nomination
- off-set
- on-set
- Oscar
- premiere
- release date
- remake
- rushes
- screenplay
- screen test
- script
- scene
- sequence
- slow motion (*informal* slo-mo)
- sound effects
- soundtrack
- special effects
- storyboard
- subtitles
- supporting role
- titles
- trailer
- voice-over
- wide-screen

filter *VERB*
❶ *The water must be filtered before drinking.*
• strain, sieve, sift, purify, refine
❷ *Rain began to filter through the roof.*
• pass, trickle, leak, seep, ooze, percolate

filth *NOUN*
The beach was covered in filth.
• dirt, grime, muck, mess, mud, sludge, scum, sewage, refuse

filthy *ADJECTIVE*
❶ *Those trainers are filthy!*
• dirty, mucky, messy, grimy, grubby, muddy, soiled, stained, unwashed
OPPOSITE clean
❷ *Don't drink the filthy water from the well.*
• impure, polluted, contaminated, foul
OPPOSITE pure
❸ *They were telling filthy jokes.*
• obscene, rude, dirty, vulgar, crude, bawdy, lewd

final *ADJECTIVE*
❶ *The final moments of the film were very tense.*
• last, closing, finishing, concluding, terminal
OPPOSITE opening
❷ *What was the final result?*
• eventual, ultimate
❸ *The judges' decision is final.*
• definite, conclusive, absolute, decisive

finally *ADVERB*
❶ *I've finally managed to finish my book.*
• eventually, at last, in the end
IDIOM at long last
❷ *Finally, I'd like to say a few words.*
• lastly, in conclusion

finance *NOUN*

❶ *He is an expert in finance.*
• financial affairs, money matters, economics, investment, commerce, banking, accounting

❷ *Our finances are in a good state.*
• money, bank account, funds, resources, assets, wealth

financial *ADJECTIVE*

She helps people with their financial affairs.
• monetary, money, economic, fiscal, commercial, banking

find *VERB*

❶ *Did you ever find your keys?*
• locate, spot, track down, trace, recover, retrieve, detect, identify
OPPOSITE lose

❷ *We found a perfect place for a picnic.*
• come across, discover, encounter, stumble on, unearth, uncover

❸ *You might find that you feel tired.*
• become aware, realize, learn, recognize, notice, observe

➤ **find out**
At last we will find out what happened.
• learn, discover, ascertain

findings *PLURAL NOUN*

the findings of the police investigation
• conclusions, judgement, verdict, decision

fine *ADJECTIVE*

❶ *a fine example of Dutch painting*
• excellent, first-class, superb, splendid, admirable, commendable, good
OPPOSITE bad

❷ *a day of fine weather*
• sunny, fair, dry, bright, clear, cloudless, pleasant
OPPOSITE dull

❸ *Spiders spin very fine thread for their webs.*
• delicate, fragile, thin, flimsy, slender, slim
OPPOSITE thick

❹ *a layer of fine sand*
• fine-grained, dusty, powdery
OPPOSITE coarse

❺ *I've had a cold but I'm feeling fine now.*
• well, healthy, all right, in good shape

❻ *That all sounds fine to me.*
• all right, acceptable, satisfactory (*informal*) OK

fine *NOUN*

a fine for speeding
• penalty, charge, damages

finger *NOUN*

She wore a gold ring on her finger.
• digit

WORD WEB

The fingers on a hand (in order):

➤ thumb
➤ index finger
➤ middle finger
➤ ring finger
➤ little finger (*Scottish & North American* pinkie)

finger *VERB*

The old man fingered his moustache nervously.
• touch, feel, handle, fondle, caress, play with, toy with

finicky *ADJECTIVE*

Cats can be finicky about their food.
• fussy, hard to please, particular (*informal*) choosy, picky

finish *VERB*

❶ *Have you finished your homework?*
• complete, reach the end of, accomplish, round off (*informal*) wrap up

❷ *I've already finished my bag of crisps.*
• consume, use up, get through, exhaust (*informal*) polish off

❸ *The film should finish around nine o'clock.*
• end, stop, conclude, come to a stop, cease, terminate (*informal*) wind up
OPPOSITES start, begin

finish *NOUN*

❶ *We watched the film until the finish.*
• **end, close, conclusion, completion, result, termination**
OPPOSITE start
❷ *furniture with a glossy finish*
• **surface, polish, shine, gloss, glaze, sheen, lustre**

fire *NOUN*

We warmed our hands in front of the fire.
• **blaze, flames, burning, combustion**
- A very big hot fire is an **inferno**.
- A great and destructive fire is a **conflagration**.
- An open fire out of doors is a **bonfire**.
➤ **catch fire**
The leaves caught fire quickly.
• **catch light, ignite, kindle**
IDIOMS **burst into flames, go up in smoke**
➤ **on fire**
The forest was soon on fire.
• **burning, flaming, blazing, alight, in flames, aflame, ablaze**
➤ **set fire to**
They tried to set fire to the school.
• **set alight, set on fire, ignite, kindle**
– The crime of deliberately setting fire to a building is **arson**.

fire *VERB*

❶ *The pots are fired to a red colour in the kiln.*
• **bake, harden, heat**
❷ *One of the guards fired a warning shot into the air.*
• **shoot, discharge, let off, set off**
– To fire a missile is to **launch** it.
❸ (*informal*) *He was fired for being late for work.*
• **dismiss**
(*informal*) **sack**
❹ *The story fired our imagination.*
• **excite, stimulate, stir up, arouse**

firm *ADJECTIVE*

❶ *The ground was firm underfoot.*
• **hard, solid, dense, compact, rigid, inflexible, unyielding, set**
OPPOSITE soft
❷ *She kept a firm grip on the reins.*
• **secure, tight, strong, stable, fixed, rooted, sturdy, steady**
❸ *He has a firm belief in ghosts.*
• **definite, certain, sure, decided, determined, resolute, unshakeable, unwavering, unswerving**
OPPOSITE unsure
❹ *The two girls became firm friends.*
• **close, devoted, faithful, loyal, constant, steadfast, long-standing**

firm *NOUN*

a family-run firm
• **company, business, establishment, organization, enterprise, corporation**

first *ADJECTIVE*

❶ *the first chapter of a book*
• **earliest, opening, introductory, preliminary**
– The first voyage of a ship is its **maiden** voyage.
❷ *The first thing to do in an emergency is to keep calm.*
• **foremost, principal, key, main, fundamental, chief, primary**
➤ **at first**
At first, no one spoke.
• **at the beginning, to start with, initially, originally**

first-class *ADJECTIVE*

He became a first-class detective.
• **excellent, first-rate, outstanding, superb, exceptional, superior, superlative, top-notch**
OPPOSITES second-rate, mediocre

fish *NOUN*

WORD WEB

Some common fish:

➤ bream
➤ catfish
➤ cod
➤ dogfish
➤ eel
➤ flounder
➤ haddock
➤ hake
➤ halibut
➤ herring
➤ mackerel
➤ marlin
➤ minnow
➤ monkfish

- ➤ mullet
- ➤ pike
- ➤ pilchard
- ➤ roach
- ➤ salmon
- ➤ sardine
- ➤ shark
- ➤ sole
- ➤ sprat
- ➤ stickleback
- ➤ stingray
- ➤ sturgeon
- ➤ swordfish
- ➤ trout
- ➤ tuna
- ➤ turbot
- ➤ whiting

- Fish that live mainly in the sea are **marine fish** and fish that live mainly in rivers are **freshwater fish**. A tiny freshwater fish is a **minnow**.

Parts of a fish:

- ➤ backbone
- ➤ belly
- ➤ fins
- ➤ gills
- ➤ lateral line
- ➤ scales
- ➤ swim bladder
- ➤ tail

For shellfish see **crustacean**.

fish *VERB*
She fished in her pocket and pulled out a photo.
• **rummage, search, delve, ferret**

fishing *NOUN*
a fishing trip
• **angling, trawling**

fit *ADJECTIVE*
❶ *It was a meal fit for a king.*
• **suitable, appropriate, fitting, right, good enough, worthy (of)**
OPPOSITE unsuitable
❷ *Dad goes to the gym to keep fit.*
• **healthy, well, strong, robust, in good shape, in trim**
(*old use*) **hale and hearty**
OPPOSITES unfit, unhealthy
❸ *The horses were exhausted and fit to collapse.*
• **ready, liable, likely, about**

fit *VERB*
❶ *We need to fit a new lock on the door.*
• **install, put in place, position, fix**
❷ *It takes a long time to fit all the pieces together.*
• **arrange, assemble, interlock, join**
❸ *He fits the description in the paper.*
• **match, correspond to, conform to, go together with, tally with**
IDIOM **fit the bill**
❹ *I chose a dress to fit the occasion.*
• **be suitable for, be appropriate to, suit**

fit *NOUN*
❶ *The two of us had a fit of the giggles.*
• **outburst, outbreak, bout, spell, attack**
❷ *an epileptic fit*
• **seizure, spasm, convulsion, attack**

fitful *ADJECTIVE*
periods of fitful sleep
• **sporadic, intermittent, irregular, spasmodic**
OPPOSITES regular, steady

fitting *ADJECTIVE*
a fitting end to the evening
• **suitable, appropriate, apt, proper**
OPPOSITE inappropriate

fix *VERB*
❶ *She fixed the sign to the front gate.*
• **fasten, attach, secure, connect, join, link**
❷ *Let's fix a time to meet.*
• **set, agree on, decide on, arrange, settle, determine**
❸ (*informal*) *Can you fix my laptop?*
• **repair, mend, sort, put right, restore**

fix *NOUN*
(*informal*) *You've got yourself into a real fix.*
• **difficulty, mess, predicament, plight, corner**
(*informal*) **jam, hole**

fixed *ADJECTIVE*
The date is fixed for next Tuesday.
• **set, arranged, decided, agreed, settled, confirmed, definite**

fizz *VERB*
Shake the bottle to make it fizz.
• **bubble, sparkle, effervesce, froth, foam, fizzle, hiss**

fizzy *ADJECTIVE*
a bottle of fizzy water
• **sparkling, bubbly, effervescent, gassy,**

frothy, carbonated
OPPOSITE still

flabbergasted *ADJECTIVE*
She just stood there, flabbergasted.
• **astonished, amazed, astounded, staggered, stunned, taken aback**
(*British informal*) **gobsmacked**

flabby *ADJECTIVE*
A flabby white arm was flung up over his face.
• **fat, fleshy, sagging, slack, loose, floppy, limp**
OPPOSITE firm

flag *NOUN*
the Olympic flag
• **banner, pennant, streamer**
- The flag of a regiment is its **colours** or **standard**.
- Strips of small flags hung up for decoration are called **bunting**.

flag *VERB*
❶ *My enthusiasm was beginning to flag.*
• **diminish, decrease, decline, lessen, fade, dwindle, wane**
❷ *The runners were flagging towards the finish.*
• **tire, weaken, wilt, droop**
OPPOSITE revive

flair *NOUN*
❶ *a flair for drawing cartoons*
• **talent, aptitude, skill, gift, knack**
❷ *She dresses with great flair.*
• **style, elegance, panache**

flake *NOUN*
a flake of plaster from the ceiling
• **sliver, shaving, wafer, fragment, chip**

flamboyant *ADJECTIVE*
a flamboyant style of dress
• **ostentatious, exuberant, showy, flashy, colourful**
OPPOSITES restrained, modest

flammable *ADJECTIVE*
made of flammable material
• **inflammable**
OPPOSITES non-flammable, fireproof, fire-resistant, fire-retardant

The words flammable and inflammable mean the same thing. They are not opposites of each other.

flap *VERB*
❶ *The sail flapped in the wind.*
• **flutter, sway, swing, wave about, thrash about**
❷ *a bat flapping its wings*
• **beat, flutter, thrash**

flare *VERB*
A match flared suddenly in the darkness.
• **blaze, burn, flash, flame**
➤ **flare up**
❶ *The rash tends to flare up at night.*
• **break out, erupt, burst out, blow up, reappear**
❷ *Elizabeth flared up at his words.*
• **lose your temper, fly into a rage, become angry**

flash *NOUN*
❶ *the flash of lightning*
• **blaze, flare, beam, burst, gleam, glint, flicker, glimmer, sparkle**
SEE ALSO **light**
❷ *an occasional flash of genius*
• **burst, outburst, show, display**

flash *VERB*
❶ *Two searchlights flashed across the sky.*
• **shine, blaze, flare, glare, gleam, beam, glint, flicker, glimmer, sparkle**
❷ *The train flashed past us.*
• **speed, fly, rush, hurtle**

flashy *ADJECTIVE*
Fraser was wearing a flashy tie.
• **showy, ostentatious, ornate, flamboyant, gaudy**
(*informal*) **snazzy, jazzy**
OPPOSITE plain

flat *ADJECTIVE*
❶ *You need a flat surface to write on.*
• **level, even, smooth, plane**
OPPOSITE uneven
❷ *lying flat on the ground*
• **horizontal, outstretched, spread out**
- To lie flat, face downwards, is to be **prone**.

A B C D E F G H I J K L M N O P Q R S T U V W X Y Z

– To lie flat, face upwards, is to be **supine**.

OPPOSITE upright

❸ *a flat tyre*

• **deflated, punctured, burst**

OPPOSITE inflated

❹ *a flat refusal*

• **outright, straight, direct, positive, absolute, definite, point-blank**

❺ *speaking in a flat tone*

• **monotonous, droning, lifeless, dull, tedious, boring**

OPPOSITE lively

flat *NOUN*

a two-bedroom flat in the city

• **apartment, rooms**

– A luxurious flat at the top of a building is a **penthouse**.

SEE ALSO **building**

flatten *VERB*

❶ *Flatten the dough with your hands.*

• **smooth, press, roll out, iron out**

❷ *The bombing flattened most of the city.*

• **demolish, destroy, knock down, pull down, level, raze**

❸ *a track where feet had flattened the grass*

• **squash, press down, compress, crush, trample**

flatter *VERB*

❶ *He was only trying to flatter you.*

• **compliment, praise, fawn on, toady**
(informal) **butter up**

❷ *I was flattered to be invited.*

• **honour, gratify, please**
(informal) **tickle pink**

flattery *NOUN*

Flattery never works on her.

• **compliments, praise, fawning, toadying**
(informal) **sweet talk**

flaunt *VERB*

celebrities flaunting their wealth

• **show off, display, parade, exhibit**

flavour *NOUN*

❶ *a strong flavour of garlic*

• **taste, tang, savour, smack**

❷ *a city with an East European flavour*

• **quality, style, character, feeling, feel, atmosphere, air, mood, ambience**

flavour *VERB*

The sauce was flavoured with garlic and herbs.

• **season, spice**

flaw *NOUN*

❶ *His only real flaw is vanity.*

• **weakness, fault, shortcoming, failing, weak point, Achilles' heel**

OPPOSITES strength, strong point

❷ *I can see a flaw in your argument.*

• **error, inaccuracy, mistake, slip**

❸ *There is a tiny flaw in the glass.*

• **imperfection, defect, blemish, chip, crack**

flawless *ADJECTIVE*

It was a flawless performance.

• **perfect, faultless, immaculate, impeccable, spotless**

OPPOSITES imperfect, flawed

fleck *NOUN*

There were a few flecks of paint on the carpet.

• **spot, speck, mark, dot, dab**

SEE ALSO **bit**

flee *VERB*

The crowd fled in panic.

• **run away, run off, bolt, fly, escape, get away, take off, hurry off**
(*informal*) **clear off, scram, scarper**

IDIOMS **take to your heels, beat a hasty retreat**

fleet *NOUN*

a fleet of sixty ships

– A fleet of boats or small ships is a **flotilla**.

– A fleet of warships is an **armada**.

– A military fleet belonging to a country is its **navy**.

fleeting *ADJECTIVE*

a fleeting glimpse of a deer

• **brief, momentary, quick, short, short-lived, cursory, passing, transient**

OPPOSITES lengthy, lasting

flesh *NOUN*
The knife slipped and cut into his flesh.
• **skin, tissue, muscle**

flew
past tense see **fly**

flex *VERB*
a weightlifter flexing his muscles
• **bend, contract, tighten**
OPPOSITE straighten

flex *NOUN*
a long flex for the computer
• **cable, lead, wire, cord**

flexible *ADJECTIVE*
❶ *a pair of trainers with flexible soles*
• **bendable, supple, pliable, bendy, elastic, springy**
OPPOSITES rigid, inflexible
❷ *flexible working hours*
• **adjustable, adaptable, variable, open**
OPPOSITES fixed, inflexible

flick *NOUN*
a quick flick of the wrist
• **swish, twitch, jerk, snap, flip**

flick *VERB*
❶ *a horse flicking its tail*
• **swish, twitch, jerk, whip**
❷ *flicking a light switch*
• **press, flip, throw, activate**
➤ **flick through**
flicking through a magazine
• **leaf through, thumb through, browse through, skim, scan**

flicker *VERB*
❶ *candles flickering in the draught*
• **glimmer, sparkle, twinkle, shimmer, flutter, blink, wink, dance**
SEE ALSO **light**
❷ *I thought I saw her eyelids flicker.*
• **flutter, quiver, tremble, twitch**

flight *NOUN*
❶ *a book about the history of flight*
• **flying, aviation, aeronautics, air travel**
❷ *the refugees' flight to safety*
• **escape, getaway, retreat, exodus**

flimsy *ADJECTIVE*
❶ *a flimsy ladder made of rotting wood*
• **fragile, delicate, frail, brittle, weak, wobbly, shaky, rickety**
OPPOSITES sturdy, robust
❷ *She wore a flimsy white gown.*
• **thin, fine, light, lightweight**
❸ *He listened to their flimsy excuses.*
• **weak, insubstantial, feeble, unconvincing, implausible**
OPPOSITES sound, substantial

flinch *VERB*
I flinched as a stone flew past my head.
• **back off, draw back, recoil, shrink back, start, wince**

fling *VERB*
I flung a stone into the pond.
• **throw, cast, sling, toss, hurl, heave, pitch, lob**
(*informal*) **chuck**

flip *VERB*
Flip the pancake to cook the other side.
• **toss, turn, turn over, flick, spin**

flippant *ADJECTIVE*
He made a flippant remark about the war.
• **frivolous, facetious, disrespectful, irreverent, cheeky**
OPPOSITE serious

float *VERB*
❶ *The raft floated gently down the river.*
• **sail, drift, bob, glide, slip, slide, waft**
❷ *I was floating around inside the spaceship.*
• **drift, bob, glide, waft, hover**

flock *NOUN*
❶ *a flock of geese*
see **bird**
❷ *a flock of sheep*
see **animal**

flock *VERB*
Fans flocked round the stage door.
• **crowd, gather, collect, congregate, assemble, mass, throng, swarm, herd, cluster**

a b c d e f g h i j k l m n o p q r s t u v w x y z

flog *VERB*
Slaves used to be flogged for running away.
• **whip, thrash, beat, lash, scourge, flay**

flood *NOUN*
❶ *The flood swept away several cars.*
• **deluge, inundation, torrent, spate**
❷ *We received a flood of emails.*
• **succession, barrage, storm, volley, rush, torrent, spate**
OPPOSITE trickle

flood *VERB*
❶ *The river burst its banks and flooded the village.*
• **inundate, swamp, drown, submerge, immerse, engulf, drench**
❷ *Shops have been flooded with cheap imports.*
• **saturate, swamp, overwhelm**

floor *NOUN*
❶ *a rug on the floor*
• **ground, flooring, base**
❷ *the top floor of the building*
• **storey, level, tier, deck, stage**

flop *VERB*
❶ *Fiona came in and flopped onto the sofa.*
• **collapse, drop, fall, slump, sink**
❷ *His red hair flopped over his eyes.*
• **dangle, droop, hang down, sag, wilt**
❸ *(informal) The first film flopped, but the sequel was a big hit.*
• **be unsuccessful, fail, founder, fall flat**

floppy *ADJECTIVE*
a rabbit with long, floppy ears
• **drooping, droopy, hanging, dangling, limp, saggy**
OPPOSITES stiff, rigid

flounder *VERB*
❶ *The horses were floundering in the mud.*
• **struggle, stumble, stagger, fumble, wallow**
❷ *I was floundering to answer the question.*
• **struggle, falter, hesitate, blunder**
IDIOM be out of your depth

flourish *VERB*
❶ *Our strawberries are flourishing this year.*
• **grow well, thrive, bloom, blossom, flower**
OPPOSITE die
❷ *Art and music flourished in this period.*
• **be successful, do well, prosper, thrive, boom, succeed, progress, develop, increase**
OPPOSITE fail
❸ *A man appeared, flourishing an umbrella.*
• **brandish, wield, wave, shake**

flout *VERB*
Players were accused of flouting the rules.
• **disobey, disregard, defy, ignore, breach, break, contravene, infringe, violate**

flow *VERB*
❶ *A river flowed through the forest.*
• **run, pour, stream, roll, course, circulate, sweep, swirl**
– To flow slowly is to **dribble**, **drip**, **ooze**, **seep** or **trickle**.
– To flow fast is to **cascade**, **gush** or **surge**.
– To flow with sudden force is to **spurt** or **squirt**.
– When the tide flows out, it **ebbs**.
❷ *Traffic was flowing in both directions.*
• **move, go, run, stream, rush**

flow *NOUN*
❶ *a steady flow of water*
• **stream, course, current, tide, drift, circulation, flood, gush, spate**
❷ *the constant flow of traffic*
• **movement, motion, stream, circulation, rush**

flower *NOUN*
a bunch of wild flowers
• **bloom, blossom, bud**

– A bunch of cut flowers is also called a **bouquet** or **posy**.

WORD WEB

Some common flowers:

- African violet
- anemone
- aster
- bluebell
- carnation
- chrysanthemum
- cornflower
- crocus
- daffodil
- dahlia
- daisy
- delphinium
- forget-me-not
- foxglove
- freesia
- fuchsia
- geranium
- gladiolus
- hyacinth
- iris
- lilac
- lily
- lupin
- marigold
- narcissus
- orchid
- pansy
- petunia
- phlox
- poinsettia
- primrose
- rose
- snapdragon
- snowdrop
- sunflower
- sweet pea
- tulip
- violet

- The scientific study of plants and flowers is **botany**.

- A person who sells or arranges cut flowers is a **florist**.

Parts of a flower:

- anthers
- filaments
- ovary
- ovules
- petals
- pistil
- sepals
- stamen
- stigma
- style

- The parts of the **stamen** are: **anthers** (containing **pollen**) and **filaments**.

- The parts of the **pistil** are: **stigma**, **style** and **ovary** (containing **ovules**).

SEE ALSO **plant**

flower *VERB*
Our snowdrops started to flower in January.
• **bloom, blossom, bud**

flowery *ADJECTIVE*
a flowery passage from the novel
• **ornate, elaborate, florid, fancy, purple**

fluctuate *VERB*
Prices have fluctuated in the past year.
• **vary, change, alter, shift, waver, rise and fall**

fluent *ADJECTIVE*
She is a fluent speaker on almost any topic.
• **articulate, eloquent, communicative**
OPPOSITES inarticulate, uncommunicative

fluffy *ADJECTIVE*
a fluffy scarf
• **feathery, downy, furry, fuzzy, hairy, shaggy**

fluid *NOUN*
Fluid was leaking from the engine.
• **liquid, solution, juice**
OPPOSITE solid

fluid *ADJECTIVE*
❶ *Try to keep the mixture fluid.*
• **liquid, free-flowing, runny, watery, molten, melted, liquefied**
OPPOSITE solid
❷ *In one fluid movement he drew out his sword.*
• **flowing, smooth, graceful**
❸ *Our holiday plans are still fluid.*
• **changeable, variable, flexible, open**
OPPOSITES fixed, firm

fluke *NOUN*
It was a fluke that the ball went into the net.
• **chance, accident, piece of luck, stroke of luck**

flurry *NOUN*
❶ *a flurry of snow*
• **swirl, whirl, gust**
❷ *a flurry of activity*
• **burst, outbreak, spurt, fit, bout, spell**

flush *VERB*
❶ *Toby flushed with embarrassment.*
• **blush, go red, colour, redden, glow, burn**

a b c d e f g h i j k l m n o p q r s t u v w x y z

A B C D E F G H I J K L M N O P Q R S T U V W X Y Z

❷ *The rain flushed away all the dirt.*
• **wash, rinse, sluice, swill**

flustered *ADJECTIVE*
She arrived late, looking flustered.
• **confused, upset, bothered, agitated, unsettled, unnerved, ruffled**
(*informal*) **rattled**
OPPOSITE calm

flutter *VERB*
❶ *A robin fluttered its wings.*
• **flap, beat, flicker, quiver, shake, tremble, vibrate**
❷ *Flags fluttered in the breeze.*
• **waver, flap, flit, ripple, ruffle, undulate**

fly *VERB*
❶ *Two eagles flew high above our heads.*
• **glide, soar, swoop, wheel, wing, flit, flutter, hover, float**
❷ *Suddenly the hawk flew into the air.*
• **rise, soar, ascend, take off**
❸ *Everyone was flying past us in a hurry.*
• **run, speed, rush, hurry, tear, zoom, hurtle**
❹ *The morning just seemed to fly.*
• **go quickly, pass quickly, rush by**

fly *NOUN*
see **insect**

foam *NOUN*
a layer of white foam
• **bubbles, froth, suds, lather**
- Foam made by sea water is **surf** or **spume**.

foam *VERB*
Water foamed around the rocks.
• **froth, bubble, seethe, boil, lather, fizz, ferment, effervesce**

focus *NOUN*
❶ *How do you adjust the focus on this camera?*
• **clarity, sharpness**
❷ *The new lion cubs were the focus of everyone's attention.*
• **centre, focal point, target, core, heart, nucleus, pivot, hub**

focus *VERB*
➤ **focus on**
I'm trying to focus on my work.
• **concentrate on, pay attention to, centre on, zero in on, spotlight, pinpoint**

fog *NOUN*
Fog was rolling in from the sea.
- Thin fog is **mist** or **haze**.
- A thick mixture of fog and smoke is **smog**.

foggy *ADJECTIVE*
❶ *a cold and foggy morning*
• **misty, hazy, murky, cloudy, smoggy**
❷ *a foggy memory of events*
• **blurred, fuzzy, dim, indistinct**

foil *VERB*
The robbery was foiled by French police.
• **thwart, frustrate, prevent, block, obstruct, stop, check**
(*informal*) **scupper**

fold *VERB*
Fold the paper along the dotted line.
• **bend, double over, crease, pleat**

fold *NOUN*
❶ *a fold in the centre of the map*
• **crease, pleat, furrow, tuck**
❷ *a sheep fold*
• **enclosure, pen**

folder *NOUN*
I keep all my art work in a folder.
• **file, binder, wallet, portfolio**

follow *VERB*
❶ *I think that car is following us.*
• **go after, chase, pursue, track, trail, tail, stalk, shadow**
❷ *Why does thunder always follow lightning?*
• **come after, succeed, replace**
OPPOSITE precede
❸ *Follow the directions on the map.*
• **carry out, comply with, heed, obey, observe, keep to, adhere to**
❹ *I like to follow current events.*
• **take an interest in, pay attention to, keep up with, support**

❺ *We couldn't follow what she was saying.*
• **understand, comprehend, grasp, take in, catch, fathom**
❻ *If you're all here, then it follows that your house is empty.*
• **mean, happen, result, ensue, arise, come about**

follower *NOUN*
Sir John had a small band of followers.
• **supporter, adherent, disciple, admirer**

following *ADJECTIVE*
the following day
• **next, succeeding, subsequent, ensuing**

folly *NOUN*
an act of sheer folly
• **foolishness, senselessness, stupidity, foolhardiness**

fond *ADJECTIVE*
❶ *a fond farewell*
• **loving, tender, affectionate, warm, caring**
❷ *a fond hope*
• **foolish, unrealistic, fanciful, vain, naive**
➤ **be fond of**
I'm very fond of blueberry muffins.
• **be keen on, be partial to, have a liking for, like, love**
IDIOM **have a soft spot for**

fondle *VERB*
She stooped down to fondle the kitten.
• **caress, stroke, nudge, pet, play with**

food *NOUN*
The table was laid out with all kinds of delicious food.
• **foodstuffs, refreshments, eatables, nourishment, nutrition, nutriment, sustenance, rations, provisions, victuals, fare**
(*informal*) **grub, nosh**
- The food you normally eat or choose to eat is your **diet**.
- Food for farm animals is **feed** or **fodder**.
For ways to prepare food see **cook**.
For tips on describing taste see **taste**.

fool *NOUN*
❶ *Only a fool would believe that story.*
• **idiot, ass, clown, halfwit, dunce, simpleton, blockhead, buffoon, dunderhead, imbecile, moron**
(*informal*) **chump, dope, dummy, dimwit, nitwit, nincompoop, ninny**
(*British informal*) **twit, clot, wally**
❷ *a medieval fool with cap and bells*
• **jester, clown**

fool *VERB*
Don't be fooled by her friendly smile.
• **deceive, trick, mislead, delude, dupe, hoodwink, hoax**
(*informal*) **con, kid, have on, take in**
IDIOMS **pull the wool over your eyes, take you for a ride**
➤ **fool about or around**
Stop fooling around and listen!
• **play about, mess about, misbehave**

foolish *ADJECTIVE*
It was a foolish idea.
• **stupid, silly, idiotic, senseless, ridiculous, nonsensical, unwise, ill-advised, half-witted, unintelligent, absurd, crazy, mad, hare-brained, foolhardy**
(*informal*) **dim-witted, dumb**
(*British informal*) **daft, barmy**
OPPOSITE sensible

foot *NOUN*
❶ *to put one foot in front of the other*
❷ *the foot of the page*
• **bottom, base**
OPPOSITES top, head, summit

WORD WEB

Parts of a foot:

➤ ankle	➤ instep
➤ arch	➤ sole
➤ ball	➤ toes
➤ heel	

Types of animal and bird feet:

➤ claw	➤ hoof

- pad
- paw
- talon
- trotter

football *NOUN*
a friendly game of football
• (*North American & Australian*) soccer

WORD WEB

Terms used in football:

- back of the net
- booking
- captain
- corner flag
- corner kick
- crossbar
- defender
- deflection
- dugout
- far post
- forward
- foul
- free kick
- fullback
- goalkeeper
- goal kick
- goal line
- goalpost
- halftime
- hat-trick
- header
- injury time
- kick-off
- linesman
- midfield
- near post
- offside
- penalty kick
- penalty shoot-out
- penalty spot
- pitch
- possession
- red card
- referee
- relegation
- sending off
- set play
- sideline
- stadium
- striker
- substitution
- suspension
- tackle
- throw-in
- yellow card

For tips on writing about sport see **sport**.

footprint *NOUN*
We followed the footprints in the snow.
• track, print, footmark
- The tracks left by an animal are also called a **spoor**.

footstep *NOUN*
the sound of footsteps
• step, tread, footfall

forbid *VERB*
I forbid you to see her again.
• prohibit, ban, bar, rule out, proscribe, veto, debar
OPPOSITES permit, allow

forbidden *ADJECTIVE*
Taking photographs is strictly forbidden.
• prohibited, banned, barred, outlawed, vetoed
OPPOSITES permitted, allowed

forbidding *ADJECTIVE*
The prison had a grim, forbidding look.
• threatening, menacing, sinister, grim, ominous, uninviting, daunting
OPPOSITE inviting

force *NOUN*
❶ *They had to use force to open the door.*
• strength, power, might, muscle, vigour, effort, energy
❷ *The force of the explosion broke all the windows.*
• impact, shock, intensity
❸ *an international peace-keeping force*
• group, unit, team, corps, body, squad

force *VERB*
❶ *They were forced to work for low wages.*
• compel, make, coerce, drive, impel, order, pressure into, bully into
❷ *I had to force my way through the crowd.*
• push, shove, drive, propel, press, thrust
❸ *Firefighters had to force the door.*
• break open, burst open, break down, kick in

forceful *ADJECTIVE*
❶ *a forceful personality*
• strong, powerful, dynamic, vigorous, assertive, pushy
(*informal*) in-your-face
OPPOSITES weak, submissive
❷ *a forceful argument*
• convincing, compelling, strong, powerful, persuasive
OPPOSITES weak, unconvincing

forecast *VERB*
Gales have been forecast for Tuesday.
• predict, foresee, foretell, prophesy

forecast *NOUN*
the weather forecast for tomorrow
• **outlook, prediction, prognosis, prophecy**

foreign *ADJECTIVE*
❶ *Every summer the town is full of foreign tourists.*
• **overseas, international, non-native**
OPPOSITES native, domestic
❷ *I like travelling to foreign countries.*
• **overseas, distant, faraway, exotic, remote, far-flung**
❸ *The idea of cooking is foreign to him.*
• **unnatural, unfamiliar, strange, alien**

foreigner *NOUN*
Many foreigners have come to live here.
• **overseas visitor, stranger, outsider, newcomer, incomer**
(*formal*) **alien**
– A foreigner who comes to live in a country is an **immigrant**.

foremost *ADJECTIVE*
He was one of the foremost artists of his day.
• **leading, greatest, best, pre-eminent, principal, premier, supreme, chief, top**

foresee *VERB*
She could foresee many problems ahead.
• **anticipate, expect, predict, forecast, prophesy, foretell**

forest *NOUN*
see **tree**

foretell *VERB*
The witches foretold that Macbeth would be king.
• **predict, prophesy, forecast, foresee**

forever *ADVERB*
❶ *Will you love me forever?*
• **for all time, for ever and ever, for good, for eternity, until the end of time, evermore**
❷ *Cal is forever complaining about something.*
• **constantly, continually, always, perpetually, incessantly, repeatedly, regularly**

forge *VERB*
❶ *Modern horseshoes are forged from steel.*
• **fashion, cast, hammer out, beat out**
❷ *That signature has been forged.*
• **fake, copy, counterfeit**
➤ **forge ahead**
The steamship was soon forging ahead.
• **advance, make progress, make headway**

forgery *NOUN*
One of these paintings is a forgery.
• **fake, copy, counterfeit, fraud, imitation, replica**
(*informal*) **phoney**

forget *VERB*
❶ *Did you forget your phone?*
• **leave behind, leave out, overlook**
❷ *I forgot to switch off the computer.*
• **omit, neglect, fail**
OPPOSITE remember

forgetful *ADJECTIVE*
He's getting forgetful in his old age.
• **absent-minded, dreamy, inattentive, careless, oblivious**

forgive *VERB*
❶ *She never forgave him for what he did.*
• **pardon, excuse, let off, absolve, exonerate**
❷ *Please forgive my rudeness.*
• **excuse, pardon, overlook, disregard, indulge, make allowances for**
IDIOM **turn a blind eye to**

fork *VERB*
The path ahead forks into two.
• **split, branch, divide, separate, diverge**

forlorn *ADJECTIVE*
She looked so forlorn.
• **sad, unhappy, miserable, sorrowful, dejected, wretched, downcast, crestfallen**
OPPOSITE cheerful

form *NOUN*
❶ *The stones are arranged in the form of a cross.*
• **shape, structure, design, outline,**

format, layout, formation, configuration, arrangement
❷ *She is good at drawing the human form.*
• body, figure, shape, frame, physique, anatomy
❸ *Haiku is a form of poetry.*
• kind, sort, type, variety, category, class, genre
❹ *Please fill in this form.*
• questionnaire, document, sheet, slip
❺ *Which form is your sister in?*
• class, year
(*North American*) grade

form *VERB*
❶ *The bat is formed from a single piece of wood.*
• shape, mould, model, fashion, build, fabricate, construct
❷ *We decided to form a book club.*
• set up, establish, found, create, start, institute, launch
❸ *Icicles had formed on the roof of the cave.*
• appear, develop, grow, emerge, materialize, take shape

formal *ADJECTIVE*
❶ *Dinner was to be a formal occasion.*
• ceremonious, ceremonial, official, grand, solemn
OPPOSITES informal, casual, unofficial
❷ *Her manner was always very formal.*
• correct, proper, dignified, reserved, stiff, cold, aloof
(*informal*) stand-offish
OPPOSITES informal, friendly, warm

formation *NOUN*
❶ *an unusual rock formation*
• structure, construction, configuration, arrangement, grouping, pattern
❷ *the formation of a new team*
• creation, establishment, setting up, foundation, institution

former *ADJECTIVE*
❶ *the former head of the FBI*
• previous, preceding, past, ex-, one-time
(*formal*) erstwhile
❷ *a photograph of the house in former times*
• earlier, past, previous, prior, bygone, olden, of old

formerly *ADVERB*
Machines were used to do the work formerly done by hand.
• previously, earlier, before, in the past, once, at one time, until now

formidable *ADJECTIVE*
We face a formidable challenge.
• daunting, intimidating, forbidding, difficult, tough, stiff

formula *NOUN*
a formula for making invisible ink
• recipe, prescription, procedure

fort *NOUN*
the remains of a Roman fort
• fortress, fortification, stronghold, castle, citadel, tower
SEE ALSO castle

forthcoming *ADJECTIVE*
a list of forthcoming events
• upcoming, future, approaching, impending, imminent

fortify *VERB*
❶ *The wall was built to fortify the old city.*
• defend, protect, secure, strengthen, reinforce
❷ *I felt fortified after breakfast.*
• invigorate, energize, enliven, strengthen, bolster, boost
OPPOSITE weaken

fortress *NOUN*
see fort

fortunate *ADJECTIVE*
We were fortunate to have good weather.
• lucky, in luck, favoured
OPPOSITES unfortunate, unlucky

fortunately *ADVERB*
Fortunately, no one was injured.
• luckily, happily, thankfully, mercifully,

by good fortune
IDIOM as luck would have it

fortune *NOUN*

❶ *She was hoping for a change in fortune.*
• **luck, fate, destiny**
❷ *By good fortune, I stumbled across a secret doorway.*
• **chance, luck, accident, providence**
❸ *The family had built up a vast fortune.*
• **wealth, riches, assets, possessions, property, estate**
(*informal*) **millions**

fortune-teller *NOUN*

A fortune-teller offered to read my palm.
• **soothsayer, clairvoyant, psychic, seer**

forward *ADJECTIVE*

❶ *a forward dive from a springboard*
• **front-facing, front, frontal, onward**
OPPOSITES backward, rear
❷ *We need to do some forward planning for the camping trip.*
• **advance, early, future**
OPPOSITE retrospective
❸ *Would it be too forward to ask him out?*
• **bold, cheeky, brash, familiar, impudent, presumptuous**
OPPOSITE shy

forwards or forward *ADVERB*

❶ *The queue moved forwards very slowly.*
• **on, onwards, along, ahead**
❷ *Can I have a seat facing forwards?*
• **to the front, towards the front, ahead**
OPPOSITES backwards, back

foster *VERB*

❶ *My aunt has fostered several children.*
• **bring up, rear, raise, care for, look after, take care of**
– To **adopt** a child is to make them legally a full member of your family.
❷ *Reading to young children can foster a long-lasting love of books.*
• **encourage, promote, nurture, stimulate, cultivate, develop**

fought

past tense see **fight**

foul *ADJECTIVE*

❶ *the foul smell of rotting food*
• **disgusting, revolting, repulsive, repugnant, offensive, loathsome, nasty, horrible, vile, stinking, sickening, nauseating**
(*informal*) **gross**
OPPOSITE pleasant
❷ *the foul state of the kitchen*
• **dirty, unclean, filthy, mucky, messy**
OPPOSITES clean, pure
❸ *The referee sent him off for using foul language.*
• **rude, offensive, improper, indecent, coarse, crude, vulgar, obscene**
❹ *That was a foul shot.*
• **illegal, prohibited, unfair**
OPPOSITE fair

found *VERB*

The society was founded a hundred years ago.
• **establish, set up, start, begin, create, initiate, institute**
OPPOSITE dissolve

foundation *NOUN*

❶ *There is no foundation for that rumour.*
• **basis, grounds, evidence, justification**
❷ *It's a hundred years since the foundation of the museum.*
• **founding, beginning, establishment, setting up, creation, institution**

founder *NOUN*

James Hutton was the founder of modern geology.
• **originator, creator, inventor, father, architect**

founder *VERB*

❶ *The ship had foundered on the rocks.*
• **go under, sink, submerge**
❷ *The project foundered because of lack of money.*
• **fail, fall through, collapse, come to nothing**
(*informal*) **fold, flop, bomb**

fountain *NOUN*
a fountain of water
• **jet, spout, spray, spring, cascade**

fox *NOUN*
the rare sight of an Arctic fox
– A female fox is a **vixen**.
– A young fox is a **cub**.
– The burrow of a fox is an **earth**.
For tips on describing animals see **animal**.

fox *VERB*
The last question foxed everyone.
• **puzzle, baffle, bewilder, mystify, perplex, stump**
(*informal*) **flummox, floor**

fraction *NOUN*
I only paid a fraction of the full price.
• **tiny part, fragment, scrap, snippet**
SEE ALSO **bit**

fracture *VERB*
Jo fell off her bike and fractured her wrist.
• **break, crack, split, splinter, snap**

fracture *NOUN*
The X-ray showed a bone fracture.
• **break, breakage, crack, split, fissure**

fragile *ADJECTIVE*
Reptile eggs are very fragile.
• **breakable, delicate, frail, brittle, flimsy, weak**
OPPOSITES sturdy, robust

fragment *NOUN*
❶ *a fragment of broken pottery*
• **bit, piece, chip, sliver, shard, splinter**
❷ *She overheard fragments of a conversation.*
• **part, portion, scrap, snippet, snatch**

fragrance *NOUN*
the heady fragrance of jasmine
• **scent, smell, aroma, perfume, bouquet**
For tips on describing smells see **smell**.

fragrant *ADJECTIVE*
The air was fragrant with spices.
• **sweet-smelling, perfumed, scented, aromatic**
OPPOSITES foul-smelling, smelly

frail *ADJECTIVE*
❶ *My grandad is still feeling frail after his illness.*
• **weak, infirm, feeble**
❷ *That footbridge looks a bit frail.*
• **flimsy, fragile, delicate, rickety, unsound**
OPPOSITES strong, robust

frame *NOUN*
❶ *a picture frame*
• **mount, mounting, surround, border, setting, edging**
❷ *the frame of an old bicycle*
• **framework, structure, shell, skeleton, casing**
– The framework under a car is the **chassis**.

framework *NOUN*
❶ *the wooden framework of the roof*
• **frame, structure, shell, skeleton, scaffolding, support**
❷ *a new framework for teaching*
• **plan, system, scheme, strategy, programme, blueprint**

frank *ADJECTIVE*
May I be frank with you?
• **direct, candid, plain, straight, straightforward, open, honest, sincere, genuine, forthright, blunt, matter-of-fact**
(*informal*) **upfront**
OPPOSITES insincere, evasive

frantic *ADJECTIVE*
❶ *His parents were going frantic with worry.*
• **beside yourself, fraught, desperate, distraught, overwrought, hysterical, worked up, berserk**
IDIOMS **at your wits' end, in a state**
❷ *It was a scene of frantic activity.*
• **excited, hectic, frenzied, frenetic, feverish, wild, mad**
OPPOSITE calm

fraud *NOUN*
❶ *She was found guilty of fraud.*
• **deceit, deception, dishonesty, cheating, swindling, sharp practice**

❷ *The phone-in competition was a fraud.*
• **swindle, trick, hoax, pretence, sham**
(*informal*) **con, scam**
❸ *The author was later exposed as a fraud.*
• **cheat, swindler, fraudster, trickster, charlatan**
(*informal*) **con man, con artist, phoney**

frayed *ADJECTIVE*
a frayed woollen carpet
• **tattered, ragged, worn, threadbare**
(*informal*) **tatty**

freak *NOUN*
❶ *a freak of nature*
• **oddity, aberration, abnormality, anomaly**
❷ (*informal*) *a health-food freak*
• **enthusiast, fan, fanatic, devotee**
(*informal*) **fiend, nut**

free *ADJECTIVE*
❶ *You are free to do as you wish.*
• **able, allowed, permitted, at liberty**
OPPOSITE restricted
❷ *All the hostages are now free.*
• **freed, liberated, released, emancipated, at large**
IDIOM **on the loose**
OPPOSITES imprisoned, captive
❸ *I got a free drink with my sandwich.*
• **complimentary, free of charge, gratis**
IDIOM **on the house**
❹ *The bathroom is free now.*
• **available, unoccupied, vacant, empty**
OPPOSITES occupied, engaged
❺ *Are you free this weekend?*
• **available, unoccupied, not busy**
OPPOSITES busy, occupied
❻ *He is very free with his money.*
• **generous, lavish, liberal**
OPPOSITE mean
➤ **free from or free of**
food which is free of additives
• **without, clear of, rid of, unaffected by**

free *VERB*
❶ *The hostages were eventually freed.*
• **release, liberate, set free, let go, set loose, untie**
– To free slaves is to **emancipate** them.
– To free hostages by paying money to the captors is to **ransom** them.
OPPOSITES imprison, confine
❷ *Rescuers freed the driver from the wreckage.*
• **extricate, undo, untangle, work loose**

freedom *NOUN*
❶ *The prisoners were finally given their freedom.*
• **liberty, liberation**
❷ *the freedom to decide for yourself*
• **right, power, entitlement, licence**

freely *ADVERB*
❶ *Elephants roam freely in the national park.*
• **unrestricted, unrestrained, free, at large**
❷ *He freely admits to taking bribes.*
• **readily, willingly, voluntarily, openly, frankly, candidly**

freeze *VERB*
❶ *Pure water begins to freeze at 0° C.*
• **become ice, ice over, harden, solidify**
OPPOSITE thaw
❷ *Vince froze when he heard the scream.*
• **stand still, remain stationary**
IDIOM **stop dead in your tracks**
❸ *Season-ticket prices have been frozen for another year.*
• **fix, hold, keep as they are**

freezing *ADJECTIVE*
❶ *a freezing winter's day*
• **chilly, frosty, icy, wintry, raw, bitter, arctic**
❷ *Your hands are freezing!*
• **frozen, chilled, numb with cold**
IDIOM **chilled to the bone**

frenzy *NOUN*
a frenzy of last-minute preparations
• **excitement, fever, madness, mania, hysteria, panic, fury**

frequent *ADJECTIVE*
❶ *We send frequent text messages to each other.*
• **numerous, continual, constant, recurring, recurrent, repeated**
OPPOSITE infrequent

a b c d e f g h i j k l m n o p q r s t u v w x y z

❷ *She is a frequent visitor to our house.*
• **regular, habitual, common, familiar, persistent**
OPPOSITE **rare**

frequent *VERB*
We frequent the same coffee shops.
• **visit, attend, spend time in, patronize, haunt**

frequently *ADVERB*
These two words are frequently confused.
• **often, continually, repeatedly, regularly, routinely, again and again**

fresh *ADJECTIVE*
❶ *The shop bakes fresh bread every day.*
• **new**
OPPOSITES **old, stale**
❷ *We are looking for fresh ideas.*
• **original, novel, new, different, innovative**
OPPOSITES **tired, stale**
❸ *a bowl of fresh fruit*
• **natural, raw, unprocessed**
OPPOSITES **preserved, processed, tinned**
❹ *Use a fresh sheet of paper.*
• **clean, unused**
OPPOSITE **used**
❺ *She went outside to get some fresh air.*
• **cool, crisp, refreshing, bracing**
OPPOSITE **stuffy**
❻ *You'll feel fresh in the morning.*
• **refreshed, revived, restored, invigorated**
OPPOSITES **tired, weary**

fret *VERB*
She's always fretting about her school work.
• **worry, be anxious, concern yourself, agonize, lose sleep, get worked up**

friction *NOUN*
❶ *Engine oil reduces friction.*
• **rubbing, chafing, abrasion, resistance, drag**
❷ *There was friction between the two teams.*
• **conflict, disagreement, discord, hostility, antagonism, animosity, acrimony, bad feeling**

friend *NOUN*
Helen is an old friend of mine.
• **companion, comrade, ally**
(*informal*) **pal, buddy, chum**
(*British informal*) **mate**
– A friend you know only slightly is an **acquaintance**.
OPPOSITE **enemy**

friendly *ADJECTIVE*
❶ *Everyone in our street is very friendly.*
• **amiable, amicable, neighbourly, genial, sociable, convivial, affable, likeable, good-natured, warm, kind-hearted, approachable, cordial, kindly**
(*informal*) **pally, chummy**
❷ *a cafe with a friendly atmosphere*
• **warm, welcoming, hospitable, cordial, informal**
OPPOSITES **unfriendly, hostile**

friendship *NOUN*
Their friendship has lasted for many years.
• **relationship, attachment, closeness, affection, fondness, familiarity, intimacy, bond, tie, fellowship, comradeship**
OPPOSITE **hostility**

fright *NOUN*
❶ *The children were speechless with fright.*
• **fear, terror, alarm, horror, panic, dread**
❷ *The explosion gave us all a fright.*
• **scare, shock, surprise, start, turn, jolt**

frighten *VERB*
Sorry, I didn't mean to frighten you.
• **scare, terrify, alarm, startle, shock, petrify, panic**
IDIOM (*informal*) **give you the creeps**

frightened *ADJECTIVE*
Were you frightened when the lights went out?
• **afraid, scared, terrified, alarmed, fearful, panicky, petrified**

frightening *ADJECTIVE*
The climb was a frightening experience.
• **terrifying, horrifying, alarming, nightmarish, hair-raising, fearsome** (*informal*) **scary**

frill *NOUN*
❶ *The dress has a lace frill.*
• **ruffle, ruff, flounce, fringe**
❷ *Our hotel was basic with no frills.*
• **extra, luxury**

fringe *NOUN*
❶ *a scarf with a beaded fringe*
• **border, edging, frill, trimming**
❷ *a region on the fringe of the solar system*
• **edge, border, margin, rim, perimeter, periphery, outskirts**

frisky *ADJECTIVE*
Our new kittens are very frisky.
• **playful, lively, high-spirited, sprightly**

fritter *VERB*
➤ **fritter away**
He frittered away all the money he had won.
• **waste, squander, use up, get through**

frivolous *ADJECTIVE*
Don't waste my time asking frivolous questions.
• **foolish, silly, ridiculous, trifling, trivial, shallow, superficial, petty**
OPPOSITES serious, weighty

frock *NOUN*
see **clothes**

frog *NOUN*

WORD WEB

The life cycle of a frog:

➤ **frogspawn** ➤ **tadpole**
- The process whereby a tadpole develops into a frog is **metamorphosis**.

SEE ALSO **amphibian**

frolic *VERB*
Lambs frolicked in the fields.
• **jump about, leap about, bound, caper, prance, gambol, romp, skip, play**

front *NOUN*
❶ *We stood at the front of the queue.*
• **head, start, beginning, lead, top**
❷ *The front of the house was painted white.*
• **face, facing, frontage, facade**
– The front of a ship is the **bow** or **prow**.
– The front of a picture is the **foreground**.
OPPOSITES back, rear
❸ *She managed to put on a brave front.*
• **appearance, act, show, exterior, face, facade**
➤ **in front**
the team in front at the half-way stage
• **ahead, in the lead, leading**

front *ADJECTIVE*
the front page of the newspaper
• **first, leading, lead, foremost**
– The front legs of an animal are its **forelegs** (opposite **hind legs**).
OPPOSITES back, rear

frontier *NOUN*
the frontier between France and Belgium
• **border, boundary, borderline, dividing line**

frosty *ADJECTIVE*
❶ *a clear and frosty morning*
• **cold, crisp, icy, freezing, wintry**
❷ *The assistant gave us a frosty stare.*
• **unfriendly, unwelcoming, cold, cool, stony**
OPPOSITES warm, friendly

froth *NOUN*
Would you like froth on your hot chocolate?
• **foam, bubbles, head**
– The froth on top of soapy water is **lather** or **suds**.
– Dirty froth is **scum**.

frown *VERB*
She frowned as she stared at the screen.
• **scowl, grimace, glower, glare**
IDIOMS **knit your brow, look daggers**

frown *NOUN*
Benny had a frown on his face.
• **scowl, grimace, glower, glare, black look**

frozen *ADJECTIVE*
My feet are frozen!
• **freezing, chilled, numb with cold**
IDIOMS **chilled to the bone, frozen solid**

frugal *ADJECTIVE*
1 *A frugal supper was laid out.*
• **meagre, paltry, plain, simple**
OPPOSITE lavish
2 *People had to be frugal during the war.*
• **thrifty, sparing, economical, prudent**
OPPOSITES wasteful, spendthrift

fruit *NOUN*

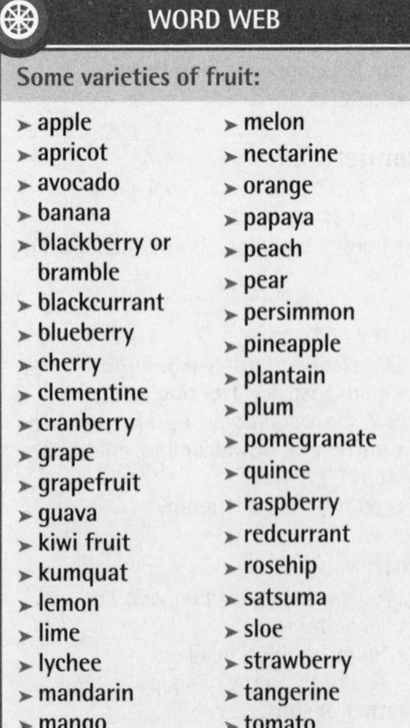

WORD WEB

Some varieties of fruit:

- apple
- apricot
- avocado
- banana
- blackberry or bramble
- blackcurrant
- blueberry
- cherry
- clementine
- cranberry
- grape
- grapefruit
- guava
- kiwi fruit
- kumquat
- lemon
- lime
- lychee
- mandarin
- mango
- melon
- nectarine
- orange
- papaya
- peach
- pear
- persimmon
- pineapple
- plantain
- plum
- pomegranate
- quince
- raspberry
- redcurrant
- rosehip
- satsuma
- sloe
- strawberry
- tangerine
- tomato

- Lemons, limes, oranges and grapefruit are **citrus fruits.**

Dried fruits:

- currant
- date
- prune
- raisin
- sultana

fruitful *ADJECTIVE*
Did you have a fruitful trip?
• **successful, productive, useful, worthwhile, profitable, rewarding**
OPPOSITE fruitless

fruitless *ADJECTIVE*
a fruitless search for clues
• **unsuccessful, unprofitable, unproductive, futile, pointless, useless, vain**
OPPOSITES fruitful, successful

frustrate *VERB*
1 *People were frustrated by the long wait.*
• **exasperate, discourage, dishearten, dispirit, irritate, infuriate**
2 *Our plans were frustrated by the weather.*
• **block, foil, thwart, defeat, hinder, prevent**

frustration *NOUN*
He banged the table in frustration.
• **exasperation, annoyance, irritation, vexation, dissatisfaction**

fry *VERB*
see **cook**

fuel *NOUN*

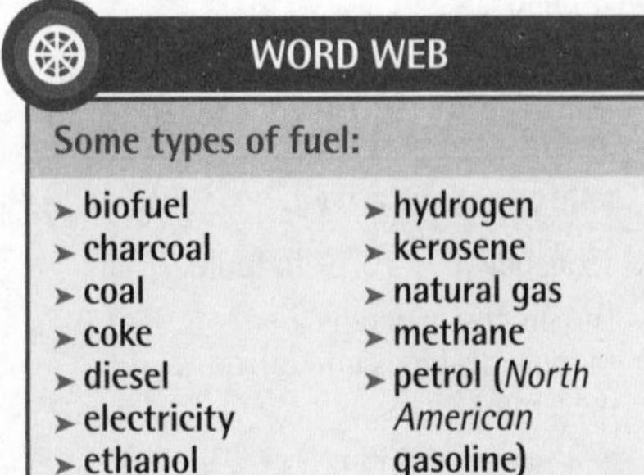

WORD WEB

Some types of fuel:

- biofuel
- charcoal
- coal
- coke
- diesel
- electricity
- ethanol
- hydrogen
- kerosene
- natural gas
- methane
- petrol (*North American* gasoline)

> ➤ petroleum or crude oil
> ➤ propane
> ➤ uranium
> ➤ wood
> - Coal, natural gas and petroleum are called **fossil fuels.**

fuel *VERB*
❶ *The rocket was fuelled by liquid hydrogen and oxygen.*
• **power, drive, fire, run**
❷ *The cinema fuelled his imagination.*
• **feed, stimulate, incite, provoke, intensify, fire, stoke, fan**

fugitive *NOUN*
Police are still searching for the fugitives.
• **runaway, escapee, outlaw, deserter**
– Someone who is a fugitive from war or persecution is a **refugee**.

fulfil *VERB*
❶ *She fulfilled her ambition to fly an aircraft.*
• **achieve, realize, accomplish, attain, carry out, complete, succeed in**
❷ *All contestants must fulfil these conditions.*
• **meet, satisfy, conform to, comply with**

full *ADJECTIVE*
❶ *My glass is already full.*
• **filled, loaded, packed, topped up, brimming**
OPPOSITE empty
❷ *The cinema is usually full on Saturdays.*
• **busy, crowded, jammed, packed, crammed, congested**
(*informal*) **jam-packed**
OPPOSITE empty
❸ *I can't eat any more—I'm full.*
• **replete, full up, sated, satiated**
(*informal*) **stuffed**
OPPOSITE hungry
❹ *You need to write a full account of what happened.*
• **complete, detailed, comprehensive, thorough, exhaustive, in-depth, unabridged**
OPPOSITES incomplete, partial, selective
❺ *They are working at full speed.*
• **top, maximum, greatest, highest**
OPPOSITE minimum
❻ *The dress has a very full skirt.*
• **wide, broad, loose-fitting, voluminous**
OPPOSITE tight

fully *ADVERB*
They were fully aware of the risks.
• **completely, totally, entirely, wholly, perfectly, quite**

fun *NOUN*
We had great fun playing in the attic.
• **amusement, enjoyment, pleasure, entertainment, recreation, diversion, merriment, sport, play, a good time**
➤ **make fun of**
Why do you always make fun of him?
• **jeer at, laugh at, mock, ridicule, taunt, tease**

function *NOUN*
❶ *Modern zoos have several functions.*
• **purpose, role, use, task, job, duty, responsibility**
❷ *The room is being used for a private function.*
• **event, occasion, party, reception**

function *VERB*
His heart isn't functioning properly.
• **work, go, operate, run, perform**

fund *NOUN*
a special emergency fund
• **collection, reserve, savings, pool, kitty**
➤ **funds**
The nature centre is running short of funds.
• **money, cash, savings, capital, reserves**

fund *VERB*
The website is funded entirely by donations.
• **finance, pay for, sponsor, subsidize, back**

fundamental *ADJECTIVE*
There are still some fundamental questions you haven't answered.
• **basic, elementary, essential, important, main, necessary, principal**

A B C D E F G H I J K L M N O P Q R S T U V W X Y Z

funeral *NOUN*
The service was followed by a private funeral.
• **burial, interment, entombment, cremation**

funny *ADJECTIVE*

OVERUSED WORD

❶ A funny joke, situation:

➤ amusing ➤ farcical
➤ humorous ➤ witty
➤ comic ➤ entertaining
➤ comical ➤ diverting
➤ hilarious ➤ droll

(*informal*) **hysterical, priceless, side-splitting, rib-tickling**

The best part of the film is the **hilarious** *car chase.*

OPPOSITES **serious, unfunny**

❷ A funny feeling, look:

➤ strange ➤ puzzling
➤ odd ➤ perplexing
➤ peculiar ➤ weird
➤ unusual ➤ bizarre
➤ curious

Being alone in the graveyard gave me a **peculiar** *feeling.*

❸ A funny taste, smell:

➤ strange ➤ puzzling
➤ odd ➤ perplexing
➤ peculiar ➤ weird
➤ unusual ➤ bizarre
➤ curious

The rattlesnake stew had a **curious** *flavour.*

fur *NOUN*
the fur of an arctic fox
• **hair, coat, hide, pelt**

furious *ADJECTIVE*
❶ *Tony was furious when he heard the news.*
• **angry, irate, enraged, infuriated, incensed, fuming, raging, seething, livid**
(*informal*) **mad**
❷ *We worked at a furious rate.*
• **frantic, hectic, frenzied, extreme, intense**
OPPOSITE **calm**

furniture *NOUN*

WORD WEB

Some items of furniture:

➤ armchair ➤ dresser
➤ bed ➤ dressing table
➤ bookcase ➤ filing cabinet
➤ bureau ➤ settee
➤ chair ➤ sideboard
➤ chest of drawers ➤ sofa
➤ coffee table ➤ sofa bed
➤ couch ➤ stool
➤ cupboard ➤ table
➤ desk ➤ wardrobe

- The soft covering on a chair or sofa is **upholstery.**
- Old and valuable pieces of furniture are **antiques.**

furrow *NOUN*
The tractor wheels had made deep furrows in the mud.
• **groove, rut, ditch, channel, trench**

furry *ADJECTIVE*
a small, furry creature
• **hairy, woolly, fleecy, fuzzy, fluffy, downy**

further *ADJECTIVE*
See our website for further information.
• **more, extra, additional, supplementary**

furtive *ADJECTIVE*
She cast a furtive glance backwards.
• **secretive, stealthy, surreptitious, conspiratorial, sneaky, sly, underhand**
IDIOM **cloak-and-dagger**
OPPOSITE **open**

fury *NOUN*
❶ *His eyes blazed with fury.*
• **anger, rage, wrath, indignation**

❷ *There was no shelter from the fury of the storm.*
• **ferocity, fierceness, intensity, severity, violence, turbulence, savagery**

fuse *VERB*
Two or more cells can be fused together.
• **merge, unite, join, combine, blend, melt**
– To fuse metals together when making or mending something is to **solder** or **weld** them.

fuss *NOUN*
You're making a fuss about nothing.
• **bother, commotion, excitement, trouble, hullabaloo, stir**
(*informal*) **to-do**
IDIOM **song and dance**

fuss *VERB*
I wish you'd stop fussing.
• **worry, fret, bother, get worked up**
IDIOMS (*informal*) **get in a flap, get in a tizzy**

fussy *ADJECTIVE*
❶ *Our cat is fussy about her food.*
• **finicky, hard to please, particular**
(*informal*) **choosy, picky, pernickety**
❷ *a carpet with a fussy design*
• **fancy, elaborate, busy, ornate, florid**

futile *ADJECTIVE*
He made a futile attempt to escape.
• **fruitless, pointless, unsuccessful, useless, ineffectual, vain, wasted**
OPPOSITES **successful, fruitful**

future *NOUN*
He has a bright future as an actor.
• **outlook, prospects**
OPPOSITE **past**

future *ADJECTIVE*
at a future date
• **later, following, ensuing, to come**
OPPOSITES **past, previous, earlier**

fuzzy *ADJECTIVE*
❶ *A fuzzy image appeared on the screen.*
• **blurred, bleary, unfocused, unclear, indistinct, hazy, cloudy**
OPPOSITE **clear**
❷ *a fuzzy ball of wool*
• **fluffy, frizzy, furry, woolly, fleecy**

Gg

gadget *NOUN*
a handy kitchen gadget
• **tool, instrument, implement, device, contraption**
(*informal*) **gizmo**

gain *VERB*
❶ *Samira gained a place at art college.*
• **get, acquire, obtain, achieve, attain, earn, win**
(*informal*) **land**
OPPOSITE lose
❷ *The car began to gain speed.*
• **increase, gather, pick up, build up**

game *NOUN*
❶ *an old-fashioned party game*
• **amusement, pastime, sport, activity, recreation**
❷ *Are you going to the game this Saturday?*
• **match, contest, competition, tournament, fixture, tie**

gang *NOUN*
❶ *a gang of bullies*
• **group, band, crowd, pack, set, mob**
❷ *a gang of builders*
• **team, unit, crew, squad, detachment, shift**

gaol *NOUN*
see **jail**

gap *NOUN*
❶ *We can go through that gap in the fence.*
• **opening, space, hole, aperture, break, breach, rift, crack**
❷ *She is back in the team after a gap of two years.*
• **break, interval, interruption, pause, lull**
❸ *The gap between rich and poor is widening.*
• **difference, disparity, separation, contrast, gulf, chasm**

gape *VERB*
Anne could only gape in surprise.
• **stare, be open-mouthed, gaze**
(*informal*) **gawp**

gaping *ADJECTIVE*
a gaping hole in the ground
• **wide, broad, yawning, vast, cavernous**

garden *NOUN*
a vegetable garden
• **plot, patch**
– A rented garden for growing vegetables is an **allotment**.
– A garden planted with trees is an **orchard**.
– A formal word for gardening is **horticulture** and a word meaning 'to do with gardens or gardening' is **horticultural**.

garment *NOUN*
see **clothes**

gas *NOUN*
The air we breathe is a mixture of gases.
• **vapour, fumes**

gash *NOUN*
a deep gash on my knee
• **cut, slash, slit, wound**

gasp *VERB*
At the end of the race we lay down, gasping for breath.
• **gulp, pant, puff, wheeze**

gate *NOUN*
Please enter by the main gate.
• **gateway, doorway, entrance, portal**

gather *VERB*
❶ *A crowd gathered to watch the fireworks.*
• **assemble, collect, come together, congregate, converge, rally**
OPPOSITE disperse
❷ *He gathered up all his papers.*
• **collect, assemble, bring together, round up, marshal**
❸ *We've been gathering sticks of wood.*
• **pick, pluck, collect, harvest**

❹ *I gather that you've been ill.*
• **understand, hear, learn, believe**

gathering *NOUN*
an annual family gathering
• **assembly, meeting, get-together, party, convention, crowd**

gaudy *ADJECTIVE*
The man on the TV was wearing a gaudy tie.
• **flashy, showy, loud, glaring, garish, lurid**
OPPOSITE subdued

gauge *VERB*
❶ *This instrument can gauge the temperature of the water.*
• **measure, calculate, work out, compute, determine, ascertain**
❷ *It was difficult to gauge the mood of the audience.*
• **judge, estimate, assess, reckon**

gaunt *ADJECTIVE*
an old woman with gaunt features
• **haggard, drawn, thin, skinny, scraggy, scrawny, wasted, skeletal**

gave
past tense see **give**

gaze *VERB*
He continued to gaze blankly out of the window.
• **stare, look, gape**

gear *NOUN*
(*informal*) *We put our camping gear in the back of the car.*
• **equipment, apparatus, materials, paraphernalia, tackle, kit**

gem *NOUN*
a silver casket studded with gems
• **jewel, gemstone, precious stone**

WORD WEB

Some common gemstones:

- agate
- amber
- amethyst
- aquamarine
- carnelian
- diamond
- emerald
- garnet
- jade
- jasper
- jet
- lapis lazuli
- malachite
- moonstone
- onyx
- opal
- pearl
- rose quartz
- ruby
- sapphire
- tiger's eye
- topaz
- tourmaline
- turquoise

general *ADJECTIVE*
❶ *There was a general feeling of relief.*
• **widespread, extensive, broad, sweeping, overall, prevalent**
IDIOM across the board
❷ *I've got a general idea of where we are.*
• **rough, approximate, vague, broad, loose, indefinite, imprecise**
OPPOSITES specific, detailed

generally *ADVERB*
❶ *I generally travel by bus.*
• **usually, normally, as a rule, chiefly, mostly, mainly, predominantly, on the whole**
❷ *He is generally considered to be the greatest player ever.*
• **widely, commonly, popularly, universally**

generate *VERB*
The website has generated a lot of interest.
• **create, produce, bring about, give rise to, prompt, stimulate, trigger, spark**

generous *ADJECTIVE*
❶ *He is always generous to his friends.*
• **unselfish, charitable, kind-hearted, magnanimous, giving**
OPPOSITES selfish, mean
❷ *We each got a generous portion of chips.*
• **ample, large, lavish, plentiful, abundant, copious**
OPPOSITE meagre

A B C D E F G H I J K L M N O P Q R S T U V W X Y Z

genial *ADJECTIVE*
He had a very pleasant, genial manner.
• **friendly, kind, warm, warm-hearted, kindly, good-natured, pleasant, agreeable, cordial, amiable, affable**
OPPOSITES unfriendly, cold

genius *NOUN*
Luke is a genius at maths.
• **expert, master, mastermind, wizard, ace, virtuoso, maestro**

gentle *ADJECTIVE*
❶ *She was shy and gentle by nature.*
• **kind, tender, good-tempered, humane, mild, placid**
OPPOSITES rough, harsh
❷ *Grasses swayed in the gentle breeze.*
• **light, slight, mild, soft, faint**
OPPOSITES strong, severe
❸ *There is a gentle slope down the hill.*
• **gradual, slight, easy**
OPPOSITE steep

genuine *ADJECTIVE*
❶ *a genuine diamond*
• **real, actual, true, authentic**
OPPOSITES fake, imitation
❷ *She seems like a very genuine person.*
• **honest, sincere, frank, earnest, natural, candid**
OPPOSITES false, insincere

gesture *NOUN*
The man raised his hands in a gesture of surrender.
• **sign, signal, motion, movement, indication**

gesture *VERB*
She gestured to us to keep quiet.
• **signal, indicate, motion, give a sign**

get *VERB*
❶ *Where did you get those trainers?*
• **acquire, obtain, come by, get hold of, buy, purchase**
❷ *She got an award for gymnastics.*
• **receive, be given, gain, earn, win, achieve**
❸ *It's starting to get dark outside.*
• **become, grow, turn, go**
❹ *What time did you get home?*
• **reach, arrive at, come to**
OPPOSITE leave
❺ *Could you get me a fork, please?*
• **bring, fetch, collect, pick up, retrieve**
❻ *You'll never get her to agree.*
• **persuade, urge, influence, coax**
❼ *We all got a stomach bug on holiday.*
• **catch, develop, contract, pick up** (*informal*) **go down with, come down with**
❽ (*informal*) *I don't get your point.*
• **understand, comprehend, follow, grasp, see**

➤ **get on or along**
❶ *How are you getting on with playing the guitar?*
• **manage, fare, cope, prosper, succeed**
❷ *We didn't get along at first.*
• **harmonize, gel, connect**
IDIOMS hit it off, see eye to eye

➤ **get out of**
I can't get out of going to the party.
• **avoid, evade, escape, dodge, shirk** (*informal*) **wriggle out of**

➤ **get over**
He never got over his disappointment.
• **recover from, get better from, shake off, survive**

➤ **have got to**
You've got to tell her the truth.
• **must, need to, should, ought to, be obliged to**

ghastly *ADJECTIVE*
The story is about a ghastly murder.
• **appalling, awful, dreadful, frightful, grim, grisly, horrible, horrifying, shocking, monstrous, terrible**

ghost *NOUN*
They say the house is haunted by ghosts.
• **spirit, spectre, phantom, ghoul, apparition, shade, wraith** (*informal*) **spook**
– A ghost or spirit that throws things about noisily is a **poltergeist**.
For tips on writing horror fiction see **horror**.

ghostly *ADJECTIVE*
the icy touch of a ghostly hand
• spectral, phantom, ghoulish, unearthly, eerie, sinister, uncanny
(*informal*) creepy, spooky

giant *NOUN*
Argus was a giant with a hundred eyes.
see **fantasy**

giant *ADJECTIVE*
the trunk of a giant redwood tree
• gigantic, huge, enormous, massive, immense, mammoth, colossal, mighty
OPPOSITES tiny, miniature
SEE ALSO **big**

giddy *ADJECTIVE*
I felt giddy when I looked down.
• dizzy, light-headed, faint, unsteady
(*informal*) woozy

gift *NOUN*
❶ *a birthday gift*
• present, offering
❷ *You have a real gift for drawing.*
• talent, ability, flair, knack, genius, aptitude, bent

gifted *ADJECTIVE*
He is a gifted pianist.
• talented, skilled, accomplished, capable, able, proficient, expert

gigantic *ADJECTIVE*
A gigantic wall surrounded the city.
• huge, giant, enormous, massive, colossal, immense, vast, mammoth, monumental, mountainous, gargantuan
(*informal*) whopping, humongous
OPPOSITES tiny, minuscule
SEE ALSO **big**

giggle *VERB*
I saw them whispering and giggling together.
• snigger, titter, chuckle, chortle, laugh

girl *NOUN*
a girl of thirteen or fourteen
• young woman, young lady, miss, lass
(*old use*) damsel, maid, maiden

give *VERB*
❶ *I gave her a brooch for her birthday.*
• present with, offer, supply with, issue with, hand over to, deliver to
❷ *We gave some money to the charity appeal.*
• contribute, donate, grant
❸ *He gave a loud yawn.*
• utter, emit, let out, produce, make
❹ *The band will be giving a free performance.*
• present, put on, lay on, organize, arrange, host, throw
❺ *The branch gave under their weight.*
• collapse, give way, bend, break, buckle
➤ **give in**
I'm not going to give in now!
• surrender, yield, submit, concede defeat
➤ **give up**
We gave up waiting for the bus.
• abandon, stop, cease, discontinue
(*informal*) quit

glad *ADJECTIVE*
I'm glad that you like your present.
• pleased, happy, delighted, thrilled
OPPOSITES sad, sorry
➤ **be glad of**
We'd be glad of your help.
• appreciate, be grateful for, value

glamorous *ADJECTIVE*
the glamorous life of a film star
• attractive, elegant, stylish, fashionable, chic, exotic, glittering
(*informal*) glitzy

glance *VERB*
❶ *Ravi glanced quickly at his watch.*
• look, peek, peep, glimpse
❷ *I glanced briefly through the papers.*
• browse, skim, scan, flick, leaf, thumb

glance *NOUN*
She gave a quick glance behind her.
• look, peek, peep, glimpse

glare *VERB*
❶ *She glared at him without speaking.*
• stare, frown, scowl, glower
IDIOM look daggers

a b c d e f g h i j k l m n o p q r s t u v w x y z

A B C D E F G H I J K L M N O P Q R S T U V W X Y Z

❷ *A bright light glared in my face.*
• **dazzle, blaze, shine, flash**

glare *NOUN*
❶ *the glare of the headlights*
• **dazzle, blaze, brightness, brilliance**
❷ *The manager gave us an angry glare.*
• **stare, scowl, glower, frown, black look**

glaring *ADJECTIVE*
There were a few glaring errors.
• **obvious, conspicuous, noticeable, unmistakable, unmissable, striking, blatant**

glasses *PLURAL NOUN*
She put on her glasses to read the letter.
• **spectacles**
(*informal*) **specs**

gleam *NOUN*
a gleam of moonlight
• **glimmer, glint, flash, ray, shaft**

gleam *VERB*
Lights gleamed on the water.
• **glimmer, glint, glisten, shimmer, shine**

glide *VERB*
The balloon glided gently over the treetops.
• **slide, slip, drift, float, coast**

glimmer *VERB*
The city lights glimmered in the distance.
• **gleam, glint, glow, glisten, shimmer, flicker, blink**

glimpse *NOUN*
We caught a glimpse of a dolphin's tail.
• **peek, peep, glance, sighting, view**

glimpse *VERB*
I glimpsed a deer running through the forest.
• **catch sight of, spot, spy, sight**

glint *VERB*
Sunlight glinted off the windows.
• **flash, glitter, sparkle, twinkle**

glisten *VERB*
The pavement glistened with frost.
• **gleam, shine, glint, shimmer, glimmer**

glitter *VERB*
The jewels glittered under the lights.
• **sparkle, twinkle, shimmer, glimmer, glint, glisten, flash, shine**

gloat *VERB*
They were still gloating about the score.
• **boast, brag, crow, show off**

global *ADJECTIVE*
The Internet is a global network of computers.
• **worldwide, international, universal**
OPPOSITE local

globe *NOUN*
❶ *She has travelled all over the globe.*
• **world, planet, earth**
❷ *The fortune teller stared into a crystal globe.*
• **ball, sphere, orb**

gloom *NOUN*
❶ *We could hardly see in the gloom of the cave.*
• **darkness, dimness, shade, shadow, murk**
– The dim light of the evening is **dusk** or **twilight**.
❷ *A feeling of gloom descended on me.*
• **depression, sadness, unhappiness, melancholy, misery, despair, dejection, woe**

gloomy *ADJECTIVE*
❶ *It was cold and gloomy in the cellar.*
• **dark, dingy, dim, shadowy, murky, dismal, dreary, sombre, cheerless**
OPPOSITE bright
❷ *I stayed in bed feeling gloomy.*
• **depressed, sad, unhappy, glum, miserable, melancholy, low, down, downcast, dejected, despondent, crestfallen**
(*informal*) **fed up**
IDIOMS (*informal*) **down in the dumps, down in the mouth**
OPPOSITE cheerful

glorious *ADJECTIVE*
the sight of a glorious sunset
• **magnificent, splendid, stunning,**

spectacular, superb, magnificent, wonderful, marvellous

glossy *ADJECTIVE*
a cat with a glossy coat
• **shiny, shining, gleaming, lustrous, sleek, silky, polished**
OPPOSITE **dull**

glove *NOUN*
a pair of sheepskin gloves
– Gloves without separate parts for the fingers are **mittens**.
– A glove with a wide cuff covering the wrist is a **gauntlet**.
SEE ALSO **clothes**

glow *NOUN*
The soft glow of candlelight lit the room.
• **shine, gleam, radiance, glimmer**

glow *VERB*
A flying saucer glowed in the night sky.
• **shine, gleam, glimmer, beam, burn, flare**
– Something that glows in the dark is **luminous** or **phosphorescent**.

glower *VERB*
The two men glowered at each other.
• **glare, scowl, frown, stare angrily**
IDIOM **look daggers**

glue *NOUN*
a tube of glue
• **adhesive, paste, gum**

glue *VERB*
Glue the edges together.
• **stick, paste, bond, seal**

glum *ADJECTIVE*
Why are you looking so glum?
• **depressed, sad, unhappy, gloomy, miserable, melancholy, low, down, downcast, dejected, despondent, crestfallen**
(*informal*) **fed up**
IDIOM (*informal*) **down in the dumps**
OPPOSITE **cheerful**

gnarled *ADJECTIVE*
a gnarled tree trunk
• **bent, twisted, crooked, distorted, knobbly, knotty**

gnaw *VERB*
A dog was gnawing at a bone.
• **chew, bite, nibble, munch**

go *VERB*
❶ *Our bus went slowly up the hill.*
• **move, progress, proceed, advance, make your way**
SEE ALSO **move**
❷ *Are you going into town today?*
• **travel, journey**
❸ *Some of the guests had already gone.*
• **leave, depart, set off, withdraw**
❹ *A path goes all the way to the summit.*
• **extend, lead, reach, stretch, run**
❺ *My fingers went blue with cold.*
• **become, turn, grow**
❻ *The cups go on the top shelf.*
• **belong, be kept, be placed**
(*informal*) **live**
❼ *By morning, all the snow had gone.*
• **disappear, vanish**
❽ *All the money has gone.*
• **be used up, be spent**
❾ *Is that old clock still going?*
• **function, operate, work, run**
❿ *The morning went quickly.*
• **pass, go by, elapse**

➤ **go back**
Let's go back to the house.
• **return, retreat, retrace your steps**

➤ **go in for**
Are you going in for the race this year?
• **enter, take part in, participate in**

➤ **go off**
❶ *A firework went off by mistake.*
• **explode, blow up, detonate**
❷ *This milk has gone off.*
• **go bad, turn sour, spoil, rot**

➤ **go on**
❶ *What's going on over there?*
• **happen, occur, take place**
❷ *Please go on with your story.*
• **carry on, continue, keep going, proceed**

A B C D E F G H I J K L M N O P Q R S T U V W X Y Z

➤ **go through**
The family were going through a hard time.
• **experience, undergo, face, suffer, endure**

➤ **go with**
Do these shoes go with my dress?
• **match, suit, blend with**

go *NOUN*
Can I have a go on your tablet?
• **turn, try, chance, opportunity, spell, stint**
(*informal*) **shot, bash, stab**

goal *NOUN*
The goal of the society is to protect wildlife.
• **aim, objective, purpose, object, end, target, ambition, intention**

god, goddess *NOUN*
the gods of ancient Greece
• **deity, divine being, immortal**
– A word meaning 'to do with a god or goddess' is **divine**.

golden *ADJECTIVE*
❶ *a golden helmet*
• **gold**
– Something that is covered with a thin layer of gold is **gilded** or **gilt**.
❷ *golden hair*
• **fair, blonde, yellow**

good *ADJECTIVE*
That's a really good idea!
• **excellent, fine, lovely, nice, wonderful**
(*informal*) **fantastic, great, super, cool**
OPPOSITES bad, poor, awful

OVERUSED WORD

❶ A good person, good deed:

➤ honest ➤ noble
➤ worthy ➤ kind
➤ honourable ➤ humane
➤ moral ➤ charitable
➤ decent ➤ merciful
➤ virtuous

Sir Lancelot is portrayed as an **honourable** *knight.*

OPPOSITES wicked, evil

❷ Good behaviour:

➤ well-behaved ➤ exemplary
➤ obedient ➤ angelic

The kittens are **well-behaved.**

OPPOSITES naughty, disobedient

❸ A good friend:

➤ true ➤ reliable
➤ loyal ➤ trusty
➤ loving ➤ trustworthy

You have always been a **true** *friend to me.*

❹ A good experience, good news:

➤ pleasant ➤ agreeable
➤ enjoyable ➤ pleasing
➤ delightful

I found the book more **enjoyable** *than the film.*

OPPOSITES unpleasant, disagreeable

❺ Good food, a good meal:

➤ delicious ➤ appetizing
➤ healthy ➤ well-cooked
➤ nourishing ➤ wholesome
➤ nutritious ➤ substantial
➤ tasty ➤ hearty

The crew ate a **hearty** *breakfast.*

❻ Good weather:

➤ fine ➤ favourable
➤ fair

We are hoping for **fine** *weather tomorrow.*

OPPOSITES harsh, adverse

❼ A good feeling, good mood:

➤ happy ➤ contented
➤ cheerful ➤ good-humoured
➤ light-hearted ➤ buoyant
➤ positive

(*informal*) **chirpy**

Ali began the day in a **buoyant** *mood.*

8 A good performer, good work:

- capable
- skilled
- talented
- able
- competent
- commendable
- sound

My grandmother was a **talented** *painter.*

OPPOSITES poor, awful

9 Good grammar, good spelling:

- accurate
- correct
- exact
- proper

Can you translate this into **correct** *French?*

OPPOSITES poor, awful

10 Good timing, a good moment:

- convenient
- suitable
- fortunate
- appropriate
- opportune

Is this a **convenient** *time for a chat?*

OPPOSITES inconvenient, unsuitable

11 A good excuse, good reason:

- acceptable
- valid
- satisfactory
- proper
- legitimate
- strong
- convincing

That is not a **valid** *excuse for being late.*

OPPOSITES poor, unacceptable

12 A good look, good clean:

- thorough
- comprehensive
- rigorous
- careful
- complete
- full

My locker needs a **thorough** *clean-out!*

OPPOSITES rough, superficial

13 Something that is good for you:

- beneficial
- advantageous
- helpful
- valuable
- rewarding
- health-giving

Eating garlic is **beneficial** *for your heart.*

OPPOSITES harmful, detrimental

goodbye *NOUN*
It was time to say goodbye.
• **farewell**
(*informal*) **cheerio, bye, bye bye, so long, see you**

good-looking *ADJECTIVE*
I think your cousin is quite good-looking.
• **attractive, handsome, pretty**
OPPOSITE ugly

goods *PLURAL NOUN*
The smugglers hid the stolen goods in a cave.
• **property, merchandise, wares, articles, produce, cargo**

gorgeous *ADJECTIVE*
a gorgeous sunset
• **beautiful, glorious, dazzling, stunning, splendid, superb, attractive, glamorous, handsome**
SEE ALSO **beautiful**

gossip *VERB*
Those two are always gossiping.
• **chatter, tell tales**
(*informal*) **natter**

gossip *NOUN*
1 *I want to hear all the gossip.*
• **chatter, rumour, hearsay, scandal**
(*informal*) **tittle-tattle**
2 *She is a dreadful gossip.*
• **busybody, chatterbox, telltale, scandalmonger**

gouge *VERB*
Glaciers gouged out valleys from the hills.
• **dig, hollow out, scoop out, excavate**

govern *VERB*
The ancient Romans governed a vast empire.
• **rule, run, administer, direct, command, manage, oversee, be in charge of**

gown *NOUN*
a silk evening gown
• **dress, frock, robe**

A B C D E F G H I J K L M N O P Q R S T U V W X Y Z

grab *VERB*
She reached out and grabbed my hand.
• seize, grasp, catch, clutch, grip, get hold of, snatch

graceful *ADJECTIVE*
the graceful stride of a gazelle
• elegant, flowing, stylish, smooth, agile, nimble, fluid
OPPOSITES clumsy, graceless

gracious *ADJECTIVE*
Thank you for being such a gracious host.
• polite, courteous, good-natured, pleasant, agreeable, civil

grade *NOUN*
A black belt is the highest grade in judo.
• class, standard, level, stage, rank, degree

grade *VERB*
Eggs are graded according to size.
• classify, class, categorize, arrange, group, sort, rank

gradual *ADJECTIVE*
There's been a gradual change in the weather.
• steady, slow, gentle, moderate, unhurried, regular, even
OPPOSITES sudden, abrupt

gradually *ADVERB*
Add the water gradually to the mixture.
• steadily, slowly, gently, bit by bit, little by little
OPPOSITES suddenly, all at once

grain *NOUN*
❶ *a field of grain*
• cereal, corn
❷ *a few grains of sand*
• bit, particle, speck, granule

grand *ADJECTIVE*
❶ *Their wedding was a grand occasion.*
• magnificent, splendid, stately, impressive, big, great, important, imposing
❷ (*informal*) *Keep going—you're doing a grand job!*
• excellent, fine, good, splendid, first-class

grant *VERB*
❶ *We have decided to grant your request.*
• give, allow, permit, award
❷ *I grant that I'm no expert.*
• admit, accept, acknowledge, confess, recognize

graphic *ADJECTIVE*
a graphic description of war
• detailed, explicit, vivid, striking, colourful, realistic

grapple *VERB*
The guards grappled the man to the ground.
• wrestle, struggle, tussle, scuffle
➤ **grapple with**
I have lots of homework to grapple with.
• tackle, deal with, confront, face
IDIOM get to grips with

grasp *VERB*
❶ *He managed to grasp the end of the rope.*
• clutch, grab, grip, seize, catch, snatch, take hold of, hang on to
❷ *The idea of infinity is difficult to grasp.*
• understand, comprehend, follow, take in
IDIOM take on board

grasp *NOUN*
❶ *You will need a good grasp of German.*
• understanding, comprehension, knowledge, mastery, command
❷ *She broke free from the creature's grasp.*
• hold, grip, clutch

grass *NOUN*
Please keep off the grass.
• lawn, turf, green

grate *VERB*
❶ *I grated some cheese onto the pizza.*
• shred, grind, mince

❷ *The keel of the boat grated on the sand.*
• scrape, scratch, rasp
➤ **grate on**
His voice grates on my nerves.
• annoy, irritate, jar on

grateful *ADJECTIVE*
I was grateful for their help.
• thankful, appreciative, obliged, indebted
OPPOSITE ungrateful

gratitude *NOUN*
We sent some flowers to show our gratitude.
• thanks, appreciation

grave *ADJECTIVE*
❶ *She told him he was in grave danger.*
• serious, important, profound, weighty, significant, terrible, dire
OPPOSITE trivial
❷ *He turned to me with a grave expression.*
• solemn, serious, grim, sombre, dour, heavy-hearted
OPPOSITE cheerful

grave *NOUN*
see **tomb**

graveyard *NOUN*
Some famous people are buried in the graveyard.
• burial ground, cemetery, churchyard

graze *VERB*
I grazed my knee when I fell off my bike.
• scrape, scratch, skin, scuff, chafe, cut

greasy *ADJECTIVE*
a plate of greasy food
• fatty, oily

great *ADJECTIVE*
❶ *Theirs is a story of great courage.*
• considerable, exceptional, outstanding, extraordinary, prodigious, tremendous, extreme
OPPOSITE little
❷ *Mozart was a great composer.*
• famous, notable, celebrated, eminent, distinguished, important, outstanding, major, leading, prominent
OPPOSITES insignificant, minor
❸ *A great canyon stretched before us.*
• large, huge, big, enormous, immense, gigantic, colossal, mighty, vast, extensive
OPPOSITE small
❹ (*informal*) *The food was great!*
• excellent, marvellous, outstanding, superb, tremendous, wonderful, enjoyable
(*informal*) brilliant, fantastic, super, smashing, terrific, fabulous
OPPOSITES bad, awful

greed *NOUN*
Midas was driven by his greed for gold.
• avarice, covetousness, acquisitiveness, hunger, craving, gluttony

greedy *ADJECTIVE*
❶ *Don't be greedy—leave some food for me!*
• gluttonous
(*informal*) piggish
❷ *a story about a greedy landowner*
• grasping, covetous, avaricious
(*informal*) money-grubbing

green *ADJECTIVE*
an awareness of green issues
• environmental, ecological, conservation, eco-
SEE ALSO **environment**

green *ADJECTIVE & NOUN*

WORD WEB

Some shades of green:

➤ emerald	➤ mint
➤ jade	➤ olive
➤ khaki	➤ pea-green
➤ lime	➤ sea-green

For tips on describing colours see **colour**.

greet *VERB*
She greeted us with a friendly wave.
• welcome, hail, receive, salute

A B C D E F G H I J K L M N O P Q R S T U V W X Y Z

grew
past tense see **grow**

grey *ADJECTIVE*
❶ *His grey beard had grown very long.*
• **silver, silvery, grizzly, hoary, whitish**
❷ *Her face was grey with worry.*
• **pale, pallid, pasty, ashen, wan**
❸ *The day began cold and grey.*
• **dull, cloudy, overcast, murky**

grief *NOUN*
Juliet is overcome with grief at Romeo's death.
• **sorrow, mourning, sadness, unhappiness, distress, anguish, heartache, heartbreak, woe**
OPPOSITE joy

grieve *VERB*
❶ *The family is still grieving over their loss.*
• **mourn, lament, sorrow, weep**
OPPOSITE rejoice
❷ *It grieves me to tell you this.*
• **sadden, upset, distress, hurt, pain, wound**
OPPOSITE please

grim *ADJECTIVE*
❶ *The judge wore a grim expression on his face.*
• **stern, severe, harsh, bad-tempered, sullen**
OPPOSITE cheerful
❷ *the grim details of the murder*
• **unpleasant, horrible, dreadful, terrible, hideous, shocking, gruesome, grisly**
OPPOSITE pleasant

grime *NOUN*
The floor was covered with grime.
• **dirt, filth, muck, mire, mess**

grimy *ADJECTIVE*
a grimy pair of overalls
• **dirty, filthy, grubby, mucky, soiled**
OPPOSITE clean

grin *NOUN & VERB*
Everyone is grinning in the photograph.
• **smile, beam, smirk**
– A large grin is a **broad, wide** or **cheesy** grin.

grind *VERB*
❶ *Grind the spices into a fine powder.*
• **crush, pound, powder, pulverize, mill**
❷ *This tool is for grinding knives.*
• **sharpen, file, hone, whet**

grip *VERB*
❶ *Grip the handle tightly.*
• **grasp, seize, clutch, clasp, hold**
❷ *I was gripped by the last chapter.*
• **fascinate, engross, enthral, absorb, captivate, rivet**

grip *NOUN*
❶ *She kept a tight grip on my hand.*
• **hold, grasp, clasp, clutch**
❷ *People on the streets were in the grip of panic.*
• **power, control, influence, clutches**

grisly *ADJECTIVE*
the grisly discovery of a human skull
• **gruesome, gory, ghastly, hideous, nasty, revolting, sickening**

grit *NOUN*
❶ *I've got a piece of grit in my shoe.*
• **gravel, dust, sand**
❷ *The contestants showed grit and stamina.*
• **bravery, courage, toughness, spirit, pluck**
(*informal*) **guts**

groan *VERB*
The wounded soldier was groaning with pain.
• **cry, moan, sigh, wail**

groove *NOUN*
The skates cut grooves in the ice.
• **channel, furrow, trench, rut, scratch**

grope *VERB*
I groped in the dark for the light switch.
• **fumble, feel about, flounder, scrabble**

gross *ADJECTIVE*
❶ *That is a gross exaggeration!*
• **extreme, glaring, obvious, sheer, blatant, outright**

❷ *I was shocked by their gross behaviour.*
• **offensive, rude, coarse, vulgar**
❸ (*informal*) *Sweaty feet smell gross!*
• **disgusting, repulsive, revolting, foul, obnoxious, sickening**

ground *NOUN*
❶ *We planted some seeds in the ground.*
• **earth, soil, land**
❷ *a football ground*
• **field, pitch, park, stadium, arena**
❸ *Both books cover the same ground.*
• **subject, topic, material, matter**

grounds *PLURAL NOUN*
❶ *a country house with extensive grounds*
• **gardens, estate, park, land**
❷ *There are grounds for suspicion.*
• **reason, basis, justification, cause, argument, excuse**

group *NOUN*
❶ *Japan consists of a group of islands.*
• **collection, set, batch, cluster, clump**
❷ *A group of fans was waiting outside.*
• **crowd, gathering, band, body, gang** (*informal*) **bunch**
❸ *The book group meets once a month.*
• **club, society, association, circle**
❹ *We sorted the fossils into different groups.*
• **category, class, type, kind, sort**
❺ For collective nouns see **collective**.

group *VERB*
Entries are grouped according to age.
• **categorize, classify, class, organize, arrange, sort, range**

grow *VERB*
❶ *I've grown an inch taller since last summer.*
• **get bigger, put on growth, spring up, shoot up, sprout**
❷ *Our website has grown over the past year.*
• **increase, develop, enlarge, expand, build up, swell, flourish**
OPPOSITE decrease
❸ *The local farm grows organic vegetables.*
• **cultivate, produce, raise, farm, propagate**
❹ *It is growing dark outside.*
• **become, get, turn, begin to be**

grown-up *ADJECTIVE*
a leopard with two grown-up cubs
• **adult, mature, fully grown**
OPPOSITES young, under age

growth *NOUN*
❶ *There's been a growth of interest in cycling.*
• **increase, rise, spread, expansion, development, enlargement, build-up**
❷ *an unusual growth on the skin*
• **lump, swelling, tumour**

grub *NOUN*
Moles feed on grubs and earthworms.
• **larva, maggot, caterpillar**

grubby *ADJECTIVE*
a set of grubby fingers
• **dirty, filthy, grimy, messy, mucky, soiled**
OPPOSITE clean

grudge *NOUN*
She isn't the sort of person who bears a grudge.
• **grievance, bitterness, resentment, hard feelings, ill-will, spite**

gruelling *ADJECTIVE*
It was a gruelling uphill climb.
• **hard, tough, demanding, exhausting, challenging, difficult, laborious, strenuous, taxing, back-breaking, punishing**
OPPOSITE easy

gruesome *ADJECTIVE*
The book is quite gruesome in places.
• **grisly, gory, ghastly, hideous, horrific, monstrous, revolting, sickening, appalling, dreadful, shocking, horrifying, frightful**

gruff *ADJECTIVE*
He spoke in a gruff voice.
• **harsh, rough, hoarse, husky, throaty**

grumble *VERB*
What are you grumbling about now?
• **complain, protest, whine, grouse, carp, make a fuss**
(*informal*) **gripe, moan, whinge**

grumpy *ADJECTIVE*
My brother is always grumpy in the morning.
• **bad-tempered, cross, irritable, testy, tetchy, grouchy, cantankerous, crotchety**
(*informal*) **ratty**
OPPOSITES **good-humoured, cheerful**

guarantee *VERB*
I guarantee that you will like this book.
• **promise, assure, pledge, vow, give your word**

guard *VERB*
The gate was guarded by men with spears.
• **protect, defend, stand guard over, patrol, safeguard, shield, watch over**

guard *NOUN*
a team of security guards
• **sentry, sentinel, warder, lookout, watchman**

guardian *NOUN*
The guardian of the treasure was a fierce dragon.
• **defender, protector, keeper, minder, custodian**

guess *NOUN*
My guess is that they have got lost.
• **theory, conjecture, opinion, belief, feeling, suspicion, speculation, estimate, hunch**

guess *VERB*
❶ *Can you guess how many sweets are in this jar?*
• **estimate, judge, work out, gauge, reckon, predict, conjecture**
❷ (*informal*) *I guess you must be feeling hungry.*
• **suppose, imagine, expect, assume, think, suspect**
(*informal*) **reckon**
IDIOMS **I take it, I dare say**

guest *NOUN*
We are expecting guests this weekend.
• **visitor, caller, company**

guide *NOUN*
❶ *Our guide met us outside the hotel.*
• **courier, escort, leader, chaperone**
❷ *We bought a pocket guide to the town.*
• **guidebook, handbook, manual, companion**

guide *VERB*
We sailed east, guided by the stars.
• **direct, lead, conduct, steer, pilot, escort, usher, shepherd, show the way**

guilt *NOUN*
❶ *She tearfully admitted her guilt.*
• **responsibility, liability, blame, wrongdoing**
OPPOSITE **innocence**
❷ *You could see the look of guilt on her face.*
• **shame, remorse, regret, contrition, shamefacedness, sheepishness**

guilty *ADJECTIVE*
❶ *The two men were found guilty of kidnapping.*
• **responsible, to blame, at fault, in the wrong, liable**
OPPOSITE **innocent**
❷ *I felt guilty about not inviting her.*
• **ashamed, guilt-ridden, remorseful, sorry, repentant, conscience-stricken, contrite, shamefaced, sheepish**
OPPOSITE **unrepentant**

gulp *VERB*
He gulped down the sandwich in one go.
• **swallow, bolt, gobble, guzzle, devour, down, wolf**
SEE ALSO **eat**

gulp *NOUN*
She drank the milk in long gulps.
• **swallow, mouthful**
(*informal*) **swig**

gun *NOUN*
see **weapon**

gurgle *VERB*
The mountain stream gurgled over the rocks.
• **burble, babble, trickle**

gush *VERB*
Water gushed from the broken pipe.
• **rush, stream, flow, pour, flood, spout, spurt, squirt**

gush *NOUN*
There was a gush of water from the pipe.
• **rush, stream, torrent, cascade, flood, jet, spout, spurt**

gust *NOUN*
a sudden gust of wind
• **blast, rush, puff, squall, flurry**

guzzle *VERB*
The seagulls guzzled all the bread.
• **gobble, gulp, bolt, devour, wolf**
SEE ALSO **eat**

A B C D E F G H I J K L M N O P Q R S T U V W X Y Z

habit *NOUN*

❶ *It's good to develop a habit of regular exercise.*

• **custom, practice, routine, rule**

❷ *My sister has an odd habit of talking to herself.*

• **mannerism, way, tendency, inclination, quirk**

hack *VERB*

We hacked our way through the dense undergrowth.

• **chop, cut, hew, slash, lop**

had

past tense see **have**

haggard *ADJECTIVE*

The survivors looked tired and haggard.

• **drawn, gaunt, thin, pinched, wasted, shrunken, wan**

haggle *VERB*

They haggled over the price for several minutes.

• **bargain, negotiate, argue, rangle**

hair *NOUN*

❶ *a girl with wavy auburn hair*

• **locks, tresses, curls**

(*informal*) **mop**

– A mass of hair is a **head of hair** or **shock of hair**.

– A single thread of hair is a **strand**.

❷ *a poodle with short hair*

• **fur, coat, wool, fleece, mane**

W WRITING TIPS

DESCRIBING HAIR

Adjectives:

- bushy
- close-cropped
- curly
- dishevelled
- fine
- frizzy
- glossy
- greasy
- lank
- luxuriant
- shaggy
- shaven
- shock-headed
- silken
- silky
- sleek
- spiky
- straggly
- straight
- stringy
- stubbly
- tangled
- thick
- thinning
- tousled
- unkempt
- wavy
- windswept
- wispy

Colour:

- auburn
- blond (male) or blonde (female)
- brown
- brunette
- dark
- dyed
- fair
- flaxen
- ginger
- grizzled
- hoary
- mousy
- platinum blonde
- raven
- red
- silver
- strawberry blonde
- streaked
- white

Hairstyles:

- Afro
- beehive
- bob
- braid
- bun
- bunches
- chignon
- cornrows
- crew cut
- curls
- dreadlocks
- French braid
- fringe (*North American* bangs)
- highlights
- Mohican
- parting
- perm
- pigtail
- plait
- ponytail
- quiff
- ringlets
- skinhead
- spikes
- topknot

Facial hair:

- beard
- bristle
- goatee beard
- moustache
- sideburns
- stubble
- whiskers

- Someone with a lot of hair is **hairy** or (*formal*) **hirsute**.

Artificial hair:

- false beard or moustache
- hairpiece
- toupee
- wig

SEE ALSO colour, texture

hairy *ADJECTIVE*

❶ *Mammoths were like elephants with thick hairy coats.*
• **shaggy, bushy, woolly, fleecy, furry, fuzzy, long-haired**
❷ *a man with a hairy chin*
• **bristly, stubbled, stubbly, bearded, unshaven**
(*formal*) **hirsute**

half-hearted *ADJECTIVE*

She made a half-hearted attempt to smile.
• **unenthusiastic, feeble, weak, indifferent, apathetic, lukewarm**
OPPOSITE enthusiastic

halfway *ADJECTIVE*

the halfway point in the race
• **midway, middle, mid, intermediate, centre**

hall *NOUN*

❶ *Leave your umbrella in the hall.*
• **entrance hall, hallway, lobby, foyer, vestibule**
❷ *The hall was full for the concert.*
• **assembly room, auditorium, concert hall, theatre**

halt *VERB*

❶ *The bus halted at the red light.*
• **stop, come to a halt, come to a standstill, draw up, pull up**
OPPOSITES start, go
❷ *A sudden noise halted us in our tracks.*
• **stop, check, stall, block, arrest, curb, stem**
❸ *Work halted when the whistle went.*
• **end, cease, terminate, break off**

hammer *VERB*

I hammered on the door, but no one came.
• **strike, beat, knock, batter, thump, pummel, pound**

hamper *VERB*

Bad weather hampered the rescuers.
• **hinder, obstruct, impede, restrict, handicap, frustrate, hold up, slow down, delay**
OPPOSITE help

hand *NOUN*

❶ *a cold and clammy hand*
• (*informal*) **paw, mitt**
– When you clench your hand you make a **fist**.
– The flat part of the inside of your hand is the **palm**.
– Work that you do with your hands is **manual** work.
– Someone who is able to use their left and right hands equally well is **ambidextrous**.
❷ *a farm hand*
• **labourer, worker, employee**

hand *VERB*

The postman handed me several letters.
• **give, pass, present, let someone have, offer**
➤ **hand something down**
This ring has been handed down from generation to generation.
• **pass down, pass on, bequeath**

handicap *NOUN*

❶ *Lack of experience may be a handicap.*
• **disadvantage, drawback, hindrance, obstacle, problem, difficulty, barrier, limitation**
IDIOM **stumbling block**
OPPOSITE advantage
❷ *He was born with a visual handicap.*
• **disability, impairment**

handicap *VERB*

The search was handicapped by bad weather.
• **hamper, hinder, impede, hold up, slow down, restrict**
OPPOSITE help

A B C D E F G H I J K L M N O P Q R S T U V W X Y Z

handle *NOUN*
He slowly turned the door handle.
• **grip, handgrip, knob, shaft**
– The handle of a sword is the **hilt**.

handle *VERB*
❶ *Please don't handle the exhibits.*
• **touch, feel, hold, stroke, fondle, finger, pick up, grasp**
❷ *I thought you handled the situation well.*
• **manage, tackle, deal with, cope with, control, see to**

handsome *ADJECTIVE*
❶ *a handsome young man*
• **attractive, good-looking, gorgeous, beautiful, striking**
(*informal*) **dishy**
OPPOSITES ugly, unattractive
❷ *We should make a handsome profit.*
• **big, large, substantial, sizeable, considerable, ample**
OPPOSITE slight

handy *ADJECTIVE*
❶ *a handy kitchen tool*
• **useful, helpful, convenient, practical, easy to use**
OPPOSITES awkward, useless
❷ *Always keep an umbrella handy.*
• **ready, available, accessible, close at hand, nearby, within reach, at the ready**
OPPOSITE inaccessible
❸ *I'm not very handy with chopsticks.*
• **skilled, adept, proficient, dexterous, deft**
OPPOSITES clumsy, inept

hang *VERB*
❶ *A chandelier was hanging from the ceiling.*
• **be suspended, dangle, swing, sway**
❷ *Her long hair was hanging down her back.*
• **droop, drape, flop, trail, cascade**
❸ *I hung the picture on the wall.*
• **fix, attach, fasten, stick, peg**
❹ *The tree was hung with lights.*
• **decorate, adorn, festoon, string, drape**
❺ *Our breath hung in the icy air.*
• **float, hover, drift, linger, cling**

➤ **hang about or around**
We had to hang about in the cold for hours.
• **wait around, linger, loiter, dawdle**
➤ **hang on**
(*informal*) *Could you hang on for a second?*
• **wait, stay, remain**
➤ **hang on to something**
❶ *I hung on to the side of the boat.*
• **hold, grip, grasp, clutch, clasp**
❷ *Hang on to your entrance ticket.*
• **keep, retain, save, keep a hold of**

haphazard *ADJECTIVE*
The books were shelved in a haphazard way.
• **random, unplanned, arbitrary, disorderly, chaotic, higgledy-piggledy**
OPPOSITE orderly

happen *VERB*
What happened on the night of the murder?
• **take place, occur, arise, come about, crop up, emerge, result**

happening *NOUN*
There have been strange happenings in the village lately.
• **event, occurrence, incident, episode, affair**

happiness *NOUN*
His little face glowed with happiness.
• **joy, joyfulness, pleasure, delight, jubilation, contentment, gladness, cheerfulness, merriment, ecstasy, bliss**
OPPOSITE sorrow

happy *ADJECTIVE*

OVERUSED WORD

❶ **A happy mood, happy person:**

➤ cheerful	➤ gleeful
➤ joyful	➤ light-hearted
➤ jolly	➤ contented
➤ merry	➤ carefree
➤ jovial	➤ upbeat

The girls look really **cheerful** *in the photograph.*

OPPOSITES unhappy, sad

❷ A very happy feeling:

- ➤ thrilled
- ➤ ecstatic
- ➤ elated
- ➤ overjoyed

(*informal*) over the moon, thrilled to bits, tickled pink

Fran was **ecstatic** *when she heard the news.*

❸ A happy time, happy experience:

- ➤ enjoyable
- ➤ pleasant
- ➤ delightful
- ➤ joyous
- ➤ glorious
- ➤ blissful
- ➤ heavenly
- ➤ idyllic

They spent a **glorious** *summer on the island.*

❹ Being happy to do something:

- ➤ glad
- ➤ pleased
- ➤ delighted
- ➤ willing
- ➤ keen

Would you be **willing** *to sign our petition?*

OPPOSITE unwilling

❺ A happy coincidence:

- ➤ lucky
- ➤ fortunate
- ➤ favourable
- ➤ timely

By a **lucky** *coincidence, we took the same train.*

OPPOSITE unfortunate

harass *VERB*

He claims he has been harassed by the police.

• **pester, trouble, bother, annoy, disturb, plague, torment, badger, hound** (*informal*) **hassle, bug**

harbour *NOUN*

an old fishing harbour

• **port, dock, mooring, quay, pier, wharf**

– A harbour for yachts is a **marina**.

harbour *VERB*

❶ *I think she still harbours a grudge against them.*

• **bear, hold, feel, nurse**

❷ *He was arrested for harbouring a criminal.*

• **shelter, protect, shield, hide, conceal**

hard *ADJECTIVE*

OVERUSED WORD

❶ Hard ground, a hard surface:

- ➤ solid
- ➤ firm
- ➤ dense
- ➤ compact
- ➤ rigid
- ➤ stiff

The core of the Moon is **solid** *rock.*

OPPOSITE soft

❷ A hard blow, hard thrust:

- ➤ strong
- ➤ forceful
- ➤ heavy
- ➤ hefty
- ➤ powerful
- ➤ violent
- ➤ mighty

The injury was caused by a **heavy** *blow to the head.*

OPPOSITE light

❸ A hard task, hard work:

- ➤ strenuous
- ➤ arduous
- ➤ tough
- ➤ difficult
- ➤ gruelling
- ➤ tiring
- ➤ exhausting
- ➤ laborious
- ➤ back-breaking

Digging the tunnel was **strenuous** *work.*

OPPOSITES easy, light

❹ A hard worker:

- ➤ industrious
- ➤ diligent
- ➤ keen
- ➤ energetic

At first, he was a **diligent** *student.*

OPPOSITE lazy

❺ A hard person, hard treatment:

- ➤ harsh
- ➤ stern
- ➤ strict
- ➤ severe
- ➤ cruel
- ➤ hard-hearted

A B C D E F G H I J K L M N O P Q R S T U V W X Y Z

➤ heartless ➤ unkind
➤ unfeeling ➤ unsympathetic

In the film, he plays a **hard-hearted** *gangster.*

OPPOSITE mild

❻ A hard problem, hard question:

➤ difficult ➤ puzzling
➤ complicated ➤ baffling
➤ complex ➤ knotty
➤ intricate ➤ thorny
➤ perplexing

No one has deciphered the **intricate** *code.*

OPPOSITE simple

hard *ADVERB*

❶ *I've been working hard all morning.*
• **diligently, industriously, energetically, keenly, intently**
(*informal*) **like mad**
❷ *It's been raining hard all afternoon.*
• **heavily, steadily**
(*informal*) **cats and dogs**
❸ *I stared hard at the screen.*
• **intently, closely, carefully, searchingly**

harden *VERB*

Leave the mixture to harden overnight.
• **set, solidify, stiffen, thicken**
OPPOSITE soften

hardly *ADVERB*

I could hardly see in the fog.
• **barely, scarcely, only just, with difficulty**
OPPOSITE easily

hardship *NOUN*

His childhood was full of hardship.
• **suffering, trouble, distress, misery, misfortune, adversity, need, want, poverty**
OPPOSITES prosperity, comfort

hardy *ADJECTIVE*

Highland cattle are hardy animals.
• **tough, strong, robust, sturdy, hearty, rugged**
OPPOSITES delicate, tender

harm *VERB*

❶ *No animals were harmed in making this film.*
• **hurt, injure, ill-treat, mistreat, wound**
IDIOM **lay a finger on**
❷ *Some of these chemicals can harm the environment.*
• **damage, spoil, ruin, impair, do harm to**

harm *NOUN*

You've done enough harm already.
• **damage, injury, hurt, pain**
OPPOSITES good, benefit

harmful *ADJECTIVE*

Ultraviolet rays are harmful to your skin.
• **damaging, detrimental, dangerous, hazardous, destructive, injurious, unhealthy**
OPPOSITES harmless, beneficial

harmless *ADJECTIVE*

❶ *The bite of a grass snake is harmless.*
• **safe, innocuous, non-poisonous, non-toxic**
OPPOSITES harmful, dangerous, poisonous
❷ *It was just a bit of harmless fun.*
• **innocent, inoffensive**

harsh *ADJECTIVE*

❶ *a harsh cry of a seagull*
• **rough, rasping, grating, jarring, discordant, shrill, strident, raucous**
OPPOSITES soft, gentle
❷ *the harsh light of a bare bulb*
• **bright, brilliant, dazzling, glaring**
OPPOSITES soft, subdued
❸ *The rescue was carried out in harsh weather conditions.*
• **severe, adverse, tough, bleak, inhospitable**
OPPOSITE mild
❹ *The prisoners suffered harsh treatment.*
• **cruel, inhumane, brutal, ruthless, heartless**
❺ *They exchanged harsh words.*
• **sharp, stern, unkind, unfriendly, critical, scathing**
OPPOSITE kind

harvest *NOUN*
There was a good harvest of rice this year.
• **crop, yield, return, produce**
– A plentiful harvest is a **bumper harvest**.

haste *NOUN*
In her haste, she forgot to lock the door.
• **hurry, rush, speed, urgency**

hasty *ADJECTIVE*
❶ *Don't make any hasty decisions.*
• **hurried, rash, reckless, impulsive, impetuous, precipitate**
IDIOM **spur-of-the-moment**
OPPOSITES **careful, considered**
❷ *We made a hasty exit.*
• **fast, hurried, quick, sudden, swift, rapid, speedy**
OPPOSITE **slow**

hat *NOUN*

WORD WEB

Some types of hat:

- balaclava
- baseball cap
- beanie
- bearskin
- beret
- bobble hat
- bonnet
- bowler
- cap
- cloche
- deerstalker
- fedora
- fez
- hard hat
- helmet
- kufi
- mitre
- mortarboard
- panama hat
- skullcap
- sombrero
- sou'wester
- stetson
- sun hat
- tam-o'shanter
- top hat
- trilby
- turban
- woolly hat

hatch *VERB*
Together they began to hatch a plan.
• **plan, develop, conceive, think up, devise**
(*informal*) **cook up, dream up**

hate *VERB*
❶ *The two families hated each other.*
• **dislike, detest, despise, loathe, be unable to bear, be unable to stand**
(*formal*) **abhor**
OPPOSITES **like, love**
❷ *I hate to disturb you.*
• **be sorry, be reluctant, be loath, regret**

hate *NOUN*
❶ *His eyes were full of hate.*
see **hatred**
❷ *Name one of your pet hates.*
• **dislike, bugbear**

hatred *NOUN*
Her heart was filled with hatred and rage.
• **hate, loathing, dislike, hostility, enmity, contempt, detestation, abhorrence**
OPPOSITE **love**

haughty *ADJECTIVE*
The butler responded with a haughty look.
• **proud, arrogant, conceited, lofty, superior, pompous, disdainful**
(*informal*) **stuck-up**
OPPOSITE **modest**

haul *VERB*
He hauled his bike out of the shed.
• **drag, pull, tow, heave, lug**

haunt *VERB*
Her words came back to haunt her.
• **torment, trouble, disturb, plague, prey on**

have *VERB*
❶ *Do you have your own computer?*
• **own, possess**
❷ *Our house has two bedrooms.*
• **contain, include, incorporate, comprise, consist of**
❸ *We're having a barbecue at the weekend.*
• **hold, organize, provide, host, throw**
❹ *I'm having some trouble with my computer.*
• **experience, go through, meet with, run into, face, suffer**

❺ *We had a great time at the party.*
• **experience, enjoy**
❻ *We've had lots of messages of support.*
• **receive, get, be given, be sent**
❼ *Who had the last piece of cake?*
• **take, eat, consume**
❽ *One of the giraffes has had a baby.*
• **give birth to, bear, produce**
❾ *I have to be home by nine o'clock.*
• **must, need to, ought to, should**

haven *NOUN*
The lake is a haven for wild birds.
• **refuge, shelter, retreat, sanctuary**

havoc *NOUN*
The floods caused havoc throughout the country.
• **chaos, mayhem, disorder, disruption**

hazard *NOUN*
Their journey was fraught with hazards.
• **danger, risk, threat, peril, trap, pitfall, snag**

hazardous *ADJECTIVE*
They made the hazardous journey to the South Pole.
• **dangerous, risky, unsafe, perilous, precarious, high-risk**
OPPOSITE **safe**

haze *NOUN*
I could hardly see through the haze.
• **mist, cloud, fog, steam, vapour**

hazy *ADJECTIVE*
❶ *The city looked hazy in the distance.*
• **blurred, misty, unclear, dim, faint**
OPPOSITES **clear, sharp**
❷ *I only have a hazy memory of that day.*
• **uncertain, vague**

head *NOUN*
❶ *He hit his head on a low beam.*
• **skull, crown**
(*informal*) **nut**
❷ *All the details are in my head.*
• **brain, mind, intellect, intelligence**
❸ *Mrs Owen is the head of the music department.*
• **chief, leader, manager, director, controller**
(*informal*) **boss**
❹ *Our friends were at the head of the queue.*
• **front, start, lead, top**
OPPOSITES **back, rear**

head *VERB*
Professor Rees headed the inquiry.
• **lead, direct, command, manage, oversee, be in charge of**
➤ **head for**
As night fell, we headed for home.
• **go towards, make for, aim for**

heading *NOUN*
Each chapter has a different heading.
• **title, caption, headline, rubric**

headlong *ADJECTIVE*
We made a headlong dash for shelter.
• **quick, hurried, hasty, breakneck**

heal *VERB*
It took a month for the wound to heal.
• **get better, recover, mend, be cured**

health *NOUN*
❶ *My gran is in excellent health.*
• **condition, constitution, shape**
❷ *I am slowly returning to health.*
• **well-being, fitness, strength, vigour, good shape**

healthy *ADJECTIVE*
❶ *She was always healthy as a child.*
• **well, fit, strong, sturdy, vigorous, robust**
(*informal*) **in good shape**
OPPOSITE **ill**
❷ *Porridge makes a healthy breakfast.*
• **health-giving, wholesome, invigorating, nourishing, nutritious, good for you**
OPPOSITE **unhealthy**

heap *NOUN*
There was an untidy heap of clothes on the floor.
• **pile, stack, mound, mountain, collection, mass**

heap *VERB*
We heaped up all the rubbish in the corner.
• **pile, stack, collect, bank, mass**

hear *VERB*
❶ *Did you hear what she said?*
• **catch, listen to, make out, pick up, overhear, pay attention to**
– A sound that you can hear is **audible**.
– A sound that you cannot hear is **inaudible**.
❷ *Have you heard the news?*
• **be told, discover, find out, learn, gather**

heart *NOUN*
❶ *Have you no heart?*
• **compassion, feeling, sympathy, tenderness, affection, humanity, kindness, love**
❷ *We wandered deep into the heart of the forest.*
• **centre, middle, core, nucleus, hub**
❸ *Let's try to get to the heart of problem.*
• **core, essence, crux, root**

heartless *ADJECTIVE*
How could she be so heartless?
• **hard-hearted, callous, cruel, inhuman, unfeeling, unkind, pitiless, ruthless**
OPPOSITES kind, compassionate

hearty *ADJECTIVE*
❶ *He gave a hearty laugh.*
• **strong, forceful, vigorous, loud, spirited**
OPPOSITE feeble
❷ *They gave us a hearty welcome.*
• **enthusiastic, wholehearted, sincere, genuine, warm, heartfelt**
OPPOSITES unenthusiastic, half-hearted
❸ *She always ate a hearty breakfast.*
• **large, substantial, ample, satisfying, filling**
OPPOSITE light

heat *NOUN*
❶ *Last summer, the heat made me feel ill.*
• **hot weather, warmth, high temperature**
– A long period of hot weather is a **heatwave**.
OPPOSITE cold
❷ *The fire gives out a lot of heat.*
• **warmth, hotness, glow**
❸ *Voices were raised in the heat of the debate.*
• **passion, intensity, fervour, vehemence**

heat *VERB*
The fire will gradually heat the room.
• **warm, heat up**
OPPOSITES cool, cool down

heave *VERB*
The men heaved the piano into position.
• **haul, drag, pull, draw, tow, tug, hoist, lug**

heavy *ADJECTIVE*
❶ *The box was too heavy to lift.*
• **weighty, massive, bulky, hefty**
OPPOSITE light
❷ *A heavy mist hung over the valley.*
• **dense, thick, solid**
OPPOSITE thin
❸ *The rain has caused heavy flooding.*
• **severe, extreme, torrential**
❹ *Both sides suffered heavy losses in the battle.*
• **large, substantial, considerable**
❺ *Digging the garden is heavy work.*
• **hard, tough, gruelling, back-breaking, strenuous, arduous**
❻ *This book makes heavy reading.*
• **serious, intense, demanding**
❼ *I was feeling sleepy after such a heavy meal.*
• **filling, stodgy, rich**

hectic *ADJECTIVE*
It's been a hectic day, getting the hall ready for the show.
• **frantic, feverish, frenzied, frenetic, chaotic, busy**
(*informal*) **manic**
OPPOSITES quiet, leisurely

heed *VERB*
They refused to heed our advice.
• **listen to, pay attention to, take notice of, attend to, regard, obey, follow, mark, mind, note**
OPPOSITE ignore

hefty *ADJECTIVE*
❶ *He was a hefty man with ginger hair.*
• **strong, sturdy, muscular, powerful, brawny, burly, beefy, hulking, strapping**
OPPOSITE slight
❷ *She lifted a hefty volume down from the shelf.*
• **weighty, large, massive, bulky**

height *NOUN*
❶ *We need to know the height of the tower.*
• **tallness, elevation, altitude**
– The natural height of your body is your **stature**.
❷ *the dizzying heights of the Himalayas*
• **summit, peak, crest, crown, cap, pinnacle**
❸ *They were at the height of their fame.*
• **peak, high point, pinnacle, zenith, climax**

held
past tense see **hold**

help *VERB*
❶ *Could you please help me with my luggage?*
• **aid, assist, give assistance to**
IDIOMS **give a hand to, lend a hand to**
❷ *The money will help victims of the earthquake.*
• **be helpful to, benefit, support, serve, be of service to**
❸ *This medicine will help your cough.*
• **make better, cure, ease, relieve, soothe, improve**
OPPOSITES aggravate, worsen
❹ *I couldn't help smiling.*
• **avoid, resist, refrain from, keep from, stop**

help *NOUN*
❶ *Thank you for your help.*
• **aid, assistance, support, guidance, cooperation, advice**
OPPOSITE hindrance
❷ *Would a torch be of any help to you?*
• **use, benefit**

helpful *ADJECTIVE*
❶ *The staff were friendly and helpful.*
• **obliging, accommodating, considerate, thoughtful, sympathetic, kind, cooperative**
OPPOSITE unhelpful
❷ *The website offers some helpful advice.*
• **useful, valuable, worthwhile, beneficial, profitable**
OPPOSITE worthless

helping *NOUN*
Would you like a second helping of trifle?
• **serving, portion, plateful, amount, share, ration**

helpless *ADJECTIVE*
The cubs are born blind and helpless.
• **powerless, weak, feeble, dependent, defenceless, vulnerable**
OPPOSITES independent, strong

hem *VERB*
➤ **hem someone in**
The bus was hemmed in by the traffic.
• **shut in, box in, encircle, enclose, surround**

herb *NOUN*

WORD WEB

Some common herbs:

➤ basil	➤ fennel
➤ camomile	➤ fenugreek
➤ caraway	➤ hyssop
➤ chervil	➤ lemon balm
➤ chicory	➤ lovage
➤ chive	➤ marjoram
➤ coriander	➤ mint
➤ cumin	➤ oregano
➤ dill	➤ parsley

➤ peppermint
➤ rosemary
➤ sage
➤ tarragon
➤ thyme

herd *NOUN*
For groups of animals see **collective noun**.

heritage *NOUN*
She has been exploring her African heritage.
• **ancestry, background, descent, history, roots, tradition, culture**

hero or **heroine** *NOUN*
❶ *She is one of my sporting heroines.*
• **idol, role model, star, celebrity, legend**
❷ *The film has no real hero.*
• **protagonist, main character, lead**

heroic *ADJECTIVE*
The firefighters made heroic efforts to put out the blaze.
• **bold, brave, courageous, daring, fearless, intrepid, valiant**
(*informal*) **gutsy**
OPPOSITE cowardly

hesitant *ADJECTIVE*
She took a hesitant step through the entrance.
• **uncertain, unsure, doubtful, cautious, tentative, wary, undecided**
OPPOSITE confident

hesitate *VERB*
I hesitated before picking up the phone.
• **pause, delay, wait, hold back, falter, stall, dither, waver**
(*informal*) **dilly-dally**
IDIOM **think twice**

hidden *ADJECTIVE*
❶ *a hidden camera*
• **concealed, secret, unseen, out of sight, invisible, camouflaged**
OPPOSITE visible
❷ *The poem has a hidden meaning.*
• **obscure, mysterious, secret, coded, cryptic**
OPPOSITE obvious

hide *VERB*
❶ *We hid in the bushes until they had gone.*
• **go into hiding, take cover, take refuge, keep out of sight**
IDIOMS **lie low, go to ground**
❷ *She hid the letters in a secret drawer.*
• **conceal, secrete, bury, stow, put out of sight**
(*informal*) **stash**
OPPOSITE expose
❸ *The mist hid our view of the hills.*
• **cover, obscure, screen, mask, shroud, veil, blot out**
OPPOSITE uncover
❹ *I tried to hide my true feelings.*
• **disguise, conceal, keep secret, suppress, camouflage, cloak**
IDIOM **keep a lid on**
OPPOSITES show, reveal

hideous *ADJECTIVE*
The legend tells of a hideous beast.
• **ugly, grotesque, monstrous, revolting, repulsive, ghastly, gruesome, horrible, appalling, dreadful, frightful**
OPPOSITE beautiful

high *ADJECTIVE*
❶ *The castle was surrounded by a high wall.*
• **tall, towering, elevated, lofty**
OPPOSITE low
❷ *an officer of high rank*
• **senior, top, leading, important, prominent, powerful**
OPPOSITES low, junior
❸ *the high cost of living*
• **expensive, dear, costly, excessive, exorbitant**
(*informal*) **steep**
OPPOSITE low
❹ *a warning of high winds*
• **strong, powerful, forceful, extreme**
OPPOSITES light, gentle
❺ *She spoke in a high voice.*
• **high-pitched, squeaky, shrill, piercing**
– A high singing voice is **soprano** or **treble**.
OPPOSITES deep, low

a b c d e f g h i j k l m n o p q r s t u v w x y z

A B C D E F G H I J K L M N O P Q R S T U V W X Y Z

highlight *NOUN*
What was the highlight of your trip?
• **high point, high spot, best moment, climax**
OPPOSITES low point, nadir

highly *ADVERB*
He is a highly experienced doctor.
• **very, extremely, exceptionally, considerably, decidedly**

hike *VERB*
We often go hiking across the moors.
• **walk, trek, ramble, tramp, backpack**

hilarious *ADJECTIVE*
a hilarious joke
• **funny, amusing, comical, uproarious** (*informal*) **hysterical, priceless**
SEE ALSO **funny**

hill *NOUN*
❶ *a valley between two hills*
• **mount, peak, ridge, fell**
– A small hill is a **hillock**, **knoll** or **mound**.
❷ *Their house is at the top of the hill.*
• **slope, rise, incline, ascent, gradient**

hinder *VERB*
Bad weather is hindering the rescue attempt.
• **hamper, obstruct, impede, handicap, restrict, hold up, slow down, get in the way of, interfere with**
OPPOSITE help

hindrance *NOUN*
Parked cars can be a hindrance to cyclists.
• **obstacle, obstruction, inconvenience, handicap, disadvantage, drawback**
OPPOSITE help

hint *NOUN*
❶ *Can you give me a hint?*
• **clue, indication, sign, suggestion, inkling, intimation**
❷ *The website offers some handy hints on taking good photos.*
• **tip, pointer, suggestion, guideline**

hint *VERB*
He hinted that he might be retiring soon.
• **give a hint, suggest, imply, intimate**

hire *VERB*
❶ *We hired a boat for the afternoon.*
• **rent, lease, charter**
❷ *They will be hiring extra staff for Christmas.*
• **employ, engage, recruit, take on**
OPPOSITE dismiss

historic *ADJECTIVE*
The Moon landing was a historic event.
• **famous, important, notable, celebrated, renowned, momentous, significant, major, ground-breaking**
OPPOSITES unimportant, minor
The words **historic** and **historical** do not mean the same thing. A historical event took place in the past, but a historic event is famous or important in history.

historical *ADJECTIVE*
❶ *The old library is full of useful historical documents.*
• **past, former, old, ancient, bygone, olden**
OPPOSITES contemporary, recent
❷ *Was King Arthur a historical figure?*
• **real, real-life, true, actual, authentic, documented**
OPPOSITES fictitious, legendary

WRITING TIPS

WRITING HISTORICAL FICTION
Clothes:

➤ bodice	➤ gauntlet
➤ bonnet	➤ gown
➤ breeches	➤ hose
➤ bustle	➤ petticoat
➤ cape	➤ raiment
➤ cloak	➤ robe
➤ corset	➤ ruff
➤ cravat	➤ shawl
➤ crinoline	➤ toga
➤ doublet	➤ top hat
➤ drawers	➤ tricorn hat
➤ farthingale	➤ tunic
➤ frock coat	

Occupations:

- apothecary
- barrow boy
- blacksmith
- chimney sweep
- clerk
- cobbler
- costermonger
- draper
- dressmaker
- executioner
- governess
- housemaid
- innkeeper
- kitchen maid
- laundress
- merchant
- pedlar
- seamstress
- spinner
- tanner
- weaver
- wheelwright
- wigmaker

Setting:

- battlefield
- frontier
- imperial court
- industrial town
- inn
- market
- monastery
- orphanage
- outpost
- tavern
- workhouse

Transport:

- airship
- chariot
- galleon
- hansom cab
- horse-drawn carriage
- penny-farthing
- sedan chair
- stagecoach
- steamboat
- steam train

Weapons:

- ballista
- blunderbuss
- bow and arrow
- broadsword
- cannon
- catapult
- claymore
- cutlass
- dagger
- gunpowder
- lance
- longbow
- mace
- musket
- sabre
- samurai sword
- siege tower
- shield
- spear
- sword
- trebuchet

Other details:

- candlelight
- farthing
- flagon
- gallows
- gaslight
- goblet
- groat
- guinea
- lantern
- oil lamp
- parasol
- parchment
- plague
- powdered wig
- quill pen
- shilling
- telegraph

For words in old and poetic use see **old**.

history *NOUN*

❶ *Dr Sachs is an expert on American history.*
• **heritage, past, antiquity, past times, olden days**
❷ *He is writing a history of the First World War.*
• **account, chronicle, record**
– The history of a person's life is their **biography**.
– The history of your own life is your **autobiography** or **memoirs**.

hit *VERB*

OVERUSED WORD

❶ Hit **a person, animal:**

- strike
- beat
- thump
- punch
- slap
- smack
- swipe
- slog
- cuff

(*informal*) **whack, thump, wallop, clout, clobber, sock, belt, biff**

– To hit someone with a stick is to **club** them.

In judo, you are not allowed to **strike** *your opponent.*

❷ Hit **an object, surface:**

- knock
- bang
- bump
- bash
- strike
- thump
- rap
- crack
- slam

(*informal*) **whack**

– To hit your toe on something is to **stub** it.

Mind you don't **bump** *your head on the ceiling.*

❸ Hit something in an accident:

- crash into
- smash into
- collide with
- run into
- plough into
- meet head on

A lorry had **ploughed into** *the side of their house.*

❹ Hit gently, lightly:

- tap
- pat
- patter
- rap

Pat *the dough with your hands on a floured surface.*

❺ Hit repeatedly:

- batter
- buffet
- pound
- pummel
- drum

She **drummed** *her fingers impatiently on the desk.*

❻ Hit a note, target:

- reach
- attain

Can you **reach** *the high notes in this song?*

OPPOSITES miss, fall short of

❼ Hit a problem, difficulty:

- run into
- come across
- encounter
- face
- confront

I **encountered** *a snag while installing the program.*

hit *NOUN*

❶ *He got a nasty hit on the head.*
• **bump, blow, bang, strike, knock, whack, punch, slap, smack, swipe**
❷ *The book was an instant hit.*
• **success, triumph**
(*informal*) **winner**
OPPOSITES failure, flop

hitch *NOUN*

The evening went without a hitch.
• **problem, difficulty, snag, complication, obstacle, setback**
(*informal*) **hiccup, glitch**

hitch *VERB*

She hitched up her skirt and waded into the river.
• **pull, lift, raise, hoist, draw**

hoard *NOUN*

The tomb contained a hoard of gold.
• **cache, store, stock, supply, pile, stockpile**
(*informal*) **stash**
– A hoard of treasure is a **treasure trove**.

hoard *VERB*

Squirrels hoard nuts for the winter.
• **store, collect, gather, save, pile up, stockpile, put aside, put by**
(*informal*) **stash away**

hoarse *ADJECTIVE*

Her voice was hoarse from shouting.
• **rough, harsh, husky, croaky, throaty, gruff, rasping, gravelly**

hoax *NOUN*

The email was just a hoax.
• **joke, practical joke, prank, trick, spoof, fraud**
(*informal*) **con, scam**

hobby *NOUN*

My favourite hobby is photography.
• **pastime, pursuit, interest, activity, recreation, amusement**

hoist *VERB*

The women hoisted the bundles onto their heads.
• **lift, raise, heave, pull up, haul up, winch up**

hold *VERB*

❶ *Hold the reins loosely in your left hand.*
• **clasp, grasp, grip, cling to, hang on to, clutch, seize, squeeze**
❷ *Can I hold the baby?*
• **embrace, hug, cradle**
❸ *The tank should hold ten litres.*
• **contain, take, have space for, accommodate**
❹ *Will the ladder hold my weight?*
• **bear, support, carry, take**

⑤ *If our luck holds, we could reach the final.*
• continue, last, carry on, persist, stay
⑥ *She has always held strong opinions.*
• believe in, maintain, stick to
⑦ *We will be holding a public meeting.*
• host, put on, organize, arrange, convene, call
⑧ *Three suspects are being held in prison.*
• confine, detain, keep
➤ **hold out**
① *The stranger held out his hand in greeting.*
• extend, reach out, stick out, stretch out
② *Our supplies won't hold out much longer.*
• keep going, last, carry on, continue, endure
➤ **hold up**
① *Hold up your hand if you know the answer.*
• lift, put up, raise, elevate, hoist
② *Roadworks were holding up the traffic.*
• delay, hinder, impede, slow down

hold *NOUN*
① *Keep a firm hold on the leash.*
• grip, grasp, clutch, clasp
② *The myth had a strange hold on my imagination.*
• influence, power, dominance, pull, sway

hole *NOUN*
① *The men were digging a large hole in the ground.*
• pit, hollow, crater, dent, depression, cavity, chasm, abyss
② *The rabbits escaped through a hole in the fence.*
• gap, opening, breach, break, cut, slit, gash, split, tear, rift, vent
③ *a rabbit hole*
• burrow, lair, den, earth

holiday *NOUN*
We spent our summer holiday in France.
• vacation, break, leave, time off

hollow *ADJECTIVE*
① *a hollow tube*
• empty, unfilled
OPPOSITE solid
② *hollow cheeks*
• sunken, wasted, deep-set, concave
OPPOSITES plump, chubby
③ *a hollow promise*
• insincere, empty, meaningless
OPPOSITE sincere

hollow *NOUN*
The ball rolled into a hollow in the ground.
• hole, pit, crater, cavity, depression, dent, dip

hollow *VERB*
We hollowed out a pumpkin to make a Halloween lantern.
• dig, excavate, gouge, scoop

holy *ADJECTIVE*
① *a pilgrimage to a holy shrine*
• sacred, blessed, revered, venerated, sanctified
② *The pilgrims were holy people.*
• religious, spiritual, devout, pious, godly, saintly

home *NOUN*
The cottage was their home for ten years.
• residence, house, dwelling, abode, lodging
– A home for the sick is a **convalescent home** or **nursing home**.
– A place where a bird or animal lives is its **habitat**.

homely *ADJECTIVE*
The hotel was small with a homely atmosphere.
• friendly, informal, cosy, familiar, relaxed, easy-going, comfortable, snug

honest *ADJECTIVE*
① *He's an honest boy, so he gave the money back.*
• good, honourable, upright, virtuous, moral, decent, law-abiding, scrupulous, trustworthy
OPPOSITE dishonest

A B C D E F G H I J K L M N O P Q R S T U V W X Y Z

❷ *Please give me your honest opinion.*
• **sincere, genuine, truthful, direct, frank, candid, plain, straightforward, unbiased**
OPPOSITE insincere

honour *NOUN*
❶ *Her success brought honour to the school.*
• **reputation, good name, credit, repute, standing**
❷ *I believe he is a man of honour.*
• **integrity, honesty, fairness, morality, decency, principles**
❸ *She knew that playing for her country was an honour.*
• **privilege, distinction, glory, prestige, kudos**

honour *VERB*
There will be a memorial service to honour the dead.
• **pay tribute to, salute, recognize, celebrate, praise, acclaim**

honourable *ADJECTIVE*
❶ *an honourable man*
• **honest, virtuous, good, upright, moral, principled, decent, fair, noble, worthy, righteous**
❷ *It was an honourable thing to do.*
• **noble, admirable, praiseworthy, decent**
OPPOSITE unworthy

hook *NOUN*
She hung her coat on one of the hooks.
• **peg, nail**

hook *VERB*
❶ *Dad hooked the trailer to the car.*
• **attach, fasten, hitch, connect, couple**
❷ *I managed to hook a small fish.*
• **catch, land, take**

hop *VERB*
The goblins were hopping about in excitement.
• **jump, leap, skip, spring, bound, caper, prance, dance**

hope *NOUN*
❶ *Her dearest hope was to see her family again.*
• **ambition, wish, dream, desire, aspiration**
❷ *There was little hope of escape.*
• **prospect, expectation, likelihood**

hope *VERB*
I hope to see you again soon.
• **wish, trust, expect, look forward**

hopeful *ADJECTIVE*
❶ *I am feeling hopeful about tomorrow's match.*
• **optimistic, confident, positive, buoyant, expectant**
OPPOSITE pessimistic
❷ *Our chances are looking more hopeful.*
• **promising, encouraging, favourable, reassuring**
OPPOSITE discouraging

hopeless *ADJECTIVE*
❶ *The plight of the crew was hopeless.*
• **desperate, wretched, impossible, futile, beyond hope**
OPPOSITE hopeful
❷ *I'm hopeless at ice-skating.*
• **bad, poor, incompetent, awful** (*informal*) **useless, rubbish, lousy, pathetic**
OPPOSITES good, competent

horde *NOUN*
Hordes of people thronged the streets.
• **crowd, mob, throng, mass, swarm, gang, pack**

horizontal *ADJECTIVE*
Draw a horizontal line.
• **flat, level**
OPPOSITES vertical, upright

horrible *ADJECTIVE*
What a horrible smell!
• **awful, terrible, dreadful, appalling, unpleasant, disagreeable, offensive, objectionable, disgusting, repulsive, revolting, horrendous, horrid, nasty, hateful, odious, loathsome, ghastly**
OPPOSITE pleasant

horrific *ADJECTIVE*
The film starts with a horrific battle scene.
• **horrifying, terrifying, shocking,**

gruesome, dreadful, appalling, ghastly, hideous, atrocious, grisly, sickening

horrify *VERB*

She was horrified when she discovered the truth.

• appal, shock, outrage, scandalize, disgust, sicken

horror *NOUN*

❶ *His eyes filled with horror.*

• terror, fear, fright, alarm, panic, dread

❷ *The film depicts the full horror of war.*

• awfulness, hideousness, gruesomeness, ghastliness, grimness

WRITING TIPS

WRITING HORROR FICTION

Characters:

➤ ghost
➤ ghoul
➤ mummy
➤ necromancer
➤ phantom
➤ poltergeist
➤ spectre
➤ spirit
➤ vampire
➤ werewolf
➤ wraith
➤ zombie

Setting:

➤ catacombs
➤ cemetery
➤ crypt
➤ dungeon
➤ graveyard
➤ haunted mansion
➤ mausoleum
➤ necropolis
➤ tomb

Useful words and phrases:

➤ accursed
➤ afterlife
➤ apparition
➤ beyond the grave
➤ coffin
➤ corpse
➤ curse
➤ dark side
➤ eerie
➤ exorcism
➤ ghostly
➤ ghoulish
➤ gore
➤ Halloween
➤ haunting
➤ hex
➤ living dead
➤ lycanthropy
➤ macabre
➤ malediction
➤ mortal remains
➤ necromancy
➤ nightmare
➤ occult
➤ other-worldly
➤ paranormal
➤ possession
➤ reanimation
➤ sarcophagus
➤ seance
➤ shroud
➤ soul
➤ spectral
➤ supernatural
➤ trance
➤ uncanny
➤ undead
➤ unearthly
➤ vampirism
➤ voodoo

horse *NOUN*

a horse pulling a carriage

• mount, nag

(*poetic*) steed

WORD WEB

Some types of horse:

➤ bronco
➤ carthorse
➤ Clydesdale
➤ mustang
➤ pony
➤ racehorse
➤ Shetland pony
➤ shire horse
➤ warhorse

- A male horse is a **stallion** and a female is a **mare**.
- A young horse is a **foal**, **colt** (male) or **filly** (female).
- A cross between a donkey and a horse is a **mule**.

Parts of a horse's body:

➤ coat
➤ fetlock
➤ flank
➤ hoof
➤ mane
➤ withers

Colours of a horse's coat:

➤ bay
➤ chestnut
➤ dappled
➤ dun
➤ grey
➤ palomino
➤ piebald
➤ pinto
➤ roan

Noises made by a horse:

➤ neigh
➤ snicker
➤ snort
➤ whinny

Ways a horse can move:

➤ canter
➤ gallop
➤ trot
➤ walk

- **Equine** means 'to do with horses' and

a b c d e f g h i j k l m n o p q r s t u v w x y z

equestrian means 'to do with horse-riding'.
- A person who rides a horse in a race is a **jockey**.
- Soldiers who fight on horseback are **cavalry**.

hospital *NOUN*
a small community hospital
• **clinic, infirmary, sanatorium**
SEE ALSO **medicine**

hostile *ADJECTIVE*
❶ *The men glared at us in a hostile manner.*
• **aggressive, antagonistic, confrontational, unfriendly, unwelcoming, warlike, belligerent**
OPPOSITE friendly
❷ *The North Pole has a hostile climate.*
• **harsh, adverse, unfavourable, inhospitable**
OPPOSITE favourable

hostility *NOUN*
The hostility between the two players was obvious.
• **dislike, enmity, unfriendliness, aggression, antagonism, hate, hatred, bad feeling, ill-will, malice**
OPPOSITE friendship

hot *ADJECTIVE*
❶ *a hot summer's day*
• **warm, balmy, blazing, scorching, blistering, roasting, baking, sweltering, stifling**
OPPOSITES cold, cool
❷ *a bowl of hot soup*
• **burning, boiling, scalding, searing, sizzling, steaming, red-hot, piping hot**
OPPOSITES cold, cool
❸ *a hot curry sauce*
• **spicy, peppery, fiery**
OPPOSITE mild
❹ *a hot temper*
• **fierce, fiery, violent, passionate, raging, intense**
OPPOSITES calm, mild

house *NOUN*
❶ *She still lives in the family house.*
• **residence, home, dwelling, abode, lodging**
SEE ALSO **accommodation**
❷ *He was related to the House of Stuart.*
• **family, dynasty, clan, line**

house *VERB*
The cabins are able to house twenty people.
• **accommodate, lodge, shelter, take in, quarter, board**

hover *VERB*
❶ *A helicopter hovered overhead.*
• **hang, float, drift, be suspended, be poised**
❷ *I hovered just outside the door.*
• **linger, pause, wait about, dally, loiter** (*informal*) **hang about**

however *ADVERB*
❶ *I can't remember, however hard I try.*
• **no matter how**
❷ *Spiders' silk is thin; however, it is also strong.*
• **nevertheless, nonetheless, yet, still, even so, for all that**

howl *VERB*
❶ *A baby was howling in its pram.*
• **cry, wail, bawl, scream, yell, shriek** (*informal*) **holler**
❷ *They heard wolves howling in the night.*
• **bay, yowl, yelp**

huddle *VERB*
❶ *We huddled around the fire to get warm.*
• **crowd, gather, congregate, flock, cluster, pack, squeeze**
❷ *I huddled under the blankets and tried to sleep.*
• **curl up, nestle, cuddle, snuggle**

hue *NOUN*
The leaves were various hues of red and gold.
• **colour, shade, tint, tone, tinge**

hug *VERB*
The two friends laughed and hugged each other.
• embrace, clasp, cuddle, squeeze, cling to, hold tight

hug *NOUN*
Izzie gave her dad a huge hug.
• embrace, clasp, cuddle, squeeze

huge *ADJECTIVE*
Woolly mammoths were huge creatures.
• enormous, gigantic, massive, colossal, giant, immense, vast, mighty, mammoth, monumental, hulking, great, big, large
(*informal*) whopping, humongous
(*literary*) gargantuan
OPPOSITES small, tiny

hum *VERB*
Insects were humming in the sunshine.
• drone, buzz, murmur, purr, whirr

hum *NOUN*
the hum of an engine
• drone, whirr, throb, murmur, purr

humane *ADJECTIVE*
A humane society should treat animals well.
• kind, compassionate, sympathetic, civilized, benevolent, kind-hearted, charitable, loving, merciful
OPPOSITE cruel

humans *PLURAL NOUN*
Humans have smaller brains than whales.
• human beings, the human race, people, humanity, humankind, mankind, Homo sapiens

humble *ADJECTIVE*
❶ *The book is about a humble watchmaker.*
• modest, meek, unassuming, self-effacing, unassertive, submissive
OPPOSITE proud
❷ *a painting of a humble domestic scene*
• simple, modest, plain, ordinary, commonplace, lowly
OPPOSITE grand

humid *ADJECTIVE*
It was a hot and humid day.
• muggy, clammy, close, sultry, sticky, moist, steamy
OPPOSITE fresh

humiliate *VERB*
He humiliated her in front of her friends.
• embarrass, disgrace, shame, make ashamed, humble, crush, degrade, demean, mortify
(*informal*) put someone in their place, take someone down a peg

humiliating *ADJECTIVE*
The team suffered a humiliating defeat.
• embarrassing, crushing, degrading, demeaning, humbling, undignified, ignominious, mortifying
OPPOSITE glorious

humorous *ADJECTIVE*
a humorous anecdote
• amusing, funny, comic, comical, witty, entertaining, droll
OPPOSITE serious

humour *NOUN*
❶ *I liked the humour in the film.*
• comedy, wit, hilarity, satire, irony, jokes, witticisms
OPPOSITE seriousness
❷ *She is in a good humour today.*
• mood, temper, disposition, frame of mind, spirits

hump *NOUN*
Camels have humps on their backs.
• bump, lump, bulge, swelling

hunch *NOUN*
I have a hunch that she won't come.
• feeling, intuition, inkling, guess, impression, suspicion, idea, notion
IDIOM gut feeling

hung
past tense see **hang**

hunger *NOUN*
I was feeling faint with hunger.
• lack of food, starvation, undernourishment

A B C D E F G H I J K L M N O P Q R S T U V W X Y Z

– A severe shortage of food in an area is **famine**.
– Bad health caused by not having enough food is **malnutrition**.

hungry *ADJECTIVE*
❶ *I was hungry again by 3 o'clock.*
• **starving, starved, famished, ravenous**
(*informal*) **peckish**
❷ *He was hungry for power.*
• **eager, keen, longing, yearning, craving, greedy**
(*informal*) **itching**

hunt *VERB*
❶ *Some Native American tribes used to hunt buffalo.*
• **chase, pursue, track, trail, hound, stalk**
– An animal which hunts other animals for food is a **predator**.
❷ *I hunted in the attic for our old photo albums.*
• **search, seek, look, rummage, ferret, root around, scour around**
IDIOM **look high and low**

hunt *NOUN*
Police have begun the hunt for clues.
• **search, quest, chase, pursuit (of), forage**

hurdle *NOUN*
❶ *The runners cleared the first hurdle.*
• **fence, barrier, jump, barricade, obstacle**
❷ *Our biggest hurdle was our lack of experience.*
• **difficulty, problem, handicap, obstacle, hindrance, impediment, snag**
IDIOM **stumbling block**

hurl *VERB*
I hurled the ball as far as I could.
• **throw, fling, pitch, toss, cast, sling, launch**
(*informal*) **chuck**

hurried *ADJECTIVE*
He gave the clock a hurried glance.
• **quick, hasty, speedy, swift, rapid, rushed, brisk, cursory**

hurry *VERB*
❶ *We'd better hurry or we'll miss the bus.*
• **be quick, hasten, make speed**
(*informal*) **get a move on, step on it**
IDIOM (*informal*) **get your skates on**
OPPOSITE dawdle
❷ *An ambulance crew hurried to the scene.*
• **rush, dash, race, fly, speed, sprint, hurtle, scurry**
OPPOSITES amble, stroll
❸ *I don't mean to hurry you.*
• **hasten, hustle, speed up, urge on**
OPPOSITE slow down

hurry *NOUN*
In my hurry, I forgot the tickets.
• **rush, haste, speed, urgency**

hurt *VERB*
❶ *I hurt my wrist playing hockey.*
• **injure, wound, damage, harm, maim, bruise, cut**
❷ *My feet hurt.*
• **be sore, be painful, ache, throb, sting, smart**
❸ *Your letter hurt me deeply.*
• **upset, distress, offend, grieve, sadden, pain, wound, sting**

hurtful *ADJECTIVE*
That was a very hurtful remark.
• **upsetting, distressing, unkind, cruel, mean, spiteful, wounding, nasty, malicious**

hurtle *VERB*
The train hurtled along at top speed.
• **rush, speed, race, dash, fly, charge, tear, shoot, zoom**

husband *NOUN*
She lives with her husband and two sons.
• **spouse, partner**
IDIOM **other half**

hush *VERB*
The speaker tried to hush the crowd.
• **silence, quieten, settle, still, calm**
(*informal*) **shut up**
➤ **hush something up**
They tried to hush up the scandal.
• **cover up, hide, conceal, keep quiet,**

keep secret, suppress
IDIOM sweep under the carpet

hush *NOUN*
There was a sudden hush in the room.
• **silence, quiet, stillness, calm, tranquillity**

husky *ADJECTIVE*
a husky voice
• **hoarse, throaty, gruff, rasping, gravelly, rough, croaky**

hut *NOUN*
They came across a little hut in the woods.
• **shed, shack, cabin, den, shelter, shanty, hovel**

hygienic *ADJECTIVE*
Always use a hygienic surface for preparing food.
• **sanitary, clean, disinfected, sterilized, sterile, germ-free**
OPPOSITES unhygienic, insanitary

hysterical *ADJECTIVE*
1 *The fans became hysterical when the band finally appeared.*
• **crazy, frenzied, mad, delirious, raving, wild, uncontrollable**
2 (*informal*) *Some of the scenes in the film are hysterical.*
• **hilarious, funny, amusing, comical, uproarious**
(*informal*) **priceless, side-splitting**

ice *NOUN*

WORD WEB

Various forms of ice:

- ➤ black ice
- ➤ floe
- ➤ frost
- ➤ glacier
- ➤ iceberg
- ➤ ice cap
- ➤ ice field
- ➤ icicle
- ➤ pack ice
- ➤ sheet ice

- A permanently frozen layer of soil is permafrost.

icy *ADJECTIVE*
❶ *There was an icy wind.*
• cold, freezing, frosty, wintry, arctic, bitter, biting, raw
❷ *Icy roads can be dangerous.*
• frozen, slippery, glacial, glassy

idea *NOUN*
❶ *I've got a great idea!*
• plan, scheme, proposal, suggestion, proposition, inspiration
❷ *He has some odd ideas about life.*
• belief, opinion, view, theory, notion, concept, conception, hypothesis
❸ *What's the central idea of the poem?*
• point, meaning, intention, thought
❹ *Have you any idea what will happen?*
• clue, hint, inkling, impression, sense, suspicion, hunch

ideal *ADJECTIVE*
These are ideal conditions for sailing.
• perfect, excellent, suitable, faultless, the best

identical *ADJECTIVE*
All the houses looked identical.
• matching, alike, indistinguishable, interchangeable, the same
OPPOSITE different

identify *VERB*
❶ *The suspect was identified by three witnesses.*
• recognize, name, distinguish, pick out, single out
❷ *The doctors couldn't identify what was wrong.*
• diagnose, discover, spot
(*informal*) put a name to
➤ **identify with**
Can you identify with the hero of the film?
• sympathize with, empathize with, feel for, relate to, understand
(*informal*) put yourself in someone's shoes

idiot *NOUN*
I felt like such an idiot.
• fool, ass, clown, halfwit, dunce, blockhead, buffoon, dunderhead, imbecile, moron
(*informal*) chump, dope, dummy, dimwit, nitwit, nincompoop

idiotic *ADJECTIVE*
That was an idiotic thing to say.
• stupid, foolish, senseless, silly, ridiculous, nonsensical, unwise, half-witted, unintelligent, absurd, crazy, mad, hare-brained, foolhardy
(*informal*) dim-witted, dumb, daft, barmy
OPPOSITE sensible

idle *ADJECTIVE*
❶ *He's such an idle fellow.*
• lazy, indolent, slothful, work-shy
OPPOSITES hard-working, industrious
❷ *The machines lay idle all week.*
• inactive, unused, inoperative
OPPOSITES active, in use
❸ *She never makes idle threats.*
• pointless, aimless, meaningless, empty, trivial, frivolous
OPPOSITE serious

idol *NOUN*
❶ *He was a pop idol of the 1980s.*
• star, superstar, celebrity, icon
(*informal*) pin-up

❷ *an ancient clay idol*
• **god, deity, effigy, statue, figurine**

idolize *VERB*
He idolizes his big brother.
• **adore, love, worship, be devoted to, look up to**

ignite *VERB*
❶ *These sparks then ignite the gunpowder.*
• **light, set fire to, set alight**
❷ *The bonfire would not ignite.*
• **catch fire, light, burn, kindle, spark**

ignorant *ADJECTIVE*
What an ignorant lot you are!
• **uneducated, uninformed, illiterate, stupid**
➤ **ignorant of**
I'm ignorant of the facts in the case.
• **unaware of, unfamiliar with, unacquainted with**
OPPOSITE aware of

ignore *VERB*
❶ *Why are you ignoring me?*
• **take no notice of, pay no attention to, neglect, spurn, snub**
IDIOM **give you the cold shoulder**
❷ *I'll ignore that remark.*
• **disregard, overlook, brush aside**
IDIOM **turn a blind eye to**

ill *ADJECTIVE*
❶ *She was ill with flu for three weeks.*
• **unwell, sick, poorly, sickly, ailing, infirm, unfit, indisposed**
IDIOM **under the weather**
– Someone who feels ill may be **nauseous** or **queasy**.
– Someone who looks ill may be **peaky** or **off colour**.
OPPOSITES healthy, well
SEE ALSO **illness**
❷ *He suffered no ill effects from the fall.*
• **bad, harmful, adverse, damaging, detrimental**
OPPOSITES good, beneficial

illegal *ADJECTIVE*
Under-age drinking is illegal.
• **unlawful, illicit, criminal, banned, prohibited, forbidden, outlawed, against the law**
OPPOSITE legal

illegible *ADJECTIVE*
The signature was illegible.
• **unreadable, indecipherable, unintelligible, unclear, indistinct**
OPPOSITES legible, readable

illness *NOUN*
She is suffering from a mysterious illness.
• **sickness, ailment, disease, disorder, complaint, condition, affliction, malady, infirmity, infection, virus**
(*informal*) **bug**
– A sudden illness is an **attack** or **fit**.
– A period of illness is a **bout**.
– A general outbreak of illness in a particular area is an **epidemic**.

WORD WEB

Some common illnesses:

➤ allergy
➤ anaemia
➤ appendicitis
➤ asthma
➤ bronchitis
➤ chickenpox
➤ chill
➤ cold
➤ cough
➤ diarrhoea
➤ eczema
➤ fever
➤ flu
➤ glandular fever
➤ hay fever
➤ headache
➤ indigestion
➤ influenza
➤ jaundice
➤ laryngitis
➤ measles
➤ migraine
➤ mumps
➤ pneumonia
➤ stomach ache
➤ tonsillitis
➤ ulcer
➤ whooping cough

illusion *NOUN*
❶ *The trick was a clever illusion created by mirrors.*
• **deception, apparition, mirage, fantasy, hallucination**
IDIOM **figment of your imagination**
❷ *He had no illusions about the danger he was in.*
• **delusion, misapprehension, misconception**

illustrate *VERB*
❶ *These drawings illustrate scenes from 'The Hobbit'.*
• **depict, picture, portray**
❷ *To illustrate my point, let me tell you a little story.*
• **show, demonstrate, explain, make clear, get across**
IDIOM **bring home**

illustration *NOUN*
❶ *The book has beautiful colour illustrations.*
• **picture, photograph, print, plate, figure, drawing, sketch, diagram**
❷ *Let me give you an illustration of what I mean.*
• **example, instance, demonstration, specimen, case**

image *NOUN*
❶ *The film contains graphic images of war.*
• **picture, portrayal, depiction, representation**
❷ *Amy frowned at her image in the mirror.*
• **reflection, likeness**
❸ *Kabir is the image of his father.*
• **double, twin**
❹ *The company is trying to improve its image.*
• **reputation, profile, impression, perception**

imaginary *ADJECTIVE*
The story is set in an imaginary world.
• **imagined, non-existent, unreal, made-up, invented, fanciful, fictitious, fictional, make-believe, pretend**
OPPOSITE real

imagination *NOUN*
❶ *It's all in your imagination.*
• **mind, fancy, dreams**
❷ *The writing shows plenty of imagination.*
• **creativity, inventiveness, ingenuity, inspiration, originality, vision**

imaginative *ADJECTIVE*
Roald Dahl wrote highly imaginative stories.
• **creative, inventive, inspired, original, innovative, fanciful**
OPPOSITES unimaginative, dull

imagine *VERB*
❶ *Can you imagine life without computers?*
• **picture, visualize, envisage, conceive of**
IDIOM **see in your mind's eye**
❷ *I imagine you'd like something to eat.*
• **suppose, assume, presume, expect, guess, take it**

imitate *VERB*
❶ *At first, he imitated the style of other authors.*
• **copy, reproduce, echo, ape, simulate, follow, mirror, match**
❷ *He is good at imitating famous people.*
• **mimic, impersonate, do an impression of**
(*informal*) **send up, take off**

imitation *ADJECTIVE*
The rug is made from imitation fur.
• **artificial, synthetic, fake, sham, mock, man-made**
OPPOSITES real, genuine

imitation *NOUN*
This is an imitation of a Roman coin.
• **copy, replica, reproduction, duplicate**
– An imitation made to deceive someone is a **fake** or **forgery**.

immature *ADJECTIVE*
He is quite immature for his age.
• **childish, babyish, infantile, juvenile**
OPPOSITE mature

immediate *ADJECTIVE*
❶ *They sent an immediate response.*
• **instant, instantaneous, prompt, speedy, swift, urgent, quick, direct**
(*informal*) **snappy**
OPPOSITE slow
❷ *Are you friends with your immediate neighbours?*
• **closest, nearest, adjacent, next**
OPPOSITE distant

immediately *ADVERB*

❶ *Call an ambulance immediately!*
• at once, now, straight away, right away, without delay, instantly, promptly

❷ *I was sitting immediately behind you.*
• right, exactly, directly, just

immense *ADJECTIVE*

At the top of the cliff was an immense boulder.
• huge, enormous, gigantic, massive, colossal, giant, vast, mighty, mammoth, monumental, great
(*informal*) whopping
OPPOSITE tiny
SEE ALSO big

imminent *ADJECTIVE*

By now, war was imminent.
• near, close, approaching, impending, forthcoming, looming

immobile *ADJECTIVE*

A figure stood immobile at the window.
• unmoving, motionless, stationary, still
OPPOSITE mobile

immoral *ADJECTIVE*

She believes that animal testing is immoral.
• wrong, unethical, bad, wicked, sinful, dishonest, corrupt, unprincipled
OPPOSITES moral, right

immortal *ADJECTIVE*

❶ *the immortal gods of Mount Olympus*
• undying, deathless, ageless, eternal
OPPOSITE mortal

❷ *the immortal words of Shakespeare*
• everlasting, enduring, timeless, perennial

immune *ADJECTIVE*

➤ **immune from**
No one is immune from the law.
• exempt from, not subject to, not liable to
OPPOSITE liable to

➤ **immune to**
Make your computer immune to viruses.
• resistant to, protected from, safe from, secure against
OPPOSITE susceptible to

impact *NOUN*

❶ *The crater was caused by the impact of a meteor.*
• crash, collision, smash, bump, blow, knock, bang, jolt

❷ *The Internet has had a huge impact on our lives.*
• effect, influence

impair *VERB*

Very loud noise can impair your hearing.
• damage, harm, injure, weaken, diminish

impartial *ADJECTIVE*

Referees must be impartial.
• unbiased, neutral, unprejudiced, disinterested, detached, objective, independent, non-partisan, even-handed
OPPOSITES biased, partisan

impatient *ADJECTIVE*

❶ *As time went on, I grew more and more impatient.*
• restless, agitated, anxious, edgy, fidgety, irritable, snappy, tetchy, testy
OPPOSITE patient

❷ *We were impatient for the show to begin.*
• anxious, eager, keen, in a hurry
(*informal*) itching
OPPOSITE reluctant

imperfect *ADJECTIVE*

The items on this shelf are imperfect.
• damaged, faulty, defective, flawed, substandard, incomplete
OPPOSITE perfect

impertinent *ADJECTIVE*

I've had enough of your impertinent questions.
• rude, cheeky, impolite, impudent, insolent, disrespectful
OPPOSITES respectful, polite

implement *NOUN*

The shed was full of garden implements.
• tool, appliance, device, utensil, gadget, instrument, contraption

implore *VERB*
I implore you to reconsider.
• **beg, entreat, plead with, appeal to, urge**

imply *VERB*
Are you implying that I am a liar?
• **suggest, hint, indicate, insinuate, make out**
The words imply and infer are not synonyms.

impolite *ADJECTIVE*
It would be impolite to refuse the invitation.
• **rude, bad-mannered, discourteous, disrespectful, insulting**
OPPOSITE polite

import *VERB*
The UK imports tea and coffee.
• **bring in, ship in**
OPPOSITE export

important *ADJECTIVE*
❶ *It is an important moment for our country.*
• **major, significant, momentous, big, central, historic**
❷ *I have some important business to attend to.*
• **serious, urgent, pressing, weighty, vital, essential, crucial**
❸ *Abraham Lincoln is an important figure in American history.*
• **prominent, influential, powerful, high-ranking, notable, eminent, distinguished**
OPPOSITES unimportant, minor

impose *VERB*
A new tax was imposed on fuel.
• **introduce, enforce, fix, inflict, prescribe, set**
➤ **impose on**
Are you sure I'm not imposing on you?
• **inconvenience, intrude on, take advantage of, put out**

imposing *ADJECTIVE*
The castle is an imposing building.
• **grand, great, impressive, stately, magnificent, splendid, majestic, dignified, striking**
OPPOSITE insignificant

impossible *ADJECTIVE*
It's impossible to get there and back in a day.
• **impractical, unrealistic, unworkable, unthinkable, unachievable, unattainable, not viable, out of the question**
OPPOSITES possible, realistic

impress *VERB*
She tried hard to impress the judges.
• **make an impression on, influence, leave your mark on, stick in the mind of**

impression *NOUN*
❶ *The book made a big impression on me.*
• **impact, influence, effect, mark**
❷ *I had the impression that something was wrong.*
• **feeling, sense, idea, notion, suspicion, hunch**
❸ *My sister does a good impression of the Queen.*
• **imitation, impersonation**
(*informal*) **send-up, take-off**

impressive *ADJECTIVE*
The film includes some impressive special effects.
• **striking, effective, powerful, spectacular, stunning, breathtaking, awesome, grand, imposing, prodigious**
OPPOSITES unimpressive, uninspiring

imprison *VERB*
Galileo was arrested and imprisoned for his ideas.
• **send to prison, jail, lock up, incarcerate, confine, detain**
(*informal*) **put away, send down**
IDIOM **put under lock and key**
OPPOSITE release

improve *VERB*
❶ *My playing has improved this year.*
• **get better, advance, progress, develop, move on**
OPPOSITE deteriorate
❷ *How can I improve this story?*
• **make better, refine, enhance, amend, revise, correct, upgrade**

❸ *Her health is slowly improving.*
• get better, recover, recuperate, pick up, rally, revive
IDIOM be on the mend
OPPOSITE get worse

improvement *NOUN*
❶ *Your handwriting is showing signs of improvement.*
• getting better, advance, progress, development, recovery, upturn
❷ *We have made some improvements to the website.*
• amendment, correction, revision, modification, enhancement

impudent *ADJECTIVE*
The boy had an impudent grin on his face.
• cheeky, insolent, rude, impolite, impertinent, disrespectful
OPPOSITES respectful, polite

impulse *NOUN*
I had a sudden impulse to laugh out loud.
• desire, instinct, urge, compulsion, whim

impulsive *ADJECTIVE*
She regretted her impulsive decision to dye her hair.
• hasty, rash, reckless, sudden, spontaneous, unplanned, unpremeditated, thoughtless, unthinking, impetuous, impromptu, spur-of-the-moment
OPPOSITES deliberate, premeditated

inaccessible *ADJECTIVE*
The caves are in an inaccessible part of the island.
• unreachable, isolated, remote, out-of-the-way, hard to find
OPPOSITE accessible

inaccurate *ADJECTIVE*
The information you gave is inaccurate.
• wrong, incorrect, inexact, imprecise, mistaken, false, erroneous, untrue
OPPOSITES accurate, correct

inadequate *ADJECTIVE*
They had an inadequate supply of water.
• insufficient, deficient, not enough, poor, limited, scarce, scanty, meagre, paltry
OPPOSITE adequate

inappropriate *ADJECTIVE*
Some scenes are inappropriate for very young children.
• unsuitable, unfitting, out of place, ill-suited, improper, unseemly
OPPOSITE appropriate

inaudible *ADJECTIVE*
From that distance the voices were inaudible.
• indistinct, muffled, muted, faint
OPPOSITE audible

incapable *ADJECTIVE*
➤ **incapable of**
They seem incapable of making a decision.
• unable to, incompetent at, unfit to, unsuited to, ineffective at
(*informal*) not up to
OPPOSITE capable of

incident *NOUN*
There was an amusing incident at school today.
• event, happening, occurrence, episode, affair

incidental *ADJECTIVE*
Some of these details are incidental to the plot.
• unimportant, inessential, secondary, minor, subordinate, subsidiary, peripheral
OPPOSITES essential, key

incite *VERB*
They were accused of inciting rebellion.
• provoke, instigate, arouse, stir up, whip up, kindle, inflame

inclination *NOUN*
❶ *The child shows a strong inclination towards music.*
• tendency, leaning, propensity, predisposition, bent

a b c d e f g h i j k l m n o p q r s t u v w x y z

(*formal*) penchant
❷ *That night, I felt no inclination for sleep.*
• desire, taste, liking, preference, urge

incline *NOUN*
The house was at the top of a steep incline.
• slope, hill, rise, gradient, ascent, ramp

inclined *ADJECTIVE*
➤ **be inclined to**
❶ *I'm inclined to agree with her.*
• be disposed to, be of a mind to
❷ *My brother is inclined to say the wrong thing.*
• tend to, be in the habit of, be liable to, be prone to, be given to, be apt to

include *VERB*
The cost includes postage and packing.
• contain, incorporate, cover, comprise, encompass, involve, take in, allow for, take into account
OPPOSITE exclude

income *NOUN*
Her income has gone up in the last year.
• earnings, pay, salary, wages, takings, revenue
OPPOSITE expenditure

incompetent *ADJECTIVE*
He is an incompetent buffoon!
• inept, unskilful, inexpert, amateurish, bungling
(*informal*) useless
OPPOSITE competent

incomplete *ADJECTIVE*
The new stadium is still incomplete.
• unfinished, uncompleted, not ready
OPPOSITE complete

incomprehensible *ADJECTIVE*
He left an incomprehensible message.
• unintelligible, unclear, indecipherable, unfathomable
OPPOSITES comprehensible, intelligible

inconsiderate *ADJECTIVE*
Some drivers are inconsiderate to cyclists.
• selfish, unthinking, thoughtless, insensitive, uncaring, tactless
OPPOSITE considerate

inconsistent *ADJECTIVE*
❶ *Their performance has been inconsistent this season.*
• changeable, variable, unreliable, unpredictable, erratic, fickle
❷ *The stories of the two witnesses are inconsistent.*
• contradictory, conflicting, irreconcilable, at odds, at variance
OPPOSITE consistent

inconspicuous *ADJECTIVE*
He stood in the corner, trying to remain inconspicuous.
• unnoticed, unobtrusive, camouflaged, out of sight
OPPOSITE conspicuous

inconvenient *ADJECTIVE*
I'm sorry if I've arrived at an inconvenient moment.
• awkward, difficult, bad, unsuitable, unfortunate, untimely, inopportune
OPPOSITE convenient

incorporate *VERB*
The show incorporates some well-known tunes.
• include, contain, embrace, take in
OPPOSITE exclude

incorrect *ADJECTIVE*
The next three answers were incorrect.
• wrong, mistaken, inaccurate, false, untrue
OPPOSITE correct

increase *VERB*
❶ *They have increased the size of the page.*
• make bigger, enlarge, expand, widen, broaden
❷ *We are increasing our efforts to reduce waste.*
• intensify, strengthen, develop, enhance, add to, step up

❸ *The train company will be increasing ticket prices soon.*
• **put up, raise**
❹ *How do you increase the volume on the TV?*
• **turn up, amplify, boost**
❺ *The population continues to increase.*
• **grow, mount, go up, build up, rise, soar, escalate, multiply**
❻ For opposites see **decrease**.

increase *NOUN*
There has been an increase in demand.
• **rise, growth, expansion, enlargement, leap, surge**
(*informal*) **hike**
OPPOSITE decrease

incredible *ADJECTIVE*
❶ *I find her story incredible.*
• **unbelievable, unlikely, improbable, implausible, unconvincing, far-fetched**
OPPOSITE credible
❷ *The new bridge is an incredible feat of engineering.*
• **extraordinary, marvellous, amazing, astounding, phenomenal, spectacular, magnificent, breathtaking, prodigious**

independence *NOUN*
The islanders value their independence.
• **freedom, liberty, autonomy, self-rule**
OPPOSITE dependence

independent *ADJECTIVE*
❶ *My granny is a very independent person.*
• **self-sufficient, self-reliant**
OPPOSITE dependent
❷ *Luxembourg is an independent country.*
• **autonomous, self-governing**
❸ *We need an independent opinion.*
• **impartial, unbiased, neutral, objective, disinterested**
OPPOSITE biased

indicate *VERB*
❶ *Please indicate your preference.*
• **specify, point out, show, reveal, make known**
❷ *A red light indicates danger.*
• **mean, stand for, denote, express, signal, signify, communicate, convey**

indication *NOUN*
He gave no indication of his feelings.
• **sign, signal, hint, clue, inkling, evidence, token, warning, symptom, pointer**

indifferent *ADJECTIVE*
❶ *Her voice showed how indifferent she was.*
• **uninterested, unconcerned, detached, impassive, uncaring, unmoved, unenthusiastic**
OPPOSITE enthusiastic
❷ *The food in the restaurant was indifferent.*
• **mediocre, ordinary, average, unexciting, uninspired, middle-of-the-road**
OPPOSITE excellent

indignant *ADJECTIVE*
The voice at the end of the phone was indignant.
• **annoyed, displeased, angry, resentful, affronted, offended, outraged, aggrieved, piqued**
(*informal*) **peeved**

indirect *ADJECTIVE*
The bus took an indirect route into town.
• **roundabout, circuitous, winding, meandering, tortuous, zigzag**
OPPOSITE direct

indistinct *ADJECTIVE*
❶ *In the photocopies, some of the numbers were indistinct.*
• **unclear, blurred, blurry, fuzzy, indefinite, vague, obscure, hazy**
OPPOSITE clear
❷ *I could hear indistinct sounds of people talking.*
• **muffled, mumbled, muted, faint, weak, inaudible, unintelligible, incoherent**
OPPOSITES distinct, clear

individual *ADJECTIVE*
❶ *Count each individual word.*
• **single, separate, discrete**

A B C D E F G H I J K L M N O P Q R S T U V W X Y Z

❷ *Her singing has an individual style.*
• **characteristic, distinct, distinctive, special, unique, personal, singular**

individual *NOUN*
He is a rather odd individual.
• **person, character, man, woman**
(*informal*) **sort, type**

induce *VERB*
❶ *Nothing would induce me to live there.*
• **persuade, convince, prompt, coax, tempt, prevail upon**
❷ *Some headaches are induced by stress.*
• **cause, produce, generate, provoke, bring on, lead to, give rise to**

indulge *VERB*
❶ *She could not be accused of indulging her children.*
• **spoil, pamper, pander to, mollycoddle, cosset**
❷ *Her husband indulged her every wish.*
• **satisfy, gratify, fulfil, meet, yield to, give in to**
➤ **indulge in**
On the journey we indulged in jokes and bad puns.
• **enjoy, treat yourself to, revel in**

indulgent *ADJECTIVE*
They are very indulgent towards their grandchildren.
• **tolerant, patient, permissive, lenient, easy-going, generous, liberal**
OPPOSITE **strict**

industry *NOUN*
❶ *Many people in the area work in the car industry.*
• **business, trade, commerce, manufacturing, production**
❷ *The workshop was a hive of industry.*
• **hard work, effort, energy, endeavour, industriousness, diligence, application**
OPPOSITE **laziness**

ineffective *ADJECTIVE*
❶ *Her protests were ineffective.*
• **unsuccessful, ineffectual, unproductive**
OPPOSITES **effective, successful**
❷ *He was an ineffective captain of the team.*
• **incompetent, inept, incapable, unfit, inadequate**
(*informal*) **useless**

inefficient *ADJECTIVE*
❶ *It is an inefficient way of doing things.*
• **ineffective, unproductive, unsystematic, disorganized, inept, slow, sloppy**
❷ *The car is inefficient in its use of fuel.*
• **wasteful, uneconomical, extravagant**
OPPOSITE **efficient**

inequality *NOUN*
Is there still inequality between men and women?
• **imbalance, inequity, disparity, discrepancy, unfairness, bias**
OPPOSITE **equality**

inevitable *ADJECTIVE*
It was inevitable that they would meet one day.
• **unavoidable, inescapable, certain, sure, definite**

inexpensive *ADJECTIVE*
You can buy inexpensive clothes in the market.
• **cheap, low-priced, low-cost, cut-price, affordable, economical, bargain, budget**
OPPOSITE **expensive**

infamous *ADJECTIVE*
Jesse James was an infamous outlaw.
• **notorious, villainous, disreputable, scandalous**

infant *NOUN*
On the wall there's a picture of me as an infant.
• **baby, newborn, small child, tot, toddler**

infect *VERB*
A virus had infected the water supply.
• **contaminate, pollute, poison**

infection *NOUN*
The infection spread rapidly.
• **disease, virus, contagion, contamination**

infectious *ADJECTIVE*
Chickenpox is highly infectious.
• **contagious, communicable**
(*informal*) **catching**
OPPOSITE non-infectious

infer *VERB*
What can we infer from this letter?
• **conclude, deduce, gather, work out**
SEE ALSO imply

inferior *ADJECTIVE*
❶ *The goods were of inferior quality.*
• **poor, bad, second-rate, low-grade, substandard, cheap, shoddy**
❷ *Officers can give orders to those of inferior rank.*
• **lesser, lower, junior, subordinate**
OPPOSITE superior

infested *ADJECTIVE*
The cellar was infested with mice.
• **swarming, teeming, crawling, overrun, plagued**

infinite *ADJECTIVE*
You need infinite patience to train a puppy.
• **unlimited, endless, limitless, boundless, never-ending, unending, inexhaustible, immeasurable**
OPPOSITES finite, limited

infirm *ADJECTIVE*
Most of the patients are elderly and infirm.
• **frail, weak, feeble, poorly, ill, unwell**
– People who have to stay in bed are **bedridden**.
OPPOSITE healthy

inflammable *ADJECTIVE*
see **flammable**

inflammation *NOUN*
This ointment will soothe the inflammation.
• **swelling, redness, soreness, infection**

inflate *VERB*
We have ten minutes to inflate fifty balloons.
• **blow up, pump up**
OPPOSITE deflate

inflict *VERB*
They inflicted a heavy defeat on us last season.
• **administer, deal out, mete out, exact, impose, force**

influence *NOUN*
❶ *Jazz had a major influence on his music.*
• **effect, impact, hold, pull, sway**
❷ *Europe had no influence in the region.*
• **power, authority, dominance, control, leverage, weight**
(*informal*) **clout**

influence *VERB*
Did anything influence your decision?
• **affect, have an impact on, guide, shape, direct, control, govern, determine**

influential *ADJECTIVE*
She knows some very influential people.
• **important, leading, powerful, significant**
OPPOSITE unimportant

inform *VERB*
Please inform us if you move house.
• **tell, let someone know, notify, advise, send word to**

informal *ADJECTIVE*
❶ *The dinner will be very informal.*
• **casual, relaxed, easy-going, friendly, homely**
(*informal*) **laid-back**
❷ *Emails are usually written in an informal style.*
• **colloquial, vernacular, familiar, everyday, popular, chatty**
OPPOSITE formal

information *NOUN*
There is more information on our website.
• **details, particulars, facts, data,**

advice, guidance, knowledge
(*informal*) info

informative *ADJECTIVE*
It's a very informative website.
• **helpful, useful, instructive, illuminating, revealing**
OPPOSITE unhelpful

infuriate *VERB*
My answer just infuriated her.
• **anger, enrage, incense, madden, exasperate**

ingenious *ADJECTIVE*
It seemed like an ingenious plan.
• **clever, brilliant, inspired, inventive, imaginative, original, crafty, cunning, shrewd**

inhabit *VERB*
People once inhabited these caves.
• **live in, occupy, dwell in, reside in, populate, settle in**

inhabitant *NOUN*
The island has fewer than a hundred inhabitants.
• **resident, dweller, native, occupier, occupant**
– An inhabitant of a particular city or country is a **citizen**.
– The inhabitants of a place are its **population**.

inhabited *ADJECTIVE*
Is the island inhabited?
• **occupied, lived-in**
OPPOSITE uninhabited

inherit *VERB*
She inherited the farm from her uncle.
• **succeed to, be left, come into**

inherited *ADJECTIVE*
Eye colour is an inherited characteristic.
• **hereditary, passed down, genetic**

inhuman *ADJECTIVE*
It was an act of inhuman cruelty.
• **barbaric, inhumane, savage, cruel, merciless, heartless**
OPPOSITE humane

initial *ADJECTIVE*
❶ *My initial reaction was to run away.*
• **first, earliest, immediate**
OPPOSITES final, eventual
❷ *The initial part of the poem is about the sea.*
• **opening, preliminary, introductory, preparatory**
OPPOSITES final, closing

initially *ADVERB*
Initially, I thought the book was boring.
• **at first, in the beginning, to begin with, to start with, at the outset**

initiative *NOUN*
They had to use their initiative to survive.
• **resourcefulness, inventiveness, originality, ingenuity, enterprise**

injection *NOUN*
The nurse gave me an injection.
• **inoculation, vaccination, immunization**
(*informal*) **jab, shot**

injure *VERB*
Some passengers were seriously injured.
• **hurt, wound, harm**
– To injure someone causing permanent damage is to **maim** them.

injury *NOUN*
We all escaped without any serious injury.
• **wound, harm, hurt**

WORD WEB

Some types of injury:

➤ bite	➤ graze
➤ bruise	➤ scald
➤ burn	➤ scratch
➤ cut	➤ sprain
➤ fracture	➤ sting
➤ gash	➤ strain

inner *ADJECTIVE*
❶ *A passageway leads to the inner chamber.*
• **central, inside, interior, internal, inward, middle**

❷ *She kept her inner feelings to herself.*
• innermost, personal, private, intimate, secret, hidden, concealed
OPPOSITE outer

innocent *ADJECTIVE*
❶ *He was found innocent of murder.*
• guiltless, blameless, faultless, free from blame
OPPOSITE guilty
❷ *She looks so sweet and innocent.*
• angelic, virtuous, pure, inexperienced, naive
OPPOSITES wicked, cunning
❸ *It was just a bit of innocent fun.*
• harmless, innocuous, inoffensive

innumerable *ADJECTIVE*
The sun is just one of innumerable stars.
• countless, numberless, uncountable, untold

inquire *VERB*
➤ **inquire into**
The police are inquiring into the case.
• look into, investigate, examine, explore

inquiry *NOUN*
There will be an official inquiry into the accident.
• investigation, inspection, examination

inquisitive *ADJECTIVE*
Chimpanzees are naturally inquisitive.
• curious, questioning, inquiring, probing
– An uncomplimentary word is **nosy**.

insane *ADJECTIVE*
❶ *It was rumoured that the king had gone insane.*
• mentally ill, mad, crazy, deranged, demented, unhinged
(*informal*) nuts, bonkers
IDIOMS off your head, stark raving mad
IDIOMS (*informal*) off your rocker, off your trolley
OPPOSITE sane
❷ *The whole idea seems insane now.*
• crazy, mad, senseless, stupid, foolish, idiotic, foolhardy, absurd, ludicrous, preposterous, hare-brained
(*informal*) nutty, daft, barmy
OPPOSITES sensible, wise

inscription *NOUN*
I tried to read the inscription on the tomb.
• engraving, carving, writing, lettering

insect *NOUN*
night-flying insects
• bug
(*informal*) creepy-crawly, minibeast

WORD WEB

Some types of insect:

➤ ant
➤ aphid
➤ bee
➤ beetle
➤ bluebottle
➤ bumblebee
➤ butterfly
➤ cicada
➤ cockroach
➤ crane fly (*informal* daddy-long-legs)
➤ cricket
➤ dragonfly
➤ earwig
➤ firefly
➤ flea
➤ fly
➤ glow-worm
➤ gnat
➤ grasshopper
➤ greenfly
➤ hornet
➤ horsefly
➤ lacewing
➤ ladybird
➤ locust
➤ louse
➤ mantis
➤ mayfly
➤ midge
➤ mosquito
➤ moth
➤ stick insect
➤ termite
➤ tsetse fly
➤ wasp
➤ weevil

Life stages of insects:

➤ caterpillar
➤ chrysalis
➤ grub
➤ larva
➤ maggot
➤ pupa

Parts of an insect's body:

➤ head
➤ thorax
➤ abdomen; antennae
➤ legs
➤ mandibles
➤ wings

– The scientific study of insects is entomology.

insecure *ADJECTIVE*
I used to feel insecure around people.
• **unconfident, uncertain, self-conscious, diffident, hesitant, anxious, nervous, apprehensive, uneasy**
OPPOSITES secure, self-confident

insensitive *ADJECTIVE*
I'm sorry if my comments were insensitive.
• **thoughtless, tactless, unfeeling, uncaring, unsympathetic, callous**
OPPOSITE sensitive

insert *VERB*
Please insert a coin in the slot.
• **put in, place, push in, slide in, slot in, install, implant, load**
(*informal*) **pop in, stick in**

inside *NOUN*
❶ *The inside of the nest was lined with feathers.*
• **interior, inner surface, centre, core, heart, middle**
OPPOSITE outside
❷ (*informal*) *I felt a pain in my insides.*
• **stomach, belly, gut, bowels, intestines**
(*informal*) **innards**

inside *ADJECTIVE*
The inside walls of the house were damp.
• **interior, inner, internal, innermost, indoor**
OPPOSITES outside, outer

insignificant *ADJECTIVE*
These changes may seem insignificant to you.
• **unimportant, minor, trivial, trifling, negligible, slight, insubstantial, paltry, petty**
OPPOSITES significant, major

insincere *ADJECTIVE*
The waiter welcomed us with an insincere smile.
• **false, pretended, feigned, hollow, hypocritical, disingenuous**
(*informal*) **two-faced, phoney, put-on**
OPPOSITE sincere

insist *VERB*
He insisted that no one else was to blame.
• **declare, state, assert, maintain, protest, stress, emphasize, swear, vow, claim**
➤ **insist on**
I insist on seeing the manager.
• **demand, require**

insistent *ADJECTIVE*
There was an insistent tapping on the window.
• **persistent, unrelenting, unremitting, dogged, tenacious**

insolent *ADJECTIVE*
The boy gave him an insolent stare.
• **rude, impudent, disrespectful, impolite, impertinent, arrogant, brazen**
(*informal*) **cheeky**
OPPOSITES polite, respectful

inspect *VERB*
We inspected the damage done by the storm.
• **examine, investigate, check, look over, study, survey, scrutinize, monitor, vet**
(*informal*) **check out**
IDIOM (*informal*) **give the once-over**

inspection *NOUN*
There will be a safety inspection this afternoon.
• **check, check-up, examination, review, survey, scrutiny, investigation**

inspiration *NOUN*
❶ *I had a sudden inspiration.*
• **idea, bright idea, thought, revelation**
(*informal*) **brainwave**
❷ *What was the inspiration behind your story?*
• **impulse, motivation, stimulus, influence, spur**

inspire *VERB*
❶ *I felt inspired to write a poem.*
• **motivate, stimulate, prompt, encourage, stir, rouse, spur on**

❷ *He's a manager who inspires loyalty in his players.*
• **arouse, induce, awaken, kindle, trigger, bring out**

install *VERB*
We are having a new cooker installed.
• **put in, set up, fix, place, position, establish**
OPPOSITE remove

instalment *NOUN*
I missed the first instalment of the new series.
• **episode, part, programme, issue, section**

instance *NOUN*
Give me an instance of what you mean.
• **example, illustration, case, sample**

instant *ADJECTIVE*
The show was an instant success.
• **immediate, instantaneous, quick, rapid, fast, prompt, snappy, speedy, swift, direct**

instant *NOUN*
I only saw the figure for an instant.
• **moment, second, flash**
(*informal*) **tick, jiffy**
IDIOMS **split second, twinkling of an eye**

instinct *NOUN*
Good detectives should always follow their instincts.
• **impulse, inclination, intuition, hunch, feeling, urge**

instinctive *ADJECTIVE*
Many people have an instinctive fear of snakes.
• **intuitive, natural, innate, inherent, automatic, involuntary, reflex, spontaneous, impulsive, unconscious, unthinking**
OPPOSITES deliberate, conscious

instruct *VERB*
❶ *All the staff are instructed in first aid.*
• **teach, train, coach, tutor, educate, school**
❷ *The guide instructed us to wait.*
• **tell, order, direct, command**

instructions *PLURAL NOUN*
Please follow the instructions carefully.
• **directions, guidelines, orders, commands**

instructor *NOUN*
She is a qualified skiing instructor.
• **teacher, trainer, tutor, coach**

instrument *NOUN*
They use a special instrument for measuring wind speed.
• **tool, implement, utensil, appliance, device, gadget, contraption**
(*informal*) **gizmo**
For musical instruments see **music**.

insufficient *ADJECTIVE*
The plants had an insufficient amount of water.
• **inadequate, deficient, not enough, too little, scant, scanty**
OPPOSITES enough, excessive

insult *VERB*
I apologize if I have insulted you.
• **offend, outrage, be rude to, hurt, injure, slight, snub**

insult *NOUN*
Would it be an insult to refuse her offer?
• **affront, slight, slur, snub**
(*informal*) **put-down**

insulting *ADJECTIVE*
She made an insulting comment about my hair.
• **offensive, rude, impolite, derogatory, disparaging, scornful, uncomplimentary**
OPPOSITE complimentary

intact *ADJECTIVE*
The skeleton was largely intact.
• **unbroken, whole, undamaged, unharmed, complete, perfect**
(*informal*) **in one piece**

integrate *VERB*
They decided to integrate the two classes.
• **combine, join, merge, unite, unify, amalgamate, bring together**
OPPOSITE separate

a b c d e f g h i j k l m n o p q r s t u v w x y z

A B C D E F G H I J K L M N O P Q R S T U V W X Y Z

integrity *NOUN*
Is there any reason to doubt his integrity?
• **honesty, honour, loyalty, trustworthiness, reliability, sincerity, fidelity, virtue**
OPPOSITE dishonesty

intelligence *NOUN*
❶ *The robot shows signs of intelligence.*
• **cleverness, understanding, comprehension, reason, sense, wisdom, insight, intellect, brainpower, wits**
(*informal*) **brains**
❷ *He was sent on a spying mission to gather secret intelligence.*
• **information, knowledge, data, facts, reports**

intelligent *ADJECTIVE*
He was an intelligent boy for his age.
• **clever, bright, smart, quick-witted, sharp, perceptive, shrewd, able, brilliant, rational, thinking**
(*informal*) **brainy**
OPPOSITES unintelligent, stupid

intelligible *ADJECTIVE*
The message was barely intelligible.
• **understandable, comprehensible, clear, plain, unambiguous, coherent, lucid**
OPPOSITE incomprehensible

intend *VERB*
What do you intend to do?
• **plan, aim, mean, have in mind, plot, propose**
➤ **be intended for**
The class is intended for beginners.
• **be aimed at, be designed for, be meant for, be set up for**

intense *ADJECTIVE*
❶ *I felt a sudden, intense pain in my chest.*
• **extreme, acute, severe, sharp, great, strong, violent**
OPPOSITES slight, mild
❷ *The debate aroused intense feelings.*
• **deep, passionate, powerful, strong, profound**
OPPOSITE mild

intensive *ADJECTIVE*
Police carried out an intensive search of the area.
• **detailed, thorough, rigorous, exhaustive, concentrated, in-depth, methodical, painstaking**
OPPOSITE superficial

intent *ADJECTIVE*
He read the letter with an intent look of concentration.
• **attentive, focused, absorbed, engrossed, preoccupied, rapt**
➤ **intent on**
Why are you intent on leaving?
• **determined to, resolved to, committed to, set on, fixed on, bent on**

intention *NOUN*
Our only intention is to win.
• **aim, objective, target, goal, ambition, plan, intent**

intentional *ADJECTIVE*
It was clearly an intentional foul.
• **deliberate, conscious, calculated, planned, intended, meant, wilful, done on purpose**
OPPOSITE accidental

intercept *VERB*
A defender intercepted the pass.
• **check, stop, block, catch, cut off, head off, deflect**

interest *NOUN*
❶ *He listened with increasing interest.*
• **curiosity, attention, involvement, attentiveness, regard, notice**
❷ *The information is of no interest to anyone.*
• **importance, significance, concern, consequence, relevance, note, value**
❸ *My interests include painting and photography.*
• **hobby, pastime, pursuit, activity, diversion, amusement**

interest *VERB*
Astronomy has always interested me.
• **appeal to, be of interest to, attract, excite, fascinate, absorb, capture your imagination**
OPPOSITE **bore**
➤ **be interested in**
Are you interested in fashion?
• **be keen on, care about, follow**

interesting *ADJECTIVE*
She is full of interesting ideas.
• **fascinating, stimulating, intriguing, absorbing, captivating, engrossing, entertaining, diverting**
OPPOSITES **boring, dull**

interfere *VERB*
➤ **interfere in**
Please stop interfering in my affairs!
• **intervene in, intrude in, meddle in, pry into, encroach on, butt in on**
IDIOM (*informal*) **poke your nose into**
➤ **interfere with**
The weather interfered with our plans.
• **hamper, hinder, get in the way of, obstruct**

interior *ADJECTIVE & NOUN*
see **inside**

intermediate *ADJECTIVE*
Should I join the intermediate or the advanced class?
• **middle, midway, halfway, in-between, transitional**

internal *ADJECTIVE*
This is a diagram of the internal parts of the engine.
• **inner, inside, interior**
OPPOSITE **external**

international *ADJECTIVE*
An international rescue team was put together.
• **global, worldwide, multinational, intercontinental**

interpret *VERB*
Can you interpret this old writing?
• **explain, make sense of, clarify, translate, decipher, decode**

interrogate *VERB*
The police interrogated the two suspects for several hours.
• **question, interview, examine, cross-examine, quiz**
(*informal*) **grill**

interrupt *VERB*
❶ *Please don't interrupt while I am speaking.*
• **intervene, interject, break in, butt in, cut in**
❷ *Heavy rain interrupted the match.*
• **stop, suspend, disrupt, break off, cut short**

interruption *NOUN*
I worked for an hour without any interruption.
• **break, pause, stop, gap, halt, disruption, suspension**

interval *NOUN*
❶ *There will be a short interval after the first act.*
• **intermission, interlude, recess, break, pause, time-out**
(*informal*) **breather**
❷ *There are signs at regular intervals along the road.*
• **space, gap, distance**

intervene *VERB*
A man intervened to stop the fight.
• **intercede, step in, interfere, interrupt, butt in**

interview *VERB*
The actress was being interviewed about her new film.
• **question, talk to, interrogate, examine, quiz, sound out**
(*informal*) **grill**

intimate *ADJECTIVE*
❶ *They have been intimate friends for years.*
• **close, cherished, dear, bosom**
OPPOSITE **distant**
❷ *The restaurant has an intimate atmosphere.*
• **friendly, warm, welcoming, informal, cosy**

❸ *They printed intimate details about her life.*
• personal, private, confidential, secret
❹ *He has an intimate knowledge of this area.*
• detailed, thorough, deep, profound, exhaustive, in-depth

intimidate *VERB*
He was accused of trying to intimidate a witness.
• bully, threaten, frighten, menace, scare, terrify, terrorize, persecute

intrepid *ADJECTIVE*
The intrepid explorers finally reached the North Pole.
• daring, bold, fearless, courageous, brave, valiant, heroic, plucky

intricate *ADJECTIVE*
The clock has an intricate mechanism.
• complex, complicated, elaborate, sophisticated, involved, convoluted
OPPOSITE simple

intriguing *ADJECTIVE*
The results of the experiment are intriguing.
• interesting, fascinating, absorbing, captivating, beguiling

introduce *VERB*
❶ *When was printing introduced in Europe?*
• establish, institute, bring in, set up, create, start, begin, initiate, launch, inaugurate
❷ *Let me introduce you to my friend.*
• present, make known, acquaint (with)
❸ *The director stood up to introduce the film.*
• announce, give an introduction to, lead into

introduction *NOUN*
The plot is outlined in the introduction.
• preface, foreword, preamble, prelude (*informal*) intro
– An introduction to a play is a **prologue**.
– An introduction to an opera or a ballet is an **overture**.

intrude *VERB*
I hope I'm not intruding.
• interrupt, intervene, break in, butt in
➤ **intrude on**
I don't mean to intrude on your privacy.
• encroach on, infringe on, trespass on, violate, invade

intruder *NOUN*
Some intruders broke into the building.
• trespasser, interloper, prowler, burglar

invade *VERB*
The Vikings invaded many parts of Europe.
• attack, raid, occupy, overrun, conquer, capture, seize

invalid *ADJECTIVE*
❶ *Your ticket is invalid because it is out of date.*
• unacceptable, illegitimate, void
❷ *That is an invalid argument.*
• false, unsound, unjustifiable, spurious, fallacious
OPPOSITE valid

invaluable *ADJECTIVE*
She is an invaluable member of the team.
• indispensable, irreplaceable, crucial, essential, vital, all-important
OPPOSITES dispensable, worthless

invasion *NOUN*
the Viking invasion of Ireland
• attack, raid, occupation, capture, seizure, conquest

invent *VERB*
❶ *Who invented the telescope?*
• create, design, devise, originate, think up, conceive
❷ *He had to invent an excuse quickly.*
• make up, fabricate, concoct, dream up

invention *NOUN*
❶ *The recipe is my own invention.*
• creation, design, discovery, innovation (*informal*) brainchild
❷ *The newspaper article was mostly invention.*
• fantasy, fiction, fabrication, lies, deceit, falsehood

inventive *ADJECTIVE*
She has an inventive mind.
• creative, original, imaginative, ingenious, inspired, innovative

inventor *NOUN*
James Watt was the inventor of the steam engine.
• creator, designer, originator, discoverer, author, architect

investigate *VERB*
Police are investigating the cause of the accident.
• examine, explore, inquire into, look into, study, scrutinize, consider, follow up, probe, research
(*informal*) go into

investigation *NOUN*
There will be an investigation into the accident.
• examination, inquiry, inspection, study, review, survey

invigorating *ADJECTIVE*
We had an invigorating walk before breakfast.
• refreshing, stimulating, reviving, bracing

invisible *ADJECTIVE*
These creatures are so tiny that they are invisible to the human eye.
• out of sight, unseen, undetectable, unnoticeable, unnoticed, unobserved, inconspicuous, hidden, concealed, covered, obscured
OPPOSITE visible

invitation *NOUN*
I received an invitation to attend the ceremony.
• request, call, summons
(*informal*) invite

invite *VERB*
❶ *Who are you inviting to your party?*
• ask, summon, have someone round
(*formal*) request someone's company
❷ *That sort of thing just invites trouble.*
• ask for, lead to, bring about, encourage, induce, provoke

inviting *ADJECTIVE*
An inviting smell came from the kitchen.
• attractive, appealing, pleasant, welcoming, agreeable, appetizing, tempting, enticing
OPPOSITE repulsive

involve *VERB*
❶ *Her job involves a lot of travel.*
• include, comprise, require, demand, necessitate, mean
❷ *These are decisions that involve everybody.*
• affect, concern, interest, touch

involved *ADJECTIVE*
The plot is too involved to summarize.
• complex, complicated, elaborate, intricate, convoluted
OPPOSITE simple
➤ **be involved in**
Are you involved in the theatre?
• associated with, connected with, concerned with, caught up in, mixed up in

irrational *ADJECTIVE*
I have an irrational fear of spiders.
• unreasonable, illogical, senseless, groundless, unfounded, nonsensical, absurd
OPPOSITE rational

irregular *ADJECTIVE*
❶ *The bricks were arranged in an irregular pattern.*
• varying, variable, erratic, unpredictable, uneven, random, haphazard, fitful, patchy
OPPOSITES regular, orderly
❷ *The suggestion is highly irregular!*
• abnormal, unusual, exceptional, unconventional, improper
OPPOSITES normal, usual

irrelevant *ADJECTIVE*
Don't waste time on irrelevant details.
• inappropriate, unnecessary, inessential, pointless, immaterial, unrelated, unconnected, extraneous
IDIOM beside the point
OPPOSITE relevant

A B C D E F G H I J K L M N O P Q R S T U V W X Y Z

irresistible *ADJECTIVE*
I had an irresistible urge to giggle.
• **overwhelming, overpowering, uncontrollable, unavoidable, powerful, compelling**

irresponsible *ADJECTIVE*
It's irresponsible to drive too fast.
• **reckless, rash, thoughtless, inconsiderate, uncaring, unthinking, negligent**
OPPOSITE **responsible**

irritable *ADJECTIVE*
He arrived in an irritable mood.
• **bad-tempered, grumpy, short-tempered, cross, impatient, irascible, snappy, touchy, testy, grouchy, prickly, peevish, quarrelsome**
OPPOSITES **good-humoured, cheerful**

irritate *VERB*
❶ *The noise began to irritate me.*
• **annoy, bother, exasperate, anger, provoke, madden, vex**
(*informal*) **bug, rile, get to**
IDIOM **get on your nerves**
❷ *Soap may irritate sensitive skin.*
• **inflame, itch, burn**

island *NOUN*
Fiji is an island in the South Pacific.
• (*literary*) **isle**
– A small island is an **islet**.
– A coral island is an **atoll**.
– A group of islands is an **archipelago**.
– An uninhabited island is a **desert island**.

isolated *ADJECTIVE*
❶ *They found their way to an isolated village in the mountains.*
• **remote, secluded, out-of-the-way, outlying, inaccessible, cut off**
OPPOSITE **accessible**
❷ *There was an isolated sighting of a UFO.*
• **single, solitary, lone, unique, uncommon, unusual, exceptional**
(*informal*) **one-off**
OPPOSITE **common**

issue *VERB*
❶ *They issued blankets to the refugees.*
• **give out, distribute, supply, furnish, equip**
❷ *The ambassador issued a strongly-worded statement.*
• **put out, send out, bring out, produce, publish, release, circulate, print, broadcast**
❸ *Black smoke issued from the chimneys.*
• **come out, emerge, appear, flow out, gush, erupt**

issue *NOUN*
❶ *The paper mainly covers local issues.*
• **matter, subject, topic, affair, concern, question, problem, situation**
❷ *There will be a special issue of the magazine next month.*
• **edition, number, instalment, copy**

itch *NOUN*
❶ *I had an annoying itch on my foot.*
• **tickle, tingling, prickle**
❷ *You've always had an itch to travel.*
• **desire, longing, yearning, craving, hankering, urge, wish, ache, thirst, hunger**

item *NOUN*
❶ *I bought a few items in the sale.*
• **thing, object, article**
❷ *There was an item about our school in the paper.*
• **article, piece, report, feature, write-up**

jab *VERB*
A passer-by jabbed me in the ribs.
• **poke, prod, elbow, nudge, stab, dig**

jagged *ADJECTIVE*
Holly leaves have jagged edges.
• **spiky, toothed, serrated, prickly, thorny, barbed, ragged**
OPPOSITE smooth

jail *NOUN*
see **prison**

jam *NOUN*
1 *We got stuck in a jam on the motorway.*
• **traffic jam, hold-up, tailback, blockage, congestion, bottleneck**
2 (*informal*) *I'm in a bit of a jam.*
• **difficulty, mess, predicament, plight**
(*informal*) **fix**
IDIOM **tight corner**

jam *VERB*
1 *Someone had jammed the door open.*
• **prop, wedge, stick**
2 *The paper has jammed in the printer.*
• **become stuck, stick, catch**
3 *I jammed my things into a backpack.*
• **cram, pack, stuff, squeeze, squash, crush, ram, crowd**
4 *The roads are jammed at rush hour.*
• **block, clog, obstruct, congest**
(*informal*) **bung up**

jangle *NOUN & VERB*
His keys jangled in his pocket.
• **jingle, tinkle, ring, chink, clink**

jar *NOUN*
an earthenware jar
• **pot, container, vase, crock**

jar *VERB*
1 *I jarred my wrist when I fell.*
• **jolt, jerk, shake, vibrate**
2 *Those colours jar with each other.*
• **clash, conflict, be incompatible, be at odds**
OPPOSITES harmonize, go together

jealous *ADJECTIVE*
1 *Some people were jealous of her popularity.*
• **envious, resentful, grudging**
IDIOM **green with envy (at)**
2 *In the story she is locked away by her jealous lover.*
• **suspicious, distrustful, possessive**

jealousy *NOUN*
1 *I couldn't help feeling a twinge of jealousy at his good fortune.*
• **envy, resentment, bitterness**
2 *She could no longer stand her lover's jealousy.*
• **suspicion, distrust, possessiveness**

jeer *VERB*
Some of the audience whistled and jeered.
• **boo, hiss, sneer, taunt, mock, scoff, ridicule**
OPPOSITE cheer

jerk *VERB*
1 *The train suddenly jerked to a halt.*
• **jolt, lurch, judder, shudder, bump, bounce**
2 *I just managed to jerk my arm free.*
• **pull, tug, yank, pluck, wrench**

jerky *ADJECTIVE*
The stagecoach drew to a jerky halt.
• **jolting, jumpy, shaky, bouncy, bumpy, twitchy, uneven**
OPPOSITES steady, smooth

jet *NOUN*
A jet of water shot high in the air.
• **spout, spurt, spray, squirt, gush, stream, fountain**

jewel *NOUN*
see gem

jewellery *NOUN*

WORD WEB

Some items of jewellery:

- anklet
- bangle
- beads
- bindi
- body jewel
- bracelet
- brooch
- cameo
- chain
- charm
- choker
- clasp
- crown
- cufflinks
- diadem
- earring
- engagement ring
- lapel pin
- locket
- necklace
- necklet
- pendant
- pin
- ring
- tiara
- tiepin
- toe ring
- wedding ring

- A person who sells or makes jewellery is a **jeweller**.
- A person who makes gold or silver jewellery is a **goldsmith** or **silversmith**.

SEE ALSO **gem**

jingle *NOUN & VERB*
We heard the sound of sleigh bells jingling.
• **tinkle, jangle, ring, chink, clink**

job *NOUN*
❶ *My sister has a job as a teaching assistant.*
• **post, position, profession, occupation, employment, trade, work, career, vocation, calling**
For types of job see **occupation**.
❷ *Whose job is it to do the washing-up?*
• **duty, task, assignment, chore, errand**

jog *VERB*
❶ *He jogs round the park every morning.*
• **run, trot**
❷ *I jogged his elbow by accident.*
• **nudge, prod, jolt, jostle, jar, knock, bump**
❸ *The photograph may jog your memory.*
• **prompt, stir, arouse, stimulate, spark, set off**

join *VERB*
❶ *The two roads join here.*
• **come together, meet, converge, merge, unite, combine, amalgamate**
OPPOSITES **divide, separate**
❷ *Join the two pieces of rope together.*
• **put together, connect, fasten, attach, fix, link, couple, bond**
OPPOSITES **detach, separate**
❸ *I joined the crowd going into the cinema.*
• **follow, go with, accompany**
(*informal*) **tag along with**
❹ *We have joined a local sports club.*
• **become a member of, enrol in, sign up for**
– To join the army is to **enlist**.
OPPOSITES **leave, resign from**

join *NOUN*
If you look hard, you can still see the join.
• **joint, connection, link, mend, seam**

joint *ADJECTIVE*
Putting on the show was a joint effort.
• **combined, shared, common, communal, cooperative, united, collective, mutual, concerted**
OPPOSITE **individual**

joke *NOUN*
Do you know any good jokes?
• **jest, quip, witticism, wisecrack**
(*informal*) **gag, crack**

joke *VERB*
Those two are always laughing and joking.
• **jest, clown, have a laugh, make jokes, tease**

jolly *ADJECTIVE*
He was in his usual, jolly mood.
• **cheerful, good-humoured, happy, merry, joyful, cheery, bright, sunny, chirpy**
(*informal*) **upbeat**
OPPOSITE **gloomy**

jolt *VERB*
The car jolted over the bumps in the road.
• **jerk, lurch, judder, shudder, bump, bounce**

jostle *VERB*
People jostled to get a better view.
• **push, shove, elbow, barge, press, scramble, jockey**

jot *VERB*
➤ **jot down**
I quickly jotted down a few ideas.
• **make a note of, write down, take down, note, scribble**

journal *NOUN*
❶ *She has had a few articles published in academic journals.*
• **magazine, periodical, newspaper, review, bulletin, gazette**
❷ *He kept a journal of the voyage.*
• **diary, log, logbook, record, account, chronicle**

journalist *NOUN*
She works as a journalist on the local paper.
• **reporter, correspondent, columnist, writer**

journey *NOUN*
The journey takes you through three countries.
• **voyage, trip, expedition, passage, tour, route, travels**

jovial *ADJECTIVE*
A jovial old man greeted them.
• **cheerful, happy, jolly, merry, good-humoured, joyful, cheery**
OPPOSITE sad

joy *NOUN*
My heart leaped with joy.
• **happiness, joyfulness, delight, cheerfulness, gladness, glee, jubilation, rejoicing, bliss, ecstasy, elation, exultation, euphoria, rapture**
OPPOSITE sorrow

joyful *ADJECTIVE*
The wedding was a joyful occasion.
• **happy, cheerful, merry, joyous, jolly, good-humoured**
OPPOSITE sad

judge *NOUN*
The judges could not agree on a winner.
• **adjudicator, assessor, referee, umpire**

judge *VERB*
❶ *The umpire judged that the ball was out.*
• **rule, decide, decree, pronounce, adjudicate**
❷ *Entries will be judged by a panel of experts.*
• **assess, evaluate, appraise, rate, examine**
❸ *She judged the helmet to be about a thousand years old.*
• **gauge, estimate, reckon, deduce, guess**

judgement *NOUN*
❶ *What is the judgement of the court?*
• **decision, verdict, finding, ruling, pronouncement, decree**
❷ *In my judgement, you're making a big mistake.*
• **opinion, view, belief, assessment, appraisal, estimate**
❸ *His comments show a lack of judgement.*
• **wisdom, sense, common sense, understanding, perception, discrimination, discernment**

juice *NOUN*
Add the juice of a lemon.
• **liquid, fluid, sap, extract**

jumble *VERB*
Please don't jumble the pages.
• **muddle, mix up, mess up, disorganize, disorder, shuffle, tangle**
OPPOSITES arrange, order

jumble *NOUN*
His clothes were in a jumble on the floor.
• **mess, muddle, clutter, chaos, confusion, disarray, disorder**
(*informal*) **hotchpotch**

A B C D E F G H I J K L M N O P Q R S T U V W X Y Z

jump *VERB*
❶ *Suddenly a deer jumped in front of us.*
• leap, spring, bound, hop, skip, prance, pounce
❷ *All the horses jumped the first hurdle.*
• leap over, vault, clear
❸ *The loud bang made everyone jump.*
• start, flinch, jolt

jump *NOUN*
❶ *With a jump she reached the other side.*
• leap, spring, bound, vault, hop, skip
❷ *I awoke with a jump.*
• start, jolt, jerk, spasm, judder
❸ *There has been a sharp jump in prices.*
• increase, rise, leap, surge
(*informal*) hike

junction *NOUN*
Turn left at the junction.
• intersection, crossroads, interchange

junior *ADJECTIVE*
❶ *I play for the junior hockey team.*
• younger
❷ *He's a junior officer in the army.*
• low-ranking, minor, lesser, subordinate
OPPOSITE senior

junk *NOUN*
The garage is full of old junk.
• rubbish, clutter, jumble, trash, garbage, waste, refuse, scrap, odds and ends

just *ADJECTIVE*
❶ *It was a just decision.*
• fair, impartial, unbiased, even-handed, honourable, upright, principled
OPPOSITES unjust, unfair
❷ *I think it was a just punishment for the crime.*
• deserved, fair, fitting, merited, appropriate, due, rightful, reasonable, proper
OPPOSITE undeserved

just *ADVERB*
❶ *The colour is just right.*
• exactly, precisely, absolutely
❷ *She was just a child then.*
• only, simply, merely
❸ *It's just after nine o'clock.*
• slightly, barely, scarcely

justice *NOUN*
❶ *We demand to be treated with justice.*
• fairness, justness, right, honesty, impartiality, even-handedness, equity, fair play
OPPOSITE injustice
❷ *They were tried in a court of justice.*
• law

justify *VERB*
How can you justify the cost?
• defend, excuse, account for, explain, vindicate

jut *VERB*
➤ **jut out**
A large nail jutted out from the wall.
• stick out, project, protrude, extend, overhang

juvenile *ADJECTIVE*
❶ *The bookshop sells a range of juvenile fiction.*
• children's, young people's
OPPOSITE adult
❷ *His jokes are really juvenile.*
• childish, babyish, immature
OPPOSITE mature

Kk

keen *ADJECTIVE*
❶ *Layla is a keen photographer.*
• **enthusiastic, eager, fervent, avid, devoted, committed, motivated**
OPPOSITE unenthusiastic
❷ *A carving knife should have a keen edge.*
• **sharp, razor-sharp, honed**
OPPOSITE blunt
❸ *Owls have keen eyesight.*
• **sharp, acute, piercing**
OPPOSITE poor
❹ *A keen wind was blowing from the east.*
• **bitter, cold, icy, biting, penetrating**
OPPOSITE mild
➤ **be keen on**
I'm not very keen on flying.
• **be fond of, like, enjoy, be partial to**
(*informal*) **be mad on, be into**
IDIOM **have a soft spot for**

keep *VERB*
❶ *I've kept all of her letters.*
• **save, conserve, preserve, retain, hang on to, hold on to, guard, store**
❷ *It costs money to keep a pet.*
• **support, maintain, provide for, pay for**
❸ *She tried to keep calm.*
• **stay, remain**
❹ *I won't keep you long.*
• **delay, detain, hold up, keep waiting**
❺ *Why do you keep asking me questions?*
• **persist in, go on, carry on, continue, insist on**
❻ *The milk will keep until tomorrow.*
• **last, be usable, stay good**
❼ *Where do you keep the knives and forks?*
• **store, house, put, stow**
➤ **keep off**
❶ *Let's hope the rain keeps off.*
• **stay away**
❷ *Please keep off the grass.*
• **avoid, stay away from, steer clear of**
➤ **keep to**
❶ *Keep to the cycle path.*
• **stay on, stay within**
❷ *You must keep to your promise.*
• **abide by, adhere to, hold to, carry out, make good, honour**
➤ **keep something up**
Keep up the good work!
• **carry on, continue, maintain**

keeper *NOUN*
For years he was the keeper of the lighthouse.
• **guardian, curator, custodian, caretaker, steward**

key *NOUN*
At last I found the key to the riddle.
• **answer, solution, explanation, clue**

keyboard *NOUN*
For musical instruments see **music**.

kick *VERB*
❶ *He kicked the ball over the wall.*
• **strike, boot, drive, send, propel, punt**
❷ *The beetle was kicking its legs in the air.*
• **wave, flail, swing, shake**

kick *NOUN*
❶ *She gave the door a kick.*
• **strike, boot, hit, blow, punt, flick**
❷ (*informal*) *I still get a kick out of watching this film.*
• **thrill, excitement, tingle**
(*informal*) **buzz**

kidnap *VERB*
This is a story about a boy who is kidnapped by bandits.
• **abduct, capture, seize, carry off, snatch, take hostage**

kill *VERB*
The victim was killed by an unknown poison.
• (*informal*) **bump off, do away with**
(*old use*) **slay**
– To kill someone deliberately is to **murder** them.
– To kill someone brutally is to **butcher** them.
– To kill large numbers of people is to

massacre or **slaughter** them.
– To kill someone as a punishment is to **execute** them or **put them to death**.
– To kill someone for political reasons is to **assassinate** them.

kind *NOUN*
What kind of music do you like?
• **sort, type, variety, style, category, class, genre**

kind *ADJECTIVE*
It was very kind of you to help me.
• **kind-hearted, caring, good-natured, kindly, affectionate, warm, genial, loving, sweet, gentle, amiable, friendly, generous, sympathetic, thoughtful, obliging, considerate, understanding, compassionate, unselfish, giving, gracious, merciful, benevolent, charitable, humane, neighbourly**
OPPOSITES unkind, cruel

kindness *NOUN*
The family treated me with great kindness.
• **kind-heartedness, benevolence, compassion, generosity, warmth, affection, sympathy, good nature**
OPPOSITE cruelty

king *NOUN*
Neptune is the King of the Sea.
• **monarch, sovereign, ruler**

kingdom *NOUN*
One day the prince will rule over a vast kingdom.
• **realm, monarchy, empire, dominion, domain**

kiss *NOUN*
She gave him a kiss on the cheek.
• (*informal*) **peck**

kit *NOUN*
❶ *The box contains an emergency repair kit.*
• **equipment, apparatus, materials, paraphernalia, tools, tackle**
❷ *I've forgotten my football kit.*
• **clothing, clothes, outfit, strip** (*informal*) **gear, get-up**

kitchen *NOUN*
He worked in the kitchen of a large hotel.
– A small kitchen is a **kitchenette**.
– The kitchen on a ship or aircraft is the **galley**.

knack *NOUN*
You have a knack for taking unusual photographs.
• **skill, talent, gift, flair, instinct**

knead *VERB*
Knead the dough until it is smooth.
• **work, press, squeeze, pummel**

knew
past tense see **know**

knife *NOUN*
a sharp kitchen knife
• **blade, cutter**
– A large heavy knife used by a butcher is a **cleaver**.
– A sharp thin knife used by a surgeon is a **scalpel**.
SEE ALSO **weapon**

knight *NOUN*
a medieval knight
– A boy training to be a knight was first a **page** and then a **squire**.
For tips on writing historical fiction see **historical**.

knit *VERB*
❶ *The broken bones will eventually knit together.*
• **join, fuse, bond, unite, combine**
❷ *Mrs Oliphant knitted her brows.*
• **furrow, wrinkle, gather**

knob *NOUN*
❶ *a old wooden door knob*
• **handle**
❷ *Melt a small knob of butter in a pan.*
• **piece, bit, pat, lump, chunk**

knobbly *ADJECTIVE*
I picked up a knobbly piece of wood.
• **lumpy, bumpy, gnarled**

knock *VERB*
❶ *Someone is knocking at the door.*
• **rap, tap, pound, pummel, hammer, bang, thump**
❷ *Don't knock your head on the way out.*
• **bump, bang, bash, hit, strike, crack**
(*informal*) **whack**
SEE ALSO **hit**

knock *NOUN*
❶ *We heard a knock at the door.*
• **rap, tap, pounding, pummelling, hammering, banging**
❷ *The bike has had a few knocks over the years.*
• **bump, bang, bash, hit, strike, blow, crash, collision**

knot *NOUN*
❶ *I was combing the knots out of my hair.*
• **tangle, snarl, lump, mass**
❷ *We were surrounded by a knot of people.*
• **cluster, group, huddle, circle, ring, band, bunch**

knot *VERB*
Knot the two threads together.
• **tie, bind, fasten, join, lash, entwine**
OPPOSITE untie

know *VERB*
❶ *None of us knew how to speak Russian.*
• **understand, comprehend, have knowledge of, be versed in**
OPPOSITE be ignorant of
❷ *Do you know where we are?*
• **recognize, realize, appreciate, be aware of**
OPPOSITE be unaware of
❸ *I know her sister quite well.*
• **be acquainted with, be familiar with, be a friend of**
OPPOSITE be unfamiliar with

knowledge *NOUN*
❶ *She has a good knowledge of Italian.*
• **understanding, grasp, command, mastery, familiarity (with), grounding (in)**
– a slight knowledge of a subject is a **smattering** of it
❷ *There is much ancient knowledge contained in this book.*
• **learning, wisdom, scholarship, erudition**
(*informal*) **know-how**

knowledgeable *ADJECTIVE*
We were shown around by a knowledgeable guide.
• **well-informed, learned, erudite, scholarly, educated, cultured**
OPPOSITE ignorant
➤ **be knowledgeable about**
My dad is surprisingly knowledgeable about rap music.
• **be well informed about, know a lot about, be familiar with**
(*informal*) **be up on**

A B C D E F G H I J K L M N O P Q R S T U V W X Y Z

label *NOUN*
an address label
• **tag, ticket, sticker, tab**

label *VERB*
❶ *I've labelled all the boxes.*
• **tag, mark, name, identify**
❷ *He was soon labelled as a troublemaker.*
• **categorize, classify, mark out, stamp, brand, dub**

laborious *ADJECTIVE*
It was a laborious climb to the top of the hill.
• **strenuous, arduous, hard, tough, difficult, stiff, tiring, exhausting, gruelling, punishing, back-breaking**
OPPOSITES easy, effortless

labour *NOUN*
❶ *It took hours of painstaking labour to restore the painting.*
• **work, effort, industry, exertion, toil, drudgery**
(*informal*) **slog**
❷ *The factory had to take on extra labour.*
• **workers, employees**

labour *VERB*
Rescuers laboured through the night to reach survivors.
• **work hard, exert yourself, toil**
(*informal*) **slave away**

lack *NOUN*
I was suffering from lack of sleep.
• **absence, shortage, scarcity, want, dearth, deficiency, shortfall**
– A general lack of food is a **famine**.
– A general lack of water is a **drought**.
OPPOSITE abundance

lack *VERB*
The match lacked excitement.
• **be without, be short of, be deficient in, be low on, miss**
OPPOSITE possess

lady *NOUN*
see **woman**

lag *VERB*
One runner lagged behind the others.
• **straggle, trail, fall behind, drop behind, dawdle**

laid
past tense see **lay**

lair *NOUN*
The hunters tracked the beast back to its lair.
• **den, refuge, shelter, hideout, hiding place**

lake *NOUN*
We rowed across the lake.
• **pond, pool**
– A lake in Scotland is a **loch**.
– A salt-water lake is a **lagoon**.
– A lake used to supply water is a **reservoir**.

lame *ADJECTIVE*
❶ *a lame horse*
• **disabled, crippled, limping, hobbling**
❷ *What a lame excuse!*
• **feeble, flimsy, poor, unconvincing, inadequate, weak, tame**

lamp *NOUN*
see **light**

land *NOUN*
❶ *It's a large house, surrounded by several acres of land.*
• **grounds, estate, property**
❷ *The land here is good for growing strawberries.*
• **ground, soil, earth**
❸ *China is a land with an ancient history.*
• **country, nation, state, region, territory, province, realm**

land *VERB*
❶ *The plane landed exactly on time.*
• **touch down, arrive**
OPPOSITE take off
❷ *The ship will land at Dover.*
• **dock, berth, come ashore, put in**

❸ *How did these papers land on my desk?*
• **arrive, turn up, end up, wind up, settle**

landmark *NOUN*
❶ *The tower is a landmark that can be seen for miles around.*
• **feature, sight, monument**
❷ *This was a landmark in the history of science.*
• **milestone, turning point, watershed**

landscape *NOUN*
The best way to see the landscape is on foot or by bike.
• **countryside, scenery, terrain, view, scene, outlook, prospect, panorama**

WRITING TIPS

DESCRIBING LANDSCAPE

Areas of landscape:

- bush
- desert
- grassland
- island
- marsh
- moor
- peninsula
- plain
- plateau
- prairie
- rainforest
- savannah
- steppe
- swamp
- tundra
- wasteland
- wetland

Landscape features:

- beach
- bog
- brae
- cave
- cavern
- copse
- crag
- crevasse
- crevice
- dell
- dune
- escarpment
- fell
- fen
- forest
- glen
- gorge
- gully
- hill
- hillock
- hillside
- hummock
- knoll
- ledge
- meadow (*poetic* lea)
- mountain
- pass
- peak
- precipice
- range
- ridge
- rise
- riverbank
- slope
- wood
- valley

Areas of water:

- bay
- bayou
- billabong
- cove
- creek
- estuary (*Scottish* firth)
- fjord
- geyser
- glacier
- ice floe
- inlet
- lagoon
- lake
- loch
- oasis
- pond
- pool
- ravine
- river
- rivulet
- sound
- spring
- stream
- waterhole

Man-made features:

- bridge
- canal
- dam
- dyke
- field
- furrow
- path
- track

Adjectives:

- arid
- bare
- barren
- bleak
- craggy
- enclosed
- exposed
- fallow
- farmed
- fenced
- fertile
- furrowed
- hilly
- inhospitable
- irrigated
- jagged
- lunar
- lush
- mountainous
- open
- patchwork
- pitted
- ploughed
- rocky
- rugged
- shady
- sheltered
- steep
- sun-drenched
- wooded

lane *NOUN*
a narrow country lane
• **track, path, trail, walk, passageway, alley**

language *NOUN*
❶ *The scroll was written in an ancient language.*
• **tongue, speech, dialect** (*informal*) **lingo**

A B C D E F G H I J K L M N O P Q R S T U V W X Y Z

❷ *In this piece of writing, the author uses very poetic language.*
• wording, phrasing, vocabulary, expression, style, turn of phrase, terminology

lap *NOUN*
❶ *Rachael was happy to have the baby on her lap for the evening.*
• knees, thighs
❷ *The runners were on the last lap of the race.*
• circuit, round, leg

lapse *NOUN*
❶ *I made a mistake because of a short lapse in concentration.*
• failure, error, fault, slip, flaw, weakness, shortcoming
❷ *After a lapse of six months work began again.*
• interval, gap, break, interlude, lull, pause

lapse *VERB*
❶ *Your membership has lapsed.*
• expire, become void, run out
❷ *He lapsed into unconsciousness.*
• drift, slip, slide, sink

large *ADJECTIVE*
❶ *Elephants have large skulls.*
• big, huge, enormous, gigantic, great, immense, giant, colossal, massive, mammoth, bulky, hefty, weighty, mighty (*informal*) whopping
❷ *I had a large helping of pudding.*
• ample, generous, plentiful, abundant, lavish
❸ *The living room is the largest room in the house.*
• spacious, extensive, sizeable, roomy
❹ *We were flying over a large area of desert.*
• wide, broad, extensive, widespread, vast
❺ *The programme received a large number of complaints.*
• considerable, substantial, high
OPPOSITES **small, tiny**
SEE ALSO **big**

largely *ADVERB*
The abbey was largely destroyed by fire.
• mainly, chiefly, mostly, principally, to a large extent

lash *VERB*
❶ *Rain was lashing against the window.*
• beat, pound, pelt, batter
❷ *The crocodile started lashing its tail.*
• swish, flick, whip
❸ *During the storm they lashed the boxes to the mast.*
• tie, fasten, bind, tether, knot, hitch

last *ADJECTIVE*
❶ *I have just started the last chapter.*
• final, closing, concluding, terminating, ultimate
OPPOSITE **first**
❷ *Did you see her last film?*
• latest, most recent
OPPOSITE **next**

last *NOUN*
➤ at last
At last someone was listening to me.
• finally, eventually, in the end

last *VERB*
❶ *Let's hope our luck will last.*
• carry on, continue, keep on, stay, remain, persist, endure, hold
OPPOSITES **end, wear out**
❷ *The plants won't last long without water.*
• hold out, keep going, live, survive

lasting *ADJECTIVE*
The Australian landscape left a lasting impression on me.
• enduring, abiding, long-lasting, long-lived, undying, everlasting, permanent, durable

late *ADJECTIVE*
❶ *My bus was late again.*
• delayed, overdue
OPPOSITES **early, punctual, on time**
❷ *There was a portrait of his late wife on the wall.*
• dead, deceased, departed, former

lately *ADVERB*
It has been a lot warmer lately.
• recently, latterly, of late

later *ADJECTIVE*
The mystery is revealed in a later chapter.
• subsequent, future, following, succeeding, upcoming, ensuing, to come

later *ADVERB*
❶ *The letter arrived a week later.*
• afterwards, after that, subsequently
❷ *I'll phone you later.*
• in a while, at a later date, in the future, in due course

latter *ADJECTIVE*
We played better in the latter part of the year.
• later, more recent, second, last, final

laugh *VERB*
That story always makes me laugh.
• chuckle, chortle, guffaw, giggle, titter, burst out laughing, roar with laughter, fall about laughing
(*informal*) crack up,
IDIOMS be in stitches, have hysterics, be rolling in the aisles
➤ **laugh at**
Many people laughed at Newton's ideas.
• make fun of, mock, ridicule, scoff at, jeer at, deride, poke fun at
IDIOM (*informal*) take the mickey out of

laughter *NOUN*
We heard laughter coming from the next room.
• laughing, amusement, humour, hilarity, mirth, merriment

launch *VERB*
❶ *The space rocket will be launched next month.*
• send off, set off, blast off
❷ *She sprinted up and launched a javelin into the air.*
• throw, propel, hurl, pitch, fling, let fly, fire, shoot
❸ *Their website was launched last year.*
• begin, start, set up, open, establish, found, initiate, inaugurate, introduce

lavatory *NOUN*
a public lavatory
• toilet, bathroom, WC, convenience, cloakroom, washroom
(*informal*) loo

lavish *ADJECTIVE*
❶ *The wedding was followed by a lavish feast.*
• sumptuous, luxurious, extravagant, opulent, rich, grand, splendid
OPPOSITES meagre, paltry
❷ *He had been spending lavish amounts of money.*
• abundant, copious, generous, plentiful, extravagant

law *NOUN*
a law against child labour
• regulation, statute, rule, ruling, decree, edict, order, commandment, directive
– A law passed by parliament is an **act**.
– A proposed law to be discussed by parliament is a **bill**.

lay *VERB*
❶ *She laid the book down carefully on her desk.*
• put down, set down, place, position, deposit, rest, leave
❷ *I was laying the table for dinner.*
• set out, set, arrange
❸ *He laid the blame on his sister.*
• assign, attach, attribute, ascribe, fix
❹ *We began to lay our plans for the future.*
• devise, prepare, plan, conceive, concoct, formulate, work out, hatch
➤ **lay something on**
Our hosts had laid on entertainment.
• provide, supply, furnish, prepare, organize, line up

layer *NOUN*
❶ *The walls needed two layers of paint.*
• coat, coating, covering, film, skin, blanket, sheet
❷ *You can see various layers of rock in the cliff.*
• seam, stratum, tier, thickness

A B C D E F G H I J K L M N O P Q R S T U V W X Y Z

laze *VERB*
We spent all day lazing in the garden.
• **be lazy, idle, loaf, lounge, relax, take it easy, lie about**

lazy *ADJECTIVE*
He was too lazy to walk to the shops.
• **idle, indolent, slothful, inactive, lethargic, sluggish**

lead *VERB*
❶ *Our guide led us through the underground caves.*
• **guide, conduct, escort, usher, steer, pilot, shepherd**
OPPOSITE follow
❷ *She led from the start of the race.*
• **be in front, be in the lead, head the field**
❸ *He was chosen to lead the expedition.*
• **be in charge of, direct, command, head, manage, supervise, preside over**
(*informal*) **head up**
❹ *This path leads to the beach.*
• **go, run, make its way**
❺ *I prefer to lead a quiet life.*
• **live, pass, spend, experience, enjoy**
➤ **lead to**
Their carelessness led to the accident.
• **result in, cause, bring about, give rise to, occasion, generate, spark**

lead *NOUN*
❶ *Our team were in the lead.*
• **first place, front position**
❷ *Detectives are following up a new lead.*
• **clue, pointer, tip-off**
❸ *The older students provide a lead for the younger ones.*
• **example, model, pattern, guidance, leadership, direction**
❹ *My sister is playing the lead in the school play.*
• **principal part, starring role, title role**
❺ *Keep your dog on a lead.*
• **leash, strap, chain, tether, rein**
❻ *The toaster needs a new lead.*
• **cable, flex, wire**

leader *NOUN*
The leader of the gang was called Redbeard.
• **head, chief, commander, captain, director, principal, ruler**
(*informal*) **boss**
– The leader of a group of wrongdoers is the **ringleader**.
OPPOSITE follower

leaf *NOUN*
❶ *the leaf of a maple tree*
– A mass of leaves is **foliage** or **greenery**.
❷ *A single leaf had been torn from the book.*
• **page, sheet**

leak *NOUN*
❶ *The plumber came to mend a leak in one of the pipes.*
• **crack, hole, opening, split, rupture, perforation**
– A leak in a tyre is a **puncture**.
❷ *We had a gas leak.*
• **escape, discharge, leakage, drip**

leak *VERB*
❶ *Gallons of oil leaked from the tanker.*
• **escape, seep, ooze, drain, drip, dribble, trickle**
❷ *Details of the plan were leaked to the press.*
• **reveal, disclose, divulge, pass on, let out, make known, make public**

lean *VERB*
❶ *Two boys were leaning against the front wall.*
• **recline, rest, prop yourself, support yourself**
❷ *The Tower of Pisa leans to one side.*
• **slope, tilt, tip, incline, slant, list, bank**

lean *ADJECTIVE*
a dancer with a strong, lean figure
• **slim, slender, thin, trim, wiry**
OPPOSITES fat, plump
For tips on describing bodies see **body**.

leap *VERB*
❶ *The dog leapt in the air to catch the ball.*
• **jump, spring, bound, vault**
❷ *The price of fuel has leapt in the last*

few months.
• **rise sharply, jump, soar, rocket, shoot up**

leap *NOUN*
With one leap he cleared the stream.
• **jump, spring, bound, vault**

learn *VERB*
❶ *We have started to learn French.*
• **acquire, master, pick up, absorb** (*informal*) **get the hang of**
❷ *I need to learn the words of this song.*
• **learn by heart, memorize, master**
❸ *I later learned that we had met before.*
• **discover, find out, hear, gather, grasp**

learner *NOUN*
The swimming class is for learners only.
• **beginner, starter, novice**
– Someone learning things at school or college is a **pupil** or **student**.
– Someone learning a trade is an **apprentice** or **trainee**.
OPPOSITE expert

learning *NOUN*
The city became a centre of learning.
• **study, education, knowledge, erudition, scholarship**

least *ADJECTIVE*
❶ *Who got the least number of points?*
• **fewest, lowest**
❷ *I found the house without the least difficulty.*
• **slightest, smallest, tiniest**

leave *VERB*
❶ *We'll be leaving tomorrow morning.*
• **go, go away, depart, withdraw, take your leave, go out, set off, say goodbye** (*informal*) **take off, disappear**
OPPOSITE arrive
❷ *She left the room suddenly.*
• **exit, go out of, depart from, quit, vacate**
OPPOSITE enter
❸ *Don't leave me here on my own!*
• **abandon, desert, forsake**
❹ *You can leave your coat in here.*
• **place, position, put down, set down, deposit**
❺ *My sister has left her job at the bank.*
• **give up, quit, resign from, step down from**
❻ *I'll leave all the arrangements to you.*
• **pass on, hand over, refer, entrust**
❼ *She left all her money to charity.*
• **bequeath, hand down, will, endow**
➤ **leave someone or something out**
You've left out the best part of the story.
• **miss out, omit, exclude, overlook, pass over, skip, drop**

leave *NOUN*
❶ *The doctor is away on leave for two weeks.*
• **holiday, vacation, time off**
❷ *Will you give me leave to speak?*
• **permission, authorization, consent, approval**

lecture *NOUN*
❶ *There is a lecture on dinosaurs at the museum today.*
• **talk, speech, address, lesson, presentation**
❷ *He got a stern lecture about being late.*
• **reprimand, warning, scolding** (*informal*) **telling-off, talking-to, dressing-down**

led
past tense see **lead**

ledge *NOUN*
She was standing on a narrow ledge of rock.
• **shelf, projection**
– A ledge under a window is a **windowsill**.

left *ADJECTIVE*
on the left side of the road
• **left-hand**
– The left side of a ship when you face forwards is the **port** side.
OPPOSITE right

leg *NOUN*
❶ *Callum fell and bruised his leg.*
see **body**

A B C D E F G H I J K L M N O P Q R S T U V W X Y Z

❷ *We were on the final leg of the journey.*
• part, stage, section, phase, stretch

legal *ADJECTIVE*
Is it legal to download this file?
• lawful, legitimate, within the law, permissible, permitted, allowed
OPPOSITE illegal

legend *NOUN*
the legend of the Loch Ness Monster
• myth, story, folk tale, fairy tale, fable, saga, tradition
For tips on writing fantasy fiction see **fantasy**.

legendary *ADJECTIVE*
❶ *the legendary city of Camelot*
• mythical, mythological, fabulous, fabled, fairy-tale
OPPOSITE real
❷ *Her cooking is legendary.*
• famous, well-known, celebrated, renowned, acclaimed

legible *ADJECTIVE*
The inscription is now barely legible.
• readable, clear, distinct, neat
OPPOSITE illegible

legitimate *ADJECTIVE*
Many people believed he had a legitimate claim to the throne.
• legal, proper, rightful, authorized, permitted

leisure *NOUN*
His busy life leaves little time for leisure.
• free time, spare time, relaxation, recreation, rest

leisurely *ADJECTIVE*
We went for a leisurely stroll in the park.
• unhurried, relaxed, relaxing, gentle, easy, restful, slow
OPPOSITE fast

lend *VERB*
❶ *Could you lend me some money?*
• loan, advance, let someone have
OPPOSITE borrow
❷ *Moonlight lent an air of mystery to the scene.*
• give, add, impart, bestow, confer, contribute

length *NOUN*
❶ *My heart sank when I saw the length of the queue.*
• extent, size, distance, expanse, range, span
❷ *We only had to wait a short length of time.*
• period, duration, space, stretch

lengthen *VERB*
❶ *Maya deliberately lengthened her stride.*
• extend, make longer, elongate, stretch
OPPOSITE shorten
❷ *The afternoon shadows began to lengthen.*
• draw out, get longer, stretch out

lengthy *ADJECTIVE*
There was a lengthy argument over who was to blame.
• long, drawn-out, extended, prolonged, protracted, time-consuming, long-running
OPPOSITES short, brief

lenient *ADJECTIVE*
I think the referee was too lenient.
• easy-going, soft-hearted, tolerant, forgiving, indulgent, charitable, merciful
OPPOSITE strict

lessen *VERB*
❶ *He was given medicine to lessen the pain.*
• minimize, reduce, relieve
❷ *Her fear gradually lessened.*
• diminish, decrease, dwindle, subside, weaken, ease off, tail off, die down, ebb, wane, recede
OPPOSITE increase

lesson *NOUN*
I have a piano lesson every week.
• class, period, session, tutorial, instruction

let *VERB*

❶ *My parents would not let me go on the trip.*
• **allow, permit, give permission to, consent to, agree to, authorize**
OPPOSITE forbid
❷ *A microscope lets you see tiny objects.*
• **enable, allow, equip**
❸ *Our neighbours are letting their house for the summer.*
• **lease, rent out, hire out**
➤ **let someone off**
We were let off classes for the day.
• **excuse from, exempt from, spare from**
➤ **let something out**
Suddenly Molly let out a scream.
• **utter, emit, give, produce, express**
➤ **let up**
The rain didn't let up.
• **ease, subside, abate, slacken, diminish**

lethal *ADJECTIVE*

He had been given a lethal dose of poison.
• **deadly, fatal, mortal, life-threatening, poisonous, toxic**

letter *NOUN*

❶ *The sign was written in large letters.*
• **character, symbol, sign, figure**
– The letters a, e, i, o, u and sometimes y are **vowels.**
– The other letters are **consonants.**
❷ *Did you remember to sign your letter?*
• **note, message, communication**
– Letters people send each other are **correspondence.**

level *ADJECTIVE*

❶ *Put the tent up on a level piece of ground.*
• **even, flat, horizontal, plane, smooth, flush**
OPPOSITE uneven
❷ *At half-time the scores were level.*
• **equal, even, the same, matching, tied, drawn**
IDIOMS all square, neck and neck

level *NOUN*

❶ *The water rose to a dangerous level.*
• **height, position**
❷ *The lift takes you up to the sixth level.*
• **floor, storey, tier**
❸ *She has reached a high level of skill.*
• **grade, standard, stage, rank, degree**

lever *VERB*

Slowly, they levered open the coffin.
• **prise, wrench, force**

liable *ADJECTIVE*

❶ *You're liable to make mistakes when you're tired.*
• **likely, inclined, disposed, prone, apt, given**
OPPOSITE unlikely
❷ *We are not liable for any loss or damage.*
• **responsible, answerable, accountable**

liberal *ADJECTIVE*

❶ *Apply a liberal amount of hair gel.*
• **generous, abundant, copious, ample, plentiful, lavish, unstinting**
OPPOSITES meagre, miserly
❷ *She has a liberal attitude towards such things.*
• **broad-minded, open-minded, tolerant, permissive, enlightened, lenient, easy-going**
OPPOSITE strict

liberate *VERB*

The prisoners were liberated at the end of the war.
• **free, set free, release, emancipate, discharge, let go, set loose**
OPPOSITE imprison

liberty *NOUN*

❶ *The king granted the prisoners their liberty.*
• **liberation, release, emancipation**
OPPOSITES imprisonment, slavery
❷ *You have the liberty to come and go as you please.*
• **freedom, independence**
OPPOSITE constraint

licence *NOUN*

He has a licence to practise as a vet.
• **permit, certificate, authorization, warrant, pass**

license *VERB*
Are you licensed to drive this vehicle?
• **permit, allow, authorize, entitle, certify**

lid *NOUN*
Can you help me get the lid off this jar?
• **cover, covering, cap, top**

lie *NOUN*
She can't help telling lies.
• **untruth, falsehood, fib, fabrication, deception**
(*informal*) **whopper**
OPPOSITE truth

lie *VERB*
1 *Why would he lie about his past?*
• **tell a lie, fib, bluff**
OPPOSITE tell the truth
2 *He was lying on the grass.*
• **recline, stretch out, sprawl, lounge, rest, repose**
– To lie face downwards is to **be prone** or **be prostrate**.
– To lie face upwards is to **be supine**.
3 *The village lies ten miles from the coast.*
• **be sited, be situated, be located, be placed, be found**

life *NOUN*
1 *I owe you my life.*
• **existence, being, survival**
2 *Our dog leads a very easy life.*
• **way of life, lifestyle**
3 *You seem to be full of life today!*
• **energy, liveliness, vigour, vitality, vivacity, spirit, sprightliness, animation, exuberance, dynamism**
4 *I'm reading a life of Charles Dickens.*
• **life story, biography, autobiography**
5 *The battery has a life of two years.*
• **duration, lifetime, lifespan**

lift *VERB*
1 *The box is too heavy to lift.*
• **raise, pick up, pull up, elevate, hoist**
2 *One by one, the balloons lifted off the ground.*
• **rise, ascend, soar**
3 *The ban has finally been lifted.*
• **remove, withdraw, cancel, revoke**

light *NOUN*

WORD WEB

Some kinds of natural light:

- daylight
- moonlight
- starlight
- sunlight
- twilight

Sources of artificial light:

- bulb
- candle
- chandelier
- flambeau
- floodlight
- fluorescent lamp
- headlamp or headlight
- lamp
- lantern
- laser
- LED or light-emitting diode
- neon light
- searchlight
- spotlight
- street light
- torch

WRITING TIPS

DESCRIBING LIGHT
Effects of light:

- beam
- blaze
- burn
- dazzle
- flame
- flare
- flash
- flicker
- glare
- gleam
- glimmer
- glint
- glisten
- glitter
- glow
- lustre
- radiance
- ray
- reflection
- shaft
- shimmer
- shine
- sparkle
- twinkle
- wink

Adjectives:

- bright
- brilliant
- dappled
- diffused
- dim
- harsh

- luminous
- lustrous
- muted
- pale
- radiant
- scintillating
- soft
- sparkling
- strong
- warm
- weak

light *ADJECTIVE*

❶ *Artists like to work in light and airy studios.*
• **bright, well-lit, illuminated, sunny**
OPPOSITES dim, gloomy
❷ *My new scarf is a light shade of grey.*
• **pale, faint, delicate, subtle**
OPPOSITES dark, deep
❸ *The cart was only carrying a light load.*
• **lightweight, portable, weightless, slight**
OPPOSITES heavy, weighty
❹ *A light breeze rippled the water.*
• **gentle, faint, slight, soft**
OPPOSITES strong, forceful
❺ *We ate a light breakfast before setting out.*
• **small, modest, simple, insubstantial**
OPPOSITES heavy, substantial
❻ *Are you well enough to do some light housework?*
• **easy, undemanding, effortless**
OPPOSITES heavy, demanding
❼ *I bought a magazine for some light reading.*
• **undemanding, entertaining, lightweight, superficial**
OPPOSITE serious

light *VERB*

❶ *Let's light the candles on your cake.*
• **ignite, set alight, set fire to, kindle, switch on**
OPPOSITE extinguish
❷ *The stage was lit by a bright spotlight.*
• **light up, illuminate, brighten, shine on, shed light on**
OPPOSITE darken

like *VERB*

OVERUSED WORD

❶ To like a person, animal or possession:

- admire
- adore
- love
- be attached to
- be fond of
- care for
- cherish
- esteem
- hold dear
- be attracted to
- be interested in

(*informal*) fancy

IDIOM have a soft spot for

He is very attached to *his new puppy.*

❷ To like a taste, book, film, etc.:

- be partial to
- have a taste for
- have a liking for
- have a preference for
- be keen on
- enjoy
- appreciate
- prefer

(*informal*) be mad on

My mum is partial to *chocolate cake.*

I used to enjoy *fantasy, but now I* prefer *science fiction.*

OPPOSITE dislike

❸ To like doing something:

- delight in
- take pleasure in
- enjoy
- relish
- savour
- revel in

My brother delights in *telling rude jokes.*

like *PREPOSITION*

He made a noise like a strangled cat.
• **similar to, the same as, resembling, identical to, akin to, in the manner of**
OPPOSITE unlike

likeable *ADJECTIVE*

The main character is a likeable lad called Seth.
• **pleasant, appealing, attractive, agreeable, amiable, engaging, charming**

A B C D E F G H I J K L M N O P Q R S T U V W X Y Z

likely *ADJECTIVE*
❶ *Heavy rain and high winds are likely this afternoon.*
• **probable, expected, anticipated, predictable, foreseeable**
OPPOSITE unlikely
❷ *I can think of a more likely reason for their defeat.*
• **plausible, credible, reasonable, feasible, believable**
OPPOSITE implausible

likeness *NOUN*
❶ *There is a strong likeness between the two sisters.*
• **resemblance, similarity, correspondence**
OPPOSITE difference
❷ *This photo is a good likeness of my grandfather.*
• **image, representation, picture, portrait, depiction, portrayal**

liking *NOUN*
She has a liking for large earrings and flowery hats.
• **fondness, taste, love, passion, affection, preference, partiality, penchant**
OPPOSITES dislike, distaste

limb *NOUN*
see **body**

limit *NOUN*
❶ *This stone marks the limit of the old city.*
• **border, boundary, edge, perimeter, frontier**
❷ *The course has a limit of twenty places.*
• **maximum, restriction, threshold, ceiling, cut-off point**
– A limit on time is a **deadline** or **time limit**.

limit *VERB*
I had to limit the invitations to my party.
• **put a limit on, restrict, ration, curb, cap**

limited *ADJECTIVE*
❶ *We only had a limited supply of water.*
• **restricted, short, inadequate, insufficient, rationed, finite, fixed**
OPPOSITE limitless
❷ *It was hard to move about in the limited space.*
• **small, cramped, restricted, narrow, tight, confined**

limp *VERB*
She limped off the pitch with a twisted ankle.
• **hobble, hop, falter, stumble**

limp *ADJECTIVE*
The child's hand was quite limp and cold.
• **floppy, drooping, droopy, sagging, wilting, soft, flabby, slack**
OPPOSITES rigid, firm

line *NOUN*
❶ *I drew a pencil line across the page.*
• **stroke, rule, dash, underline, stripe, strip, streak, band, bar, belt**
– A line cut into a surface is a **groove**, **score** or **scratch**.
– A line on a person's skin is a **wrinkle**.
– A deep groove or wrinkle is a **furrow**.
– A line on fabric is a **crease**.
❷ *There was a long line of people at the bus stop.*
• **queue, row, file, column, rank, procession, chain**
– A line of schoolchildren walking in pairs is a **crocodile**.
❸ *Clothes were drying on a washing line.*
• **cord, rope, string, thread, wire, cable, flex, lead**

linger *VERB*
❶ *The smell of burning lingered in the air.*
• **continue, remain, stay, last, persist, endure**
OPPOSITE disappear
❷ *We mustn't linger any longer.*
• **hang about, wait about, loiter, dawdle, dally, delay**
(*old use*) **tarry**
OPPOSITE hurry

link *NOUN*
The two schools have close links with each other.
• **relationship, association, connection, bond, tie**

link *VERB*
❶ *The two trains were linked together.*
• **connect, attach, fasten, join, couple, hook up**
OPPOSITE separate
❷ *Police are linking this death with a series of other murders.*
• **connect, associate, relate, bracket**

lion *NOUN*
Lions usually stalk their prey.
– A female lion is a **lioness**.
– A young lion is a **cub**.
– A group of lions is a **pride**.
– The fur collar on a male lion is its **mane**.
SEE ALSO **cat**
For tips on describing animals see **animal**.

liquid *NOUN*
Stir the liquid until it thickens.
• **fluid, solution, juice, liquor**
– The liquid inside a plant is **sap**.
OPPOSITE solid

liquid *ADJECTIVE*
Pour the liquid jelly into a mould.
• **runny, watery, fluid, flowing, running, sloppy**
– To make food into a liquid or pulp is to **liquidize** it.
– To make something liquid by heating it is to **melt** it.
– Liquid metal or rock is **molten**.
OPPOSITE solid

list *NOUN*
I'll add your name to the list.
• **register, roll, rota, catalogue, directory, inventory, checklist**
– A list of topics mentioned in a book is an **index**.
– A list of things to choose from is a **menu**.

list *VERB*
❶ *She spent an hour listing the books in in alphabetical order.*
• **record, register, write down, catalogue, index, itemize**
❷ *The ship was listing dangerously to one side.*
• **lean, tilt, tip, pitch, incline, slant, slope**

listen *VERB*
Do you think anyone is listening?
• **pay attention, attend**
IDIOMS **keep your ears open, be all ears**
– To listen secretly to a private conversation is to **eavesdrop**.
➤ **listen to someone**
Nobody ever listens to me.
• **pay attention to, take notice of, attend to, heed**

literature *NOUN*
The publisher specializes in children's literature.
• **writing, books**
For types of literature see **drama, fiction, poetry**.

litter *NOUN*
The street was covered with litter.
• **rubbish, refuse, waste, garbage, junk, clutter, mess**

litter *VERB*
The desk was littered with scraps of paper.
• **scatter, strew, clutter**

little *ADJECTIVE*

OVERUSED WORD

❶ **Little in size, scale:**

➤ **small**	➤ **mini**
➤ **tiny**	➤ **miniature**
➤ **minute**	➤ **minuscule**
➤ **petite**	➤ **midget**
➤ **compact**	➤ **diminutive**

(*informal*) **teeny, titchy**
(*Scottish*) **wee**
Microbes are so **minute** *they can only be seen through a microscope.*
OPPOSITES big, large

❷ **Little in age:**

➤ young ➤ small

(*Scottish*) wee

My granny lived in India when she was **young**.

OPPOSITES old, big

❸ **A little time, a little while:**

➤ brief ➤ passing
➤ short ➤ cursory
➤ fleeting

It was a **short** *while before our friends arrived.*

OPPOSITES lengthy, long

❹ **A little problem:**

➤ slight ➤ insignificant
➤ minor ➤ trivial
➤ unimportant ➤ trifling

I have a **slight** *problem with my bike.*

OPPOSITE major

❺ **Little left of something:**

➤ hardly any ➤ paltry
➤ insufficient ➤ scarcely any
➤ meagre

There was **scarcely any** *food left by the time we arrived.*

OPPOSITES ample, plenty

❻ **A little amount of something:**

➤ some ➤ a touch of
➤ a bit of ➤ a dash of
➤ a drop of ➤ a pinch of
➤ a spot of

Would you like **a drop of** *milk in your tea?*

OPPOSITES plenty of, lots of

❼ **A little:**

➤ a bit ➤ somewhat
➤ slightly ➤ to some degree
➤ rather

I'm feeling **slightly** *tired now.*

live *VERB*

❶ *Giant tortoises can live for over a hundred years.*
• **stay alive, survive, exist**
OPPOSITE die
❷ *She has lived a happy life.*
• **lead, experience, go through, spend, pass**
❸ *Where do you live?*
• **reside, dwell**
➤ **live in**
We used to live in a basement flat.
• **inhabit, occupy, dwell in, reside in**
➤ **live on**
Some whales live entirely on plankton.
• **eat, feed on, subsist on**

live *ADJECTIVE*

The fishermen caught a live octopus in their nets.
• **alive, living, breathing**
OPPOSITE dead

lively *ADJECTIVE*

❶ *The toddlers were in a lively mood.*
• **active, energetic, vigorous, dynamic, animated, spirited, vibrant, vivacious, buoyant, exuberant, sprightly, frisky, chirpy, perky**
IDIOM **full of beans**
OPPOSITE inactive
❷ *The city centre is always lively at night.*
• **busy, bustling, crowded, exciting, buzzing, vibrant**
OPPOSITES quiet, dead

livid *ADJECTIVE*

He was livid when he saw the damage to his bike.
• **angry, furious, fuming, incensed, enraged, seething, raging**

living *ADJECTIVE*

❶ *Miss Cooper had no living relatives.*
• **alive, surviving**
OPPOSITES dead, deceased
❷ *Basque is a living language.*
• **current, existing, in use**
OPPOSITES dead, extinct

living *NOUN*

❶ *He makes a living from painting.*
• **income, livelihood, subsistence**

❷ *What does she do for a living?*
• **job, occupation, profession, trade, career**

load *NOUN*
❶ *Camels can carry heavy loads.*
• **burden, weight**
❷ *The lorry was picking up a load for delivery.*
• **cargo, consignment, goods, freight**
➤ **loads of**
(*informal*) *We had loads of time to spare.*
• **plenty of, lots of**
(*informal*) **tons of, masses of**

load *VERB*
❶ *We loaded the suitcases into the car.*
• **pack, stack, pile, heap, stow**
❷ *The men were loading a van with furniture.*
• **fill up, pack, stock**
❸ *She arrived loaded with shopping bags.*
• **weigh down, burden, saddle, encumber**

loan *NOUN*
They needed a loan from the bank.
• **advance**
– A system which allows you to pay for something later is **credit**.
– A loan to buy a house is a **mortgage**.

loath *ADJECTIVE*
I'm loath to ask for their help again.
• **reluctant, unwilling, disinclined**
OPPOSITES willing, keen

loathe *VERB*
My brother loathes the colour pink.
• **hate, detest, despise, can't bear, can't stand**
(*formal*) **abhor**
OPPOSITES love, adore

local *ADJECTIVE*
There are story-telling sessions at our local library.
• **neighbourhood, community, nearby, neighbouring**

locate *VERB*
❶ *I can't locate the book you asked for.*
• **find, discover, track down, detect, pinpoint, unearth**
IDIOM **lay your hands on**
OPPOSITE lose
❷ *The gallery is located in the city centre.*
• **place, position, site, situate, set up, establish, station, base**

location *NOUN*
What is the exact location of the submarine?
• **position, situation, place, site, spot, setting, whereabouts, locality, locale**

lock *NOUN*
❶ *There was a heavy lock on the door.*
• **fastening, clasp, catch, padlock, bolt, latch**
❷ *The princess gave him a lock of her hair.*
• **tress, curl, tuft, wisp, coil, ringlet**

lock *VERB*
Remember to lock the door.
• **fasten, secure, bolt, latch, padlock, chain, seal**

lodge *VERB*
❶ *Where are you lodging at present?*
• **reside, stay, board, live, dwell**
(*North American*) **room**
❷ *The animals are lodged indoors in the winter.*
• **house, accommodate, board, put up**
❸ *The bullet had lodged in his chest.*
• **get caught, become stuck, jam, wedge, fix, embed**

log *NOUN*
Keep a log of your computer time.
• **record, register, account, tally, diary, journal, logbook**

logical *ADJECTIVE*
❶ *Holmes used logical methods of deduction.*
• **rational, analytical, methodical, systematic, sound, valid**
OPPOSITE illogical
❷ *That would be the logical thing to do.*
• **sensible, reasonable, natural, understandable**

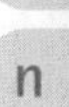

a b c d e f g h i j k l m n o p q r s t u v w x y z

lone *ADJECTIVE*

A lone figure appeared on the horizon.

• **single, solitary, unaccompanied, isolated, solo**

lonely *ADJECTIVE*

❶ *I felt lonely in the house by myself.*

• **alone, friendless, lonesome, abandoned, neglected, forlorn, forsaken**

❷ *She took me to a lonely place by the river.*

• **deserted, isolated, remote, secluded, out-of-the-way**

long *ADJECTIVE*

There was a long and awkward silence.

• **lengthy, prolonged, extended, extensive, long-lasting, drawn-out, interminable**

OPPOSITES **short, brief**

long *VERB*

➤ **long for something**

We were all longing for a rest.

• **yearn for, crave, wish for, desire, hunger for, pine for, hanker after, itch for, be desperate for**

(*informal*) **be dying for**

look *VERB*

❶ *A woman was looking in our direction.*

• **gaze, peer, glance, watch, stare**

❷ *You look a bit sad.*

• **appear, seem, come across as**

➤ **look after someone or something**

Would you look after my cat while I'm away?

• **care for, take care of, tend, mind, watch over, guard, protect**

IDIOM **keep an eye on**

– To look after sick people is to **nurse** them.

➤ **look for something**

I spent ages looking for my keys.

• **search for, hunt for, seek**

➤ **look into something**

We've been looking into our family history.

• **investigate, inquire into, find out about, examine, explore**

➤ **look out for something**

Look out for sharp bends in the road.

• **beware of, watch out for, be careful of, pay attention to**

IDIOM **keep an eye open for**

➤ **look something up**

If you don't know what a word means, look it up in the dictionary.

• **find, search for, track down, research, locate**

OVERUSED WORD

❶ To look at something:

➤ watch
➤ observe
➤ view
➤ regard
➤ contemplate
➤ inspect
➤ take in
➤ eye

He **inspected** *himself in the mirror.*

❷ To look quickly:

➤ glance
➤ glimpse
➤ peek
➤ peep
➤ sneak a look

I thought I **glimpsed** *the fin of a shark.*

❸ To look carefully, look intently:

➤ stare
➤ peer
➤ squint
➤ study
➤ scrutinize
➤ examine
➤ inspect
➤ take a good look at

She knelt down and **peered** *at the footprints.*

❹ To look angrily:

➤ glare
➤ glower
➤ grimace
➤ frown
➤ scowl

Mr Davies merely **glowered** *at us in silence.*

❺ To look in amazement:

➤ gape
➤ stare wide-eyed
➤ stare open-mouthed
➤ goggle

(*informal*) **gawk, gawp**

IDIOM **have your eyes on stalks**

I found myself **gaping** *in genuine surprise.*

look *NOUN*
❶ *Take a look at this website.*
• glance, gaze, glimpse, peek, peep, sight, view, squint
(*informal*) eyeful
❷ *I don't like the look of this place.*
• appearance, air, aspect, bearing, manner
❸ *The girl turned to us with a look of horror.*
• expression, face, countenance

lookout *NOUN*
Lookouts were posted along the wall.
• sentry, guard, sentinel, watchman

loom *VERB*
❶ *A figure loomed out of the mist.*
• appear, emerge, arise, take shape
❷ *A sheer cliff face loomed before us.*
• rise, tower, stand out, hang over

loop *NOUN*
Make a loop in the string.
• coil, ring, hoop, circle, noose, bend, curl, twist, kink

loop *VERB*
Loop the thread around your finger.
• coil, wind, twist, curl, bend, turn, snake

loose *ADJECTIVE*
❶ *Some of the roof tiles are loose.*
• insecure, unfixed, movable, unsteady, shaky, wobbly
OPPOSITES firm, secure
❷ *She likes to wear her hair loose.*
• untied, free, down
OPPOSITE tied
❸ *These jeans are loose around the waist.*
• slack, baggy, roomy, loose-fitting
OPPOSITE tight
❹ *The chickens wander loose about the farm.*
• free, at large, at liberty, on the loose, unconfined, unrestricted
OPPOSITE confined
❺ *Here is a loose translation of the poem.*
• rough, general, vague, inexact
OPPOSITES exact, literal

loosen *VERB*
❶ *Can you loosen this knot?*
• undo, unfasten, untie, free, loose, slacken
OPPOSITE tighten
❷ *I loosened my grip on the rope.*
• relax, slacken, ease, release, let go
OPPOSITE tighten

loot *NOUN*
Under the floorboards was a bag full of stolen loot.
• spoils, plunder, stolen goods, booty, haul

loot *VERB*
Rioters looted the shops.
• raid, ransack, rob, steal from, pillage, plunder

lorry *NOUN*
see **vehicle**

lose *VERB*
❶ *I've lost one of my gloves.*
• mislay, misplace
OPPOSITE find
❷ *By now, we had lost a lot of time.*
• waste, squander, let pass
❸ *Our team lost 3-0.*
• be defeated, get beaten, suffer a defeat
OPPOSITE win

loss *NOUN*
❶ *She is suffering from a loss of memory.*
• failure, disappearance, deprivation, depletion
❷ *I want to report the loss of my phone.*
• disappearance, misplacement, theft
❸ *They were devastated by the loss of their dear friend.*
• death, decease, passing

lost *ADJECTIVE*
❶ *I eventually found my lost keys.*
• missing, mislaid, misplaced
OPPOSITE found
❷ *He appeared to be lost in thought.*
• absorbed, engrossed, preoccupied, deep, immersed, rapt

lot *NOUN*

We are having another lot of visitors this weekend.

• **group, batch, set, crowd, collection**

➤ **a lot of**

These patients need a lot of care.

• **a large amount of, a good deal of, a great deal of, plenty of**

➤ **lots of**

I got lots of cards on my birthday.

• **a great number of, many, numerous, plenty, plenty of, a wealth of, an abundance of, galore**

(*informal*) **loads of, tons of, masses of, stacks of, oodles of, hundreds of, umpteen**

The word *galore* comes after a noun: *a film that offers action and stunts galore.*

loud *ADJECTIVE*

❶ *That music is too loud!*

• **noisy, blaring, booming, deafening, resounding, thunderous, penetrating, piercing, ear-splitting**

– A noise which is loud enough to hear is **audible**.

OPPOSITES **quiet, soft**

❷ *He was wearing a very loud shirt.*

• **bright, gaudy, garish, showy**

(*informal*) **flashy**

OPPOSITES **muted, subdued**

lounge *VERB*

She lounged on the sofa all morning.

• **laze, idle, loaf, relax, take it easy, sprawl, slouch, lie around, loll**

lovable *ADJECTIVE*

Our neighbours have a lovable new cat.

• **adorable, dear, sweet, charming, likeable, lovely, appealing, attractive, cuddly, enchanting, endearing**

OPPOSITE **hateful**

love *NOUN*

❶ *the love between Romeo and Juliet*

• **adoration, infatuation, affection, fondness, attachment, tenderness, passion, warmth, intimacy**

❷ *She had a love of the outdoors.*

• **liking, fondness, taste, passion, enthusiasm, keenness**

❸ *Emma was his true love.*

• **sweetheart, beloved, loved one, darling, dearest**

love *VERB*

❶ *It's obvious that those two love each other.*

• **be in love with, adore, care for, cherish, hold dear, treasure, worship, idolize, be infatuated with, be besotted with, be smitten with**

(*informal*) **be crazy about**

– A relationship between two people who love each other is a **romance**.

❷ *My brother loves anything to do with football.*

• **like, be fond of, be partial to, have a weakness for, have a passion for, delight in, enjoy**

IDIOMS **have a soft spot for,** (*informal*) **have a thing about**

OPPOSITE **hate**

lovely *ADJECTIVE*

OVERUSED WORD

❶ **A lovely person:**

➤ **charming** ➤ **sweet**
➤ **delightful** ➤ **enchanting**
➤ **lovable** ➤ **endearing**
➤ **likeable** ➤ **adorable**
➤ **dear**

She is a **charming** *girl.*

❷ **A lovely day, lovely weather:**

➤ **fine** ➤ **fair**
➤ **glorious** ➤ **sunny**
➤ **bright**

It was **glorious** *weather for a bike ride.*

❸ **A lovely view:**

➤ **scenic** ➤ **glorious**
➤ **picturesque** ➤ **splendid**
➤ **pleasing**

You get a **splendid** *view from the cable car.*

❹ A lovely experience, a lovely time:

➤ pleasant
➤ pleasing
➤ enjoyable
➤ delightful
➤ marvellous
➤ wonderful

(*informal*) **fantastic, terrific, brilliant, smashing**

I had an **enjoyable** *time doing absolutely nothing!*

❺ Looking lovely:

➤ appealing
➤ attractive
➤ good-looking
➤ beautiful
➤ pretty
➤ glamorous
➤ alluring
➤ ravishing

(*informal*) **cute**

(*Scottish*) **bonny**

You look particularly **attractive** *in that hat.*

lover *NOUN*

❶ *Some lovers send each other Valentine cards.*
• **boyfriend, girlfriend, sweetheart, beloved**
❷ *He is a great lover of musicals.*
• **admirer, fan, devotee, enthusiast**

loving *ADJECTIVE*

She grew up in a loving family.
• **affectionate, kind, friendly, warm, tender, fond, devoted, passionate**
OPPOSITE unfriendly

low *ADJECTIVE*

❶ *The garden is surrounded by a low wall.*
• **short, shallow, sunken, squat**
OPPOSITES high, tall
❷ *You can tell from his uniform that he was a soldier of low rank.*
• **junior, inferior, lowly, modest, humble**
OPPOSITES high, senior
❸ *This work is of low quality.*
• **poor, inferior, substandard, unsatisfactory**
OPPOSITES high, superior
❹ *The tuba plays low notes.*
• **bass, deep, sonorous**
OPPOSITE high
❺ *We spoke in low whispers.*
• **quiet, soft, muted, subdued, muffled, hushed**
OPPOSITE loud

lower *VERB*

❶ *Some shops have lowered their prices.*
• **reduce, cut, drop, decrease, lessen, bring down**
(*informal*) **slash**
❷ *Please lower your voices.*
• **quieten, soften, turn down, tone down, muffle, hush**
❸ *At the end of the ceremony, soldiers lower the flag.*
• **take down, let down, dip, let fall**
OPPOSITE raise

loyal *ADJECTIVE*

He has always been a loyal supporter of the club.
• **faithful, devoted, true, steadfast, constant, staunch, reliable, dependable, trusty**
OPPOSITE disloyal

luck *NOUN*

❶ *I found the hidden entrance by pure luck.*
• **chance, accident, fortune, fate, fluke**
❷ *She had a bit of luck today.*
• **good fortune, good luck, success**

lucky *ADJECTIVE*

❶ *It was just a lucky guess.*
• **accidental, chance, fortuitous, providential**
❷ *Are you feeling lucky today?*
• **fortunate, favoured, charmed, blessed, in luck**
OPPOSITE unlucky

ludicrous *ADJECTIVE*

The film has a ludicrous plot.
• **ridiculous, absurd, laughable, idiotic, nonsensical, foolish, preposterous, crazy**
(*informal*) **daft**

luggage *NOUN*

Put your luggage on the trolley.
• **baggage, cases, suitcases, bags**

lull *VERB*
She lulled the baby to sleep by rocking it gently.
• **soothe, calm, hush, quieten, pacify, subdue**

lull *NOUN*
There was a brief lull in the conversation.
• **pause, break, gap, interval, respite, calm**
(*informal*) **let-up**

lumber *VERB*
❶ *A rhinoceros lumbered past our jeep.*
• **trundle, shamble, trudge, tramp, blunder, clump**
❷ (*informal*) *Why am I lumbered with all the washing-up?*
• **burden, encumber, saddle, land**

lump *NOUN*
❶ *Lumps of sticky clay stuck to his boots.*
• **chunk, piece, cluster, clump, wad, mass, hunk, wedge, block**
– A lump of gold is a **nugget**.
– A lump of earth is a **clod**.
– A lump of blood is a **clot**.
❷ *I could feel a lump where I'd banged my head.*
• **bump, swelling, bulge, protrusion**

lump *VERB*
➤ **lump things together**
The newspaper reports lumped together two different incidents.
• **put together, combine, merge, bunch up**

lunge *VERB*
The creature lunged forward and grabbed my leg.
• **thrust, charge, rush, dive, spring, pounce, throw yourself, launch yourself**

lurch *VERB*
❶ *It looked like a zombie lurching towards us.*
• **stagger, stumble, totter, sway, reel, roll, rock**
❷ *The bus suddenly lurched to one side.*
• **veer, swerve, swing, lean, list**

lure *VERB*
It was a trick to lure him into the forest.
• **attract, entice, tempt, coax, draw, invite, persuade, seduce**
– Something used to lure an animal into a trap is **bait**.
OPPOSITES deter, put off

lurk *VERB*
I had the feeling that someone was lurking in the shadows.
• **skulk, loiter, prowl, crouch, hide, lie in wait, lie low**

lush *ADJECTIVE*
Rainforests have lush vegetation.
• **rich, dense, thick, profuse, abundant, rampant, luxuriant**

luxurious *ADJECTIVE*
He was shown into a room with luxurious furnishings.
• **rich, expensive, costly, lavish, lush, sumptuous, opulent, de luxe, magnificent, splendid, extravagant**
(*informal*) **plush, swanky**
The words *luxurious* and *luxuriant* do not mean the same thing. A *luxurious hair salon* is expensive and comfortable, but *luxuriant hair* is thick and abundant.
OPPOSITES simple, austere

luxury *NOUN*
❶ *Dining out is a luxury these days.*
• **indulgence, extravagance, treat, frill**
OPPOSITE necessity
❷ *Only the nobility lived in luxury.*
• **affluence, wealth, richness, splendour, opulence, sumptuousness**
OPPOSITE poverty

machine *NOUN*
Do you know how this machine works?
• **appliance, device, apparatus, engine, contraption, mechanism**

mad *ADJECTIVE*
❶ *Have you gone completely mad?*
• **insane, crazy, deranged, demented, unbalanced**
(*informal*) **nuts, bonkers, loopy, crackers, potty**
IDIOMS (*informal*) **off your head, round the bend, round the twist**
OPPOSITE **sane**
❷ *It is a mad idea but it might just work.*
• **foolish, idiotic, senseless, crazy, stupid, silly, absurd, hare-brained**
(*informal*) **crackpot, cockeyed, daft**
❸ (*informal*) *Shami is mad about football.*
• **fanatical, enthusiastic, passionate, fervent, wild**
(*informal*) **crazy, nuts**
❹ (*informal*) *Please don't get mad when you hear this.*
• **angry, furious, infuriated, annoyed, cross, beside yourself, frenzied, hysterical**

made
past tense see **make**

magazine *NOUN*
I bought a magazine to read on the train.
• **journal, periodical, supplement, comic**
(*informal*) **mag**

magic *NOUN*
❶ *The wizard used magic to make himself invisible.*
• **sorcery, witchcraft, wizardry, enchantment, black magic, the black arts, white magic, the supernatural, the occult**
For tips on writing fantasy fiction see **fantasy**.
❷ *She is good at performing magic with a pack of cards.*
• **conjuring, illusion, sleight of hand**
❸ *The place has lost none of its magic.*
• **charm, allure, fascination, mystery, enchantment, wonder**

magic *ADJECTIVE*
❶ *The castle was surrounded by a magic spell.*
• **magical, supernatural, mystical, occult**
❷ *My uncle taught me some magic tricks.*
• **conjuring**

magical *ADJECTIVE*
❶ *The ring had magical powers.*
• **supernatural, magic, mystical, occult**
❷ *It was a magical evening.*
• **enchanting, entrancing, captivating, spellbinding, bewitching, charming, alluring, enthralling, delightful**

magician *NOUN*
❶ *The magician performed card tricks at our table.*
• **conjuror, illusionist**
❷ *Merlin, the legendary magician.*
• **sorcerer, sorceress, witch, wizard, warlock, enchanter, enchantress**

magnificent *ADJECTIVE*
❶ *The mountain scenery was magnificent.*
• **splendid, spectacular, glorious, superb, impressive, striking, dazzling, breathtaking, awe-inspiring**
OPPOSITES **uninspiring, ordinary**
❷ *They lived in a magnificent mansion.*
• **grand, imposing, stately, majestic, palatial, luxurious**
❸ *What a magnificent goal!*
• **excellent, first-class, outstanding, wonderful, marvellous, superb**
(*informal*) **fabulous, fantastic, terrific, brilliant**

magnify *VERB*
This image has been magnified many times.
• **enlarge, make larger, amplify, boost**
(*informal*) **blow up**
OPPOSITES **reduce, minimize**

mail *NOUN*
Have we had a delivery of mail yet?
• **post, letters, correspondence**

mail *VERB*
Can you mail this letter for me?
• **post, send, dispatch, ship**

maim *VERB*
Many people were killed or maimed in the attack.
• **injure, wound, mutilate, disfigure**

main *ADJECTIVE*
What is the main theme of the play?
• **principal, chief, major, central, leading, dominant, key, basic, essential, fundamental, primary, prime, predominant, pre-eminent, foremost**
OPPOSITES minor, secondary

mainly *ADVERB*
Vitamin C is found mainly in fruits and vegetables.
• **mostly, chiefly, principally, primarily, predominantly, largely, on the whole, for the most part**

maintain *VERB*
❶ *The referee tried to maintain order.*
• **keep, preserve, sustain, retain, perpetuate**
❷ *A team of gardeners maintain the grounds.*
• **look after, take care of, keep in order**
❸ *He still maintains that he's innocent.*
• **claim, insist, assert, declare, state, affirm, contend, profess**

majestic *ADJECTIVE*
These are the ruins of what was once a majestic city.
• **grand, magnificent, splendid, impressive, imposing, stately, noble**

major *ADJECTIVE*
❶ *Winning the Oscar was a major achievement.*
• **big, great, considerable, significant, important, serious, weighty**
OPPOSITES minor, trivial
❷ *There are delays on all the major roads into the city.*
• **chief, principal, primary, leading, foremost**
OPPOSITES minor, lesser

majority *NOUN*
➤ **the majority of**
The majority of Americans live in cities.
• **the greater number of, the bulk of, most**
IDIOM the lion's share of
OPPOSITE minority

make *VERB*
❶ *We were making a model aeroplane.*
• **build, construct, assemble, put together, manufacture, fashion**
❷ *Try not to make a noise.*
• **cause, produce, create, generate**
❸ *The company made a huge profit last year.*
• **gain, get, obtain, acquire, earn, win**
❹ *They made me do it.*
• **force to, compel to, drive to, order to, press into**
❺ *We should make the coast before nightfall.*
• **reach, arrive at, get to, get as far as**
❻ *I think she'll make a good actress.*
• **become, grow into, turn into, change into**
❼ *What time do you make it?*
• **calculate, estimate, reckon**
❽ *5 and 8 make 13.*
• **add up to, come to, total**
❾ *He stood up and made a little bow.*
• **perform, execute, carry out, give, do**
❿ *I'm just making my bed.*
• **arrange, tidy**
⓫ *I'll make you an offer.*
• **propose, suggest**
➤ **make for**
We made for the nearest exit.
• **go towards, head for**
IDIOM make a beeline for
➤ **make off**
The gang made off in a stolen car.
• **leave, escape, get away, run away, disappear**
(*informal*) **clear off, scarper**
➤ **make something out**

❶ *Can you make out a figure in the background?*
• **see, detect, discern, distinguish, recognize, spot**
❷ *I can't make out what you're saying.*
• **understand, follow, grasp, work out, comprehend, fathom, make sense of**
❸ *My brother always makes out that he's some kind of genius.*
• **claim, allege, suggest, imply, insinuate, pretend**

➤ **make something up**
She was good at making up stories.
• **create, invent, think up, concoct, fabricate**

➤ **make up for something**
The acting makes up for the far-fetched plot.
• **compensate for, cancel out, offset**

make *NOUN*
What make of phone do you have?
• **brand, model, label**

male *ADJECTIVE*
a male model
• **masculine**
– Something that is suitable for a man is **manly**.
OPPOSITE female
SEE ALSO **man**

malicious *ADJECTIVE*
Someone has been spreading malicious rumours.
• **malevolent, hostile, malign, spiteful, vindictive, vicious, hurtful**

mammal *NOUN*

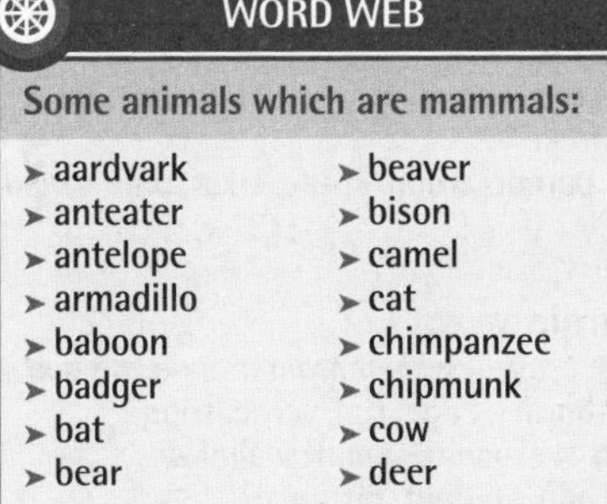

WORD WEB

Some animals which are mammals:

➤ aardvark
➤ anteater
➤ antelope
➤ armadillo
➤ baboon
➤ badger
➤ bat
➤ bear
➤ beaver
➤ bison
➤ camel
➤ cat
➤ chimpanzee
➤ chipmunk
➤ cow
➤ deer
➤ dog
➤ dolphin
➤ dormouse
➤ echidna
➤ elephant
➤ elk
➤ ferret
➤ fox
➤ gazelle
➤ gibbon
➤ giraffe
➤ goat
➤ gorilla
➤ hare
➤ hedgehog
➤ hippopotamus
➤ horse
➤ hyena
➤ lemming
➤ lemur
➤ leopard
➤ lion
➤ lynx
➤ manatee
➤ meerkat
➤ mole
➤ mongoose
➤ monkey
➤ moose
➤ mouse
➤ narwhal
➤ orang-utan
➤ otter
➤ panda
➤ pig
➤ polar bear
➤ porcupine
➤ porpoise
➤ rabbit
➤ raccoon
➤ rat
➤ reindeer
➤ rhinoceros
➤ seal
➤ sea lion
➤ sheep
➤ shrew
➤ skunk
➤ sloth
➤ squirrel
➤ tapir
➤ tiger
➤ vole
➤ walrus
➤ weasel
➤ whale
➤ wildebeest
➤ wolf
➤ yak
➤ zebra

- A related adjective is **mammalian**.
- When a female mammal produces milk she is **lactating**.

SEE ALSO **cat, dog, horse, rodent**

For tips on describing animals see **animal**.

man *NOUN*
❶ *The man at the ticket desk was very helpful.*
• **gentleman, male, fellow**
(*informal*) **guy, gent, bloke, chap**
– An unmarried man is a **bachelor**.
– A man whose wife has died is a **widower**.
❷ *Early man lived by hunting.*
• **mankind, humankind, the human race, humanity, Homo sapiens**

A B C D E F G H I J K L M N O P Q R S T U V W X Y Z

manage *VERB*
❶ *His son manages the business now.*
• be in charge of, run, direct, lead, control, govern, rule, supervise, oversee, preside over
❷ *I can't manage any more work just now.*
• cope with, deal with, take on, carry out
❸ *I don't know how we'll manage without you.*
• cope, make do, get along, get by, survive, fare
(*informal*) muddle through

manager *NOUN*
She is the manager of a bookshop.
• director, head, chief, proprietor
(*informal*) boss

mania *NOUN*
A mania for this new hobby swept the country.
• craze, enthusiasm, passion, obsession (with), fixation (with), fad, rage

manipulate *VERB*
❶ *She began to manipulate the controls and levers.*
• work, handle, pull, push, turn, twist
(*informal*) twiddle
❷ *He uses his charm to manipulate people.*
• take advantage of, use, exploit, impose on

man-made *ADJECTIVE*
a man-made fibre
• synthetic, artificial, imitation, mock, fake
OPPOSITES natural, real

manner *NOUN*
❶ *They dealt with the problem in a very efficient manner.*
• way, style, fashion, method, mode, means, system, technique
❷ *I was put off by her frosty manner.*
• behaviour, conduct, attitude, air, aspect, demeanour, bearing

➤ **manners**
Some people have no manners at all!
• politeness, courtesy, civility, etiquette, social graces

manoeuvre *NOUN*
Parking a bus is a difficult manoeuvre.
• move, operation

manoeuvre *VERB*
She manoeuvred the boat through the gap in the rocks.
• guide, move, pilot, steer, navigate

manufacture *VERB*
The factory manufactures tyres.
• make, build, construct, assemble, put together, turn out

many *DETERMINER*
I've been on a boat many times.
• numerous, a lot of, plenty of, countless, innumerable, untold
(*informal*) umpteen, lots of, masses of
OPPOSITE few

map *NOUN*
She had a map of France on the wall.
• chart, diagram, plan
– A book of maps is an **atlas**.
– A person who draws maps is a **cartographer**.

mar *VERB*
The film is marred by a terrible soundtrack.
• spoil, ruin, wreck, damage, impair, tarnish
OPPOSITE enhance

march *VERB*
A brass band was marching down the street.
• parade, troop, stride, strut, pace, tread, file

margin *NOUN*
❶ *Leave a wide margin around the text.*
• border, edge, rim, verge, fringe
❷ *We won by a narrow margin.*
• gap, amount, distance

marginal *ADJECTIVE*
I can see a marginal improvement.
• **slight, small, minimal, minor, unimportant, negligible, borderline**
OPPOSITES **great, marked**

mark *NOUN*
❶ *The dog left muddy paw marks on the floor.*
• **spot, stain, blemish, blotch, blot, smear, smudge, streak, speck**
(*informal*) **splodge**
❷ *What mark did you get in the test?*
• **score, grade**
❸ *They stood in silence as a mark of respect.*
• **sign, token, indication, symbol, emblem**

mark *VERB*
❶ *Please try not to mark the pages.*
• **stain, dirty, blot, smudge, smear, streak**
❷ *He had exam papers to mark that evening.*
• **correct, grade, assess**
❸ *She'll be back, you mark my words!*
• **mind, heed, attend to, listen to, note, take note of**

marked *ADJECTIVE*
You can see a marked improvement in his health.
• **noticeable, considerable, pronounced, clear, obvious, distinct, decided, striking**
OPPOSITES **slight, marginal**

marriage *NOUN*
❶ *My grandparents are celebrating forty years of marriage.*
• **matrimony, wedlock**
❷ *Today is the anniversary of their marriage.*
• **wedding, union**
(*formal*) **nuptials**

marry *VERB*
In what year did your grandparents marry?
• **get married, wed**
IDIOMS (*informal*) **tie the knot, get hitched**
– A couple who have promised to marry are **engaged** to each other.
– A man who is engaged to be married is a **fiancé** and a woman who is engaged to be married is a **fiancée**.

marsh *NOUN*
Wading birds are found in coastal marshes.
• **swamp, bog, wetland, marshland, fen**

marvel *NOUN*
the marvels of modern science
• **wonder, miracle, phenomenon, sensation**

marvel *VERB*
➤ **marvel at**
Audiences marvelled at the acrobats' skill.
• **admire, wonder at, be amazed by, be astonished by**

marvellous *ADJECTIVE*
What a marvellous achievement!
• **excellent, superb, splendid, magnificent, glorious, sublime, wonderful, tremendous, amazing, remarkable, extraordinary, incredible, phenomenal**
(*informal*) **brilliant, fantastic, terrific, super, smashing**
OPPOSITES **terrible, awful**

masculine *ADJECTIVE*
The singer had a deep, masculine voice.
• **male, manly, macho, virile**
OPPOSITE **feminine**

mash *VERB*
Mash the potatoes with a little butter.
• **crush, pound, pulp, smash, squash**
– To make something into powder is to **grind** or **pulverize** it.

mask *VERB*
The entrance was masked by a curtain.
• **conceal, hide, cover, obscure, screen, veil, shroud, camouflage**

mass *NOUN*
She sifted through the mass of papers on her desk.
• **heap, pile, mound, stack, collection,**

A B C D E F G H I J K L M N O P Q R S T U V W X Y Z

quantity, accumulation
(*informal*) load

massacre *VERB*
see kill

massive *ADJECTIVE*
Near the entrance stood a massive bronze statue.
• enormous, huge, gigantic, colossal, giant, immense, vast, mighty, mammoth, monumental, great, big, large
(*informal*) whopping
(*literary*) gargantuan
OPPOSITES small, tiny
SEE ALSO big

master *NOUN*
❶ *a computer game called Masters of the Universe*
• lord, ruler, sovereign, governor
❷ *Sherlock Holmes was a master of disguise.*
• expert, genius, ace, wizard, virtuoso, maestro
(*informal*) whizz

master *VERB*
❶ *Have you mastered the guitar yet?*
• grasp, learn, understand, become proficient in, pick up
(*informal*) get the hang of, get to grips with
❷ *She succeeded in mastering her fear of heights.*
• overcome, conquer, defeat, triumph over, get the better of, control, curb, subdue, tame
OPPOSITES succumb to, give in to

match *NOUN*
❶ *We lost the first match of the season.*
• game, contest, competition, fixture, tournament, tie
❷ *Those colours are a good match.*
• combination, pairing
OPPOSITE contrast

match *VERB*
Does this tie match my shirt?
• go with, suit, fit with, blend with, tone in with
OPPOSITES contrast with, clash with

matching *ADJECTIVE*
She wore a red hat with a matching scarf.
• coordinating, corresponding, complementary, equivalent, twin, paired
OPPOSITES contrasting, clashing

mate *NOUN*
❶ (*informal*) *Jermaine is one of my best mates.*
• friend
(*informal*) pal, chum, buddy
❷ *I could hear a bird calling for its mate.*
• partner
❸ *He got a job as a plumber's mate.*
• assistant, helper, apprentice

material *NOUN*
❶ *I'm collecting material for the school magazine.*
• information, facts, data, ideas, notes, details
❷ *We have a range of art materials in the cupboard.*
• supplies, stuff, substances, things
❸ *The curtains are made of heavy material.*
• cloth, fabric, textile
SEE ALSO fabric

mathematics *NOUN*
a professor of mathematics
• (*informal*) maths
(*North American*) math

WORD WEB

Branches of mathematics:

- algebra
- arithmetic
- calculus
- geometry
- set theory
- statistics
- trigonometry

Terms used in mathematics:

- acute angle
- addition
- calculation
- calculator
- cardinal number
- constant
- cosine
- decimal
- diameter
- digit
- division
- equation

- exponent
- factor
- formula
- fraction
- hypotenuse
- index
- integer
- locus
- long division
- matrix
- median
- multiplication
- obtuse angle
- ordinal number
- pi
- power
- prime number
- product
- quotient
- reciprocal
- remainder
- sector
- sine
- square root
- subtraction
- symbol
- symmetry
- tangent
- vector
- whole number

matted *ADJECTIVE*
The dog's coat was dirty and matted.
• tangled, knotted, uncombed

matter *NOUN*
❶ *This is a matter of great importance.*
• affair, concern, issue, business, situation, incident, subject, topic, thing
❷ *What's the matter with the car?*
• problem, difficulty, trouble, worry
❸ *Peat consists mainly of plant matter.*
• material, stuff, substance

matter *VERB*
Will it matter if I'm late?
• be important, count, make a difference

mature *ADJECTIVE*
❶ *The zoo has two mature gorillas.*
• adult, fully grown, well developed
OPPOSITE young
❷ *He is very mature for his age.*
• grown-up, responsible, sensible
OPPOSITES immature, childish

maximum *NOUN*
The heat is at its maximum at midday.
• highest point, peak, top, upper limit, ceiling

maximum *ADJECTIVE*
The ship has a maximum speed of 40 knots.
• greatest, top, highest, biggest, largest, fullest, utmost
OPPOSITE minimum

maybe *ADVERB*
Maybe they've got lost.
• perhaps, possibly
OPPOSITE definitely

maze *NOUN*
We were lost in a maze of underground tunnels.
• labyrinth, network, web, tangle, warren

meadow *NOUN*
Cows were grazing in the meadow.
• field, pasture

meagre *ADJECTIVE*
The prisoners were given meagre rations of rice and water.
• scant, sparse, poor, scanty, inadequate, insufficient, skimpy, paltry
(*informal*) measly, stingy
OPPOSITES generous, ample

meal *NOUN*
a simple meal of bread and cheese
• (*informal*) bite
(*formal*) repast

WORD WEB

Some types of meal:

- afternoon tea
- barbecue
- breakfast
- banquet
- brunch
- buffet
- dinner
- (*informal*) elevenses
- feast
- high tea
- lunch
- (*formal*) luncheon
- picnic
- snack
- supper
- takeaway
- tea
- tea break

SEE ALSO **food**

mean *VERB*
❶ *Do you know what this symbol means?*
• indicate, signify, denote, symbolize, represent, stand for, express, convey, communicate, suggest, imply

A B C D E F G H I J K L M N O P Q R S T U V W X Y Z

❷ *I didn't mean to cause any harm.*
• **intend, aim, plan, set out, propose, want, have in mind**

mean *ADJECTIVE*
❶ *Scrooge was too mean to buy any presents.*
• **selfish, miserly, uncharitable, penny-pinching**
(*informal*) **stingy, tight, tight-fisted**
OPPOSITE generous
❷ *That was a mean thing to say.*
• **unkind, unpleasant, spiteful, vicious, cruel, malicious, horrible, nasty**
(*informal*) **rotten**
OPPOSITE kind

meaning *NOUN*
What is the meaning of this word?
• **sense, explanation, interpretation, definition, significance, import, gist**

meaningful *ADJECTIVE*
The two friends exchanged a meaningful look.
• **pointed, significant, expressive, suggestive, revealing**
OPPOSITES insignificant, inconsequential

meaningless *ADJECTIVE*
It was a meaningless promise.
• **empty, hollow, insincere, pointless, worthless, ineffectual**
OPPOSITES serious, worthwhile

means *PLURAL NOUN*
❶ *Camels are used as a means of transport.*
• **method, mode, medium, channel, course, way**
❷ *They don't have the means to buy a house.*
• **money, resources, assets, funds, finance, capital, wherewithal**

measure *VERB*
Now measure the height of the wall.
• **calculate, gauge, determine, quantify, assess**

measure *NOUN*
❶ *You can't use money alone as a measure of success.*
• **gauge, standard, scale, indicator, yardstick, barometer**
❷ *At least we know the measure of the problem.*
• **size, extent, magnitude**
❸ *They are taking measures to improve the park.*
• **step, action, course, procedure, initiative**

WORD WEB

Metric weights and measures:

➤ centimetre
➤ gram
➤ hectare
➤ kilo or kilogram
➤ kilolitre
➤ kilometre
➤ litre
➤ metre
➤ milligram
➤ millilitre
➤ millimetre
➤ tonne

Imperial weights and measures:

➤ acre
➤ foot
➤ gallon
➤ inch
➤ mile
➤ ounce
➤ pint
➤ pound
➤ quart
➤ stone
➤ ton
➤ yard

- The depth of the sea is measured in **fathoms**.
- The speed of a boat or ship is measured in **knots**.
- The distance of an object in space is measured in **light years**.

For measurements used in cooking see **cook**.

measurement *NOUN*
What are the measurements of the room?
• **dimensions, size, extent, proportions**

meat *NOUN*
Dad was carving the meat from the turkey.
• **flesh**

WORD WEB

Some kinds of meat:

- bacon
- beef
- chicken
- duck
- game
- gammon
- goose
- ham
- lamb
- mutton
- offal
- pork
- turkey
- veal
- venison

medal *NOUN*

We won the bronze medal in the relay race.

• **award, prize, trophy**

– A person who wins a medal is a **medallist**.

meddle *VERB*

❶ *He's always meddling in other people's affairs.*

• **interfere, intrude, intervene, pry**

IDIOMS (*informal*) **poke your nose in, stick your oar in**

❷ *Someone has been meddling with my phone.*

• **fiddle about, tinker, tamper**

medicine *NOUN*

❶ *Have you taken your cough medicine?*

• **drug, medication, treatment, remedy, cure**

– An amount of medicine taken at one time is a **dose**.

– Medicine which a doctor gives you is a **prescription**.

❷ *The plant is used in herbal medicine.*

• **therapy, treatment, healing**

WORD WEB

Some types of medicine:

- anaesthetic
- antibiotic
- antidote
- antiseptic
- expectorant
- painkiller
- sedative
- stimulant
- tonic
- tranquillizer

Methods of taking medicine:

- capsule
- eardrops
- eyedrops
- gargle
- inhaler
- injection
- lotion
- lozenge
- ointment
- pill
- tablet

Medical instruments:

- forceps
- scalpel
- stethoscope
- syringe
- thermometer
- tweezers

Some forms of alternative therapy:

- acupuncture
- aromatherapy
- herbal medicine or herbalism
- homeopathy
- reflexology

People involved in health and medicine:

- anaesthetist
- cardiologist
- chiropodist
- dentist
- dermatologist
- doctor
- GP
- gynaecologist
- herbalist
- homeopath
- midwife
- neurologist
- nurse
- obstetrician
- oncologist
- ophthalmologist
- optician
- orthodontist
- osteopath
- paediatrician
- paramedic
- pharmacist
- physician
- physiotherapist
- podiatrist
- psychiatrist
- psychologist
- radiographer
- speech therapist
- surgeon

mediocre *ADJECTIVE*

I thought the film was rather mediocre.

• **ordinary, average, commonplace, indifferent, second-rate, run-of-the-mill, undistinguished, uninspiring, forgettable, lacklustre, pedestrian** (*informal*) **so-so**

OPPOSITES **outstanding, exceptional**

medium *ADJECTIVE*

She is of medium height.

• **average, middle, middle-sized, middling, standard, moderate, normal**

A B C D E F G H I J K L M N O P Q R S T U V W X Y Z

medium *NOUN*
The Internet is a powerful medium of communication.
• **means, mode, method, way, channel, vehicle**

meek *ADJECTIVE*
That cat looks meek but she has sharp claws.
• **gentle, mild, docile, tame, obedient, submissive**
OPPOSITE aggressive

meet *VERB*
❶ *We're meeting outside the cinema.*
• **assemble, gather, get together, congregate, convene**
❷ *I met an old friend from university at the party.*
• **encounter, run into, come across, stumble across, chance on, happen on**
(*informal*) **bump into**
❸ *When did you two first meet?*
• **become acquainted (with), be introduced (to), get to know**
❹ *The two roads meet here at the crossroads.*
• **come together, converge, connect, touch, join, cross, intersect, link up**
❺ *My parents met me at the arrivals hall at the airport.*
• **greet, pick up, welcome**
❻ *She meets all the requirements for the job.*
• **fulfil, satisfy, match, answer, comply with**

meeting *NOUN*
❶ *We held a meeting to discuss our plans.*
• **gathering, assembly, council, forum, congress, conference**
– A large outdoor public meeting is a **rally**.
– A formal meeting with an important person is an **audience**.
❷ *It is a story about the meeting of two cultures.*
• **coming together, convergence, intersection, confluence, union**

melancholy *ADJECTIVE*
She was playing a melancholy tune.
• **sad, sorrowful, mournful, doleful, unhappy, gloomy, wistful, sombre**
OPPOSITE cheerful
SEE ALSO **sad**

melody *NOUN*
The song has a simple melody.
• **tune, air, theme**

melt *VERB*
❶ *The snow has already begun to melt.*
• **thaw, defrost, soften, liquefy**
– To melt ore to extract its metal is to **smelt** it.
– Rock or metal that has melted through great heat is **molten**.
OPPOSITE freeze
❷ *Soon the crowd began to melt away.*
• **disperse, break up, drift away, disappear, vanish, fade**

member *NOUN*
➤ **be a member of something**
Are you a member of the sports club?
• **belong to, subscribe to**

memorable *ADJECTIVE*
It was a memorable holiday.
• **unforgettable, notable, remarkable, noteworthy, significant, outstanding**
OPPOSITE ordinary

memorize *VERB*
He is good at memorizing long numbers.
• **learn, learn by heart, commit to memory, remember**
OPPOSITE forget

memory *NOUN*
My earliest memory is of watching the sea.
• **recollection, remembrance, reminiscence, reminder, impression**

menace *NOUN*
❶ *Sharks can be a menace to divers.*
• **danger, threat, risk, hazard, peril**
❷ *That cat is an absolute menace!*
• **nuisance, annoyance, irritation, inconvenience**
(*informal*) **pest**

a b c d e f g h i j k l m n o p q r s t u v w x y z

mend *VERB*
Workmen were mending a hole in the road.
• **repair, fix, put right, restore, renovate, patch**

mention *VERB*
❶ *Please don't mention this to anyone.*
• **refer to, speak about, touch on, hint at, allude to**
❷ *She mentioned that she had been ill.*
• **say, remark, reveal, disclose, divulge**
(*informal*) **let out**
❸ *The programme mentioned all the cast.*
• **name, acknowledge, list**

mercy *NOUN*
The queen showed no mercy to her enemies.
• **compassion, humanity, sympathy, pity, leniency, kindness, charity, clemency**
OPPOSITE **cruelty**

merge *VERB*
❶ *They plan to merge the two schools.*
• **join together, combine, integrate, unite, amalgamate, conflate, consolidate**
❷ *Two smaller rivers merge to form the Danube.*
• **come together, converge, join, meet**
OPPOSITE **separate**

merit *NOUN*
❶ *She's a writer of great merit.*
• **excellence, quality, calibre, distinction, worth, talent**
❷ *I can see the merits of this argument.*
• **benefit, advantage, virtue, asset, value, good point**

merit *VERB*
This suggestion definitely merits further discussion.
• **deserve, justify, warrant, be worthy of, be entitled to, earn, rate**

merry *ADJECTIVE*
A boy sat on a wall, whistling a merry tune.
• **cheerful, happy, light-hearted, joyful, jolly, bright, sunny, cheery, lively, chirpy**
OPPOSITES **sad, gloomy**

mess *NOUN*
❶ *Please clear up this mess.*
• **untidiness, clutter, jumble, muddle, chaos, disorder, disarray, litter**
(*informal*) **shambles, tip**
❷ *I've made a real mess of things, haven't I?*
• **disaster, botch**
(*informal*) **hash**
❸ *How can we get out of this mess?*
• **difficulty, problem, predicament, plight, trouble**
(*informal*) **fix, jam**
IDIOMS **tight spot, tight corner**

mess *VERB*
➤ **mess about or around**
I spent the day messing about at home.
• **potter about, lounge about, play about, fool around**
(*informal*) **muck about**
➤ **mess something up**
❶ *I don't want to mess up my hair.*
• **make a mess of, mix up, muddle, jumble, tangle, dishevel**
❷ *I think I messed up my audition.*
• **make a mess of, bungle**
(*informal*) **botch, make a hash of**

message *NOUN*
❶ *Did you get my message?*
• **note, letter, communication, memo, dispatch**
(*formal*) **missive**
❷ *What is the main message of the poem?*
• **meaning, sense, import, idea, point, moral, gist, thrust**

messy *ADJECTIVE*
This kitchen is really messy!
• **untidy, disorderly, chaotic, muddled, dirty, filthy, grubby, mucky**
(*informal*) **higgledy-piggledy**
OPPOSITES **neat, tidy, clean**

met
past tense see **meet**

metal *NOUN*

WORD WEB

Some common metals:

- aluminium
- brass
- bronze
- copper
- gold
- iron
- lead
- magnesium
- mercury
- nickel
- pewter
- platinum
- silver
- steel
- tin
- zinc

- A metal formed by mixing two or more metals is an **alloy**.
- Rock which contains a particular metal is **ore**.
➤ *iron ore*
- Something that looks or sounds like metal is **metallic**.

method *NOUN*
They practised new methods of farming.
• **technique, way, procedure, process, system, approach, routine**

methodical *ADJECTIVE*
She has a methodical way of working.
• **orderly, systematic, structured, organized, well-ordered, disciplined, deliberate, efficient, businesslike**
OPPOSITES **disorderly, haphazard**

middle *NOUN*
❶ *There is an island in the middle of the lake.*
• **centre, midpoint, core, heart, hub**
❷ *Tie the rope around your middle.*
• **waist, midriff, stomach, belly**
(*informal*) **tummy**

middle *ADJECTIVE*
❶ *I keep my paints in the middle drawer.*
• **central, midway, mid, inner**
❷ *a middle size of egg*
• **medium, average, moderate**

might *NOUN*
I banged at the door with all my might.
• **strength, power, force, energy, vigour**

mighty *ADJECTIVE*
The creature let out a mighty roar.
• **powerful, forceful, vigorous, ferocious, violent, hefty, great**
OPPOSITES **weak, feeble**

mild *ADJECTIVE*
❶ *Her horse has a mild temper.*
• **easy-going, gentle, docile, placid, good-tempered, kind, soft-hearted**
❷ *There is a mild flavour of garlic.*
• **slight, faint, subtle, light**
OPPOSITES **strong, pronounced**
❸ *It was a mild form of the disease.*
• **light, gentle, slight, soft**
OPPOSITES **severe, harsh**
❹ *The weather should turn mild this week.*
• **pleasant, warm, balmy, temperate, clement**
OPPOSITES **harsh, inclement**

milky *ADJECTIVE*
Rubber trees produce a milky sap.
• **whitish, cloudy, misty, chalky, opaque**
OPPOSITE **clear**

mimic *VERB*
My brother is good at mimicking other people.
• **do impressions of, imitate, impersonate, pretend to be, caricature, parody**
(*informal*) **take off**

mind *NOUN*
❶ *Her mind was as sharp as ever.*
• **brain, intelligence, intellect, head, sense, understanding, wits, judgement, mental powers, reasoning**
❷ *Are you sure you won't change your mind?*
• **wishes, intention, fancy, inclination, thoughts, opinion, point of view**

mind *VERB*
❶ *Would you mind my bag for a minute?*
• **guard, look after, watch, care for**
IDIOM **keep an eye on**
❷ *Mind the step.*
• **look out for, watch out for, beware of, pay attention to, heed, note**

❸ *They won't mind if I'm late.*
• **bother, care, worry, be upset, take offence, object, disapprove**

mine *NOUN*
The village was next to an abandoned coal mine.
• **pit, colliery**
– A place where coal is removed from the surface is an **opencast mine.**
– A place where stone or slate is removed is a **quarry.**

mingle *VERB*
I tried to mingle with the other guests.
• **mix in, circulate, blend, combine, merge, fuse**

miniature *ADJECTIVE*
His glasses were fitted with a miniature camera.
• **tiny, minute, diminutive, small-scale, baby, mini**
SEE ALSO **small**

minimum *ADJECTIVE*
Set the oven to the minimum temperature.
• **least, smallest, lowest, bottom**
OPPOSITE maximum

minor *ADJECTIVE*
I only had a minor part in the play.
• **small, unimportant, insignificant, inferior, lesser, subordinate, trivial, trifling, petty**
OPPOSITE major

minute *ADJECTIVE*
❶ *You can hardly see the minute crack.*
• **tiny, minuscule, microscopic, negligible**
OPPOSITE large
❷ *Each flower is drawn in minute detail.*
• **exhaustive, thorough, meticulous, painstaking**
OPPOSITE rough

miraculous *ADJECTIVE*
The patient made a miraculous recovery.
• **amazing, astonishing, astounding, extraordinary, incredible, inexplicable, phenomenal**

misbehave *VERB*
The puppies have been misbehaving again!
• **behave badly, be naughty, be disobedient, get up to mischief**
OPPOSITE behave

miscellaneous *ADJECTIVE*
The box contained miscellaneous musical instruments.
• **assorted, various, varied, different, mixed, sundry, diverse**

mischief *NOUN*
The twins are always getting up to mischief.
• **naughtiness, bad behaviour, misbehaviour, disobedience, playfulness**

miser *NOUN*
The old miser kept his money hidden under the floorboards.
• **penny-pincher, Scrooge**
(*informal*) **skinflint**

miserable *ADJECTIVE*
❶ *You look miserable. What's the matter?*
• **sad, unhappy, sorrowful, gloomy, glum, downhearted, despondent, dejected, depressed, melancholy, mournful, tearful**
IDIOMS (*informal*) **down in the mouth, down in the dumps**
OPPOSITES cheerful, happy
❷ *The animals lived in miserable conditions.*
• **distressing, uncomfortable, wretched, pitiful, pathetic, squalid**
OPPOSITE comfortable
❸ *The weather was cold and miserable.*
• **dismal, dreary, bleak, depressing, cheerless, drab**
OPPOSITES fine, mild

miserly *ADJECTIVE*
He was too miserly to donate any money.
• **mean, selfish, penny-pinching**
(*informal*) **stingy, tight, tight-fisted**
OPPOSITE generous

misery *NOUN*
They thought they were doomed to a life of misery.
• **unhappiness, wretchedness, sorrow, sadness, gloom, grief, distress, despair, anguish, suffering, torment, heartache, depression**
OPPOSITE happiness

misfortune *NOUN*
I heard about her family's misfortune.
• **bad luck, trouble, hardship, adversity, affliction, setback, mishap**
OPPOSITE good luck

mishap *NOUN*
I had a slight mishap with my computer.
• **accident, problem, difficulty, setback**

mislay *VERB*
I seem to have mislaid my watch.
• **lose, misplace**
OPPOSITE find

misleading *ADJECTIVE*
The directions they gave us were misleading.
• **confusing, unreliable, deceptive, ambiguous, unclear**

miss *VERB*
❶ *I don't want to miss the start of the film.*
• **be too late for**
❷ *The bullet missed him by inches.*
• **fall short of, go wide of, overshoot**
❸ *If we leave now, we should miss the traffic.*
• **avoid, evade, bypass, beat**
❹ *I missed my friends over the holidays.*
• **long for, yearn for, pine for**
➤ **miss something out**
Don't miss out the gory details!
• **leave out, omit, exclude, cut out, pass over, overlook, ignore, skip**

missile *NOUN*
see **weapon**

missing *ADJECTIVE*
❶ *She found the missing keys in a drawer.*
• **lost, mislaid, misplaced, absent, astray**
❷ *What is missing from this photograph?*
• **absent, lacking, wanting, left out, omitted**

mission *NOUN*
❶ *The mission of the society is to protect wildlife.*
• **aim, purpose, objective, task, job, vocation, calling**
❷ *The astronauts are on a mission to Mars.*
• **expedition, journey, voyage, exploration, quest**

mist *NOUN*
❶ *The hills were enveloped in mist.*
• **fog, haze, cloud, drizzle**
❷ *I wiped the mist from the window.*
• **condensation, steam, vapour**

mistake *NOUN*
This article is full of mistakes.
• **error, fault, inaccuracy, miscalculation, blunder, lapse, slip, slip-up**
(*informal*) **howler**
– A spelling mistake is a **misspelling**.
– A mistake made during printing is a **misprint**.
– A mistake where something is left out is an **omission** or **oversight**.
➤ **make a mistake**
You've made a mistake in the formula.
• **err, miscalculate, blunder, slip up**

mistake *VERB*
At first, I mistook the meaning of her letter.
• **misunderstand, misinterpret, misconstrue, misread, get wrong**
➤ **mistake someone for someone**
People often mistake him for his brother.
• **confuse someone with, take someone for, mix someone up with**

mistrust *VERB*
Do you have any reason to mistrust him?
• **distrust, have doubts about, suspect, be wary of, have misgivings about, have reservations about**
OPPOSITE trust

misty *ADJECTIVE*

❶ *It was a cold and misty morning.*
• **foggy, hazy**
❷ *I couldn't see through the misty windows.*
• **steamy, cloudy, smoky, opaque**
❸ *I have misty memories of that day.*
• **indistinct, vague, faint, dim, hazy, fuzzy, blurred**
OPPOSITE clear

misunderstand *VERB*

I think you misunderstood what I said.
• **mistake, misinterpret, misconstrue, misread, get wrong, miss the point of**
IDIOM **get the wrong end of the stick**
OPPOSITE understand

mix *VERB*

Mix the ingredients in a bowl.
• **combine, blend, mingle, amalgamate, fuse**
➤ **mix something up**
Please don't mix up my DVDs.
• **muddle, jumble, shuffle, confuse**
➤ **mix with**
She's been mixing with the wrong sort of people.
• **associate with, socialize with, keep company with, consort with**
IDIOM **rub shoulders with**

mix *NOUN*

The style is a strange mix of ancient and modern.
• **mixture, blend, combination, compound, mingling, amalgamation, fusion, union**

mixed *ADJECTIVE*

Add a teaspoon of mixed herbs.
• **assorted, varied, various, different, miscellaneous, sundry, diverse**
OPPOSITE separate

mixture *NOUN*

❶ *I felt a mixture of fear and excitement.*
• **mix, blend, combination, compound, mingling**
– A mixture of metals is an **alloy**.
– A mixture of two different species of plant or animal is a **hybrid**.
❷ *The book contains an odd mixture of stories.*
• **assortment, collection, variety, miscellany, medley, jumble, ragbag**
– A confused mixture is a **mishmash**.

mix-up *NOUN*

There was a mix-up with our tickets.
• **confusion, misunderstanding, mistake, error, blunder, muddle**

moan *VERB*

❶ *He lay on the ground, moaning in pain.*
• **cry, groan, sigh, wail, howl, whimper**
❷ (*informal*) *My sister is always moaning about something.*
• **complain, grumble, grouse, carp, bleat, whine**
(*informal*) **gripe, whinge**

mob *NOUN*

There was an angry mob of protesters outside the gate.
• **crowd, horde, throng, mass, multitude, rabble, gang, pack, herd**

mob *VERB*

The singer was mobbed by fans as he left the hotel.
• **surround, crowd round, besiege, hem in, jostle**

mobile *ADJECTIVE*

❶ *A mobile library visits once a fortnight.*
• **movable, transportable, portable, travelling**
OPPOSITES stationary, fixed
❷ *You should be mobile again in a day or two.*
• **moving about, active**
(*informal*) **up and about**
OPPOSITE immobile

mock *VERB*

It was mean of them to mock his singing.
• **ridicule, laugh at, make fun of, jeer at, scoff at, sneer at, scorn, deride**
IDIOM (*informal*) **take the mickey out of**

mock *ADJECTIVE*
He held up his hands in mock surprise.
• imitation, pretend, simulated, fake, artificial, sham
OPPOSITES real, genuine

mode *NOUN*
The normal mode of transport on the island is horse and cart.
• way, manner, method, system, means, style, approach

model *NOUN*
❶ *I'm building a model of the Eiffel Tower.*
• replica, copy, reproduction, miniature, toy, dummy
❷ *Her dad always has the latest model of car.*
• design, type, version
❸ *He is a model of good behaviour.*
• example, ideal

model *ADJECTIVE*
❶ *We went to an exhibition of model railways.*
• miniature, replica, toy, dummy
❷ *She is a model student.*
• ideal, perfect, exemplary, faultless

model *VERB*
We learnt how to model figures in clay.
• make, mould, shape, construct, fashion

moderate *ADJECTIVE*
Her first book was a moderate success.
• average, fair, modest, medium, reasonable, passable, tolerable
OPPOSITES exceptional, great

moderately *ADVERB*
I'm moderately happy with my score.
• fairly, reasonably, relatively, quite, rather, somewhat
(*informal*) pretty

modern *ADJECTIVE*
❶ *The speed of modern computers is amazing.*
• present-day, current, contemporary, the latest, recent, advanced
OPPOSITE past
❷ *She has a very modern hairstyle.*
• fashionable, up to date, stylish, modish, trendsetting
(*informal*) trendy, hip
OPPOSITES old-fashioned, out of date, retro

modest *ADJECTIVE*
❶ *He's very modest about his work.*
• humble, unassuming, self-effacing, diffident, reserved, shy, bashful, coy
OPPOSITES conceited, boastful
❷ *There has been a modest increase in sales.*
• moderate, reasonable, average, medium, limited
OPPOSITE considerable
❸ *She always dressed in a modest style.*
• demure, decent, decorous, proper, seemly
OPPOSITES immodest, indecent

modify *VERB*
We've had to modify our travel plans.
• adapt, alter, change, adjust, refine, revise, vary
(*informal*) tweak

moist *ADJECTIVE*
❶ *a current of warm, moist air*
• damp, dank, wet, humid, muggy, clammy, steamy
❷ *a rich and moist fruitcake*
• juicy, soft, tender, succulent
OPPOSITE dry

moisture *NOUN*
There was a patch of moisture on the wall.
• wetness, dampness, damp, wet, condensation, humidity, dew

moment *NOUN*
❶ *I'll be ready in a moment.*
• short while, minute, second, instant, flash
(*informal*) jiffy, tick
❷ *It was a great moment in the history of science.*
• time, occasion, point

momentary *ADJECTIVE*
There was a momentary pause.
• brief, short, short-lived, temporary, fleeting, passing
OPPOSITES lengthy, long-lived

momentous *ADJECTIVE*
We have reached a momentous decision.
• very important, significant, historic, major, far-reaching, pivotal
(*informal*) earth-shattering
OPPOSITES insignificant, trivial

monarch *NOUN*
see **ruler**

money *NOUN*
❶ *How much money do you have with you?*
• cash, currency, change, coins, notes
(*informal*) dough, dosh
❷ *The family lost all their money when the business collapsed.*
• funds, finance, capital, wealth, riches, fortune, means, wherewithal

monster *NOUN*
A sea monster reared its head above the waves.
• beast, giant, ogre, brute, fiend, demon
(*literary*) leviathan

monstrous *ADJECTIVE*
❶ *The volcano triggered a monstrous tidal wave.*
• huge, gigantic, enormous, massive, immense, colossal, great, mighty, towering, vast
❷ *The whole country was shocked by this monstrous crime.*
• horrifying, shocking, wicked, evil, hideous, vile, atrocious, abominable, dreadful, horrible, gruesome, grisly, outrageous, scandalous

mood *NOUN*
He arrived in a foul mood.
• temper, humour, state of mind, frame of mind, disposition

moody *ADJECTIVE*
She slumped on the chair, looking moody.
• sulky, sullen, grumpy, bad-tempered, temperamental, touchy, miserable, gloomy, glum, morose
OPPOSITE cheerful

moon *NOUN*
Saturn has a large number of moons.
• satellite

WORD WEB

Phases of the moon:

➤ new moon
➤ crescent moon
➤ half moon
➤ gibbous moon
➤ full moon

- The Moon **waxes** when it appears gradually bigger before a full moon.
- The Moon **wanes** when it appears gradually smaller after a full moon.
- A landscape on the Moon is a **moonscape**.
- A word meaning 'to do with the Moon' is **lunar**.

➤ *a lunar eclipse*

SEE ALSO **planet, space**

moor *NOUN*
The tower stands on a windswept moor.
• moorland, heath, fell

moor *VERB*
Several yachts were moored in the harbour.
• tie up, secure, fasten, anchor, berth, dock

moral *ADJECTIVE*
She tried her best to lead a moral life.
• good, virtuous, upright, honourable, principled, honest, just, truthful, decent, ethical, righteous
OPPOSITE immoral

moral *NOUN*
The moral of this story is to be careful what you wish for.
• lesson, message, meaning, teaching

morale *NOUN*
A win would improve the team's morale.
• confidence, self-esteem, spirit, mood, attitude, motivation, state of mind

A B C D E F G H I J K L M N O P Q R S T U V W X Y Z

more *DETERMINER*
We need more light in this room.
• **extra, further, added, additional, supplementary**
OPPOSITES less, fewer

morning *NOUN*
We set off in the early morning.
• **daybreak, dawn, first light, sunrise**

morsel *NOUN*
You haven't eaten a morsel of food.
• **bite, crumb, mouthful, taste, nibble, piece, scrap, fragment**

mortal *ADJECTIVE*
❶ *All of us are mortal.*
OPPOSITE immortal
❷ *I believe you are in mortal danger.*
• **deadly, lethal, fatal**
❸ *The brothers became mortal enemies.*
• **bitter, deadly, irreconcilable**

mostly *ADVERB*
❶ *The account is written mostly from memory.*
• **mainly, largely, chiefly, primarily, principally, predominantly, in the main, for the most part**
❷ *Floods mostly occur during monsoon season.*
• **generally, usually, normally, typically, ordinarily, as a rule**

mother *NOUN*
My mother uses her maiden name.
• (*informal*) **mum, mummy, ma** (*North American informal*) **mom, mommy**
– A word meaning 'to do with a mother' is **maternal**.
For other members of a family see **family**.

motion *NOUN*
He silenced the audience with a motion of his hand.
• **gesture, movement, gesticulation**

motivate *VERB*
What motivated you to write a book?
• **prompt, drive, stimulate, influence, inspire, urge, induce, impel, provoke, spur**

motive *NOUN*
The police can find no motive for the crime.
• **cause, motivation, reason, rationale, purpose, grounds**

motor *NOUN*
see **engine**

motto *NOUN*
Her motto has always been 'Keep it simple'.
• **slogan, proverb, saying, maxim, adage, axiom, golden rule**

mould *VERB*
The little figures on the cake are moulded out of marzipan.
• **shape, form, fashion, model, sculpt, work, cast**

mouldy *ADJECTIVE*
At the back of the fridge was a lump of mouldy cheese.
• **rotten, rotting, decaying, musty**

mound *NOUN*
❶ *The letter was buried under a mound of paper.*
• **heap, pile, stack, mountain, mass**
❷ *There used to be a castle on top of that mound.*
• **hill, hillock, rise, hump**
– An ancient mound of earth over a grave is a **barrow**.

mount *VERB*
❶ *She slowly mounted the stairs.*
• **go up, climb, ascend, scale**
OPPOSITE descend
❷ *He mounted his bicycle and rode off.*
• **get on, climb onto, jump onto, hop onto**
OPPOSITE dismount
❸ *Tension began to mount in the audience.*
• **grow, increase, rise, escalate, intensify, build up**
OPPOSITES fall, lessen
❹ *The library is mounting a new exhibition.*
• **put on, set up, display, install, stage, present**

mountain *NOUN*

❶ *They had to make their way through the mountains.*

• **mount, peak, summit**

– A line of mountains is a **range**.

– A long narrow hilltop or mountain range is a **ridge**.

– An area of land with many mountains is said to be **mountainous**.

❷ *I have a mountain of work to get through.*

• **heap, pile, mound, stack, mass**

mourn *VERB*

He was still mourning the loss of his dear friend.

• **grieve for, lament for**

mouth *NOUN*

❶ *He was staring into the mouth of a crocodile.*

• **jaws, muzzle, maw**
(*informal*) **chops, trap**

– A word meaning 'to do with your mouth' is **oral**.

❷ *They lived in a village at the mouth of the river.*

• **outlet, estuary, delta**
(*Scottish*) **firth**

❸ *The mouth of the cave was hidden by trees.*

• **entrance, opening**

move *VERB*

❶ *The robot can move in any direction.*

• **go, walk, step, proceed, travel, change position, budge, stir, shift**

❷ *We need to move the piano to the front of the stage.*

• **shift, lift, carry, push, slide, transport, remove, transfer**

❸ *I heard you were moving to Cardiff.*

• **move house, move away, relocate, transfer, decamp**

– To move abroad permanently is to **emigrate**.

❹ *Her sad story moved me deeply.*

• **affect, touch, stir, shake, impress, inspire**

OVERUSED WORD

❶ To move **forwards**, move **towards a place:**

➤ **advance**
➤ **approach**
➤ **proceed**
➤ **progress**
➤ **press on**
➤ **make headway**
➤ **gain ground**

They saw a pirate ship **approaching**.

❷ To move **back**, move **away:**

➤ **retreat**
➤ **withdraw**
➤ **reverse**
➤ **retire**
➤ **back away**
➤ **fall back**
➤ **give way**

The werewolves **fell back** *as dawn began to break.*

❸ To move **upwards:**

➤ **rise**
➤ **ascend**
➤ **climb**
➤ **mount**
➤ **soar**

I looked out of the window as we **climbed** *above the clouds.*

❹ To move **downwards:**

➤ **drop**
➤ **descend**
➤ **fall**
➤ **dive**
➤ **plunge**
➤ **sink**
➤ **swoop**
➤ **nosedive**

The film captures a falcon **swooping** *down on its prey.*

❺ To move **from side to side:**

➤ **sway**
➤ **swing**
➤ **wave**
➤ **rock**
➤ **wag**
➤ **swish**
➤ **flourish**
➤ **brandish**
➤ **undulate**

The knight stepped forward, **swinging** *his sword.*

❻ To move **quickly:**

➤ **hurry**
➤ **dash**
➤ **race**
➤ **run**
➤ **rush**
➤ **hasten**

➤ hurtle
➤ career
➤ fly
➤ speed
➤ sweep
➤ shoot
➤ zoom

A boy went **careering** *past on a skateboard.*

❼ To move slowly, aimlessly:

➤ amble
➤ stroll
➤ saunter
➤ dawdle
➤ crawl
➤ drift
➤ wander
➤ meander

(*informal*) mosey

The cat yawned and **strolled** *over to her basket.*

❽ To move clumsily:

➤ stumble
➤ stagger
➤ shuffle
➤ lurch
➤ lumber
➤ flounder
➤ reel
➤ totter
➤ trundle
➤ trip

He **stumbled** *up the narrow steps.*

❾ To move gracefully:

➤ flow
➤ glide
➤ dance
➤ drift
➤ flit
➤ float
➤ slide
➤ slip

Swans **glided** *gently across the pond.*

❿ To move restlessly:

➤ toss
➤ turn
➤ stir
➤ twist
➤ shake
➤ fidget
➤ twitch
➤ jerk
➤ flap

The children kept **fidgeting** *in their seats.*

⓫ To move stealthily:

➤ creep
➤ crawl
➤ edge
➤ inch
➤ slink
➤ slither
➤ tiptoe

Agent 007 **edged** *carefully along the window ledge.*

move *NOUN*

❶ *Someone was watching our every move.*
• **movement, motion, action, gesture, step, deed, manoeuvre**
❷ *It's your move next.*
• **turn, go**

movement *NOUN*

❶ *The robot made a sudden, jerky movement.*
• **motion, move, action, gesture**
❷ *Has there been any movement in their attitude?*
• **progress, advance, development, change, shift**
❸ *Her mother was involved in the peace movement.*
• **organization, group, party, faction, campaign**

movie *NOUN*

see **film**

moving *ADJECTIVE*

The story was so moving that I started to cry.
• **emotional, affecting, touching, poignant, heart-rending, stirring, inspiring**
(*informal*) **tear-jerking**

much *DETERMINER*

There is still much work to be done.
• **a lot of, a great deal of, plenty of, ample**
OPPOSITE **little**

much *ADVERB*

I find messaging much quicker than email.
• **a great deal, a lot, considerably, substantially, markedly, greatly, far**

muck *NOUN*

❶ *We had to clear the muck out of the stable.*
• **dung, manure, droppings**
❷ (*informal*) *I'll just scrape the muck off the windscreen.*
• **dirt, filth, grime, mud, sludge, mess**
(*informal*) **gunge, gunk**

mucky *ADJECTIVE*
She took off her mucky football boots.
• **dirty, messy, muddy, grimy, grubby, filthy, foul, soiled**
OPPOSITE **clean**

mud *NOUN*
He slipped and fell in the mud.
• **dirt, muck, mire, sludge, clay, soil, silt**

muddle *NOUN*
❶ *There was a muddle over the invitations.*
• **confusion, misunderstanding**
(*informal*) **mix-up**
❷ *These files are all in a muddle.*
• **jumble, mess, tangle, disorder, disarray**

muddle *VERB*
❶ *The words to the song are all muddled.*
• **mix up, mess up, disorder, jumble up, shuffle, tangle**
OPPOSITE **tidy**
❷ *I got muddled trying to follow the instructions.*
• **confuse, bewilder, puzzle, perplex, baffle, mystify**

muddy *ADJECTIVE*
❶ *Take off your muddy trainers before you come in.*
• **dirty, messy, mucky, filthy, grimy, caked, soiled**
OPPOSITE **clean**
❷ *The ground was very muddy.*
• **boggy, marshy, swampy, waterlogged, wet, sodden, squelchy**
OPPOSITES **dry, firm**

muffle *VERB*
❶ *We muffled ourselves up to play in the snow.*
• **wrap up, cover up, swathe, cloak, enfold**
❷ *I closed the door to muffle the noise.*
• **deaden, dampen, dull, stifle, smother, soften, mask**

muffled *ADJECTIVE*
We heard muffled voices from the next room.
• **faint, indistinct, unclear, muted, deadened, stifled**
OPPOSITE **clear**

muggy *ADJECTIVE*
The weather is often muggy before a storm.
• **humid, close, clammy, sticky, moist, damp, oppressive**
OPPOSITE **fresh**

multiply *VERB*
❶ *Multiply the remaining number by ten.*
– To multiply a number by two is to **double** it; to multiply it by three is to **triple** it; and to multiply it by four is to **quadruple** it.
OPPOSITE **divide**
❷ *The problems seemed to be multiplying.*
• **increase, grow, spread, proliferate, mount up, accumulate, mushroom, snowball**
OPPOSITE **decrease**

mumble *VERB*
He mumbled an apology.
• **mutter, murmur**
IDIOM **talk under your breath**

munch *VERB*
We munched popcorn all through the film.
• **chew, chomp, crunch**

murder *VERB*
The woman is accused of murdering her husband.
• **kill, assassinate**
(*informal*) **bump off, do away with**

murder *NOUN*
Detectives are treating the case as murder.
• **homicide, killing, assassination**

murky *ADJECTIVE*
❶ *The sky was murky and drizzle was falling.*
• **dark, dull, clouded, overcast, foggy, misty, grey, leaden, dismal, dreary, dingy**
OPPOSITES **fine, bright**

A B C D E F G H I J K L M N O P Q R S T U V W X Y Z

❷ *The water in the well was green and murky.*
• **muddy, cloudy, dirty**
OPPOSITE clear

murmur *VERB*
The crowd murmured their approval.
• **mutter, mumble, whisper**

muscular *ADJECTIVE*
He's tall and muscular.
• **brawny, beefy, burly, well built, athletic, sinewy, strapping, strong**
OPPOSITES puny, weak

music *NOUN*

WORD WEB

Musical styles and genres:

- bebop
- bhangra
- blues
- bluegrass
- classical music
- country music
- dance music
- disco music
- early music
- flamenco
- folk music
- funk
- gospel
- heavy metal
- hip-hop
- jazz
- pop music
- punk
- ragtime
- rap
- reggae
- rock
- ska
- soul
- swing

Musical forms and compositions:

- anthem
- ballad
- carol
- concerto
- folk song
- fugue
- hymn
- lullaby
- march
- mass
- musical
- opera
- operetta
- oratorio
- prelude
- raga
- requiem
- sonata
- song
- suit
- symphony
- tune

Families of musical instruments:

- brass
- keyboard
- percussion
- strings
- woodwind

Stringed instruments:

- acoustic guitar
- balalaika
- banjo
- bass guitar
- bouzouki
- cello
- double bass
- dulcimer
- electric guitar
- harp
- hurdy gurdy
- lute
- lyre
- mandolin
- pedal steel guitar
- sitar
- ukulele
- viol or viola da gamba
- viola
- violin (*informal* fiddle)
- zither

Wind and brass instruments:

- bagpipes
- bassoon
- bugle
- clarinet
- cor anglais
- cornet
- euphonium
- flugelhorn
- flute
- French horn
- harmonica
- oboe
- panpipes
- piccolo
- recorder
- saxophone
- tin whistle
- trombone
- trumpet
- tuba
- uilleann pipes

Keyboard instruments:

- accordion
- clavichord
- harmonium
- harpsichord
- keyboard
- organ
- piano
- spinet
- synthesizer

Percussion instruments:

- bass drum
- bongo drum
- castanets
- cymbals
- drum
- gamelan
- glockenspiel
- gong
- maracas
- marimba
- mbira or thumb piano
- rattle
- snare drum
- steel drum or steelpan
- tabla
- tambourine
- timpani or kettledrums
- triangle
- tubular bells
- vibraphone
- xylophone

Other terms used in music:

- chord
- clef
- counterpoint
- crotchet (*North American* quarter note)
- discord
- flat
- harmony
- key signature
- melody
- metronome
- minim
- natural
- note
- octave
- pitch
- quaver (*North American* eighth note)
- rhythm
- scale
- semibreve (*North American* whole note)
- semiquaver (*North American* sixteenth note)
- semitone
- sharp
- stave
- tempo
- theme
- time signature
- tone

musical *ADJECTIVE*
My mum has a very musical voice.
• **tuneful, melodic, melodious, harmonious, sweet-sounding**
OPPOSITE discordant

musician *NOUN*
a musician in an orchestra
• **performer, instrumentalist**

WORD WEB

Some types of musician:

- bassist or bass player
- bugler
- cellist
- chorister
- clarinettist
- composer
- conductor
- drummer
- fiddler
- flautist
- guitarist
- harpist or harper
- lutenist
- oboist
- organist
- percussionist
- pianist
- piper
- singer
- timpanist
- trombonist
- trumpeter
- violinist (*informal* fiddler)
- vocalist

- A musican who plays music or sings alone is a **soloist**.
- A musician who plays music to support a singer or another musician is an **accompanist**.

Groups of musicians:

- band
- choir or chorus
- duet or duo
- ensemble
- group
- orchestra
- quartet
- quintet
- trio

musty *ADJECTIVE*
There is a musty smell in the cellar.
• **damp, dank, mouldy, stale, stuffy, airless**
OPPOSITE fresh

mute *ADJECTIVE*
She could only stare, mute with terror.
• **silent, speechless, unspeaking, dumb, tongue-tied**

mutilate *VERB*
His right hand was mutilated by a firework.
• **maim, disfigure, injure, wound, mangle**

mutiny *NOUN*
The ship's crew were plotting a mutiny.
• **rebellion, revolt, uprising**

mutter *VERB*
She sat muttering to herself in the corner.
• **mumble, murmur, whisper**
IDIOM **talk under your breath**

mutual *ADJECTIVE*
It is in our mutual interest to work together.
• **joint, common, shared, reciprocal**

mysterious *ADJECTIVE*
The letter contained a mysterious message.
• **puzzling, strange, baffling, perplexing, mystifying, bizarre, curious, weird, obscure, unexplained, incomprehensible, inexplicable**

mystery *NOUN*
What really happened remains a mystery.
• **puzzle, riddle, secret, enigma, conundrum**

mystify *VERB*
I was completely mystified by the plot.
• **puzzle, baffle, bewilder, perplex**

myth *NOUN*
My story is based on the ancient myth of the Minotaur.
• **legend, fable, saga, folklore**

mythical *ADJECTIVE*
The unicorn is a mythical beast.
• **fabulous, fanciful, imaginary, invented, fictional, legendary, mythological**
OPPOSITE real

nag *VERB*

He was always nagging her to work harder.

• **badger, pester, hound, harass, keep on at**

naive *ADJECTIVE*

She was still hopelessly naive about life.

• **innocent, inexperienced, unsophisticated, immature, unworldly, artless, gullible, green**

IDIOM **wet behind the ears**

naked *ADJECTIVE*

He walked naked into the bathroom.

• **bare, nude, unclothed, undressed, stripped, with nothing on**

IDIOMS (*humorous*) **without a stitch on, in the buff, in your birthday suit**

OPPOSITE clothed

name *NOUN*

What's your name?

– The official names you have are your **first names** or **forenames** and **surname**.

– Names a Christian is given at baptism are **Christian names**.

– A false name is an **alias**.

– A name people use instead of your real name is a **nickname**.

– A false name an author uses is a **pen name** or **pseudonym**.

– The name of a book or film is its **title**.

name *VERB*

❶ *They named the puppy Ricky.*

• **call, label, dub, term, title**

– To name someone at the ceremony of baptism is to **baptize** or **christen** them.

❷ *The victim has not been named.*

• **identify, specify**

nap *NOUN*

She was on the sofa, taking a nap.

• **rest, sleep, doze, lie-down**

(*informal*) **snooze**

IDIOM **forty winks**

narrate *VERB*

The story is narrated by the main character.

• **tell, recount, relate, report**

– The person who narrates a story is the **narrator**.

narrative *NOUN*

We were spellbound by his narrative of the voyage.

• **account, history, story, tale, chronicle**

(*informal*) **yarn**

narrow *ADJECTIVE*

❶ *We had to crawl through a narrow tunnel.*

• **thin, slender, slight, slim, tight, constricted, confined**

OPPOSITES wide, broad

❷ *He has a narrow outlook on life.*

• **limited, restricted, close-minded, inadequate, deficient**

OPPOSITES broad, open-minded

nasty *ADJECTIVE*

❶ *This medicine has a nasty taste.*

• **unpleasant, offensive, disgusting, revolting, repulsive, repellent, obnoxious, horrible, horrid, foul, vile, rotten, sickening**

(*informal*) **yucky**

OPPOSITES pleasant, agreeable

❷ *That was a nasty thing to say.*

• **unkind, unpleasant, unfriendly, disagreeable, malicious, cruel, spiteful, vicious, mean**

OPPOSITES likeable, agreeable

❸ *She's had a nasty accident.*

• **serious, dreadful, awful, terrible, severe, painful**

OPPOSITE slight

nation *NOUN*

People from many nations compete in the Olympic Games.

• **country, state, land, realm, race, people**

A B C D E F G H I J K L M N O P Q R S T U V W X Y Z

national *ADJECTIVE*
The interview will be broadcast on national television.
• **nationwide, countrywide, state**
OPPOSITE **local**

native *ADJECTIVE*
❶ *the native population of Hawaii*
• **indigenous, original, local**
OPPOSITES **immigrant, imported**
❷ *Is Urdu your native language?*
• **mother, first, home**

natural *ADJECTIVE*
❶ *Is that your natural hair colour?*
• **real, original, normal**
OPPOSITES **unnatural, fake**
❷ *Our smoothies are made with natural ingredients.*
• **unprocessed, unrefined, pure**
OPPOSITES **artificial, processed**
❸ *It's only natural to be nervous before a race.*
• **normal, common, understandable, reasonable, predictable**
OPPOSITES **abnormal, unnatural**
❹ *She has a natural gift for music.*
• **born, inborn, instinctive, intuitive, native**

nature *NOUN*
❶ *I like TV programmes about nature.*
• **the natural world, wildlife, the environment, natural history**
❷ *Labradors are known for their mild nature.*
• **character, disposition, temperament, personality, manner, make-up**
❸ *I collect coins, medals and things of that nature.*
• **kind, sort, type, order, description, variety, category**

naughty *ADJECTIVE*
He had been the naughtiest kid in his class.
• **badly behaved, disobedient, bad, troublesome, mischievous, uncontrollable, unmanageable, wayward, unruly**
OPPOSITE **well behaved**

navigate *VERB*
She managed to navigate her boat through the rocks.
• **steer, pilot, guide, direct, manoeuvre**

navy *NOUN*
see **fleet**

near *ADJECTIVE*
❶ *We get on well with our near neighbours.*
• **nearby, next-door, close, adjacent, accessible**
OPPOSITES **far, remote**
❷ *The message warned us that danger was near.*
• **imminent, approaching, coming, looming, impending, on its way**
(*old use*) **nigh**
IDIOMS **round the corner, in the offing**
OPPOSITE **far off**
❸ *We sent cards to all our near relatives.*
• **close, dear, familiar, intimate**
OPPOSITE **distant**

nearby *ADVERB*
A photographer happened to be standing nearby.
• **close by, not far off, close at hand, within reach**
IDIOMS **a stone's throw away, within spitting distance**
OPPOSITES **far away, far off**

nearly *ADVERB*
You're nearly as tall as I am.
• **almost, practically, virtually, just about**

neat *ADJECTIVE*
❶ *Please leave the room as neat as possible.*
• **clean, tidy, orderly, uncluttered, immaculate, trim, in good order**
IDIOM **spick and span**
OPPOSITES **untidy, messy**
❷ *He always looks very neat in his school uniform.*
• **smart, elegant, spruce, trim, dapper, well turned out**
OPPOSITE **scruffy**

❸ *That is the neatest handwriting I've ever seen.*
• **clear, precise, well formed, elegant**
❹ *She produced a neat pass into the penalty area.*
• **skilful, deft, clever, adroit, adept, well executed**
OPPOSITE clumsy

necessary *ADJECTIVE*
Are all these forms strictly necessary?
• **essential, required, needed, requisite, compulsory, obligatory, mandatory, unavoidable, imperative**
OPPOSITE unnecessary

need *VERB*
❶ *I need a pound coin for the locker.*
• **require, want, be short of, lack**
❷ *It's a charity which needs our support.*
• **depend on, rely on**
➤ **need to**
We need to leave by 6 o'clock.
• **have to, must, be required to, be supposed to, be expected to**

need *NOUN*
There's definitely a need for more shops in our area.
• **call, demand, requirement, necessity, want**

needless *ADJECTIVE*
They went to a lot of needless expense.
• **unnecessary, unwanted, uncalled for, excessive, superfluous, redundant, gratuitous**

needlework *NOUN*
see **textiles**

needy *ADJECTIVE*
They set up a fund to help needy children.
• **poor, deprived, underprivileged, disadvantaged, poverty-stricken, penniless, destitute, in need**
OPPOSITES wealthy, privileged

negative *ADJECTIVE*
❶ *Why are you being so negative?*
• **pessimistic, defeatist, fatalistic, unenthusiastic, gloomy, cynical, downbeat**
OPPOSITES positive, optimistic, upbeat
❷ *Stress can have a negative effect on your health.*
• **bad, adverse, unfavourable, detrimental, harmful, damaging**
OPPOSITES positive, beneficial

neglect *VERB*
❶ *She's been neglecting her work recently.*
• **ignore, overlook, disregard, pay no attention to, shirk, abandon**
❷ *You neglected to mention a few things.*
• **fail, omit, forget**

negligible *ADJECTIVE*
There is a negligible difference in price.
• **slight, insignificant, unimportant, minor, trivial, trifling, minimal**
OPPOSITES considerable, significant

negotiate *VERB*
❶ *They refused to negotiate with the kidnappers.*
• **bargain, haggle, deal, confer, discuss terms**
❷ *They finally negotiated a treaty.*
• **work out, agree on, broker (*informal*) thrash out**
❸ *We first had to negotiate a five-metre wall.*
• **get past, get round, get over, manoeuvre round**

neighbourhood *NOUN*
They lived in a run-down neighbourhood.
• **area, district, community, locality, locale, quarter, vicinity**

neighbouring *ADJECTIVE*
We went on a tour of the neighbouring villages.
• **nearby, bordering, adjacent, adjoining, surrounding, nearest, next-door**

neighbourly *ADJECTIVE*
It was neighbourly of her to offer to feed the cat.
• **friendly, helpful, obliging, kind, sociable**
OPPOSITE unfriendly

nerve *NOUN*

❶ *It takes nerve to be a trapeze artist.*
• **bravery, courage, daring, fearlessness, pluck, grit**
(*informal*) **guts, bottle**
❷ *He had the nerve to ask me to leave!*
• **cheek, impudence, audacity, effrontery, impertinence, presumption**

nervous *ADJECTIVE*

Do you get nervous before you go on stage?
• **anxious, worried, apprehensive, concerned, uneasy, fearful, edgy, fraught, tense, worked up, keyed up**
(*informal*) **uptight, jittery, twitchy**
IDIOMS (*informal*) **in a flap, in a state**
OPPOSITES calm, confident

nestle *VERB*

She nestled her head on his shoulder.
• **snuggle, nuzzle, cuddle, huddle, curl up**

neutral *ADJECTIVE*

❶ *A referee has to be neutral.*
• **impartial, detached, uninvolved, disinterested, objective, unbiased, even-handed**
OPPOSITE biased
❷ *The room was decorated in neutral colours.*
• **dull, drab, cool, muted, colourless, indefinite, nondescript**
OPPOSITES colourful, vibrant

new *ADJECTIVE*

❶ *Start on a new sheet of paper.*
• **fresh, unused, pristine, brand new**
– Something new and unused is **in mint condition.**
OPPOSITES old, used
❷ *Have you read the new issue of the magazine?*
• **latest, current, recent, up-to-date**
❸ *I've added a new paragraph to my story.*
• **additional, extra, further, supplementary**
❹ *He introduced a whole new style of acting.*
• **fresh, original, novel, innovative, cutting-edge, state-of-the-art, contemporary**
❺ *Flying was a new experience for me.*
• **unfamiliar, unknown, different, alternative, strange**
OPPOSITE familiar

news *NOUN*

Have you heard the news?
• **information, word, report, bulletin**
(*old use*) **tidings**

next *ADJECTIVE*

❶ *What time is the next train?*
• **following, subsequent, succeeding, upcoming**
OPPOSITE previous
❷ *I could hear people laughing in the next room.*
• **adjacent, closest, nearest, next door**
OPPOSITE distant

nice *ADJECTIVE*

❶ *That's not a very nice thing to say!*
• **pleasant, agreeable**
OPPOSITES unpleasant, nasty
❷ *There's a nice distinction between telling a lie and not telling the whole truth.*
• **fine, subtle, delicate, precise**

OVERUSED WORD

❶ A nice person:

➤ good
➤ kind
➤ pleasant
➤ friendly
➤ agreeable
➤ likeable
➤ amiable
➤ genial
➤ personable
➤ charming
➤ engaging
➤ sympathetic
➤ polite
➤ civil
➤ courteous

The film features a cast of likeable *characters.*

❷ A nice experience, nice feeling:

➤ enjoyable
➤ pleasant
➤ good
➤ delightful
➤ satisfying
➤ agreeable
➤ entertaining
➤ amusing

➤ wonderful
➤ splendid
➤ marvellous

Did you have an **enjoyable** *time on holiday?*

❸ **Looking nice:**

➤ beautiful
➤ fine
➤ attractive
➤ handsome
➤ pleasing
➤ striking
➤ lovely

There is an **attractive** *view from the upstairs window.*

❹ **A nice smell:**

➤ fragrant
➤ perfumed
➤ pleasant
➤ aromatic
➤ sweet

The **fragrant** *scent of lavender filled the garden.*

OPPOSITE smelly

❺ **A nice taste, nice food:**

➤ appetizing
➤ delicious
➤ tasty
➤ delectable
➤ flavoursome
➤ mouth-watering

(*informal*) **yummy, scrumptious**

Slow cooking will make the dish more **flavoursome.**

❻ **Nice weather, a nice day:**

➤ fine
➤ mild
➤ sunny
➤ balmy
➤ warm
➤ dry

The weather has been **fine** *all week.*

SEE ALSO **good, lovely**

night *NOUN*

Badgers usually come out at night.

• **night-time, dark, the hours of darkness**

– The time immediately after sunset when the sky is still light is **twilight**.

– The time when the evening twilight ends is **dusk** or **nightfall**.

– A **nightly** event happens every night.

– Animals which are active at night are **nocturnal**.

OPPOSITES day, daytime

nil *NOUN*

The score was nil all at half-time.

• **zero, nought, nothing, none**

– A score of nil in cricket is a **duck**.

– A score of nil in tennis is **love**.

nimble *ADJECTIVE*

You need nimble fingers for that job.

• **agile, skilful, quick, deft, dexterous, adroit**

OPPOSITE clumsy

nip *VERB*

❶ *Frost had begun to nip at our toes.*

• **bite, nibble, peck, pinch, tweak, catch**

❷ (*informal*) *I'm just nipping out to the shops.*

• **dash, run, rush**

(*informal*) **pop**

noble *ADJECTIVE*

❶ *The count came from an ancient noble family.*

• **aristocratic, high-born, upper-class, titled**

OPPOSITES low-born, humble, base

❷ *Their noble sacrifice will be remembered.*

• **brave, heroic, courageous, valiant, honourable, worthy, virtuous, gallant**

OPPOSITES cowardly, unworthy

❸ *The oak is a noble tree.*

• **grand, stately, magnificent, impressive, imposing, dignified, proud, majestic**

noble *NOUN*

A group of nobles were loyal to the king.

• **aristocrat, nobleman, noblewoman, lord, lady, peer**

OPPOSITE commoner

nod *VERB*

The others nodded their heads in agreement.

• **bob, bow, dip, lower, incline**

➤ **nod off**

She sometimes nods off in front of the fire.

• **fall asleep, doze off, drop off, have a nap**

A B C D E F G H I J K L M N O P Q R S T U V W X Y Z

noise *NOUN*
My computer is making a peculiar noise.
• **sound, racket, din, row, uproar, commotion, clamour, hullabaloo**
For tips on describing sounds see **sound**.

noisy *ADJECTIVE*
❶ *It was noisy in the classroom.*
• **rowdy, raucous, clamorous, uproarious**
OPPOSITES quiet, silent
❷ *The plane completed its noisy take-off.*
• **loud, blaring, booming, deafening, ear-splitting, thunderous**
OPPOSITES quiet, soft

nominate *VERB*
His latest novel has been nominated for several prizes.
• **propose, put forward, recommend, select, choose, name, elect**

nonsense *NOUN*
Stop talking such nonsense!
• **rubbish, drivel, gibberish, claptrap, garbage**
(*informal*) **gobbledegook, baloney, rot, tripe, twaddle, piffle**
(*old use*) **balderdash, poppycock**
OPPOSITES sense, reason

nonsensical *ADJECTIVE*
It was a nonsensical suggestion.
• **absurd, ridiculous, ludicrous, senseless, irrational, illogical, preposterous, crazy, laughable, silly, stupid, foolish, idiotic**
(*British informal*) **daft**
OPPOSITES sensible, reasonable

non-stop *ADJECTIVE*
❶ *All he could hear was the sound of non-stop traffic.*
• **constant, continual, continuous, endless, ceaseless, incessant, never-ending, unending, perpetual, round-the-clock**
❷ *We took a non-stop train from Paris to Nice.*
• **direct, express**

normal *ADJECTIVE*
❶ *It began as just a normal day.*
• **ordinary, average, typical, usual, common, standard, regular, routine, familiar, habitual, customary, conventional**
IDIOM **run-of-the-mill**
OPPOSITE abnormal
❷ *It can't be normal to feel this way.*
• **healthy, natural, rational, reasonable, sane**
OPPOSITES unhealthy, unnatural

north *NOUN, ADJECTIVE & ADVERB*
The Sahara is in the north of Africa.
– The parts of a country or continent in the north are the **northern** parts.
– To travel towards the north is to travel **northward** or **northwards**.
– A wind from the north is a **northerly** wind.
– A person who lives in the north of a country is a **northerner**.

nose *NOUN*
❶ *Someone punched me on the nose.*
– The openings in your nose are your **nostrils**.
– An animal's nose is its **muzzle** or **snout**.
– A long flexible snout is a **trunk** or **proboscis**.
– A word meaning 'to do with your nose' is **nasal**.
❷ *I was sitting in the nose of the boat.*
• **front, bow, prow**

nosy (*informal*) *ADJECTIVE*
A nosy reporter was asking a lot of questions.
• **inquisitive, curious, prying, snooping, intrusive**

notable *ADJECTIVE*
❶ *It was a notable date in American history.*
• **memorable, noteworthy, significant, major, important, well known, famous, celebrated, renowned, noted, prominent**
OPPOSITES insignificant, minor
❷ *He was showing a notable lack of enthusiasm.*
• **distinct, definite, obvious, conspicuous, marked, pronounced, striking, remarkable**

notch *NOUN*
She cut a small notch in the tree trunk.
• cut, nick, groove, score, scratch, incision

note *NOUN*
❶ *Someone had written a note in the margin.*
• comment, annotation, jotting, entry, record, memo
❷ *I sent her a brief thank-you note.*
• message, letter, line, communication
❸ *There was a note of warning in his voice.*
• tone, feeling, quality, sense, hint, suggestion

note *VERB*
❶ *I noted the address on a scrap of paper.*
• jot down, make a note of, write down, take down, scribble, record, list, enter, pencil in
❷ *Did you note what she was wearing?*
• notice, take note of, pay attention to, heed, mark, register, observe

nothing *NOUN*
❶ *There's nothing more we can do.*
• not a thing
(*informal*) zilch
IDIOM (*humorous*) not a sausage
❷ *They scored nothing in the first round.*
• nought, zero, nil
SEE ALSO nil

notice *NOUN*
❶ *There was a notice pinned to the wall.*
• sign, advertisement, poster, placard
❷ *Some islands received no notice of the tsunami.*
• warning, notification, announcement
➤ **take notice of something**
They took no notice of the warning.
• pay attention to, heed, mark

notice *VERB*
❶ *Did you notice the tattoo on his arm?*
• note, take note of, heed, mark, register, observe, spot
❷ *I noticed a funny smell in the room.*
• become aware of, detect, discern

noticeable *ADJECTIVE*
❶ *There has been a noticeable improvement in the weather.*
• notable, distinct, definite, measurable, perceptible, appreciable, significant, marked, pronounced, salient, unmistakable, striking
❷ *She spoke with a noticeable foreign accent.*
• obvious, conspicuous, visible, detectable, discernible, evident, apparent
OPPOSITE imperceptible

notion *NOUN*
He has some old-fashioned notions about women.
• belief, idea, view, thought, opinion, theory, concept

notorious *ADJECTIVE*
They were the most notorious criminal gang in the country.
• infamous, disreputable, disgraceful

nought *NOUN*
see nil

nourish *VERB*
Plants are nourished by water drawn up through their roots.
• feed, sustain, support, nurture

nourishing *ADJECTIVE*
She used to make us bowls of hot, nourishing soup.
• nutritious, wholesome, healthy, health-giving

novel *ADJECTIVE*
They came up with a novel method of filming underwater.
• original, new, innovative, fresh, different, imaginative, creative, unusual, unconventional, unorthodox
OPPOSITES traditional, familiar

now *ADVERB*
❶ *My sister is now living in Melbourne.*
• at present, at the moment, at this time, currently, nowadays
❷ *I'll send them an email now.*
• immediately, at once, straight away,

a b c d e f g h i j k l m n o p q r s t u v w x y z

right away, without delay, instantly, directly, this instant

nude *ADJECTIVE*
On the wall was a painting of a nude figure.
• **naked, bare, unclothed, undressed**
OPPOSITE clothed

nudge *VERB*
❶ *She nudged me with her elbow.*
• **poke, prod, dig, elbow, jab, jolt, bump**
❷ *We nudged the piano into position.*
• **ease, inch, manoeuvre**

nuisance *NOUN*
Mosquitoes can be a nuisance in the summer.
• **annoyance, irritation, inconvenience, bother, menace, pest, drawback**
(*informal*) **bind, hassle, pain, headache, drag**

numb *ADJECTIVE*
My toes were numb with cold.
• **unfeeling, deadened, frozen, insensitive, paralysed**
OPPOSITE sensitive

number *NOUN*
❶ *The paper had a line of numbers written on it.*
• **figure, numeral**
– Any of the numbers from 0 to 9 is a **digit**.
– A negative or positive whole number is an **integer**.
– An amount used in measuring or counting is a **unit**.
❷ *We received a large number of emails.*
• **amount, quantity, collection, quota, total, tally**
❸ *I've ordered the latest number of the magazine.*
• **edition, issue**
❹ *The musical features some well-known numbers.*
• **song, piece, tune**

numerous *ADJECTIVE*
The book contains numerous errors.
• **many, a lot of, plenty of, abundant, copious, countless, innumerable, untold, myriad**
(*informal*) **umpteen, lots of, masses of**
OPPOSITE few

nurse *NOUN*
see **medicine**

nurse *VERB*
She nursed her sick mother for years.
• **look after, care for, take care of, tend, treat**

nut *NOUN*

WORD WEB

Some edible nuts:

- almond
- Brazil
- cashew
- chestnut
- coconut
- hazelnut
- macadamia
- peanut
- pecan
- pine nut
- pistachio
- walnut

- The part inside the shell of a nut is the **kernel**.

oath *NOUN*
❶ *The knights swore an oath of allegiance.*
• **pledge, promise, vow, word of honour**
❷ *He banged his head, letting out a stream of oaths.*
• **swear word, curse, expletive, profanity**

obedient *ADJECTIVE*
Your dog seems very obedient.
• **well-behaved, disciplined, manageable, dutiful, docile, compliant**
OPPOSITE disobedient

obey *VERB*
❶ *The robot will obey any command.*
• **follow, carry out, execute, implement, observe, heed, comply with, adhere to, submit to**
❷ *Do you always obey without question?*
• **do what you are told, take orders, be obedient, conform**
OPPOSITE disobey

object *NOUN*
❶ *There were reports of a strange object in the sky.*
• **article, item, thing**
❷ *What is the object of this experiment?*
• **point, purpose, aim, goal, intention, objective**
❸ *He has become an object of pity.*
• **target, focus**

object *VERB*
➤ **object to something**
Only one person objected to the plan.
• **oppose, be opposed to, disapprove of, take exception to, take issue with, protest against, complain about**
OPPOSITES accept, agree to

objection *NOUN*
Has anybody got any objections?
• **protest, complaint, opposition, disapproval, disagreement, dissent**

objectionable *ADJECTIVE*
He can be thoroughly objectionable when he wants to be.
• **unpleasant, disagreeable, disgusting, foul, offensive, repellent, revolting, obnoxious, nasty**
OPPOSITE acceptable

objective *NOUN*
My main objective is to tell a good story.
• **aim, goal, intention, target, ambition, object, purpose, plan**

objective *ADJECTIVE*
She tried to give an objective account of what happened.
• **impartial, neutral, unbiased, unprejudiced, even-handed, disinterested, dispassionate, detached**
OPPOSITE subjective

obligatory *ADJECTIVE*
The wearing of seat belts is obligatory.
• **compulsory, mandatory, required, prescribed, necessary**
OPPOSITE optional

oblige *VERB*
Would you oblige me by delivering this letter?
• **do someone a favour, help, assist, indulge**

obliged *ADJECTIVE*
❶ *I felt obliged to accept the invitation.*
• **bound, compelled, expected, required, constrained**
❷ *I'm much obliged to you for your help.*
• **thankful, grateful, appreciative, indebted**

oblong *NOUN*
The garden was simply an oblong of grass.
• **rectangle**
SEE ALSO **shape**

obscene *ADJECTIVE*
The film contains some obscene language.
• **indecent, offensive, explicit, rude, vulgar, coarse, lewd**
OPPOSITES clean, decent

a b c d e f g h i j k l m n o p q r s t u v w x y z

obscure *ADJECTIVE*
❶ *The origins of the stone circle remain obscure.*
• **uncertain, unclear, mysterious, vague, hazy, shadowy, murky, dim**
OPPOSITE clear
❷ *The poem is full of obscure references.*
• **oblique, enigmatic, cryptic, puzzling, perplexing**
OPPOSITE obvious
❸ *He is an obscure Russian poet.*
• **unknown, unheard of, little known, minor, unrecognized, forgotten**
OPPOSITES famous, well known

obscure *VERB*
A tall hedge obscured the view.
• **block out, cover, hide, conceal, mask, screen, veil, shroud**
OPPOSITE reveal

observant *ADJECTIVE*
If you're observant, you might see a badger tonight.
• **alert, attentive, sharp-eyed, vigilant, watchful**
OPPOSITE inattentive

observation *NOUN*
❶ *You will need a telescope for observation of the Moon.*
• **study, watching, scrutiny, surveillance, monitoring**
❷ *The author makes some interesting observations.*
• **comment, remark, statement, reflection**

observe *VERB*
❶ *He has spent his life observing elephants in the wild.*
• **watch, look at, view, study, survey, monitor, scrutinize, regard**
IDIOMS **keep an eye on, keep tabs on**
❷ *I observed her putting the letter into her bag.*
• **notice, note, see, detect, spot, discern, perceive, witness**
❸ *You must observe the rules of the game.*
• **comply with, abide by, keep to, adhere to, obey, honour, respect, follow, heed**
❹ *'This is a most curious case,' observed Holmes.*
• **remark, comment, mention, say, state, declare**
SEE ALSO say

obsessed *ADJECTIVE*
Raheem is completely obsessed with cars.
• **infatuated, fixated, preoccupied, besotted, smitten**
IDIOM (*informal*) **have a thing about**

obsession *NOUN*
She seems to have an obsession with aliens.
• **passion, fixation, infatuation, preoccupation, mania, compulsion**
IDIOMS **a bee in your bonnet,** (*informal*) **a thing about**

obsolete *ADJECTIVE*
That piece of software is now obsolete.
• **out of date, outdated, outmoded, passé, antiquated, dated, archaic, defunct, extinct**
IDIOM **past its sell-by date**
OPPOSITES current, modern

obstacle *NOUN*
❶ *I cycled around the obstacles in the road.*
• **obstruction, barrier, barricade, block**
❷ *Your age should not be an obstacle.*
• **problem, difficulty, hindrance, hurdle, snag, catch, disadvantage, drawback, stumbling block, impediment**
IDIOMS **a fly in the ointment, a spanner in the works**
OPPOSITES aid, advantage

obstinate *ADJECTIVE*
He's too obstinate to admit that he's wrong.
• **stubborn, uncooperative, wilful, self-willed, headstrong, pig-headed, inflexible, unyielding**
OPPOSITES cooperative, compliant

obstruct *VERB*
The path was obstructed by a fallen tree.
• **block, jam, clog, choke,**

make impassable
(*informal*) bung up

obstruction *NOUN*
A fallen tree was causing an obstruction.
• blockage, barrier, obstacle, hindrance, impediment, stoppage, hold-up, check

obtain *VERB*
You must obtain a permit to park here.
• get, get hold of, acquire, pick up, procure, come by
IDIOM lay your hands on

obvious *ADJECTIVE*
❶ *There were no obvious marks on the body.*
• noticeable, conspicuous, visible, prominent, pronounced, distinct, glaring
OPPOSITES inconspicuous, imperceptible
❷ *It was obvious that the woman was lying.*
• clear, evident, apparent, plain, manifest, patent, undeniable, unmistakable
OPPOSITE unclear

obviously *ADVERB*
There has obviously been some mistake.
• clearly, plainly, evidently, apparently, patently, of course, needless to say
OPPOSITES perhaps, arguably

occasion *NOUN*
❶ *We met on a number of occasions.*
• time, moment, instance
❷ *Is the dress for a special occasion?*
• event, affair, function, happening, incident, occurrence

occasional *ADJECTIVE*
The forecast is for occasional showers.
• intermittent, infrequent, irregular, periodic, sporadic, odd, scattered
OPPOSITES frequent, regular

occasionally *ADVERB*
He nodded occasionally to show he was listening.
• sometimes, every so often, once in a while, now and again, from time to time, on occasion, periodically
OPPOSITES frequently, often

occupant *NOUN*
The only occupants of the castle were a family of bats.
• resident, inhabitant, occupier, tenant

occupation *NOUN*
❶ *The birth certificate lists his father's occupation.*
• job, employment, profession, post, position, trade, work, line of work, calling
❷ *My favourite occupation is reading.*
• activity, pastime, hobby, pursuit, recreation
❸ *the Roman occupation of Gaul*
• capture, seizure, conquest, invasion, takeover, colonization

WORD WEB

Some occupations:

- accountant
- actor or actress
- architect
- artist
- astronaut
- banker
- barber
- bookseller
- builder
- bus driver
- care worker
- chef
- cleaner
- coach
- cook
- curator
- dancer
- dentist
- detective
- diver
- doctor
- editor
- electrician
- engineer
- farmer
- film-maker
- firefighter
- fisherman
- flight attendant
- florist
- footballer
- gardener
- hairdresser
- imam
- janitor
- joiner
- journalist
- lawyer
- lecturer
- lexicographer
- librarian
- mechanic
- midwife
- miner
- minister
- model
- musician
- nurse
- office worker
- optician
- painter
- paramedic
- pharmacist
- photographer
- pilot
- plumber
- police officer
- politician

- postal worker
- priest
- professor
- programmer
- psychiatrist
- psychologist
- rabbi
- receptionist
- reporter
- sailor
- scientist
- secretary
- security guard
- shepherd
- shopkeeper
- singer
- soldier
- solicitor
- stockbroker
- surgeon
- tailor
- teacher
- traffic warden
- train driver
- TV presenter
- undertaker
- vet
- vicar
- waiter or waitress
- web designer
- writer
- zookeeper

For occupations in the past see **historical**.
For medical occupations see **medicine**.

occupied *ADJECTIVE*
❶ *This game will keep you occupied for hours.*
• **busy, engaged, absorbed, engrossed, involved, active, tied up**
OPPOSITE idle
❷ *Is this seat occupied?*
• **in use, taken, engaged, full**
OPPOSITES free, vacant

occupy *VERB*
❶ *A young couple occupy the flat upstairs.*
• **live in, reside in, dwell in, inhabit**
❷ *The piano occupies most of the room.*
• **fill, take up, use up**
❸ *This game should occupy them for a few hours.*
• **keep you busy, engage your attention, divert, amuse, absorb, engross**
❹ *The Romans occupied Britain for nearly 400 years.*
• **capture, seize, take over, conquer, colonize**

occur *VERB*
❶ *She told them what had occurred.*
• **happen, take place, come about, arise**
❷ *It is a disease which occurs mainly in childhood.*
• **appear, develop, be found, crop up, turn up**
➤ **occur to**
Just then an idea occurred to me.
• **cross your mind, enter your head**

occurrence *NOUN*
Highway robbery was once a common occurrence.
• **event, happening, incident, phenomenon**

ocean *NOUN*

WORD WEB

The oceans of the world:

- Antarctic
- Arctic
- Atlantic
- Indian
- Pacific

SEE ALSO **sea**

odd *ADJECTIVE*
❶ *Her behaviour seems rather odd.*
• **strange, unusual, abnormal, peculiar, curious, puzzling, extraordinary, funny, weird, bizarre, eccentric, quirky, outlandish**
IDIOM (*informal*) **off the wall**
OPPOSITES normal, ordinary
❷ *I could only find one odd sock.*
• **unmatched, unpaired, single, lone, leftover, spare**
❸ *He does odd jobs around the house.*
• **occasional, casual, irregular, various, sundry**

odour *NOUN*
There's a strange odour coming from the kitchen.
• **smell, aroma, scent, perfume, fragrance, bouquet**
(*informal*) **whiff**
– An unpleasant odour is a **reek, stench** or **stink**.
For tips on describing smells see **smell**.

offence *NOUN*
❶ *They were only charged with minor offences.*
• **crime, wrongdoing, misdeed, misdemeanour, felony, sin**
– In sports, an offence is a **foul** or an **infringement**.
❷ *I didn't mean to cause any offence.*
• **annoyance, anger, displeasure, resentment, hard feelings, animosity**

offend *VERB*
❶ *I hope my email didn't offend you.*
• **upset, hurt your feelings, annoy, anger, displease, insult, affront**
❷ *Some criminals are likely to offend again.*
• **break the law, commit a crime, do wrong**

offensive *ADJECTIVE*
❶ *He apologized for his offensive remarks.*
• **insulting, rude, impolite, disrespectful, abusive, upsetting, hurtful**
OPPOSITE complimentary
❷ *The gas produces an offensive smell.*
• **unpleasant, disagreeable, distasteful, objectionable, off-putting, repellent, repulsive, disgusting, obnoxious, revolting, nasty**
OPPOSITES pleasant, agreeable

offer *VERB*
❶ *May I offer a suggestion?*
• **propose, put forward, suggest, submit, present, proffer**
OPPOSITES withdraw, retract
❷ *A few people offered to help me clear up.*
• **volunteer, come forward**
OPPOSITE refuse

offer *NOUN*
Thank you for your offer of help.
• **proposal, suggestion, proposition**

office *NOUN*
❶ *Over the summer he is working in a newspaper office.*
• **workplace, bureau, department**
❷ *She took up the office of vice president immediately.*
• **post, position, appointment, job, role, function**

officer *NOUN*
a customs officer
• **official, office-holder, executive**

official *ADJECTIVE*
The official opening of the museum is next month.
• **formal, authorized, legitimate, approved, recognized, proper, valid**
OPPOSITES unofficial, unauthorized

official *NOUN*
We spoke to a high-ranking official in the ministry.
• **officer, office-holder, executive, representative, agent**

often *ADVERB*
It often rains in April.
• **frequently, regularly, commonly, constantly, repeatedly, again and again, time after time, many times**

oil *VERB*
She was oiling her bicycle chain.
• **lubricate, grease**

oily *ADJECTIVE*
I'm cutting down on oily foods.
• **greasy, fatty**

ointment *NOUN*
Here's some ointment for your rash.
• **cream, lotion, salve, liniment, balm**

OK or **okay** (*informal*) *ADJECTIVE*
see **all right**

old *ADJECTIVE*

OVERUSED WORD

❶ **An old person:**

➤ **elderly** ➤ **senior**
➤ **aged**

Bus tickets are free for **elderly** *people.*

OPPOSITE young

❷ An old building, old document:

➤ historical	➤ archaic
➤ early	➤ antiquarian
➤ ancient	

The church stands on the site of an **ancient** *Celtic monastery.*

OPPOSITE modern

❸ An old machine, old vehicle:

➤ old-fashioned	➤ vintage
➤ out of date	➤ veteran
➤ antiquated	➤ early
➤ antique	➤ obsolete

My uncle collects and restores **vintage** *motorcycles.*

OPPOSITES up to date, current

❹ Old clothes, old furnishings:

➤ worn	➤ frayed
➤ scruffy	➤ threadbare
➤ shabby	➤ (*informal*) tatty

IDIOM falling to pieces

I was wearing a pair of **scruffy** *jeans and a t-shirt.*

OPPOSITE new

❺ The old days, old times:

➤ past	➤ previous
➤ former	➤ bygone
➤ earlier	➤ olden

– Times before written records were kept are **prehistoric** times.

We did a project on how children lived in **former** *times.*

OPPOSITES modern, recent

old-fashioned *ADJECTIVE*
The illustrations look old-fashioned now.
• **out of date, dated, outdated, outmoded, unfashionable, antiquated, passé**
(*informal*) **old hat**
IDIOM **behind the times**
OPPOSITES modern, up to date

omit *VERB*
❶ *These scenes were omitted from the final film.*
• **exclude, leave out, cut, drop, eliminate, miss out, skip**
OPPOSITE include
❷ *You omitted to mention the author's name.*
• **forget, fail, neglect**
OPPOSITE remember

once *ADVERB*
❶ *California was once part of Mexico.*
• **formerly, at one time, previously, in the past**
❷ *We spoke only once on the phone.*
• **one time, on one occasion**

once *CONJUNCTION*
The show will begin once everyone is seated.
• **as soon as, when, after**

one-sided *ADJECTIVE*
❶ *The game has been one-sided so far.*
• **uneven, unequal, unbalanced**
❷ *This book gives a one-sided account of the conflict.*
• **biased, prejudiced, partisan, partial, slanted, distorted**

only *ADVERB*
❶ *There is only room for one passenger.*
• **just, no more than, at most, at best**
❷ *This email is for your eyes only.*
• **solely, purely, exclusively**

ooze *VERB*
The jam was oozing from my doughnut.
• **seep, leak, escape, dribble, drip**

opaque *ADJECTIVE*
The window was fitted with opaque glass.
• **cloudy, dull, obscure**
OPPOSITES transparent, translucent

open *ADJECTIVE*
❶ *Just leave the door open.*
• **unlocked, unfastened, ajar, gaping**
OPPOSITES closed, shut

❷ *There was an open packet of crisps on the table.*
• **opened, unsealed, uncovered, unwrapped**
OPPOSITES closed, sealed
❸ *Several maps were open on the desk.*
• **unfolded, spread out, unrolled, unfurled**
❹ *Through the window was a view of open countryside.*
• **clear, unrestricted, unenclosed, extensive, rolling, sweeping**
OPPOSITE enclosed
❺ *He was open about his mistakes.*
• **frank, honest, candid, direct, forthcoming, unreserved, outspoken** (*informal*) **upfront**
OPPOSITES secretive, evasive
❻ *The idea was met with open hostility.*
• **plain, undisguised, unconcealed, overt, manifest, blatant, public**
OPPOSITES hidden, suppressed
➤ **be open to**
❶ *I am always open to suggestions.*
• **receptive to, willing to listen to, responsive to**
❷ *Computers are open to online attacks.*
• **vulnerable to, susceptible to, exposed to, liable to, subject to**

open *VERB*
❶ *Let me open a window.*
• **unfasten, unlock, unbolt**
❷ *I can't wait to open my presents.*
• **undo, unwrap, untie, unseal, unfold, unroll**
– To open an umbrella is to **unfurl** it.
– To open a wine bottle is to **uncork** it.
❸ *The exhibition opens next Friday.*
• **begin, start, commence, get under way** (*informal*) **kick off**
OPPOSITE close

opening *NOUN*
❶ *The sheep got through an opening in the fence.*
• **gap, hole, breach, break, split**
❷ *The film has a very dramatic opening.*
• **beginning, start, commencement** (*informal*) **kick-off**
❸ *We are invited to the opening of the new sports centre.*
• **launch, inauguration**
– The opening of a new play or film is the **first night** or **premiere**.
❹ *The job offers a good opening for a keen young person.*
• **chance, opportunity**

opening *ADJECTIVE*
Can you remember the opening lines of the song?
• **first, initial, introductory, preliminary**
OPPOSITES final, closing

operate *VERB*
❶ *Do you know how to operate this camera?*
• **use, work, run, drive, handle, control, manage**
❷ *This watch operates even underwater.*
• **work, function, go, run, perform**
❸ *They had to operate to save his life.*
• **carry out an operation, perform surgery**

operation *NOUN*
❶ *This lever controls the operation of the robot.*
• **performance, working, functioning, running, action**
❷ *Defusing a bomb is a dangerous operation.*
• **task, activity, action, exercise, manoeuvre, process, procedure**
❸ *I had an operation to remove my appendix.*
• **surgery**

opinion *NOUN*
What was your honest opinion of the film?
• **view, judgement, impression, assessment, estimation, point of view, thought, belief, feeling, attitude, idea, notion**

opponent *NOUN*
He was one of the main opponents of slavery.
• **critic, objector, challenger, rival, adversary, enemy, foe**
– Your opponents in a game are the **opposition**.
OPPOSITES supporter, ally

opportunity *NOUN*
There weren't many opportunities to relax.
• **chance, possibility, occasion, moment, time**

oppose *VERB*
Many people opposed the plans for a new runway.
• **object to, be against, disapprove of, disagree with, argue against, be hostile towards, fight against, resist, challenge**
OPPOSITES **support, defend**

opposite *ADJECTIVE*
❶ *My friend lives on the opposite side of the street.*
• **facing**
❷ *They hold opposite opinions on the subject.*
• **contrasting, conflicting, contradictory, opposed, opposing, different, contrary**
OPPOSITES **the same, similar**

opposite *NOUN*
She always says one thing and does the opposite.
• **reverse, converse, contrary, antithesis**

opposition *NOUN*
❶ *There was fierce opposition to the new road.*
• **resistance, objection, disapproval, hostility, antagonism, dissent**
OPPOSITE **support**
❷ *Our team easily beat the opposition.*
• **opponents, rivals**

optimistic *ADJECTIVE*
I'm feeling optimistic about the future.
• **positive, confident, cheerful, buoyant, hopeful, expectant**
(*informal*) **upbeat**
OPPOSITE **pessimistic**

option *NOUN*
We had the option to walk or take the bus.
• **choice, alternative, selection, possibility**

optional *ADJECTIVE*
Art is an optional subject at the school.
• **voluntary, non-compulsory, discretionary**
OPPOSITE **compulsory**

oral *ADJECTIVE*
Students take an oral exam in each language.
• **spoken, verbal, unwritten**
OPPOSITE **written**

orange *ADJECTIVE*
a bright orange colour
For tips on describing colours see **colour**.

orbit *VERB*
The earth orbits the sun in about 365 days.
• **circle, travel round, go round**

ordeal *NOUN*
One of the survivors gave an account of their ordeal.
• **suffering, hardship, trial, trauma, torment, anguish, torture, nightmare**

order *NOUN*
❶ *The captain gave the order to abandon ship.*
• **command, instruction, direction, decree, edict**
❷ *You can put in an advance order for the DVD.*
• **request, demand, reservation, booking**
❸ *The films are listed in alphabetical order.*
• **arrangement, sequence, series, succession**
❹ *She keeps her bike in good order.*
• **condition, state, shape, repair**
❺ *The police eventually restored order to the streets.*
• **peace, calm, control, quiet, harmony, law and order**
OPPOSITE **chaos**

order *VERB*
❶ *The crew were ordered to return.*
• **command, instruct, direct, tell, require, charge**
❷ *I ordered the tickets over the Internet.*
• **request, reserve, apply for, book**

❸ *He needed a few minutes to order his thoughts.*
• arrange, organize, sort, put in order

orderly *ADJECTIVE*
❶ *Plants are named according to an orderly system.*
• organized, well ordered, systematic, methodical, neat, tidy
OPPOSITES untidy, haphazard
❷ *Please form an orderly queue.*
• well behaved, controlled, disciplined
OPPOSITE disorderly

ordinary *ADJECTIVE*
❶ *It began as just an ordinary day.*
• normal, typical, usual, customary, habitual, regular, routine
❷ *The picture was taken with an ordinary camera.*
• standard, average, common, conventional, run-of-the-mill, everyday
IDIOM common or garden
OPPOSITES special, unusual

organization *NOUN*
❶ *The UN is an international organization.*
• institution, operation, enterprise, company
(*informal*) outfit, set-up
❷ *She is responsible for the organization of this year's parade.*
• coordination, planning, arrangement, running

organize *VERB*
❶ *Can you help me to organize the party?*
• coordinate, plan, see to, set up, put together, run
❷ *I'm trying to organize all my notebooks.*
• arrange, put in order, sort out, tidy up, classify, collate

origin *NOUN*
❶ *We know very little about the origin of life on Earth.*
• beginning, start, creation, birth, dawn, emergence, source, cause, root
OPPOSITE end
❷ *He was proud of his humble origins.*
• background, ancestry, descent, parentage, pedigree, lineage, roots, stock, birth, family, extraction

original *ADJECTIVE*
❶ *The settlers drove out the original inhabitants.*
• earliest, first, initial, native, indigenous
❷ *It's certainly an original idea for a story.*
• inventive, innovative, new, novel, fresh, creative, imaginative, unusual, unconventional, unorthodox
❸ *Is that an original painting or a copy?*
• genuine, real, authentic, true

originate *VERB*
❶ *Rock music originated in the 1950s.*
• begin, start, arise, emerge, emanate, spring up, crop up
❷ *He originated his own style of playing the guitar.*
• invent, create, design, conceive, dream up, devise, formulate, develop, pioneer

ornament *NOUN*
The shelf was covered with ornaments.
• decoration, bauble, trinket, knick-knack

ornamental *ADJECTIVE*
There was an ornamental fountain in the garden.
• decorative, fancy, ornate, decorated

ornate *ADJECTIVE*
The frame around the mirror was very ornate.
• elaborate, decorative, fancy, showy, fussy
OPPOSITE plain

orthodox *ADJECTIVE*
She wasn't taught to play the piano in the orthodox way.
• conventional, accepted, customary, usual, standard, traditional, regular, established, approved, recognized, official
OPPOSITES unorthodox, unconventional

a b c d e f g h i j k l m n o p q r s t u v w x y z

other *ADJECTIVE*

❶ *It is more expensive than other brands.*
• **alternative, different, separate, distinct**
❷ *I have some other questions.*
• **more, further, additional, supplementary, extra**

outbreak *NOUN*

❶ *People in the town fear an outbreak of violence.*
• **outburst, eruption, flare-up, upsurge (in), spate, wave, rash**
– An outbreak of disease that spreads quickly is an **epidemic**.
❷ *They left the country a year after the outbreak of the war.*
• **beginning, start, onset, commencement**

outburst *NOUN*

There was an outburst of laughter from the next room.
• **explosion, eruption, outbreak, fit, storm, surge**

outcome *NOUN*

What was the outcome of your experiment?
• **result, consequence, effect, upshot, end result**

outcry *NOUN*

There was a massive outcry over the closure of the hospital.
• **protest, protestation, complaints, objections, uproar, fuss, furore, dissent**

outdoor *ADJECTIVE*

The hotel has an outdoor swimming pool.
• **open-air, out of doors, outside, al fresco**
OPPOSITE **indoor**

outer *ADJECTIVE*

They finally broke through the outer walls of the city.
• **external, exterior, outside, outermost, outward**
OPPOSITE **inner**

outfit *NOUN*

❶ *She was wearing her new outfit.*
• **clothes, costume, suit, ensemble** (*informal*) **get-up**
❷ *Do you have a puncture repair outfit?*
• **equipment, apparatus, kit** (*informal*) **set-up, gear**

outing *NOUN*

We went on a family outing to the coast.
• **trip, excursion, expedition, jaunt, day out**

outlaw *NOUN*

A band of outlaws held up the train.
• **bandit, fugitive, wanted criminal, highwayman, brigand**

outlet *NOUN*

❶ *The basin has an outlet for excess water.*
• **opening, way out, exit, vent, channel, conduit, duct**
OPPOSITE **inlet**
❷ *The company has outlets throughout Europe.*
• **shop, store, branch, market**

outline *NOUN*

❶ *He first drew the outline of a face.*
• **profile, silhouette, shape, form, contour**
❷ *Write a brief outline of the plot.*
• **summary, sketch, synopsis, precis, résumé, rough idea, rundown, gist**
IDIOM **bare bones**

outline *VERB*

She quickly outlined her plan.
• **summarize, sketch out, rough out**

outlook *NOUN*

❶ *The cottage has a beautiful outlook over the lake.*
• **view, vista, prospect, panorama**
❷ *She has a gloomy outlook on life.*
• **point of view, view, attitude, frame of mind, standpoint, stance**
❸ *The outlook for tomorrow is bright and sunny.*
• **forecast, prediction, prospect, prognosis**

out of date *ADJECTIVE*
❶ *The information in the article is already out of date.*
• **outdated, dated, old-fashioned, obsolete, obsolescent**
IDIOMS behind the times, past its sell-by date
OPPOSITES modern, up to date
❷ *Your library card is out of date.*
• **expired, invalid, void, lapsed**
OPPOSITES valid, current

outrage *NOUN*
❶ *There was public outrage at the government's decision.*
• **anger, fury, indignation, rage, disgust, horror**
❷ *Such a waste of public money is an outrage.*
• **disgrace, scandal, crime, atrocity**

outrage *VERB*
He was outraged at the way he had been treated.
• **shock, anger, enrage, infuriate, affront**

outrageous *ADJECTIVE*
❶ *It was an outrageous way to behave.*
• **disgraceful, scandalous, shocking, atrocious, appalling, monstrous, shameful**
OPPOSITES acceptable, reasonable
❷ *They charge outrageous prices at that shop.*
• **excessive, exorbitant, extortionate, inflated, unreasonable, preposterous**

outset *NOUN*
The plan was doomed from the outset.
• **start, beginning, starting point**
IDIOM the word go

outside *NOUN*
Insects have their skeletons on the outside of their bodies.
• **exterior, shell, surface, case, skin, facade**
OPPOSITE inside

outside *ADJECTIVE*
We have an outside light above the front door.
• **exterior, external, outer**
OPPOSITE inside

outsider *NOUN*
She's lived in the village for years, but still feels like an outsider.
• **newcomer, stranger, alien, foreigner, immigrant, incomer**

outskirts *PLURAL NOUN*
We live on the outskirts of town.
• **edges, fringes, periphery, outer areas**
– The outskirts of a large town or city are the **suburbs**.
OPPOSITE centre

outspoken *ADJECTIVE*
He's always been outspoken in his views.
• **frank, open, forthright, direct, candid, plain-spoken, blunt, straightforward**

outstanding *ADJECTIVE*
❶ *She is an outstanding athlete.*
• **excellent, exceptional, first-rate, first-class, tremendous, marvellous, wonderful, superb, great, fine, superior, superlative, top-notch**
(*informal*) **brilliant, fantastic, terrific, fabulous, sensational, super**
OPPOSITES ordinary, second-rate, unexceptional
❷ *There are still some outstanding bills to pay.*
• **unpaid, unsettled, overdue, owing**

outward *ADJECTIVE*
His outward manner was bright and cheerful.
• **external, exterior, outside, outer, surface, superficial**
OPPOSITE inward

outwit *VERB*
Somehow she always manages to outwit her opponents.
• **outsmart, outfox, get the better of, beat, defeat**

oval *ADJECTIVE*
Our garden has an oval lawn.
• **egg-shaped, elliptical**

oven *NOUN*
The meat was roasting in the oven.
• **cooker, stove, range**

– A special oven for firing pottery is a **kiln**.

overcast *ADJECTIVE*
The sky has been overcast all day.
• **cloudy, dull, grey, sunless, dark, leaden**
For tips on describing the weather see **weather**.

overcome *VERB*
❶ *He managed to overcome his fear of flying.*
• **conquer, defeat, master, get the better of, prevail over**
❷ *Rescuers were overcome by the fumes.*
• **overpower, overwhelm**

overflow *VERB*
I left the tap on and the bath overflowed.
• **spill over, pour over, brim over, run over, flood**

overgrown *ADJECTIVE*
The back garden was completely overgrown.
• **unkempt, untidy, tangled, weedy, wild**

overhaul *VERB*
The engine has been completely overhauled.
• **service, check over, inspect, repair, restore, refit, refurbish**

overhead *ADVERB*
A flock of geese flew overhead.
• **above, high up, in the sky, above your head**

overlook *VERB*
❶ *You have overlooked one important fact.*
• **miss, fail to see, fail to notice**
❷ *I am willing to overlook the error.*
• **disregard, ignore, pay no attention to, forget about, pass over**
IDIOM **turn a blind eye to**
❸ *The villa overlooks an olive grove.*
• **have a view of, look on to, look out on, face**

overpowering *ADJECTIVE*
❶ *The stench was overpowering.*
• **overwhelming, strong, intense, pungent, oppressive, suffocating, unbearable**
❷ *I felt an overpowering urge to giggle.*
• **overwhelming, powerful, compelling, irresistible, uncontrollable**

overrun *VERB*
The barn was overrun with rats and mice.
• **invade, take over, spread over, swarm over, inundate, overwhelm**

overtake *VERB*
We overtook the car in front.
• **pass, go past, pull ahead of, leave behind**

overthrow *VERB*
The rebels planned to overthrow the president.
• **depose, bring down, topple, defeat, remove, oust, drive out, unseat**

overturn *VERB*
❶ *Our canoe overturned.*
• **capsize, turn over, keel over, turn turtle**
❷ *I accidentally overturned a milk jug.*
• **knock over, tip over, topple, upset, upend**
❸ *The court overturned the judge's decision.*
• **cancel, reverse, repeal, rescind, revoke, overrule**

overwhelm *VERB*
❶ *We have been overwhelmed by the response.*
• **affect deeply, move deeply, overcome**
IDIOMS **bowl you over, leave you speechless**
❷ *The attackers overwhelmed us with sheer numbers.*
• **defeat, overcome, overpower, crush, trounce**
❸ *A huge tidal wave overwhelmed the village.*
• **engulf, flood, inundate, submerge, swallow up, bury**

overwhelming *ADJECTIVE*
❶ *It was another overwhelming defeat.*
• **decisive, devastating, crushing, massive, monumental**

– An overwhelming victory at an election is a **landslide**.

❷ *I had an overwhelming desire to see him again.*

• **strong, powerful, overpowering, irresistible, compelling**

owe *VERB*

How much do you owe her?

• **be in debt (to), be in arrears (to)**

owing *ADJECTIVE*

➤ **owing to**

It was a difficult journey owing to the heavy snow and ice.

• **because of, on account of, as a result of, thanks to, due to**

own *VERB*

It was the first bike she had owned.

• **be the owner of, have, possess**

➤ **own up to**

No one owned up to breaking the window.

• **confess to, admit to, tell the truth about**

IDIOM **come clean about**

A B C D E F G H I J K L M N O P Q R S T U V W X Y Z

Pp

pace *NOUN*
❶ *Take a pace backwards.*
• **step, stride**
❷ *The runners set off at a fast pace.*
• **speed, rate, velocity, tempo**

pace *VERB*
She was pacing anxiously around the room.
• **walk, step, stride, march, pound**
SEE ALSO **walk**

pacify *VERB*
It was too late to pacify her now and she stormed off.
• **calm, quieten, soothe, humour, appease**
OPPOSITES anger, annoy

pack *NOUN*
❶ *He took out a pack of chewing gum.*
• **packet, box, carton, package, bundle**
❷ *The hikers picked up their packs and trudged off.*
• **bag, rucksack, backpack, haversack, knapsack**
❸ *Wolves hunt in packs.*
• **group, herd, troop, band**

pack *VERB*
❶ *She was packing a suitcase.*
• **fill, load up**
❷ *I packed everything away in the cupboards.*
• **stow, store, put away**
❸ *Over a hundred people packed into the hall.*
• **cram, crowd, squeeze, stuff, jam, wedge**

package *NOUN*
The postman delivered a huge package.
• **parcel, packet, bundle**

pad *NOUN*
❶ *She put a pad of cotton wool over the wound.*
• **wad, dressing, cushion, pillow**
❷ *There's a pad for messages next to the phone.*
• **notebook, notepad, jotter**

pad *VERB*
❶ *The seats are padded with foam rubber.*
• **stuff, fill, pack, wad**
– To put covers and padding on furniture is to **upholster** it.
❷ *He padded along to the bathroom.*
see **walk**

padding *NOUN*
The padding is coming out of this cushion.
• **stuffing, filling, wadding**
– The covers and padding on furniture is **upholstery**.

paddle *VERB*
The children were paddling in rock pools.
• **splash about, dabble**
– To walk through deep water is to **wade**.

page *NOUN*
❶ *The last page had been torn from the book.*
• **sheet, leaf, folio**
❷ *I wrote two whole pages of notes.*
• **side**

paid
past tense see **pay**

pain *NOUN*
❶ *I felt a sharp pain in my ankle.*
• **soreness, ache, pang, stab, throbbing, twinge**
– A slight pain is **discomfort**.
❷ *She had suffered the pain of losing her husband.*
• **anguish, agony, suffering, torment, torture**

painful *ADJECTIVE*
❶ *Is your knee still painful?*
• **sore, aching, tender, hurting, smarting, stinging, throbbing**
OPPOSITES painless, pain-free
❷ *We looked at the photographs and it*

brought back painful memories.
• **unpleasant, upsetting, distressing, disagreeable, traumatic, agonizing, harrowing**
OPPOSITE pleasant

painless *ADJECTIVE*
❶ *The treatment is quite painless.*
• **comfortable, pain-free**
OPPOSITE painful
❷ *This is a quick and painless way to make a cake.*
• **easy, simple, effortless, trouble-free, undemanding**

painstaking *ADJECTIVE*
He showed a painstaking attention to detail.
• **meticulous, thorough, careful, conscientious, rigorous, scrupulous**

paint *VERB*
❶ *Each wall was painted a different colour.*
• **colour, decorate, dye, stain, tint**
❷ *Cézanne often painted apples.*
• **depict, portray, represent**

painting *NOUN*
Most of his paintings are landscapes.
• **picture, artwork, canvas, oil painting, watercolour**
– *A painting of a person or an animal is a* **portrait**.
– *A picture painted on a wall is a* **mural** *or* **fresco**.
– *A painting by a famous artist of the past is an* **old master**.
SEE ALSO **picture**

pair *NOUN*
Next to the bowl were a pair of chopsticks.
• **couple, brace, set**
– *Two people who sing or play music together are a* **duet** *or* **duo**.
– *Two people who work or play together are* **partners** *or a* **partnership**.

palace *NOUN*
The palace once belonged to the royal family.
• **mansion, stately home, castle, chateau**

pale *ADJECTIVE*
❶ *His face suddenly turned pale.*
• **white, pallid, pasty, wan, ashen, sallow, anaemic, colourless**
– *To go pale with fear is to* **blanch**.
OPPOSITES rosy-cheeked, flushed
❷ *Her jacket was a pale shade of blue.*
• **light, pastel, faint, subtle, faded, muted, bleached**
OPPOSITES bright, dark
❸ *It was difficult to see much in the pale moonlight.*
• **dim, faint, low, weak, feeble**
OPPOSITES bright, strong

pamper *VERB*
The twins' grandparents liked to pamper them.
• **spoil, indulge, cosset, mollycoddle, humour**

pamphlet *NOUN*
She had several pamphlets on bee-keeping.
• **leaflet, booklet, brochure, circular**

pan *NOUN*
Heat some milk in a pan.
• **pot, saucepan, frying pan**

panel *NOUN*
❶ *He stared at the control panel, looking for the right switch.*
• **board, unit, console, array**
❷ *The contest was judged by a panel of experts.*
• **group, team, body, board, committee**

panic *NOUN*
People fled the streets in panic.
• **alarm, fear, fright, terror, frenzy, hysteria**
OPPOSITE calm

panic *VERB*
If the alarm goes off, don't panic.
• **be alarmed, take fright, become hysterical, be panic-stricken** (*informal*) **freak out**
IDIOM **lose your head**

pant *VERB*
He stood panting at the top of the hill.
• **gasp, wheeze, puff, breathe heavily**
IDIOM **huff and puff**

pants *PLURAL NOUN*
see **clothes**

paper *NOUN*
❶ *We are out of printing paper.*
– A single piece of paper is a **leaf** or **sheet**.
– Paper and other writing materials are **stationery**.
❷ *The story made the front page of the local paper.*
• **newspaper, journal, gazette, bulletin**
❸ *Excuse me, there are some papers I need to sign.*
• **document, deed, certificate, paperwork**

WORD WEB

Some types of paper:

- blotting paper
- card
- cardboard
- cartridge paper
- crêpe paper
- graph paper
- greaseproof paper
- papyrus
- parchment
- recycled paper
- rice paper
- tissue paper
- toilet paper
- tracing paper
- wallpaper
- wrapping paper
- vellum

parade *NOUN*
The circus parade passed along the street.
• **procession, march, spectacle, show, display**
– A parade of people in costume is a **pageant**.
– A parade of vehicles or people on horseback is a **cavalcade**.

parade *VERB*
❶ *A brass band paraded past our window.*
• **march, troop, file**
❷ *My sister paraded round the room in her new dress.*
• **strut, stride, swagger**

parallel *ADJECTIVE*
The two main characters have led parallel lives.
• **similar, corresponding, comparable, analogous, matching, twin**
OPPOSITES **divergent, contrasting**

paralyse *VERB*
❶ *Scorpions paralyse their prey with venom.*
• **disable, immobilize, incapacitate, deaden, numb**
❷ *I stood and stared, paralysed with fear.*
• **immobilize, freeze, petrify**

parcel *NOUN*
I received a parcel in the post this morning.
• **package, packet**

parched *ADJECTIVE*
❶ *Nothing was growing in the parched fields.*
• **dry, arid, baked, scorched, barren, sterile, waterless**
❷ (*informal*) *I need a drink of water – I'm parched!*
• **thirsty, dry**

pardon *VERB*
❶ *Pardon me for asking.*
• **excuse, forgive**
❷ *One of the conspirators was later pardoned.*
• **exonerate, reprieve, let off, spare, forgive**

parent *NOUN*
see **family**

park *NOUN*
❶ *In the afternoon we went for a walk in the park.*
• **recreation ground, public garden**
❷ *The house and surrounding park are open to visitors.*
• **parkland, gardens, grounds, estate**

park *VERB*
You may park your car outside.
• leave, position, station

parliament *NOUN*
The Isle of Man has its own parliament.
• assembly, legislature, congress, senate, chamber, house

part *NOUN*
❶ *All the parts of the engine are now working properly.*
• component, constituent, bit, element, module
❷ *I missed the first part of the film.*
• section, piece, portion, bit, division, instalment
❸ *Our friends are moving to another part of town.*
• area, district, region, neighbourhood, sector, quarter
❹ *She has the lead part in the school play.*
• character, role

part *VERB*
❶ *The clouds parted to reveal a full moon.*
• separate, divide, move apart, split
OPPOSITE join
❷ *We parted on friendly terms.*
• part company, say goodbye, take your leave, go your separate ways
OPPOSITE meet
➤ **part with**
I couldn't bear to part with any of my books.
• discard, get rid of, give away, dispense with, throw out, hand over, surrender

partial *ADJECTIVE*
The show was only a partial success.
• limited, imperfect, incomplete, qualified
OPPOSITES complete, total
➤ **be partial to**
My sister has always been partial to chocolate.
• like, love, enjoy, be fond of, be keen on
IDIOMS have a soft spot for, have a taste for, have a weakness for

participate *VERB*
Twenty-two choirs will be participating in the event.
• take part, join in, be involved, contribute, play a part
IDIOM have a hand in

particle *NOUN*
There were particles of dust on the camera lens.
• speck, grain, fragment, bit, piece, scrap, shred, sliver
SEE ALSO bit

particular *ADJECTIVE*
❶ *Do you have a particular date in mind?*
• specific, certain, distinct, definite, exact, precise
❷ *Please take particular care with this package.*
• special, exceptional, unusual, extreme, marked, notable
❸ *My cat's very particular about her food.*
• fussy, finicky, fastidious, faddy, hard to please
(*informal*) choosy, picky

particularly *ADVERB*
❶ *The view is particularly good from here.*
• especially, exceptionally, remarkably, outstandingly, unusually, uncommonly, uniquely
❷ *I particularly asked for front-row seats.*
• specifically, explicitly, expressly, specially, in particular

particulars *PLURAL NOUN*
A police officer took down all the particulars.
• details, facts, information, circumstances

partition *NOUN*
A partition separates the two classrooms.
• room divider, screen, barrier, panel

A B C D E F G H I J K L M N O P Q R S T U V W X Y Z

partly *ADVERB*

The accident was partly my own fault.

• **in part, to some extent, up to a point**

OPPOSITE entirely

partner *NOUN*

❶ *The two women had been business partners for years.*

• **colleague, associate, collaborator, ally**

❷ *Staff were encouraged to bring their partners to the party.*

• **spouse, husband, wife, boyfriend, girlfriend, lover**

– An animal's partner is its **mate**.

party *NOUN*

❶ *We're all going to a New Year party.*

• **celebration, festivity, function, gathering, reception**

(*informal*) **get-together, bash, do**

❷ *A party of tourists was going round the museum.*

• **group, band, crowd, company**

(*informal*) **bunch, gang**

❸ *They have formed a new political party.*

• **alliance, association, faction, league**

pass *VERB*

❶ *A crowd watched as the parade passed.*

• **go by, move past**

❷ *The soldiers passed over the bridge.*

• **go, advance, proceed, progress, travel, make your way**

❸ *We tried to pass the car in front.*

• **overtake, go past, go ahead of**

❹ *Three years passed before we met again.*

• **go by, elapse, roll by**

❺ *Could you pass me the sugar, please?*

• **hand, give, deliver, offer, present**

❻ *Did you pass your audition?*

• **be successful in, get through, succeed in**

– To pass something easily is to **sail through** and to pass it barely is to **scrape through**.

OPPOSITE fail

❼ *They passed the time playing cards.*

• **spend, occupy, fill, use, employ, while away**

❽ *The pain will soon pass.*

• **go away, come to an end, disappear, fade**

IDIOMS **run its course, blow over**

➤ **pass out**

One of the runners passed out in the heat.

• **faint, lose consciousness, black out**

pass *NOUN*

❶ *You'll need a pass to go backstage.*

• **permit, licence, ticket**

❷ *We went through a narrow mountain pass.*

• **gap, gorge, ravine, canyon, valley**

passage *NOUN*

❶ *A secret passage leads to the inner chamber.*

• **passageway, corridor, hallway, tunnel**

❷ *The ship managed to force a passage through the ice.*

• **path, route, way**

❸ *They finally reached land after a long sea passage.*

• **journey, voyage, crossing**

❹ *We all had to read out a passage from the book.*

• **excerpt, extract, quotation, piece, section**

❺ *He hadn't changed at all, despite the passage of time.*

• **passing, progress, advance**

passenger *NOUN*

The bus has seats for 30 passengers.

• **traveller**

– Passengers who travel regularly to work are **commuters**.

passion *NOUN*

❶ *It is a story about youthful passion.*

• **love, emotion, desire**

❷ *She has a passion for sports.*

• **enthusiasm, eagerness, appetite, craving, urge, zest, thirst, mania, obsession**

passionate *ADJECTIVE*
❶ *He gave a passionate speech before the battle.*
• **emotional, intense, impassioned, heartfelt, vehement, fervent**
OPPOSITE unemotional
❷ *She is a passionate collector of art.*
• **eager, keen, avid, enthusiastic, fanatical**
OPPOSITE apathetic

passive *ADJECTIVE*
Owls are normally passive during the daytime.
• **inactive, docile, submissive**
OPPOSITE active

past *ADJECTIVE*
❶ *Things were very different in past centuries.*
• **earlier, former, previous, old, olden, bygone, of old, gone by**
OPPOSITE future
❷ *The road has been closed for the past month.*
• **last, preceding, recent**
OPPOSITE next

past *NOUN*
❶ *The story is set in the distant past.*
• **past times, old days, olden days, days gone by**
OPPOSITE future
❷ *I knew nothing about her colourful past.*
• **history, background, past life**
OPPOSITE future

paste *NOUN*
❶ *Mix the powder with water to make a paste.*
• **pulp, mash, purée**
❷ *We were both covered in wallpaper paste.*
• **glue, gum, adhesive**

pastime *NOUN*
Ice skating is a popular winter pastime.
• **activity, hobby, recreation, pursuit, amusement, interest, diversion, entertainment, relaxation, game, sport**

pasture *NOUN*
Sheep were grazing on the hill pastures.
• **grassland, field, meadow**

pat *VERB*
I reached down and patted the horse's neck.
• **tap, touch, stroke, pet**
– To touch something quickly and lightly is to **dab** it.
– To stroke someone with an open hand is to **caress** them.

pat *NOUN*
He gave me a reassuring pat on the shoulder.
• **tap, touch, stroke**

patch *NOUN*
❶ *There is a damp patch on the carpet.*
• **mark, area, spot, blotch, stain, blemish**
❷ *Harry had a small vegetable patch.*
• **plot, area, piece, strip, parcel, bed, allotment**

patch *VERB*
I need some material to patch a hole in my jeans.
• **mend, repair, stitch up, darn**

patchy *ADJECTIVE*
There will be patchy outbreaks of rain overnight.
• **irregular, uneven, varying, inconsistent, unpredictable**

path *NOUN*
❶ *A path winds through the forest.*
• **pathway, track, trail, footpath, walk, walkway, lane**
– A path for horse-riding is a **bridleway**.
– A path along a canal is a **towpath**.
❷ *The tornado destroyed everything in its path.*
• **way, route, course**
❸ *He is now surely on the path to success.*
• **course of action, approach, method, line, tack**

A B C D E F G H I J K L M N O P Q R S T U V W X Y Z

pathetic *ADJECTIVE*

❶ *The girl came in, a pathetic little creature in rags.*
• **pitiful, wretched, sorry, heartbreaking, moving, touching, plaintive**
❷ (*informal*) *What a pathetic excuse!*
• **hopeless, useless, weak, feeble, inadequate, incompetent**

patience *NOUN*

Bird-watching requires great patience.
• **perseverance, persistence, endurance, tenacity, staying power, forbearance, tolerance, restraint**
OPPOSITE **impatience**

patient *ADJECTIVE*

❶ *Please be patient while we connect you.*
• **calm, composed, uncomplaining, forbearing, tolerant, understanding, long-suffering**
❷ *It took hours of patient work to restore the painting.*
• **persevering, persistent, unhurried, untiring, dogged, determined, tenacious**
OPPOSITE **impatient**

patrol *VERB*

A security guard patrols the grounds at night.
• **guard, keep watch over, stand guard over, do the rounds of, inspect**

patrol *NOUN*

An armed military patrol was guarding the gates.
• **guard, force, party, squad, detail**

patter *NOUN & VERB*

For tips on describing sounds see **sound**.

pattern *NOUN*

❶ *Do you like the pattern on this wallpaper?*
• **design, decoration, motif**
❷ *His films follow a set pattern.*
• **example, model, standard, norm**
❸ *How do you explain this strange pattern of behaviour?*
• **system, structure, scheme, plan, arrangement**

WORD WEB

Some types of pattern:

- checked
- criss-cross
- dotted
- floral or flowery
- geometric
- herringbone
- mosaic
- paisley
- pinstriped
- polka dot
- spiral
- spotted or spotty
- striped or stripy
- swirling
- symmetrical
- tartan
- wavy
- zigzag

pause *NOUN*

There was a long pause before she answered.
• **break, gap, halt, rest, lull, stop, wait, interruption, stoppage**
(*informal*) **let-up**
– A pause in the middle of a performance is an **interlude** or **interval**.
– A pause in the middle of a cinema film is an **intermission**.
– A pause for rest is a **breathing space** or (*informal*) **breather**.

pause *VERB*

❶ *I paused at the door before knocking.*
• **hesitate, wait, delay, hang back**
❷ *The speaker paused to sip some water.*
• **halt, stop, break off, rest, take a break**
(*informal*) **take a breather**

paw *NOUN*

She stroked the cat's paw.
• **foot, pad**
– A horse's foot is a **hoof**
– A pig's feet are its **trotters**
– A bird's feet are its **claws**

pay *VERB*

❶ *How much did you pay for your new phone?*
• **spend, give out, hand over**
(*informal*) **fork out, shell out, cough up**
❷ *Who's going to pay the bill?*
• **pay off, repay, settle, clear**
❸ *Sometimes it pays to complain.*
• **be worthwhile, be beneficial, be to your advantage, be profitable**

❹ *I'll make you pay for this!*
• **suffer**

pay *NOUN*
You should get an increase in pay next year.
• **wages, salary, income, earnings, revenue, remuneration**
– A payment for doing a single job is a **fee**.

payment *NOUN*
❶ *She never received any payment for her work.*
• **earnings, pay, income, fee, revenue, remuneration, reimbursement**
– A voluntary payment to a charity is a **contribution** or **donation**.
– Money that is paid back to you is a **refund**.
❷ *We require prompt payment of all bills.*
• **settlement, clearance, remittance**

peace *NOUN*
❶ *After the war there was a period of peace.*
• **agreement, harmony, friendliness, truce, ceasefire**
OPPOSITES war, conflict
❷ *She enjoys the peace of the countryside.*
• **calm, peacefulness, quiet, tranquillity, stillness, serenity, silence, hush**
OPPOSITES noise, bustle

peaceful *ADJECTIVE*
We found a peaceful spot by the water's edge.
• **calm, quiet, relaxing, tranquil, restful, serene, undisturbed, untroubled, gentle, placid, soothing, still**
OPPOSITES noisy, busy

peak *NOUN*
❶ *There was a stunning view of snow-capped mountain peaks.*
• **summit, cap, crest, crown, pinnacle, top, tip, point**
❷ *She is at the peak of her career as a gymnast.*
• **top, height, high point, climax, pinnacle, culmination, zenith**

peculiar *ADJECTIVE*
❶ *What's that peculiar smell?*
• **strange, unusual, odd, curious, puzzling, extraordinary, abnormal, funny, weird, bizarre**
OPPOSITES normal, ordinary
❷ *Her way of writing is peculiar to her.*
• **characteristic, distinctive, individual, particular, personal, special, unique, identifiable**

pedigree *NOUN*
This horse has an impressive pedigree.
• **ancestry, lineage, descent, bloodline, parentage, background**

peek *VERB*
see **look**

peel *NOUN*
a strip of lemon peel
• **rind, skin, zest**

peel *VERB*
❶ *I peeled a banana.*
• **pare, skin**
❷ *You can see the paintwork starting to peel.*
• **fall off, flake off, be shed**

peep *VERB*
❶ *I found her peeping through the keyhole.*
• **peek, glance, squint**
❷ *The sun was just peeping out from the clouds.*
• **emerge, appear, issue, come into view**

peer *VERB*
see **look**

peg *NOUN*
I hung my coat and scarf on the peg.
• **hook, knob, pin, nail**

pelt *VERB*
❶ *We pelted each other with snowballs.*
• **attack, bombard, shower**
❷ *It's still pelting down outside.*
• **rain hard, pour, teem**
(*informal*) **bucket**
❸ *Two lads came pelting down the street.*
see run

pen *NOUN*
❶ *My pen has run out of ink.*
see **writing**
❷ *The dog drove the sheep into the pen.*
• **enclosure, fold**

penalize *VERB*
You will be penalized if you handle the ball.
• **punish, discipline**

penalty *NOUN*
The penalty for murder is life imprisonment.
• **punishment, sanction, sentence, fine**
OPPOSITE reward

penetrate *VERB*
❶ *The bullet had penetrated the man's chest.*
• **pierce, puncture, perforate, bore through, enter**
❷ *Your mission is to penetrate deep into enemy territory.*
• **get through, enter, infiltrate**

penetrating *ADJECTIVE*
❶ *She gave him a penetrating look.*
• **piercing, searching, probing, intent, keen, sharp**
❷ *The students asked some penetrating questions.*
• **perceptive, insightful, sharp, acute, astute**

penniless *ADJECTIVE*
The family was left penniless and homeless.
• **poor, impoverished, poverty-stricken, destitute**
OPPOSITE rich

people *PLURAL NOUN*
❶ *How many people are you inviting?*
• **persons, individuals**
(*informal*) **folk**
– People as opposed to animals are **humans, human beings** or **mankind**.
❷ *the people of the United States*
• **population, citizens, populace, public, inhabitants, society, nation, race**

perceive *VERB*
❶ *I perceived a change in her voice.*
• **notice, become aware of, recognize, detect, discern, make out**
❷ *I began to perceive what she meant.*
• **realize, understand, comprehend, grasp**

perceptive *ADJECTIVE*
❶ *It was very perceptive of you to spot my mistake.*
• **observant, sharp, quick, alert**
IDIOM (*informal*) **on the ball**
OPPOSITE unobservant
❷ *She asked some perceptive questions.*
• **insightful, penetrating, discerning, shrewd, astute, intelligent**
OPPOSITE obtuse

perch *VERB*
A robin was perching on the fence.
• **sit, settle, rest, balance**

percussion *NOUN*
see **music**

perfect *ADJECTIVE*
❶ *The guitar is in perfect condition.*
• **faultless, flawless, intact, undamaged, complete, whole, mint, pristine, immaculate**
(*informal*) **tip-top**
OPPOSITES imperfect, flawed
❷ *He produced a perfect copy of my signature.*
• **exact, faithful, accurate, precise, correct**
❸ *That dress is perfect on you.*
• **ideal, just right**
(*informal*) **spot on, just the job**
❹ *Today I received a letter from a perfect stranger.*
• **complete, absolute, total, utter**

perfect *VERB*
She spent months perfecting some new magic tricks.
• **make perfect, improve, refine, polish, hone, fine-tune**

perfectly *ADVERB*
❶ *Please stand perfectly still.*
• **completely, absolutely, totally, utterly,**

entirely, wholly, altogether
❷ *The TV works perfectly now.*
• superbly, faultlessly, flawlessly, immaculately, to perfection

perform *VERB*
❶ *Do you enjoy performing on stage?*
• act, appear, play, dance, sing
❷ *We performed the play in the school hall.*
• present, stage, produce, put on
❸ *The robot is programmed to perform simple tasks.*
• do, carry out, execute, fulfil, accomplish

performance *NOUN*
❶ *This evening's performance is already sold out.*
• show, production, presentation, showing, screening, staging, concert, recital
❷ *It was the team's best performance of the season.*
• effort, work, endeavour, exertion, behaviour, conduct

performer *NOUN*
We stopped to watch a group of street performers.
• actor, actress, musician, singer, dancer, artist, entertainer, player
SEE ALSO **drama, music**

perfume *NOUN*
The perfume of roses filled the room.
• smell, scent, fragrance, aroma, bouquet

perhaps *ADVERB*
Perhaps no one will notice.
• maybe, possibly, conceivably, for all you know
OPPOSITE definitely

peril *NOUN*
The crew faced many perils on their voyage.
• danger, hazard, risk, menace, threat
OPPOSITE safety

perimeter *NOUN*
The dotted line marks the perimeter of the old city.
• edge, border, boundary, limits, bounds
– The distance round the edge of something round is the **circumference**.

period *NOUN*
❶ *After a period of silence he spoke again.*
• time, span, interval, spell, stretch, phase
❷ *These rocks date from the Jurassic Period.*
• age, era, epoch

perish *VERB*
❶ *Without sunlight, the plants will perish.*
• die, be killed, pass away
❷ *The rubber ring has started to perish.*
• rot, decay, disintegrate, decompose, crumble away

permanent *ADJECTIVE*
❶ *Sugar can do permanent damage to your teeth.*
• lasting, long-lasting, long-term, irreparable, irreversible, everlasting, enduring
❷ *Pollution is a permanent problem in the city.*
• never-ending, perpetual, persistent, chronic, perennial
❸ *She has been offered a permanent job in the firm.*
• fixed, long-term, stable, secure
OPPOSITE temporary

permission *NOUN*
Do you have permission to leave early?
• authorization, consent, agreement, approval, leave, licence
(*informal*) go-ahead, say-so

permit *VERB*
The gallery doesn't permit photographs.
• allow, consent to, give permission for, authorize, license, grant

permit *NOUN*
You need a permit to fish in the river.
• licence, pass, ticket

A B C D E F G H I J K L M N O P Q R S T U V W X Y Z

perpetual *ADJECTIVE*
The machine produces a perpetual hum.
• **constant, continual, continuous, never-ending, non-stop, endless, ceaseless, incessant, persistent, unceasing, unending**
OPPOSITES intermittent, short-lived

perplexing *ADJECTIVE*
It is one of the most perplexing problems in science.
• **puzzling, confusing, bewildering, baffling, mystifying**

persecute *VERB*
❶ *Galileo and his followers were persecuted for their beliefs.*
• **oppress, discriminate against, victimize**
❷ *She claimed she was being persecuted by the media.*
• **harass, hound, intimidate, bully, pick on, pester, torment**

persevere *VERB*
The rescuers persevered despite the conditions.
• **continue, carry on, keep going, persist**
(*informal*) **keep at it, stick at it**
OPPOSITE give up

persist *VERB*
If the pain persists, you should see a doctor.
• **continue, carry on, last, linger, remain, endure**
OPPOSITES stop, cease
➤ **persist in**
Why do you persist in arguing with me?
• **keep on, insist on**
OPPOSITE give up

persistent *ADJECTIVE*
❶ *There was a persistent drip from the tap.*
• **constant, continual, incessant, never-ending, steady, non-stop**
OPPOSITE intermittent
❷ *The interviewer was very persistent.*
• **determined, persevering, insistent, tenacious, obstinate, stubborn, dogged, resolute, unrelenting, tireless**

person *NOUN*
Not a single person has replied to my email.
• **individual, human being, man, woman, character, soul**

personal *ADJECTIVE*
❶ *The book is based on her personal experience.*
• **own, individual, particular, special, unique**
❷ *The contents of the letter are personal.*
• **confidential, private, secret, intimate**

personality *NOUN*
❶ *She has a warm and cheerful personality.*
• **character, nature, disposition, temperament, make-up**
❷ *He is a well-known TV personality.*
• **celebrity, star**
(*informal*) **celeb**

persuade *VERB*
I persuaded my friends to sign the petition.
• **convince, coax, induce, talk into, prevail on, win over, bring round**
OPPOSITE dissuade

persuasive *ADJECTIVE*
She used some very persuasive arguments.
• **convincing, compelling, effective, telling, strong, powerful, forceful, valid, sound**
OPPOSITE unconvincing

pessimistic *ADJECTIVE*
I'm pessimistic about our chances of winning.
• **negative, gloomy, downbeat, despairing, unhopeful, resigned, cynical**
OPPOSITES optimistic, hopeful

pest *NOUN*
❶ *Here are some tips to help you get rid of garden pests.*
- Pests in general are **vermin**.
- An informal word for insect pests is **bugs**.
- A pest which lives on or in another creature is a **parasite**.

❷ (*informal*) *My cousin can be a pest at times.*
• nuisance, bother, annoyance
IDIOM (*informal*) pain in the neck

pester *VERB*
Please stop pestering me with questions!
• annoy, bother, trouble, harass, badger, hound, nag, plague
(*informal*) bug, hassle

pet *ADJECTIVE*
❶ *My brother keeps a pet snake in his bedroom.*
• tame, domesticated
❷ *Have I told you my pet theory about UFOs?*
• favourite, favoured, cherished, personal

petrified *ADJECTIVE*
I stood for a moment petrified, then turned and fled.
• terrified, horrified, terror-struck, paralysed, frozen
IDIOM rooted to the spot

petty *ADJECTIVE*
❶ *There was a long list of petty rules and regulations.*
• minor, trivial, trifling, unimportant, insignificant, inconsequential, footling
OPPOSITE important
❷ *It was a petty act of revenge.*
• small-minded, mean, mean-spirited, spiteful, ungracious

phase *NOUN*
This was the start of a new phase in my life.
• period, time, stage, step, spell, episode, chapter

phenomenal *ADJECTIVE*
She was blessed with a phenomenal memory.
• exceptional, remarkable, extraordinary, outstanding, incredible, miraculous, amazing, astonishing, astounding, staggering, awesome
OPPOSITE ordinary

phenomenon *NOUN*
❶ *A solar eclipse is an extraordinary natural phenomenon.*
• happening, occurrence, event, fact
❷ *The band soon became a worldwide phenomenon.*
• sensation, wonder, marvel, prodigy

phobia *NOUN*

WORD WEB

Some types of phobia:

- acrophobia (fear of heights)
- agoraphobia (fear of open or crowded spaces)
- arachnophobia (fear of spiders)
- claustrophobia (fear of enclosed spaces)
- xenophobia (fear or dislike of foreigners)

phone *VERB*
I'll phone you later this evening.
• telephone, call, ring, give someone a call
(*informal*) give someone a ring, give someone a bell

photograph *NOUN*
I have an old photograph of my great grandmother.
• photo, picture, snap, snapshot, shot, print, still

photograph *VERB*
He loves photographing the night sky.
• take a picture of, shoot, snap

phrase *NOUN*
She liked the sound of the phrase 'the bee's knees'.
• expression, saying, construction, idiom

phrase *VERB*
I tried to phrase my email carefully.
• express, put into words, formulate, couch, frame

A B C D E F G H I J K L M N O P Q R S T U V W X Y Z

physical *ADJECTIVE*
❶ *Rugby is a game with a lot of physical contact.*
• **bodily, corporeal, corporal**
OPPOSITES mental, spiritual
❷ *There was no physical evidence of the crime.*
• **material, concrete, solid, substantial, tangible**

pick *VERB*
❶ *We picked some flowers from the garden.*
• **pluck, gather, collect, cut, harvest**
❷ *Pick a number from one to twenty.*
• **choose, select, decide on, settle on, opt for, single out, nominate, elect**
❸ *She was picking the polish off her fingernails.*
• **pull off, scrape, remove, extract**
➤ **pick on**
Why are they always picking on me?
• **victimize, bully, persecute, torment, single out**
➤ **pick up**
Sales have started to pick up.
• **improve, recover, rally, bounce back, perk up**
➤ **pick something up**
❶ *It took two men to pick up the wardrobe.*
• **lift, raise, hoist**
❷ *I'll pick up some milk on the way home.*
• **get, collect, fetch, call for**
❸ *You'll pick up the language in no time.*
• **acquire, learn**
❹ *We have picked up a distress signal from a ship.*
• **receive, detect, hear**

picture *NOUN*
❶ *There's a picture of a volcano on the cover.*
• **illustration, image, painting, drawing, sketch, print**
– A picture which represents a particular person is a **portrait**.
– A picture which represents the artist himself or herself is a **self-portrait**.
– A picture which represents a group of objects is a **still life**.
– A picture which represents a country scene is a **landscape**.
– Pictures on a computer are **graphics**.
SEE ALSO **painting**
❷ *I took a lot of pictures on holiday.*
• **photograph, photo, snapshot, snap**

picture *VERB*
❶ *She is pictured here with her two brothers.*
• **depict, illustrate, represent, show, portray, paint, photograph**
❷ *He pictured himself holding up the trophy.*
• **imagine, visualize**
IDIOM **see in your mind's eye**

picturesque *ADJECTIVE*
❶ *We stayed in a picturesque thatched cottage.*
• **attractive, pretty, charming, quaint, scenic**
OPPOSITE ugly
❷ *She wrote a picturesque account of her travels.*
• **colourful, descriptive, imaginative, expressive, lively, poetic, vivid**

piece *NOUN*
❶ *They collected pieces of wood to build a raft.*
• **bar, block, length, stick, chunk, lump, hunk, bit, chip, fragment, particle, scrap, shred**
❷ *Who wants the last piece of chocolate?*
• **bit, portion, part, section, segment, share, slice**
❸ *There wasn't a single piece of furniture in the room.*
• **item, article**
❹ *I've lost one of the pieces of this jigsaw.*
• **part, element, unit, component, constituent**
❺ *There's a piece about our school in the local paper.*
• **article, item, report, feature**

pier *NOUN*
Fishing boats were tied up at the pier.
• **quay, wharf, jetty, landing stage**

pierce *VERB*
The arrow pierced his armour.
• **penetrate, perforate, puncture, enter, make a hole in, go through, bore through**
– To pierce someone with a spear or spike is to **impale** them.

piercing *ADJECTIVE*
❶ *From the wood came a piercing screech.*
• **high-pitched, shrill, strident, penetrating, ear-splitting, deafening**
❷ *The girl had piercing blue eyes.*
• **penetrating, intense, sharp, keen, searching, probing**

pig *NOUN*
The farm rears free-range pigs.
– An old word for pigs is **swine**.
– A wild pig is a **wild boar**.
– A male pig is a **boar** or **hog**.
– A female pig is a **sow**.
– A young pig is a **piglet**.
– A family of piglets is a **litter**.
– The smallest piglet in a litter is the **runt**.

pile *NOUN*
❶ *In the corner was a pile of old newspapers.*
• **heap, stack, mound, mass, collection, accumulation, stockpile, hoard**
❷ (*informal*) *I still have piles of work to do.*
• **plenty, a lot, a great deal**
(*informal*) **lots, masses, loads, heaps, a stack, a ton**

pile *VERB*
Just pile the dirty dishes in the sink.
• **heap, stack**
➤ **pile up**
The bills are beginning to pile up.
• **build up, mount up, accumulate, multiply, grow**

pill *NOUN*
Take one pill every four hours.
• **tablet, capsule, pellet, lozenge**

pillar *NOUN*
The dome was supported by marble pillars.
• **column, post, support, upright, pier, prop**

pillow *NOUN*
She rested her head on a pillow.
• **cushion, pad**
– A long kind of pillow is a **bolster**.

pilot *NOUN*
see **aircraft**

pilot *VERB*
He piloted the little plane to the island.
• **navigate, steer, guide, control, manoeuvre, captain, fly**

pimple *NOUN*
I had a pimple on the end of my nose.
• **spot, boil, swelling**
(*informal*) zit

pin *NOUN*
She wore a shawl fastened with a pin.
• **brooch, fastener, tack, staple, nail**

pin *VERB*
❶ *I pinned the list on the noticeboard.*
• **attach, fasten, secure, tack, nail**
❷ *He was pinned under the wreckage for hours.*
• **hold down, press, pinion**

pinch *VERB*
❶ *Pinch the dough between your fingers.*
• **nip, squeeze, press, tweak, grip**
❷ (*informal*) *Who pinched my calculator?*
• **steal, take, snatch, pilfer**
(*informal*) **swipe, lift, nick, make off with**

pine *VERB*
The dog pined when its master died.
• **mope, languish, sicken, waste away**
➤ **pine for**
She was pining for the sight of the sea again.
• **long for, yearn for, miss, crave, hanker after**

pink *ADJECTIVE & NOUN*

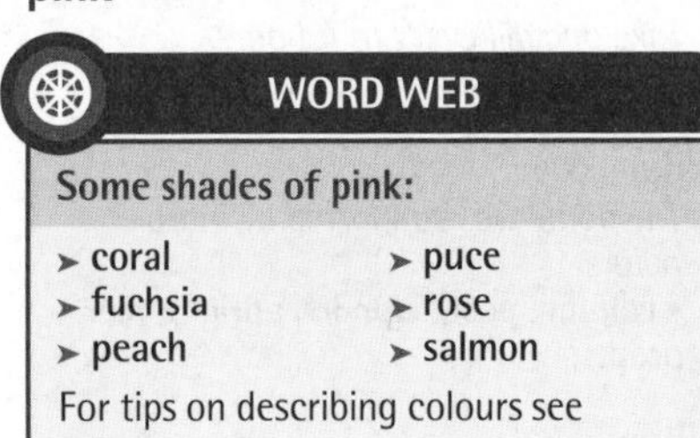
WORD WEB

Some shades of pink:

- coral
- fuchsia
- peach
- puce
- rose
- salmon

For tips on describing colours see **colour**.

pip *NOUN*
Remove the pips from the grapes.
• **seed**
– To remove pips from fruit is to **deseed** it.

pipe *NOUN*
The water flows away along this pipe.
• **tube, duct, conduit, channel**
– A pipe used for watering the garden is a **hose**.
– A pipe in the street which supplies water for fighting fires is a **hydrant**.
– A pipe for carrying oil or gas over long distances is a **pipeline**.
– The system of water pipes in a house is the **plumbing**.

pipe *VERB*
Water is piped from the reservoir to the town.
• **carry, convey, run, channel, funnel, siphon**

pirate *NOUN*
Pirates attacked the ship.
• **buccaneer, marauder, freebooter**

pit *NOUN*
❶ *We first dug a deep pit.*
• **hole, crater, cavity, hollow, depression, pothole, chasm, abyss**
❷ *The town is next to a disused coal pit.*
• **mine, colliery, quarry**

pitch *NOUN*
❶ *The football pitch was covered in snow.*
• **ground, field, playing field, park**
❷ *Dogs can hear at a higher pitch than humans.*
• **tone, frequency**
❸ *a roof with a steep pitch*
• **slope, slant, gradient, incline, angle, tilt**

pitch *VERB*
❶ *Boys were pitching pebbles into the pond.*
• **throw, toss, fling, hurl, sling, cast, lob** (*informal*) **chuck**
❷ *This is a perfect place to pitch a tent.*
• **erect, put up, set up**
❸ *She tripped and pitched headlong into the water.*
• **plunge, dive, drop, topple, plummet**
❹ *The little boat pitched about in the storm.*
• **lurch, toss, rock, roll, reel**

pitfall *NOUN*
Being famous has some serious pitfalls.
• **difficulty, problem, hazard, danger, snag, catch, trap**

pitiful *ADJECTIVE*
❶ *We could hear pitiful cries for help.*
• **sad, sorrowful, mournful, pathetic, plaintive, piteous, heart-rending, moving, touching**
❷ *What a pitiful excuse!*
• **feeble, weak, pathetic, hopeless, useless, inadequate, incompetent**

pity *NOUN*
They showed no pity towards their captives.
• **mercy, compassion, sympathy, humanity, kindness, concern, feeling**
OPPOSITE cruelty
➤ **a pity**
It's a pity you have to leave so soon.
• **a shame, unfortunate, bad luck, too bad**

pity *VERB*
I pity anyone who has to live there.
• **feel sorry for, feel for, sympathize with, take pity on, commiserate with**

pivot *NOUN*
The wheel on the barrow acts as a pivot.
– The point on which a lever turns is

called the **fulcrum**.
– The point on which a spinning object turns is its **axis**.
– The point on which a wheel turns is the **axle** or **hub**.

place *NOUN*
❶ *This is a good place to park.*
• **site, spot, location, position, situation, venue**
❷ *They are looking for a quiet place to live.*
• **area, district, locality, neighbourhood, region, vicinity, locale**
❸ *Save me a place on the bus.*
• **seat, space**
❹ *She was offered a place as a trainee.*
• **job, position, post, appointment**
❺ *Let's go back to my place.*
• **home, house, flat, apartment, quarters**
(*informal*) **pad**
➤ **in place of**
You can use honey in place of sugar.
• **instead of, rather than, in exchange for, in lieu of**

place *VERB*
❶ *Our table was placed next to the window.*
• **locate, situate, position, station**
❷ *You can place your coats on the bed.*
• **put down, set down, lay, deposit, stand, leave**

placid *ADJECTIVE*
❶ *Her pony has a very placid nature.*
• **calm, composed, unexcitable, even-tempered**
OPPOSITE excitable
❷ *The sea was placid at that time of the day.*
• **calm, quiet, tranquil, peaceful, undisturbed, unruffled**
OPPOSITE stormy

plague *NOUN*
❶ *Millions of people died of the plague.*
• **pestilence, epidemic, pandemic, contagion, outbreak**
❷ *There was a plague of wasps this summer.*
• **invasion, infestation, swarm**

plague *VERB*
❶ *Stop plaguing me with questions!*
• **pester, bother, annoy, badger, harass, hound**
(*informal*) **nag, hassle, bug**
❷ *I've been plagued by bad luck recently.*
• **afflict, beset, trouble, torment, dog, curse**

plain *ADJECTIVE*
❶ *The furniture in the room was very plain.*
• **simple, modest, basic, unelaborate**
OPPOSITES elaborate, ornate
❷ *Jodie was rather plain compared with her sister.*
• **unattractive, ordinary**
OPPOSITE attractive
❸ *It is plain to me that you are not interested.*
• **clear, evident, obvious, apparent, unmistakable**
OPPOSITE unclear
❹ *Let me tell you what I think in plain terms.*
• **direct, frank, candid, blunt, honest, sincere, straightforward, forthright, outspoken**
OPPOSITE obscure

plain *NOUN*
He missed the wide open plains of Wyoming.
• **grassland, prairie, pampas, savannah, steppe, veld**

plan *NOUN*
❶ *We'd better come up with a plan quickly!*
• **scheme, strategy, proposal, idea, suggestion, proposition, stratagem**
– A plan to do something bad is a **plot**.
❷ *On the wall were the plans for the new sports centre.*
• **design, diagram, chart, map, drawing, blueprint**

plan *VERB*
❶ *Some of us are planning a surprise party.*
• **organize, arrange, devise, design, scheme, plot, work out, map out, formulate**

A B C D E F G H I J K L M N O P Q R S T U V W X Y Z

❷ *What do you plan to do next?*
• **aim, intend, propose, mean**

plane *NOUN*
see **aircraft**

planet *NOUN*
Could there be life on planets beyond our solar system?
• **world**

WORD WEB

The planets of our solar system (in order from the sun):

➤ **Mercury**
➤ **Venus**
➤ **Earth**
➤ **Mars**
➤ **Jupiter**
➤ **Saturn**
➤ **Uranus**
➤ **Neptune**

- The path followed by a planet is its **orbit.**
- Pluto is classified as a **dwarf planet.**
- Minor planets orbiting the Sun are **asteroids** or **planetoids.**
- Something which orbits a planet is a **satellite.**
- The Earth's large satellite is the **Moon.**

SEE ALSO **space**

plant *NOUN*
Most of these plants are native to Australia.
• **vegetation, greenery, plantlife**
– The plants of a particular place or time are its **flora.**

WORD WEB

Some types of plant:

➤ **algae**
➤ **bush**
➤ **cactus**
➤ **cereal**
➤ **evergreen**
➤ **fern**
➤ **flower**
➤ **grass**
➤ **herb**
➤ **house plant**
➤ **lichen**
➤ **moss**
➤ **pot plant**
➤ **shrub**
➤ **tree**
➤ **vegetable**
➤ **vine**
➤ **weed**
➤ **wild flower**

SEE ALSO **flower, fruit, herb, tree, vegetable**

Parts of a plant:

➤ **bloom**
➤ **blossom**
➤ **branch**
➤ **bud**
➤ **bulb**
➤ **flower**
➤ **fruit**
➤ **leaf**
➤ **petal**
➤ **pod**
➤ **root**
➤ **seed**
➤ **shoot**
➤ **stalk**
➤ **stem**
➤ **trunk**
➤ **twig**

- A young plant is a **seedling.**
- A piece cut off a plant to form a new plant is a **cutting.**
- The scientific study of plants and flowers is **botany.**
- A word meaning 'to do with plants' is **botanical.**

➤ *an exhibition of botanical art*

plant *VERB*
❶ *Plant the seeds in September.*
• **sow, put in the ground**
– To move a growing plant to a new position is to **transplant** it.
❷ *He planted his feet on the ground and took hold of the rope.*
• **place, set, position**

plaster *NOUN*
You should put a plaster on your finger.
• **dressing, sticking plaster, bandage**

plate *NOUN*
❶ *They piled their plates with food.*
• **dish, platter, salver**
❷ *The design is first etched on a metal plate.*
• **panel, sheet**
❸ *The book includes thirty two full-page colour plates.*
• **illustration, picture, photograph, print**

platform *NOUN*
People gathered round as he made a speech from the platform.
• **dais, podium, stage, stand, rostrum**

play *VERB*
❶ *Children were playing in the street.*
• **amuse yourself, have fun, romp about**
❷ *Do you like playing basketball?*
• **take part in, participate in, compete in**
❸ *We are playing the defending champions.*
• **compete against, oppose, challenge, take on**
❹ *I am learning to play the piano.*
• **perform on**
❺ *Who is going to play the lead role?*
• **act, perform, take the part of, portray, represent**

play *NOUN*
❶ *We both had parts in the school play.*
• **drama, theatrical work, piece, performance, production**
SEE ALSO **drama**
❷ *The weekend was a mixture of work and play.*
• **recreation, amusement, leisure, fun, games, sport**

player *NOUN*
❶ *You need four players for this game.*
• **contestant, participant, competitor, contender**
❷ *We have some experienced players in the band.*
• **performer, musician, artist, instrumentalist**
– Someone who plays music on their own is a **soloist**.

playful *ADJECTIVE*
❶ *The kittens are in a playful mood.*
• **lively, spirited, frisky, frolicsome, mischievous, roguish, impish**
❷ *He made a few a playful remarks.*
• **light-hearted, joking, teasing, frivolous, flippant**
OPPOSITE serious

plea *NOUN*
The emperor ignored his plea for mercy.
• **appeal, request, call, entreaty, petition**

plead *VERB*
➤ **plead with**
They pleaded with us to listen to them.
• **beg, entreat, implore, appeal to, ask, petition**

pleasant *ADJECTIVE*
❶ *We spent a pleasant afternoon in the park.*
• **enjoyable, agreeable, pleasing, pleasurable, delightful, lovely, entertaining**
OPPOSITES unpleasant, disagreeable
❷ *The staff there are always pleasant.*
• **kind, friendly, likeable, charming, amiable, amicable, cheerful, genial, good-natured, good-humoured, approachable, hospitable, welcoming**
❸ *The forecast is for a spell of pleasant weather.*
• **fine, mild, sunny, warm**

please *VERB*
❶ *I wish I knew how to please her.*
• **make happy, satisfy, gratify, delight, amuse, entertain, charm**
❷ *Everyone just does as they please.*
• **like, want, wish, choose, prefer, see fit**

pleased *ADJECTIVE*
I'm very pleased to meet you.
• **happy, glad, delighted, content, contented, satisfied, gratified, thankful, grateful, elated, thrilled**
OPPOSITES unhappy, dissatisfied, discontented

pleasure *NOUN*
❶ *My aunt gets a lot of pleasure from her garden.*
• **enjoyment, happiness, delight, satisfaction, gratification, comfort, contentment, gladness, joy, fun**
– Very great pleasure is **bliss** or **ecstasy**.
❷ *He talked of the pleasures of living in the country.*
• **joy, comfort, delight**

pleat *NOUN*
It takes ages to iron the pleats in this skirt.
• **crease, fold, tuck**

pledge *NOUN*
The knights swore a pledge of allegiance to the king.
• **oath, vow, promise, word, commitment, guarantee**

plentiful *ADJECTIVE*
There is a plentiful supply of berries in the forest.
• **abundant, ample, copious, profuse, generous, lavish, bountiful, prolific**
OPPOSITE scarce

plenty *NOUN*
There should be plenty for everyone.
• **an ample supply, a sufficiency, quite enough, more than enough**
OPPOSITE a shortage
➤ **plenty of**
We've still got plenty of time.
• **a lot of, lots of, a great deal of, many, ample, abundant**
(*informal*) **loads of, masses of, stacks of, tons of**

plight *NOUN*
He was concerned about the plight of the homeless.
• **predicament, trouble, difficulty, problem, dilemma**
IDIOM **dire straits**

plod *VERB*
❶ *We plodded back through the snow.*
• **tramp, trudge, lumber**
❷ *I'm still plodding through all the paperwork.*
• **slog, plough, wade, toil, labour**

plot *NOUN*
❶ *They were part of a plot against the government.*
• **conspiracy, scheme, secret plan, intrigue**
❷ *It was hard to follow the plot of the film.*
• **story, storyline, narrative, thread**
❸ *He bought a small plot of land.*
• **area, piece, lot, patch**
– A plot of ground for growing flowers or vegetables is an **allotment**.
– A large plot of land is a **tract** of land.

plot *VERB*
❶ *The men were plotting a daring escape from prison.*
• **plan, devise, concoct, hatch**
(*informal*) **cook up**
❷ *They were accused of plotting against the queen.*
• **conspire, intrigue, scheme**
❸ *The captain plotted the course of the ship.*
• **chart, map, mark**

plough *VERB*
❶ *A tractor was ploughing the field.*
• **cultivate, till, turn over**
❷ *Are you still ploughing through that book?*
• **wade, labour, toil, slog, plod**

ploy *NOUN*
It was a clever ploy to attract publicity.
• **scheme, plan, ruse, trick, tactic, stratagem, manoeuvre**

pluck *VERB*
❶ *We started plucking berries off the bush.*
• **pick, pull off, remove, gather, collect, harvest**
❷ *A seagull plucked the sandwich out of her hand.*
• **grab, seize, snatch, jerk, pull, tug, yank**
❸ *The guitarist plucked the strings very gently.*
– To run your finger or plectrum across the strings of a guitar is to **strum**.

plug *NOUN*
She took the plug out of the side of the barrel.
• **stopper, cork, bung**

plug *VERB*
❶ *We managed to plug the leak in the pipe.*
• **stop up, block, close, fill, seal, bung up**
❷ (*informal*) *The author was there to plug her new book.*
• **advertise, publicize, promote, market, push**

plump *ADJECTIVE*
He was a plump little man with a bald head.
• **chubby, dumpy, fat, tubby, podgy, round, stout, portly**
OPPOSITE **skinny**

plunder *VERB*
Viking raiders plundered the villages near the coast.
• **loot, pillage, raid, ransack, rob, steal from**

plunge *VERB*
❶ *One by one, the girls plunged into the pool.*
• **dive, jump, leap, throw yourself**
❷ *Temperatures have plunged overnight.*
• **drop, fall, tumble, plummet, nosedive**
❸ *I plunged my hand in the cold water.*
• **dip, lower, dunk, sink, immerse, submerge**
❹ *You must plunge a stake into the vampire's heart.*
• **thrust, stab, stick, push, shove, sink, force, drive, ram**

poem *NOUN*
I was reading a poem about winter.
• **rhyme, verse, lyric**
SEE ALSO **poetry**

poetic *ADJECTIVE*
The book is written in a poetic style.
• **expressive, imaginative, lyrical, poetical**
– An uncomplimentary synonym is **flowery**.

poetry *NOUN*
This is a book of First World War poetry.
• **poems, verse, rhyme, lyrics**

WORD WEB

Some forms of poetry:

➤ **acrostic**
➤ **ballad**
➤ **blank verse**
➤ **cinquain**
➤ **clerihew**
➤ **concrete poetry**
➤ **elegy**
➤ **epic**
➤ **free verse**
➤ **haiku**
➤ **limerick**
➤ **lyric**
➤ **narrative poetry**
➤ **nonsense verse**
➤ **nursery rhyme**
➤ **ode**
➤ **rap**
➤ **sonnet**
➤ **tanka**

- A group of lines forming a section of a poem is a **stanza**.
- A pair of rhyming lines within a poem is a **couplet**.
- The rhythm of a poem is its **metre**.

point *NOUN*
❶ *That knife has a very sharp point.*
• **tip, end, nib, spike, prong, barb**
❷ *The stars looked like points of light in the sky.*
• **dot, spot, speck, fleck**
❸ *We headed for the point where the two rivers meet.*
• **location, place, position, site, spot**
❹ *Just at that point, the doorbell rang.*
• **moment, instant, second, time, stage**
❺ *His sense of humour is one of his good points.*
• **characteristic, feature, attribute, trait, quality, side, aspect**
❻ *I agree with your last point.*
• **idea, argument, thought**
❼ *I didn't get the point of that film at all.*
• **meaning, essence, core, gist, nub, crux**
❽ *There is no point in phoning at this hour.*
• **purpose, reason, aim, object, use, usefulness, sense, advantage**

point *VERB*
❶ *An arrow points the way to the exit.*
• **indicate, show, signal**
❷ *Can you point me in the right direction?*
• **direct, aim, guide, lead, steer**
➤ **point out**
I'd like to point out that this was your idea.
• **make known, mention, indicate, specify, detail, draw someone's attention to**

pointed *ADJECTIVE*
❶ *I used the pointed end of the stick.*
• **sharp, spiked, spiky, barbed**

(*informal*) **pointy**
OPPOSITES rounded, blunt
❷ *It was a rather pointed remark.*
• **deliberate, clear, unmistakable, obvious, conspicuous**
OPPOSITES oblique, obscure

pointless *ADJECTIVE*
It would be pointless to continue the experiment.
• **useless, senseless, futile, idle, vain**
OPPOSITE worthwhile

poise *NOUN*
She shows great poise for her age.
• **calmness, composure, calm, assurance, self-confidence, dignity, aplomb**

poised *ADJECTIVE*
He raised his arm, poised to strike.
• **ready, prepared, waiting, all set, set**

poison *NOUN*
He had been given a lethal dose of poison.
• **toxin, venom**
– A poison to kill plants is **herbicide** or **weedkiller.**
– A poison to kill insects is **insecticide** or **pesticide**.
– A substance which counteracts the effects of a poison is an **antidote**.

poisonous *ADJECTIVE*
This particular mushroom is poisonous.
• **toxic, deadly, lethal, fatal**
– Snakes and other animals which produce a toxic venom are said to be **venomous**.

poke *VERB*
Someone poked me in the back with an umbrella.
• **prod, dig, jab, stab, nudge**
➤ **poke out**
Bits of straw were poking out of the mattress.
• **stick out, jut out, project, protrude**

poke *NOUN*
She gave me a poke in the back.
• **prod, dig, jab, stab, nudge**

polar *ADJECTIVE*
Sea ice is melting in the polar regions.
• **Arctic or Antarctic**
SEE ALSO **ice**

pole *NOUN*
The huts are supported on wooden poles.
• **post, pillar, stick, rod, shaft, stake, staff, prop**
– A strong pole to support sails on a ship is a **mast** or **spar**.

police *NOUN*
I think you'd better call the police.
• **police force, constabulary**
(*informal*) **the law, the cops, the fuzz**

police officer *NOUN*
Two police officers arrived in a patrol car.
• **policeman or policewoman, officer, constable**
(*informal*) **cop, copper**
– Police officers of higher rank are **sergeant, inspector** and **superintendent**.
– The head of a police force is the **chief constable.**
– Someone training for the police force is a **cadet**.
– A person who investigates crimes is a **detective**.

policy *NOUN*
What is the school's policy on bullying?
• **approach, strategy, plan of action, guidelines, code, line, position, stance**

polish *VERB*
❶ *I need to polish my shoes.*
• **rub down, shine, buff, burnish, wax**
❷ *She sat down to polish the final draft of the script.*
• **refine, improve, perfect, hone, revise, edit, touch up**
➤ **polish something off**
We polished off a whole plate of sandwiches.
• **finish, get through, eat up**

polish *NOUN*
Marble can be given a high polish.
• **shine, sheen, gloss, lustre, sparkle, brightness, glaze, finish**

polished *ADJECTIVE*
❶ *She could see her face in the polished surface.*
• **shining, shiny, bright, gleaming, glossy, lustrous**
OPPOSITES dull, tarnished
❷ *The cast gave a polished performance.*
• **accomplished, skilful, masterly, expert, adept**

polite *ADJECTIVE*
They were too polite to complain.
• **courteous, well mannered, respectful, civil, well behaved, gracious, gentlemanly or ladylike, chivalrous, gallant**
OPPOSITES rude, impolite

politics *NOUN*

WORD WEB

Some terms used in uk politics:

- alliance
- AM (Assembly Member)
- assembly
- ballot
- bill
- cabinet
- campaign
- coalition
- conservative
- constituency
- constitution
- devolution
- election
- electorate
- executive
- First Minister
- general election
- government
- House of Commons
- House of Lords
- liberal
- left-wing
- lobby
- local election
- lower house
- majority
- manifesto
- Member of Parliament or MP
- minister
- ministry
- minority
- MLA (Member of the Legislative Assembly)
- MSP (Member of the Scottish Parliament)
- opinion poll
- parliament
- party
- policy
- politician
- Prime Minister
- proportional representation
- radical
- referendum
- right-wing
- socialist
- speaker
- upper house
- vote

Some terms used in other political systems:

- congress
- congressman or congresswoman
- House of Representatives
- president
- senate
- senator
- vice-president

poll *NOUN*
The results of a nationwide poll have been published.
• **election, vote, ballot**
– A vote on a particular question by all the people in a country is a **referendum**.
– An official survey to find out about the population is a **census**.

pollute *VERB*
Industrial waste has polluted the lake.
• **contaminate, poison, infect, dirty, foul**
OPPOSITE purify

pompous *ADJECTIVE*
He sounded so pompous I couldn't help smiling.
• **arrogant, self-important, haughty, conceited, pretentious, puffed up**
OPPOSITE modest

pond *NOUN*
see **pool**

pool *NOUN*
❶ *The surface of the pool was covered with frogspawn.*
• **pond**
– A larger area of water is a **lake** or (in Scotland) a **loch**.
– A salt-water lake is a **lagoon**.
– A pool of water in the desert is an **oasis**.
– A pool among rocks on a seashore is a **rock pool**.
❷ *On the floor was a pool of spilled milk.*
• **puddle, patch**
❸ *The sports centre has an indoor and an outdoor pool.*
• **swimming pool, swimming bath**

a b c d e f g h i j k l m n o p q r s t u v w x y z

A B C D E F G H I J K L M N O P Q R S T U V W X Y Z

poor *ADJECTIVE*

❶ *He was the son of a poor farm labourer.*
• **impoverished, poverty-stricken, penniless, impecunious, needy, destitute, badly off**
(*informal*) **hard up**
OPPOSITES rich, affluent

❷ *Her handwriting is very poor.*
• **bad, inferior, inadequate, unsatisfactory, substandard, deficient, imperfect, incompetent, shoddy**
OPPOSITES good, superior

❸ *The poor man had to wait for ages in the rain.*
• **unlucky, unfortunate, pitiful, wretched**
OPPOSITE lucky

poorly *ADJECTIVE*

I've been feeling poorly for weeks.
• **ill, unwell, unfit, ailing**
IDIOMS **off colour, under the weather**
OPPOSITE well

pop *NOUN & VERB*

For tips on describing sounds see **sound**.

popular *ADJECTIVE*

❶ *She is a popular children's author.*
• **well liked, well loved, celebrated, favourite**
OPPOSITES unpopular, little known

❷ *These hats have suddenly become popular.*
• **fashionable, widespread, current, in demand, in vogue**
(*informal*) **trendy, hot, big**
IDIOM **all the rage**
OPPOSITES unpopular, out of fashion

population *NOUN*

China has the largest population of any country in the world.
• **inhabitants, residents, occupants, citizens, people, populace, community**

pore *VERB*

➤ **pore over**
I've pored over the letter a hundred times.
• **examine, study, inspect, look closely at, scrutinize, peruse**

port *NOUN*

Rotterdam is a major European port.
• **harbour, docks, seaport**
– A harbour for yachts and pleasure boats is a **marina**.

portable *ADJECTIVE*

They took a portable TV on holiday.
• **transportable, mobile, compact, lightweight**

portion *NOUN*

❶ *He ordered a large portion of chips.*
• **helping, serving, ration, share, quantity, measure, serving, plateful, slice**

❷ *The central portion of the bridge collapsed.*
• **part, piece, section, division, segment**

portrait *NOUN*

This is a portrait of the artist's mother.
• **picture, image, likeness, representation, painting, drawing, photograph**
– A portrait which shows a side view of someone is a **profile**.
– A portrait which shows someone in outline is a **silhouette**.
– A portrait which exaggerates some aspect of a person is a **caricature**.

portray *VERB*

❶ *The book portrays life in rural Australia.*
• **depict, represent, show, describe, illustrate**

❷ *In the film, he portrays a notorious gangster.*
• **play, act the part of, appear as**

pose *VERB*

❶ *She loves posing in front of the camera.*
• **model, posture**

❷ *Flooding poses a serious threat at this time of year.*
• **present, put forward, offer, constitute**

➤ **pose as someone**
He posed as a newspaper reporter.
• **impersonate, pretend to be, pass yourself off as, masquerade as**

posh (*informal*) ADJECTIVE
❶ *We went to a posh restaurant.*
• **smart, stylish, high-class, upmarket, fancy, elegant, fashionable, chic, exclusive, luxury, de luxe**
(*informal*) **classy, swanky, swish, snazzy**
❷ *She has a very posh accent.*
• **upper-class, aristocratic**

position NOUN
❶ *Mark the position on the map.*
• **location, place, point, spot, site, situation, whereabouts, locality**
❷ *My arms were aching so I shifted my position slightly.*
• **pose, posture, stance**
❸ *What would you do in my position?*
• **situation, state, condition, circumstances, predicament**
❹ *He made his position on nuclear energy very clear.*
• **opinion, attitude, outlook, view, viewpoint, thinking, stand**
❺ *She now has a senior position in the government.*
• **job, post, appointment, situation, rank, status, standing**

positive ADJECTIVE
❶ *Are you positive this is the man you saw?*
• **certain, sure, convinced, assured, confident, satisfied**
OPPOSITES uncertain, doubtful
❷ *We received a positive reply.*
• **favourable, affirmative**
OPPOSITE negative
❸ *Don't you have anything positive to say?*
• **constructive, supportive, encouraging, helpful, useful, productive**
OPPOSITE negative

possess VERB
❶ *The gallery possesses a number of his early paintings.*
• **own, have**
❷ *My brother does not really possess a sense of humour.*
• **have, be blessed with, be endowed with, enjoy, boast**
❸ *What possessed you to take up snorkelling?*
• **make you think of, come over you**

possession NOUN
The photograph is no longer in my possession.
• **ownership, keeping, care, custody, charge, hands**
➤ **possessions**
The refugees had lost all of their possessions.
• **belongings, property, things, worldly goods, personal effects**

possibility NOUN
There's a possibility of snow tomorrow.
• **chance, likelihood, hope, danger, risk**

possible ADJECTIVE
❶ *Is it possible that life exists on other planets?*
• **likely, probable, conceivable, credible, plausible, imaginable**
OPPOSITES impossible, unlikely
❷ *It's not possible to get there before nightfall.*
• **feasible, practicable, viable, attainable, workable**
(*informal*) **doable**
OPPOSITES impossible, out of the question

possibly ADVERB
❶ *This is possibly the best film ever made.*
• **maybe, perhaps, arguably**
OPPOSITES definitely, without a doubt
❷ *I couldn't possibly accept the money.*
• **in any way, under any circumstances, conceivably, at all, ever**

post NOUN
❶ *The fence is supported by wooden posts.*
• **pole, pillar, shaft, stake, support, prop, strut**
❷ *I am expecting a package in the post.*
• **mail, letters, delivery**

❸ *Are you thinking of applying for the post?*
• **job, position, situation, appointment, vacancy, opening**

post *VERB*
❶ *The timetable will be posted on the noticeboard.*
• **display, put up, pin up, announce, advertise**
❷ *Did you post those letters?*
• **mail, send, dispatch**
❸ *Guards were posted along the wall.*
• **station, position, place, mount**

poster *NOUN*
He collects old film posters.
• **advertisement, notice, bill, sign, placard**

postpone *VERB*
The match has been postponed because of bad weather.
• **put off, defer, delay, put back, hold over**
– To stop a game or meeting that you intend to start again later is to **adjourn** or **suspend** it.
OPPOSITE **bring forward**

posture *NOUN*
He tried to raise himself into a sitting posture.
• **pose, position, stance, attitude**

pot *NOUN*
On the table were little pots of jam and honey.
• **jar, dish, bowl, pan, vessel**

potent *ADJECTIVE*
❶ *The local wine is potent.*
• **strong, powerful, pungent, heady, intoxicating**
❷ *She persuaded us with her potent arguments.*
• **effective, forceful, strong, compelling, persuasive, convincing**
OPPOSITE **weak**

potential *ADJECTIVE*
❶ *He is a potential Wimbledon champion.*
• **prospective, budding, future, likely, possible, probable, promising**
❷ *These floods are a potential disaster.*
• **looming, threatening**

potential *NOUN*
She is a young actress with great potential.
• **prospects, promise, capability, future**

potion *NOUN*
The witch gave him a magic potion to drink.
• **concoction, brew, compound, medicine, drug, draught**

pottery *NOUN*

WORD WEB

Some types of pottery:

- **bone china**
- **china**
- **earthenware**
- **porcelain**
- **raku**
- **slipware**
- **stoneware**
- **terracotta**

- Pottery used to serve food and drink is **crockery**.
- A formal word for pottery is **ceramics**.
- A person who creates pottery is a **potter** or **ceramic artist**.

pouch *NOUN*
He kept his coins in a leather pouch.
• **bag, purse, sack**

poultry *NOUN*
see **bird**

pounce *VERB*
A tiger will stalk its prey before pouncing.
• **jump, leap, spring, swoop down, lunge, attack, ambush**

pound *VERB*
❶ *Huge waves pounded against the sea wall.*
• **batter, buffet, beat, hit, smash, dash**

❷ *I heard heavy footsteps pounding up the stairs.*
• **stamp, stomp, tramp, thud, thump, clump, clomp**
❸ *She felt her heart pounding faster.*
• **beat, thump, hammer, pulse, race**

pour *VERB*
❶ *Sunlight poured through the front window.*
• **flow, stream, run, gush, spill, flood**
❷ *I poured some milk into a saucer.*
• **tip, splash, spill**
(*informal*) **slosh**
– To pour wine or other liquid from one container to another is to **decant** it.
❸ *It's absolutely pouring outside!*
• **rain heavily, teem, lash down, tip down, pelt down**
(*informal*) **bucket down**
❹ *Crowds poured through the gate.*
• **surge, stream, crowd, swarm, throng**

poverty *NOUN*
Bad harvests have caused widespread poverty and famine.
• **pennilessness, hardship, need, want, destitution**
– Extreme poverty is known as **abject poverty**.
OPPOSITES wealth, affluence

powder *NOUN*
Ginger root is dried and then ground to powder.
• **dust, particles, grains**

powdery *ADJECTIVE*
The ground was covered with powdery snow.
• **powder-like, fine, light, loose, dusty, grainy, sandy, chalky**

power *NOUN*
❶ *The film shows the immense power of a tsunami.*
• **strength, force, might, energy, vigour**
❷ *As a storyteller he has the power to move an audience to tears.*
• **skill, talent, ability, capacity, capability**
❸ *Roman slave-owners had absolute power over their slaves.*
• **authority, command, control, dominance, domination, sway**

powerful *ADJECTIVE*
❶ *He has one of the most powerful serves in tennis.*
• **strong, forceful, hard, mighty, vigorous, formidable, potent**
OPPOSITES weak, ineffective
❷ *Persia was once a powerful empire.*
• **influential, leading, commanding, dominant, high-powered, formidable**
OPPOSITES powerless, weak
❸ *She used some powerful arguments.*
• **strong, convincing, compelling, effective, persuasive, impressive**

powerless *ADJECTIVE*
❶ *A normal bullet is powerless against a werewolf.*
• **ineffective, impotent, useless, weak, feeble**
❷ *The citizens were powerless to defend themselves.*
• **helpless, defenceless, vulnerable**

practical *ADJECTIVE*
❶ *We need a practical person to lead the team.*
• **down-to-earth, matter-of-fact, sensible, level-headed, commonsensical, no-nonsense**
OPPOSITE impractical
❷ *The idea was not practical from the start.*
• **workable, realistic, sensible, feasible, viable, achievable**
(*informal*) **doable**
OPPOSITE impractical
❸ *Do you have any practical experience of sailing?*
• **real, actual, hands-on**
OPPOSITE theoretical

practically *ADVERB*
The place was practically deserted.
• **almost, just about, nearly, virtually, as good as**

practice *NOUN*

❶ *We have extra football practice this week.*
• **training, exercises, drill, preparation, rehearsal, run-through**
❷ *His usual practice was to work until midnight.*
• **custom, habit, convention, routine, procedure**
➤ **in practice**
What will the plan involve in practice?
• **in effect, in reality, actually, really**

practise *VERB*

❶ *I've spent weeks practising for my music exam.*
• **do exercises, rehearse, train, drill, prepare**
IDIOM **go through your paces**
– To practise just before the start of a performance is to **warm up.**
❷ *Let's practise that scene again.*
• **rehearse, go over, go through, run through, work at**
❸ *She was accused of practising witchcraft.*
• **do, perform, carry out, observe, follow, pursue**

praise *VERB*

The judge praised her for her bravery.
• **commend, applaud, pay tribute to, compliment, congratulate, speak highly of**
(*informal*) **rave about**
IDIOM **sing the praises of**
OPPOSITES **criticize, condemn**

praise *NOUN*

His performance has received a lot of praise.
• **approval, acclaim, admiration, commendation, compliments, congratulations, plaudits**
IDIOM **a pat on the back**

prance *VERB*

The lead guitarist was prancing about on stage.
• **leap, skip, romp, cavort, caper, frolic**

precarious *ADJECTIVE*

❶ *She was in a precarious position on the ledge.*
• **dangerous, perilous, risky, hazardous**
OPPOSITE **safe**
❷ *That chimney looks a bit precarious.*
• **unsafe, unstable, unsteady, insecure, shaky, wobbly, rickety**
OPPOSITE **secure**

precaution *NOUN*

Always wear a helmet as a precaution.
• **safeguard, safety measure, preventative measure**

precede *VERB*

A firework display preceded the concert.
• **come before, go before, lead into, lead up to**
IDIOM **pave the way for**
OPPOSITES **follow, succeed**

precious *ADJECTIVE*

❶ *Trading ships arrived carrying precious silks and spices.*
• **valuable, costly, expensive, priceless**
OPPOSITE **worthless**
For precious stones see **gem**.
❷ *Her most precious possession was a faded letter.*
• **treasured, cherished, valued, prized, dearest, beloved**

precise *ADJECTIVE*

❶ *Can you tell me the precise time?*
• **exact, accurate, correct, true, right**
OPPOSITE **rough**
❷ *We were given precise instructions.*
• **careful, detailed, specific, particular, definite, explicit**
OPPOSITES **vague, imprecise**

predict *VERB*

Scientists try to predict when earthquakes will happen.
• **forecast, foresee, foretell, prophesy**

predictable *ADJECTIVE*

The outcome of the match was predictable.
• **foreseeable, to be expected, likely, unsurprising, inevitable**
OPPOSITE **unpredictable**

prediction *NOUN*
What is your prediction for next year?
• **forecast, prophecy, prognosis**

preface *NOUN*
The title of the book is explained in the preface.
• **introduction, prologue**

prefer *VERB*
Would you prefer rice or pasta?
• **rather have, sooner have, go for, opt for, plump for, choose, fancy**

preferable *ADJECTIVE*
➤ **preferable to**
She finds country life preferable to living in the city.
• **better than, superior to, more suitable than, more desirable than**
OPPOSITE inferior to

preference *NOUN*
I have a slight preference for the red one.
• **liking, fondness, taste, fancy, partiality, inclination, penchant**

pregnant *ADJECTIVE*
She was six months pregnant at the time.
• **expectant, carrying a baby** (*informal*) **expecting**
– A pregnant woman is an **expectant mother**.

prehistoric *ADJECTIVE*

WORD WEB

Prehistoric remains:

➤ barrow or tumulus
➤ cromlech or stone circle
➤ dolmen
➤ hill fort
➤ menhir or standing stone

- A person who studies prehistory by examining remains is an archaeologist.

Prehistoric periods:

➤ Stone Age
➤ Bronze Age
➤ Iron Age
➤ Ice Age

- Formal names for the Old, Middle and New Stone Ages are **Palaeolithic, Mesolithic** and **Neolithic** periods.
- A prehistoric species of humans who lived during the Stone Age were the Neanderthals.

Some prehistoric animals:

➤ cave bear
➤ dinosaur
➤ glyptodon
➤ ground sloth
➤ macrauchenia
➤ sabre-toothed cat or smilodon
➤ sabre-toothed squirrel
➤ woolly mammoth
➤ woolly rhino

- A person who studies fossils of prehistoric life is a **palaeontologist**.

prejudice *NOUN*
The school has a policy against any form of racial prejudice.
• **discrimination, intolerance, bigotry, narrow-mindedness, bias, partiality**
– Prejudice against other races is **racism**.
– Prejudice against other nations is **xenophobia**.
– Prejudice against the other sex is **sexism**.
– Prejudice against older or younger people is **ageism**.
OPPOSITES impartiality, tolerance

preliminary *ADJECTIVE*
Our team was knocked out in the preliminary round.
• **first, initial, introductory, early, opening, preparatory**

prelude *NOUN*
The award was a prelude to a glittering career.
• **introduction, precursor, preamble, lead-in, opening**
OPPOSITE swansong

premises *PLURAL NOUN*
No one is allowed on the premises after dark.
• **property, grounds, site, buildings**

A B C D E F G H I J K L M N O P Q R S T U V W X Y Z

preoccupied *ADJECTIVE*
➤ **preoccupied with something**
She was so preoccupied with her work that she forgot the time.
• **absorbed in, engrossed in, wrapped up in, concerned with, involved with, obsessed with**

preparation *NOUN*
An event like this requires months of preparation.
• **planning, organization, arrangement, setting-up, development, groundwork**

prepare *VERB*
❶ *The city is preparing to host the Olympics.*
• **get ready, plan, make preparations, make arrangements, make provisions**
– To prepare for a play is to **rehearse**.
– To prepare to take part in a sport is to **train**.
❷ *We are preparing a surprise party for her.*
• **arrange, organize, make arrangements for, plan, set up**
❸ *He was in the kitchen preparing lunch.*
• **make, produce, put together, make ready, get ready, assemble**

prepared *ADJECTIVE*
❶ *I don't feel prepared for this exam at all.*
• **ready, all set**
❷ *Are you prepared to take the risk?*
• **willing, disposed, inclined, of a mind**

presence *NOUN*
Your presence is required upstairs.
• **attendance, appearance, existence**

present *ADJECTIVE*
❶ *Is everyone present?*
• **here, in attendance, at hand**
❷ *He is the present world record holder.*
• **current, existing**
OPPOSITES past, former

present *NOUN*
❶ *The opening chapter takes place in the present.*
• **now, today, the here and now, the present time, nowadays**
OPPOSITES past, future
❷ *I have a birthday present for you.*
• **gift, offering, donation**

present *VERB*
❶ *A local celebrity was asked to present the prizes.*
• **hand over, award, bestow**
❷ *I'd like to present my latest invention.*
• **introduce, put forward, show, display, exhibit, make known**
❸ *Our drama group is presenting a series of one-act plays.*
• **put on, perform, stage, mount**
❹ *Translating a poem presents a number of problems.*
• **offer, provide, set out, open up**

preserve *VERB*
❶ *Salt was used to preserve meat and fish.*
• **keep, save, store**
❷ *We are campaigning to preserve the rainforest.*
• **look after, protect, conserve, defend, safeguard, maintain**
OPPOSITE destroy

press *VERB*
❶ *The olives are then pressed to extract their oil.*
• **push, squeeze, squash, crush, cram, compress, hold down, force down**
❷ *She pressed her blouse for the party.*
• **iron, flatten, smooth**
❸ *I must press you for an answer.*
• **urge, push, force, implore** (*informal*) **lean on**

press *NOUN*
❶ *The story has been reported in the press.*
• **newspapers, magazines**
❷ *All the press came to the opening night of the show.*
• **journalists, reporters, the media**

pressure *NOUN*

❶ *Apply steady pressure to the wound.*
• **force, compression, squeezing, weight, load**
❷ *I've been under a lot of pressure lately.*
• **stress, strain, tension**
❸ *The newspapers are putting pressure on her to resign.*
• **influence, persuasion, intimidation, coercion, duress**

prestige *NOUN*

There's a lot of prestige in winning an Oscar.
• **glory, honour, credit, renown, distinction, status, kudos**

prestigious *ADJECTIVE*

Her books have won several prestigious awards.
• **distinguished, respected, renowned, highly regarded**

presume *VERB*

❶ *I presume you know how to use a camera.*
• **assume, suppose, imagine, expect**
IDIOM **I take it**
❷ *I wouldn't presume to doubt your word.*
• **dare, venture, be so bold as, go so far as**

pretend *VERB*

❶ *Let's pretend we're snakes.*
• **act like, make as if, make believe, play at**
❷ *Is he really crying or just pretending?*
• **bluff, sham, pose, fake it**
(*informal*) **kid on, put it on**

pretend *ADJECTIVE* (*informal*)

That's just a pretend spider, not a real one.
• **fake, false, artificial, made-up, imaginary**

pretty *ADJECTIVE*

That's a pretty brooch you're wearing.
• **attractive, beautiful, lovely, nice, appealing, pleasing, charming, dainty, picturesque**
(*informal*) **cute**
OPPOSITE **ugly**

prevent *VERB*

❶ *The driver could do nothing to prevent the accident.*
• **avert, avoid, stop, forestall, head off**
IDIOM **nip in the bud**
❷ *Her illness prevented her from travelling.*
• **stop, bar, block, obstruct, impede, inhibit, thwart**
❸ *Some people say that garlic prevents colds.*
• **stave off, ward off, fend off**
IDIOM **keep at bay**

previous *ADJECTIVE*

❶ *The couple had met on a previous occasion.*
• **earlier, former, prior, past**
❷ *There had been a storm the previous night.*
• **preceding, former, last, most recent**
OPPOSITE **subsequent**

prey *NOUN*

The eagle swooped down on its prey.
• **quarry, kill, victim**
OPPOSITE **predator**

prey *VERB*

➤ **prey on**
Owls prey on small animals.
• **hunt, kill, feed on**

price *NOUN*

❶ *What's the price of a return ticket to Sydney?*
• **cost, charge, fee, fare, rate, expense, amount, figure, sum**
– The price you pay to send a letter is the **postage**.
– The price you pay to use a private road, bridge or tunnel is a **toll**.
❷ *He was paying the price of failure.*
• **consequence, result, penalty, cost, downside**

priceless *ADJECTIVE*

❶ *The museum contains many priceless works of art.*
• **precious, rare, invaluable,**

irreplaceable, expensive, costly
OPPOSITE worthless
❷ (*informal*) *The joke she told at the end was priceless.*
• funny, amusing, comic, hilarious, witty

prick *VERB*
Prick the pastry all over with a fork.
• pierce, puncture, stab, jab, perforate, spike

prickle *NOUN*
A hedgehog uses its prickles for defence.
• spike, spine, needle, barb, thorn
– The prickles on a hedgehog or porcupine are also called **quills**.

prickly *ADJECTIVE*
❶ *Holly leaves are very prickly.*
• spiky, spiked, thorny, spiny, bristly
❷ *He's quite a prickly character.*
• bad-tempered, irritable, grumpy, tetchy, testy

pride *NOUN*
❶ *She takes great pride in her work.*
• satisfaction, pleasure, delight, joy, fulfilment, gratification
❷ *My heart swelled with pride.*
• self-esteem, self-respect, dignity, honour
OPPOSITE shame
❸ *Finally, the hero is forced to swallow his pride.*
• arrogance, conceitedness, vanity, self-importance, big-headedness, egotism, snobbery
OPPOSITE humility

priest *NOUN*
see **religion**

prim *ADJECTIVE*
She was a rather prim and proper young lady.
• prudish, strait-laced, formal, demure

primarily *ADVERB*
The website is aimed primarily at teenagers.
• chiefly, especially, mainly, mostly, largely, predominantly, principally, above all, first and foremost

primary *ADJECTIVE*
The primary aim of a website is to communicate.
• main, chief, principal, foremost, most important, key, central
OPPOSITE secondary

prime *ADJECTIVE*
❶ *The bad weather was the prime cause of the accident.*
• main, chief, top, principal, foremost, leading
(*informal*) number-one
❷ *The dish is made from prime cuts of meat.*
• best, superior, first-class, choice, select, top-quality, finest

primitive *ADJECTIVE*
❶ *Primitive humans were hunters rather than farmers.*
• ancient, early, prehistoric, primeval
OPPOSITES civilized, advanced
❷ *It was a primitive type of computer.*
• crude, basic, simple, rudimentary, undeveloped
OPPOSITES advanced, sophisticated

principal *ADJECTIVE*
What is the principal aim of the experiment?
• main, chief, primary, foremost, most important, key, central, predominant, pre-eminent, leading, supreme, major, top
OPPOSITES secondary, minor

principle *NOUN*
❶ *He follows the principles of Buddhism.*
• rule, standard, code, ethic, precept, doctrine, creed
❷ *She taught me the principles of good design.*
• basics, fundamentals, essentials

print *NOUN*
❶ *The tiny print was difficult to read.*
• type, printing, lettering, letters, characters
❷ *Detectives searched the building for prints.*
• mark, impression, footprint,

fingerprint
❸ *On the wall was a full-size print of the Mona Lisa.*
• **copy, reproduction, duplicate, photograph**

priority *NOUN*
❶ *Traffic on the main road has priority.*
• **precedence, right of way**
❷ *Emergency cases are given priority in hospital.*
• **preference, precedence, favour, first place**

prise *VERB*
Slowly, we began to prise the lid off the chest.
• **lever, force, wrench**

prison *NOUN*
He was sentenced to six months in prison.
• **jail, imprisonment, confinement, custody**

prisoner *NOUN*
Two escaped prisoners are on the run.
• **convict, inmate, captive**
(*informal*) **jailbird, con**
– A person who is held prisoner until some demand is met is a **hostage**.
– A person who is captured by the opposite side during a war is a **prisoner-of-war**.

private *ADJECTIVE*
❶ *Always keep your password private.*
• **secret, confidential, personal, intimate**
– Secret official documents are **classified** documents.
OPPOSITES **public, known**
❷ *Can we go somewhere a little more private?*
• **quiet, secluded, hidden, concealed**
OPPOSITES **public, open**

privilege *NOUN*
Club members enjoy special privileges.
• **advantage, benefit, concession, right, entitlement**

privileged *ADJECTIVE*
❶ *She comes from a privileged family background.*
• **affluent, wealthy, prosperous, rich, well off, well-to-do**
OPPOSITES **disadvantaged, poor**
❷ *I feel privileged to be here.*
• **honoured, fortunate, lucky, favoured**

prize *NOUN*
Our team won first prize in the relay race.
• **award, reward, trophy**
– Money that you win as a prize is your **winnings**.
– Prize money that keeps increasing until someone wins it is a **jackpot**.

prize *VERB*
They prize their freedom above all else.
• **treasure, value, cherish, hold dear, esteem, revere**
IDIOM **set great store by**
OPPOSITE **disdain**

probable *ADJECTIVE*
A burst pipe was the most probable cause of the flood.
• **likely, feasible, possible, expected, predictable**
OPPOSITE **improbable**

probe *VERB*
❶ *The inquiry will probe the circumstances surrounding the accident.*
• **investigate, inquire into, examine, study, scrutinize, look into, go into**
❷ *This small spacecraft will probe the outer solar system.*
• **explore, penetrate, see into, plumb**

problem *NOUN*
❶ *I'm having problems with my computer.*
• **difficulty, trouble, complication, snag, hitch, hiccup, setback**
(*informal*) **headache**
❷ *I was struggling with a complicated maths problem.*
• **puzzle, question, riddle, conundrum**
(*informal*) **brain-teaser, poser**

procedure *NOUN*
What is the procedure for making a complaint?
• **method, process, system, mechanism, practice, routine, technique, way**

proceed *VERB*
❶ *The sheep proceeded slowly along the lane.*
• **go forward, move forward, make your way, advance, progress**
❷ *NASA has decided to proceed with the launch.*
• **go ahead, carry on, continue, get on, press on, push on**
❸ *The stranger proceeded to tell me his life story.*
• **go on to, move on to, begin to, start to**

proceedings *PLURAL NOUN*
A thunderstorm interrupted the day's proceedings.
• **events, happenings, activities, affairs** (*informal*) **goings-on**

proceeds *PLURAL NOUN*
All proceeds from the auction will go to charity.
• **income, takings, money, earnings, profit, revenue, returns**

process *NOUN*
This is a new process for storing solar energy.
• **method, procedure, operation, system, technique, way, means**

process *VERB*
We are still processing your application.
• **deal with, attend to, see to, handle, treat, prepare**

procession *NOUN*
The procession made its way slowly down the hill.
• **parade, march, column, line**
– A procession of mourners at a funeral is a **cortège**.

proclaim *VERB*
Two teams were proclaimed joint winners of the title.
• **declare, announce, pronounce, state**

prod *VERB*
He prodded the worm to see if it was alive.
• **poke, dig, jab, nudge, push**

produce *VERB*
❶ *Some lorries produce a lot of fumes.*
• **create, generate, emit, give out, yield**
❷ *The company produces computer games.*
• **make, manufacture, construct, fabricate, put together, assemble, turn out**
❸ *The writers have produced an award-winning comedy.*
• **create, compose, invent, think up, come up with**
❹ *His speech produced boos and whistles from the crowd.*
• **provoke, arouse, stimulate, prompt, give rise to, result in, trigger**
❺ *Brandon produced a letter from his pocket.*
• **bring out, pull out, fish out, extract, present, show, reveal**

produce *NOUN*
She works in a shop which sells organic produce.
• **food, foodstuffs, crops, fruit and vegetables**

product *NOUN*
❶ *The company launched a new range of beauty products.*
• **article, commodity, merchandise, goods**
❷ *The famine is the product of years of drought.*
• **result, consequence, outcome, upshot**

production *NOUN*
❶ *The firm is famous for the production of luxury cars.*
• **manufacture, making, construction, creation, assembly, building, fabrication**
❷ *Production at the factory has increased thus year.*
• **output, yield**
❸ *We went to see a production of 'Oliver'.*
• **performance, show, staging, presentation**

productive *ADJECTIVE*
❶ *She had a long and productive literary career.*
• **prolific, creative, fruitful, fertile**
❷ *It wasn't a very productive meeting.*
• **useful, valuable, worthwhile, constructive, profitable**
OPPOSITE unproductive

profession *NOUN*
Why did you chose acting as a profession?
• **career, job, occupation, vocation, business, trade, line of work**

professional *ADJECTIVE*
❶ *His ambition is to be a professional footballer.*
• **paid, full-time**
OPPOSITES amateur, non-professional
❷ *The plans were drawn by a professional architect.*
• **qualified, chartered, skilled, trained, experienced**
❸ *This is a very professional piece of work.*
• **skilled, expert, proficient, accomplished, competent, polished**
OPPOSITE incompetent

proficient *ADJECTIVE*
It takes years to become proficient in judo.
• **skilful, skilled, accomplished, capable, expert, able**
OPPOSITE incompetent

profile *NOUN*
❶ *He was a handsome man with a strong profile.*
• **silhouette, side view, outline, shape**
❷ *Write a short profile of a famous person.*
• **biography, portrait, sketch, study, account**

profit *NOUN*
The business made a small profit last year.
• **gain, surplus, excess**
– The extra money you get on your savings is **interest**.
OPPOSITE loss

programme *NOUN*
❶ *There was a really good programme on TV last night.*
• **broadcast, show, production, transmission**
❷ *We worked out a varied programme of events.*
• **plan, schedule, timetable, calendar, line-up**
– A list of things to be done at a meeting is an **agenda**.
– A list of places to visit on a journey is an **itinerary**.

progress *NOUN*
❶ *Scientists monitored the progress of the hurricane.*
• **journey, route, movement, travels**
❷ *I'm not making much progress with the trumpet.*
• **advance, development, improvement, growth, headway, step forward**
– An important piece of progress is a **breakthrough**.

progress *VERB*
❶ *You can now progress to the next level of the game.*
• **go forward, move forward, proceed, advance**
❷ *The chicks are progressing at a steady rate.*
• **develop, grow, improve**
(*informal*) **come along**

prohibit *VERB*
Taking photographs is prohibited here.
• **ban, forbid, disallow, outlaw, rule out, veto**
OPPOSITES permit, allow

project *NOUN*
❶ *We did a history project on the Victorians.*
• **assignment, task, activity, piece of research**
❷ *There is a project to create a bird sanctuary in the area.*
• **plan, scheme, undertaking, enterprise, venture, proposal, bid**

project *VERB*
❶ *A narrow ledge projects from the cliff.*
• **extend, protrude, stick out, jut out, overhang**
❷ *The laser projects a narrow beam of light.*
• **emit, throw out, cast, shine**
❸ *He likes to project an image of absent-minded brilliance.*
• **give out, send out, convey, communicate**

prolong *VERB*
There is no point in prolonging the argument.
• **extend, lengthen, protract, stretch out, draw out, drag out, spin out**
OPPOSITES **shorten, curtail**

prominent *ADJECTIVE*
❶ *She had a long nose and prominent teeth.*
• **noticeable, conspicuous, striking, eye-catching, protruding**
OPPOSITE **inconspicuous**
❷ *He became a prominent member of the government.*
• **well-known, famous, celebrated, major, leading, notable, distinguished, eminent**
OPPOSITES **unknown, obscure**

promise *NOUN*
❶ *We had promises of help from many people.*
• **assurance, pledge, guarantee, commitment, vow, oath, word of honour**
❷ *This group of young actors show great promise.*
• **potential, talent, ability, aptitude**

promise *VERB*
❶ *Do you promise not to tell anyone?*
• **give your word, guarantee, swear, take an oath, vow, pledge**
❷ *I promise you I'll be there.*
• **assure, swear to, give your word to**

promising *ADJECTIVE*
❶ *The weather looks promising for tomorrow.*
• **encouraging, hopeful, favourable, auspicious**
❷ *She is a promising young singer.*
• **talented, gifted, budding, aspiring** (*informal*) **up-and-coming**

promote *VERB*
❶ *Rory has been promoted to captain.*
• **move up, advance, upgrade, elevate**
❷ *The band are here to promote their new album.*
• **advertise, publicize, market, push** (*informal*) **plug, hype**
❸ *The school launched a campaign to promote healthy eating.*
• **encourage, foster, advocate, back, support, boost**

prompt *ADJECTIVE*
I received a prompt reply to my email.
• **quick, speedy, swift, rapid, punctual, immediate, instant, direct**
OPPOSITES **late, belated**

prompt *VERB*
What prompted you to start writing a diary?
• **induce, lead, cause, motivate, persuade, inspire, stimulate, encourage, provoke, spur**

prone *ADJECTIVE*
❶ *My sister is prone to exaggerate things.*
• **inclined, apt, liable, likely, given**
❷ *The victim was lying prone on the floor.*
• **face down, on the front**

pronounce *VERB*
❶ *Try to pronounce the words clearly.*
• **say, speak, utter, articulate, enunciate, sound**
❷ *The man was pronounced dead on arrival.*
• **declare, announce, proclaim, judge**

pronounced *ADJECTIVE*
She spoke with a pronounced Australian accent.
• **marked, strong, clear, distinct, definite, noticeable, obvious, striking, unmistakable, prominent**
OPPOSITE **imperceptible**

proof *NOUN*
Do you have any proof of your identity?
• **evidence, confirmation, verification, authentication**

prop *NOUN*
The tunnel roof is supported by metal props.
• **support, strut, pole, post, upright**
– A stick used to support an injured leg is a **crutch**.
– Part of a building which props up a wall is a **buttress**.

prop *VERB*
I propped my bike against the railing.
• **lean, rest, stand, balance**
➤ **prop something up**
The old tree was propped up with posts.
• **support, hold up, reinforce, shore up**

propel *VERB*
The steamboat was propelled by a huge paddle wheel.
• **drive, push, power, move forward**

proper *ADJECTIVE*
❶ *This is the proper way to hold a tennis racket.*
• **correct, right, accepted, established, conventional, appropriate, suitable**
OPPOSITES **wrong, incorrect**
❷ *He looks just like a proper movie star.*
• **real, actual, genuine, true**
OPPOSITE **fake**
❸ *I could do with a proper meal.*
• **good, decent, adequate, substantial**
OPPOSITE **inadequate**
❹ *Her whole family is very proper and polite.*
• **formal, correct, respectable, conventional, polite**
OPPOSITES **informal, unconventional**
❺ (*informal*) *I must have looked a proper idiot!*
• **complete, total, utter, absolute, thorough, downright**
(*informal*) **right**

property *NOUN*
❶ *This box contains lost property.*
• **belongings, possessions, goods, personal effects**
❷ *The newspaper has lists of property for sale.*
• **buildings, houses, land, premises**
❸ *Many herbs have healing properties.*
• **quality, characteristic, feature, attribute, trait**

prophecy *NOUN*
The witch's prophecy came true.
• **prediction, forecast**

prophesy *VERB*
Many people have been prophesying disaster.
• **predict, forecast, foresee, foretell**

proportion *NOUN*
❶ *A large proportion of the earth's surface is covered by sea.*
• **part, section, portion, segment, share, fraction, percentage**
❷ *What is the proportion of girls to boys in the class?*
• **ratio, balance, distribution, relationship**
➤ **proportions**
The dining hall was a room of large proportions.
• **size, dimensions, measurements, area, expanse**

proposal *NOUN*
There is a proposal to build a new skate park.
• **plan, project, scheme, suggestion, proposition, recommendation**

propose *VERB*
❶ *We are proposing a change in the rules.*
• **suggest, ask for, put forward, submit, recommend**
❷ *How do you propose to pay for this?*
• **intend, mean, plan, aim**

proprietor *NOUN*
Who is the proprietor of the bicycle shop?
• **manager, owner, landlord or landlady**
(*informal*) **boss**

prosecute *VERB*
Anyone caught shoplifting will be prosecuted.
• **charge, take to court, bring to trial, indict**
– To take someone to court to try to get money from them is to **sue** them.

prospect *NOUN*
❶ *There is little prospect of success.*
• **chance, hope, promise, expectation, likelihood, possibility, probability**
❷ *The terrace outside has a prospect over the sea.*
• **outlook, view, vista, panorama**

prosper *VERB*
Over time, the settlement prospered.
• **do well, be successful, flourish, thrive, grow, progress, boom**
OPPOSITES fail, flounder

prosperity *NOUN*
Tourism has brought prosperity to the region.
• **wealth, affluence, growth, success**

prosperous *ADJECTIVE*
She was the daughter of a prosperous farmer.
• **wealthy, rich, well-off, well-to-do, affluent, successful, thriving, booming**
OPPOSITE poor

protect *VERB*
❶ *The magpie was protecting its nest.*
• **guard, defend, keep safe, safeguard, secure, keep from harm**
OPPOSITE neglect
❷ *Sunscreen will protect your skin from harmful rays.*
• **shield, shade, shelter, screen, insulate**
OPPOSITE expose

protection *NOUN*
The trees gave some protection from the rain.
• **shelter, cover, defence, insulation, security, refuge, sanctuary**

protest *NOUN*
❶ *There were protests at the plan to close the cinema.*
• **complaint, objection**
– A general protest is an **outcry**.
❷ *Supporters staged a protest outside parliament.*
• **demonstration, march, rally, sit-in**
(*informal*) **demo**

protest *VERB*
We wrote a letter protesting about the programme.
• **complain, make a protest, object (to), take exception (to), take issue (with), express disapproval (of)**

protrude *VERB*
His tongue protruded from his lips.
• **stick out, poke out, bulge, swell, project, stand out, jut out**

proud *ADJECTIVE*
❶ *You should be proud of your work this year.*
• **delighted (with), pleased (with), satisfied, gratified**
OPPOSITE ashamed (of)
❷ *He's too proud to admit his mistakes.*
• **conceited, arrogant, vain, haughty, superior, self-important, pompous**
(*informal*) **stuck-up, big-headed**
OPPOSITE humble

prove *VERB*
❶ *Can you prove you were at home on the night of the murder?*
• **demonstrate, provide proof, provide evidence, establish, confirm, verify**
OPPOSITE disprove
❷ *The idea proved unpopular with the public.*
• **turn out to be, be found to be**

proverb *NOUN*
see **saying**

provide *VERB*
❶ *We'll provide the tea and coffee.*
• **supply, contribute, arrange for, lay on, come up with**
– To provide food and drink for people is to **cater** for them.

❷ *Our website should provide you with all the information you need.*
• **equip, supply, furnish, issue**

provisions *PLURAL NOUN*
We have enough provisions for a week.
• **supplies, food and drink, rations, stores**

provoke *VERB*
❶ *Rattlesnakes are dangerous if provoked.*
• **annoy, irritate, anger, enrage, incense, infuriate, exasperate, madden, nettle, rile, taunt, goad**
(*informal*) **wind up**
OPPOSITE pacify
❷ *The decision provoked anger from the crowd.*
• **arouse, produce, prompt, cause, generate, instigate, induce, stimulate, trigger, kindle, spark off, stir up**

prowl *VERB*
Dogs prowled about at night.
• **creep, sneak, slink, steal, skulk, roam**

prudent *ADJECTIVE*
❶ *It would be prudent to get some advice first.*
• **wise, sensible, shrewd**
OPPOSITES unwise, rash
❷ *She has always been prudent with her money.*
• **careful, cautious, thoughtful, thrifty**
OPPOSITES wasteful, reckless

prune *VERB*
Roses should be pruned every spring.
• **cut back, trim, clip, shear**

pry *VERB*
I don't mean to pry, but I overheard your conversation.
• **be curious, be inquisitive, interfere**
(*informal*) **be nosy, nose around, snoop**
➤ **pry into something**
She was always prying into other people's affairs.
• **interfere in, meddle in, spy on**
IDIOM (*informal*) **poke your nose into**

psychological *ADJECTIVE*
The doctor thinks her illness is psychological.
• **mental, emotional**
OPPOSITE physical

public *ADJECTIVE*
❶ *The public entrance is at the front.*
• **common, communal, general, open, shared, collective**
OPPOSITE private
❷ *The name of the author is now public knowledge.*
• **known, acknowledged, published, available, open, general, universal**
OPPOSITE secret

public *NOUN*
➤ **the public**
This part of the house is not open to the public.
• **people, everyone, the community, society, the nation**

publication *NOUN*
❶ *She is celebrating the publication of her first novel.*
• **issuing, printing, production, appearance**
❷ *Here is a list of our latest publications.*
• **book, newspaper, magazine, periodical, title, work**

publicity *NOUN*
❶ *The band got some free publicity for their latest album.*
• **advertising, advertisements, promotion**
(*informal*) **hype, build-up**
❷ *He is an actor who shies away from publicity.*
• **attention, exposure, the limelight**
IDIOM **the public eye**

publish *VERB*
❶ *The magazine is published twice a month.*
• **issue, print, produce, bring out, release, circulate**
❷ *When will they publish the results?*
• **announce, declare, disclose, make known, make public, report, reveal**

– To publish information on radio or TV is to **broadcast** it.

pudding *NOUN*
There is strawberry ice cream for pudding.
• **dessert, sweet**
(*informal*) **afters**

puff *NOUN*
❶ *A puff of wind caught his hat.*
• **gust, draught, breath, flurry**
❷ *A puff of smoke rose from the chimney.*
• **cloud, whiff, waft, wisp**

puff *VERB*
❶ *High chimneys puffed clouds of black smoke.*
• **blow out, send out, emit, belch**
❷ *A red-faced man stood puffing in the doorway.*
• **breathe heavily, pant, gasp, wheeze**
❸ *The sails puffed out as the wind rose.*
• **become inflated, billow, swell**

pull *VERB*
❶ *Can you pull your chair a bit closer?*
• **drag, draw, haul, lug, trail, tow**
OPPOSITE **push**
❷ *Be careful, you nearly pulled my arm off!*
• **tug, rip, wrench, jerk, pluck**
(*informal*) **yank**
➤ **pull off**
They've pulled off an amazing stunt.
• **achieve, accomplish, manage, fulfil, bring off**
➤ **pull out**
❶ *The dentist pulled out one of my teeth.*
• **extract, take out, remove**
❷ *One team had to pull out of the race.*
• **back out, withdraw, retire, step down, bow out**
(*informal*) **quit**
➤ **pull through**
It was a bad accident, but the doctors expect him to pull through.
• **get better, recover, revive, rally, survive**
➤ **pull up**
A taxi pulled up at the door.
• **draw up, stop, halt**

pulse *NOUN*
❶ *See if you can feel your own pulse.*
• **heartbeat, heart rate**
❷ *I love the pulse of Brazilian samba music.*
• **beat, rhythm, throb, drumming**

pump *VERB*
The crew had to pump water out of the boat.
• **drain, draw off, empty**
– To move liquid between containers through a tube is to **siphon** it.
➤ **pump up**
You need to pump up the tyre.
• **inflate, blow up**
OPPOSITES **deflate, let down**

punch *VERB*
❶ *She punched him on the nose.*
• **strike, hit, jab, poke, prod, thump, smash**
(*informal*) **biff, slug, sock**
SEE ALSO **hit**
❷ *I need to punch a hole through the card.*
• **bore, pierce, puncture**

punch *NOUN*
He received a punch on the nose.
• **blow, hit, box, jab, poke, thump, smash**
(*informal*) **biff, slug, sock**

punctual *ADJECTIVE*
Please be punctual so we can start early.
• **prompt, on time, on schedule, in good time**
OPPOSITE **late**

punctuation *NOUN*

WORD WEB

Punctuation marks:

- ➤ apostrophe
- ➤ brackets
- ➤ colon
- ➤ comma
- ➤ dash
- ➤ exclamation mark
- ➤ full stop
- ➤ hyphen
- ➤ question mark
- ➤ inverted commas or speech marks
- ➤ semicolon
- ➤ square brackets

Other marks used in writing:

- ➤ accent
- ➤ asterisk
- ➤ at sign
- ➤ bullet point
- ➤ capital letters
- ➤ emoticon
- ➤ forward slash

For tips on using punctuation see the Young Writer's Toolkit.

puncture *NOUN*

❶ *I found the puncture in my tyre.*
• **hole, perforation, rupture, leak**
❷ *I had a puncture on the way home.*
• **burst tyre, flat tyre**

puncture *VERB*

A nail must have punctured the tyre.
• **perforate, pierce, rupture**

punish *VERB*

Anyone who breaks the rules will be punished.
• **penalize, discipline, chastise**

punishment *NOUN*

The punishment for dropping litter is a fine.
• **penalty, sentence**
– Punishing someone by taking their life is **capital punishment** or **execution**.

puny *ADJECTIVE*

He was rather a puny child.
• **delicate, weak, feeble, frail, slight, undersized**
(*informal*) **weedy**
OPPOSITES strong, sturdy

pupil *NOUN*

How many pupils are in the class?
• **schoolchild, student, learner, scholar**
– Someone who follows a great teacher is a **disciple**.

purchase *VERB*

The library has purchased new computers.
• **buy, pay for, get, obtain, acquire, procure**

purchase *NOUN*

❶ *Keep the receipt as proof of your purchase.*
• **acquisition, buying, shopping**
❷ *I couldn't get any purchase on the slippery rock.*
• **grasp, grip, hold, leverage, traction**

pure *ADJECTIVE*

❶ *The coin is made of pure gold.*
• **solid, genuine, unadulterated, undiluted**
OPPOSITES impure, adulterated
❷ *All our dishes are made from pure ingredients.*
• **natural, unprocessed, unrefined, wholesome**
OPPOSITE processed
❸ *She loved the pure mountain air.*
• **clean, clear, fresh, unpolluted, uncontaminated**
OPPOSITES polluted, stale
❹ *This book is pure nonsense.*
• **complete, absolute, utter, sheer, total, out-and-out**

purify *VERB*

A filter is used to purify the rainwater.
• **clean, make pure, decontaminate**
– You destroy germs by **disinfecting** or **sterilizing** things.
– You take solid particles out of liquids by **filtering** them.
– To purify water by boiling it and condensing the vapour is to **distil** it.
– To purify crude oil is to **refine** it.

purple *ADJECTIVE & NOUN*

WORD WEB

Some shades of purple:

- ➤ lavender
- ➤ lilac
- ➤ magenta
- ➤ mauve
- ➤ plum
- ➤ violet

For tips on describing colours see **colour**.

purpose *NOUN*

❶ *What was your purpose in coming here?*
• **intention, motive, aim, objective, goal, end, target**

A B C D E F G H I J K L M N O P Q R S T U V W X Y Z

❷ *She began to feel that her life had no purpose.*
• **point, use, usefulness, value**
➤ **on purpose**
Did you trip me up on purpose?
• **deliberately, intentionally, purposely, knowingly, consciously**

purposeful *ADJECTIVE*
She set off with a purposeful look on her face.
• **determined, decisive, resolute, positive, committed**
OPPOSITE aimless

purse *NOUN*
I always keep some change in my purse.
• **money bag, pouch, wallet**

pursue *VERB*
❶ *The thief ran off, pursued by two police officers.*
• **chase, follow, run after, tail, track, hunt, trail, shadow**
❷ *She plans to pursue a career as a musician.*
• **follow, undertake, practise, conduct, take up, carry on, continue, maintain**

pursuit *NOUN*
❶ *The film is about one man's pursuit of happiness.*
• **hunt (for), search (for), striving (for), chase, quest**
❷ *Guests can enjoy a range of outdoor pursuits.*
• **activity, pastime, hobby, recreation, amusement, interest**

push *VERB*
❶ *Push the red button.*
• **press, depress, hold down**
❷ *She pushed a chair against the door.*
• **shove, thrust, drive, propel, send**
OPPOSITE pull
❸ *Push the mixture down with the back of a spoon.*
• **pack, press, cram, crush, compress, ram, squash, squeeze**
❹ *We pushed our way through the large crowd.*
• **force, barge, shove, thrust, elbow, jostle**
❺ *I think she pushes herself too hard.*
• **pressurize, press, drive, urge, compel, bully**
(*informal*) **lean on**
❻ *They are really pushing the new TV series.*
• **promote, publicize, advertise**
(*informal*) **plug, hype**

put *VERB*
❶ *Just put the parcels by the door.*
• **place, set down, leave, deposit, stand**
(*informal*) **dump, stick, park, plonk**
❷ *Maria put her head on my shoulder.*
• **lay, lean, rest**
❸ *I was putting a picture on the wall.*
• **attach, fasten, fix, hang**
❹ *Where are you planning to put the piano?*
• **locate, situate**
❺ *They always put a lifeguard on duty.*
• **position, post, station**
❻ *I'm not sure of the best way to put this.*
• **express, word, phrase, say, state**
➤ **put someone off**
The stench put me off eating.
• **deter, discourage, dissuade**
➤ **put something off**
We can't put off the decision any longer.
• **delay, postpone, defer, shelve**
➤ **put something out**
It took three hours to put out the blaze.
• **extinguish, quench, smother, douse, snuff out**
➤ **put something up**
❶ *We put up the tent in the garden.*
• **set up, construct, erect, raise**
❷ *They have put up their prices.*
• **increase, raise, inflate**
➤ **put up with something**
How do you put up with that racket?
• **bear, stand, tolerate, endure, stomach, abide**

puzzle *NOUN*
Has anyone managed to solve the puzzle?
• **mystery, riddle, conundrum, problem,**

enigma
(*informal*) **brain-teaser, poser**

puzzle *VERB*

❶ *Your response puzzled me.*
• **confuse, baffle, bewilder, bemuse, mystify, perplex**
(*informal*) fox

❷ *We spent all night puzzling over the problem.*
• **ponder, think, meditate, worry, brood**

puzzled *ADJECTIVE*

Why are you looking so puzzled?
• **confused, baffled, bewildered, mystified, perplexed**

puzzling *ADJECTIVE*

There was something puzzling about the photograph.
• **confusing, baffling, bewildering, mystifying, perplexing, mysterious, inexplicable**
OPPOSITES clear, straightforward

Qq

quaint *ADJECTIVE*
We stayed in a quaint thatched cottage.
• **charming, picturesque, sweet, old-fashioned, old-world**

quake *VERB*
The whole building quaked with the blast.
• **shake, shudder, tremble, quiver, rock, sway, wobble**

qualification *NOUN*
❶ *She has a qualification in healthcare.*
• **diploma, certificate, degree, licence, training, skill**
❷ *I'd like to add a qualification to what I said.*
• **condition, reservation, limitation, proviso**

qualified *ADJECTIVE*
❶ *This job needs a qualified electrician.*
• **certified, chartered, licensed, experienced, skilled, trained, professional**
OPPOSITE amateur
❷ *The plan has been given qualified approval.*
• **conditional, limited, partial, guarded, cautious, half-hearted**

qualify *VERB*
❶ *The course will qualify you to administer first aid.*
• **authorize, certify, license, permit, allow, entitle**
❷ *The first three runners will qualify for the final.*
• **be eligible, be entitled, get through, pass**
❸ *I'd like to qualify that statement.*
• **limit, modify, restrict, moderate**

quality *NOUN*
❶ *We only use ingredients of the highest quality.*
• **grade, class, standard, calibre, merit**
❷ *It has all the qualities of a good detective story.*
• **characteristic, feature, property, attribute, trait**

quantity *NOUN*
❶ *Add a very small quantity of baking powder.*
• **amount, mass, volume, bulk, weight** *(informal)* **load**
❷ *We received a large quantity of emails.*
• **number, sum, total**

quarrel *NOUN*
My brother and I have quarrels all the time.
• **argument, disagreement, dispute, difference of opinion, row, tiff, fight, squabble, wrangle, clash**
– *Continuous quarrelling is* **strife**.
– *A long-lasting quarrel is a* **feud** *or* **vendetta**.
– *A quarrel in which people become violent is a* **brawl**.

quarrel *VERB*
What are you two quarrelling about?
• **argue, disagree, fight, row, squabble, bicker, clash, fall out**
IDIOM **cross swords**
➤ **quarrel with something**
I won't quarrel with your decision.
• **disagree with, object to, oppose, take exception to, take issue with, criticize, fault**

quarrelsome *ADJECTIVE*
They were a quarrelsome family.
• **argumentative, belligerent, confrontational, aggressive, bad-tempered, irritable**
OPPOSITES placid, peacable

quarry *NOUN*
He filmed a leopard stalking its quarry.
• **prey, victim, kill**

quarters *PLURAL NOUN*
The attic was originally the servants' quarters.
• **accommodation, lodging, rooms, housing**

quaver *VERB*
I was so nervous my voice began to quaver.
• **shake, tremble, waver, quake, quiver, falter**

quay *NOUN*
Boats were moored alongside the quay.
• **dock, harbour, pier, wharf, jetty, landing stage, marina**

queasy *ADJECTIVE*
Long bus journeys make me feel queasy.
• **sick, nauseous, ill, unwell, groggy**

queen *NOUN*
The infant Mary was crowned Queen of Scots.
• **monarch, sovereign, ruler**

queer *ADJECTIVE*
There's a queer smell in here.
• **odd, peculiar, strange, unusual, abnormal, curious, funny, weird, bizarre, mysterious, puzzling**
OPPOSITES normal, ordinary

quench *VERB*
❶ *They gave us water to quench our thirst.*
• **satisfy, ease, relieve, cool**
IDIOM **take the edge off**
OPPOSITE intensify
❷ *Firefighters are struggling to quench a forest fire.*
• **extinguish, put out, smother, snuff out**
OPPOSITE kindle

query *NOUN*
Please email your queries to this address.
• **question, enquiry, problem**

query *VERB*
No one queried the referee's decision.
• **question, challenge, dispute, argue over, quarrel with, object to**
OPPOSITE accept

quest *NOUN*
He set off on a quest for adventure.
• **search, hunt, expedition, mission**

question *NOUN*
❶ *Does anyone have any questions?*
• **enquiry, query**
– A question which someone sets as a puzzle is a **brain-teaser, conundrum** or **riddle.**
– A series of questions asked as a game is a **quiz.**
– A set of questions which someone asks to get information is a **questionnaire** or **survey.**
❷ *There's some question over his fitness to play.*
• **uncertainty, doubt, argument, debate, dispute**
❸ *There is also the question of cost.*
• **matter, issue, topic, subject, concern, problem**

question *VERB*
❶ *Detectives have been questioning the suspect.*
• **interrogate, cross-examine, interview, quiz**
(*informal*) **grill, pump for information**
❷ *She never questioned his right to be there.*
• **query, challenge, dispute, argue over, quarrel with, object to**
OPPOSITE accept

queue *NOUN*
There was a queue of people waiting for tickets.
• **line, file, column, string, procession, train**
– A long queue of traffic on a road is a **tailback.**

queue *VERB*
Please queue at the door.
• **line up, form a queue**

quick *ADJECTIVE*
❶ *You need to be quick when applying the paint.*
• **fast, swift, rapid, speedy, snappy, brisk**
(*informal*) **nippy**
OPPOSITES slow, unhurried
❷ *Do you mind if I make a quick phone call?*
• **short, brief, momentary, hurried, hasty, cursory**
OPPOSITES long, lengthy

❸ *I would appreciate a quick reply.*
• **prompt, immediate, instant, direct**
OPPOSITE delayed
❹ *She's very quick at mental arithmetic.*
• **bright, sharp, clever, acute, alert, perceptive**
IDIOM (*informal*) **on the ball**
OPPOSITES slow, dull

quicken *VERB*
The pace quickens as the story unfolds.
• **accelerate, speed up, step up, pick up speed**

quickly *ADVERB*
❶ *She began to walk more quickly.*
• **fast, hurriedly, swiftly, rapidly, speedily, briskly, at speed**
IDIOMS **at the double, at full tilt**
OPPOSITES slowly, unhurriedly
❷ *I had to come up with a plan quickly.*
• **immediately, at once, soon, straight away, right away, directly, instantly**
(*informal*) **pronto, asap**
IDIOM **in a heartbeat**

quiet *ADJECTIVE*
❶ *Suddenly the whole room went quiet.*
• **silent, still, noiseless, soundless, mute**
OPPOSITE noisy
❷ *He spoke in a quiet voice.*
• **hushed, low, soft, faint, muted, muffled, whispered**
– Something that is too quiet to hear clearly is **inaudible**.
OPPOSITE loud
❸ *She has always been a quiet child.*
• **shy, reserved, subdued, placid, uncommunicative, retiring, withdrawn**
OPPOSITE talkative
❹ *I found a quiet place to sit and read.*
• **peaceful, tranquil, secluded, restful, calm, serene**
OPPOSITE busy

quieten *VERB*
➤ **quieten down**
Eventually the audience quietened down.
• **fall silent, calm down, settle**

quietly *ADVERB*
❶ *I crept quietly along the corridor.*
• **silently, noiselessly, without a sound, inaudibly**
OPPOSITE noisily
❷ *A voice whispered quietly into my ear.*
• **softly, faintly, in a whisper, under your breath**
OPPOSITE loudly

quit *VERB*
❶ *He decided to quit his job and go abroad.*
• **leave, give up, resign from**
(*informal*) **pack in**
❷ (*informal*) *Quit asking me all these questions!*
• **stop, cease**
(*informal*) **leave off**

quite *ADVERB*
❶ *His sisters have quite different personalities.*
• **completely, totally, utterly, entirely, wholly, absolutely, altogether**
OPPOSITE slightly
❷ *It's still quite dark outside.*
• **fairly, reasonably, moderately, comparatively, rather, somewhat**
(*informal*) **pretty**

quiver *VERB*
The dog was wet through and quivering with cold.
• **shiver, shake, shudder, tremble, quake, quaver, wobble**

quiz *NOUN*
We took part in a general knowledge quiz.
• **test, competition**

quiz *VERB*
Detectives quizzed him about his missing wife.
• **question, interrogate, cross-examine, interview**
(*informal*) **grill**

quota *NOUN*
We are given a quota of work to get through each week.
• **allocation, allowance, ration, share, portion**

quotation *NOUN*
The title is a quotation from Shakespeare.
• **extract, excerpt, passage, piece, quote**
– A piece taken from a newspaper is a **cutting.**
– A piece taken from a film or TV programme is a **clip.**

quote *VERB*
He ended by quoting a few lines from a poem.
• **recite, repeat**

Rr

race *NOUN*
❶ *We had a race across the field.*
• **competition, contest, chase**
– A race to decide who will take part in the final is a **heat**.
❷ *People of many different races lived together in the city.*
• **ethnic group, people, nation**

race *VERB*
❶ *I'll race you to the corner.*
• **have a race with, run against, compete with**
❷ *I raced home to tell them the exciting news.*
• **run, rush, hurry, dash, sprint, fly, tear, whizz, zoom**

rack *NOUN*
Cooking pots hung from a rack on the wall.
• **frame, framework, support, holder, stand, shelf**

racket *NOUN*
The chickens are making a terrible racket!
• **noise, din, row, commotion, clamour, uproar, rumpus, hubbub**

radiant *ADJECTIVE*
She gave him a radiant smile.
• **bright, dazzling, happy, cheerful, joyful, warm**

radiate *VERB*
❶ *All stars radiate light.*
• **give off, send out, emit**
❷ *She is a woman who radiates confidence.*
• **show, exhibit, exude, ooze**
❸ *The city's streets radiate from the central square.*
• **spread out, fan out, branch out**

radical *ADJECTIVE*
❶ *We had to make radical changes to the script.*
• **fundamental, drastic, thorough, comprehensive, extensive, sweeping, wide-ranging, far-reaching**
OPPOSITE superficial
❷ *She has radical views on education.*
• **extreme, revolutionary, militant**
OPPOSITE moderate

rage *NOUN*
He let out a cry of rage.
• **anger, fury, wrath, temper, outrage, indignation, pique**

rage *VERB*
❶ *She just sat there, raging inwardly.*
• **be angry, be enraged, fume, seethe, rant, rave**
❷ *The storm was still raging outside.*
• **blow, storm, rampage**

ragged *ADJECTIVE*
❶ *A man came to the door wearing ragged clothes.*
• **tattered, torn, frayed, threadbare, ripped, patched, shabby, worn out** (*informal*) **tatty**
❷ *A ragged line of people waited in the rain.*
• **irregular, uneven, rough**

raid *NOUN*
The bombing raids continued for weeks.
• **attack, assault, strike, onslaught, invasion, foray, blitz**

raid *VERB*
❶ *The monastery was raided by Vikings in 795.*
• **attack, invade, ransack, plunder, loot, pillage**
❷ *Police raided the house at dawn.*
• **descend on, break into, rush, storm, swoop on**

rail *NOUN*
The track is made of steel rails.
• **bar, rod, spar**
– A fence made of rails is also called **railings**.

railway *NOUN*
see **transport**

rain *NOUN*
We were caught in a shower of rain.
• **rainfall, raindrops, drizzle**
(*formal*) **precipitation**
– The rainy season in south and south-east Asia is the **monsoon**.
– A long period without rain is a **drought**.
– A fall of rain is a **shower** or **downpour**.
– A heavy fall of rain is a **deluge**.
For tips on describing weather see **weather**.

rain *VERB*
Is it still raining outside?
• **pour, teem, bucket, pelt, spit, drizzle**

rainy *ADJECTIVE*
It was a cold and rainy day.
• **wet, showery, drizzly, damp**
OPPOSITES dry, fine
For tips on describing weather see **weather**.

raise *VERB*
❶ *Raise your hand if you need help.*
• **put up, hold up, lift**
❷ *The box was too heavy for him to raise.*
• **lift, pick up, elevate, hoist**
❸ *The company was forced to raise its prices.*
• **increase, put up, push up, inflate**
(*informal*) **bump up**
❹ *They raised thousands of pounds for charity.*
• **collect, gather, take in, make**
❺ *She raised three children on her own.*
• **bring up, care for, look after, nurture, rear**
❻ *Several objections have been raised.*
• **put forward, bring up, mention, present, air**
❼ *I don't want to raise your hopes.*
• **encourage, build up, arouse**
❽ *The accident raises questions about rail safety.*
• **produce, create, give rise to, prompt**

rally *NOUN*
Demonstrators held a rally in the town square.
• **demonstration, meeting, march, protest**
(*informal*) **demo**

rally *VERB*
They tried to rally support for the campaign.
• **gather, collect, amass, raise**

ram *VERB*
❶ *He quickly rammed the wallet into his pocket.*
• **thrust, force, push, jam, stuff, plunge, stick**
❷ *The car skidded and rammed into a lamp post.*
• **hit, strike, bump, crash into, collide with, smash into**

ramble *VERB*
❶ *We both enjoy rambling in the countryside.*
• **walk, hike, trek, backpack, roam, rove, range**
❷ *The speaker rambled on for hours.*
• **chatter, babble, prattle**
(*informal*) **rabbit, witter**

rambling *ADJECTIVE*
It was a long rambling speech.
• **confused, disorganized, unfocused, roundabout, meandering**
OPPOSITE focused

rampage *VERB*
An angry mob rampaged through the streets.
• **run riot, run amok, go berserk, storm, charge**

ran
past tense see **run**

random *ADJECTIVE*
Make the longest word you can out of a random selection of letters.
• **arbitrary, unplanned, haphazard, chance, casual, indiscriminate**
OPPOSITE deliberate

A B C D E F G H I J K L M N O P Q R S T U V W X Y Z

rang
past tense see **ring**

range *NOUN*
❶ *Supermarkets sell a wide range of goods.*
• **variety, assortment, mixture, collection, selection, choice**
❷ *The competition is open to children in the age range 8 to 12.*
• **span, scope, spectrum, compass**
❸ *There is a range of mountains in the south.*
• **chain, line, row, series, string**

range *VERB*
❶ *Prices range from fifteen to twenty pounds.*
• **vary, differ, extend, run, fluctuate**
❷ *Jars of preserves were ranged on the shelf.*
• **arrange, order, lay out, set out, line up**
❸ *Wild deer range over the hills.*
• **wander, ramble, roam, rove, stray**

rank *NOUN*
❶ *Ranks of marching soldiers approached the town.*
• **row, line, file, column**
❷ *He holds the rank of sergeant.*
• **grade, level, position, status**
– To raise someone to a higher rank is to **promote** them.
– To reduce someone to a lower rank is to **demote** them.

ransack *VERB*
❶ *She ransacked the wardrobe for something to wear.*
• **search, scour, rummage through, comb**
(*informal*) **turn upside down**
❷ *Thieves had ransacked the building.*
• **loot, pillage, plunder, rob, wreck**

rap *VERB*
❶ *Someone rapped urgently on the door.*
• **knock, tap**
❷ *She rapped her knuckles on the desk.*
• **strike, hit, drum**

rapid *ADJECTIVE*
They set off at a rapid pace.
• **fast, quick, speedy, swift, brisk**
OPPOSITE slow

rare *ADJECTIVE*
❶ *This is a rare species of orchid.*
• **uncommon, unusual, infrequent, scarce, sparse**
OPPOSITE common
❷ *She has a rare talent for storytelling.*
• **exceptional, remarkable, outstanding, special**

rarely *ADVERB*
He is rarely seen in public.
• **seldom, infrequently, hardly ever**
OPPOSITE often

rash *ADJECTIVE*
Don't make any rash promises.
• **reckless, foolhardy, hasty, hurried, impulsive, impetuous, unthinking**
OPPOSITES prudent, considered

rash *NOUN*
❶ *I had an itchy red rash on my leg.*
• **spots**
❷ *There has been a rash of break-ins lately.*
• **series, succession, wave, flurry, outbreak, flood, spate**

rate *NOUN*
❶ *The boys were pedalling at a furious rate.*
• **speed, pace, velocity, tempo**
❷ *What's the usual rate for washing a car?*
• **charge, cost, fee, payment, price, figure, amount**

rate *VERB*
How do you rate your chances of winning?
• **assess, judge, estimate, evaluate, gauge, weigh up**

rather *ADVERB*
❶ *It's rather chilly today.*
• **slightly, fairly, moderately, somewhat, quite, a bit, a little**
❷ *I'd rather not discuss it on the phone.*
• **preferably, sooner**

➤ **rather than**
We decided to walk rather than wait for the bus.
• **as opposed to, instead of**

ratio *NOUN*
Mix oil and vinegar in the ratio of three to one.
• **proportion, balance**
– You can express a ratio as a **percentage**.

ration *NOUN*
Each of us was allowed a daily ration of water.
• **allowance, allocation, quota, share, portion, helping, measure**
➤ **rations**
We took plenty of rations for our camping trip.
• **provisions, food, supplies, stores**

ration *VERB*
Food had to be rationed during the war.
• **limit, restrict, share out, allocate, allot**

rational *ADJECTIVE*
There was no rational explanation for what had happened.
• **logical, reasonable, sensible, sane, common-sense**
OPPOSITE irrational

rattle *VERB*
Something rattled inside the parcel.
• **clatter, clink, clunk**
For tips on describing sounds see **sound**.

rave *VERB*
❶ *Liz started raving at me down the phone.*
• **rage, rant, storm, fume, shout, yell**
❷ *Everyone is raving about the new book.*
• **enthuse, be excited, talk wildly**

ravenous *ADJECTIVE*
By evening we were all ravenous.
• **hungry, famished, starving, starved**

raw *ADJECTIVE*
❶ *He was eating a piece of raw carrot.*
• **uncooked**
OPPOSITE cooked
❷ *The factory imports most of its raw materials from abroad.*
• **unprocessed, crude, natural, untreated**
OPPOSITES manufactured, processed
❸ *She started as a raw trainee reporter.*
• **inexperienced, untrained, new, green**
OPPOSITE experienced
❹ *The fall had left a patch of raw skin on my knee.*
• **red, rough, sore, tender, inflamed**
❺ *There was a raw north-east wind blowing.*
• **bitter, cold, chilly, biting, freezing, piercing**

ray *NOUN*
A ray of sunlight shone through the branches.
• **beam, shaft, stream**

reach *VERB*
❶ *After a while we reached a small village.*
• **arrive at, go as far as, get to, make, end up at**
❷ *The appeal fund has reached its target.*
• **achieve, attain, hit**
OPPOSITES miss, fall short of
❸ *I can't reach the top shelf.*
• **get hold of, grasp, touch**
❹ *You can reach me on my mobile.*
• **contact, get in touch with, get through to, speak to, get hold of**
➤ **reach out**
Reach out your hands.
• **extend, hold out, stretch out, thrust out, stick out**

reach *NOUN*
❶ *The lower branches were just out of my reach.*
• **grasp, range, stretch**
❷ *The island is within easy reach of the mainland.*
• **distance, range**

react *VERB*
The woman reacted oddly when I gave my name.
• **respond, behave, answer, reply**

A B C D E F G H I J K L M N O P Q R S T U V W X Y Z

reaction *NOUN*
What was your immediate reaction to the news?
• **response, answer, reply**

read *VERB*
❶ *Can you read this signature?*
• **make out, understand, decipher**
❷ *I read through my notes again quickly.*
• **look over, study, scan, leaf through, peruse**
IDIOM **cast your eye over**
– To read through something very quickly is to **skim through** it.
– To read here and there in a book is to **dip into** it.
– To read something intently is to **pore over** it.

readily *ADVERB*
❶ *My friends readily agreed to help.*
• **willingly, gladly, happily, eagerly**
OPPOSITES **reluctantly, grudgingly**
❷ *All the ingredients are readily available.*
• **easily, conveniently, without any difficulty**

ready *ADJECTIVE*
❶ *When will tea be ready?*
• **prepared, all set, done, organized, arranged, available, in place**
OPPOSITE **not ready**
❷ *He's always ready to help a friend.*
• **willing, glad, pleased, happy, keen, eager**
OPPOSITES **reluctant, unwilling**
❸ *She has a ready answer for everything.*
• **prompt, swift, immediate**
OPPOSITE **slow**

real *ADJECTIVE*
❶ *The play is based on a real story.*
• **actual, true, factual, verifiable**
OPPOSITES **fictitious, imaginary**
❷ *Is that a real diamond?*
• **genuine, authentic, natural**
OPPOSITES **artificial, imitation**
❸ *She doesn't often show her real feelings.*
• **sincere, honest, genuine, true, heartfelt**
OPPOSITES **insincere, put on**

realistic *ADJECTIVE*
❶ *It's a very realistic portrait.*
• **lifelike, true to life, faithful, authentic, convincing, natural**
❷ *It's not realistic to expect a puppy to be quiet.*
• **feasible, practical, sensible, possible, workable**
(*informal*) **doable**
OPPOSITES **unrealistic, impractical**

reality *NOUN*
You need to stop daydreaming and face reality.
• **the facts, the real world, real life, the truth**
OPPOSITE **fantasy**

realize *VERB*
❶ *Don't you realize what this means?*
• **understand, appreciate, comprehend, perceive, recognize, grasp, see**
(*informal*) **catch on to, tumble to, twig**
❷ *She realized her ambition to become a racing driver.*
• **fulfil, achieve, accomplish, attain**

really *ADVERB*
❶ *Can there really be life on other planets?*
• **actually, definitely, genuinely, honestly, certainly, truly, in fact, in truth, in reality**
❷ *I thought that was a really good film.*
• **very, extremely, exceptionally**

realm *NOUN*
❶ *Hobbits live in the mythical realm of Middle-earth.*
• **country, kingdom, domain, empire**
❷ *Perhaps the answer lies beyond the realm of science.*
• **sphere, domain, field, area**

rear *NOUN*
The buffet car is at the rear of the train.
• **back, end, tail end**

– The rear of a ship is the **stern**.
OPPOSITES front, head

rear *ADJECTIVE*
Our seats were in the rear coach of the train.
• **back, end, last**
– The rear legs of an animal are its **hind** legs.
OPPOSITES front, leading

rear *VERB*
❶ *The couple have reared three children.*
• **bring up, raise, nurture**
❷ *The cobra reared its head.*
• **hold up, lift, raise**
❸ *Ahead of us reared the Himalayas.*
• **rise up, tower, loom, soar**

rearrange *VERB*
❶ *Someone has rearranged the furniture.*
• **reorganize, reorder, reposition**
(*informal*) **rejig**
❷ *Let's rearrange our meeting.*
• **reschedule**

reason *NOUN*
❶ *What was the reason for the delay?*
• **cause, grounds, explanation, motive, justification, basis, excuse**
❷ *He never listens to reason.*
• **sense, common sense, logic, rationality**
❸ *It was clear that the poor woman had lost her reason.*
• **sanity, mind, senses, wits**
(*informal*) **marbles**

reason *VERB*
➤ **reason with someone**
It's no use reasoning with him.
• **argue with, persuade, talk round**

reasonable *ADJECTIVE*
❶ *That seems like a reasonable plan.*
• **sensible, intelligent, realistic, rational, logical, sane, sound, valid**
OPPOSITES irrational, illogical
❷ *It's a reasonable price for a camera.*
• **fair, moderate, affordable, respectable, acceptable**
OPPOSITES excessive, exorbitant
❸ *The bike is in reasonable condition.*
• **satisfactory, acceptable, adequate, average, tolerable, passable, not bad, fairly good**
(*informal*) **OK**

reassure *VERB*
She tried hard to reassure us.
• **calm, comfort, encourage, hearten, give confidence to**
IDIOM **put your mind at rest**
OPPOSITE alarm

rebel *VERB*
The people of the south rebelled.
• **revolt, rise up**
– To rebel against the captain of a ship is to **mutiny**.
OPPOSITE obey

rebellion *NOUN*
❶ *The protest soon became a widespread rebellion.*
• **revolt, revolution, uprising, insurgence, insurrection**
– A rebellion on a ship is a **mutiny**.
❷ *She was showing signs of teenage rebellion.*
• **resistance, defiance, disobedience, insubordination**

rebellious *ADJECTIVE*
My sister is going through a rebellious phase.
• **defiant, disobedient, insubordinate, mutinous, unruly, obstreperous**

rebound *VERB*
The ball rebounded off the keeper's chest.
• **bounce back, spring back, ricochet**

recall *VERB*
Can you recall any of their names?
• **remember, recollect, think back to**
OPPOSITE forget

recede *VERB*
❶ *The flood water slowly receded.*
• **go back, retreat, withdraw, subside, ebb**
OPPOSITE advance
❷ *His fear began to recede.*
• **lessen, diminish, decline, subside, ebb, fade, dwindle**
OPPOSITES grow, intensify

receive *VERB*
❶ *I went up to the stage to receive the trophy.*
• **be given, be presented with, be awarded, take, accept, collect**
OPPOSITES give, present
❷ *Some passengers received minor injuries.*
• **experience, suffer, undergo, sustain**
OPPOSITE inflict
❸ *He received the news in complete silence.*
• **react to, respond to**
❹ *We went to the front door to receive our visitors.*
• **greet, meet, welcome**

recent *ADJECTIVE*
She tries to keep up with recent fashion trends.
• **current, contemporary, new, fresh, modern, the latest, up to date, up to the minute**
OPPOSITE old

recently *ADVERB*
I've not heard from her recently.
• **lately, of late, latterly**

reception *NOUN*
❶ *The landlady gave us a frosty reception.*
• **greeting, welcome, treatment**
❷ *The wedding reception will be held at a nearby hotel.*
• **party, function, gathering, get-together, celebration**
(*informal*) **do**

recipe *NOUN*
Here is a simple recipe for carrot cake.
• **directions, instructions**
– The items you use for a recipe are the **ingredients**.

recital *NOUN*
❶ *There will be a short piano recital at noon.*
• **concert, performance**
❷ *He stood up to give a recital of one of his poems.*
• **recitation, reading**

recite *VERB*
She recited the whole poem from memory.
• **say aloud, read out, narrate, deliver, declaim**

reckless *ADJECTIVE*
A man has been charged with reckless driving.
• **careless, thoughtless, rash, irresponsible, heedless, foolhardy, negligent**
OPPOSITE careful

reckon *VERB*
❶ (*informal*) *I reckon it's going to rain.*
• **think, believe, guess, imagine, feel**
❷ *I tried to reckon how much she owed me.*
• **calculate, work out, add up, assess, estimate**
(*informal*) **tot up**
➤ **reckon on**
They hadn't reckoned on it being so expensive.
• **be prepared for, plan for, anticipate, foresee, expect, consider, bargain on**

recline *VERB*
She reclined lazily on the sofa.
• **lean back, lie back, lounge, rest, stretch out, sprawl, loll**

recognize *VERB*
❶ *I didn't recognize the voice at first.*
• **identify, know, distinguish, recall, recollect, put a name to, place**
❷ *They refuse to recognize that there is a problem.*
• **acknowledge, admit, accept, grant, concede, confess, realize**

recoil *VERB*
She recoiled at the sight of blood.
• **draw back, shrink back, flinch, quail, wince**

recollect *VERB*
Do you recollect what happened?
• **remember, recall, have a memory of**
OPPOSITE forget

recommend *VERB*
❶ *I recommend that you book in advance.*
• **advise, counsel, propose, suggest, advocate, prescribe, urge**
OPPOSITE advise against
❷ *I recommend the strawberry ice cream.*
• **endorse, praise, commend, vouch for, speak favourably of**
IDIOM **put in a good word for**

reconsider *VERB*
Would you like to reconsider your answer?
• **rethink, review, reassess, re-evaluate**
IDIOM **have second thoughts about**

record *NOUN*
I keep a record of my dreams.
• **account, report, register, diary, journal, log, chronicle**
– The records of what happened at a meeting are the **minutes**.
– Records consisting of historical documents are **archives**.

record *VERB*
❶ *He recorded everything he heard in a notebook.*
• **write down, note, document, set down, put down, enter, register, log**
❷ *The concert is being recorded live.*
• **tape, film, video**

recover *VERB*
❶ *She is still recovering from her illness.*
• **get better, recuperate, convalesce, heal, mend, improve, pick up, revive, bounce back**
OPPOSITE deteriorate
❷ *The police have recovered the stolen painting.*
• **get back, retrieve, regain, reclaim, recoup, repossess, find, trace**
OPPOSITE lose

recovery *NOUN*
We all wish you a speedy recovery.
• **recuperation, improvement, convalescence, healing, revival**

recreation *NOUN*
❶ *What do you do for recreation around here?*
• **leisure, fun, relaxation, enjoyment, amusement, entertainment, pleasure, diversion, play**
❷ *Curling is a popular recreation in Canada.*
• **pastime, hobby, leisure activity**

recruit *NOUN*
The centre is where new recruits are trained in fire fighting.
• **trainee, apprentice, learner, novice**
– A recruit training to be in the armed services is a **cadet**.

recruit *VERB*
We have recruited two new members for our book club.
• **bring in, take on, enrol, sign up, hire**
– To be recruited into the armed services is to **enlist**.

rectangle *NOUN*
You will need a rectangle of fabric.
– A rectangle with adjacent sides of unequal length is also called an **oblong**.

recur *VERB*
Go to the doctor if the symptoms recur.
• **reappear, be repeated, come back, happen again, return**

recycle *VERB*
We recycle all our plastic and glass.
• **reuse, reprocess, salvage, reclaim**

red *ADJECTIVE*
❶ *He wore a bright red T-shirt.*
see **red** adjective
❷ *She had flaming red hair.*
• **ginger, auburn, chestnut, coppery** (*informal*) **carroty**
For tips on describing hair see **hair**.
❸ *My eyes were red from lack of sleep.*
• **bloodshot, inflamed, red-rimmed**
❹ *Xiang went red with embarrassment.*
• **flushed, blushing, rosy, ruddy**

A B C D E F G H I J K L M N O P Q R S T U V W X Y Z

red *ADJECTIVE & NOUN*

WORD WEB

Some shades of red:

➤ brick red
➤ burgundy
➤ cherry
➤ crimson
➤ maroon
➤ pillar-box red
➤ pink
➤ rose
➤ ruby
➤ scarlet
➤ vermilion
➤ wine

For tips on describing colours see **colour**.

reduce *VERB*

I have reduced the amount of sugar in my diet.
• **decrease, lessen, lower, diminish, minimize, cut, cut back, slash**
– To reduce something by half is to **halve** it.
– To reduce the width of something is to **narrow** it.
– To reduce the length of something is to **shorten** or **trim** it.
– To reduce speed is to **decelerate**.
– To reduce the strength of a liquid is to **dilute** it.
OPPOSITE increase
➤ **reduce to**
The audience were reduced to tears.
• **drive to, bring to**

reel *NOUN*

I bought a reel of black cotton thread.
• **spool**

reel *VERB*

❶ *He reeled as if he was going to faint.*
• **stagger, lurch, sway, rock, totter, stumble, wobble**
❷ *All these questions are making my head reel.*
• **spin, whirl, swirl, swim, feel dizzy**
➤ **reel off**
The chef reeled off a long list of ingredients.
• **recite, rattle off, fire off**

refer *VERB*

Your doctor may refer you to a specialist.
• **hand over, pass on, direct, send**
➤ **refer to**
❶ *Which book are you referring to?*
• **allude to, make reference to, mention, comment on, touch on, call attention to, bring up**
❷ *Refer to our website for more information.*
• **look up, consult, go to, turn to, call up**
➤ **refer to as**
Junk email is often referred to as 'spam'.
• **call, term, style, dub, describe as**

referee *NOUN*

The referee blew his whistle.
• **umpire, adjudicator, judge**
(*informal*) **ref**

refill *VERB*

Can I refill your glass?
• **top up**
– To refill a fuel tank is to **refuel**.

refine *VERB*

❶ *This chapter explains the process of refining sugar.*
• **purify, filter, process, distil**
❷ *I'm trying to refine my juggling skills.*
• **improve, perfect, polish, hone, fine-tune**

reflect *VERB*

❶ *Mirrored surfaces reflect sunlight.*
• **send back, throw back, shine back**
❷ *Her love of adventure is reflected in her writing.*
• **show, indicate, demonstrate, exhibit, reveal**
➤ **reflect on**
I have been reflecting on the events of the past week.
• **think about, contemplate, consider, ponder, mull over**

reflection *NOUN*

❶ *I could see my reflection in the pond.*
• **image, likeness**
❷ *His art is a reflection of his passion for life.*
• **indication, demonstration, evidence, expression, manifestation, result**
❸ *We need more time for reflection.*
• **thinking, contemplation,**

consideration, deliberation, meditation, musing

reform *VERB*
❶ *We need to reform the way we live on this planet.*
• improve, better, rectify, revise, refine, revamp, modify, adapt
❷ *He promised to reform in the future.*
• change for the better, mend your ways
IDIOM turn over a new leaf
Note that re-form, spelled with a hyphen, is a different word meaning 'get back together': *The band are re-forming after twenty years.*

reform *NOUN*
They are making reforms to the school curriculum.
• improvement, amendment, refinement, revision, modification

refrain *VERB*
➤ **refrain from**
I found it hard to refrain from smiling.
• stop yourself, avoid, hold back from, abstain from

refresh *VERB*
❶ *Maybe a walk will refresh me.*
• revive, revitalize, reinvigorate, restore, freshen, wake up, perk up
OPPOSITE weary
❷ *Let me refresh your memory.*
• jog, prompt, prod

refreshing *ADJECTIVE*
We went for a refreshing dip in the pool.
• reviving, invigorating, restorative, bracing, stimulating, fortifying

refuge *NOUN*
❶ *A cave provided refuge from the blizzard.*
• shelter, cover, protection, safety
❷ *The outlaws hid in their secret mountain refuge.*
• hideaway, hideout, retreat, haven, sanctuary

refund *VERB*
She asked them to refund her money.
• repay, pay back, give back, return

refusal *NOUN*
❶ *I sent them a polite refusal.*
• non-acceptance, rejection
OPPOSITE acceptance
❷ *I can't understand her refusal to cooperate.*
• unwillingness, reluctance, disinclination
OPPOSITE willingness

refuse *VERB*
❶ *He refused all offers of help.*
• decline, reject, turn down, say no to, rebuff, spurn
(*informal*) pass up
OPPOSITE accept
❷ *We were refused permission to take photos inside.*
• deny, deprive of
OPPOSITES grant, allow

refuse *NOUN*
We recycle most of our household refuse.
• rubbish, waste, litter, junk
(*North American*) trash, garbage

regain *VERB*
Mike slowly began to regain consciousness.
• get back, get back to, return to

regard *VERB*
❶ *I still regard it as a great film.*
• think of, consider, judge, value, estimate, rate, look on
❷ *The boy regarded us suspiciously.*
• look at, gaze at, stare at, eye, view, observe, scrutinize, watch, contemplate

regard *NOUN*
➤ **regards**
Give my regards to your family.
• best wishes, greetings, compliments, respects

regarding *PREPOSITION*
For more information regarding our products, visit our website.
• about, concerning, on the subject of, with reference to, with regard to, with respect to, in connection with

regardless *ADJECTIVE*

➤ **regardless of**

I kept on reading, regardless of the time.

• **indifferent to, not caring about, unconcerned about, irrespective of, without regard to, disregarding**

region *NOUN*

They lived in a remote region of northern Australia.

• **area, district, territory, province, sector, quarter, zone, neighbourhood**

register *VERB*

❶ *You need to register your username.*

• **record, enter, submit, lodge**

❷ *This dial registers the oven temperature.*

• **indicate, display, read, show**

❸ *His face registered deep suspicion.*

• **show, express, display, exhibit, reveal**

regret *VERB*

Do you now regret your decision?

• **be sorry about, feel remorse for, repent, rue**

regular *ADJECTIVE*

❶ *Try to eat regular meals.*

• **evenly spaced, fixed**

OPPOSITES irregular, haphazard

❷ *The drummer kept up a regular rhythm.*

• **steady, even, uniform, unvarying, constant, consistent**

OPPOSITES irregular, erratic, uneven

❸ *Is this your regular route to school?*

• **normal, usual, customary, habitual, ordinary, routine, standard**

OPPOSITE unusual

❹ *She is one of our regular customers.*

• **frequent, familiar, habitual, persistent**

OPPOSITES rare, occasional

regulate *VERB*

❶ *Turn the dial to regulate the temperature.*

• **control, set, adjust, alter, moderate**

❷ *The broadcasting industry is strictly regulated.*

• **manage, direct, control, govern, monitor, supervise, police**

regulation *NOUN*

There are new regulations on school uniform.

• **rule, order, law, directive, decree, statute**

rehearsal *NOUN*

This morning we have a rehearsal for the school concert.

• **practice, run-through, dry run, drill**

– A rehearsal in which the cast wear costumes is a **dress rehearsal.**

rehearse *VERB*

We need to rehearse the final scene again.

• **go over, practise, run over, read through**

reign *VERB*

How long did Queen Victoria reign?

• **be king or queen, sit on the throne, govern, rule**

reject *VERB*

❶ *Why did you reject their offer?*

• **decline, refuse, turn down, say no to, spurn, rebuff**

OPPOSITE accept

❷ *Faulty parts are rejected at the factory.*

• **discard, get rid of, throw out, scrap**

OPPOSITE keep

rejoice *VERB*

Everyone rejoiced when the fighting ceased.

• **be happy, celebrate, delight, exult**

OPPOSITE grieve

relate *VERB*

They have many stories to relate about their adventures abroad.

• **tell, narrate, recount, report, describe**

➤ **relate to**

❶ *The rest of the letter relates to her family.*

• **be about, refer to, have to do with, concern**

❷ *How does this scene relate to the rest of the play?*

• **fit in with, connect to, be linked to**

❸ *I find it hard to relate to any of the characters.*
• empathize with, identify with, feel for, get on with

related *ADJECTIVE*
Do you think the murders are related?
• connected, linked, interconnected, allied
OPPOSITES unrelated, unconnected

relation *NOUN*
❶ *The stolen car has no relation to the robbery.*
• connection, relationship, association, link, bond
❷ *Are you a relation of hers?*
• relative, member of the family
(*old use*) kinsman or kinswoman
SEE ALSO family

relationship *NOUN*
❶ *There is a relationship between your diet and your health.*
• connection, relation, association, link, bond
– The relationship between two numbers is a **ratio**.
❷ *She has a good relationship with her stepmother.*
• friendship, attachment (to), understanding (of), rapport (with)

relative *NOUN*
see **relation**

relax *VERB*
❶ *I like to relax by listening to music.*
• unwind, rest, take it easy
(*informal*) chill out
IDIOM put your feet up
❷ *A warm bath always relaxes me.*
• calm down, soothe
❸ *Try to relax your grip on the racket.*
• slacken, loosen, unclench, ease, soften
OPPOSITES tighten, tense

relaxed *ADJECTIVE*
The cafe had a relaxed atmosphere.
• informal, casual, carefree, leisurely, easy-going, peaceful, restful, unhurried, calm
(*informal*) laid-back, chilled-out
OPPOSITES tense, stressful

release *VERB*
❶ *All the hostages have been released.*
• free, let go, discharge, liberate, set free
OPPOSITES capture, imprison
❷ *What if they release the guard dogs?*
• let loose, set loose, unfasten, unleash, untie
❸ *Her new album will be released in April.*
• issue, publish, put out

relent *VERB*
In the end Mum and Dad relented and let me go to the party.
• give in, give way, yield, soften, weaken

relentless *ADJECTIVE*
He faced relentless criticism.
• constant, continuous, never-ending, incessant, perpetual, persistent, unrelenting, unremitting

relevant *ADJECTIVE*
Make sure your answer is relevant to the question.
• applicable, pertinent, to the point, appropriate, suitable, related
OPPOSITE irrelevant

reliable *ADJECTIVE*
❶ *This website is a reliable source of information.*
• dependable, valid, trustworthy, safe, sound, steady, sure
OPPOSITES unreliable, untrustworthy
❷ *He's a reliable boy and won't let you down.*
• faithful, dependable, trustworthy, loyal, constant, devoted, staunch, true

relief *NOUN*
❶ *The pills gave some relief from the pain.*
• comfort, easing, soothing, alleviation
❷ *I watched TV for some light relief.*
• relaxation, rest, respite, diversion
❸ *The charity is involved in famine relief.*
• aid, assistance, help

relieve *VERB*

❶ *The doctor said the pills would relieve the pain.*

• **alleviate, ease, soothe, lessen, diminish, dull**

OPPOSITE intensify

❷ *We played cards to relieve the boredom.*

• **reduce, lighten, dispel, counteract**

religion *NOUN*

Prayers are used in many religions.

• **faith, belief, creed, denomination, sect**

WORD WEB

Major world religions:

- Buddhism
- Christianity
- Hinduism
- Islam
- Judaism
- Shintoism
- Sikhism
- Taoism
- Zen

- The study of religion is **divinity** or **theology**.

Major religious festivals:

- (*Buddhist*) Buddha Day, Nirvana Day
- (*Christian*) Lent, Easter, Christmas
- (*Hindu*) Holi, Diwali
- (*Muslim*) Ramadan, Eid
- (*Jewish*) Passover, Rosh Hashana, Yom Kippur, Hanukkah
- (*Sikh*) Baisakhi, Birth of Guru Nanak

Religious leaders:

- cleric, clergyman or clergywoman
- (*Buddhist*) lama
- (*Christian*) priest, minister, vicar, bishop, cardinal, pope, chaplain
- (*Hindu or Sikh*) guru
- (*Muslim*) imam
- (*Jewish*) rabbi

Places of religious worship:

- temple
- shrine
- (*Christian*) church, chapel, cathedral
- (*Muslim*) mosque
- (*Jewish*) synagogue

religious *ADJECTIVE*

❶ *The choir sang a selection of religious music.*

• **sacred, spiritual, holy, divine**

OPPOSITE secular

❷ *My grandparents were very religious.*

• **devout, pious, reverent, god-fearing, churchgoing**

relish *VERB*

Many people would relish the chance to be on TV.

• **enjoy, delight in, appreciate, savour, revel in**

reluctant *ADJECTIVE*

I was reluctant to admit defeat.

• **unwilling, disinclined, loath, resistant, hesitant, grudging**

OPPOSITES eager, willing

rely *VERB*

➤ **rely on**

Can I rely on you to keep a secret?

• **depend on, count on, have confidence in, trust in, be sure of**

(*informal*) **bank on**

remain *VERB*

❶ *A few people remained in their seats.*

• **stay, wait, linger, stay put**

(*informal*) **hang about**

❷ *The heatwave is forecast to remain all week.*

• **continue, persist, last, keep on, carry on**

❸ *Little remained of the house after the fire.*

• **be left, survive, endure, abide**

remainder *NOUN*

We watched a film for the remainder of the afternoon.

• **rest, what is left, surplus, residue**

remains *PLURAL NOUN*

They cleared away the remains of the picnic.

• **leftovers, remnants, residue, fragments, traces, scraps, debris**

– The remains at the bottom of a cup are **dregs**.

– Remains still standing after a building has collapsed are **ruins**.
– Historic remains are **relics**.

remark *NOUN*
We exchanged a few remarks about the weather.
• **comment, observation, word, statement, reflection, mention**

remark *VERB*
He remarked that it was very quiet in the room.
• **say, state, comment, note, declare, mention, observe**
SEE ALSO **say**

remarkable *ADJECTIVE*
❶ *This was a remarkable stroke of good luck.*
• **extraordinary, astonishing, amazing, incredible, wonderful**
❷ *She has a remarkable ear for music.*
• **exceptional, outstanding, striking, notable, noteworthy, impressive, phenomenal**
OPPOSITE ordinary

remedy *NOUN*
❶ *This is a traditional remedy for sore throats.*
• **cure, treatment, medicine, medication, therapy**
– A remedy for the effects of poison is an **antidote**.
❷ *I may have found the remedy to all your problems.*
• **solution, answer, relief**

remember *VERB*
❶ *Can you remember what she looked like?*
• **recall, recollect, recognize, place**
OPPOSITE forget
❷ *I'll never remember all this information.*
• **memorize, retain, learn, keep in your head**
❸ *My granny likes to remember the old days.*
• **reminisce about, think back to, look back on**

remind *VERB*
Remind me to buy a newspaper.
• **prompt, jog someone's memory**
➤ **remind you of**
What does this tune remind you of?
• **make you think of, be reminiscent of, take you back to**

reminder *NOUN*
❶ *The photos are a reminder of our holiday.*
• **souvenir, memento**
❷ *I sent round a reminder about the party.*
• **prompt, cue, hint, nudge**

reminiscent *ADJECTIVE*
➤ **be reminiscent of something**
The tune is reminiscent of an old folk song.
• **remind you of, make you think of, call to mind, evoke, conjure up**

remnants *PLURAL NOUN*
Remnants of the meal lay on the floor.
• **remains, remainder, residue, traces, scraps, debris, dregs**

remorse *NOUN*
He showed no remorse for causing the accident.
• **regret, repentance, guilt, contrition, sorrow, shame**

remote *ADJECTIVE*
❶ *They went on an expedition to a remote part of Brazil.*
• **isolated, faraway, distant, inaccessible, cut off, secluded, out of the way, unfrequented**
IDIOM **off the beaten track**
OPPOSITE accessible
❷ *There is only a remote chance of us winning.*
• **unlikely, improbable, slight, slim, faint, doubtful**
OPPOSITES likely, strong

remove *VERB*
❶ *Please remove your rubbish.*
• **clear away, take away**
❷ *The dentist removed my bad tooth.*
• **extract, take out, pull out, withdraw**

A B C D E F G H I J K L M N O P Q R S T U V W X Y Z

❸ *Some protesters were removed from the building.*
• **throw out, turn out, eject, expel, evict** (*informal*) **kick out**
– To remove someone from power is to **depose** them.
❹ *I decided to remove the last paragraph.*
• **get rid of, delete, cut, cut out, erase, do away with, eliminate, abolish**
❺ *The divers removed their wetsuits.*
• **take off, peel off, strip off, shed, cast off**

render *VERB*
❶ *The shock rendered her speechless.*
• **make, leave, cause to be**
❷ *We are asking the public to render their support.*
• **give, provide, offer, furnish, supply**

renew *VERB*
❶ *The paintwork has been completely renewed.*
• **repair, renovate, restore, replace, rebuild, reconstruct, revamp, refurbish, overhaul**
(*informal*) **do up**
❷ *We stopped for a snack to renew our energy.*
• **refresh, revive, restore, replenish, revitalize, reinvigorate**
❸ *I need to renew my bus pass.*
• **bring up to date, update**

renowned *ADJECTIVE*
Venice is renowned for its canals.
• **famous, celebrated, well known, famed, noted, notable, acclaimed**
OPPOSITE **unknown**

rent *VERB*
We rented bikes to tour the island.
• **hire, charter, lease**

repair *VERB*
Will you be able to repair the damage?
• **mend, fix, put right, patch up**

repair *NOUN*
❶ *The ceiling is badly in need of repair.*
• **restoration, renovation, mending, fixing**
❷ *Keep your bike in good repair.*
• **condition, working order, state, shape**

repay *VERB*
❶ *You can repay me later.*
• **pay back, refund, reimburse**
❷ *How can I ever repay their kindness?*
• **return, reciprocate**

repeat *VERB*
❶ *Could you please repeat your name?*
• **say again, restate, reiterate, go through again, echo**
❷ *We will have to repeat the experiment.*
• **do again, redo, replicate**

repeatedly *ADVERB*
I knocked repeatedly, but there was no answer.
• **again and again, over and over, time after time, frequently, regularly, often, many times**

repel *VERB*
❶ *They fought bravely and repelled the attackers.*
• **drive back, beat back, fight off, fend off, hold off, resist**
❷ *You can use this spray to repel insects.*
• **keep away, ward off, deter, scare off**
OPPOSITE **attract**
❸ *I was repelled by the awful smell.*
• **disgust, revolt, sicken, nauseate, offend**
(*informal*) **turn off**
OPPOSITE **tempt**

repellent *ADJECTIVE*
The villain is portrayed as truly repellent.
• **repulsive, revolting, hideous, horrible, loathsome, vile, objectionable, offensive, foul, disgusting**
OPPOSITE **attractive**

replace *VERB*
❶ *Please replace books on the correct shelf.*
• **put back, return, restore, reinstate**

❷ *Who will replace the coach next season?*
• **follow, succeed, take over from, take the place of**
IDIOM **step into someone's shoes**
❸ *I need to replace one of the tyres on my bike.*
• **change, renew, swap, exchange**

replacement *NOUN*
They needed to find a replacement for the injured player.
• **substitute, standby, stand-in, reserve**
– Someone who can take the place of an actor is an **understudy**.

replica *NOUN*
He built a replica of the Statue of Liberty.
• **copy, reproduction, model, duplicate, imitation**
– An exact copy of a document is a **facsimile**.

reply *NOUN*
I got an immediate reply to my email.
• **response, answer, reaction, acknowledgement**
– An angry reply is a **retort**.

reply *VERB*
➤ **reply to**
I'd better reply to her text.
• **answer, respond to, send a reply to, react to, acknowledge**

report *VERB*
❶ *We had to report our findings to the rest of the group.*
• **communicate, give an account of, describe, announce, publish, broadcast, disclose**
❷ *He threatened to report us to the police.*
• **complain about, inform on, denounce**
(*informal*) **tell on, rat on, shop**
❸ *Please report to reception when you arrive.*
• **present yourself, make yourself known, check in**

report *NOUN*
❶ *There is a full report of the incident in the paper.*
• **account, description, story, record, article, piece, bulletin**
❷ *We heard the loud report of a rifle.*
• **bang, crack, noise, explosion**

reporter *NOUN*
She is a reporter for the local newspaper.
• **journalist, correspondent**

represent *VERB*
❶ *The dove usually represents peace.*
• **stand for, symbolize, personify, epitomize, embody**
❷ *The statue represents the god Zeus.*
• **depict, portray, illustrate, picture, show**
❸ *He appointed a lawyer to represent him.*
• **speak for, appear for, speak on someone's behalf, stand in for**

reprimand *VERB*
They were reprimanded for their bad behaviour.
• **reproach, rebuke, scold**
(*informal*) **tell off, tick off**
OPPOSITE praise

reproduce *VERB*
❶ *The robot can reproduce a human voice.*
• **copy, duplicate, replicate, imitate, simulate, mimic**
❷ *Rats and mice reproduce quickly.*
• **breed, procreate, produce offspring, multiply**
– Fish reproduce by **spawning**.
– To reproduce plants is to **propagate** them.

reproduction *NOUN*
❶ *Is that an original painting or a reproduction?*
• **copy, replica, imitation, duplicate, likeness**
– An exact reproduction of a document is a **facsimile**.
– A reproduction which is intended to deceive people is a **fake** or **forgery**.
❷ *The programme is all about the cycle of animal reproduction.*
• **breeding, procreation, propagation**

reptile *NOUN*

WORD WEB

Some animals which are reptiles:

➤ alligator	➤ salamander
➤ chameleon	➤ skink
➤ crocodile	➤ slow-worm
➤ gecko	➤ snake
➤ iguana	➤ terrapin
➤ Komodo dragon	➤ tortoise
➤ lizard	➤ turtle

- A **basilisk** is a reptile found in myths and legends.

repulsive *ADJECTIVE*
We were put off eating by the repulsive smell.
• **disgusting, revolting, offensive, repellent, disagreeable, foul, repugnant, obnoxious, sickening, nauseating, loathsome, objectionable, nasty, vile**
OPPOSITE attractive

reputation *NOUN*
She is a singer with an international reputation.
• **fame, celebrity, name, renown, eminence, standing, stature**

request *VERB*
❶ *Several players are requesting a transfer.*
• **ask for, appeal for, call for, seek, apply for, beg for, demand**
❷ *They requested us to stop.*
• **ask, call on, invite, entreat, implore, beg, beseech**

request *NOUN*
❶ *They have ignored our request for help.*
• **appeal, plea, entreaty, call, cry, demand**
– A request for a job or membership is an **application**.
– A request signed by a lot of people is a **petition**.
❷ *It was her last request before she died.*
• **wish, desire, requirement**

require *VERB*
❶ *These patients require immediate treatment.*
• **need, must have, demand, depend on**
❷ *Visitors are required to sign the register.*
• **instruct, oblige, request, direct, order, command**
❸ *Is there anything in particular that you require?*
• **want, desire, be short of, lack**

rescue *VERB*
❶ *A helicopter was sent to rescue the climbers.*
• **free, liberate, release, save, set free**
❷ *The divers rescued some items from the sunken ship.*
• **retrieve, recover, salvage**

resemblance *NOUN*
He bears a remarkable resemblance to my brother.
• **likeness, similarity, closeness, correspondence, comparability**
OPPOSITES difference, dissimilarity

resemble *VERB*
She closely resembles my sister.
• **look like, be similar to, remind you of, mirror, echo**
(*informal*) **take after**
OPPOSITE differ from

resent *VERB*
She resents having to work such long hours.
• **feel bitter about, feel aggrieved about, take exception to, be resentful of, object to, begrudge, grudge**

reservation *NOUN*
❶ *We have a reservation for bed and breakfast.*
• **booking**
❷ *I still have reservations about the idea.*
• **doubt, misgiving, hesitation, qualm, scruple**
– If you have reservations about something, you are **sceptical** about it.

reserve *VERB*
❶ *The astronauts had to reserve fuel for the return voyage.*
• **set aside, put aside, save, keep, preserve, retain, hold back**
❷ *Have you reserved your seats on the train?*
• **book, order, secure**

reserve *NOUN*
❶ *The climbers had a week's reserve of food.*
• **stock, store, supply, hoard, stockpile, pool, fund**
❷ *He was named as a reserve for the semi-final.*
• **substitute, standby, stand-in, replacement**
– Someone who can take the place of an actor is an **understudy**.
❸ *We visited a wild bird reserve.*
• **reservation, park, preserve, sanctuary**
❹ *She has a natural air of reserve.*
• **shyness, timidity, reticence, inhibition, modesty, diffidence**

reserved *ADJECTIVE*
❶ *These seats are reserved.*
• **booked, set aside, ordered, taken, spoken for**
❷ *He was unusually reserved that evening.*
• **shy, timid, taciturn, quiet, uncommunicative, withdrawn, reticent, inhibited, diffident**
OPPOSITE **outgoing**

residence *NOUN*
The palace is the official residence of the queen.
• **home, house, address, dwelling**
(*old use*) **abode**

resident *NOUN*
The residents of the town love their new sports centre.
• **inhabitant, citizen, native, occupant, householder**
– A temporary resident in a hotel is a **guest**.
– A resident in rented accommodation is a **boarder, lodger** or **tenant**.

resign *VERB*
The team manager has been forced to resign.
• **leave, stand down, step down, give in your notice, quit, bow out**
– When a monarch resigns from the throne, he or she **abdicates**.

resist *VERB*
❶ *They were too weak to resist the sorcerer's magic.*
• **stand up to, withstand, defend yourself against, fend off, combat, oppose, defy**
OPPOSITES **succumb to, give in to**
❷ *Some residents are resisting the plan.*
• **oppose, object to, fight against, defy**
OPPOSITES **agree to, welcome**
❸ *I couldn't resist taking a peek.*
• **refrain from, hold back from, restrain yourself from**
OPPOSITE **allow yourself to**

resolve *VERB*
❶ *We resolved to press on until nightfall.*
• **decide, determine, make up your mind**
❷ *They held a meeting to try to resolve the dispute.*
• **settle, sort out, straighten out, end, overcome**

resort *VERB*
➤ **resort to**
In the end, they resorted to violence.
• **turn to, fall back on, stoop to**

resort *NOUN*
As a last resort, we could always walk.
• **option, alternative, choice, course of action**

resound *VERB*
Frantic screams resounded through the crowd.
• **echo, reverberate, resonate, ring, boom**

resources *PLURAL NOUN*
❶ *It is a country rich in natural resources.*
• **materials, raw materials, reserves**

❷ *The business had to survive on limited resources.*
• **funds, money, capital, assets, means, wealth**

respect *NOUN*
❶ *Her colleagues have the deepest respect for her.*
• **admiration, esteem, regard, reverence, honour**
❷ *Have some respect for other people's feelings.*
• **consideration, politeness, courtesy, thought**
❸ *In some respects, he's a better player than I am.*
• **aspect, way, sense, regard, detail, feature, point, particular**

respect *VERB*
❶ *He was highly respected as a songwriter.*
• **admire, esteem, think highly of, look up to, honour, revere**
OPPOSITES scorn, despise
❷ *You must respect other people's privacy.*
• **show consideration for, be mindful of, have regard for**
OPPOSITE disregard
❸ *She tried to respect the wishes of her dead husband.*
• **obey, follow, observe, adhere to, comply with**
OPPOSITES ignore, defy

respectable *ADJECTIVE*
❶ *He came from a very respectable family.*
• **decent, honest, upright, honourable, reputable, worthy**
❷ *What would be a respectable score?*
• **reasonable, satisfactory, acceptable, passable, adequate, fair, tolerable**

respective *ADJECTIVE*
The pets were returned to their respective owners.
• **own, personal, individual, separate, particular, specific**

respond *VERB*
➤ **respond to**
He responded to each question with a shrug.
• **reply to, answer, react to, acknowledge**

response *NOUN*
Did you get a response to your letter?
• **reply, answer, reaction, acknowledgement**
– An angry response is a **retort**.

responsible *ADJECTIVE*
❶ *Miss Kumar is responsible for the school's website.*
• **in charge (of), in control (of)**
❷ *You seem to be a responsible sort of person.*
• **reliable, sensible, trustworthy, dependable, conscientious, dutiful**
OPPOSITE irresponsible
❸ *Looking after people's money is a responsible job.*
• **important, serious**
❹ *I hope they find whoever is responsible.*
• **to blame, guilty (of), at fault, culpable**

rest *NOUN*
❶ *The actors had a short rest in the middle of the rehearsal.*
• **break, pause, respite, breathing space, nap, lie-down**
(*informal*) **breather**
❷ *Try to get as much rest as you can.*
• **relaxation, inactivity, leisure, ease, quiet, time off**
➤ **the rest**
I spent the rest of the money on clothes.
• **the remainder, the surplus, the remains, the others**

rest *VERB*
❶ *Let's stop and rest for a while.*
• **have a rest, take a break, relax, have a nap, take it easy, lie down**
(*informal*) **have a breather**
IDIOM **put your feet up**
❷ *Rest the ladder against the wall.*
• **lean, prop, stand, place, support**

restaurant *NOUN*

WORD WEB

Some types of restaurant:

- bistro
- brasserie
- buffet
- cafe
- cafeteria
- canteen
- carvery
- chip shop
- coffee shop
- diner
- grill room
- ice cream parlour
- pizzeria
- snack bar
- steakhouse
- takeaway
- tea room
- wine bar

restful *ADJECTIVE*

What I needed was a restful night's sleep.
• **peaceful, undisturbed, quiet, relaxing, leisurely, calm, tranquil**
OPPOSITES stressful, disturbed

restless *ADJECTIVE*

❶ *I'd been feeling strangely restless all morning.*
• **agitated, nervous, anxious, uneasy, edgy, jumpy, jittery, tense**
(*informal*) **uptight, nervy**
OPPOSITE relaxed
❷ *She spent a restless night worrying.*
• **sleepless, wakeful, troubled, disturbed, unsettled**
OPPOSITES restful, peaceful

restore *VERB*

❶ *Please restore the book to its proper place on the shelf.*
• **put back, return, replace**
❷ *They are restoring the Sunday bus service.*
• **bring back, reinstate**
❸ *My uncle loves restoring old motorcycles.*
• **renew, repair, renovate, recondition, fix, mend, rebuild**
(*informal*) **do up**

restrain *VERB*

❶ *Dogs must be restrained on a lead in the park.*
• **hold back, keep back, keep under control, restrict**
❷ *She tried to restrain her anger.*
• **control, check, curb, suppress, contain, hold in**
IDIOM **keep the lid on**

restrict *VERB*

❶ *The new law restricts the sale of fireworks.*
• **control, limit, regulate, moderate, keep within bounds**
❷ *Dancers wear clothes that don't restrict their movement.*
• **hinder, impede, obstruct, block**

result *NOUN*

❶ *The forest fires were the result of a long drought.*
• **consequence, effect, outcome, upshot, sequel (to)**
OPPOSITE cause
❷ *What was the result of the match?*
• **score, tally**

result *VERB*

The bruising on his leg resulted from a bad fall.
• **come about, develop, emerge, happen, occur, follow, ensue**
➤ **result in**
The flooding resulted in chaos on the roads.
• **cause, bring about, give rise to, lead to, develop into**

resume *VERB*

The class will resume after lunch.
• **restart, start again, recommence, proceed, continue, carry on**
OPPOSITES discontinue, cease

retain *VERB*

❶ *Please retain your ticket for inspection.*
• **hold on to, keep, preserve, reserve, save**
(*informal*) **hang on to**
OPPOSITE surrender

A B C D E F G H I J K L M N O P Q R S T U V W X Y Z

❷ *This type of soil is good at retaining water.*
• **hold in, keep in, hold back**
OPPOSITE release

retire *VERB*
❶ *He retired two years ago after a long career in teaching.*
• **give up work, stop working, bow out**
– To leave your job voluntarily is to **resign**.
❷ *She retired to her room with a headache.*
• **withdraw, retreat, adjourn**

retort *NOUN*
see **reply**

retreat *VERB*
❶ *We retreated to a safe distance from the bonfire.*
• **move back, draw back, fall back, withdraw, retire**
OPPOSITE advance
❷ *The snail retreated into its shell.*
• **shrink back, recoil**

retrieve *VERB*
I had to climb over the fence to retrieve the ball.
• **get back, bring back, recover, rescue, salvage**

return *VERB*
❶ *I hope to return to New Zealand some day.*
• **go back, revisit**
❷ *I'll see you when I return.*
• **get back, come back, come home**
❸ *Take these pills if the symptoms return.*
• **reappear, come back, recur**
❹ *I returned the cat to its rightful owner.*
• **give back, send back, restore**
❺ *Faulty goods may be returned to the shop.*
• **send back, take back**

return *NOUN*
❶ *She was looking forward to her friends' return.*
• **homecoming, reappearance**
❷ *The museum is hoping for the safe return of the stolen painting.*
• **retrieval, recovery**
❸ *We are all waiting for the return of spring.*
• **reappearance, recurrence**
❹ *He gets a good return on his savings.*
• **profit, interest, gain**

reveal *VERB*
❶ *The bookcase swung out to reveal a secret room.*
• **uncover, unveil, expose**
OPPOSITES hide, conceal
❷ *She never revealed her real identity.*
• **disclose, make known, divulge, confess, admit, make public, give away, let slip**

revel *VERB*
➤ **revel in**
My sister revelled in all the attention.
• **enjoy, delight in, love, adore, relish, savour, lap up**

revenge *NOUN*
The story is about a man who seeks revenge for his brother's murder.
• **vengeance, reprisal, retribution, retaliation**
➤ **take revenge on someone**
He swore to take revenge on them all.
• **get even with, make someone pay** (*informal*) **get your own back on**

revere *VERB*
The painter was greatly revered by his fellow artists.
• **admire, respect, esteem, think highly of, look up to, venerate**
OPPOSITE despise

reverse *NOUN*
❶ *This is the reverse of what I expected.*
• **opposite, contrary, converse, antithesis**
❷ *The letter had a handwritten note on the reverse.*
• **other side, back**

reverse *VERB*

❶ *You can use tracing paper to reverse a drawing.*
• **turn round, swap round, turn back to front, transpose, invert, flip**
❷ *The driver was reversing into a parking space.*
• **back, move backwards, go backwards**
❸ *The referee refused to reverse his decision.*
• **go back on, overturn, overrule, cancel, revoke**

review *NOUN*

❶ *After the accident they carried out a review of safety procedures.*
• **study, survey, examination, inspection, enquiry, probe**
❷ *The reviews of her latest film aren't good.*
• **report, commentary, appraisal, assessment**
(*informal*) **crit**

review *VERB*

❶ *The judge began to review the evidence.*
• **examine, go over, study, survey, consider, assess, evaluate, appraise, weigh up, size up**
❷ *On Friday they always review the latest films.*
• **write a review of, comment on, criticize**

revise *VERB*

❶ *We revised the work we did last term.*
• **go over, review, reread, study, cram**
❷ *The last chapter has been revised by the author.*
• **correct, amend, edit, rewrite, update**
❸ *I have revised my opinion about that.*
• **change, modify, alter, reconsider, re-examine**

revive *VERB*

❶ *He fainted but soon revived.*
• **come round, come to, recover, regain consciousness**
❷ *A cup of tea should revive you.*
• **refresh, restore, reinvigorate, revitalize, bring back to life**

revolt *VERB*

❶ *The stench in the dungeon revolted him.*
• **disgust, repel, sicken, nauseate, offend, appal, put off**
(*informal*) **turn off**
IDIOM **turn your stomach**
❷ *The people revolted against their Roman masters.*
• **rebel, riot, rise up**
– To revolt on a ship is to **mutiny**.

revolt *NOUN*

Boudicca led a revolt against the Romans.
• **rebellion, riot, uprising, revolution**
– A revolt on a ship is a **mutiny**.

revolting *ADJECTIVE*

What is that revolting smell?
• **disgusting, foul, horrible, nasty, loathsome, offensive, obnoxious, repulsive, repugnant, sickening, nauseating, vile, unpleasant**
OPPOSITES **pleasant, attractive**

revolution *NOUN*

❶ *The Russian Revolution took place in 1917.*
• **rebellion, revolt, uprising**
❷ *Computers brought about a revolution in the way people work.*
• **change, transformation, shift**
(*informal*) **shake-up**
❸ *One revolution of the Earth takes 24 hours.*
• **rotation, turn, circuit, cycle, orbit, lap**

revolutionary *ADJECTIVE*

He invented a revolutionary type of battery.
• **new, novel, innovative, unconventional, unorthodox, radical**

revolve *VERB*

❶ *The Earth revolves once every 24 hours.*
• **rotate, turn, spin**
❷ *The Moon revolves around the Earth.*
• **circle, go around, orbit**

reward *NOUN*
❶ *You deserve a reward for all your hard work.*
• **award, bonus, treat**
(*informal*) **pay-off**
OPPOSITE punishment
❷ *The dog's owners have offered a reward for its safe return.*
• **payment, bounty**

reward *VERB*
It is good to reward your pet for good behaviour.
• **recompense, give a treat to, give a bonus to, repay**
OPPOSITE punish

rewarding *ADJECTIVE*
Being a vet must be a rewarding job.
• **satisfying, gratifying, fulfilling, pleasing, worthwhile**
OPPOSITE thankless

rhyme *NOUN*
I have a book of nonsense rhymes.
• **poem, verse**
SEE ALSO **poem**

rhythm *NOUN*
Everyone clapped to the rhythm of the music.
• **beat, pulse, tempo**
– The rhythm of a poem is its **metre**.

rich *ADJECTIVE*
❶ *He came from a rich family.*
• **wealthy, affluent, prosperous, well-off, well-to-do**
(*informal*) **flush, loaded, well-heeled**
OPPOSITES poor, impoverished
❷ *The room was decorated with rich fabrics.*
• **luxurious, lavish, sumptuous, opulent, ornate, splendid, expensive, costly**
❸ *She has hair of a rich chestnut colour.*
• **deep, strong, vivid, intense**
❹ *I'm cutting down on rich foods.*
• **fatty, creamy, heavy**
❺ *Plant the bulbs in moist rich soil.*
• **fertile, fruitful, productive**
➤ **be rich in**
The islands are rich in animal and plant species.
• **be full of, abound in, teem with, overflow with, be well supplied with, be well stocked with**

riches *PLURAL NOUN*
They acquired riches beyond their wildest dreams.
• **wealth, money, affluence, prosperity, fortune, treasure**

rickety *ADJECTIVE*
She pulled out a rickety old step ladder.
• **shaky, unsteady, unstable, wobbly, flimsy**
OPPOSITES solid, firm

rid *VERB*
He rid the town of rats.
• **clear, free, empty, strip, purge**
➤ **get rid of**
She decided to get rid of her old guitar.
• **dispose of, throw away, throw out, discard, scrap, dump, jettison**
(*informal*) **ditch, chuck out**

riddle *NOUN*
They had to solve the riddle to find the treasure.
• **puzzle, question, conundrum, problem, mystery**
(*informal*) **brain-teaser, poser**

ride *VERB*
❶ *My little brother is learning to ride a bike.*
• **control, handle, manage, steer**
❷ *She used to ride around on a scooter.*
• **travel, drive, cycle, pedal**

ride *NOUN*
We took a ride on a snowmobile.
• **drive, run, journey, trip**
(*informal*) **spin**

ridicule *VERB*
People have often ridiculed great inventors at first.
• **laugh at, make fun of, mock, scoff at, jeer at, sneer at, taunt, tease, deride**
OPPOSITE respect

ridiculous *ADJECTIVE*
❶ *You look ridiculous in those trousers.*
• **silly, stupid, foolish, absurd, laughable, farcical**
OPPOSITE sensible
❷ *That is a ridiculous price for a pair of shoes.*
• **ludicrous, senseless, nonsensical, preposterous, outrageous, absurd, unreasonable**
OPPOSITE reasonable

right *ADJECTIVE*
❶ *The entrance is on the right side of the building.*
• **right-hand**
– The right side of a ship when you face forwards is the **starboard** side.
OPPOSITE left
❷ *That is the right answer.*
• **correct, accurate, true, exact**
OPPOSITE wrong
❸ *She was waiting for the right moment to tell him.*
• **proper, appropriate, fitting, suitable, ideal, perfect**
OPPOSITE wrong
❹ *It's not right to cheat.*
• **fair, honest, moral, just, honourable, decent, upright, virtuous, ethical**
OPPOSITE wrong

right *ADVERB*
❶ *Turn right at the corner.*
OPPOSITE left
❷ *Go right ahead.*
• **directly, straight**
❸ *We had walked right round in a circle.*
• **all the way, completely**
❹ *There is a dot right in the centre of the screen.*
• **exactly, precisely, squarely, dead**
(*informal*) **bang**
❺ *Did I do that right?*
• **correctly, properly, accurately, perfectly**
❻ (*informal*) *I'll be right back.*
• **immediately, promptly, soon**

right *NOUN*
❶ *Take the turning on the right.*
OPPOSITE left
❷ *We both know the difference between right and wrong.*
• **goodness, fairness, virtue, morality, truth, justice**
OPPOSITE wrong
❸ *People over 18 have the right to vote in elections.*
• **entitlement, privilege, prerogative, freedom, liberty, licence, power**

rigid *ADJECTIVE*
❶ *The tent was supported by a rigid framework.*
• **stiff, firm, hard, inflexible, unbending**
OPPOSITES flexible, pliable
❷ *The referee was rigid in applying the rules.*
• **strict, inflexible, uncompromising**
OPPOSITES flexible, lenient

rigorous *ADJECTIVE*
Detectives carried out a rigorous investigation.
• **thorough, careful, meticulous, painstaking, conscientious, scrupulous**

rim *NOUN*
She peered at us over the rim of her glasses.
• **brim, edge, lip, brink**

ring *NOUN*
❶ *Mushrooms were growing in a ring.*
• **circle, round, loop, circuit**
❷ *Each bird is tagged with a metal ring.*
• **band, hoop**
❸ *Four gladiators entered the ring.*
• **arena, circus, enclosure**

ring *VERB*
❶ *The whole area was ringed by barbed wire.*
• **surround, encircle, enclose, circle**
❷ *Church bells rang all morning.*
• **chime, peal, toll, clang**
❸ *The doorbell rang unexpectedly.*
• **sound, buzz, jangle, tinkle**
❹ *Ring me later this evening.*
• **phone, call, telephone, give someone a call**
(*informal*) **give someone a ring, give someone a bell**

rinse *VERB*
Rinse the wound carefully with clean water.
• **wash, clean, cleanse, bathe, swill, flush out**

riot *NOUN*
The incident sparked a riot in the capital.
• **disturbance, commotion, turmoil, disorder, uproar, uprising**

riot *VERB*
Students rioted in the streets of the capital.
• **run riot, run wild, run amok, rampage, revolt, rise up, rebel**

rip *VERB*
❶ *She read the note and ripped it into little pieces.*
• **tear**
❷ *He ripped the letter out of my hands.*
• **pull, tug, wrench, snatch, tear**

ripe *ADJECTIVE*
❶ *You need ripe berries for making jam.*
• **mature, ready to eat**
– To become ripe is to **ripen**.
❷ *I feel that the time is ripe for change.*
• **ready, right, suitable, favourable**

ripple *VERB*
A light breeze rippled the tree tops.
• **ruffle, stir, disturb, make waves on**

rise *VERB*
❶ *A plume of smoke rose high into the air.*
• **climb, mount, ascend, soar, fly up, take off, lift off**
OPPOSITE **descend**
❷ *The castle walls rose above us.*
• **tower, loom, soar, reach up**
❸ *Prices are set to rise again.*
• **go up, increase, escalate, jump, leap**
OPPOSITE **fall**
❹ *I rose to greet our visitor.*
• **stand up, get up, leap up, get to your feet**
OPPOSITE **sit down**
❺ *They rose early winter and summer.*
• **awake, get up, stir**
OPPOSITES **go to bed, retire**

rise *NOUN*
❶ *There will be a rise in temperature over the next few days.*
• **increase, jump, leap, hike**
OPPOSITE **fall**
❷ *The hill fort sits at the top of a rise.*
• **hill, slope, ascent, incline**

risk *NOUN*
❶ *She was aware of the risks involved in mountaineering.*
• **danger, hazard, peril**
❷ *There is a risk of further delays.*
• **chance, likelihood, possibility, prospect**

risk *VERB*
❶ *I decided to risk taking a look outside.*
• **chance, dare, gamble, venture**
❷ *She risked her life to save others.*
• **endanger, put at risk, jeopardize, imperil**

risky *ADJECTIVE*
Bungee jumping is a risky activity.
• **dangerous, hazardous, perilous, unsafe, precarious**
(*informal*) **dicey**
IDIOM **touch and go**
OPPOSITE **safe**

ritual *NOUN*
The temple was used for ancient religious rituals.
• **ceremony, rite**

rival *NOUN*
The two players became friendly rivals.
• **opponent, adversary, challenger, competitor, contender**

rival *VERB*
This scenery can rival any in the world.
• **compete with, contend with, vie with, compare with, match, equal**

rivalry *NOUN*
There was intense rivalry between the two local teams.
• **competition, competitiveness, opposition**
OPPOSITE **cooperation**

river *NOUN*
We took a ferry across the river.
– A small river is a **stream, brook, rivulet** or (*Scottish*) **burn**.
– A small river which flows into a larger river is a **tributary**.
– The place where a river begins is its **source**.
– The place where a river goes into the sea is its **mouth**.
– A wide river mouth is an **estuary** or (*Scottish*) **firth**.
– The place where the mouth of a river splits before going into the sea is a **delta**.

road *NOUN*
We have to cross a busy road.
• **street, lane, alley, avenue, boulevard, highway, motorway, bypass**
– A road which is closed at one end is a **dead end**.
– A private road up to a house is a **drive**.

roam *VERB*
❶ *We roamed about town aimlessly.*
• **wander, drift, stroll, amble, traipse**
❷ *Herds of buffalo used to roam the plains.*
• **range, rove**

roar *NOUN*
❶ *It sounded like the roar of a wild animal.*
• **bellow, howl, cry**
❷ *Outside the stadium we heard the roars of the crowd.*
• **shout, cry, yell, clamour**

roar *VERB*
The monster lifted its head and roared.
• **bellow, cry, howl, thunder, bawl, yell**

rob *VERB*
Masked highwaymen used to rob stagecoaches.
• **steal from, break into, burgle, hold up, raid, loot, ransack, rifle**
➤ **be robbed of something**
We were robbed of victory in the last minute of the match.
• **be deprived of, be denied, be cheated out of**

robber *NOUN*
The money was stolen by a gang of armed robbers.
• **thief, burglar, housebreaker, looter**

robbery *NOUN*
He planned a daring robbery on a jewellery store.
• **theft, stealing, burglary, housebreaking, looting**

robe *NOUN*
He wore the ceremonial robes of a chief.
• **gown, vestments**

robot *NOUN*
In the future, housework will be done by robots.
• **automaton, android**
– A robot which is part-human is a **cyborg**.

robust *ADJECTIVE*
❶ *He is in a robust state of health.*
• **strong, vigorous, fit, hardy, healthy, rugged**
OPPOSITE weak
❷ *Bring a robust pair of boots.*
• **sturdy, tough, durable, hard-wearing**
OPPOSITE flimsy

rock *NOUN*
We clambered over the rocks on the seashore.
• **stone, boulder, pebble**

WORD WEB

Some rocks and minerals:

➤ basalt	➤ marble
➤ chalk	➤ pumice
➤ flint	➤ quartz
➤ granite	➤ sandstone
➤ gypsum	➤ shale
➤ limestone	➤ slate

- Rock from which metal or valuable minerals can be extracted is **ore**.
- A layer of rock is a **stratum**.

a b c d e f g h i j k l m n o p q r s t u v w x y z

- The scientific study of rocks and rock formations is **geology**.
- The scientific study of minerals is **mineralogy**.

rock *VERB*
❶ *At each turn, the bus rocked from side to side.*
• **roll, toss, lurch, pitch, tilt, reel**
❷ *I rocked the baby's cradle to and fro.*
• **sway, swing**

rocky *ADJECTIVE*
❶ *Nothing was growing in the rocky ground.*
• **stony, pebbly, rough, craggy, shingly**
❷ *I wish this chair wasn't so rocky.*
• **unsteady, unstable, rickety, shaky, wobbly, tottery**

rod *NOUN*
He was putting up a metal curtain rod.
• **bar, rail, pole, strut, shaft, stick, spoke, staff**

rode
past tense see **ride**

rodent *NOUN*

WORD WEB

Some animals which are rodents:

- beaver
- chinchilla
- chipmunk
- coypu
- gerbil
- gopher
- groundhog
- guinea pig
- hamster
- jerboa
- lemming
- marmot
- mouse
- muskrat
- porcupine
- prairie dog
- rat
- squirrel
- vole
- water vole or water rat

rogue *NOUN*
What a rogue he turned out to be!
• **rascal, scoundrel, villain, cheat, fraud, swindler**

role *NOUN*
❶ *Who played the lead role in the film?*
• **part, character**
❷ *Each player has an important role in the team.*
• **job, task, function, position, responsibility, duty**

roll *VERB*
❶ *Slowly the wheels began to roll.*
• **move round, turn, revolve, rotate, spin, whirl**
❷ *Roll the ribbon around your finger.*
• **curl, wind, wrap, twist, coil, twirl**
- To roll up a sail is to **furl** it.
❸ *Roll out the pastry into a large circle.*
• **flatten, level out, smooth**
❹ *A tiny boat was rolling about in the storm.*
• **rock, sway, pitch, toss, lurch**

romantic *ADJECTIVE*
❶ *Do you think they had a romantic relationship?*
• **amorous, loving, passionate, affectionate, tender**
❷ *The film had a very romantic ending.*
• **sentimental, emotional**
(*informal*) **soppy, mushy**
❸ *She has a romantic view of life in the countryside.*
• **idealistic, unrealistic, fanciful, fairy-tale**

roof *NOUN*
The shed has a sloping roof.
- The sloping beams in the framework of a roof are **rafters**.
- The overhanging edges of a roof are the **eaves**.
- The triangular section of wall under a sloping roof is the **gable**.

room *NOUN*
❶ *There is a small room at the top of the stairs.*
• (*old use*) **chamber**
❷ *Do you have room for another passenger?*
• **space, capacity**

❸ *There is still room for improvement.*
• **scope, opportunity**

WORD WEB

Some types of room:

- ➤ anteroom
- ➤ bathroom
- ➤ bedroom
- ➤ box room
- ➤ classroom
- ➤ cloakroom
- ➤ conservatory
- ➤ dining room
- ➤ dormitory
- ➤ drawing room
- ➤ dressing room
- ➤ games room
- ➤ guest room
- ➤ hall
- ➤ kitchen
- ➤ kitchenette
- ➤ landing
- ➤ lavatory or toilet
- ➤ library
- ➤ living room
- ➤ lounge
- ➤ music room
- ➤ nursery
- ➤ pantry
- ➤ parlour
- ➤ playroom
- ➤ scullery
- ➤ sitting room
- ➤ spare room
- ➤ staffroom
- ➤ storeroom
- ➤ study
- ➤ utility room

- A sleeping room on a ship is a **cabin**.
- A small room in a monastery or prison is a **cell**.
- An underground room is a **basement** or **cellar**. In a church it is a **vault**.
- The space in the roof of a house is the **attic** or **loft**.
- A room where an artist works is a **studio**.
- A room where you wait to see a doctor or dentist is a **waiting room**.

roomy *ADJECTIVE*
The flat is surprisingly roomy inside.
• **spacious, extensive, big, sizeable**

root *NOUN*
We need to get to the root of the problem.
• **source, cause, basis, origin, starting point**

rope *NOUN*
He lowered down a length of rope.
• **cable, cord, line**
- The ropes which support a ship's mast and sails are the **rigging**.
- The ropes which hold down a tent are the **guy ropes**.
- A rope with a loop at one end used for catching cattle is a **lasso**.

rose
past tense see **rise**

rot *VERB*
The floorboards had begun to rot.
• **decay, decompose, become rotten, disintegrate, crumble**
- If metal rots it is said to **corrode**.
- If rubber rots it is said to **perish**.
- If food rots it is said to **go bad** or **putrefy**.

rotate *VERB*
A day is the time it takes the Earth to rotate once on its axis.
• **revolve, turn, spin, pivot, gyrate, wheel, swivel, twirl, whirl**

rotten *ADJECTIVE*
❶ *The window frame is rotten.*
• **decayed, decaying, decomposed, crumbling, disintegrating**
OPPOSITE sound
❷ *The fridge smelled of rotten eggs.*
• **bad, mouldy, putrid, rancid, gone off**
OPPOSITE fresh
❸ (*informal*) *I've had a rotten week!*
• **bad, unpleasant, disagreeable, awful, dreadful, terrible, abysmal**
(*informal*) **lousy**
OPPOSITE good

rough *ADJECTIVE*
❶ *A rough track led to the farm.*
• **uneven, irregular, rugged, bumpy, rocky, stony**
OPPOSITES even, level
❷ *Feel the rough texture of this handmade paper.*
• **coarse, harsh, scratchy, bristly**
OPPOSITES smooth, soft
❸ *She pushed him away with a rough shove.*
• **hard, forceful, violent, severe,**

A B C D E F G H I J K L M N O P Q R S T U V W X Y Z

tough, brutal
OPPOSITES gentle, mild
❹ *The sea was rough that day.*
• **stormy, choppy, turbulent, heaving**
OPPOSITES calm, smooth
❺ *He's been having a rough time.*
• **hard, difficult, troublesome, bad, disagreeable, unpleasant**
OPPOSITES good, easy
❻ *I had only a rough idea of where we were.*
• **approximate, vague, inexact, imprecise**
OPPOSITES exact, precise
❼ *I've written a rough draft of the first chapter.*
• **preliminary, basic, rudimentary, unfinished, unpolished, sketchy**
OPPOSITES finished, final

roughly *ADVERB*
The cinema seats roughly a hundred people.
• **approximately, about, around, close to, nearly**

round *ADJECTIVE*
❶ *The room had a little round window.*
• **circular, disc-shaped**
❷ *Holly bushes have small round berries.*
• **spherical, ball-shaped, globular**

round *NOUN*
❶ *We got through to the second round of the competition.*
• **stage, level, heat, game, bout, contest**
❷ *My brother does a morning paper round.*
• **route, circuit, tour**
– The regular round of a police officer is their **beat**.

round *VERB*
A large van slowly rounded the corner.
• **go round, travel round, turn**
➤ **round something off**
We rounded off the meal with coffee and cake.
• **finish off, conclude, complete, end, crown, cap**
➤ **round someone up**
The teacher was rounding up the children.
• **gather together, assemble, collect, muster, rally**

roundabout *ADJECTIVE*
That is a very roundabout way of answering the question.
• **indirect, circuitous, winding, meandering**
OPPOSITE direct

rouse *VERB*
❶ *The doorbell roused her from her daydream.*
• **awaken, wake up, arouse**
❷ *My curiosity was roused by a flashing light in the sky.*
• **excite, arouse, stir up, stimulate, activate, galvanize, provoke, agitate**

route *NOUN*
We took the quickest route home.
• **way, course, path, road, direction**

routine *NOUN*
❶ *A morning run is part of her daily routine.*
• **procedure, practice, regime, drill, pattern, custom, habit, programme, schedule**

❷ *I've been practising a new dance routine.*
• **act, programme, performance, number**

row (rhymes with go) *NOUN*
Across the road was a neat row of houses.
• **line, column, file, series, sequence, string, chain**
– A row of people waiting for something is a **queue**.

row (rhymes with cow) *NOUN*
❶ *The people next door were making a terrible row.*
• **noise, din, racket, commotion, clamour, uproar, rumpus, hubbub**
❷ *Some of the players were having a row with the referee.*
• **argument, fight, disagreement, dispute, quarrel, squabble, tiff**

rowdy *ADJECTIVE*
A rowdy group of men got on the train.
• **noisy, unruly, wild, disorderly,**

boisterous, riotous
OPPOSITE quiet

royal *ADJECTIVE*
These pyramids were built as royal tombs.
• **regal, kingly, queenly, princely**

royalty *NOUN*

WORD WEB

Some members of a royal family:

- ➤ king
- ➤ monarch
- ➤ prince
- ➤ princess
- ➤ queen
- ➤ queen mother
- ➤ sovereign

- The way to address a king or queen is **Your Majesty**.
- The way to address a prince or princess is **Your Highness**.
- The husband or wife of a royal person is a **consort**.
- A person who rules while a monarch is too young or unable to rule is a **regent**.

rub *VERB*
❶ *Try not to rub your eyes.*
• **stroke, knead, massage, pat**
❷ *Rub some suncream on your arms.*
• **spread, smear, apply (to), smooth**
❸ *I rubbed the window to see outside.*
• **wipe, polish, shine, buff**
❹ *These boots are rubbing against my ankles.*
• **graze, scrape, chafe**
➤ **rub something out**
I just need to rub out the pencil marks.
• **erase, wipe out, delete, remove**

rubbish *NOUN*
❶ *Dad took the rubbish out to the bin.*
• **refuse, waste, junk, litter, scrap**
(*North American*) **trash, garbage**
❷ *Don't talk rubbish!*
• **nonsense, drivel, gibberish, claptrap,**
(*North American*) **garbage**
(*informal*) **gobbledegook, baloney, rot, tripe, twaddle, piffle, codswallop**
(*old use*) **balderdash, poppycock**
OPPOSITE sense

rude *ADJECTIVE*
❶ *It was rude of me to interrupt.*
• **impolite, discourteous, bad-mannered, impertinent, impudent, insolent, offensive, insulting, abusive**
OPPOSITE polite
❷ *He's always telling rude jokes.*
• **indecent, coarse, crude, dirty, smutty, vulgar, lewd, obscene**
OPPOSITE clean

ruffle *VERB*
❶ *A light breeze ruffled the waters of the lake.*
• **stir, disturb, ripple**
❷ *Lukasz's dad leaned over and ruffled his hair.*
• **tousle, mess up, rumple, dishevel**

ruin *NOUN*
❶ *The city was in a state of ruin.*
• **destruction, disintegration, decay, collapse**
❷ *They now face financial ruin.*
• **failure, loss, bankruptcy, insolvency, destitution**
➤ **ruins**
Archaeologists discovered the ruins of an ancient Mayan city.
• **remains, remnants, fragments**

ruin *VERB*
❶ *A sudden rainstorm could ruin the entire harvest.*
• **destroy, wreck, devastate, demolish, ravage, lay waste, wipe out**
❷ *The ending ruined the whole film for me.*
• **spoil, mar, blight, mess up**
(*informal*) **scupper**

ruined *ADJECTIVE*
Bats flew in and out of the ruined abbey.
• **wrecked, crumbling, derelict, dilapidated, tumbledown, ramshackle**

rule *NOUN*
❶ *Players must stick to the rules of the game.*
• **regulation, law, principle, statute**

❷ *The country was formerly under French rule.*
• **control, authority, command, power, government, jurisdiction**
❸ *The usual rule is to leave a tip.*
• **custom, convention, practice, habit, norm**

rule *VERB*
❶ *The Romans ruled a vast empire.*
• **govern, control, command, direct, lead, manage, run, administer**
❷ *Queen Elizabeth I ruled for over 40 years.*
• **reign, be ruler**
❸ *The umpire ruled that the ball was out.*
• **judge, decree, pronounce, decide, determine, find**
➤ **rule something out**
We can't rule out the possibility of sabotage.
• **eliminate, exclude, disregard, disallow**

ruler *NOUN*

WORD WEB

Some titles of ruler:

➤ emir
➤ emperor
➤ empress
➤ governor
➤ head of state
➤ king
➤ monarch
➤ potentate
➤ premier
➤ president
➤ prince
➤ princess
➤ queen
➤ sovereign
➤ viceroy

- A person who rules while a monarch is too young or unable to rule is a **regent**.
- A single ruler with unlimited power is an **autocrat** or a **dictator**.

Historical rulers:

➤ caesar
➤ caliph
➤ kaiser
➤ maharaja
➤ maharani
➤ pharaoh
➤ raja
➤ rani
➤ shah
➤ sultan
➤ tsar
➤ tsarina

rummage *VERB*
She started rummaging in her bag for her keys.
• **search, hunt, root about**

rumour *NOUN*
All kinds of rumours were flying round the school.
• **gossip, hearsay, talk, speculation, story**
(*informal*) **tittle-tattle**

run *VERB*
❶ *We ran at full speed down the hill.*
• **race, sprint, dash, speed, rush, hurry, tear, bolt, fly, streak, whizz, zoom, zip, pelt, hurtle, scurry, scamper, career**
(*informal*) **scoot**
– To run at a gentle pace is to **jog**.
❷ *Beads of sweat ran down his face.*
• **stream, flow, pour, gush, flood, cascade, spill, trickle, dribble**
❸ *My old laptop still runs well.*
• **function, operate, work, go, perform**
❹ *Her dream is to run her own restaurant.*
• **manage, be in charge of, direct, control, supervise, oversee, govern, rule**
❺ *The river Amazon runs through seven countries.*
• **go, extend, pass, stretch, reach**
❻ *Could you please run me to the station?*
• **give someone a lift, drive, take, transport, convey**
➤ **run away or off**
The boys ran off when they saw me.
• **flee, take flight, take off, escape, fly, bolt**
(*informal*) **make off, clear off, scarper**
IDIOM **take to your heels**
➤ **run into**
❶ *Guess who I ran into at the weekend?*
• **meet, come across, encounter**
(*informal*) **bump into**
❷ *Two lorries nearly ran into each other.*
• **hit, collide with**

run *NOUN*
❶ *She likes to go for a morning run along the beach.*
• **jog, trot, sprint, race, dash**

❷ *We went for a run in the car.*
• **drive, journey, ride, trip, outing, excursion**
(*informal*) **spin**
❸ *They've had a run of good luck recently.*
• **sequence, stretch, series**
❹ *The farmer had to build a new chicken run.*
• **enclosure, pen, coop**

runaway *NOUN*
We watched a film about three teenage runaways.
• **missing person**
– A person who has run away from the army is a **deserter**.
– A person who is running away from the law is a **fugitive** or an **outlaw**.

runner *NOUN*
Over a thousand runners will take part in the marathon.
• **athlete, competitor, racer**
– Someone who runs fast over short distances is a **sprinter**.
– Someone who runs to keep fit is a **jogger**.

runny *ADJECTIVE*
This sauce is too runny.
• **watery, thin, liquid, fluid**
OPPOSITE thick

rural *ADJECTIVE*
They live in a remote rural area.
• **country, rustic, agricultural, pastoral**
OPPOSITE urban

rush *VERB*
❶ *I rushed home with the good news.*
• **hurry, hasten, race, run, dash, fly, bolt, charge, speed, sprint, tear, hurtle, scurry**
❷ *Don't rush me – I'm thinking.*
• **push, hurry, press, hustle**

rush *NOUN*
❶ *What's the rush?*
• **hurry, haste, urgency**
❷ *There was a sudden rush of water.*
• **flood, gush, spurt, stream, spate**
❸ *I was surprised by the rush for tickets.*
• **demand, call, clamour, run (on)**

rustic *ADJECTIVE*
On the wall was a painting of a rustic scene.
• **country, rural, pastoral**

rustle *VERB*
The trees rustled in the breeze.
• **crackle, swish, whisper**

rut *NOUN*
There were deep ruts made by a tractor.
• **furrow, groove, channel, trough**

ruthless *ADJECTIVE*
He was a ruthless dictator who terrorized his people.
• **merciless, pitiless, heartless, hard-hearted, cold-blooded, callous, cruel, vicious, brutal**
OPPOSITE merciful

A B C D E F G H I J K L M N O P Q R S T U V W X Y Z

Ss

sack *NOUN*
In the corner was a large sack of potatoes.
• bag, pack, pouch
➤ **the sack**
(*informal*) *If the boss finds out, he'll get the sack.*
• dismissal, discharge, redundancy
(*informal*) the boot, the axe

sack *VERB*
They threatened to sack the whole workforce.
• dismiss, discharge, let go
(*informal*) fire, give someone the sack

sacred *ADJECTIVE*
The Koran is the sacred book of Muslims.
• holy, religious, hallowed, divine, heavenly
OPPOSITE secular

sacrifice *VERB*
❶ *She sacrificed her career to bring up the children.*
• give up, surrender, forfeit, go without
❷ *Animals were sacrificed on this altar.*
• offer up, slaughter, kill

sad *ADJECTIVE*

OVERUSED WORD

❶ A sad mood, sad feeling:

➤ unhappy
➤ sorrowful
➤ miserable
➤ depressed
➤ downcast
➤ downhearted
➤ despondent
➤ crestfallen
➤ dismal
➤ gloomy
➤ glum
➤ blue
➤ low
➤ down
➤ dejected
➤ forlorn
➤ morose
➤ desolate
➤ doleful
➤ wretched
➤ woeful
➤ woebegone
➤ tearful
➤ heartbroken
➤ broken-hearted

(*informal*) down in the dumps, down in the mouth
He has been miserable *since his dog died.*
OPPOSITES happy, cheerful

❷ A sad situation, sad news:

➤ unfortunate
➤ upsetting
➤ distressing
➤ painful
➤ disheartening
➤ discouraging
➤ regrettable
➤ lamentable
➤ deplorable
➤ grim
➤ serious
➤ grave
➤ desperate
➤ tragic
➤ grievous

I'm afraid I have some upsetting *news.*
OPPOSITES fortunate, good

❸ A sad story, sad tune:

➤ depressing
➤ melancholy
➤ mournful
➤ moving
➤ touching
➤ heartbreaking
➤ heart-rending
➤ pitiful
➤ pathetic
➤ plaintive
➤ wistful

She stayed in her room, listening to mournful *music.*
OPPOSITES cheering, uplifting

sadden *VERB*
I was saddened by how much the town had changed.
• depress, upset, dispirit, dishearten, discourage, grieve
IDIOM break your heart
OPPOSITE cheer up

sadness *NOUN*
There was sadness and despair in her eyes.
• unhappiness, sorrow, grief, misery, depression, dejection, melancholy, gloom
OPPOSITES happiness, joy

safe *ADJECTIVE*

❶ *The missing hillwalkers were found safe and well.*
• **unharmed, unhurt, uninjured, undamaged, unscathed, sound, intact** (*informal*) **in one piece**
OPPOSITES hurt, damaged
❷ *He felt safe up in the tree.*
• **protected, defended, secure, out of danger, out of harm's way**
OPPOSITES vulnerable, insecure
❸ *She knew she was leaving her dog in safe hands.*
• **reliable, trustworthy, dependable, sound**
OPPOSITES dangerous, risky
❹ *Is the tap water safe to drink?*
• **harmless, uncontaminated, innocuous, non-poisonous**
OPPOSITE harmful

safety *NOUN*

These rules are for your own safety.
• **protection, security, well-being**
OPPOSITE danger

sag *VERB*

❶ *The tent began to sag under the weight of the rain.*
• **sink, slump, bulge, dip**
❷ *His shoulders sagged.*
• **hang down, droop, flop**

said

past tense see **say**

sail *VERB*

❶ *Tall ships used to sail right into the harbour.*
• **travel, voyage, cruise**
– To begin a sea voyage is to **put to sea** or **set sail**.
❷ *They learned how to sail a yacht.*
• **pilot, steer, navigate**
❸ *The ball sailed over the fence.*
• **glide, drift, float, flow, sweep**

sailor *NOUN*

We have a crew of experienced sailors.
• **seaman, seafarer, mariner, hand**
– A person who sails a yacht is a **yachtsman** or **yachtswoman**.

sake *NOUN*

➤ **for the sake of**
He was told to lose weight for the sake of his health.
• **for the good of, in the interests of, to benefit, to help**

salary *NOUN*

The job has an annual salary of £30,000.
• **income, pay, earnings, wages**

sale *NOUN*

They made a lot of money from the sale of the painting.
• **selling, dealing, trading, marketing, vending**
OPPOSITE purchase

salvage *VERB*

The crew tried to salvage some supplies from the wreck.
• **save, rescue, recover, retrieve, reclaim**

same *ADJECTIVE*

➤ **the same**
❶ *My sister and I like the same kinds of music.*
• **similar, alike, equivalent, comparable, matching, identical**
– Words which mean the same are **synonymous**.
OPPOSITES different, contrasting
❷ *Our recipe has remained the same for years.*
• **unaltered, unchanged, constant**
OPPOSITES different, new

sample *NOUN*

The detective asked for a sample of her handwriting.
• **specimen, example, illustration, snippet, taster**

sample *VERB*

Would you like to sample the new flavour?
• **try out, test, taste**

sands *PLURAL NOUN*

The children played on the sands for hours.
• **beach, shore**
– Hills of sand along the coast are **dunes**.

sane *ADJECTIVE*
He was the only sane member of an eccentric family.
• **sensible, rational, reasonable, balanced, level-headed**
OPPOSITE insane

sang
past tense see **sing**

sank
past tense see **sink**

sarcastic *ADJECTIVE*
It's hard to tell if the author is being sarcastic.
• **mocking, satirical, ironic, sneering, cutting**

sat
past tense see **sit**

satisfaction *NOUN*
He looked at his work with a sense of satisfaction.
• **pleasure, contentment, enjoyment, gratification, fulfilment, sense of achievement, pride**
OPPOSITE dissatisfaction

satisfactory *ADJECTIVE*
That is not a satisfactory explanation.
• **acceptable, adequate, passable, tolerable, sufficient, competent, good enough**
IDIOMS **up to scratch, up to the mark**
OPPOSITE unsatisfactory

satisfied *ADJECTIVE*
❶ *Are you satisfied with your score?*
• **pleased, contented, happy**
OPPOSITES dissatisfied, discontented
❷ *The police are satisfied that the death was accidental.*
• **certain, sure, convinced**

satisfy *VERB*
❶ *Some days, nothing seemed to satisfy him.*
• **please, content, gratify, make you happy**
– To satisfy your thirst is to **quench** or **slake** it.
OPPOSITES dissatisfy, frustrate
❷ *I think this should satisfy your requirements.*
• **meet, fulfil, answer**

saturate *VERB*
❶ *Several days of rain have saturated the soil.*
• **soak, drench, waterlog**
❷ *The Internet is saturated with cat photos.*
• **flood, inundate, overwhelm, overload**

saunter *VERB*
We sauntered slowly along the footpath.
• **amble, stroll, wander, ramble**

savage *ADJECTIVE*
❶ *It was a savage attack on a defenceless young man.*
• **vicious, cruel, barbaric, brutal, bloodthirsty, pitiless, ruthless, merciless, inhuman**
OPPOSITE humane
❷ *A pack of savage dogs roamed the streets.*
• **wild, feral, untamed, ferocious, fierce**
OPPOSITE domesticated

save *VERB*
❶ *Firefighters managed to save most of the building.*
• **preserve, protect, safeguard, rescue, recover, retrieve, reclaim, salvage**
❷ *You saved me from making a big mistake!*
• **stop, prevent, spare, deter**
❸ *I saved you a piece of cake.*
• **keep, reserve, set aside, retain, hold on to, store, hoard**
❹ *Here are some ways to save household energy.*
• **conserve, be sparing with, use wisely**

savings *PLURAL NOUN*
The couple have lost all of their savings.
• **reserves, funds, capital, resources, investments**
IDIOM **nest egg**

savour *VERB*
He was savouring every mouthful.
• **relish, enjoy, appreciate, delight in, revel in**

saw
past tense see **see**

say *VERB*
❶ *He found it hard to say what he meant.*
• **express, communicate, articulate, put into words, convey**
❷ *I'd like to say a few words before we start.*
• **utter, speak, voice, recite, read**

OVERUSED WORD

❶ To say something loudly:

➤ call	➤ bawl
➤ cry	➤ shout
➤ exclaim	➤ yell
➤ bellow	➤ roar

'Not much farther to go!' he **yelled** *above the roar of the engine.*

❷ To say something quietly:

➤ whisper	➤ mutter
➤ mumble	

'Now would be a good time to leave,' I **whispered.**

❸ To say something casually:

➤ remark	➤ note
➤ comment	➤ mention
➤ observe	➤ blurt out

'Lovely morning,' a passer-by **remarked.**

❹ To say something strongly:

➤ state	➤ declare
➤ announce	➤ pronounce
➤ assert	➤ insist
➤ maintain	➤ command
➤ profess	➤ demand
➤ order	

His wife **maintains** *that he is innocent.*

❺ To say something angrily:

➤ snap	➤ bark
➤ snarl	➤ rasp
➤ growl	➤ rant
➤ thunder	➤ rave

'I don't have time to talk to you!' **barked** *the voice on the phone.*

❻ To say something unclearly:

➤ babble	➤ stammer
➤ burble	➤ stutter
➤ gabble	

The stranger kept **babbling** *about an ancient prophecy.*

❼ To say something again:

➤ repeat	➤ echo
➤ reiterate	

Could you please **repeat** *your email address?*

❽ To say something in reply:

➤ answer	➤ respond
➤ reply	➤ retort

'Certainly not!' **retorted** *the judge.*

saying *NOUN*
There is an old saying, 'look before you leap'.
• **proverb, motto, maxim, aphorism, phrase, expression**
– An overused saying is a **cliché**.

scamper *VERB*
The rabbits scampered away to safety.
• **scurry, scuttle, hurry, dash, dart, run, rush, hasten**

scan *VERB*
❶ *The lookout scanned the horizon, hoping to see land.*
• **search, study, survey, examine, inspect, scrutinize, scour, stare at, eye**

❷ *I scanned through some magazines in the waiting room.*
• **skim, glance at, flick through, browse through**
IDIOM **cast your eye over**

scandal *NOUN*
❶ *He discovered a scandal in his family's past.*
• **disgrace, shame, embarrassment**
IDIOMS **skeleton in the cupboard,** (*North American*) **skeleton in the closet**
❷ *The amount of money wasted was a scandal.*
• **outrage, disgrace**
❸ *The papers were full of the latest scandal.*
• **gossip, rumours, muckraking**
(*informal*) **dirt**

scanty *ADJECTIVE*
Details of his life are scanty.
• **meagre, paltry, inadequate, insufficient, sparse, scarce**
(*informal*) **measly**
OPPOSITES **abundant, plentiful**

scar *NOUN*
He had a scar on his left cheek.
• **mark, blemish, disfigurement**

scar *VERB*
The victim may be scarred for life.
• **mark, disfigure**

scarce *ADJECTIVE*
Food was becoming scarce.
• **hard to find, in short supply, sparse, scanty, uncommon, rare**
(*informal*) **thin on the ground, few and far between**
OPPOSITES **plentiful, abundant**

scarcely *ADVERB*
She was so tired that she could scarcely speak.
• **barely, hardly, only just**

scare *VERB*
You scared me creeping up like that!
• **frighten, terrify, petrify, alarm, startle, panic, unnerve**

scare *NOUN*
You gave me quite a scare!
• **fright, shock, start, turn**

scared *ADJECTIVE*
Were you scared of the dark when you were little?
• **frightened, afraid, terrified, petrified, alarmed, fearful, panicky**

scary (*informal*) *ADJECTIVE*
It's quite a scary film.
• **frightening, terrifying, chilling, hair-raising, spine-tingling, spine-chilling, blood-curdling, eerie, sinister, nightmarish**
(*informal*) **creepy, spooky**

scatter *VERB*
❶ *She scattered breadcrumbs on the ground.*
• **spread, strew, distribute, sprinkle, shower, sow**
OPPOSITE **collect**
❷ *The crowd scattered in all directions.*
• **break up, separate, disperse, disband**
OPPOSITE **gather**

scene *NOUN*
❶ *Police were called to the scene of the accident.*
• **location, position, site, place, situation, spot**
❷ *We were rehearsing a scene from the play.*
• **episode, part, section, sequence, extract**
❸ *On the wall was a painting of a winter scene.*
• **landscape, view, outlook, prospect, vista, sight, spectacle, setting, scenery, backdrop**
❹ *He didn't want to create a scene in the restaurant.*
• **fuss, commotion, disturbance, quarrel, row**
(*informal*) **to-do, carry-on**

scenery *NOUN*
We stopped to admire the scenery.
• **landscape, outlook, prospect, scene, view, vista, panorama**

scent *NOUN*

There was an overpowering scent of vanilla.

• **smell, fragrance, perfume, aroma, odour**

SEE ALSO **smell**

sceptical *ADJECTIVE*

At first, I was sceptical about these results.

• **disbelieving, doubtful, doubting, dubious, incredulous, unconvinced, suspicious**

OPPOSITES certain, convinced

schedule *NOUN*

We have a busy training schedule.

• **programme, timetable, plan, calendar, diary**

– A schedule for a meeting is an **agenda**.

– A schedule of places to visit is an **itinerary**.

scheme *NOUN*

They worked out a scheme to raise more money.

• **plan, proposal, project, strategy, tactic, method, procedure, system**

scheme *VERB*

She felt they were all scheming against her.

• **plot, conspire, intrigue**

school *NOUN*

He goes to a school for international students.

• **academy, college, institute**

science *NOUN*

He is an expert in the science of genetics.

• **discipline, subject, field of study, branch of knowledge**

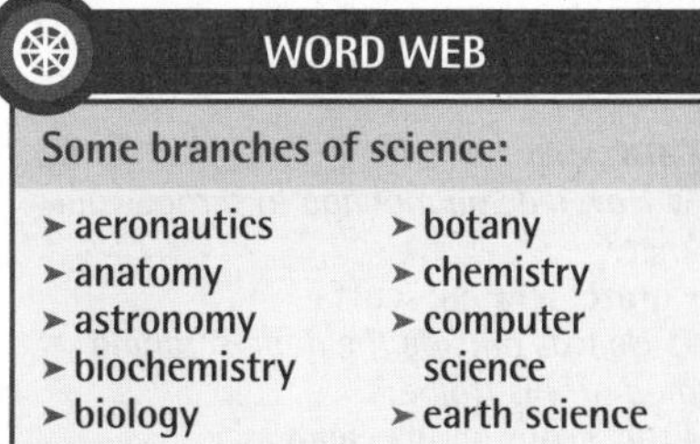

WORD WEB

Some branches of science:

- aeronautics
- anatomy
- astronomy
- biochemistry
- biology
- botany
- chemistry
- computer science
- earth science
- ecology
- electronics
- engineering
- environmental science
- food science
- forensic science
- genetics
- geography
- geology
- information technology
- mathematics
- mechanical engineering
- medical science
- meteorology
- nuclear science
- oceanography
- pathology
- physics
- psychology
- robotics
- space technology
- veterinary science
- zoology

science fiction *NOUN*

WRITING TIPS

WRITING SCIENCE FICTION

Characters:

- alien life-form
- android
- artificial life-form
- astronaut
- cyborg
- robot
- space traveller
- time traveller

Setting:

- alien planet
- deep space
- mother ship
- outer space
- parallel universe
- space colony
- spacecraft
- spaceship
- space shuttle
- space station
- starship
- time machine

Useful words and phrases:

- bionic
- black hole
- extraterrestrial
- force field
- futuristic
- galactic
- home planet
- humanoid
- hyperspace
- intelligent life
- inter-galactic
- inter-planetary
- inter-stellar
- light year
- orbit
- portal
- post-apocalyptic
- spacesuit
- space-time continuum
- space walk
- suspended animation
- telepathic

➤ teleport
➤ time warp
➤ UFO
➤ wormhole

SEE ALSO moon, planet, space

scoff *VERB*
➤ scoff at
Everyone scoffed at her ideas.
• **mock, ridicule, sneer at, deride, make fun of, poke fun at**

scold *VERB*
She scolded us for being late.
• **reprimand, reproach**
(*informal*) **tell off, tick off**

scoop *VERB*
❶ *Scoop out the middle of the pineapple.*
• **dig, gouge, scrape, excavate, hollow**
❷ *She scooped the kitten up in her arms.*
• **lift, pick, gather, take, snatch**

scope *NOUN*
❶ *There is plenty of scope for new ideas.*
• **opportunity, space, room, capacity, freedom, leeway**
❷ *Those questions are outside the scope of this essay.*
• **range, extent, limit, reach, span**

scorch *VERB*
The sand was so hot, it scorched our feet.
• **burn, singe, sear, blacken, char**

score *NOUN*
What was your final score?
• **mark, points, total, tally, count, result**

score *VERB*
❶ *How many goals did you score?*
• **win, get, gain, earn, make, notch up, chalk up**
❷ *Someone had scored their initials on the tree.*
• **cut, gouge, notch, scratch, scrape**

scorn *NOUN*
She dismissed my suggestion with scorn.
• **contempt, derision, disrespect, mockery, ridicule, sneers**
OPPOSITES admiration, respect

scour *VERB*
❶ *He was at the sink, scouring pots and pans.*
• **scrub, rub, clean, polish, burnish, buff**
❷ *They scoured the room for clues.*
• **search, hunt through, ransack, comb, turn upside-down**

scowl *VERB*
❶ *She scowled and folded her arms across her chest.*
• **frown, glower**
IDIOM **knit your brows**
❷ For facial expressions see **face**.

scramble *VERB*
❶ *The quickest route is to scramble over the rocks.*
• **clamber, climb, crawl, scrabble**
❷ *Everyone scrambled to get the best seats.*
• **push, jostle, struggle, fight, scuffle**

scrap *NOUN*
❶ *He wrote his number on a scrap of paper.*
• **bit, piece, fragment, snippet, oddment**
– Scraps of cloth are **rags** or **shreds**.
❷ *They fed scraps of food to the birds.*
• **remnant, leftovers, morsel, crumb, speck**
❸ *The lorry was loaded with scrap.*
• **rubbish, waste, junk, refuse, litter**
❹ *There was a scrap between rival fans.*
• **fight, brawl, scuffle, tussle, squabble**

scrap *VERB*
❶ *I decided to scrap the last paragraph.*
• **discard, throw away, throw out, abandon, cancel, delete, drop**
(*informal*) **dump, ditch**
❷ *The cubs enjoy scrapping with each other.*
• **fight, brawl, tussle, scuffle**

scrape *VERB*
❶ *How did you manage to scrape your knee?*
• **graze, scratch, scuff**
❷ *He was outside the door, scraping mud off his trainers.*
• **rub, scour, scrub, clean**

scrape *NOUN*
My little brother is always getting into scrapes.
• **trouble, mischief**
(*informal*) **jam, pickle**

scratch *VERB*
❶ *Try not to scratch the paintwork.*
• **mark, score, scrape, gouge, graze**
❷ *The dog was scratching at the door.*
• **claw**

scratch *NOUN*
There was a tiny scratch on the surface.
• **score, line, mark, gash, groove, scrape, graze**

scrawl *VERB*
He scrawled his name on a piece of paper.
• **jot down, scribble, write**

scream *NOUN*
He let out a scream of pain.
• **shriek, screech, shout, yell, cry, bawl, howl, wail, squeal, yelp**

scream *VERB*
People screamed and ran in all directions.
• **shriek, screech, shout, yell, cry, bawl, howl, wail, squeal, yelp**

screen *NOUN*
❶ *The room was divided into two by a screen.*
• **partition, divider, curtain**
❷ *Look at the image on the screen.*
• **monitor, display**

screen *VERB*
❶ *She used her hand to screen her eyes from the sun.*
• **shield, protect, shelter, shade, cover, hide, mask, veil**
❷ *All employees are screened before being appointed.*
• **examine, investigate, check, test, vet**
❸ *The match will be screened live on Saturday.*
• **show, broadcast, transmit, air, put out**

screw *VERB*
❶ *Screw the lid on tightly.*
• **twist, wind, turn, tighten**
❷ *Nail or screw the panel to the wall.*
• **fasten, secure, fix, attach**

scribble *VERB*
She was always scribbling ideas on scraps of paper.
• **scrawl, write, jot down, note, dash off**
– To scribble a rough drawing is to **doodle**.

script *NOUN*
She rewrote the original script for the film version.
– The script for a film is a **screenplay**.
– A handwritten or typed script is a **manuscript**.

scrub *VERB*
She was scrubbing the kitchen floor.
• **scour, rub, brush, clean, wash**

scruffy *ADJECTIVE*
He was wearing an old T-shirt and scruffy jeans.
• **untidy, messy, ragged, tatty, tattered, worn-out, shabby**
OPPOSITE smart

scrutinize *VERB*
They scrutinized her passport for a few minutes.
• **examine, inspect, look at, study, peruse, investigate, explore**

scuffle *NOUN*
A scuffle broke out between rival fans.
• **fight, brawl, tussle, scrap, squabble**

sculpture *NOUN*
The temple was full of marble sculptures.
• **carving, figure, statue, effigy, model**
– A sculpture of a person's head, shoulders and chest is a **bust**.
– A small sculpture of a person is a **figurine** or **statuette**.

sea *NOUN*
❶ *70 per cent of the Earth's surface is covered by sea.*
• **ocean, waves**
(*literary*) **the deep**

❷ *She looked out at a sea of adoring fans.*
• **expanse, stretch, mass, host, swathe, carpet**

WORD WEB

- An area of sea partly enclosed by land is a **bay** or **gulf**.
- A wide inlet of the sea is a **sound**.
- A wide inlet where a river joins the sea is an **estuary** or in Scotland a **firth**.
- A narrow stretch of water linking two seas is a **strait**.
- The bottom of the sea is the **seabed**.
- The land near the sea is the **coast** or the **seashore**.
- Creatures that live in the sea are **marine** creatures.
- People who work or travel on the sea are **seafaring** people.

Creatures that live in the sea:

➤ coral	➤ sea cucumber
➤ dogfish	➤ seahorse
➤ dolphin	➤ seal
➤ eel	➤ sea lion
➤ fish	➤ sea otter
➤ jellyfish	➤ sea turtle
➤ killer whale	➤ sea urchin
➤ manta ray	➤ shark
➤ octopus	➤ squid
➤ plankton	➤ starfish
➤ porpoise	➤ stingray
➤ sea anemone	➤ whale

seal *VERB*
The entrance to the burial chamber had been sealed.
• **close, fasten, shut, secure, lock**
– To seal a leak is to **plug** it or **stop** it.

seam *NOUN*
❶ *The seam on his trousers split.*
• **join, stitching**
❷ *Geologists discovered a rich seam of coal.*
• **layer, stratum, vein**

search *VERB*
❶ *He was searching for the book he had lost.*
• **hunt, look, seek**
IDIOM **look high and low**
– To search for gold or other minerals is to **prospect**.
❷ *Police searched the house for clues.*
• **explore, scour, ransack, rummage through, go through, comb**
IDIOM **turn upside down**
❸ *Security staff searched all the passengers.*
• **check, inspect, examine, scrutinize** (*informal*) **frisk**

search *NOUN*
After a long search, she found her keys.
• **hunt, look, exploration, check**
– A long journey in search of something is a **quest**.

seashore *NOUN*
We explored the seashore, looking for fossils.
• **seaside, beach, shore, coast, sands**

seaside *NOUN*
On Saturday we had a trip to the seaside.
• **beach, sands, seashore, coast**

season *NOUN*
Autumn is traditionally the season for harvest.
• **period, time, time of year, term**

seat *NOUN*
There were two empty seats in the front row.
• **chair, place**
– A long seat for more than one person is a **bench**.
– A long wooden seat in a church is a **pew**.
– A seat on a bicycle or horse is a **saddle**.

seat *VERB*
❶ *Please seat yourselves in a circle.*
• **place, position, sit down, settle**
❷ *The theatre can seat two hundred people.*
• **accommodate, have room for, hold, take**

secluded *ADJECTIVE*
The path leads down to a secluded beach.
• **quiet, isolated, private, lonely, remote, cut off, sheltered, hidden**
OPPOSITES **crowded, busy**

second *ADJECTIVE*
Would anyone like a second helping?
• **another, additional, extra, further**

second *NOUN*
I'll be with you in a second.
• **moment, little while, instant, flash**
(*informal*) **jiffy, tick**

second *VERB*
Will anyone second the proposal?
• **support, back, approve, endorse**

secondary *ADJECTIVE*
She loves to run and winning is of secondary importance to her.
• **lesser, lower, minor, subordinate, subsidiary**
OPPOSITES **primary, main**

second-hand *ADJECTIVE*
The shop sells second-hand computers.
• **used, pre-owned, handed-down, cast-off**
OPPOSITE **new**

secret *ADJECTIVE*
❶ *It's important to keep your password secret.*
• **private, confidential, personal, undisclosed, classified, restricted**
IDIOM **under wraps**
OPPOSITE **public**
❷ *The detectives are part of a secret operation.*
• **undercover, covert, clandestine**
(*informal*) **hush-hush**
IDIOM **cloak-and-dagger**
❸ *We were shown a secret entrance to an underground cave.*
• **hidden, concealed, disguised**
OPPOSITE **open**
❹ For secret agents see **spy**.

➤ **in secret**
Talks were held in secret.
• **in private, privately, on the quiet**
IDIOM **behind closed doors**

secretive *ADJECTIVE*
He was very secretive about his past.
• **uncommunicative, reticent, reserved, tight-lipped, mysterious, quiet**
(*informal*) **cagey**
OPPOSITES **communicative, open**

section *NOUN*
The website has a section on wind energy.
• **part, division, bit, sector, segment, portion, compartment, module, chapter**
– A section from a piece of classical music is a **movement**.

sector *NOUN*
❶ *This is the residential sector of the city.*
• **area, part, district, region, section, zone**
❷ *People from all sectors of the music industry attend the awards ceremony.*
• **branch, part, division, department, area, arm**

secure *ADJECTIVE*
❶ *They bolted all the doors and windows to make the house secure.*
• **safe, protected, defended, guarded**
OPPOSITES **insecure, vulnerable**
❷ *Tie the ropes together with a secure knot.*
• **steady, firm, solid, fixed, fast, immovable**
OPPOSITE **loose**
❸ *She is trying to find a secure job.*
• **permanent, regular, steady, reliable, dependable, settled**

secure *VERB*
❶ *The door wasn't properly secured.*
• **fasten, lock, seal, bolt**
❷ *They secured their place in the semi-final.*
• **make certain of, gain, acquire, obtain**
(*informal*) **land**

A B C D E F G H I J K L M N O P Q R S T U V W X Y Z

security *NOUN*
❶ *You must wear a seat belt for your own security.*
• **safety, protection**
❷ *There was increased security at the airport.*
• **safety measures, surveillance, policing**

see *VERB*
❶ *If you look closely, you might see a dragonfly.*
• **catch sight of, spot, sight, notice, observe, make out, distinguish, note, perceive, spy, glimpse, witness**
(*informal*) **clap eyes on**
SEE ALSO **look**
❷ *Did you see the news last night?*
• **watch, look at, view, catch**
❸ *You should see a doctor about that cough.*
• **consult, call on, visit, report to**
❹ *I see what you mean.*
• **understand, appreciate, comprehend, follow, grasp, realize, take in**
(*informal*) **get**
❺ *Can you see yourself as a teacher?*
• **imagine, picture, visualize, view**
❻ *I'll see what I can do.*
• **think about, consider, ponder, reflect on, weigh up**
❼ *Please see that the lights are switched off.*
• **make sure, make certain, ensure, check, verify, confirm**
❽ *She went to see what all the fuss was about.*
• **find out, discover, learn, establish, ascertain**
❾ *I'll see you to the door.*
• **escort, conduct, accompany, guide, lead, take**
➤ **see to something**
Will you see to the invitations?
• **deal with, attend to, take care of, sort out**

seed *NOUN*
The fruit was full of seeds.
– The seeds in an orange, lemon, etc. are the **pips**.
– The seed in a date, plum, etc. is the **stone**.

seek *VERB*
❶ *For many years he sought his long-lost brother.*
• **search for, hunt for, look for, try to find**
❷ *We always seek to please our customers.*
• **try, attempt, strive, want, wish, desire**

seem *VERB*
Everything seems to be in working order.
• **appear, look, give the impression of being, strike you as**

seep *VERB*
Water began to slowly seep through the roof.
• **leak, ooze, escape, drip, dribble, trickle, flow, soak**

seethe *VERB*
❶ *The mixture in the cauldron began to seethe.*
• **boil, bubble, foam, froth up**
❷ *Inwardly he was seething with indignation.*
• **be angry, be furious, rage, storm**

segment *NOUN*
Divide the orange into segments.
• **section, portion, piece, part, bit, wedge, slice**

seize *VERB*
❶ *He stretched out to seize the rope.*
• **grab, catch, snatch, take hold of, grasp, grip, clutch**
❷ *The town was seized by rebels last year.*
• **capture, take over, conquer, occupy, overrun**
❸ *Customs officers seized the smuggled goods.*
• **take possession of, confiscate, impound, commandeer**
➤ **seize up**
Without oil, the engine will seize up.
• **become jammed, become clogged, become stuck**

seldom *ADVERB*
He seldom spoke.
• **rarely, infrequently, hardly ever, scarcely**
IDIOM **once in a blue moon**
OPPOSITE often

select *VERB*
We have to select a new team captain.
• **choose, pick, decide on, opt for, settle on, appoint, elect**

select *ADJECTIVE*
Only a select few were invited to the party.
• **chosen, special, hand-picked, privileged**

selection *NOUN*
❶ *Have you made your selection?*
• **choice, option, pick, preference**
❷ *They stock a wide selection of games.*
• **range, variety, assortment, array**

selfish *ADJECTIVE*
It was selfish of him to keep all the chocolate for himself.
• **self-centred, thoughtless, inconsiderate, uncharitable, mean, miserly**
OPPOSITES unselfish, generous

sell *VERB*
The corner shop sells newspapers and sweets.
• **deal in, trade in, stock, market**
– Uncomplimentary synonyms are **peddle** and **hawk**.
OPPOSITE buy

send *VERB*
❶ *I'll send you a text message.*
• **dispatch, post, mail, transmit, forward**
OPPOSITE receive
❷ *They are sending a satellite into orbit.*
• **launch, propel, direct, fire, shoot**
❸ *This computer is sending me crazy!*
• **drive, make, turn**
➤ **send for someone**
I think we should send for a doctor.
• **call, summon, fetch**
➤ **send something out**
The device was sending out weird noises.
• **emit, discharge, give off, issue, release**

senior *ADJECTIVE*
❶ *She is one of the senior players in the squad.*
• **older, long-standing**
OPPOSITES younger, junior
❷ *He is a senior officer in the navy.*
• **high-ranking, superior**
OPPOSITES junior, subordinate

sensation *NOUN*
❶ *She had a tingling sensation in her fingers.*
• **feeling, sense, perception**
❷ *The unexpected news caused a sensation.*
• **stir, thrill, commotion, fuss, furore, to-do**

sensational *ADJECTIVE*
❶ *The newspaper printed a sensational account of the murder.*
• **shocking, horrifying, scandalous, lurid** (*informal*) **juicy**
❷ (*informal*) *Wow, that was a sensational goal!*
• **amazing, extraordinary, stunning, spectacular, stupendous, tremendous, wonderful, fantastic, fabulous, terrific**

sense *NOUN*
❶ *A baby learns about the world through its senses.*
– The five human senses are **hearing**, **sight**, **smell**, **taste** and **touch**.
❷ *He has a good sense of rhythm.*
• **appreciation, awareness, consciousness, feeling (for)**
❸ *At least she had the sense to keep quiet.*
• **common sense, wisdom, wit, intelligence, brains**
❹ *The sense of the word is not clear.*
• **meaning, significance, import, definition**
➤ **make sense of something**
No one could make sense of the code.
• **understand, make out, interpret, decipher**

sense *VERB*
❶ *We sensed that we were not welcome.*
• **be aware, realize, perceive, feel, notice, observe**
❷ *This device can sense any change in temperature.*
• **detect, respond to, pick up, recognize**

senseless *ADJECTIVE*
❶ *It was a senseless act of violence.*
• **pointless, mindless, futile, foolish, stupid, irrational, illogical, mad, crazy**
OPPOSITE **sensible**
❷ *His attackers left him senseless on the ground.*
• **unconscious, knocked out**
OPPOSITE **conscious**

sensible *ADJECTIVE*
❶ *She gave me some sensible advice.*
• **wise, shrewd, reasonable, rational, logical, sane, sound, prudent, level-headed**
OPPOSITES **foolish, unwise**
❷ *Bring a pair of sensible shoes.*
• **comfortable, practical**
OPPOSITE **impractical**

sensitive *ADJECTIVE*
❶ *This cream is for sensitive skin.*
• **delicate, tender, fine, soft**
❷ *Don't be so sensitive!*
• **touchy, defensive, thin-skinned**
OPPOSITES **insensitive, thick-skinned**
❸ *This is still a sensitive subject.*
• **difficult, delicate, tricky, awkward**
❹ *She's very sensitive towards other people.*
• **tactful, considerate, thoughtful, sympathetic, understanding**
OPPOSITES **insensitive, thoughtless**

sentence *NOUN*
The judge will decide on a sentence next week.
• **judgement, verdict, decision, ruling**

sentence *VERB*
Both men were sentenced to five years in prison.
• **condemn, convict**

sentimental *ADJECTIVE*
❶ *The song has sentimental value to me.*
• **emotional, nostalgic**
❷ *The film is spoiled by a sentimental ending.*
• **romantic, saccharine, mawkish**
(*informal*) **soppy, mushy**

sentry *NOUN*
A sentry was on duty at the gate.
• **guard, lookout, sentinel, watchman**

separate *ADJECTIVE*
❶ *Raw food and cooked food should be kept separate.*
• **apart, separated, detached, isolated, segregated**
OPPOSITE **together**
❷ *Contestants have to cook three separate dishes.*
• **different, distinct, discrete, independent, unrelated**
OPPOSITES **related, shared**

separate *VERB*
❶ *The two sides of the city are separated by a river.*
• **divide, split, beak up, part**
– To separate something which is connected to something else is to **detach** or **disconnect** it.
OPPOSITES **combine, mix**
❷ *Separate the yolks of the eggs from the whites.*
• **keep apart, set apart, isolate, cut off, remove**
❸ *The trail separates from here onwards.*
• **branch, fork, split, divide, diverge**
OPPOSITE **merge**
❹ *Her friend's parents have separated.*
• **split up, break up, part company**
– To end a marriage legally is to **divorce**.

sequence *NOUN*
We tried to piece together the sequence of events.
• **order, progression, series, succession, course, flow, chain, train**

serene *ADJECTIVE*
A serene smile spread across her face.
• **calm, contented, untroubled, peaceful,**

quiet, placid, tranquil
OPPOSITE agitated

series *NOUN*
I had to answer a series of questions.
• **succession, sequence, string, set, round, chain, train**

serious *ADJECTIVE*
❶ *She wore a serious expression.*
• **solemn, sombre, sober, earnest, grave, grim, unsmiling, humourless**
OPPOSITES light-hearted, cheerful
❷ *We need a serious talk.*
• **important, significant, momentous, weighty, major**
OPPOSITES unimportant, insignificant
❸ *He was writing a serious book about global warming.*
• **learned, intellectual, scholarly, heavy, in-depth**
OPPOSITES light, casual
❹ *Are you serious about wanting to help?*
• **sincere, genuine, in earnest, committed, wholehearted**
❺ *She was recovering from a serious illness.*
• **severe, grave, bad, major, acute, critical, dangerous**
OPPOSITES minor, trivial

seriously *ADVERB*
❶ *Erin nodded seriously.*
• **solemnly, soberly, earnestly, gravely, grimly**
OPPOSITE cheerfully
❷ *Are you seriously interested?*
• **genuinely, truly, honestly, sincerely**
❸ *No one was seriously injured.*
• **severely, badly, gravely, acutely, critically**
OPPOSITES slightly, mildly
❹ *(informal) a seriously bad film*
• **extremely, exceptionally, extraordinarily**

seriousness *NOUN*
❶ *I saw the seriousness in her eyes.*
• **solemnity, gravity, sobriety, humourlessness**
OPPOSITES cheerfulness, levity
❷ *You must understand the seriousness of the situation.*
• **gravity, severity, importance, weight**

servant *NOUN*
A servant entered with a tray of food.
• **attendant, domestic, maid, retainer, minion**

serve *VERB*
❶ *Is anyone waiting to be served?*
• **help, assist, attend to, deal with**
❷ *Serve the rice in separate bowls.*
• **give out, dish up, present, pass round, distribute**
❸ *He served the school for 40 years until his retirement.*
• **work for, contribute to**
❹ *An old crate served as a table.*
• **be used, act, function**

service *NOUN*
❶ *Let me know if I can be of any service.*
• **help, assistance, aid, use, usefulness, benefit**
❷ *The funeral service was held in the local church.*
• **ceremony, ritual, rite**
❸ *Treat your bike to an annual service.*
• **check-up, overhaul, maintenance, servicing**

service *VERB*
A local garage services their car.
• **maintain, check, go over, overhaul**

session *NOUN*
❶ *We have a training session on Saturday mornings.*
• **period, time**
❷ *The Queen will open the next session of Parliament.*
• **meeting, sitting, assembly**

set *VERB*
❶ *He set the microphone on its stand.*
• **place, put, stand, position, lay**
❷ *Have they set a date for the wedding?*
• **appoint, specify, name, decide, determine, choose, fix, establish, settle**
❸ *She set the alarm for five the next morning.*
• **adjust, regulate, correct**

A B C D E F G H I J K L M N O P Q R S T U V W X Y Z

❹ *Leave the jelly to set in the fridge.*
• **become firm, solidify, harden, stiffen**
❺ *The sun was just beginning to set.*
• **go down, sink**
➤ **set about something**
We set about clearing the table immediately.
• **begin, start, commence**
➤ **set off**
❶ *They set off early for the airport.*
• **depart, get going, leave, set out, start out**
❷ *I set off the smoke alarm by mistake.*
• **activate, start, trigger**
➤ **set something out**
The information is clearly set out on the page.
• **lay out, arrange, display, present**
➤ **set something up**
❶ *Can you set up the table-tennis table?*
• **put up, erect, construct, build**
❷ *A few of us are setting up a film club.*
• **create, establish, institute, start, found**

set *NOUN*
❶ *There is a set of measuring spoons in the drawer.*
• **collection, batch, kit, series**
❷ *There is a quick change of set after Act One.*
• **scenery, backdrop, setting**

set *ADJECTIVE*
❶ *The evening meal is served at a set time.*
• **fixed, established, definite**
OPPOSITE variable
❷ *Everything is set for the big finale.*
• **ready, prepared, organized, primed**

setback *NOUN*
We ran into a setback before we even started.
• **difficulty, problem, complication, snag, hitch, hiccup, glitch**

setting *NOUN*
The abbey stands in a rural setting.
• **surroundings, location, situation, position, place, site, environment, background**

settle *VERB*
❶ *It's time to settle our differences.*
• **resolve, sort out, work out, clear up, iron out, end**
❷ *I had just settled down on the sofa when the doorbell rang.*
• **sit, get comfortable**
❸ *A crow settled on a nearby branch.*
• **land, alight, perch, come to rest**
❹ *The family settled in Canada after the war.*
• **emigrate (to), move (to), set up home (in)**
IDIOM **put down roots**
❺ *Wait until the mud settles.*
• **sink to the bottom, clear, subside**
❻ *We can settle the bill in the morning.*
• **pay, clear, square**
➤ **settle on**
Have you settled on a name for the puppy?
• **agree on, decide on, choose, pick, determine, establish, fix**

settlement *NOUN*
This was the site of an old Viking settlement.
• **community, colony, encampment, outpost, village**

settler *NOUN*
a book about early European settlers in America
• **colonist, immigrant, pioneer, incomer**

sever *VERB*
❶ *The builders accidentally severed a water pipe.*
• **cut through, shear through**
– To sever a limb is to **amputate** it.
❷ *He threatened to sever all ties with his family.*
• **break off, end, terminate**

several *ADJECTIVE*
I made several attempts to contact them.
• **a number of, many, some, a few, various**

severe *ADJECTIVE*
❶ *Mum gave me one of her severe looks.*
• **harsh, strict, stern, hard, disapproving,**

withering
OPPOSITES gentle, lenient
❷ *He suffered a severe neck injury in the accident.*
• **bad, serious, acute, grave**
OPPOSITE mild
❸ *Siberia has a severe climate.*
• **extreme, tough, harsh, hostile, sharp, intense**
OPPOSITE mild

sew *VERB*
She sewed a name tag on to my coat.
• **stitch, tack, embroider**
– To sew a picture or design is to **embroider** it.

sewing *NOUN*
She always had a piece of sewing tucked in her belt.
• **embroidery, mending, needlepoint, needlework**

sex *NOUN*
❶ *What sex is the hamster?*
• **gender**
❷ *education about sex and relationships*
• **sexual intercourse, lovemaking**

shabby *ADJECTIVE*
❶ *He was wearing a shabby pair of slippers.*
• **ragged, scruffy, tattered, frayed, worn out, threadbare**
(*informal*) **tatty**
OPPOSITE smart
❷ *They lived in a shabby boarding house.*
• **dilapidated, run down, seedy, dingy, squalid, sordid**
❸ *That was a shabby trick!*
• **mean, nasty, unfair, unkind, dishonest, shameful, low, cheap**

shade *NOUN*
❶ *They were sitting in the shade of a palm tree.*
• **shadow, cover**
❷ *The porch had a shade to keep out the sun.*
• **screen, blind, canopy, awning**
– A type of umbrella used as a sun shade is a **parasol**.
❸ *The walls are a pale shade of blue.*
• **hue, tinge, tint, tone, colour**

shade *VERB*
❶ *She used her hand to shade her eyes from the sun.*
• **shield, screen, protect, hide, mask**
❷ *Use small pencil strokes to shade the edges.*
• **fill in, darken**

shadow *NOUN*
❶ *The candlelight cast weird shadows on the wall.*
• **silhouette, shape, figure, outline**
❷ *Her face was deep in shadow.*
• **shade, darkness, semi-darkness, gloom**
❸ *Not a shadow of doubt remained.*
• **trace, hint, flicker, suggestion, suspicion**

shadow *VERB*
Police have been shadowing the suspect for weeks.
• **follow, pursue, stalk, track, trail**
(*informal*) **tail**

shady *ADJECTIVE*
❶ *We found a shady spot under a tree.*
• **shaded, shadowy, sheltered, dark, sunless**
OPPOSITE sunny
❷ *He was involved in some shady business deals.*
• **dishonest, disreputable, suspicious, dubious, suspect, untrustworthy**
(*informal*) **fishy, dodgy**
OPPOSITE honest

shaft *NOUN*
❶ *The arrow has a wooden shaft.*
• **pole, rod, stick, staff, spine**
❷ *A shaft of moonlight shone through the window.*
• **beam, ray, gleam, streak**
❸ *He nearly fell into an old mine shaft.*
• **pit, tunnel, hole**

shaggy *ADJECTIVE*
Highland cows have long shaggy coats.
• **bushy, woolly, fleecy, hairy, thick**

A B C D E F G H I J K L M N O P Q R S T U V W X Y Z

shake *VERB*

❶ *The walls and floor shook with the blast.*

• **quake, shudder, vibrate, rattle, rock, sway, totter, wobble, judder**

❷ *The driver shook his fist as he overtook us.*

• **wave, brandish, flourish, wield, wag, waggle, joggle**

❸ *She was so upset that her voice was shaking.*

• **tremble, quaver, quiver**

❹ *They were shaken by the terrible news.*

• **shock, distress, upset, disturb, unsettle, unnerve, startle, alarm, agitate, rattle, fluster**

shaky *ADJECTIVE*

❶ *We sat at a shaky table.*

• **unsteady, wobbly, unstable, insecure, rickety**

OPPOSITES steady, stable

❷ *He was so nervous that his hands were shaky.*

• **trembling, quavering, quivering, faltering**

OPPOSITE steady

shallow *ADJECTIVE*

No diving in the shallow end of the pool.

OPPOSITE deep

sham *NOUN*

I later found out that her illness was a sham.

• **pretence, deception, lie, act**

shame *NOUN*

❶ *He hung his head in shame.*

• **remorse, contrition, guilt**

❷ *Their actions brought shame to our community.*

• **disgrace, dishonour, ignominy, humiliation, embarrassment**

➤ **a shame**

It's a shame you have to leave.

• **a pity, unfortunate**

shameful *ADJECTIVE*

It was a shameful incident involving eight players.

• **disgraceful, deplorable, reprehensible, discreditable, dishonourable, contemptible, despicable, outrageous, scandalous**

OPPOSITES admirable, honourable

shape *NOUN*

❶ *He sent her a Valentine card in the shape of a heart.*

• **form, figure, outline**

– A dark outline seen against a light background is a **silhouette**.

❷ *For his age he was feeling in good shape.*

• **condition, health, form, order, fettle, trim**

WORD WEB

Two-dimensional geometric shapes:

➤ circle
➤ decagon (10 sides)
➤ diamond
➤ ellipse
➤ heptagon (7 sides)
➤ hexagon (6 sides)
➤ nonagon (9 sides)
➤ oblong
➤ octagon (8 sides)
➤ oval
➤ parallelogram
➤ pentagon (5 sides)
➤ polygon
➤ quadrilateral
➤ rectangle
➤ rhombus
➤ ring
➤ semicircle
➤ square
➤ trapezium
➤ triangle

Three-dimensional geometric shapes:

➤ cone
➤ cube
➤ cuboid
➤ cylinder
➤ hemisphere
➤ polyhedron
➤ prism
➤ pyramid
➤ sphere

shape *VERB*

Shape the dough into a ball.

• **form, mould, fashion, make**

– To shape metal or plaster in a mould is to **cast** it.

share *NOUN*

Everyone gets a fair share of computer time.

• **portion, quota, allocation, allowance,**

ration, helping
(*informal*) cut

share *VERB*
❶ *We shared the cost of a taxi between us.*
• **divide, split**
❷ *They finally got round to sharing out the prizes.*
• **distribute, deal out, ration out, allocate, allot**

sharp *ADJECTIVE*
❶ *Use a pair of sharp scissors.*
• **keen, sharpened, razor-sharp**
OPPOSITE blunt
❷ *Many species of cactus have sharp spines.*
• **pointed, spiky, jagged**
OPPOSITE rounded
❸ *I felt a sharp pain in my ankle.*
• **acute, piercing, stabbing**
OPPOSITE dull
❹ *I'm trying to make the image on the screen sharper.*
• **clear, distinct, well defined, crisp**
OPPOSITE blurred
❺ *She has a sharp eye for detail.*
• **keen, observant, perceptive**
OPPOSITE unobservant
❻ *He had a quick wit and a sharp mind.*
• **clever, quick, shrewd, perceptive**
OPPOSITES dull, slow
❼ *Just ahead there's a sharp bend in the road.*
• **abrupt, sudden, steep**
– A bend that doubles back on itself is a **hairpin** bend.
OPPOSITE gradual
❽ *There is likely to be a sharp overnight frost.*
• **severe, extreme, intense, serious**
OPPOSITES slight, mild
❾ *This salad dressing is a bit sharp.*
• **sour, tart, bitter**
OPPOSITES mild, sweet

sharpen *VERB*
You will need to sharpen the knife.
• **make sharp, grind, whet, hone**

shatter *VERB*
❶ *The mirror fell and shattered into tiny pieces.*
• **smash, break, splinter, fracture, fragment, disintegrate**
❷ *Her dreams of being a writer were shattered.*
• **destroy, wreck, ruin, demolish, crush, dash**
(*informal*) scupper

sheaf *NOUN*
He handed me a sheaf of handwritten pages.
• **bunch, bundle**

sheath *NOUN*
Keep the thermometer in its plastic sheath.
• **casing, covering, sleeve**
– A sheath for a sword or dagger is a **scabbard**.

shed *NOUN*
We have a shed full of garden tools.
• **hut, shack, outhouse, cabin**

shed *VERB*
All the trees had shed their leaves.
• **drop, let fall, spill, scatter**

sheen *NOUN*
He waxed the table to give it a sheen.
• **shine, gloss, lustre, polish**

sheep *NOUN*
We could see a flock of sheep on the hill.
– A female sheep is a **ewe**.
– A male sheep is a **ram**.
– A young sheep is a **lamb**.
– Meat from sheep is **mutton** or **lamb**.
– The woolly coat of a sheep is its **fleece**.

sheer *ADJECTIVE*
❶ *That story he told was sheer nonsense.*
• **complete, total, utter, absolute, pure, downright, out-and-out**
❷ *The path ran alongside a sheer cliff.*
• **vertical, perpendicular, precipitous**
– A sheer or steep cliff face is a **precipice**.
❸ *She wore a scarf of sheer silk.*
• **fine, thin, transparent, see-through**

sheet *NOUN*
❶ *Start on a fresh sheet of paper.*
• **page, leaf, piece**
❷ *We need to fit a new sheet of glass.*
• **pane, panel, plate**
❸ *The pond was covered with a thin sheet of ice.*
• **layer, film, coating, covering, surface**

shelf *NOUN*
Please put the books back on the shelf.
• **ledge, rack**
– A shelf above a fireplace is a **mantelpiece**.

shell *NOUN*
Tortoises have hard shells.
• **covering, case, casing, outside, exterior**

shellfish *NOUN*

WORD WEB

Some types of shellfish:

- **barnacle**
- **clam**
- **cockle**
- **conch**
- **crab**
- **crayfish**
- **cuttlefish**
- **limpet**
- **lobster**
- **mussel**
- **oyster**
- **prawn**
- **razor shell**
- **scallop**
- **shrimp**
- **whelk**
- **winkle**

- Shellfish with legs, such as crabs, lobsters and shrimps, are **crustaceans**.
- Shellfish such as clams and oysters, with soft bodies and often an external shell, are **molluscs**.

shelter *NOUN*
The tents provide shelter from the desert winds.
• **cover, protection, safety, security, refuge**

shelter *VERB*
❶ *An overhanging rock sheltered us from the rain.*
• **protect, shield, screen, guard, defend, safeguard, cushion**
❷ *They sheltered in a cave until morning.*
• **take shelter, take refuge, take cover**

shelve *VERB*
The news is that the film has been shelved.
• **postpone, put off, put back, defer, suspend, put to one side**
IDIOMS **put on ice, put on the back burner**

shield *NOUN*
The trees act as an effective wind shield.
• **screen, barrier, defence, guard, protection, cover, shelter**
– The part of a helmet that shields your face is the **visor**.

shield *VERB*
A hat will shield your eyes from the sun.
• **protect, screen, cover, shelter, guard, safeguard, defend, keep safe**

shift *VERB*
❶ *Do you need help to shift the furniture?*
• **move, rearrange, reposition**
❷ *These stains won't be easy to shift.*
• **remove, get off, lift, get rid of**
❸ *Attitudes have shifted in recent years.*
• **change, alter, modify**

shine *VERB*
❶ *A light shone from an upstairs window.*
• **beam, gleam, glow, glare, blaze, radiate**
For tips on describing light see **light**.
❷ *He shines his shoes every morning.*
• **polish, brush, buff**
❸ *She's good at all sports, but she shines at tennis.*
• **excel, stand out, be outstanding**

shiny *ADJECTIVE*
She polished the mirror until it was shiny.
• **shining, gleaming, glistening, polished, glossy, burnished, lustrous**
OPPOSITES matt, dull

ship *NOUN*
❶ *Another big wave hit the ship.*
• **boat, craft, vessel**
– A large passenger ship is a **liner**.
– Ships that travel long distances at sea are **ocean-going** or **seagoing** ships.
– A word that means 'to do with ships' is **nautical**.
❷ For types of boat or ship see **boat**.

ship *VERB*
Your parcel was shipped on Tuesday.
• **dispatch, send, post, mail, deliver**

shirk *VERB*
He promised not to shirk his fair share of the work.
• **avoid, evade, get out of, dodge, duck**

shiver *VERB*
A boy stood on the doorstep, shivering with cold.
• **tremble, quiver, shake, shudder, quake**

shock *NOUN*
❶ *News of his death came as a great shock.*
• **blow, surprise, fright, upset**
IDIOM **bolt from the blue**
❷ *The driver is still in a state of shock.*
• **trauma, distress**
❸ *The shock of the explosion was felt for miles.*
• **impact, jolt, reverberation**

shock *VERB*
The whole town was shocked by the news.
• **horrify, appal, startle, stun, stagger, astonish, astound, shake, rock, scandalize, outrage**

shocking *ADJECTIVE*
❶ *There were shocking scenes of violence on the news.*
• **appalling, horrifying, horrific, dreadful, horrendous, atrocious, horrible, terrible, distressing, sickening**
❷ (*informal*) *It is a shocking waste of money.*
• **very bad, awful, terrible, deplorable, disgraceful, dreadful**
(*informal*) **abysmal**

shoes *PLURAL NOUN*
The shop sells fancy shoes and bags.
• **footwear**

WORD WEB

Some types of shoe or boot:

- ankle boots
- ballet shoes
- baseball boots
- brogues
- clogs
- court shoes
- espadrilles
- flip-flops
- football boots
- gym shoes
- high heels
- moccasins
- mules
- platform shoes
- plimsolls
- pumps
- sandals
- slippers
- stilettos
- tap shoes
- tennis shoes
- trainers (*North American* sneakers)
- wellingtons (*informal* wellies)

shone
past tense see **shine**

shook
past tense see **shake**

shoot *VERB*
❶ *She shot an arrow into the air.*
• **fire, discharge, launch, aim, propel**
❷ *It is now illegal to hunt and shoot tigers.*
• **fire at, hit, open fire on, gun down**
❸ *An ambulance shot past with its lights flashing.*
• **race, speed, dash, rush, tear, streak, hurtle, fly, whizz, zoom**
❹ *He shot the penalty into the corner of the net.*
• **kick, strike, hit, drive, boot**
❺ *Most of the film was shot in New Zealand.*
• **film, photograph, record**

A B C D E F G H I J K L M N O P Q R S T U V W X Y Z

shop *NOUN*
The high street has a good range of shops.
• **store, boutique**
(*old use*) **emporium**

WORD WEB

Some types of shop and shopkeeper:

- antique shop
- bakery
- bookshop
- butcher
- cheesemonger
- chemist or pharmacy (*North American* drugstore)
- clothes shop
- confectioner
- corner shop
- delicatessen
- department store
- fishmonger
- florist
- garden centre
- greengrocer
- grocer
- haberdasher
- hardware shop
- health-food shop
- hypermarket
- ironmonger
- jeweller
- music shop
- newsagent
- off-licence
- pharmacy
- post office
- shoe shop
- shopping arcade
- shopping centre (*North American* shopping mall)
- stationer
- supermarket
- toyshop
- watchmaker

shopping *NOUN*
We put our shopping in the back of the car.
• **goods, purchases**

shore *NOUN*
see **seashore**

short *ADJECTIVE*
❶ *They live a short distance from the shops.*
• **little, small**
OPPOSITE long
❷ *We had to write a short summary of the story.*
• **concise, brief, succinct, condensed, pithy**
OPPOSITES long, lengthy
❸ *It was a very short visit.*
• **brief, quick, fleeting, hasty, cursory**
OPPOSITES long, lengthy
❹ *My brother is short for his age.*
• **small, tiny, little, diminutive, petite**
– Someone who is short and fat is **squat** or **dumpy**.
OPPOSITE tall
❺ *Our food supplies were running short.*
• **low, meagre, scant, sparse, inadequate, insufficient**
OPPOSITE plentiful
❻ *The receptionist was short with me.*
• **abrupt, rude, sharp, curt, brusque, terse, blunt, snappy**
OPPOSITES polite, courteous

shortage *NOUN*
There is a severe shortage of basic medicines.
• **scarcity, deficiency, lack, want, dearth, shortfall**
– A shortage of water is a **drought**.
– A shortage of food is a **famine**.

shortcoming *NOUN*
She was aware of her own shortcomings.
• **fault, failing, imperfection, defect, flaw, weakness, limitation, weak point**
OPPOSITES strength, strong point

shorten *VERB*
Most people shorten Janet's name to Jan.
• **cut down, reduce, cut, trim, abbreviate, abridge, condense, compress, curtail**
OPPOSITE lengthen

shortly *ADVERB*
The guests will be arriving shortly.
• **soon, before long, in a little while, in no time, any minute, presently, by and by**

shot *NOUN*
❶ *We heard a noise like the shot of a rifle.*
• **crack, report, bang, blast**
❷ *He had an easy shot at goal.*
• **strike, kick, hit, stroke**
❸ *This is an unusual shot which is taken*

from the air.
• photograph, photo, picture, snap, snapshot
❹ (*informal*) *We each had a shot at solving the puzzle.*
• try, go, attempt
(*informal*) bash, crack, stab

shout *VERB*
She had to shout to be heard above the din.
• call, cry out, yell, roar, bellow, bawl, raise your voice
(*informal*) holler
OPPOSITE whisper

shove *VERB*
❶ *I shoved my bag into the locker.*
• push, thrust, force, ram, cram
❷ *Stop shoving at the back!*
• barge, push, elbow, jostle

shovel *VERB*
We shovelled the snow into a huge heap.
• dig, scoop, shift, clear, move

show *VERB*
❶ *You promised to show me your photos.*
• present, display, exhibit, set out
❷ *The painting shows a hunting scene.*
• portray, picture, depict, illustrate, represent
❸ *Can you show me how to do it?*
• explain to, make clear to, instruct, teach, tell
❹ *The evidence shows that he was right.*
• reveal, make plain, demonstrate, prove, confirm, verify
❺ *We were shown into the waiting room.*
• guide, direct, conduct, escort, accompany, usher
❻ *The dots show where to put your fingers.*
• indicate, point out
❼ *Does my T-shirt show through the blouse?*
• be seen, be visible, appear
➤ **show off**
Ignore him: he's just showing off.
• boast, brag, swagger, posture
IDIOM blow your own trumpet
➤ **show up**
The lines don't show up on the screen.
• appear, be visible, be evident

show *NOUN*
❶ *We have tickets for tonight's show.*
• performance, production, entertainment
❷ *There is a show of students' artwork at the end of term.*
• display, exhibition, presentation

shower *NOUN*
There was a sudden shower of rain.
• fall, downpour, sprinkling, drizzle
For tips on describing weather see **weather**.

shower *VERB*
The eruption showered a wide area with volcanic ash.
• spray, spatter, sprinkle, splash

showy *ADJECTIVE*
Is this tie too showy?
• gaudy, flashy, bright, loud, garish, conspicuous
OPPOSITES plain, restrained

shred *NOUN*
There's not a shred of evidence against her.
• bit, piece, scrap, trace, jot
➤ **shreds**
The gale ripped the tent to shreds.
• tatters, ribbons, rags, strips

shrewd *ADJECTIVE*
That was a shrewd decision.
• clever, astute, sharp, quick-witted, intelligent, smart, canny, perceptive
OPPOSITE stupid

shriek *NOUN & VERB*
see **shriek**

shrill *ADJECTIVE*
I could hear the shrill sound of a whistle.
• high, high-pitched, piercing, sharp, screechy
OPPOSITES low, soft

A B C D E F G H I J K L M N O P Q R S T U V W X Y Z

shrink *VERB*
❶ *My jeans have shrunk in the wash.*
• **become smaller, contract, narrow, reduce, decrease**
OPPOSITE expand
❷ *The creature shrank back instinctively from the light.*
• **recoil, flinch, shy away**

shrivel *VERB*
Many plants shrivelled in the heat.
• **wilt, wither, droop, dry up, wrinkle, shrink**

shroud *VERB*
The summit was shrouded in clouds.
• **cover, envelop, wrap, blanket, cloak, mask, hide, conceal, veil**

shrub *NOUN*
This shrub grows in northern Chile.
• **bush**
– An area planted with shrubs is a **shrubbery**.

shudder *VERB*
He shuddered at the thought of being left alone.
• **tremble, quake, quiver, shiver, shake, judder**

shuffle *VERB*
❶ *The old man shuffled over to the fireplace.*
• **shamble, hobble, scuffle, scrape, drag your feet**
❷ *Did you remember to shuffle the cards?*
• **mix, mix up, jumble, rearrange**

shut *VERB*
Please shut the door behind you.
• **close, fasten, seal, secure, lock, bolt, latch**
– To shut a door with a bang is to **slam** it.
➤ **shut down**
The hotel shut down years ago.
• **close down, go out of business**
OPPOSITE open up
➤ **shut something down**
I'll show you the best way to shut down the computer.
• **switch off, shut off, close down**
OPPOSITE start up
➤ **shut up**
(*informal*) *I wish those people behind us would shut up!*
• **be quiet, be silent, stop talking, hush up**
IDIOM **hold your tongue**
➤ **shut someone up**
❶ *I hate to see animals shut up in cages.*
• **imprison, confine, detain**
❷ (*informal*) *This should shut them up for a while.*
• **silence, quieten, quiet down, hush up**

shy *ADJECTIVE*
At first, she was too shy to say anything.
• **bashful, timid, coy, reserved, hesitant, self-conscious, inhibited, modest**
OPPOSITES bold, confident

sick *ADJECTIVE*
❶ *She was sick with a chest infection all last week.*
• **ill, unwell, poorly, sickly, ailing, infirm, indisposed**
IDIOM **under the weather**
OPPOSITES healthy, well
❷ *The sea was rough and I felt sick.*
• **nauseous, queasy**
➤ **be sick**
He suddenly felt he was going to be sick.
• **vomit, heave**
(*informal*) **throw up, puke**
➤ **be sick of**
I'm sick of all this miserable weather.
• **be fed up with, be tired of, be weary of, have had enough of**

sicken *VERB*
Many people were sickened by the violence in the film.
• **disgust, revolt, repel, nauseate, make you sick**
IDIOM **turn your stomach**

sickly *ADJECTIVE*
❶ *He had always been a sickly child.*
• **unhealthy, weak, delicate, frail**
OPPOSITES healthy, strong

❷ *The air was thick with a sickly, sweet smell.*
• **nauseating, sickening, cloying, stomach-turning**

sickness *NOUN*
❶ *A deadly sickness swept across the continent.*
• **illness, disease, ailment, malady, infection, virus**
(*informal*) **bug**
❷ *A sudden wave of sickness came over her.*
• **nausea, queasiness, vomiting**

side *NOUN*
❶ *A cube has six sides.*
• **face, surface**
❷ *He had a scar on the right side of his face.*
• **half, part**
❸ *The path runs along the side of a large playing field.*
• **edge, border, boundary, fringe, perimeter, verge, margin**
❹ *I could see both sides of the argument.*
• **point of view, viewpoint, standpoint, position, perspective, angle, slant**
❺ *We have the best side in the league.*
• **team, squad, line-up**

side *VERB*
➤ **side with someone**
Why do you always side with her?
• **support, favour, take the side of, back, agree with, stand by**

siege *NOUN*
The city was under siege for a year.
• **blockade**

sift *VERB*
Sift the flour to get rid of any lumps.
• **sieve, strain, filter**
➤ **sift through something**
Police have been sifting through piles of evidence.
• **look through, examine, inspect, pore over, analyse, scrutinize, review**

sigh *VERB*
'Not again,' he sighed.
• **moan, complain, lament, grumble**

sight *NOUN*
❶ *Owls have sharp sight and excellent hearing.*
• **eyesight, vision, eyes**
– Words meaning 'to do with sight' are **optical** and **visual**.
❷ *Later that day they had their first sight of land.*
• **view, glimpse, look (at)**
❸ *Niagara Falls is a breathtaking sight.*
• **spectacle, display, show, scene**
❹ *We spent the week seeing the sights of New York.*
• **attraction, landmark**
➤ **be in sight**
❶ *Not a single person was in sight.*
• **be visible, be in view, be in range**
❷ *At last victory was in sight.*
• **approach, loom, be imminent**

sight *VERB*
After eight days at sea we sighted land.
• **see, catch sight of, spot, spy, glimpse, make out, notice, observe, distinguish, recognize**

sign *NOUN*
❶ *A sign pointed to the exit.*
• **notice, placard, poster, signpost**
– The sign belonging to a particular business or organization is a **logo**.
– The sign on a particular brand of goods is a **trademark**.
❷ *There are no signs yet of a change in the weather.*
• **indication, hint, clue, suggestion, warning**
❸ *I'll give you the sign when I'm ready.*
• **signal, gesture, cue, reminder**

sign *VERB*
❶ *Please sign your name here.*
• **write, inscribe, autograph**
❷ *The club signed two new players this month.*
• **take on, engage, recruit, enrol**

signal *NOUN*
Don't move until I give the signal.
• **sign, gesture, cue, prompt, indication**

signal *VERB*
The photographer signalled that she was ready.
• **give a sign, indicate, gesture, motion**

A B C D E F G H I J K L M N O P Q R S T U V W X Y Z

significance *NOUN*
❶ *The significance of these carvings is not clear.*
• **meaning, message, import, importance, point, relevance**
❷ *Their discovery was of major significance.*
• **importance, consequence, seriousness, magnitude**
OPPOSITE insignificance

significant *ADJECTIVE*
❶ *Here is a list of some significant events in French history.*
• **important, major, noteworthy, notable, influential**
OPPOSITES insignificant, minor
❷ *Climate change is having a significant effect on wildlife.*
• **noticeable, considerable, substantial, perceptible, striking**
OPPOSITE negligible

signify *VERB*
❶ *A red light signifies danger.*
• **indicate, denote, mean, symbolize, represent, stand for**
❷ *Everyone nodded to signify agreement.*
• **show, express, indicate, communicate, convey**

silence *NOUN*
An eerie silence filled the room.
• **quiet, quietness, hush, stillness, calm, peace, tranquillity**
OPPOSITE noise

silence *VERB*
She silenced him with a glare.
• **quieten, quiet, hush, muffle**
– To silence someone by putting something over their mouth is to **gag** them.

silent *ADJECTIVE*
❶ *Outside, the night was cold and silent.*
• **quiet, noiseless, soundless, still, hushed**
– A sound you cannot hear is **inaudible**.
OPPOSITE noisy
❷ *He was silent for a few minutes.*
• **speechless, quiet, mute**
(*informal*) **mum**
– To be too shy to speak is to be **tongue-tied**.
OPPOSITE talkative

silky *ADJECTIVE*
This breed of rabbit has long silky fur.
• **smooth, soft, fine, sleek, velvety**

silly *ADJECTIVE*
That was a really silly idea!
• **foolish, stupid, idiotic, foolhardy, senseless, brainless, thoughtless, unwise, unintelligent, half-witted, hare-brained, scatterbrained**
(*informal*) **daft**
OPPOSITE sensible

similar *ADJECTIVE*
The two species are similar in appearance.
• **alike, nearly the same, comparable**
OPPOSITES dissimilar, different
➤ **similar to**
Her views are similar to my own.
• **like, close to, comparable to**
OPPOSITES unlike, different from

similarity *NOUN*
Notice the similarity between the paintings.
• **likeness, resemblance, correspondence, parallel**
OPPOSITE difference

simple *ADJECTIVE*
❶ *Can you answer this simple question?*
• **easy, elementary, straightforward**
OPPOSITE difficult
❷ *The forms are written in simple language.*
• **clear, plain, uncomplicated, understandable, intelligible**
OPPOSITE complicated
❸ *She was wearing a simple cotton dress.*
• **plain, undecorated**
OPPOSITES elaborate, showy
❹ *He enjoys simple pleasures like walking and gardening.*
• **ordinary, unsophisticated, humble,**

modest, homely
OPPOSITE sophisticated

simply *ADVERB*
❶ *I'll try to put it simply.*
• **clearly, plainly, straighforwardly, in simple terms**
❷ *It is simply the best book I've ever read.*
• **absolutely, wholly, completely, totally, utterly**
❸ *She was silenced simply for telling the truth.*
• **only, just, merely, purely, solely**

sin *NOUN*
They believed that the plague was a punishment for their sins.
• **wrong, evil, wickedness, wrongdoing, immorality, vice**

sincere *ADJECTIVE*
Please accept our sincere apologies.
• **genuine, honest, true, real, earnest, wholehearted, heartfelt**
OPPOSITE insincere

sing *VERB*
❶ *They started singing an old folk song.*
• **chant, croon, chorus**
❷ *A small bird was singing outside the window.*
• **chirp, trill, warble**

singe *VERB*
The flames singed the inside of the roof.
• **burn, scorch, sear, blacken, char**

singer *NOUN*
The band comprises two guitarists and a singer.
• **vocalist**
– A singer who sings alone is a **soloist**.
– A group of singers is a **choir** or **chorus**.
– A member of a church choir is a **chorister**.

single *ADJECTIVE*
❶ *A single tree stood out against the sky.*
• **solitary, isolated, sole, lone**
– When only a single example of something exists, it is **unique**.
❷ *She listened to every single word.*
• **individual, distinct, separate**
❸ *He had remained single all his life.*
• **unmarried, unattached**
(*old use*) **unwed**
– An unmarried man is a **bachelor**.
– An old-fashioned word for an unmarried woman is a **spinster**.
OPPOSITE married

single *VERB*
➤ **single someone out**
A few of us were singled out for special training.
• **pick out, select, choose, identify, earmark, target**

sinister *ADJECTIVE*
There was something sinister about the housekeeper.
• **menacing, threatening, malevolent, dark, evil, disturbing, unsettling, eerie**
(*informal*) **creepy**

sink *VERB*
❶ *The ship sank off the coast of Florida.*
• **submerge, go down, founder**
– To sink a ship deliberately by letting in water is to **scuttle** it.
❷ *The sun began to sink below the horizon.*
• **go down, fall, drop, dip, descend, subside, set**
❸ *She sank back in her chair.*
• **slump, flop, collapse**

sister *NOUN*
She has a younger sister.
• (*informal*) sis
– A formal name for a sister or brother is a **sibling**.
For other members of a family see **family**.

sit *VERB*
❶ *She sat on the sofa reading a magazine.*
• **be seated, take a seat, settle down, rest, perch**
– To sit on your heels is to **squat**.
– To sit for a photograph or portrait is to **pose**.
❷ *The house sits on top of a hill.*
• **stand, lie, rest, is situated, is set**

❸ *When are you sitting your music exam?*
• **take**
(*informal*) **go in for**

site *NOUN*
This is the site of an ancient burial ground.
• **location, place, position, situation, setting, whereabouts, venue**

situated *ADJECTIVE*
➤ **be situated**
This small village is situated in a valley.
• **be located, be positioned, sit in**

situation *NOUN*
❶ *I found myself in an awkward situation.*
• **position, circumstances, condition, state of affairs**
– A bad situation is a **plight** or **predicament**.
❷ *The house is in a pleasant situation.*
• **location, locality, place, position, setting, site, spot**
❸ *She applied for a situation in advertising.*
• **job, post, position, appointment**

size *NOUN*
❶ *What size is the garden?*
• **dimensions, proportions, measurements, area, extent**
❷ *They were amazed by the sheer size of the pyramids.*
• **scale, magnitude, immensity**

sizeable *ADJECTIVE*
The bullet left a sizeable hole in the wall.
• **large, considerable, substantial, fair-sized, appreciable, noticeable**
OPPOSITES small, unnoticeable

sizzle *VERB*
Heat the oil until it begins to sizzle.
• **crackle, sputter, spit, hiss**

skeleton *NOUN*
The model shows the skeleton of the building.
• **frame, framework, shell**
IDIOM **bare bones**

sketch *NOUN*
❶ *She drew a quick sketch of the scene.*
• **drawing, outline, plan, doodle**
❷ *They performed a short comic sketch.*
• **play, scene, skit, routine**

sketch *VERB*
Sketch your design on a piece of paper first.
• **draw, draft, outline, rough out**

skid *VERB*
Several cars skidded on the icy road.
• **slide, slip**

skilful *ADJECTIVE*
He was a skilful writer of detective stories.
• **expert, skilled, accomplished, able, capable, talented, brilliant, clever, masterly, deft, dexterous**
OPPOSITE incompetent

skill *NOUN*
Balancing on a snowboard requires a lot of skill.
• **expertise, ability, accomplishment, talent, competence, proficiency, mastery, deftness, dexterity, prowess**

skilled *ADJECTIVE*
see **skilful**

skim *VERB*
❶ *Dragonflies skimmed across the still water.*
• **glide, slide, slip, flit**
❷ *I only had time to skim the papers.*
• **scan, glance through, flick through, leaf through**
IDIOM **cast your eye over**

skin *NOUN*
❶ *Drinking water is good for your skin.*
– The appearance of the skin of your face is your **complexion**.
❷ *The drums were originally made from animal skins.*
• **hide, pelt, fur**
❸ *He nearly slipped on a banana skin.*
• **peel, rind**
❹ *When it cools the mixture will form a*

thin skin on the top.
• **film, coating, membrane, crust**

skinny *ADJECTIVE*
A skinny girl in bare feet answered the door.
• **thin, lean, bony, gaunt, lanky, scrawny, scraggy**
OPPOSITE plump

skip *VERB*
❶ *The little boy was skipping along the pavement.*
• **hop, jump, leap, bound, caper, dance, prance**
❷ *I skipped most of the first chapter.*
• **pass over, miss out, ignore, omit, leave out**

skirt *VERB*
The path skirts the east side of the lake.
• **go past, go round, border, edge**

sky *NOUN*
Clouds drifted slowly across the sky.
• **air, heavens, atmosphere**
IDIOM (*literary*) **blue yonder**

slab *NOUN*
The words were inscribed on a slab of marble.
• **block, piece, tablet, slice, chunk, hunk, lump**

slack *ADJECTIVE*
❶ *Suddenly the rope went slack.*
• **loose, limp**
OPPOSITES tight, taut
❷ *This is usually a slack time of year.*
• **slow, quiet, sluggish**
OPPOSITES busy, hectic
❸ *Standards of hygiene in the restaurant are slack.*
• **lax, careless, negligent, slapdash, sloppy**
OPPOSITE strict

slacken *VERB*
❶ *He undid his collar and slackened his tie.*
• **loosen, relax, release, ease off**
OPPOSITE tighten
❷ *Her pace gradually slackened.*
• **lessen, reduce, decrease, slow down**
OPPOSITE increase

slam *VERB*
He stormed out and slammed the door.
• **bang, shut loudly**

slant *VERB*
❶ *Italic text usually slants to the right.*
• **lean, slope, tilt, incline, be at an angle, be angled**
❷ *They slanted the story to suit themselves.*
• **skew, twist, distort, bias**

slant *NOUN*
❶ *Here, the graph shows a steep slant upwards.*
• **slope, angle, tilt, incline, gradient**
– The slant of a roof is its **pitch**.
❷ *The film brings a new slant to an old story.*
• **point of view, angle, viewpoint, perspective, bias**

slap *VERB*
He slapped his forehead and groaned.
• **smack, strike, hit, spank, clout, cuff**
(*informal*) **whack**

slap *NOUN*
The cold air hit me like a slap in the face.
• **smack, blow, spank, clout, cuff**
(*informal*) **whack**

slash *VERB*
❶ *Several cars had their tyres slashed overnight.*
• **cut, gash, slit, knife, nick**
❷ *Shops are slashing prices even further.*
• **reduce, lower, cut, drop, bring down**

slaughter *VERB*
Waves of soldiers were slaughtered as they advanced.
• **kill, butcher, massacre, cull**

slaughter *NOUN*
The battle ended in terrible slaughter.
• **bloodshed, killing, butchery, carnage, massacre, bloodbath**

slave *VERB*
He's been slaving away in the kitchen.
• **work hard, labour, toil, grind, sweat**

slavery *NOUN*
The central character is kidnapped and sold into slavery.
• **captivity, bondage, servitude**
OPPOSITE freedom

sledge *NOUN*
We pulled our sledges up the snowy slope.
• **toboggan**
(*North American*) **sled**
– A large sledge pulled by horses is a **sleigh**.
– A sledge used in winter sports is a **bobsleigh**.

sleek *ADJECTIVE*
Seal pups are born with sleek coats.
• **smooth, glossy, shiny, silky, silken**
OPPOSITES coarse, matted

sleep *NOUN*
He usually has a short sleep after lunch.
• **nap, rest, doze, catnap, siesta**
(*informal*) **snooze, kip**
(*literary*) **slumber**
IDIOM (*informal*) **forty winks**
➤ **go to sleep**
That night I was too restless to go to sleep.
• **fall asleep, doze, drop off, nod off**

sleep *VERB*
The baby is sleeping in the next room.
• **be asleep, doze, take a nap**
(*informal*) **snooze**
(*literary*) **slumber**

sleepless *ADJECTIVE*
We spent a sleepless night waiting for news.
• **restless, wakeful, troubled, disturbed**
– The formal name for sleeplessness is **insomnia**.
OPPOSITE restful

sleepy *ADJECTIVE*
I didn't feel sleepy, so I decided to walk round for a bit.
• **drowsy, tired, lethargic, heavy-eyed**
(*informal*) **dopey**
– Something that makes you feel sleepy is **soporific**. *the soporific warmth of the fire*
OPPOSITE wide awake

slender *ADJECTIVE*
❶ *He was a slender youth with dark hair.*
• **slim, lean, slight, thin, trim, svelte, willowy**
OPPOSITE fat
❷ *The spider dangled on a slender thread.*
• **thin, fine, fragile, delicate**
OPPOSITE thick
❸ *We only have a slender chance of winning.*
• **poor, slight, slim, faint, negligible, remote**
OPPOSITES good, strong
❹ *They won by a slender margin.*
• **narrow, small, slim**
OPPOSITE wide

slice *NOUN*
Would you like a slice of cheesecake?
• **piece, bit, wedge, slab, portion**
– A thin slice is a **sliver**.

slice *VERB*
Slice the vegetables into thick chunks.
• **cut, carve, chop**

slick *ADJECTIVE*
The team have a slick passing style.
• **skilful, artful, clever, cunning, smooth, deft**
OPPOSITE clumsy

slide *VERB*
The spoon slid across the table.
• **glide, slip, slither, skim, skate, skid**

slight *ADJECTIVE*
❶ *I have a slight problem with my computer.*
• **small, minor, modest, negligible, trivial, insignificant**
OPPOSITE large

❷ *There was a slight pause before anyone spoke.*
• **short, brief, fleeting**
OPPOSITE long
❸ *There is a slight chance of rain tomorrow.*
• **slim, slender, faint, remote**
OPPOSITE strong
❹ *A slight figure emerged from the shadows.*
• **slender, slim, petite, delicate, fragile, frail**
OPPOSITE stout

slightly *ADVERB*
He was slightly hurt in the accident.
• **a little, a bit, somewhat, rather, moderately**
OPPOSITES very, seriously

slim *ADJECTIVE*
❶ *She is tall and slim.*
• **slender, thin, lean, spare, trim, svelte**
OPPOSITES fat, plump
❷ *Their chances of winning are slim at best.*
• **poor, faint, slight, slender, negligible, remote**
OPPOSITES good, strong
❸ *He won the election by a slim margin.*
• **narrow, small, slender**
OPPOSITE wide

slimy *ADJECTIVE*
The floor of the tunnel was covered in slimy mud.
• **slippery, slithery, sticky, oozy**
(*informal*) **gooey, icky**

sling *VERB*
❶ *He slung his rucksack over his shoulder.*
• **swing, hang, suspend**
❷ (*informal*) *She slung the letter away in disgust.*
• **throw, fling, hurl, cast, toss, pitch, lob**
(*informal*) **chuck**

slink *VERB*
I tried to slink away from the party unnoticed.
• **slip, sneak, steal, creep, edge, sidle**

slip *VERB*
❶ *I slipped on a patch of ice outside.*
• **skid, slide, slither, lose your balance**
❷ *One by one, the seals slipped into the water.*
• **glide, slide**
❸ *He slipped out while the others were talking.*
• **sneak, steal, slink, sidle, creep, tiptoe**

slip *NOUN*
❶ *The rehearsal went off without any slips.*
• **mistake, error, fault, blunder, gaffe, lapse**
❷ *A name was written on a slip of paper.*
• **piece, scrap**
➤ **give someone the slip**
It won't be easy to give your friends the slip.
• **escape from, get away from, run away from**

slippery *ADJECTIVE*
The stone steps were worn and slippery.
• **slithery, slick, smooth, glassy, slimy, greasy, oily**
(*informal*) **slippy**

slit *NOUN*
Daylight shone through a slit in the tent.
• **cut, split, tear, gash, rent, chink, gap, opening, slot**

slit *VERB*
She used her nail to slit open the envelope.
• **cut, split, slice, slash, gash**

slither *VERB*
A snake slithered through the grass.
• **slip, slide, glide, slink, snake**

slogan *NOUN*
We need a catchy slogan for the poster.
• **motto, catchphrase, jingle**

slope *VERB*
The beach slopes gently down to the sea.
• **tilt, slant, incline, fall, drop, rise, climb, bank, shelve**

slope *NOUN*
❶ *It was hard work pushing my bike up the slope.*
• **hill, rise, bank, ramp**
– An upward slope is an **ascent** and a downward slope is a **descent**.
❷ *Rain runs down the roof because of the slope.*
• **tilt, slant, pitch, gradient, incline**

sloppy *ADJECTIVE*
❶ *The batter should have a sloppy texture.*
• **runny, watery, liquid, slushy, mushy**
(*informal*) **gloopy**
OPPOSITE stiff
❷ *That was a sloppy performance from the team.*
• **careless, slapdash, slack, messy, untidy, slovenly, slipshod**
OPPOSITE careful

slot *NOUN*
❶ *Insert a coin or token in the slot.*
• **slit, opening, aperture, chink, gap**
❷ *The show has been moved to a late-night slot.*
• **time, spot, space, place**

slouch *VERB*
She sat slouched over her laptop.
• **hunch, stoop, slump, droop, flop**

slow *ADJECTIVE*
❶ *They walked on at a slow pace.*
• **unhurried, leisurely, steady, sedate, plodding, dawdling, sluggish**
❷ *Erosion is usually a slow process.*
• **lengthy, prolonged, protracted, gradual, drawn-out**
❸ *She's often slow to reply to emails.*
• **tardy, late, sluggish, hesitant, reluctant**
OPPOSITE quick

slow *VERB*
➤ **slow down**
❶ *The boat slowed down as it approached the island.*
• **go slower, reduce speed, brake, decelerate**
OPPOSITES speed up, accelerate
❷ *The storm slowed us down.*
• **make slower, delay, hold up, impede, set back**

sludge *NOUN*
They cleared a lot of sludge out of the pond.
• **muck, mud, ooze, slime**
(*informal*) **gunge, gunk**

slump *VERB*
❶ *I slumped exhausted into an armchair.*
• **flop, collapse, sink, sag, slouch**
❷ *CD sales continue to slump.*
• **fall, decline, drop, plummet, tumble, plunge**

slump *NOUN*
There was a slump in trade after Christmas.
• **collapse, drop, fall, decline, downturn, slide**
– A general slump in trade is a **depression** or **recession**.
OPPOSITE boom

sly *ADJECTIVE*
❶ *Foxes are traditionally portrayed as sly creatures.*
• **crafty, cunning, artful, clever, wily, tricky, sneaky, devious, furtive, secretive, stealthy, underhand**
OPPOSITES straightforward, honest
❷ *He looked up with a sly grin on his face.*
• **mischievous, playful, impish, roguish, knowing, arch**

smack *VERB*
She groaned and smacked her forehead in dismay.
• **slap, strike, hit, cuff, clip, spank**
(*informal*) **whack**

small *ADJECTIVE*

OVERUSED WORD

❶ **Small in size, scale:**

➤ **little**	➤ **compact**
➤ **tiny**	➤ **miniature**
➤ **minute**	➤ **microscopic**

➤ minuscule
➤ mini
➤ baby

(*informal*) teeny, titchy, dinky

(*Scottish*) wee

He spotted a **minuscule** *speck of dirt on his collar.*

OPPOSITES big, large

2 A small person, creature:

➤ little
➤ short
➤ squat
➤ petite
➤ dainty
➤ diminutive
➤ miniature
➤ undersized

(*informal*) pint-sized

The fossil belonged to a **diminutive** *species of dinosaur.*

OPPOSITES giant, tall, well-built

3 Small inside:

➤ cramped
➤ confined
➤ restricted
➤ narrow
➤ poky

The cabin was a bit **cramped** *for three people plus luggage.*

OPPOSITES spacious, roomy

4 A small amount, small portion:

➤ meagre
➤ inadequate
➤ insufficient
➤ paltry
➤ scanty
➤ skimpy
➤ mean
➤ stingy

(*informal*) measly

For breakfast there was stale bread with a **meagre** *scraping of butter.*

OPPOSITES ample, substantial

5 A small change, small problem:

➤ minor
➤ slight
➤ unimportant
➤ insignificant
➤ trivial
➤ trifling
➤ negligible

We made some **minor** *changes to the script.*

OPPOSITES major, significant

smart *ADJECTIVE*

1 *He looked smart in his new suit.*
• **well-dressed, elegant, stylish, fashionable, chic, spruce, neat, dapper, well-groomed**
(*informal*) **natty**
– To make yourself smart is to **smarten up.**
OPPOSITE scruffy

2 *They booked a table at a smart restaurant in the city centre.*
• **fashionable, upmarket, high-class, exclusive, fancy**
(*informal*) **posh, swanky, swish**

3 *That was a very smart move!*
• **clever, ingenious, intelligent, shrewd, astute, crafty**
OPPOSITE stupid

4 *They set off at a smart pace.*
• **fast, quick, rapid, speedy, swift, brisk**
(*informal*) **cracking**
OPPOSITES slow, gentle

smart *VERB*

Chopping onions makes my eyes smart.
• **sting, prick, prickle, tingle, burn**

smash *VERB*

1 *Every window in the building had been smashed.*
• **break, crush, shatter, splinter, crack**

2 *He smashed the ball past the keeper.*
• **hit, strike, kick, shoot, drive, slam**

➤ **smash into**
The truck left the road and smashed into a wall.
• **crash into, collide with, bang into, bump into, hit**

smear *VERB*

Smear butter over the inside of the dish.
• **spread, rub, wipe, plaster, smother, coat, smudge, dab, daub**

smear *NOUN*

There was a smear of blood on the carpet.
• **streak, smudge, daub, patch, splodge, mark, blotch**

smell *VERB*

1 *I could smell something baking in*

the oven.
• **scent, sniff**
(*informal*) **get a whiff of**
❷ *My shoes were beginning to smell.*
• **stink, reek**
(*informal*) **pong**

smell *NOUN*
❶ *Don't you love the smell of fresh popcorn?*
• **scent, aroma, perfume, fragrance, bouquet**
❷ *What is that awful smell?*
• **odour, stench, stink, reek, whiff**
(*informal*) **pong, niff**

WRITING TIPS

DESCRIBING SMELLS
Pleasant:

➤ aromatic
➤ delicate
➤ fragrant
➤ perfumed
➤ scented
➤ sweet-smelling

Unpleasant:

➤ evil-smelling
➤ fetid
➤ foul
➤ foul-smelling
➤ musty
➤ nauseating
➤ odorous
➤ (*informal*) pongy
➤ rancid
➤ rank
➤ reeking
➤ rotten
➤ sickly
➤ smelly
➤ stinking
➤ (*informal*) stinky
➤ (*informal*) whiffy

Strong:

➤ choking
➤ heady
➤ overpowering
➤ pungent
➤ rich
➤ sharp

smile *VERB & NOUN*
The woman smiled and waved at us from the window.
• **grin, beam**
– To smile in a silly way is to **simper**.
– To smile in a self-satisfied way is to **smirk**.
– To smile in an insulting way is to **sneer**.

smoke *NOUN*
Thick smoke billowed from the roof.
• **fumes**
– The smoke given out by a vehicle is **exhaust**.
– A mixture of smoke and fog is **smog**.

smoke *VERB*
❶ *The bonfire was still smoking next morning.*
• **smoulder**
❷ *A man stood silently smoking a cigar.*
• **puff at**

smooth *ADJECTIVE*
❶ *Roll out the dough on a smooth surface.*
• **flat, even, level**
OPPOSITE uneven
❷ *In the early morning, the lake was perfectly smooth.*
• **calm, still, unruffled, undisturbed, glassy**
OPPOSITE rough
❸ *Otters have smooth and shiny coats.*
• **silky, sleek, velvety**
OPPOSITE coarse
❹ *Stir the mixture until it is smooth.*
• **creamy, velvety, silky**
OPPOSITE lumpy
❺ *The take-off was surprisingly smooth.*
• **comfortable, steady**
OPPOSITES bumpy, rocky
❻ *Installing the software was a smooth operation.*
• **straightforward, easy, effortless, trouble-free**
OPPOSITES difficult, troublesome

smooth *VERB*
She stood up and smoothed her dress.
• **flatten, level, even out**
– To smooth cloth you can **iron** or **press** it.
– To smooth wood you can **plane** or **sand** it.

smother *VERB*
❶ *Pythons smother their prey to death.*
• **suffocate, choke, stifle**
❷ *Rescuers tried to smother the flames.*
• **extinguish, put out, snuff out, douse**
❸ *The chips were smothered in ketchup.*
• **cover, coat, spread, smear, daub**

❹ *She managed to smother a yawn.*
• **suppress, stifle, muffle, hold back, conceal**

smoulder *VERB*
❶ *The fire was still smouldering a week later.*
• **smoke, glow, burn slowly**
❷ *She was smouldering with rage.*
• **fume, seethe, burn, boil**

smudge *NOUN*
There were smudges of ink all over the page.
• **smear, blot, streak, stain, mark, splodge**

smug *ADJECTIVE*
Why are you looking so smug all of a sudden?
• **self-satisfied, pleased with yourself, complacent, superior**

snack *NOUN*
They had a quick snack before leaving.
• **refreshments, bite to eat**
(*informal*) **nibbles**
– A mid-morning snack is sometimes called **elevenses**.

snag *NOUN*
Our holiday plans have hit a snag.
• **problem, difficulty, obstacle, hitch, complication, setback, catch**
(*informal*) **hiccup, glitch**

snake *NOUN*

WORD WEB

Some types of snake:

➤ adder
➤ anaconda
➤ asp
➤ boa constrictor
➤ cobra
➤ garter snake
➤ grass snake
➤ mamba
➤ puff adder
➤ python
➤ rattlesnake
➤ sand snake
➤ sea snake
➤ sidewinder
➤ viper

- A literary word for a snake is a serpent.

snap *VERB*
❶ *One of the ropes snapped under the strain.*
• **break, split, crack, fracture**
❷ *The dogs were snapping at them.*
• **bite, nip**
❸ *'Leave me alone!' the boy snapped.*
• **snarl, bark, retort**

snare *NOUN*
A rabbit was caught in a snare.
• **trap, wire, net**
(*old use*) gin
– To catch an animal in a snare is to **ensnare** or **snare** it.

snarl *VERB*
❶ *A guard dog snarled as we approached.*
• **growl, bare its teeth**
❷ *'What do you want?' snarled a voice.*
• **snap, bark, growl, thunder**

snatch *VERB*
She snatched the letter from my hand.
• **grab, seize, grasp, pluck, wrench away, wrest away**

sneak *VERB*
I managed to sneak in without anyone noticing.
• **slip, steal, creep, slink, tiptoe, sidle, skulk**

sneaky *ADJECTIVE*
That was a really sneaky trick.
• **sly, underhand, cunning, crafty, devious, furtive, dishonest**
OPPOSITE honest

sneer *VERB*
➤ **sneer at**
He sneered at my attempts to build a sandcastle.
• **make fun of, mock, ridicule, scoff at, jeer at, deride**

snigger *VERB*
Someone sniggered at the back of the room.
• **giggle, titter, chuckle, laugh**

snip *VERB*
She snipped off a lock of her hair.
• **cut, clip, trim, chop**

snippet *NOUN*
We could hear snippets of their conversation.
• **piece, fragment, bit, scrap, morsel, snatch**

snivel *VERB*
For goodness' sake, stop snivelling!
• **cry, sob, weep, sniff, whimper, whine**

snobbish *ADJECTIVE*
I didn't like the snobbish atmosphere in the club.
• **arrogant, pompous, superior, haughty** (*informal*) **stuck-up, snooty, toffee-nosed**
IDIOM **high and mighty**
OPPOSITE humble

snoop *VERB*
A man was seen snooping round the building at night.
• **sneak, pry, poke, rummage, spy**

snout *NOUN*
Aardvarks have long, narrow snouts.
• **muzzle, nose**

snub *VERB*
She felt snubbed by not being invited.
• **insult, offend, slight, spurn, brush off**

snug *ADJECTIVE*
❶ *These boots will keep your feet snug through the winter.*
• **cosy, comfortable, warm, relaxed** (*informal*) **comfy**
❷ *Choose a smaller size for a snug fit.*
• **tight, close-fitting, figure-hugging**
OPPOSITES loose, roomy

soak *VERB*
❶ *You'll get soaked without a raincoat!*
• **wet through, drench, saturate**
❷ *Leave the beans to soak in water overnight.*
• **steep, immerse, submerge**

➤ **soak something up**
The roots act like a sponge, soaking up rainwater.
• **take in, absorb, suck up**

soaking *ADJECTIVE*
They arrived at the campsite soaking and exhausted.
• **wet through, drenched, dripping, wringing, saturated, sodden, sopping, soggy**
– Ground that has been soaked by rain is **waterlogged**.

soar *VERB*
❶ *A seagull soared into the air.*
• **climb, rise, ascend, fly up**
❷ *The number of complaints has soared recently.*
• **go up, rise, increase, escalate, shoot up**
IDIOMS **go through the roof, go sky-high**
OPPOSITE plummet

sob *VERB*
She threw herself on the bed, sobbing uncontrollably.
• **cry, weep, bawl, snivel, shed tears** (*informal*) **blubber**

sober *ADJECTIVE*
❶ *He drank a little wine, but he stayed sober.*
• **clear-headed**
OPPOSITE drunk
❷ *The funeral was a sober occasion.*
• **serious, solemn, sombre, grave, dignified, sedate, subdued**
OPPOSITES light-hearted, frivolous

sociable *ADJECTIVE*
Our new neighbours seem very sociable.
• **friendly, outgoing, gregarious, neighbourly, amiable**
OPPOSITE unfriendly

social *ADJECTIVE*
❶ *Chimpanzees live in social groups.*
• **communal, collective, community, group**
OPPOSITES individual, solitary

❷ *Here is a list of this month's social events.*
• **recreational, leisure**
OPPOSITE work-related

society *NOUN*
❶ *We live in a multiracial society.*
• **community, culture, civilization, people**
❷ *She is a member of the local music society.*
• **association, group, organization, club, league, union**
❸ *He shunned the society of his fellow students.*
• **company, companionship, fellowship, friendship**

soft *ADJECTIVE*
❶ *My head sank into the soft pillow.*
• **supple, pliable, springy, spongy, yielding, flexible, squashy**
OPPOSITES firm, hard
❷ *The rabbit's fur felt very soft.*
• **smooth, silky, velvety, fleecy, feathery, downy**
OPPOSITES coarse, rough
❸ *We spoke in soft whispers.*
• **quiet, muted, muffled, hushed, low, faint**
OPPOSITE loud
❹ *A soft breeze stirred the leaves.*
• **gentle, light, mild, delicate**
OPPOSITES strong, forceful
❺ *Through the window came the soft light of early morning.*
• **pale, muted, subdued, dim, low**
OPPOSITES bright, dazzling
❻ *You're being too soft with that puppy.*
• **lenient, easy-going, tolerant, indulgent**
OPPOSITES strict, tough

soggy *ADJECTIVE*
The pitch was still soggy underfoot.
• **wet, moist, soaked, saturated, sodden, drenched, waterlogged**
OPPOSITE dry

soil *NOUN*
❶ *These plants grow best in well-drained soil.*
• **earth, ground, land**
– Good fertile soil is **loam**.
– The upper layer of soil is **topsoil**.
❷ *We were glad to be back on home soil.*
• **territory, turf, ground, country**

sold
past tense see **sell**

soldier *NOUN*
Two soldiers stood guard outside the gate.
• **serviceman or servicewoman**
– A soldier paid to fight for a foreign country is a **mercenary**.
– An old word for a soldier is **warrior**.
– Soldiers who use large guns are **artillery**.
– Soldiers who fight on horseback or in armoured vehicles are **cavalry**.
– Soldiers who fight on foot are **infantry**.

sole *ADJECTIVE*
She was the sole survivor of the shipwreck.
• **only, single, one, solitary, lone, unique**

solemn *ADJECTIVE*
❶ *Both men wore a solemn expression.*
• **serious, grave, sober, sombre, unsmiling, grim, dour**
OPPOSITE cheerful
❷ *The coronation was a solemn occasion.*
• **formal, dignified, ceremonial, grand, stately, majestic**
OPPOSITE frivolous

solid *ADJECTIVE*
❶ *These bars are made of solid steel.*
OPPOSITE hollow
❷ *Leave the plaster to turn solid.*
• **hard, firm, dense, compact, rigid, unyielding**
OPPOSITES soft, liquid
❸ *He slept for a solid nine hours.*
• **continuous, uninterrupted, unbroken**
❹ *The crown was made of solid gold.*
• **pure, genuine**

❺ *The house is built on solid foundations.*
• **firm, robust, sound, strong, stable, sturdy**
OPPOSITES weak, flimsy
❻ *She got solid support from her team mates.*
• **firm, reliable, dependable, united, unanimous**
OPPOSITES weak, divided

solidify *VERB*
The lava solidifies as it cools.
• **harden, become solid, set, stiffen**
OPPOSITES soften, liquefy

solitary *ADJECTIVE*
❶ *He leads a solitary existence.*
• **unaccompanied, on your own, reclusive, withdrawn, isolated, friendless, unsociable**
OPPOSITE sociable
❷ *There was a solitary light in the distance.*
• **single, sole, lone, individual, one, only**

solitude *NOUN*
She longed for peace and solitude.
• **privacy, seclusion, isolation, loneliness**

solve *VERB*
There's a mystery we've been trying to solve.
• **interpret, explain, answer, work out, find the solution to, unravel, decipher** (*informal*) **crack**

sombre *ADJECTIVE*
❶ *The hall was painted in sombre shades of grey.*
• **dark, dull, dim, dismal, dingy, drab, cheerless**
OPPOSITE bright
❷ *Everyone was in a sombre mood that night.*
• **gloomy, serious, sober, grave, grim, sad, melancholy, mournful**
OPPOSITE cheerful

song *NOUN*

WORD WEB

Some types of song:

- anthem
- aria
- ballad
- calypso
- carol
- chant
- ditty
- folk song
- hymn
- jingle
- lament
- lay
- love song
- lullaby
- madrigal
- nursery rhyme
- pop song
- psalm
- rap
- round
- shanty
- spiritual

- A play or film that includes many songs is a **musical.**
- A song from a musical is a **number.**
- The words for a song are the **lyrics.**

Types of singing voice:

- alto
- baritone
- bass
- contralto
- soprano
- tenor
- treble

soon *ADVERB*
The others will be back soon.
• **before long, in a minute, shortly, presently, quickly**

soothe *VERB*
❶ *The soft music soothed her nerves.*
• **calm, comfort, settle, quieten, pacify, relax**
❷ *This cream should soothe the pain.*
• **ease, alleviate, relieve, lessen, reduce**

soothing *ADJECTIVE*
Soothing music played in the background.
• **calming, relaxing, restful, peaceful, gentle**

sophisticated *ADJECTIVE*

❶ *She looks quite sophisticated with her hair up.*
• **grown-up, mature, cultivated, cultured, refined**
OPPOSITE naive
❷ *He has a sophisticated digital camera.*
• **advanced, high-level, complex, intricate, elaborate**
OPPOSITES simple, basic

sore *ADJECTIVE*

My feet are still sore from the walk.
• **painful, aching, hurting, smarting, throbbing, tender, sensitive, inflamed, raw**

sore *NOUN*

The dog had a sore on its paw.
• **wound, inflammation, swelling, ulcer**

sorrow *NOUN*

❶ *The song expresses the sorrow of parting.*
• **sadness, unhappiness, misery, woe, grief, anguish, heartache, heartbreak, melancholy, gloom, wretchedness, despair**
– Sorrow because of someone's death is **mourning**.
– Sorrow at being away from home is **homesickness**.
OPPOSITES happiness, joy
❷ *She expressed her sorrow for what she had done.*
• **regret, remorse, repentance, apologies**

sorry *ADJECTIVE*

I'm sorry if I upset you in any way.
• **apologetic, regretful, remorseful, contrite, ashamed (of), repentant**
OPPOSITE unapologetic
➤ **feel sorry for someone**
I actually began to feel sorry for him.
• **sympathize with, pity, feel compassion for**

sort *NOUN*

What sort of music do you like?
• **kind, type, variety, style, form, class, category, genre**
– A sort of animal is a **breed** or **species**.

sort *VERB*

The books are sorted according to size.
• **arrange, organize, class, group, categorize, classify**
OPPOSITE mix
➤ **sort something out**
• **resolve, settle, deal with, put right, fix, clear up, straighten out**

sought

past tense see **seek**

sound *NOUN*

I heard the sound of approaching footsteps.
• **noise, tone**
– A loud, harsh sound is a **din** or **racket**.
– Words meaning 'to do with sound' are **acoustic** and **sonic**.
➤ **sonic waves**

WRITING TIPS

DESCRIBING SOUNDS
Types of sound:

➤ bang
➤ beep
➤ blare
➤ bleep
➤ boom
➤ buzz
➤ chime
➤ chug
➤ clang
➤ clank
➤ clap
➤ clash
➤ clatter
➤ click
➤ clink
➤ clunk
➤ crack
➤ crackle
➤ crash
➤ creak
➤ crunch
➤ ding
➤ drone
➤ drum
➤ fizz
➤ gurgle
➤ jangle
➤ jingle
➤ hiss
➤ honk
➤ hoot
➤ knock
➤ patter
➤ peal
➤ ping
➤ plop
➤ pop
➤ putter
➤ rap
➤ rasp
➤ rattle
➤ ring
➤ roar
➤ rumble
➤ rustle
➤ scrape
➤ scrunch
➤ sizzle
➤ snap
➤ sputter

A B C D E F G H I J K L M N O P Q R S T U V W X Y Z

- squeak
- squelch
- swish
- tap
- thud
- thunder
- tick
- tinkle
- toot
- trill
- twang
- whirr
- whistle
- whoosh

Sounds made by people:

- bawl
- bellow
- boo
- boom
- cackle
- chortle
- croak
- cry
- gasp
- groan
- hiccup
- hiss
- howl
- hum
- moan
- murmur
- puff
- scream
- shout
- shriek
- sigh
- sing
- sniff
- snort
- sob
- splutter
- squeal
- stammer
- stutter
- wail
- wheeze
- whimper
- whine
- whisper
- whoop
- yell
- yodel

Adjectives describing sounds:

- blaring
- brittle
- croaky
- deafening
- discordant
- droning
- dulcet
- ear-splitting
- grating
- gruff
- harmonious
- harsh
- high-pitched
- hoarse
- husky
- jarring
- lilting
- mellifluous
- melodious
- piercing
- piping
- rasping
- raucous
- shrill
- squeaky
- sweet
- thin
- throaty
- tinny

sound *VERB*

A siren sounds when a shark is spotted.
• **make a noise, resound, go off, be heard**

sound *ADJECTIVE*

❶ *Parts of the outer wall are still sound.*
• **firm, solid, stable, safe, secure, intact, undamaged, in good condition**
OPPOSITES unsound, unstable
❷ *The travellers returned safe and sound.*
• **well, fit, healthy, in good shape**
OPPOSITES unhealthy, unfit
❸ *She gave us a piece of sound advice.*
• **good, sensible, wise, reasonable, reliable, trustworthy, valid**
OPPOSITES unwise, unreliable
❹ *He fell into a sound sleep.*
• **thorough, deep, undisturbed, peaceful**
OPPOSITES broken, fitful

sour *ADJECTIVE*

❶ *These apples are a bit sour.*
• **tart, bitter, sharp, acidic**
OPPOSITE sweet
❷ *The milk has gone sour.*
• **bad, off, rancid, curdled**
OPPOSITE fresh
❸ *He gave me a sour look.*
• **cross, bad-tempered, grumpy, resentful, bitter**

source *NOUN*

They've found the source of the infection.
• **origin, start, starting point, root, cause, head**
– The source of a river or stream is usually a **spring**.

south *NOUN, ADJECTIVE & ADVERB*

Portugal is in the south of Europe.
– The parts of a country or continent in the south are the **southern** parts.
– To travel towards the south is to travel **southward** or **southwards**.
– A wind from the south is a **southerly** wind.
– A person who lives in the south of a country is a **southerner**.

sow *VERB*

Sow the seeds in parallel rows.
• **plant, scatter, disperse, distribute**
– To sow an area of ground with seeds is to **seed** it.

space *NOUN*
❶ *The spacecraft's mission was to explore deep space.*
• **outer space, the cosmos, the universe**
❷ *There wasn't much space to move about.*
• **room, capacity, area, volume, expanse**
❸ *There is a space at the back of the cupboard.*
• **gap, hole, cavity, opening, aperture**
– A space without any air in it is a **vacuum.**
❹ *We moved house twice in the space of a year.*
• **period, span, interval, duration, stretch**

WORD WEB

Natural objects found in space:

➤ asteroid or planetoid
➤ black hole
➤ comet
➤ constellation
➤ dwarf planet
➤ galaxy
➤ meteor (*informal* shooting star)
➤ meteor shower
➤ Milky Way
➤ moon
➤ nebula
➤ nova
➤ planet
➤ red dwarf
➤ red giant
➤ solar system
➤ star
➤ sun
➤ supernova

SEE ALSO **planet, moon**

- A word that means 'to do with space' is **cosmic.**

➤ *cosmic rays*

- The scientific study of natural objects in space is **astronomy.**

Terms used in space exploration:

➤ astronaut
➤ heat shield
➤ intergalactic
➤ interplanetary
➤ interstellar
➤ launch
➤ mission
➤ orbit
➤ orbiter
➤ probe
➤ re-entry
➤ rover
➤ satellite
➤ spacecraft
➤ space shuttle
➤ space station
➤ spacesuit
➤ spacewalk

spacious *ADJECTIVE*
The front room is bright and spacious.
• **big, large, roomy, sizeable**
OPPOSITES **small, cramped**

span *NOUN*
❶ *The bridge has a span of 200 metres.*
• **breadth, length, width, extent, distance, reach**
– The length between the wing tips of a bird or an aircraft is its **wingspan.**
❷ *His novels were published over a span of forty years.*
• **period, time, space, interval, duration, stretch**

span *VERB*
A rickety footbridge spanned the river.
• **cross, extend across, pass over, stretch over, straddle, bridge, traverse**

spare *VERB*
❶ *Can you spare any money for a good cause?*
• **afford, part with, give, provide, do without, manage without**
❷ *The duke agreed to spare their lives.*
• **pardon, have mercy on, reprieve, let off, release, free**

spare *ADJECTIVE*
❶ *The spare tyre is in the boot.*
• **additional, extra, supplementary, reserve, standby, backup, relief, substitute**
❷ *Have you any spare change?*
• **surplus, leftover, unused, unwanted, excess, superfluous**
❸ *The figure in the doorway was tall and spare.*
• **lean, thin, skinny, gaunt, spindly**

spark *NOUN*
One firework exploded in a shower of sparks.
• **flash, gleam, glint, flicker, twinkle, sparkle**

sparkle *VERB & NOUN*
Her earrings sparkled in the lamplight.
• **glitter, glisten, glint, flash, twinkle, shimmer**
For tips on describing light see **light.**

a b c d e f g h i j k l m n o p q r s t u v w x y z

sparse *ADJECTIVE*
Vegetation is more sparse in the dry season.
• **scarce, scanty, patchy, thinly scattered** (*informal*) **thin on the ground**
OPPOSITES plentiful, abundant

spatter *VERB*
The bus spattered mud all over us.
• **splash, spray, sprinkle, scatter, shower**

speak *VERB*
❶ *Mitchell was too nervous to speak.*
• **talk, communicate, say something, express yourself**
❷ *Speak the words clearly into the microphone.*
• **say, utter, voice, pronounce, articulate, enunciate**

speaker *NOUN*
We have a line-up of guest speakers.
• **lecturer**
– A person who makes formal speeches is an **orator**.
– A person who speaks on behalf of an organization is a **spokesperson**.

spear *NOUN*
The gladiator was armed with a spear and shield.
– A spear used in whaling is a **harpoon**.
– A spear thrown as a sport is a **javelin**.
– A spear carried by a medieval knight on horseback was a **lance**.

special *ADJECTIVE*
❶ *Today we are celebrating a special occasion.*
• **important, significant, memorable, noteworthy, momentous, historic, out-of-the-ordinary**
OPPOSITES ordinary, everyday
❷ *Early autumn has its own special beauty.*
• **unique, individual, characteristic, distinctive, peculiar**
❸ *You need a special camera to film underwater.*
• **specific, particular, specialized, tailor-made, purpose-built**

speciality *NOUN*
As an actor, his speciality is playing villains.
• **strength, strong point, expertise, forte**

specific *ADJECTIVE*
Can you give us some specific examples?
• **detailed, particular, definite, precise, exact, explicit, clear-cut**
OPPOSITES general, vague

specify *VERB*
Please specify your shoe size.
• **state, identify, name, detail, define**

specimen *NOUN*
The police asked for a specimen of his handwriting.
• **sample, example, illustration, instance, model**

speck *NOUN*
She brushed a speck of dust from her shoes.
• **bit, dot, spot, fleck, grain, particle, trace**

speckled *ADJECTIVE*
A brown, speckled egg lay on the nest.
• **flecked, speckly, spotted, spotty, mottled**
- If you have a lot of brown spots on your skin you are **freckled** or **freckly**.
- Something with patches of colour is **dappled** or **patchy**.

spectacle *NOUN*
The Mardi Gras parade is a colourful spectacle.
• **display, show, sight, performance, exhibition, extravaganza**

spectacles *PLURAL NOUN*
see **glasses**

spectacular *ADJECTIVE*
❶ *The film opens with a spectacular action sequence.*
• **dramatic, exciting, impressive, thrilling, breathtaking, sensational**

❷ *The tulips are spectacular at this time of year.*
• **eye-catching, showy, striking, stunning, glorious, magnificent**

spectator *NOUN*
Spectators lined the streets.
• **watcher, viewer, observer, onlooker**
– The spectators at a show are the **audience**.
– The spectators at a sporting event are the **crowd**.
– A person who sees an accident or a crime is a **witness** or an **eyewitness**.

speech *NOUN*
❶ *His speech was slurred.*
• **speaking, talking, articulation, pronunciation, enunciation, diction**
❷ *She was invited to give a short speech.*
• **talk, address, lecture, oration**
– A talk given as part of a religious service is a **sermon**.
– The art of making speeches in public is **oratory**.
❸ *I had learned a speech from Shakespeare.*
– Speech between actors in a play is **dialogue**.
– A speech delivered by a single actor is a **monologue** or **soliloquy**.

speechless *ADJECTIVE*
She was speechless with surprise.
• **dumbstruck, dumbfounded, tongue-tied**

speed *NOUN*
❶ *Could a spaceship travel faster than the speed of light?*
• **pace, rate, velocity**
– The speed of a piece of music is its **tempo**.
– To increase speed is to **accelerate**.
– To reduce speed is to **decelerate**.
❷ *The rumour spread with astonishing speed.*
• **quickness, rapidity, swiftness, alacrity**
OPPOSITE slowness

speed *VERB*
The train sped by.
• **race, rush, dash, dart, hurry, hurtle, career, fly, streak, tear, shoot, zoom, zip**
➤ **speed up**
The car behind us started to speed up.
• **go faster, hurry up, accelerate, pick up speed**
OPPOSITE slow down

speedy *ADJECTIVE*
We wish you a speedy recovery.
• **fast, quick, swift, rapid, prompt, brisk, hasty**
OPPOSITE slow

spell *NOUN*
❶ *The spell was believed to ward off evil.*
• **charm, incantation**
❷ *We are hoping for a spell of dry weather.*
• **period, interval, time, stretch, run**
➤ **put a spell on someone**
An evil sorcerer had put a spell on her.
• **enchant, bewitch**

spend *VERB*
❶ *How much money did you spend today?*
• **pay out, use up, expend, get through** (*informal*) **fork out, shell out**
– To spend money unwisely is to **waste**, **squander** or **fritter** it.
OPPOSITE save
❷ *I spent the whole day working on the script.*
• **pass, occupy, fill, while away**

sphere *NOUN*
❶ *A glass sphere hung from the ceiling.*
• **ball, globe, orb**
❷ *She is an expert in the sphere of astronomy.*
• **subject, area, field, arena, realm, domain**

spherical *ADJECTIVE*
The earth is roughly spherical.
• **round, ball-shaped, globe-shaped**

A B C D E F G H I J K L M N O P Q R S T U V W X Y Z

spice *NOUN*

WORD WEB

Some spices used in cooking:

- allspice
- aniseed
- bay leaf
- black pepper
- caraway
- cardamom
- cayenne
- chilli
- cinnamon
- cloves
- coriander
- cumin
- curry powder
- fennel seed
- garam masala
- ginger
- juniper
- mace
- mustard
- nutmeg
- paprika
- pimento
- saffron
- sesame
- star anise
- turmeric
- white pepper

spicy *ADJECTIVE*
He made a spicy vegetable curry for us.
• **hot, peppery, fiery, piquant**
OPPOSITE mild

spike *NOUN*
His shirt got caught on a metal spike.
• **point, prong, spear, skewer, stake, barb, thorn**

spill *VERB*
❶ *He spilled his juice all over the table.*
• **overturn, upset, tip over**
❷ *Water spilled onto the floor.*
• **overflow, pour, splash, slop, slosh**
❸ *The coins came spilling out.*
• **pour, stream, flood, surge, swarm**

spin *VERB*
A wheel spins on an axle.
• **revolve, rotate, go round, turn, whirl, twirl**

spine *NOUN*
❶ *They took an X-ray of the patient's spine.*
• **backbone, spinal column**
– The bones in your spine are your **vertebrae**.
❷ *A porcupine has sharp spines.*
• **spike, prickle, barb, quill, needle, thorn, bristle**

spiral *NOUN*
The staircase wound upwards in a long spiral.
• **coil, twist, corkscrew, whorl, helix**
– A tight spiral of swirling air or water is a **vortex**.

spirit *NOUN*
❶ *They believe the house is haunted by an evil spirit.*
• **ghost, phantom, spectre, ghoul, demon**
❷ *The orchestra played the piece with great spirit.*
• **energy, liveliness, enthusiasm, vigour, zest, zeal, fire**
❸ *We come together today in a spirit of friendship and cooperation.*
• **feeling, mood, atmosphere**

spiritual *ADJECTIVE*
The Pope is the spiritual leader of Catholics around the world.
• **religious, holy, sacred**
OPPOSITES secular, worldly

spite *NOUN*
Someone wrote the email out of spite.
• **malice, malevolence, ill will, meanness, spitefulness, vindictiveness, nastiness, venom**
➤ **in spite of**
In spite of its name, the dogfish is a type of shark.
• **despite, notwithstanding, regardless of**

spiteful *ADJECTIVE*
Any spiteful comments will be deleted.
• **malicious, malevolent, vindictive, hateful, venomous, mean, nasty, unkind**
OPPOSITE kind

splash *VERB*
❶ *The bus splashed water over us.*
• **shower, spray, spatter, splatter, squirt, slop, spill**
(*informal*) **slosh**

② *Children splashed about in the water.*
• **wade, paddle, wallow**
(*informal*) **slosh**

splendid *ADJECTIVE*
① *There was a splendid banquet in their honour.*
• **magnificent, lavish, luxurious, grand, imposing, rich, sumptuous, gorgeous, glorious, resplendent, dazzling**
② *That's a splendid idea!*
• **excellent, first-class, admirable, superb, wonderful, marvellous**
(*informal*) **brilliant, fantastic, terrific**

splendour *NOUN*
We all admired the splendour of the palace.
• **magnificence, grandeur, richness, sumptuousness, glory, resplendence**

splinter *NOUN*
There were splinters of broken glass all over the floor.
• **fragment, sliver, shard, chip, flake**

splinter *VERB*
The boat's hull began to splinter and crack.
• **shatter, smash, fracture, crack, split**

split *VERB*
① *The rock had split into several pieces.*
• **break apart, crack open, fracture, rupture, splinter, snap**
② *He split his trousers climbing over a fence.*
• **rip open, tear**
③ *She split the class into two groups.*
• **divide, separate, part**
④ *We split the money between us.*
• **distribute, share out, divide up, parcel out**
➤ **split up**
The band announced they were splitting up.
• **break up, separate, part company, go your separate ways**

split *NOUN*
① *There was a large split in the rock.*
• **crack, break, breach, fracture, fissure, rupture**
② *He had a split in the seat of his trousers.*
• **tear, rip, slash, slit, cut, rent**

spoil *VERB*
① *If I tell you, it'll spoil the surprise.*
• **ruin, wreck, destroy, upset, mess up, scupper**
② *Overcooking will spoil the flavour of the fish.*
• **damage, impair, mar, blight**
– To spoil the look of something is to **disfigure** or **deface** it.
③ *Maybe he was spoilt as a child.*
• **indulge, pamper, cosset, make a fuss of**

spoke
past tense see **speak**

spoken *ADJECTIVE*
a long section of spoken dialogue
• **oral, unwritten**
OPPOSITE written

spongy *ADJECTIVE*
The mossy ground felt spongy to walk on.
• **soft, springy, squashy, absorbent, porous**

spontaneous *ADJECTIVE*
The audience broke into spontaneous applause.
• **unplanned, impromptu, unpremeditated, unrehearsed, impulsive, instinctive**
IDIOMS **off-the-cuff, spur-of-the-moment**
– An action done without any conscious thought is a **reflex** action.

sport *NOUN*

WORD WEB

Some team sports:

➤ American football	➤ bobsleigh
➤ baseball	➤ bowls
➤ basketball	➤ cricket
	➤ curling

- football or soccer
- hockey
- ice hockey
- lacrosse
- netball
- polo
- rounders
- rowing
- rugby
- volleyball
- water polo

Some individual sports:

- angling
- archery
- athletics
- badminton
- billiards
- bowling
- boxing
- canoeing
- climbing
- croquet
- cross-country running
- cycling
- darts
- diving
- fencing
- golf
- gymnastics
- horse racing
- ice skating
- jogging
- judo
- karate
- luge
- motor racing
- mountaineering
- orienteering
- pool
- rowing
- sailing
- showjumping
- skiing
- snooker
- snowboarding
- speed skating
- squash
- surfing
- swimming
- table tennis
- tae kwon do
- tennis
- waterskiing
- weightlifting
- windsurfing
- wrestling

- Someone who takes part in sport is a sportsman or sportswoman.

SEE ALSO **athletics**

WRITING TIPS

WRITING ABOUT SPORT
Useful words and phrases:

- amateur
- arena
- champion
- coach
- commentator
- cup tie
- draw
- extra time
- final whistle
- first half
- foul
- full time
- game plan
- half time
- hat trick
- heats
- highlights
- injury time
- in play
- key player
- kick-off
- man or woman of the match
- offside
- off target
- onside
- on target
- opponents
- out of bounds
- penalty
- player
- possession
- professional
- qualifying round
- quarter-final
- referee
- score sheet
- second half
- semi-final
- sending off
- squad
- stadium
- substitute
- supporters
- tactics
- team captain
- teammate
- turning point

Verbs:

- arc
- bowl
- catch
- chip
- curl
- dive
- dribble
- drive
- field
- flick
- head
- hurl
- kick
- lob
- miss
- pass
- pitch
- power
- save
- scoop
- score
- shoot
- slam
- smash
- spin
- strike
- swerve
- swing
- swipe
- tap
- throw
- toss
- trickle
- volley
- weave

SEE ALSO **football**

sporting *ADJECTIVE*
It was sporting of him to admit defeat.
• **sportsmanlike, fair, generous, honourable**
OPPOSITE **unsporting**

spot *NOUN*
❶ *There were a few spots of rust here and there.*
• **mark, patch, fleck, speck, dot, blot, stain, blotch, splodge**
– Small brown spots on your skin are **freckles**.

– A small dark spot on your skin is a **mole**.
– Spots on a bird's egg or plumage are **speckles**.
❷ *Her skin is prone to spots.*
• **pimple, blackhead**
– An area of spots on your skin is a **rash**.
❸ *Here's a good spot for a photograph.*
• **place, position, location, site, situation, setting, venue**
❹ *The first spots of rain began to fall.*
• **drop, blob, bead**

spot *VERB*
❶ *Did you spot your friends in the crowd?*
• **see, sight, spy, catch sight of, notice, observe, make out, recognize, detect**
❷ *My best coat was all spotted with mud.*
• **mark, stain, blot, spatter, fleck, dot, speckle, mottle**

spotless *ADJECTIVE*
The house was spotless from top to bottom.
• **clean, unmarked, immaculate, gleaming**
OPPOSITES dirty, grubby

spout *VERB*
Molten lava spouted far into the air.
• **gush, spew, pour, stream, spurt, squirt, jet**

sprawl *VERB*
❶ *We found him asleep, sprawling on the sofa.*
• **stretch out, spread out, lean back, loll, lounge, slouch, slump**
❷ *I could see the town sprawling across the hillside.*
• **spread, stretch, scatter**

spray *VERB*
A burst pipe was spraying water everywhere.
• **shower, spatter, sprinkle, splash, squirt, scatter**

spray *NOUN*
❶ *Give the plants a daily spray of water.*
• **shower, sprinkling, squirt, mist**
❷ *She took out her perfume spray.*
• **aerosol, sprinkler, atomizer, mister**
❸ *I picked a spray of spring flowers from the garden.*
• **bunch, posy**

spread *VERB*
❶ *Just spread the map on the table.*
• **lay out, open out, fan out, unfold, unfurl, unroll**
❷ *Newspapers were spread all over the floor.*
• **scatter, strew**
❸ *I spread some butter on my toast.*
• **smear, plaster, daub**
❹ *A big grin spread across the girl's face.*
• **expand, extend, stretch, broaden, enlarge, swell**
❺ *Someone has been spreading malicious rumours.*
• **communicate, circulate, distribute, transmit, disseminate, make known, pass round**

spread *NOUN*
❶ *Nothing could stop the spread of the disease.*
• **advance, expansion, diffusion, circulation, distribution, transmission, dissemination**
❷ *The bird's wings have a spread of nearly a metre.*
• **span, width, extent, stretch, reach**

sprightly *ADJECTIVE*
She still looks sprightly for her age.
• **lively, energetic, active, agile, nimble, frisky, spry**
OPPOSITE inactive

spring *VERB*
❶ *She sprang to her feet in alarm.*
• **jump, leap, bound, hop, vault, pounce**
❷ *Where did the idea for the character spring from?*
• **originate, arise, derive, stem, come**
➤ **spring up**
Weeds are springing up all over the garden.
• **appear, develop, emerge, shoot up, sprout**

A B C D E F G H I J K L M N O P Q R S T U V W X Y Z

springy *ADJECTIVE*
The bed felt soft and springy.
• **bouncy, elastic, stretchy, flexible, pliable**
OPPOSITE rigid

sprinkle *VERB*
❶ *She sprinkled a little perfume onto a handkerchief.*
• **spray, shower, splash, drizzle**
❷ *I like to sprinkle sugar over strawberries.*
• **scatter, strew, dust**

sprout *VERB*
❶ *Leave the seeds in a warm place to sprout.*
• **grow, germinate, put out shoots**
❷ *Sites like this are sprouting all over the Internet.*
• **spring up, appear, develop, emerge**

spruce *ADJECTIVE*
He looked spruce in his new uniform.
• **smart, well-dressed, well-groomed, elegant, neat, trim**
OPPOSITE scruffy

spun
past tense see **spin**

spur *VERB*
➤ **spur someone on**
We were spurred on by the thought of adventure.
• **encourage, stimulate, motivate, inspire, prompt, galvanize, urge on, egg on**

spurt *VERB*
Dirty water spurted from the pipe.
• **gush, spout, shoot out, stream, squirt, jet**

spy *NOUN*
He once worked as a spy.
• **agent, secret agent, mole**
– A spy who works for two rival countries or organizations is a **double agent**.

WRITING TIPS

WRITING SPY FICTION
Characters:

➤ agent
➤ codebreaker
➤ controller
➤ cryptographer
➤ double agent
➤ mole
➤ operative
➤ secret agent
➤ sleeper
➤ spy catcher
➤ spymaster

Useful words and phrases:

➤ behind enemy lines
➤ briefing
➤ CIA
➤ cipher
➤ clandestine operation
➤ code book
➤ code-breaking
➤ counter-espionage
➤ counter-intelligence
➤ covert
➤ debriefing
➤ decode
➤ decryption
➤ deep cover
➤ defection
➤ disinformation
➤ encode
➤ encryption
➤ espionage
➤ false identity
➤ FBI
➤ headquarters
➤ hidden camera
➤ infiltration
➤ intelligence
➤ listening device (*informal* bug)
➤ MI5
➤ MI6
➤ mission
➤ password
➤ recruitment
➤ secret service
➤ special operations
➤ spying
➤ surveillance
➤ transmitting device
➤ under cover

spy *VERB*
I thought I spied a familiar face.
• **see, sight, spot, catch sight of, notice, observe, make out, detect**

squabble *VERB*
Those two are always squabbling!
• **argue, fight, quarrel, bicker, wrangle**

squalid *ADJECTIVE*
The prisoners were kept in a squalid little room.
• **dirty, filthy, foul, dingy, degrading, nasty, unpleasant**
OPPOSITE clean

squander *VERB*
He squandered his fortune in gambling.
• **waste, throw away, fritter away, misuse**
(*informal*) **blow**
OPPOSITE save

square *ADJECTIVE*
All the tiles have square corners.
• **right-angled**
– A pattern of squares is a **chequered** pattern.

squarely *ADVERB*
The ball hit him squarely in the face.
• **directly, straight, head on**
OPPOSITE obliquely

squash *VERB*
❶ *The cake got a bit squashed in my bag.*
• **crush, flatten, press, compress, mangle, mash, pulp**
(*informal*) **squish**
❷ *Just squash everything into the suitcase.*
• **force, stuff, squeeze, cram, jam, pack, ram, wedge**

squat *VERB*
We squatted by the fire, trying to keep warm.
• **crouch, huddle, sit on your heels**

squat *ADJECTIVE*
He was a squat little man with a reddish face.
• **dumpy, stocky, plump, podgy, portly**

squeak *NOUN & VERB*
❶ *The door squeaked.*
• **creak, grate, rasp**
❷ *The bird squeaked in its cage.*
• **chirp, peep, cheep**

squeal *NOUN & VERB*
She squealed with pain.
• **cry, yell, yelp, screech, scream, shriek**

squeeze *VERB*
❶ *She squeezed my hand tightly.*
• **press, compress, crush, grip, clasp, pinch, nip**
❷ *Now squeeze the juice out of lemon.*
• **extract, press, express, force, wring**
❸ *Five of us squeezed into the back of the car.*
• **squash, cram, crowd, stuff, jam, push, ram, shove, wedge**

squeeze *NOUN*
❶ *She gave my hand a squeeze.*
• **press, grip, clasp, pinch, nip**
❷ *It was a tight squeeze in the back seat.*
• **squash, crush, jam**

squirm *VERB*
A rabbit had squirmed through a hole in the fence.
• **wriggle, writhe, twist**

squirt *VERB*
Tap water squirted all over the floor.
• **spurt, spray, shower, gush, spout, shoot, jet**

stab *VERB*
❶ *The victim had been stabbed in the chest.*
• **knife, spear, jab, pierce, impale, run through, skewer**
❷ *A man was shouting and stabbing a finger in the air.*
• **stick, thrust, push, jab**

stab *NOUN*
I felt a sudden stab of pain in my chest.
• **pang, twinge, prick, sting**

stable *ADJECTIVE*
❶ *The ladder doesn't look very stable.*
• **steady, secure, firm, balanced, solid, fixed**
OPPOSITES unstable, wobbly
❷ *He's been in a stable relationship for the last few years.*
• **steady, established, lasting, durable, strong**
OPPOSITES casual, temporary

stack *NOUN*
On the table was a stack of unanswered letters.
• **pile, heap, mound, mountain, tower**
– A stack of hay is also called a **rick** of hay.

a b c d e f g h i j k l m n o p q r s t u v w x y z

stack *VERB*
Just stack the dishes in the sink.
• **heap up, pile up**

staff *NOUN*
He knows all the staff at the local library.
• **workers, employees, personnel, workforce, team**
– The staff on a ship or an aircraft are the **crew**.

stage *NOUN*
❶ *They went up on the stage to collect their prizes.*
• **platform, podium**
❷ *This was the final stage of our journey.*
• **part, leg, step, phase, portion, section, stretch**
❸ *At this stage in her life, she wants to try something new.*
• **point, time, juncture, period, phase**

stagger *VERB*
❶ *Dad staggered in carrying a huge parcel.*
• **reel, stumble, lurch, totter, teeter, sway, waver, wobble**
❷ *I was staggered at the price of the tickets.*
• **amaze, astonish, astound, surprise, stun, startle, dumbfound, flabbergast**

stagnant *ADJECTIVE*
Mosquitoes swarmed around the pool of stagnant water.
• **still, motionless, static**
OPPOSITES flowing, fresh

stain *NOUN*
There were a few coffee stains on the tablecloth.
• **mark, spot, blot, blotch, smear, smudge**

stain *VERB*
❶ *Her trainers were stained with mud.*
• **discolour, mark, smear, smudge, soil, dirty, blacken, tarnish**
❷ *The wood can be stained a darker shade.*
• **dye, colour, tint, tinge**

stairs *PLURAL NOUN*
The stairs up to the front door were worn with age.
• **steps**
– A set of stairs from one floor to another is a **flight** of stairs or a **staircase** or **stairway**.
– A moving staircase is an **escalator**.
– A handrail at the side of a staircase is a **banister**.

stake *NOUN*
The fence was made with sharp wooden stakes.
• **pole, post, stick, spike, stave, pile**

stale *ADJECTIVE*
❶ *All he had to eat were some stale crusts of bread.*
• **old, dry, hard, mouldy, musty, rancid**
OPPOSITE fresh
❷ *He keeps coming out with the same old stale ideas.*
• **overused, tired, hackneyed, banal, clichéd**
OPPOSITES original, fresh

stalk *NOUN*
❶ *The boy was holding a sunflower stalk.*
• **stem, shoot, twig**
❷ For parts of a plant see **plant**.

stalk *VERB*
❶ *The panther began stalking its prey.*
• **hunt, pursue, track, trail, follow, shadow, tail**
❷ *She turned and stalked out of the room.*
• **stride, strut, march, stomp**

stall *NOUN*
We had a stall selling home-made jam.
• **stand, table, counter, kiosk, booth**

stall *VERB*
❶ *I could tell the assistant was stalling.*
• **play for time, delay, procrastinate, hedge**
❷ *See if you can stall them for a few days.*
• **delay, detain, hold off**

stamina *NOUN*
Do you have the stamina to run a marathon?
• **endurance, staying power, toughness, grit**

stammer *VERB*
He stammered over his opening lines.
• **stutter, falter, stumble, splutter**

stamp *NOUN*
I put a first-class stamp on the letter.
– A person who studies or collects stamps is a **philatelist**.

stamp *VERB*
❶ *Please don't stamp on the flowers.*
• **step, tread, trample, crush, flatten**
❷ *We stamped our feet to get warm.*
• **tramp, stomp**
❸ *The librarian stamped my books.*
• **print, mark**
– To stamp a postmark on a letter is to **frank** it.
– To stamp a mark on cattle with a hot iron is to **brand** them.

stampede *NOUN*
When the bell went, there was a stampede towards the door.
• **charge, rush, dash, rout**

stance *NOUN*
❶ *Try to keep a relaxed stance.*
• **posture, position, pose**
❷ *What is your stance on nuclear power?*
• **opinion, attitude, standpoint, position, policy, line**

stand *VERB*
❶ *Please stand when your name is called.*
• **get up, get to your feet, rise**
❷ *Stand the ladder against the wall.*
• **put, place, set, prop, position, station, erect**
❸ *My offer still stands.*
• **be valid, remain in force, apply, continue, hold**
❹ *How can you stand the noise?*
• **bear, abide, endure, put up with, tolerate, withstand**
➤ **stand for something**
❶ *What do these initials stand for?*
• **mean, indicate, signify, represent**
❷ *She won't stand for any arguments.*
• **put up with, tolerate, accept, allow, permit**
➤ **stand out**
The lettering really stands out.
• **catch your eye, leap out, be noticeable, be prominent**
➤ **stand up for someone**
He always stands up for his friends.
• **support, defend, side with, speak up for**
(*informal*) **stick up for**

stand *NOUN*
The trophy stood on a wooden stand.
• **base, rest, pedestal, plinth**
– A three-legged stand for a camera or telescope is a **tripod**.

standard *NOUN*
❶ *Their writing is of a very high standard.*
• **grade, level, quality, calibre**
❷ *The house was small by modern standards.*
• **criterion, measure, model, guide, benchmark, yardstick**
❸ *At dawn they raised the regimental standard for the last time.*
• **colours, flag, banner**

standard *ADJECTIVE*
❶ *This is the standard way to set out a letter.*
• **normal, usual, common, conventional, typical, customary, established, accepted, orthodox, regular, traditional**
OPPOSITES unusual, unorthodox
❷ *It is the standard guide to North American birds.*
• **definitive, authoritative, classic, ultimate, best, approved**

standstill *NOUN*
➤ **come to a standstill**
Traffic had come to a standstill.
• **stop moving, draw up, pull up, halt, stop**
IDIOM **grind to a halt**

A B C D E F G H I J K L M N O P Q R S T U V W X Y Z

staple *ADJECTIVE*
Rice is the staple food in many countries.
• **chief, main, principal, standard, basic**

star *NOUN*
❶ *The sky was full of stars.*
• **celestial body, heavenly body**
– The scientific study of stars is **astronomy.**
– A word meaning 'to do with stars' is **stellar.**
❷ *Several Hollywood stars attended the premiere of the film.*
• **celebrity, idol, superstar**

stare *VERB*
The eyes in the portrait were staring straight at me.
• **gaze, gape, peer, look**
(*informal*) **gawk, gawp**
– To stare angrily at someone is to **glare** at them.

start *VERB*
❶ *The new series will start in the autumn.*
• **begin, commence, get under way, get going**
(*informal*) **kick off**
OPPOSITES finish, end
❷ *Modern ice hockey started in Canada.*
• **originate, arise, begin, be born, come into being**
OPPOSITE stop
❸ *We're planning to start a film club.*
• **establish, set up, create, found, institute, initiate, inaugurate, launch**
OPPOSITES close down, wind up
❹ *Press here to start the computer.*
• **switch on, activate, fire up, boot up**
OPPOSITES shut down, deactivate
❺ *A crash in the kitchen made me start.*
• **jump, flinch, jerk, twitch, wince**

start *NOUN*
❶ *Try not to miss the start of the film.*
• **beginning, opening, introduction, commencement**
OPPOSITES end, close, finish
❷ *She has been with the theatre company right from the start.*
• **beginning, outset, creation, inception, origin, onset, birth, dawn**
❸ *Her voice gave me a nasty start.*
• **jump, jolt, shock, surprise**

startle *VERB*
A sudden noise startled the horses.
• **alarm, panic, frighten, scare, surprise, take someone by surprise, make someone jump**

starve *VERB*
People were left to starve in freezing conditions.
• **die of starvation, go hungry**
– To choose to go without food is to **fast.**

starving (*informal*) *ADJECTIVE*
By teatime we were all starving.
• **hungry, famished, ravenous**

state *NOUN*
❶ *Much of the building is in a rundown state.*
• **condition, shape, order**
❷ (*informal*) *He gets into a terrible state before an exam.*
• **panic, fluster**
(*informal*) **flap**
❸ *The Queen is the head of state.*
• **country, nation**

state *VERB*
The sign states that photography is allowed.
• **declare, announce, say, express, report, proclaim, pronounce, communicate**

stately *ADJECTIVE*
The funeral service was a stately affair.
• **dignified, grand, formal, ceremonious, imposing, majestic, noble**

statement *NOUN*
The prime minister made a statement to the press.
• **announcement, declaration, communication, report, testimony**

station *NOUN*
❶ *Does the train stop at the next station?*
– The station at the end of a line is the **terminus.**

❷ *He was taken to the police station for questioning.*
• **depot, office, base, headquarters**
❸ *She usually listens to the local radio station.*
• **channel, wavelength**

station *VERB*
Two guards were stationed at the entrance.
• **post, position, situate, locate, base**

stationary *ADJECTIVE*
The car was stationary when the van hit it.
• **still, static, unmoving, immobile, motionless, standing, at rest**
OPPOSITE moving

statue *NOUN*
There is a statue of Nelson Mandela in the park.
• **figure, sculpture, carving**
– A small statue is a **statuette**.

status *NOUN*
❶ *What was the status of women in Victorian society?*
• **rank, level, position, grade, place**
❷ *They were a family of wealth and status.*
• **importance, prestige, stature, standing**

staunch *ADJECTIVE*
He was a staunch ally of the President.
• **firm, strong, faithful, loyal, true, reliable, dependable, steadfast, trusty**
OPPOSITES disloyal, unreliable

stay *VERB*
❶ *I'll stay here until you get back.*
• **wait, remain, hang on, linger**
(*informal*) **hang about**
OPPOSITES leave, depart
❷ *Please try to stay calm.*
• **keep, remain, carry on being**
❸ *Do you plan to stay in America long?*
• **live, reside, dwell, lodge, settle, stop, stop over**

stay *NOUN*
Our friends are here for a short stay.
• **visit, stopover, holiday, break**

steady *ADJECTIVE*
❶ *Keep a steady grip on the handle.*
• **stable, secure, fixed, firm, fast, solid, balanced**
OPPOSITES unsteady, shaky
❷ *We had a steady stream of visitors.*
• **continuous, uninterrupted, non-stop, constant, consistent, reliable**
OPPOSITE intermittent
❸ *The runners kept up a steady pace.*
• **regular, constant, even, smooth, settled, rhythmic, unvarying**
OPPOSITE irregular

steady *VERB*
She steadied herself against the wall.
• **balance, stabilize, hold steady**

steal *VERB*
❶ *The thieves stole several valuable paintings.*
• **take, snatch, pilfer**
(*informal*) **swipe, lift, nick, pinch, make off with**
❷ *We both stole quietly out of the room.*
• **creep, sneak, tiptoe, slip, slink, slope**

stealing *NOUN*
He was found guilty of stealing from his employers.
• **robbery, theft**
– Stealing from a private house is **burglary** or **housebreaking**.
– Stealing small goods from a shop is **shoplifting**.
– Stealing things of little value is **pilfering**.

stealthy *ADJECTIVE*
She inched forward with slow, stealthy movements.
• **furtive, secretive, surreptitious, sly, sneaky, underhand**
OPPOSITES conspicuous, open

steam *NOUN*
The kitchen was full of steam.
• **vapour, mist, haze**
– Steam on a cold window is **condensation**.

steamy *ADJECTIVE*
❶ *The atmosphere in the greenhouse was warm and steamy.*
• **humid, muggy, close, damp, moist**
❷ *The bathroom mirror was steamy.*
• **misty, hazy, cloudy**

steep *ADJECTIVE*
❶ *Steep cliffs overlook the sea.*
• **abrupt, sharp, precipitous**
– A cliff or drop which is straight up and down is **sheer** or **vertical**.
OPPOSITES gradual, gentle
❷ (*informal*) *They charge very steep prices.*
• **high, overpriced, inflated, exorbitant, extortionate**

steer *VERB*
It can be tricky steering a shopping trolley.
• **guide, direct, manoeuvre, drive**
– To steer a boat is to **navigate** or **pilot** it.

stem *NOUN*
It's a plant with a woody stem.
• **stalk, shoot, twig**

stem *VERB*
She could no longer stem the flow of tears.
• **stop, check, hold back, curb, staunch**
➤ **stem from**
His love of writing stems from childhood.
• **come from, arise from, spring from, derive from, originate in, have its origins in**

step *NOUN*
❶ *We each took a step closer to the door.*
• **pace, stride**
❷ *I heard the sound of heavy steps outside.*
• **footstep, tread, footfall**
❸ *Mind the step as you go in.*
• **doorstep, stair, tread**
– The steps of a ladder are the **rungs**.
❹ *The first step in making a cake is to weigh the ingredients.*
• **stage, phase, action, operation, move**

step *VERB*
Don't step on the broken glass.
• **put your foot, tread, walk, stamp, trample, stride, pace**
➤ **step down**
He's stepping down at the end of the season.
• **resign, stand down, quit, bow out**
➤ **step something up**
They have stepped up security at the airport.
• **increase, intensify, strengthen, boost**

sterile *ADJECTIVE*
❶ *Very little grows in the sterile soil of the desert.*
• **barren, dry, arid, infertile, lifeless**
OPPOSITE fertile
❷ *The nurse put a sterile bandage on my arm.*
• **sterilized, disinfected, uncontaminated, clean, hygienic, germ-free, antiseptic**
OPPOSITE contaminated

stern *ADJECTIVE*
He gave them a stern look.
• **severe, strict, hard, harsh, grim, austere, forbidding, disapproving**
OPPOSITES kindly, lenient

stew *VERB*
see **cook**

stick *NOUN*
❶ *They collected dry sticks to make a fire.*
• **twig, branch, stalk**
❷ *He walked with a stick.*
• **cane, rod, staff, pole**
– A stick used by a conductor is a **baton**.
– A stick carried by a police officer is a **truncheon**.
– A stick used as a weapon is a **club** or **cudgel**.

stick *VERB*
❶ *He stuck a few drawing pins into the wall.*
• **poke, prod, stab, thrust, dig, jab**
❷ *Stick the label on the front of the parcel.*
• **attach, affix, fasten, join, fix, paste,**

glue, tape
❸ *The stamp won't stick to the envelope.*
• **adhere, cling, bond**
❹ *The rear wheels stuck fast in the mud.*
• **jam, wedge, catch, get trapped**
❺ (*informal*) *I can't stick it here any longer.*
• **endure, tolerate, stand, bear, abide, put up with**
➤ **stick out**
The shelf sticks out too far.
• **jut out, poke out, project, protrude**
➤ **stick up for**
(*informal*) *Thanks for sticking up for me.*
• **support, stand up for, side with, speak up for, defend**

sticky *ADJECTIVE*
❶ *There was a sticky blob of chewing gum on the seat.*
• **tacky, gummy, gluey**
(*informal*) **gooey, icky**
❷ *It was a hot sticky afternoon.*
• **humid, muggy, clammy, close, steamy, sultry**
OPPOSITE **dry**
❸ (*informal*) *The hero finds himself in a sticky situation.*
• **awkward, difficult, tricky, ticklish**
(*informal*) **hairy**

stiff *ADJECTIVE*
❶ *Use a stiff piece of cardboard as a base.*
• **rigid, inflexible, firm**
OPPOSITES **flexible, pliable**
❷ *Add flour to make a stiff dough.*
• **thick, solid, firm**
OPPOSITES **soft, loose**
❸ *My legs were stiff from crouching.*
• **aching, achy, painful, taut, tight**
OPPOSITE **supple**
❹ *They face stiff opposition in the final.*
• **strong, powerful, difficult, tough, determined**
OPPOSITE **weak**
❺ *There are stiff penalties for dropping litter.*
• **harsh, severe, tough, strict, stringent, heavy**
OPPOSITES **lenient, mild**
❻ *His stiff manner made him hard to talk to.*
• **formal, awkward, wooden, strained, stilted**
OPPOSITES **informal, casual, relaxed**

stifle *VERB*
❶ *We were nearly stifled by the midday heat.*
• **suffocate, smother, choke**
❷ *She tried to stifle a yawn.*
• **suppress, muffle, hold back, repress, restrain**
OPPOSITE **let out**

still *ADJECTIVE*
❶ *He stood still and held his breath.*
• **motionless, unmoving, immobile, stationary, static, inert**
IDIOM **rooted to the spot**
❷ *It was a crisp still morning.*
• **quiet, silent, peaceful, tranquil, calm, serene, noiseless, windless**

still *VERB*
I tried to still the trembling in my hand.
• **calm, quieten, soothe, settle, silence, hush, lull**
OPPOSITES **stir, disturb**

stimulate *VERB*
❶ *Her travels stimulated her to write a book.*
• **encourage, inspire, prompt, spur**
OPPOSITE **discourage**
❷ *What stimulated your interest in science?*
• **arouse, provoke, trigger, excite, kindle, stir up**
OPPOSITE **dampen**

sting *VERB*
❶ *I was stung by a wasp.*
• **bite, nip**
❷ *The smoke made our eyes sting.*
• **smart, burn, prick, prickle, tingle**

stingy (*informal*) *ADJECTIVE*
They're a bit stingy with their portions.
• **mean, miserly, penny-pinching**
(*informal*) **tight-fisted**
OPPOSITE **generous**

A B C D E F G H I J K L M N O P Q R S T U V W X Y Z

stink *NOUN*
The stink hits you as soon as you open the door.
• **reek, stench, odour, smell**
(*informal*) **pong**

stink *VERB*
The room stank of smoke.
• **reek, smell**

stir *VERB*
❶ *Stir the mixture until it is smooth.*
• **mix, beat, blend, whisk**
❷ *Something stirred in the bushes behind us.*
• **move slightly, shift, rustle**
➤ **stir something up**
They are always stirring up trouble.
• **arouse, encourage, provoke, set off, trigger, whip up**

stir *NOUN*
The news caused quite a stir.
• **fuss, commotion, excitement, to-do**

stock *NOUN*
❶ *Stocks of food were running low.*
• **supply, store, reserve, hoard, stockpile**
❷ *The grocer was waiting for new stock to arrive.*
• **goods, merchandise, wares**
❸ *He is descended from Italian stock.*
• **descent, ancestry, origin, lineage, family, pedigree, line**

stock *VERB*
Many supermarkets now stock organic food.
• **sell, carry, trade in, deal in, keep in stock**

stocky *ADJECTIVE*
He was a short, stocky man.
• **dumpy, squat, thickset, solid, sturdy**
OPPOSITE thin

stodgy *ADJECTIVE*
❶ *The pudding was rich and stodgy.*
• **heavy, solid, starchy, filling**
OPPOSITE light
❷ *It's quite a stodgy book, isn't it?*
• **dull, boring, uninteresting, slow, tedious**
OPPOSITES lively, interesting

stole
past tense see **steal**

stomach *NOUN*
I was hungry and my stomach started to rumble.
• **belly, abdomen, gut**
(*informal*) **tummy**
– A large rounded stomach is a **paunch**.

stomach *VERB*
She found it hard to stomach the truth.
• **stand, bear, take, accept, tolerate, put up with, endure**

stone *NOUN*
❶ *A boy was throwing stones into the sea.*
• **rock, pebble**
– A large rounded stone is a **boulder**.
– A mixture of sand and small stones is **gravel**.
– Pebbles on the beach are **shingle**.
– Round stones used to pave a path are **cobbles**.
❷ *The ring had a bright red stone.*
• **jewel, gem, gemstone, precious stone**

stony *ADJECTIVE*
❶ *We walked along a stony footpath.*
• **pebbly, rocky, shingly**
OPPOSITES smooth, sandy
❷ *We were greeted with stony silence.*
• **unfriendly, cold, hostile, frosty, icy**
OPPOSITES warm, friendly

stood
past tense see **stand**

stoop *VERB*
We had to stoop to go through the tunnel.
• **bend, duck, bow, crouch**

stop *VERB*
❶ *There was no sign of the rain stopping.*
• **come to an end, end, finish, cease, conclude, terminate**
OPPOSITE start
❷ *How do you stop this machine?*
• **switch off, turn off, shut down, halt, deactivate, immobilize**

❸ *Please stop asking me questions.*
• **give up, cease, discontinue, suspend, leave off, break off**
(*informal*) **knock off, pack in, quit**
OPPOSITES continue, resume
❹ *The bus will stop at the front gates.*
• **come to a stop, halt, pull up, draw up, come to rest**
❺ *They put a fence up to stop the dog getting out.*
• **prevent, obstruct, bar, block, hinder**
❻ *She was busy stopping a gap in the window frame.*
• **close, plug, seal, block up, bung up**

stop *NOUN*
❶ *Everything suddenly came to a stop.*
• **end, finish, conclusion, halt, standstill**
❷ *We had a short stop for lunch on the way.*
• **break, pause, rest, stay, stopover**

store *NOUN*
❶ *He kept a large store of wine in the cellar.*
• **hoard, supply, quantity, stock, stockpile, reserve**
❷ *The library has an underground book store.*
• **storeroom, storehouse, repository, vault**
– A store for food is a **larder** or **pantry**.
– A store for weapons is an **armoury** or **arsenal**.
❸ *She's the manager of the local grocery store.*
For more types of store see **shop**.

store *VERB*
Squirrels need to store food for the winter.
• **save, reserve, set aside, stow away, hoard, stockpile**
(*informal*) **stash**

storey *NOUN*
There is a restaurant on the top storey.
• **floor, level, tier**

storm *NOUN*
❶ *Heavy storms are forecast throughout the country.*
• **squall, blizzard, gale, thunderstorm, snowstorm, hurricane, typhoon**
(*literary*) **tempest**
– When a storm begins to develop it is **brewing**.
For tips on describing the weather see **weather**.
❷ *Plans to close the library caused a storm of protest.*
• **outburst, outcry, uproar, clamour, fuss, furore**

storm *VERB*
❶ *She stormed out in a rage.*
• **march, stride, stalk, stomp, flounce**
❷ *Police stormed the building.*
• **charge at, rush at, swoop on, attack**

stormy *ADJECTIVE*
❶ *It was a wild and stormy night.*
• **blustery, squally, windy, gusty, blowy, thundery, tempestuous**
OPPOSITE calm
❷ *Fighting broke out at the end of a stormy meeting.*
• **angry, heated, turbulent, violent, passionate**

story *NOUN*
❶ *Do you know any good ghost stories?*
• **tale, narrative, anecdote**
(*informal*) **yarn**
❷ *The book tells the story of her childhood.*
• **account, history, narrative, saga, plot**
– The story of a person's life is their **biography**.
– The story which a person writes of their own life is their **autobiography**.
❸ *It was the front-page story in all the papers.*
• **article, item, feature, report, piece**
❹ (*informal*) *Have you been telling stories again?*
• **lie, tale**
(*informal*) fib

stout *ADJECTIVE*
❶ *Inside was a rather stout lady dressed in black.*
• **fat, plump, dumpy, tubby, portly, podgy, rotund, overweight**
OPPOSITE thin

❷ *You will need a pair of stout walking boots.*
• **strong, sturdy, tough, robust, hard-wearing, durable**
OPPOSITE flimsy
❸ *The enemy put up a stout resistance.*
• **brave, courageous, spirited, plucky, determined, resolute, firm**
OPPOSITE weak

stow *VERB*
We stowed the boxes away in the attic.
• **store, put away, pack, hoard**

straight *ADJECTIVE*
❶ *They were driving along a straight stretch of road.*
• **direct, unbending**
OPPOSITE winding
❷ *Is this mirror straight?*
• **level, even, aligned, horizontal, vertical, upright**
OPPOSITE crooked
❸ *It took ages to get the room straight.*
• **neat, orderly, tidy, in order, shipshape**
OPPOSITE untidy
❹ *I just want a straight answer.*
• **honest, plain, frank, direct, straightforward, candid**
OPPOSITES indirect, evasive

straight *ADVERB*
❶ *She was looking straight at me.*
• **right, directly**
❷ *They left straight after breakfast.*
• **immediately, promptly, right**

straightaway or **straight away** *ADVERB*
She replied to my text straightaway.
• **immediately, at once, right away, without delay, instantly, promptly**

straightforward *ADJECTIVE*
❶ *The recipe is quite straightforward.*
• **uncomplicated, simple, easy, clear**
OPPOSITE complicated
❷ *I found him straightforward to deal with.*
• **frank, honest, straight, direct, plain, candid**
OPPOSITE evasive

strain *VERB*
❶ *The dog was straining at its lead.*
• **pull, tug, stretch**
❷ *I was straining to see what was happening.*
• **struggle, strive, make an effort, endeavour, try, attempt**
❸ *I think I've strained a muscle.*
• **sprain, injure, pull, twist, wrench**
❹ *Take it easy and don't strain yourself.*
• **overtax, overreach, exhaust, wear out, tire out**
❺ *Strain the liquid to get rid of any lumps.*
• **sieve, sift, filter**

strain *NOUN*
❶ *The ropes creaked under the strain.*
• **tension, tightness, tautness, stretch**
❷ *The strain was beginning to tell on us all.*
• **stress, tension, worry, anxiety, pressure**

strand *NOUN*
The strands of the wool began to unravel.
• **thread, filament, fibre**

stranded *ADJECTIVE*
❶ *A whale lay stranded on the beach.*
• **run aground, beached, marooned**
❷ *She found herself stranded without any money.*
• **abandoned, deserted, helpless, lost, adrift**
IDIOM **high and dry**

strange *ADJECTIVE*
❶ *A strange thing happened last night.*
• **unusual, odd, peculiar, funny, abnormal, curious, mysterious, weird, bizarre**
OPPOSITES ordinary, normal
❷ *I find it hard to get to sleep in a strange bed.*
• **unfamiliar, unknown, new, alien**
OPPOSITE familiar

stranger *NOUN*
Actually, I'm a stranger here myself.
• **newcomer, outsider, visitor, foreigner**

strangle *VERB*
The victim had been strangled.
• **throttle, choke**

strap *NOUN*
The trunk was fastened with leather straps.
• **belt, band, tie, thong**

strategy *NOUN*
The school has a strategy to deal with bullying.
• **plan, policy, procedure, approach, scheme, programme**

stray *VERB*
Don't stray too far from the shore.
• **wander off, drift, roam**

streak *NOUN*
❶ *There was a streak of bright light in the sky.*
• **band, line, stripe, strip, slash**
❷ *She had left streaks of mud on the floor.*
• **smear, stain, mark**
❸ *There is a streak of vanity in his character.*
• **element, trace, strain, vein**

streak *VERB*
❶ *His face was streaked with tears.*
• **smear, smudge, stain, mark, line**
❷ *A group of motorbikes streaked past.*
• **rush, speed, dash, fly, hurtle, flash, tear, zoom**

stream *NOUN*
❶ *They drank from a clear mountain stream.*
• **brook, rivulet**
(*North American & Australian*) **creek**
(*Scottish*) **burn**
❷ *A stream of water poured through the hole.*
• **flow, gush, jet, flood, rush, torrent, cataract, cascade**
❸ *The museum has a steady stream of visitors.*
• **series, string, line, succession**

stream *VERB*
❶ *Water streamed down the basement walls.*
• **pour, flow, run, gush, spill, cascade**
❷ *Thousands of fans streamed through the gates.*
• **swarm, surge, pile, pour, flood**

street *NOUN*
see **road**

strength *NOUN*
❶ *Hercules was known for his enormous strength.*
• **power, might, muscle, brawn, force, vigour**
❷ *We need to test the strength of the roof.*
• **toughness, sturdiness, robustness, firmness, solidity, resilience**
❸ *The real strength of the team is in defence.*
• **strong point, asset, advantage, forte, speciality**
OPPOSITE weakness

strengthen *VERB*
❶ *Regular exercise strengthens your muscles.*
• **make stronger, build up**
❷ *Steel is used to strengthen concrete.*
• **fortify, reinforce, stiffen, harden, toughen**
OPPOSITE weaken

strenuous *ADJECTIVE*
❶ *The doctor told him to avoid strenuous exercise.*
• **hard, tough, difficult, demanding, tiring, taxing, exhausting, gruelling**
OPPOSITE easy
❷ *We are making strenuous efforts to save energy.*
• **determined, strong, intense, vigorous, energetic, resolute**
OPPOSITE feeble

stress *NOUN*
❶ *There are different ways of coping with the stress of exams.*
• **strain, pressure, tension, worry, anxiety**

❷ *My piano teacher puts great stress on the need to practise.*
• **emphasis, importance, weight**

stress *VERB*
He stressed the need for absolute secrecy.
• **emphasize, draw attention to, highlight, underline**

stretch *VERB*
❶ *He stretched the rubber band until it snapped.*
• **extend, draw out, pull out, elongate, lengthen, expand**
❷ *She stretched her arms wide.*
• **extend, open out, reach out, straighten, spread out**
❸ *The sand dunes stretch for miles.*
• **continue, extend, go on**

stretch *NOUN*
❶ *It is a beautiful stretch of countryside.*
• **area, expanse, tract, sweep**
❷ *This is a dangerous stretch of the river.*
• **section, length, piece**
❸ *He had a brief stretch in the army.*
• **spell, period, time, stint**

strict *ADJECTIVE*
❶ *The sisters were brought up in a strict household.*
• **harsh, severe, stern, firm, rigid, authoritarian**
OPPOSITE lenient
❷ *He left strict instructions in his will.*
• **precise, exact, careful, meticulous**
OPPOSITES vague, loose
❸ *Please treat this in strict confidence.*
• **absolute, complete, total, utter**

stride *VERB*
She strode across the hall to greet us.
• **march, step, pace**

stride *NOUN*
He took a stride towards the door.
• **pace, step, tread**

strike *VERB*
❶ *He struck his head on the low ceiling.*
• **hit, knock, bang, bash, bump, beat, thump**
(*informal*) **wallop, whack**
❷ *The driver lost control and struck a lamp post.*
• **collide with, crash into, bang into, run into, hit**
❸ *The enemy could strike at any time.*
• **attack, pounce**
❹ *The clock struck midnight.*
• **chime, ring out, sound**

striking *ADJECTIVE*
❶ *Her eyes were her most striking feature.*
• **impressive, stunning, spectacular, outstanding, extraordinary, remarkable, astonishing, memorable, breathtaking**
OPPOSITE unremarkable
❷ *The resemblance between them is striking.*
• **conspicuous, noticeable, marked, obvious, strong, prominent, unmistakable**
OPPOSITE inconspicuous

string *NOUN*
❶ *The label was tied on with string.*
• **rope, cord, twine**
❷ *They have received a string of complaints.*
• **series, succession, chain, sequence, run**

string *VERB*
Lights were strung from tree to tree.
• **hang, suspend, sling, thread, loop**

stringy *ADJECTIVE*
The meat is very stringy.
• **chewy, fibrous, tough**
OPPOSITE tender

strip *VERB*
❶ *Deer had stripped the bark off the trees.*
• **peel, remove, scrape**
OPPOSITES cover, wrap
❷ *He stripped and got into the bath.*
• **get undressed, undress**
(*formal*) **disrobe**
OPPOSITE dress

strip *NOUN*
Tear the paper into narrow strips.
• **band, length, ribbon, piece, bit**

stripe *NOUN*
The tablecloth had a pattern of blue and white stripes.
• **line, strip, band, bar**

strive *VERB*
We strive to do the best we can.
• **try hard, aim, attempt, endeavour**

stroke *NOUN*
❶ *He split the log with a single stroke.*
• **blow, hit, action, movement, motion**
❷ *She rubbed out a few pencil strokes.*
• **line, mark**

stroke *VERB*
Cats like to be stroked under the chin.
• **pat, caress, fondle, pet, touch, rub**

stroll *VERB*
After lunch, we strolled along the beach.
• **walk slowly, amble, saunter**

strong *ADJECTIVE*

OVERUSED WORD

❶ A strong person, strong body:

- powerful
- muscular
- well-built
- beefy
- brawny
- burly
- strapping
- athletic

(*literary*) **mighty**

Swimmers need to develop **powerful** *shoulder muscles.*

OPPOSITES weak, puny

❷ Strong material:

- robust
- sturdy
- tough
- hard-wearing
- heavy-duty
- durable
- long-lasting
- stout
- substantial

The drumsticks are made from **hard-wearing** *maple.*

OPPOSITES fragile, flimsy

❸ A strong light, strong colour:

- bright
- dazzling
- glaring
- brilliant
- intense

He looked nervous under the **glaring** *camera lights.*

OPPOSITES faint, dim, pale

❹ A strong flavour, strong smell:

- intense
- pronounced
- overpowering
- pungent
- piquant
- tangy
- concentrated
- undiluted

There was the **pungent** *smell of burning rubber.*

OPPOSITES faint, mild

❺ A strong argument, strong case:

- convincing
- persuasive
- effective
- forceful
- compelling
- sound
- solid
- valid
- cogent

The police have **solid** *evidence of his guilt.*

OPPOSITES weak, feeble, flimsy

❻ A strong interest, strong supporter:

- enthusiastic
- keen
- eager
- passionate
- fervent
- avid
- zealous

I've been an **avid** *fan of the band for years.*

OPPOSITES slight, casual

struck
past tense see **strike**

structure *NOUN*
❶ *The new dam is a massive concrete structure.*
• **building, construction, edifice**
❷ *Can you explain the structure of the poem?*
• **design, plan, framework, shape, form, arrangement, organization**

struggle *VERB*

❶ *We struggled to get free.*
• **wrestle, tussle, fight, battle, grapple**
❷ *She struggled over the wet rocks.*
• **stagger, stumble, labour, flounder**
❸ *I struggled to make sense of the letter.*
• **try hard, strive, strain, make every effort**

struggle *NOUN*

❶ *There were some signs of a struggle.*
• **fight, tussle, scuffle, brawl, clash, conflict**
❷ *The book is about the struggle to get the vote for women.*
• **campaign, battle, crusade, drive, push**
❸ *I found the language a struggle at first.*
• **effort, exertion, problem, difficulty**

stubborn *ADJECTIVE*

My sister can be stubborn when she wants to be.
• **obstinate, headstrong, strong-willed, wilful, uncooperative, inflexible, pig-headed**
OPPOSITE compliant

stuck *ADJECTIVE*

❶ *The bottom drawer is stuck.*
• **jammed, immovable, wedged**
❷ *I'm completely stuck on the last question.*
• **baffled, beaten, stumped, at a loss**

stuck-up *ADJECTIVE*

(*informal*)
Our neighbours are really stuck-up.
• **arrogant, conceited, haughty, proud, snobbish, superior**
• (*informal*) **snooty, toffee-nosed**
OPPOSITE humble

stud *VERB*

➤ **studded with**
The lid of the chest was studded with jewels.
• **inlaid with, dotted with, encrusted with**

student *NOUN*

❶ *His children are students at the local school.*
• **pupil, schoolboy, schoolgirl**
❷ *She is a medical student.*
• **undergraduate**
– A person who has been awarded a university degree is a **graduate**.
– A student who is studying for a second degree is a **postgraduate**.

studious *ADJECTIVE*

He is a quiet, studious boy.
• **hard-working, diligent, scholarly, academic, bookish**
(*informal*) **swotty**

study *VERB*

❶ *She spent a year abroad studying French.*
• **learn about, read, be taught**
❷ *Scientists are studying the effects of climate change.*
• **research, investigate, examine, analyse, survey, review**
❸ *He has to study for his exams.*
• **revise, cram**
(*informal*) **swot**
❹ *She studied his face for a moment.*
• **examine, inspect, scrutinize, look closely at, peer at**

study *NOUN*

❶ *He got his degree after four long years of study.*
• **learning, education, schooling, tuition, research**
❷ *A new study of reading habits has been published.*
• **investigation, examination, analysis, review, survey, enquiry (into)**
❸ *Darwin used this room as his study.*
• **workroom, office, studio**
Words which mean 'the scientific study' of a subject often end with -logy or -ology, for example *cosmology*, *criminology* and *mineralogy*.

stuff *NOUN*

❶ *What's this stuff at the bottom of the glass?*
• **matter, substance, material**

❷ *The cupboard is crammed full of stuff.*
• **things, odds and ends, bits and pieces, paraphernalia**
❸ (*informal*) *Where can I put my stuff?*
• **belongings, possessions, things**
(*informal*) **gear**

stuff *VERB*
❶ *The cushions are stuffed with foam rubber.*
• **fill, pad, upholster**
❷ *I quickly stuffed all the papers into a drawer.*
• **shove, push, thrust, force, squeeze, jam, pack, cram, ram**

stuffy *ADJECTIVE*
❶ *Open a window – it's stuffy in here.*
• **airless, close, humid, stifling, musty, unventilated**
OPPOSITE airy
❷ *I find the writing style a bit stuffy.*
• **pompous, starchy, stodgy, staid, old-fashioned, dull, dreary**
OPPOSITES lively, fresh

stumble *VERB*
❶ *He stumbled backwards and fell over a chair.*
• **trip, lose your footing, stagger, totter, flounder, lurch**
❷ *She stumbled over her opening lines.*
• **stammer, stutter, falter, hesitate**
➤ **stumble across something**
I stumbled across some old photos.
• **come across, find, unearth, discover, happen on, chance upon**

stump *VERB*
We were all stumped by the last question.
• **baffle, bewilder, puzzle, perplex, mystify**
(*informal*) **flummox**

stun *VERB*
❶ *The pilot was alive but stunned.*
• **daze, make unconscious, knock out, knock senseless**
❷ *The whole town was stunned by the news.*
• **amaze, astonish, astound, shock, stagger, stupefy, bewilder, dumbfound**

stunning *ADJECTIVE*
Here are some stunning images of the Earth from space.
• **spectacular, breathtaking, glorious, magnificent, gorgeous, superb, sublime, awesome**

stunt *NOUN*
The acrobats performed breathtaking stunts.
• **feat, exploit, act, trick**

stupid *ADJECTIVE*
❶ *He is not as stupid as he looks.*
• **dense, dim, dim-witted, brainless, unintelligent, slow, dopey, dull, simple, feeble-minded, half-witted**
(*informal*) **thick**
OPPOSITE intelligent
❷ *It was a stupid idea anyway.*
• **foolish, silly, idiotic, senseless, mindless, foolhardy, unwise, mad, crazy, hare-brained**
(*informal*) **daft**
OPPOSITE sensible

sturdy *ADJECTIVE*
❶ *He was tall and sturdy for his age.*
• **well-built, strapping, muscular, strong, robust, brawny, burly, powerful, solid**
OPPOSITES weak, puny
❷ *She bought a pair of sturdy walking boots.*
• **robust, strong, tough, stout, hard-wearing, durable, substantial**
OPPOSITE flimsy

stutter *VERB*
He tends to stutter when he's nervous.
• **stammer, stumble, falter**

style *NOUN*
❶ *What style of shoes are you looking for?*
• **design, pattern, fashion**
❷ *The book is written in an informal style.*
• **manner, tone, way, wording**
❸ *She always dresses with great style.*
• **elegance, stylishness, taste, sophistication, flair**

A B C D E F G H I J K L M N O P Q R S T U V W X Y Z

stylish *ADJECTIVE*
He always manages to look stylish.
• **fashionable, elegant, chic, smart, sophisticated, tasteful, dapper** (*informal*) **trendy, natty, snazzy**
OPPOSITES unfashionable, dowdy

subdue *VERB*
❶ *The army quickly subdued all opposition.*
• **conquer, defeat, overcome, overpower, quell, suppress, crush, vanquish**
❷ *She struggled to subdue her true feelings.*
• **suppress, restrain, repress, check, hold back, curb, control**

subject *NOUN*
❶ *She has strong views on the subject.*
• **matter, issue, question, point, theme, topic, concern**
❷ *What is your favourite subject at school?*
• **area, field, discipline, topic**
❸ *His passport shows that he is a British subject.*
• **citizen, national**

subject *VERB*
➤ **subject someone to**
They subjected him to hours of questioning.
• **put through, force to undergo, expose to, lay open to**

submerge *VERB*
❶ *The submarine had no time to submerge.*
• **go under water, go down, sink, dive, plunge**
OPPOSITE surface
❷ *The village was now partly submerged.*
• **flood, engulf, immerse, inundate, swallow up, swamp**

submit *VERB*
❶ *He was finally forced to submit to his opponent.*
• **surrender, give in, yield, capitulate**
❷ *Submit your plans to the committee.*
• **put forward, hand in, present, enter, offer, propose**

subordinate *ADJECTIVE*
It was not easy for her to accept a subordinate role.
• **lesser, lower, inferior, junior**
OPPOSITES superior, higher

subscribe *VERB*
➤ **subscribe to something**
How do you subscribe to the mailing list?
• **become a member of, sign up to, enlist in**
OPPOSITE unsubscribe

subsequent *ADJECTIVE*
Subsequent events proved that she was right.
• **following, later, succeeding, ensuing, next**
OPPOSITE previous

subside *VERB*
❶ *One side of the old cottage has started to subside.*
• **sink, settle, give way, collapse**
❷ *The flood waters will eventually subside.*
• **recede, ebb, go down, fall, decline**
❸ *The pain should subside in a day or two.*
• **decrease, diminish, lessen, ease, die down, dwindle**

substance *NOUN*
❶ *A diamond is the hardest substance on Earth.*
• **material, matter, stuff**
❷ *What was the substance of the report?*
• **content, subject matter, essence, gist**

substantial *ADJECTIVE*
❶ *We have made substantial changes to the script.*
• **considerable, significant, sizeable, important, major, appreciable, generous, worthwhile**
OPPOSITES minor, insignificant
❷ *The farmhouse is a substantial building.*
• **strong, sturdy, solid, robust, stout, hefty, durable, sound, well-built**
OPPOSITE flimsy

substitute *NOUN*
He came on as a substitute in extra time.
• **replacement, reserve, standby, stand-in**
(*informal*) **sub**
– Someone who can take the place of an actor is an **understudy**.

substitute *VERB*
You can substitute honey for sugar in this recipe.
• **exchange, swap, switch**
You can also say: *'Honey can take the place of sugar.'* or *'You can replace sugar with honey.'*

subtle *ADJECTIVE*
❶ *The walls are a subtle shade of grey.*
• **faint, delicate, soft, gentle, pale, mild, subdued, muted**
OPPOSITES strong, bright
❷ *She noticed a subtle change in the atmosphere.*
• **slight, gradual, negligible, minute, fine**
OPPOSITE pronounced
❸ *I tried to give her a subtle hint.*
• **gentle, tactful, indirect**
OPPOSITE obvious

subtract *VERB*
Subtract this number from your final score.
• **take away, deduct, remove**
OPPOSITE add

suburbs *PLURAL NOUN*
They live in the suburbs of Melbourne.
• **outskirts, outer areas, fringes, suburbia**

succeed *VERB*
❶ *You have to work hard if you want to succeed.*
• **be successful, do well, prosper, flourish, thrive**
(*informal*) **make it**
❷ *No one thought the plan would succeed.*
• **be effective, work out, turn out well**
(*informal*) **come off**
OPPOSITE fail
❸ *Edward VII succeeded Queen Victoria.*
• **come after, follow, replace, take over from**
OPPOSITE precede

success *NOUN*
❶ *She talked about her success as an author.*
• **achievement, attainment, fame**
❷ *The team has had an incredible run of success.*
• **victory, win, triumph**
❸ *The success of the mission depends on us.*
• **effectiveness, successful outcome**
OPPOSITE failure
❹ *The show was a runaway success.*
• **hit, best-seller, winner**
(*informal*) **smash, smash hit**

successful *ADJECTIVE*
❶ *He owns a successful chain of restaurants.*
• **thriving, flourishing, booming, prosperous, profitable, popular**
❷ *A trophy is awarded to the successful team.*
• **winning, victorious, triumphant**
OPPOSITE unsuccessful

succession *NOUN*
He received a succession of mysterious emails.
• **series, sequence, run, string, chain, trail**

successive *ADJECTIVE*
We are aiming for a third successive win.
• **consecutive, uninterrupted, in succession, in a row, running**

suck *VERB*
❶ *A sponge will suck up water.*
• **soak up, draw up, absorb**
❷ *The canoe was sucked into the whirlpool.*
• **pull in, draw in**
OPPOSITE push out

sudden *ADJECTIVE*
❶ *She felt a sudden urge to burst into song.*
• **unexpected, unforeseen, impulsive, rash, quick**
OPPOSITE expected

❷ *The bus came to a sudden halt.*
• **abrupt, sharp, rapid, swift**
OPPOSITE gradual

suffer *VERB*
❶ *I hate to see animals suffer.*
• **be in pain, hurt, be in distress**
❷ *The team suffered a humiliating defeat.*
• **experience, undergo, go through, be subjected to, endure, face**
❸ *She's not sleeping and her work is suffering.*
• **be damaged, be impaired, diminish, decline, dip**
➤ **suffer from something**
He suffers from a severe nut allergy.
• **be afflicted by, be troubled with, have**

suffering *NOUN*
The people endured great suffering during the war.
• **hardship, deprivation, misery, anguish, pain, distress, affliction, trauma**

sufficient *ADJECTIVE*
Make sure you get sufficient sleep.
• **enough, adequate, ample, plenty of**
OPPOSITE insufficient

suffocate *VERB*
Most of the casualties were suffocated by smoke.
• **choke, asphyxiate, stifle, smother**

suggest *VERB*
❶ *Viewers were asked to suggest a name for the show.*
• **propose, put forward, nominate, recommend, advocate, advise**
❷ *Her smile suggested that she agreed with me.*
• **indicate, signify, show, imply, hint**

suggestion *NOUN*
❶ *Does anyone have an alternative suggestion?*
• **proposal, plan, idea, proposition, recommendation**
❷ *There was a suggestion of a sob in her voice.*
• **hint, sign, indication, trace, suspicion, implication**

suit *VERB*
❶ *Which date would suit you best?*
• **be convenient for, be suitable for, please, satisfy**
OPPOSITE displease
❷ *That colour really suits you.*
• **look good on, become, flatter**

suitable *ADJECTIVE*
❶ *Please wear clothes suitable for wet weather.*
• **appropriate, apt, fitting, fit, suited (to), right**
OPPOSITE unsuitable
❷ *Would tomorrow morning be a suitable time to meet?*
• **convenient, acceptable, satisfactory**
OPPOSITE inconvenient

sulk *VERB*
She was still sulking and wouldn't join in.
• **be sullen, mope, brood, pout**

sulky *ADJECTIVE*
He was turning into a sulky teenager.
• **moody, sullen, brooding, moping, grumpy**

sullen *ADJECTIVE*
The rest of us ate in sullen silence.
• **sulky, moody, bad-tempered, surly, sour**
OPPOSITES cheerful, good-tempered

sum *NOUN*
❶ *She can do complicated sums in her head.*
• **calculation, addition, problem**
❷ *What is the sum of the remaining numbers?*
• **total, tally, aggregate**
❸ *They lost a large sum of money.*
• **amount, quantity**

sum *VERB*
➤ **sum up**
Let me sum up the situation as I see it.
• **summarize, outline, review** (*informal*) **recap**

summarize *VERB*
Can you summarize the main points of the story?
• **sum up, outline, review, condense, abridge**
IDIOM **put in a nutshell**

summary *NOUN*
Give a brief summary of your idea.
• **synopsis, precis, abstract, outline, rundown**

summit *NOUN*
The summit of the mountain was shrouded in mist.
• **top, peak, crown, cap, tip**
OPPOSITE **base**

summon *VERB*
❶ *The king summoned his knights from far and wide.*
• **call for, send for, ask for, bid to come**
❷ *I finally summoned the courage to phone.*
• **gather, rally, muster**

sun *NOUN*
Lizards bask in the sun to get warm.
• **sunshine, sunlight**
– To sit or lie in the sun is to **sunbathe**.
– A word meaning 'to do with the sun' is **solar**.

sunlight *NOUN*
These plants need a lot of sunlight.
• **daylight, sun, sunshine**
– Rays of light from the sun are **sunbeams**.

sunny *ADJECTIVE*
❶ *It was a beautiful sunny day.*
• **bright, clear, cloudless, fine**
OPPOSITES **dull, overcast**
❷ *We sat in a sunny spot in the garden.*
• **sunlit, sun-baked, sun-drenched**
OPPOSITE **shady**
❸ *She has a naturally sunny nature.*
• **cheerful, happy, bright, joyful, merry, jolly**
(*informal*) **upbeat**
OPPOSITES **sad, melancholy**

sunrise *NOUN*
They left at sunrise.
• **dawn, daybreak, first light**
(*literary*) **break of day**
OPPOSITE **sunset**

sunset *NOUN*
At sunset the cliffs are tinted red and gold.
• **nightfall, dusk, twilight, close of day**
(*North American*) **sundown**
OPPOSITE **sunrise**

superb *ADJECTIVE*
The Brazilian scored a superb late goal.
• **excellent, outstanding, exceptional, tremendous, marvellous, wonderful, fine, superior, superlative, top-notch**
(*informal*) **brilliant, fantastic, terrific, fabulous, sensational, super**
OPPOSITES **bad, terrible**

superficial *ADJECTIVE*
❶ *Don't worry, it's only a superficial scratch.*
• **on the surface, shallow, slight**
OPPOSITE **deep**
❷ *The programme gives a rather superficial view of the subject.*
• **cursory, casual, lightweight, shallow, frivolous, trivial**
OPPOSITES **thorough, profound**

superfluous *ADJECTIVE*
Get rid of any superfluous words.
• **excess, unnecessary, redundant, surplus, spare, unwanted**
OPPOSITE **necessary**

superior *ADJECTIVE*
❶ *A soldier should salute a superior officer.*
• **senior, higher-ranking**
OPPOSITES **inferior, junior**
❷ *They make chocolates of superior quality.*
• **first-class, first-rate, top, top-notch, choice, select, finest, best**
OPPOSITES **inferior, substandard**
❸ *I don't like his superior attitude.*
• **arrogant, haughty, snobbish, self-important**

(*informal*) **snooty, stuck-up**
IDIOM **high and mighty**

supernatural *ADJECTIVE*
The old man claimed to have supernatural powers.
• **magic, magical, miraculous, mystical, paranormal, occult**
OPPOSITE **natural**

supervise *VERB*
Young children must be supervised by an adult in the park.
• **oversee, superintend, watch over, be in charge of, be responsible for, direct, manage**
IDIOM **keep an eye on**
– To supervise candidates in an exam is to **invigilate**.

supple *ADJECTIVE*
❶ *These shoes are made of supple leather.*
• **flexible, pliable, soft**
OPPOSITES **stiff, rigid**
❷ *Regular exercise helps to keep your body supple.*
• **agile, nimble, flexible, lithe**

supplementary *ADJECTIVE*
There is a supplementary charge for postage.
• **additional, extra**

supply *VERB*
❶ *The art shop can supply you with paints.*
• **provide, furnish, equip**
– To supply someone with weapons is to **arm** them.
❷ *They grow enough food to supply their needs.*
• **satisfy, meet, fulfil, cater for**

supply *NOUN*
We keep a supply of paper in the cupboard.
• **quantity, stock, store, reserve, cache, hoard**
➤ **supplies**
I bought some supplies for the trip.
• **provisions, stores, rations, food, necessities**

support *VERB*
❶ *Timber beams support the roof.*
• **hold up, prop up, buttress, reinforce**
❷ *How much weight will the bridge support?*
• **bear, carry, stand**
❸ *Not many people supported this idea.*
• **back, favour, advocate, champion, promote, endorse**
❹ *His friends supported him when he was in trouble.*
• **help, aid, assist, stand by, rally round**
❺ *She has two children to support.*
• **provide for, maintain, keep**
❻ *He supports several local charities.*
• **donate to, contribute to, give to**
❼ *Which football team do you support?*
• **be a supporter of, follow**

support *NOUN*
❶ *She thanked her family for their support.*
• **backing, encouragement, aid, help, assistance**
❷ *The stadium was built with support from local businesses.*
• **donations, contributions, sponsorship, subsidy, funds**
❸ *The shelves rest on wooden supports.*
• **prop, brace, bracket, strut, upright, post**
– A support built against a wall is a **buttress**.
– A support put under a board to make a table is a **trestle**.

supporter *NOUN*
❶ *The home supporters went wild.*
• **fan, follower**
❷ *He is a well-known supporter of animal rights.*
• **champion, advocate, backer, defender, upholder**

suppose *VERB*
❶ *I suppose you're wondering why I'm here.*
• **expect, presume, assume, guess**
IDIOMS **I take it, I dare say**
❷ *Suppose you could travel back in time.*
• **imagine, pretend, let's say**

➤ **be supposed to do something**
Traditionally, ghosts are not supposed to speak.
• **be meant to, be expected to, be due to, ought to, should**

suppress *VERB*
❶ *The army soon suppressed the rebellion.*
• **crush, quash, quell, curb, put down, stamp out, crack down on**
❷ *She could not suppress a smile.*
• **check, hold back, stifle, restrain, repress, bottle up, contain**
– To suppress ideas for political or moral reasons is to **censor** them.

supreme *ADJECTIVE*
❶ *He is the supreme commander of the armed forces.*
• **highest, superior, chief, head, top, principal, foremost, prime**
❷ *With a supreme effort, she managed not to laugh.*
• **extreme, enormous, very great, exceptional, extraordinary, remarkable**

sure *ADJECTIVE*
❶ *Are you sure this is the right address?*
• **certain, positive, confident, definite, convinced, satisfied**
OPPOSITES unsure, uncertain
❷ *She's sure to find out eventually.*
• **bound, likely, certain**
OPPOSITE unlikely
❸ *He was pacing the floor, a sure sign he was nervous.*
• **clear, definite, certain, reliable, undeniable, unambiguous**
OPPOSITES unclear, doubtful

surface *NOUN*
❶ *The surface of Mars is barren and rocky.*
• **exterior, outside, top**
OPPOSITES inside, interior
❷ *A cube has six surfaces.*
• **face, side, facet**

surface *VERB*
❶ *The submarine slowly surfaced.*
• **rise to the surface, come up, emerge**
(*informal*) **pop up**
❷ *The road is surfaced with cobbles.*
• **cover, pave, coat**

surge *VERB*
❶ *Huge waves surged over the sea wall.*
• **rise, roll, heave, billow, sweep, burst**
❷ *Without warning, the crowd surged forward.*
• **rush, push, sweep**

surge *NOUN*
❶ *I felt a surge of panic.*
• **rush, wave, upsurge, outpouring, onrush**
❷ *There has been an unexpected surge in sales.*
• **rise, increase, growth, escalation**

surly *ADJECTIVE*
The landlord muttered a surly greeting.
• **bad-tempered, unfriendly, sullen, sulky, grumpy**

surpass *VERB*
This trip has surpassed all my expectations.
• **beat, better, exceed, do better than, improve on, outdo, outshine, eclipse**

surplus *NOUN*
We have a surplus of tomatoes from our garden.
• **excess, surfeit, glut, oversupply**
OPPOSITES shortage, dearth

surplus *ADJECTIVE*
The body stores surplus food as fat.
• **excess, superfluous, spare, unneeded, unwanted, leftover**

surprise *NOUN*
❶ *The news came as a complete surprise.*
• **revelation, shock**
(*informal*) **bombshell, eye-opener**
IDIOM **bolt from the blue**
❷ *To my surprise, I passed the audition.*
• **amazement, astonishment, bewilderment, disbelief**

surprised *ADJECTIVE*
They seemed genuinely surprised to see me.
• **amazed, astonished, astounded, taken**

A B C D E F G H I J K L M N O P Q R S T U V W X Y Z

aback, startled, stunned, dumbfounded (*informal*) flabbergasted

surprising *ADJECTIVE*
Our experiment produced a surprising result.
• **unexpected, unforeseen, extraordinary, astonishing, remarkable, incredible, staggering, startling**
OPPOSITES expected, predictable

surrender *VERB*
❶ *After months of fighting, the rebels were forced to surrender.*
• **admit defeat, give in, yield, submit, capitulate**
❷ *He was asked to surrender his passport to the authorities.*
• **give, hand over, relinquish**

surround *VERB*
❶ *The garden is surrounded by a stone wall.*
• **enclose, fence in, wall in**
❷ *Armed police have surrounded the building.*
• **encircle, ring, hem in, besiege**

surroundings *PLURAL NOUN*
The hotel is set in beautiful surroundings.
• **environment, setting, location, habitat**

survey *NOUN*
❶ *We did a survey of local leisure facilities.*
• **review, enquiry, investigation, study, poll**
– A survey to count the population of an area is a **census**.
❷ *They got a detailed survey of the house before buying it.*
• **inspection, examination**

survey *VERB*
❶ *She stood at the door, surveying the mess.*
• **view, look over, look at, gaze at, scan, observe, contemplate**
❷ *The team will survey the Antarctic coastline.*
• **inspect, examine, explore, scrutinize, study, map out**

survive *VERB*
❶ *They had enough water to survive until help came.*
• **stay alive, live, last, keep going, carry on, hold out, pull through**
OPPOSITE die
❷ *Only two people survived the crash.*
• **live through, withstand, come through, endure, weather**
❸ *Few of the ancient traditions survive.*
• **remain, continue, persist, endure, abide**
❹ *She survived her husband by ten years.*
• **outlive, outlast**

suspect *VERB*
❶ *No one could possibly suspect him.*
• **doubt, mistrust, have suspicions about, have misgivings about, have qualms about**
❷ *I suspect we may never know the truth.*
• **have a feeling, think, imagine, presume, guess, sense, fancy**

suspend *VERB*
❶ *A lamp was suspended from the ceiling.*
• **hang, dangle, sling, swing**
❷ *Play was suspended until the next day.*
• **adjourn, break off, discontinue, interrupt**

suspense *NOUN*
The suspense will have you on the edge of your seat.
• **tension, uncertainty, anticipation, expectancy, drama, excitement**

suspicion *NOUN*
❶ *Something she said aroused my suspicions.*
• **distrust, doubt, misgiving, qualm, reservation**
❷ *I had a suspicion that something was wrong.*
• **feeling, hunch, inkling, intuition, impression, notion**

suspicious *ADJECTIVE*
❶ *The two men became deeply suspicious of each other.*
• **doubtful, distrustful, mistrustful, unsure, uneasy, wary**
OPPOSITE trusting
❷ *There's something suspicious about this email.*
• **questionable, suspect, dubious, irregular, funny, shady**
(*informal*) **fishy**

sustain *VERB*
❶ *Squirrels store nuts to sustain them through the winter.*
• **keep going, nurture, nourish, provide for**
❷ *Somehow the film manages to sustain your interest.*
• **maintain, preserve, keep up, hold onto, retain, prolong**
❸ *The driver sustained only minor injuries.*
• **suffer, receive, experience, undergo**

swagger *VERB*
The lead guitarist swaggered about on stage.
• **strut, parade**

swallow *VERB*
The bread was so dry that it was hard to swallow.
• **gulp down**
➤ **swallow something up**
The summit was soon swallowed up by clouds.
• **envelop, engulf, cover over, absorb**

swam
past tense see **swim**

swamp *NOUN*
The area around the lake used to be a swamp.
• **marsh, bog, mire, fen, quicksand, quagmire**

swamp *VERB*
❶ *Their boat was swamped by heavy waves.*
• **flood, engulf, inundate, deluge, submerge**
❷ *Our phone lines have been swamped with calls.*
• **overwhelm, bombard, inundate, deluge, snow under**

swan *NOUN*
In the sky was a flock of migrating swans.
– A male swan is a **cob**.
– A female swan is a **pen**.
– A young swan is a **cygnet**.
SEE ALSO **bird**

swap or **swop** (*informal*) *VERB*
We swapped seats so I could sit by the window.
• **exchange, switch, trade, substitute**
– To exchange goods for other goods without using money is to **barter**.

swarm *VERB*
Fans and photographers swarmed around her.
• **crowd, flock, mob, throng, cluster**
➤ **swarm with**
The city centre was swarming with tourists.
• **be overrun by, teem with, be inundated with, be crawling with**

sway *VERB*
The branches were swaying in the breeze.
• **move to and fro, swing, wave, rock, undulate**

swear *VERB*
❶ *Do you swear never to tell anyone?*
• **promise, pledge, vow, give your word, take an oath**
❷ *He muttered and swore under his breath.*
• **curse, blaspheme, use bad language**

sweat *NOUN*
A bead of sweat trickled down her nose.
• **perspiration**

sweat *VERB*
I began to sweat in the heat of the bus.
• **perspire**

sweaty *ADJECTIVE*
When I'm nervous, my palms get sweaty.
• **sweating, perspiring, clammy, sticky, moist**

sweep *VERB*
❶ *She was sweeping the steps with a broom.*
• **brush, clean, dust**
❷ *He was in danger of being swept out to sea.*
• **carry, pull, drag, tow**
❸ *Another bus swept past them.*
• **speed, sail, shoot, zoom, glide, breeze**
➤ **sweep something away**
The floods swept away roads and bridges.
• **carry off, clear away, remove, get rid of**

sweet *ADJECTIVE*
❶ *Would you prefer sweet or salty popcorn?*
• **sugary, sugared, sweetened, syrupy**
OPPOSITES sour, savoury
❷ *The sweet smell of roses filled the room.*
• **fragrant, aromatic, perfumed, pleasant**
OPPOSITE foul
❸ *I could hear the sweet sound of a harp.*
• **mellow, melodious, soft, pleasant, soothing, tuneful**
OPPOSITES harsh, ugly
❹ *Baby elephants are so sweet!*
• **charming, delightful, lovable, adorable, endearing, cuddly**
(*informal*) **cute**

sweet *NOUN*
❶ *He bought a packet of sweets.*
• (*North American*) **candy**
– Sweets in general are **confectionery**.
❷ *There is apple pie for sweet.*
• **dessert, pudding**
(*informal*) **afters**

swell *VERB*
❶ *My ankle was starting to swell.*
• **expand, enlarge, bulge, inflate, puff up, fill out, balloon, billow**
OPPOSITE shrink
❷ *Over time the population of the city swelled to ten million.*
• **grow, increase, expand, enlarge, rise, escalate, mushroom**
OPPOSITE shrink

swelling *NOUN*
There was a painful swelling on the horse's leg.
• **inflammation, lump, bump, growth, tumour**

swerve *VERB*
The car swerved to avoid a pedestrian.
• **turn aside, veer, dodge, swing**

swift *ADJECTIVE*
❶ *He drew out his sword in one swift movement.*
• **fast, quick, rapid, speedy, brisk, lively**
OPPOSITES slow, unhurried
❷ *Her reply was swift and to the point.*
• **prompt, quick, immediate, instant, speedy, snappy**
OPPOSITES slow, tardy

swim *VERB*
We swam in the sea every day.
• **go swimming, bathe, take a dip**

WORD WEB

Common swimming strokes:

➤ **backstroke**
➤ **breaststroke**
➤ **butterfly**
➤ **dog paddle or doggy paddle**
➤ **freestyle**
➤ **front crawl**
➤ **sidestroke**

swindle *VERB*
They were swindled out of their life savings.
• **cheat, trick, dupe, fleece**
(*informal*) **con, diddle**

swing *VERB*

❶ *The inn sign swung and creaked in the wind.*

• **sway, move to and fro, flap, rock, swivel, pivot, oscillate**

❷ *She swung her bag over her shoulder and walked away.*

• **sling, hang, suspend, string**

❸ *He swung round when I called his name.*

• **turn, twist, veer, swerve, deviate**

swipe *VERB*

❶ *The crocodile nearly swiped us with its tail.*

• **slash, lash, hit, strike, swing at**

❷ (*informal*) *Who swiped my pen?*

• **steal, snatch**

(*informal*) **make off with, nick, pinch**

swirl *VERB*

The water was now swirling around their feet.

• **whirl, spin, twirl, churn, eddy**

switch *VERB*

❶ *How do you switch off your phone?*

• **turn**

❷ *This is the story of two men who switch identities.*

• **exchange, swap, change, shift**

swivel *VERB*

She swivelled round in her chair.

• **spin, turn, twirl, pivot, revolve, rotate**

swollen *ADJECTIVE*

My feet were swollen from walking all day.

• **inflamed, bloated, puffed up, puffy**

swoop *VERB*

❶ *The owl swooped down to catch a mouse.*

• **dive, plunge, plummet, pounce, descend**

❷ *Police swooped on the house in the early hours.*

• **raid, attack, storm**

sword *NOUN*

He raised his shield and drew his sword.

• **blade, foil, rapier, sabre**

– Fighting with swords is **fencing** or **swordsmanship**.

swore

past tense see **swear**

symbol *NOUN*

❶ *The dove is a symbol of peace.*

• **sign, emblem, image, representation**

❷ *The Red Cross symbol was painted on the side of the vehicle.*

• **emblem, insignia, badge, crest, logo**

❸ *The stone was covered in strange symbols.*

• **character, letter, mark**

– The symbols used in ancient Egyptian writing were **hieroglyphics**.

symbolize *VERB*

What does the rose symbolize in the poem?

• **represent, stand for, signify, indicate, mean, denote**

sympathetic *ADJECTIVE*

He gave me a sympathetic smile.

• **understanding, compassionate, concerned, caring, comforting, kind, supportive**

OPPOSITE **unsympathetic**

sympathize *VERB*

➤ **sympathize with**

You could at least sympathize with me!

• **feel sorry for, feel for, commiserate with**

sympathy *NOUN*

It's hard to feel sympathy for any of the characters.

• **compassion, understanding, concern, fellow-feeling**

synthetic *ADJECTIVE*

Nylon is a synthetic material.

• **artificial, man-made, manufactured, imitation**

OPPOSITE **natural**

system *NOUN*

❶ *The city needs a better transport system.*

• **network, organization, structure,**

framework, arrangement
(*informal*) **set-up**
❷ *I don't understand the new cataloguing system.*
• **method, procedure, process, scheme, technique, routine**

systematic *ADJECTIVE*
Police began a systematic search of the crime scene.
• **methodical, orderly, structured, organized, logical, scientific**
OPPOSITE **unsystematic**

table *NOUN*
Here is the full table of results.
• **chart, plan, list**

tablet *NOUN*
❶ *The doctor prescribed some tablets for the pain.*
• **pill, capsule, pellet**
❷ *There was a stone tablet above the entrance to the tomb.*
• **slab, plaque**

tack *VERB*
❶ *The carpet needs to be tacked down.*
• **nail, pin**
❷ *She tacked up the hem of her skirt.*
• **sew, stitch**
➤ **tack something on**
A small conservatory has been tacked onto the house.
• **add, attach, append, join on**

tackle *VERB*
❶ *Firefighters came to tackle the blaze.*
• **deal with, attend to, handle, manage, grapple with, cope with**
❷ *You can only tackle a player with the ball.*
• **challenge, intercept, take on**

tackle *NOUN*
❶ *He kept his fishing tackle in a special case.*
• **gear, equipment, apparatus, kit**
❷ *The player was sent off for a late tackle.*
• **challenge, interception**

tactful *ADJECTIVE*
I tried to think of a tactful way to say no.
• **subtle, discreet, delicate, diplomatic, sensitive, thoughtful**
OPPOSITE tactless

tactics *PLURAL NOUN*
The team changed tactics at half-time.
• **strategy, moves, manoeuvres, plan of action**

tag *NOUN*
I'll just remove the price tag.
• **label, sticker, ticket, tab**

tag *VERB*
Every item is tagged with a barcode.
• **label, mark, identify, flag**
➤ **tag along with someone**
My sister tagged along with us for a while.
• **accompany, follow, go with, join**
➤ **tag something on**
He tagged on a PS at the end of his letter.
• **add, attach, append, join on, tack on**

tail *NOUN*
You'll have to join the tail of the queue.
• **end, back, rear**
OPPOSITES front, head

tail *VERB*
(*informal*) *They tailed the suspect to this address.*
• **follow, pursue, track, trail, shadow, stalk**
➤ **tail off**
Audiences slowly began to tail off.
• **decrease, decline, lessen, diminish, dwindle, wane**

taint *VERB*
He was forever after tainted with suspicion.
• **tarnish, stain, sully, blot, blight, damage, spoil**

take *VERB*
❶ *She took her sister's hand.*
• **clutch, clasp, take hold of, grasp, grip, seize, snatch, grab**
❷ *Many prisoners were taken.*
• **capture, seize, detain**
❸ *He took an envelope from his pocket.*
• **remove, withdraw, pull, extract**
❹ *Has someone taken my calculator?*
• **steal**
(*informal*) **swipe, make off with, pinch, nick**

A B C D E F G H I J K L M N O P Q R S T U V W X Y Z

5 *I'll take you upstairs to your room.*
• **conduct, escort, lead, accompany, guide, show, usher**
6 *Would you like me to take your luggage?*
• **carry, convey, bring, bear, transport, ferry**
7 *Take any seat you like.*
• **pick, choose, select**
8 *Each cable car can take eight passengers.*
• **hold, contain, accommodate, have room for**
9 *I can't take much more of this.*
• **bear, put up with, stand, endure, tolerate, suffer, stomach**
10 *It'll take decades for the forest to recover.*
• **need, require**
11 *Let me take you name and phone number.*
• **make a note of, record, register, write down, jot down**
12 *Take the total sum from the original number.*
• **subtract, take away, deduct, discount**
➤ **take after someone**
Do you think she takes after her mother?
• **resemble, look like, remind someone of**
➤ **take someone in**
No one was taken in by his story.
• **fool, deceive, trick, cheat, dupe, hoodwink**
➤ **take something in**
I was too tired to take it all in.
• **understand, comprehend, grasp, absorb, follow**
➤ **take off**
1 *Our plane took off on time.*
• **lift off, blast off, depart**
2 *Her business has really taken off.*
• **succeed, do well, catch on, become popular, prosper**
➤ **take something off**
Please take off your coats.
• **remove, strip off, peel off**
➤ **take part in something**
Everyone has to take part in the show.
• **participate in, be involved in, join in**
➤ **take place**
Where exactly did the accident take place?
• **happen, occur, come about**
➤ **take to something**
How are you taking to life in the city?
• **like, cope with, get on with**
➤ **take something up**
1 *I have recently taken up tap dancing.*
• **begin to do, start learning**
2 *This desk takes up a lot of space.*
• **use up, fill up, occupy, require**
3 *I decided to take up their offer.*
• **accept, agree to, say yes to**

tale *NOUN*
It is a tale of love and betrayal.
• **story, narrative, account, legend, fable, saga**
(*informal*) **yarn**

talent *NOUN*
She shows a real talent for drawing.
• **gift, ability, aptitude, skill, flair, knack, forte**
– Unusually great talent is **genius**.

talented *ADJECTIVE*
He's a very talented actor.
• **gifted, able, accomplished, capable, skilled, skilful, brilliant, expert**
– Someone who is talented in several ways is said to be **versatile**.
OPPOSITES inept, talentless

talk *VERB*
1 *When do babies start learning to talk?*
• **speak, say things, communicate, express yourself**
2 *You two must have a lot to talk about.*
• **discuss, converse, chat, chatter, gossip**
(*informal*) **natter**
3 *The prisoner refused to talk.*
• **give information, confess**
SEE ALSO **say**

talk *NOUN*
1 *I need to have a talk with you soon.*
• **conversation, discussion, chat**
– Talk between characters in a play, film or novel is **dialogue**.

❷ *There is a talk on Egyptian art at lunchtime.*
• **lecture, presentation, speech, address**
❸ *There was talk of witchcraft in the village.*
• **rumour, gossip**

talkative *ADJECTIVE*
You're not very talkative this morning.
• **chatty, communicative, vocal, forthcoming, loquacious, garrulous**
OPPOSITE taciturn

tall *ADJECTIVE*
❶ *She is tall for her age.*
• **big, giant, towering**
– Someone who is awkwardly tall and thin is **lanky** or **gangling**.
OPPOSITE short
❷ *Singapore has many tall buildings.*
• **high, lofty, towering, soaring, giant**
– Buildings with many floors are **high-rise** or **multi-storey** buildings.
OPPOSITE low

tally *VERB*
➤ **tally with**
This doesn't tally with your previous answer.
• **agree with, correspond with, match**

tame *ADJECTIVE*
❶ *These guinea pigs are tame and do not bite.*
• **domesticated, broken in, docile, gentle, manageable, trained**
OPPOSITE wild
❷ *The film seems very tame nowadays.*
• **dull, unexciting, unadventurous, boring, bland, humdrum**
OPPOSITES exciting, adventurous

tame *VERB*
He was an expert at taming wild horses.
• **domesticate, break in, subdue, master**

tamper *VERB*
➤ **tamper with something**
Someone has been tampering with the lock.
• **meddle with, tinker with, fiddle about with, interfere with, doctor**

tang *NOUN*
You can taste the tang of lemon in the soup.
• **sharpness, zest, zing**

tangle *VERB*
❶ *The tree roots were tangled into a solid mass.*
• **entangle, twist, knot, jumble, muddle**
– Tangled hair is **dishevelled** or **matted** hair.
❷ *Dolphins can get tangled in fishing nets.*
• **catch, trap, ensnare**

tangle *NOUN*
Underneath the desk was a tangle of computer cables.
• **muddle, jumble, knot, twist, confusion**

tap *NOUN*
❶ *Turn the tap to the off position.*
• **valve, stopcock**
❷ *I thought I heard a tap on the window.*
• **knock, rap, pat, strike**

tap *VERB*
He tapped three times on the door.
• **knock, strike, rap, pat, drum**

tape *NOUN*
The parcel was tied up with tape.
• **band, ribbon, braid, binding, string**

target *NOUN*
❶ *His target was to swim thirty lengths.*
• **goal, aim, objective, intention, purpose, hope, ambition**
❷ *She was the target of a hate campaign.*
• **object, victim, butt, focus**

tarnish *VERB*
❶ *The mirror had tarnished with age.*
• **discolour, corrode, rust**
❷ *The scandal tarnished his reputation.*
• **stain, taint, sully, blot, blacken, spoil, mar, damage**

tart *NOUN*
I had a slice of lemon tart.
• **flan, pie, pastry**

A B C D E F G H I J K L M N O P Q R S T U V W X Y Z

tart *ADJECTIVE*
❶ *Cranberries have a tart flavour.*
• sharp, sour, acid, tangy
OPPOSITE sweet
❷ *She gave me a tart reply.*
• sarcastic, biting, cutting, caustic

task *NOUN*
❶ *The robot can carry out simple tasks.*
• job, chore, errand, exercise
❷ *Your task is to design a logo for the company.*
• assignment, mission, duty, undertaking

taste *NOUN*
❶ *I love the taste of ginger.*
• flavour, savour
❷ *Would you like a taste of my pudding?*
• mouthful, sample, bite, bit, morsel, nibble
❸ *She dresses with impeccable taste.*
• style, elegance, discrimination, judgement
❹ *He has always had a taste for travel.*
• liking, love, fondness, desire, inclination

W **WRITING TIPS**

DESCRIBING TASTE
Pleasant:

➤ appetizing
➤ delectable
➤ delicious
➤ flavoursome
➤ luscious
➤ (*informal*) moreish
➤ mouth-watering
➤ palatable
➤ (*informal*) scrumptious
➤ succulent
➤ tasty
➤ tempting
➤ (*informal*) yummy

Unpleasant:

➤ disgusting
➤ foul
➤ inedible
➤ insipid
➤ nauseating
➤ nauseous
➤ rancid
➤ revolting
➤ sickening
➤ unappetizing
➤ uneatable
➤ unpalatable

Other:

➤ acidic
➤ acrid
➤ bitter
➤ bland
➤ burnt
➤ fiery
➤ flavourless
➤ fresh
➤ fruity
➤ hot
➤ juicy
➤ mellow
➤ metallic
➤ mild
➤ nutty
➤ peppery
➤ piquant
➤ pungent
➤ refreshing
➤ salty
➤ savoury
➤ sharp
➤ smoky
➤ sour
➤ spicy
➤ strong
➤ sugary
➤ sweet
➤ syrupy
➤ tangy
➤ tart
➤ tasteless
➤ vinegary
➤ yeasty
➤ zesty

taste *VERB*
❶ *Taste the sauce before adding salt.*
• sample, try, test, sip, savour
❷ *Can you taste any difference in flavour?*
• perceive, distinguish, discern, make out

tasteful *ADJECTIVE*
The room was decorated in a plain and tasteful style.
• refined, stylish, elegant, chic, smart, cultured, artistic
OPPOSITES tasteless, vulgar

tasteless *ADJECTIVE*
❶ *He apologized for telling a tasteless joke.*
• crude, tactless, indelicate, inappropriate, in bad taste
❷ *The fish was overcooked and tasteless.*
• flavourless, bland, insipid
OPPOSITE flavoursome

tasty *ADJECTIVE*
That pie was very tasty.
• delicious, appetizing, flavoursome
OPPOSITES flavourless, unappetizing

tattered *ADJECTIVE*
Some of the blankets were worn and tattered.
• **ragged, ripped, torn, frayed, tatty, threadbare**
OPPOSITE **smart**

taught
past tense see **teach**

taunt *VERB*
Two sets of rival fans taunted each other.
• **jeer at, jibe, insult, sneer at, scoff at, make fun of, tease, mock, ridicule**

taunt *NOUN*
He had to ignore the taunts of the crowd.
• **jeer, jibe, insult, sneer**

taut *ADJECTIVE*
Make sure the rope is taut.
• **tight, tense, stretched**
OPPOSITE **slack**

teach *VERB*
My dad is teaching me to play the guitar.
• **educate, instruct, tutor, coach, train, school**

teacher *NOUN*
She is a qualified dance teacher.
• **tutor, instructor, trainer, coach**
– A teacher at a college or university is a **lecturer**.
– In the past, a woman who taught children in a private household was a **governess**.

team *NOUN*
❶ *She's in the school hockey team.*
• **side, squad, line-up**
❷ *They were rescued by a mountain rescue team.*
• **group, force, unit, crew, detail**

tear *VERB*
❶ *The wind tore a hole in our tent.*
• **rip, split, slit, gash, rupture, shred**
❷ *A white van came tearing round the corner.*
• **race, dash, rush, hurry, sprint, speed**

tear *NOUN*
There was a tear in one of the sails.
• **rip, split, slit, gash, rent, rupture, hole, opening, gap**

tease *VERB*
I knew she was only teasing me.
• **taunt, make fun of, poke fun at, mock, ridicule, laugh at**
IDIOM (*informal*) **pull someone's leg**

technical *ADJECTIVE*
❶ *She is good with anything technical.*
• **technological, scientific, high-tech**
❷ *The manual was full of technical terms.*
• **specialist, specialized, advanced**

technique *NOUN*
❶ *He is trained in survival techniques.*
• **method, procedure, approach, means, system**
❷ *Her piano playing shows good technique.*
• **skill, expertise, proficiency, artistry, ability**

tedious *ADJECTIVE*
I found the opening chapter slow and tedious.
• **boring, dull, dreary, tiresome, monotonous, unexciting, uninteresting**
OPPOSITE **exciting**

teem *VERB*
➤ **teem with**
The pond teems with fish.
• **be full of, be bursting with, swarm with, be overrun by, be crawling with, be infested with**

teenager *NOUN*
The website is mainly aimed at teenagers.
• **adolescent, youth, young person** (*informal*) **teen**

telephone *VERB*
see **phone**

tell *VERB*
❶ *I have something important to tell you.*
• **say to, make known to, communicate**

to, report to, announce to, reveal to, notify, inform
❷ *The film tells the story of a young shepherd.*
• **relate, narrate, recount, describe**
❸ *The police told everyone to stand back.*
• **order, command, direct, instruct**
❹ *Can you tell where we are yet?*
• **make out, recognize, identify, determine, perceive**
❺ *It's impossible to tell one character from another.*
• **distinguish, differentiate**
➤ **tell someone off**
(*informal*) *We were told off for being late.*
• **scold, reprimand, reproach**
(*informal*) **tick off**

temper *NOUN*
❶ *The chef is always flying into a temper.*
• **rage, fury, tantrum, fit of anger**
❷ *He managed to keep an even temper.*
• **mood, humour, state of mind**
➤ **lose your temper**
She loses her temper at the slightest thing.
• **get angry, fly into a rage**
IDIOMS (*informal*) **blow a fuse, blow your top, flip your lid, fly off the handle, hit the roof**

temperature *NOUN*

WORD WEB

Units for measuring temperature:

➤ degrees Celsius
➤ degrees centigrade
➤ degrees Fahrenheit

- A **thermometer** is a device for measuring temperature.
- A **thermostat** is a device for keeping temperature steady.

temple *NOUN*
For places of religious worship see **religion**.

temporary *ADJECTIVE*
❶ *That will do for a temporary repair.*
• **interim, provisional, makeshift**
❷ *He suffered a temporary loss of hearing.*
• **short-lived, momentary, passing, fleeting**
OPPOSITE permanent

tempt *VERB*
Can I tempt you to try a spoonful?
• **coax, entice, persuade, attract, lure**
OPPOSITES discourage, deter

temptation *NOUN*
I resisted the temptation to laugh.
• **urge, impulse, inclination, desire**

tempting *ADJECTIVE*
It was a tempting offer.
• **enticing, attractive, appealing, inviting, beguiling**
OPPOSITES off-putting, uninviting

tend *VERB*
❶ *She tends to have a nap in the afternoon.*
• **be inclined, be liable, be likely, be apt, be prone**
❷ *He used to help his father tend the crops.*
• **take care of, look after, cultivate, manage**
❸ *Volunteers tended the wounded in makeshift hospitals.*
• **nurse, attend to, care for, minister to**

tendency *NOUN*
He has a tendency to exaggerate.
• **inclination, leaning, predisposition, propensity**

tender *ADJECTIVE*
❶ *Cook the meat until it is tender.*
• **soft, succulent, juicy**
OPPOSITE tough
❷ *Frost may damage tender plants.*
• **delicate, fragile, sensitive**
OPPOSITES hardy, strong
❸ *My gums are still a bit tender.*
• **painful, sensitive, sore**
❹ *She turned to me with a tender smile.*
• **affectionate, kind, loving, caring,**

warm-hearted, compassionate, sympathetic
OPPOSITE uncaring

tennis *NOUN*

WORD WEB

Terms used in tennis:

- ace
- advantage
- backhand
- ballboy or ballgirl
- break point
- court
- deuce
- double fault
- doubles
- drop shot
- foot fault
- forehand
- lob
- love
- match point
- net
- racket or racquet
- serve
- service
- set
- singles
- slice
- smash
- tie-break or tie-breaker
- umpire
- volley

For tips on writing about sport see **sport**.

tense *ADJECTIVE*
❶ *Every muscle in my body was tense.*
• **taut, tight, strained, stretched**
❷ *Do you feel tense before a big match?*
• **anxious, nervous, apprehensive, edgy, on edge, jumpy, keyed up, worked up**
(*informal*) **uptight, jittery, twitchy**
OPPOSITE relaxed
❸ *The film ends with an incredibly tense car chase.*
• **nerve-racking, nail-biting, stressful, fraught**

tension *NOUN*
❶ *Can you check the tension on the ropes?*
• **tightness, tautness**
❷ *The tension in the room was unbearable.*
• **anxiety, nervousness, apprehension, suspense, worry, stress, strain**

tent *NOUN*
We slept overnight in a tent.
– A large tent used for a party or other event is a **marquee**.
– To set up a tent is to **pitch** it and to take down a tent is to **strike** it.

tepid *ADJECTIVE*
The water should be tepid, not hot.
• **lukewarm, hand-hot**

term *NOUN*
❶ *He served a long term in prison.*
• **period, time, spell, stretch, stint, run**
❷ *The book includes a glossary of technical terms.*
• **word, expression, phrase, name**

terrible *ADJECTIVE*
❶ *We heard there had been a terrible accident.*
• **horrible, dreadful, appalling, shocking, horrific, horrendous, ghastly, atrocious**
OPPOSITE minor
❷ *The first half of the show was terrible!*
• **very bad, awful, dreadful, appalling, dire, abysmal**
(*informal*) **rubbish, lousy, pathetic**
OPPOSITE excellent

terribly *ADVERB*
❶ *He was missing his parents terribly.*
• **very badly, severely, intensely**
OPPOSITE slightly
❷ *I'm terribly sorry about this.*
• **very, extremely, awfully**

terrific (*informal*) *ADJECTIVE*
❶ *There was a terrific flash of lightning.*
• **very great, tremendous, mighty, huge, enormous, massive, immense, colossal, gigantic**
❷ *She's a terrific tennis player.*
• **very good, excellent, first-class, first-rate, superb, marvellous, wonderful**
(*informal*) **brilliant, fantastic, fabulous**

terrify *VERB*
The dogs were terrified by the thunder.
• **frighten, scare, horrify, petrify, panic, alarm**

a b c d e f g h i j k l m n o p q r s t u v w x y z

A B C D E F G H I J K L M N O P Q R S T U V W X Y Z

territory *NOUN*
We were now deep in enemy territory.
• **land, area, ground, terrain, country, district, region, sector, zone**
– A territory which is part of a country is a **province**.

terror *NOUN*
They ran away screaming in terror.
• **fear, fright, horror, dread, panic, alarm**

test *NOUN*
❶ *We had a maths test today.*
• **exam, examination, assessment, appraisal, evaluation**
– A test for a job as an actor or a singer is an **audition**.
❷ *This is a new test for allergies.*
• **trial, experiment, check, investigation, examination**

test *VERB*
❶ *Mum needs to have her eyes tested.*
• **examine, check, evaluate, assess, screen**
❷ *Pilots have been testing the new aircraft.*
• **try out, experiment with, trial, sample**
IDIOM **put something through its paces**

text *NOUN*
❶ *It is easy to add text to your web pages.*
• **words, wording, content, script**
❷ *For centuries scholars have studied these ancient texts.*
• **work, book, piece of writing**

textiles *PLURAL NOUN*
All their clothes are made from natural textiles.
• **fabrics, materials, cloths**

WORD WEB

Some textile arts:

- ➤ appliqué
- ➤ crochet
- ➤ dyeing
- ➤ embroidery
- ➤ felting
- ➤ knitting
- ➤ lacemaking
- ➤ needlepoint
- ➤ needlework
- ➤ patchwork
- ➤ quilting
- ➤ sewing
- ➤ spinning
- ➤ tapestry
- ➤ weaving

For types of textiles see **fabric**.

texture *NOUN*
Silk has a smooth texture.
• **feel, touch, consistency, quality, surface**

WRITING TIPS

DESCRIBING TEXTURE

Rough or hard:

- ➤ brittle
- ➤ bumpy
- ➤ coarse
- ➤ crumbly
- ➤ firm
- ➤ grainy
- ➤ gravelly
- ➤ lumpy
- ➤ ruffled
- ➤ sandy
- ➤ scaly
- ➤ wrinkled

Smooth or soft:

- ➤ creamy
- ➤ downy
- ➤ feathery
- ➤ fine
- ➤ glassy
- ➤ light
- ➤ silky
- ➤ velvety

Wet or sticky:

- ➤ (*informal*) gloopy
- ➤ glutinous
- ➤ moist
- ➤ runny
- ➤ slimy
- ➤ viscous
- ➤ watery

Other:

- ➤ chalky
- ➤ chewy
- ➤ doughy
- ➤ elastic
- ➤ fibrous
- ➤ flaky
- ➤ greasy
- ➤ leathery
- ➤ oily
- ➤ papery
- ➤ powdery
- ➤ pulpy
- ➤ rubbery
- ➤ soupy
- ➤ spongy
- ➤ springy
- ➤ (*informal*) squidgy
- ➤ stretchy
- ➤ stringy
- ➤ waxy

thank *VERB*
How can I ever thank you enough?
• **say thank you to, express your gratitude to, show your appreciation to**

thankful *ADJECTIVE*
We were thankful to be home at last.
• **grateful, appreciative, glad, pleased, relieved**

thanks *PLURAL NOUN*
Please accept this token of my thanks.
• **gratitude, appreciation**
➤ **thanks to**
People are living longer thanks to better healthcare.
• **because of, as a result of, owing to, due to, on account of**

thaw *VERB*
❶ *Polar ice caps are thawing at a faster rate than ever.*
• **melt, dissolve, liquefy**
❷ *Leave frozen food to thaw before cooking.*
• **defrost, unfreeze**
OPPOSITE **freeze**

theatre *NOUN*
see **drama**

theft *NOUN*
She reported the theft of jewels from her hotel room.
• **robbery, stealing**
SEE ALSO **stealing**

theme *NOUN*
What is the theme of the poem?
• **subject, topic, idea, argument, gist, thread**

theory *NOUN*
❶ *Do you have any theories about the murder?*
• **hypothesis, explanation, suggestion, view, belief, contention, speculation, idea, notion**
❷ *He is studying musical theory.*
• **principles, concepts, rules, laws**

therapy *NOUN*
Acupuncture is an ancient therapy.
• **treatment, remedy**

thick *ADJECTIVE*
❶ *The tree has thick roots.*
• **stout, chunky, heavy, solid, bulky, hefty, substantial**
OPPOSITES **thin, slender**
❷ *The stone walls are more than a metre thick.*
• **wide, broad, deep**
❸ *There was a thick layer of mist.*
• **dense, close, compact, opaque, impenetrable**
OPPOSITES **thin, light**
❹ *He spoke with a thick Polish accent.*
• **heavy, noticeable**
OPPOSITE **slight**
❺ *Beat the mixture into a thick paste.*
• **stiff, firm, heavy**
OPPOSITES **thin, runny**
❻ *(informal) Maybe I'm just being thick.*
• **stupid, unintelligent, brainless, dense, dim**
OPPOSITE **intelligent**

thief *NOUN*
Thieves broke in and stole valuable equipment.
• **robber, burglar**
– Someone who steals from people in the street is a **pickpocket**.
– Someone who steals small goods from a shop is a **shoplifter**.

thin *ADJECTIVE*
❶ *He was a thin little boy with a freckled face.*
• **lean, slim, slender, skinny, bony, gaunt, spare, slight**
– Someone who is thin and tall is **lanky**.
– Someone who is thin but strong is **wiry**.
– Thin arms or legs are **spindly**.
OPPOSITES **fat, plump, stout**
❷ *Her cloak was made of thin material.*
• **fine, lightweight, light, delicate, flimsy, wispy, sheer**
OPPOSITES **thick, heavy**
❸ *Draw a thin line underneath.*
• **narrow, fine**
OPPOSITES **thick, broad**
❹ *Add water to make a thin paste.*
• **runny, watery, sloppy**
OPPOSITES **firm, stiff**

thin *VERB*
You can thin the paint with a little water.
• **dilute, water down, weaken**

➤ **thin out**
Towards evening the crowd began to thin out.
• **disperse, scatter, break up, dissipate**

thing *NOUN*
❶ *Magpies are attracted by shiny things.*
• **object, article, item**
❷ *She had a lot of things to think about.*
• **matter, affair, detail, point, factor**
❸ *Odd things keep happening to me.*
• **event, happening, occurrence, incident**
❹ *I have only one thing left to do.*
• **job, task, act, action**
➤ **things**
Put your things in one of the lockers.
• **belongings, possessions**
(*informal*) **stuff, gear**

think *VERB*
❶ *Stop to think before you do anything rash.*
• **consider, contemplate, reflect, deliberate, meditate, ponder**
– To think hard about something is to **concentrate** on it.
❷ *Do you think this is a good idea?*
• **believe, feel, consider, judge, conclude, be of the opinion**
❸ *When do you think you'll be ready?*
• **reckon, suppose, imagine, estimate, guess, expect, anticipate**
➤ **think about something**
I've thought about what you said.
• **consider, reflect on, ponder on, muse on, mull over**
– To keep thinking anxiously about something is to **brood on** it.
➤ **think something up**
They thought up a good plan.
• **invent, make up, conceive, concoct, devise, dream up**

thirsty *ADJECTIVE*
Exercise always makes me thirsty.
• **dry, parched**
– Someone who has lost a lot of water from their body is **dehydrated**.

thorn *NOUN*
Rose stems have thorns on them.
• **prickle, spike, spine, needle, barb**

thorny *ADJECTIVE*
❶ *He scratched his arm on the thorny branches.*
• **prickly, spiky, spiny, bristly**
❷ *This is quite a thorny issue for a lot of people.*
• **difficult, complicated, complex, hard, tricky, perplexing**

thorough *ADJECTIVE*
❶ *The police made a thorough search of the crime scene.*
• **comprehensive, full, rigorous, detailed, close, in-depth, exhaustive, careful, meticulous, systematic, methodical, painstaking**
OPPOSITES superficial, cursory
❷ *He's making a thorough nuisance of himself.*
• **complete, total, utter, perfect, proper, absolute, downright, out-and-out**

thought *NOUN*
❶ *I've given some thought to the problem.*
• **consideration, deliberation, study**
❷ *She was lost in thought for a moment.*
• **thinking, contemplation, reflection, meditation**
❸ *Look, I've just had a thought.*
• **idea, notion, belief, view, opinion, theory, conclusion**

thoughtful *ADJECTIVE*
❶ *He looked thoughtful for a moment.*
• **pensive, reflective, contemplative, meditative, absorbed, preoccupied**
OPPOSITES blank, vacant
❷ *She added some thoughtful comments in the margin.*
• **well-thought-out, careful, conscientious, thorough**
OPPOSITE careless
❸ *It was thoughtful of you to write.*
• **considerate, kind, caring, compassionate, sympathetic, understanding**
OPPOSITE thoughtless

thoughtless *ADJECTIVE*
It was thoughtless of me to say that.
• **inconsiderate, insensitive, uncaring,**

unthinking, negligent, ill-considered, rash
OPPOSITE thoughtful

thrash *VERB*
❶ *The owner was reported for thrashing his dog.*
• **hit, beat, strike, whip, flog**
❷ *The visitors thrashed the home side.*
• **beat, defeat, trounce**
(*informal*) **hammer**
❸ *The crocodile thrashed its tail.*
• **swish, flail, toss, jerk, twitch**

thread *NOUN*
❶ *There is a loose thread hanging from your cuff.*
• **strand, fibre**
❷ *Do you sell embroidery thread?*
• **cotton, yarn, wool, silk**
❸ *I'm afraid I've lost the thread of this conversation.*
• **theme, drift, direction, train, tenor**

threat *NOUN*
❶ *She made a threat about taking revenge.*
• **warning, ultimatum**
❷ *The oil spill poses a threat to wildlife.*
• **danger, menace, hazard, risk**

threaten *VERB*
❶ *They tried to threaten him into paying.*
• **menace, intimidate, terrorize, bully, browbeat**
❷ *Uncontrolled logging is threatening the forests.*
• **endanger, jeopardize, put at risk**
❸ *The hazy sky threatened rain.*
• **warn of, indicate, signal, forecast**

three *NOUN*
People arrived in groups of two or three.
– A group of three people is a **threesome** or **trio**.
– A series of three related books, plays or films is a **trilogy**.
– To multiply a number by three is to **triple** it.

threw
past tense see **throw**

thrifty *ADJECTIVE*
She has always been thrifty with her money.
• **careful, economical, frugal, prudent, sparing**
OPPOSITE extravagant

thrill *NOUN*
I love the thrill of riding on a roller coaster.
• **excitement, stimulation, sensation, tingle**
(*informal*) **buzz, kick**

thrill *VERB*
The thought of seeing a real shark thrilled him.
• **excite, exhilarate, stir, rouse, stimulate, electrify**
IDIOM (*informal*) **give you a buzz**
OPPOSITE bore

thrilled *ADJECTIVE*
She was thrilled to see her name in print.
• **delighted, pleased, excited, overjoyed, ecstatic**

thrilling *ADJECTIVE*
The movie starts off with a thrilling car chase.
• **exciting, stirring, stimulating, electrifying, exhilarating, action-packed, gripping, riveting**

thrive *VERB*
Crops thrive in this climate.
• **do well, flourish, prosper, succeed, boom**
OPPOSITE decline

thriving *ADJECTIVE*
The region has a thriving tourist industry.
• **flourishing, successful, prosperous, booming, healthy, profitable**
OPPOSITE declining

throb *VERB*
He felt his heart throbbing in his chest.
• **beat, pound, pulse, pulsate, thump**

A B C D E F G H I J K L M N O P Q R S T U V W X Y Z

throb *NOUN*
We could hear the incessant throb of the music next door.
• **beat, pulse, pulsation, pounding, thumping**

throng *NOUN*
Throngs of onlookers turned out to watch.
• **crowd, swarm, horde, mass, drove**

throng *VERB*
Spectators thronged into the piazza.
• **swarm, flock, stream, crowd**
➤ **thronged with**
In summer Venice is thronged with tourists.
• **crowded with, packed with, full of, swarming with**

throttle *VERB*
This stiff collar is throttling me!
• **strangle, choke, suffocate**

throw *VERB*
❶ *We threw scraps of food to the birds.*
• **fling, toss, sling, cast, pitch, hurl, heave**
(*informal*) **bung, chuck**
❷ *Her question threw me for a second.*
• **disconcert, unsettle, unnerve, put off, rattle**
(*informal*) **faze**
❸ *They threw a surprise party for her.*
• **hold, host, put on, arrange, organize**
➤ **throw something away or out**
I'm throwing out a lot of my old stuff.
• **get rid of, dispose of, discard, scrap, dump**
(*informal*) **ditch, bin**

thrust *VERB*
❶ *A woman thrust a leaflet into my hands.*
• **shove, push, force**
❷ *The man thrust at me with his spear.*
• **lunge, jab, prod, stab, poke**

thump *VERB*
❶ *He stood up and thumped his fist on the table.*
• **bang, bash, pound, hit, strike, knock, hammer, punch**
(*informal*) **whack**
❷ *My heart was thumping.*
• **throb, pound, pulse, hammer**

thunder *NOUN*
We heard thunder in the distance.
– A burst of thunder is a **clap, crack, peal** or **roll** of thunder.
SEE ALSO **weather**

thunder *VERB*
❶ *Waves thundered against the rocks.*
• **boom, roar, rumble, pound**
❷ *'What do you want?' a voice thundered.*
• **shout, roar, bellow, bark, boom**

thunderous *ADJECTIVE*
The speech was greeted with thunderous applause.
• **deafening, resounding, tumultuous, loud, booming**
OPPOSITE **quiet**

tick *VERB*
A clock was ticking in the background.
• **click, make a tick, beat**
➤ **tick someone off**
(*informal*) *She ticked him off for being late.*
• **reprimand, reproach, scold**
(*informal*) **tell off**

ticket *NOUN*
❶ *We won free cinema tickets.*
• **pass, permit, token, voucher, coupon**
❷ *What does it say on the price ticket?*
• **label, tag, sticker, tab**

tide *NOUN*
Lots of seaweed gets washed up by the tide.
• **current**
– An incoming tide is a **flow tide** and an outgoing tide is an **ebb tide**.
– The tide is fully in at **high tide** and fully out at **low tide**.

tidy *ADJECTIVE*
I like to keep my room tidy.
• **neat, orderly, uncluttered, trim, spruce, in good order**
IDIOM **spick and span**
OPPOSITES **untidy, messy**

tie *VERB*
❶ *He was tying string around the parcel.*
• **bind, fasten, hitch, strap, loop, knot, lace, truss**
– To tie up a boat is to **moor** it.
– To tie up an animal is to **tether** it.
OPPOSITE **untie**
❷ *The top two players tied with each other.*
• **draw, be equal, be level**

tie *NOUN*
❶ *The final score was a tie.*
• **draw, dead heat**
❷ *They still maintain close family ties.*
• **bond, connection, link, association, relationship**

tier *NOUN*
The seats are arranged in tiers.
• **row, line, rank, level, layer, storey**

tight *ADJECTIVE*
❶ *The lid was too tight to unscrew.*
• **firm, fast, secure**
– If something is so tight that air cannot get through, it is **airtight**.
– If something is so tight that water cannot get through, it is **watertight**.
OPPOSITE **loose**
❷ *These jeans are quite tight.*
• **close-fitting, snug, figure-hugging**
OPPOSITES **loose, roomy**
❸ *Make sure that the ropes are tight.*
• **taut, tense, stretched, rigid**
OPPOSITE **slack**
❹ *We had to squeeze into a tight space.*
• **cramped, confined, compact, limited, small, narrow, poky**
OPPOSITE **spacious**
❺ *He can be very tight with his money.*
• **mean, stingy, miserly, tight-fisted**
OPPOSITE **generous**

tighten *VERB*
❶ *She tightened her grip on the rail.*
• **increase, strengthen, harden, stiffen**
❷ *You need to tighten the ropes.*
• **pull tighter, stretch, make taut, make tense**
OPPOSITE **loosen**

till *VERB*
Farmers use tractors to till the land.
• **cultivate, farm, plough, dig, work**

tilt *VERB*
He tilted his head to one side.
• **lean, incline, tip, slope, slant, angle**
– When a ship tilts to one side, it **lists**.

timber *NOUN*
❶ *He bought some timber to build a shed.*
• **wood,** (*North American*) **lumber**
❷ *I could hear the timbers of the ship creaking.*
• **beam, plank, board, spar**

time *NOUN*
❶ *Autumn is my favourite time of the year.*
• **phase, season, period**
❷ *He spent a short time living in China.*
• **period, while, term, spell, stretch**
❸ *Shakespeare lived in the time of Elizabeth I.*
• **era, age, days, epoch, period**
❹ *Is this a good time to talk?*
• **moment, occasion, opportunity**
❺ *Try to keep time with the music.*
• **tempo, beat, rhythm**
➤ **on time**
Please try to be on time.
• **punctual, prompt**

WORD WEB

Units for measuring time:

➤ second
➤ minute
➤ hour
➤ day
➤ week
➤ fortnight
➤ month
➤ quarter
➤ year
➤ decade
➤ century
➤ millennium

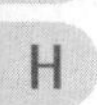

Devices used to measure time:

- ➤ calendar
- ➤ clock
- ➤ hourglass
- ➤ metronome
- ➤ pocket watch
- ➤ stopwatch
- ➤ sundial
- ➤ timer
- ➤ watch
- ➤ wristwatch

timetable *NOUN*
I have a busy timetable this week.
• **schedule, programme, rota, diary**

timid *ADJECTIVE*
He spoke in a timid little voice.
• **shy, bashful, modest, nervous, fearful, shrinking, retiring, sheepish**
OPPOSITES brave, confident

tinge *VERB*
❶ *The clouds were tinged with gold.*
• **colour, stain, tint, wash, flush**
❷ *Our relief was tinged with sadness.*
• **flavour, colour, touch**

tinge *NOUN*
❶ *The walls are white with just a tinge of blue.*
• **tint, colour, shade, hue, tone**
❷ *There was a tinge of sadness in her voice.*
• **trace, note, touch, suggestion, hint, streak**

tingle *VERB*
My ears were tingling with the cold.
• **prickle, sting**

tingle *NOUN*
❶ *She felt a tingle in her toes.*
• **prickling, stinging**
IDIOM **pins and needles**
❷ *He felt a tingle of excitement.*
• **thrill, sensation, quiver, shiver**

tinker *VERB*
He was outside, tinkering with his bike.
• **fiddle, play about, dabble, meddle, tamper**

tint *NOUN*
The paper was white with a faint tint of blue.
• **shade, tone, colour, hue, tinge**

tiny *ADJECTIVE*
On the leaf was a tiny yellow tree frog.
• **very small, minute, minuscule, miniature, mini, microscopic, diminutive** (*informal*) **teeny, titchy**
OPPOSITES huge, giant

tip *NOUN*
❶ *The arrow had a poisoned tip.*
• **end, point, nib**
❷ *The tip of the mountain was covered in snow.*
• **peak, top, summit, cap, crown, pinnacle**
❸ *Here are some tips on how to draw faces.*
• **hint, suggestion, pointer, piece of advice**
❹ *We took a load of rubbish to the tip.*
• **dump, rubbish dump**

tip *VERB*
❶ *Tip your head back to stop a nosebleed.*
• **lean, tilt, incline, slope, slant, angle**
– When a ship tips slightly to one side, it **lists**.
❷ *She tipped everything onto the counter.*
• **empty, turn out, dump, unload**
➤ **tip over**
The surfboard tipped over on top of him.
• **overturn, roll over, keel over, capsize**
➤ **tip something over**
I tipped the jug over by accident.
• **knock over, overturn, topple, upset, upend**

tire *VERB*
My legs were beginning to tire.
• **get tired, weaken, flag, droop**
OPPOSITES revive, strengthen
➤ **tire someone out**
The long walk home had tired her out.
• **exhaust, wear out, drain, weary**
OPPOSITES refresh, invigorate

tired *ADJECTIVE*
We were all feeling tired after such a long day.
• **exhausted, fatigued, weary, worn out, listless, sleepy, drowsy**
(*informal*) **all in, whacked, bushed, dead beat**
OPPOSITES energetic, refreshed
➤ **be tired of something**
I'm tired of waiting.
• **be bored with, be fed up with, be sick of, be weary of, have had enough of**

tiring *ADJECTIVE*
Digging the garden is tiring work.
• **exhausting, taxing, demanding, arduous, strenuous, laborious, gruelling, wearying**
OPPOSITE refreshing

title *NOUN*
❶ *You need a good title for your story.*
• **name, heading**
– The title above a newspaper story is a **headline**.
– A title or description next to a picture is a **caption**.
❷ *She won two Olympic titles.*
• **championship, crown**
❸ *What is your preferred title?*
• **form of address, designation, rank**

together *ADVERB*
❶ *We wrote the song together.*
• **jointly, as a group, in collaboration, with each other, side by side**
OPPOSITES independently, separately
❷ *Let's sing the first verse together.*
• **simultaneously, at the same time, all at once, in chorus, in unison**

toil *VERB*
❶ *They had been toiling in the fields all day.*
• **work hard, labour, sweat, slave**
(*informal*) **grind, slog**
❷ *Every morning he toiled up the hill.*
• **struggle, trudge, plod**

toilet *NOUN*
They have a downstairs toilet.
• **lavatory, WC, bathroom**
(*informal*) **loo**
– A toilet in a camp or barracks is a **latrine**.

token *NOUN*
❶ *You can exchange this token for a free drink.*
• **voucher, coupon, ticket, counter**
❷ *Please accept this gift as a small token of our gratitude.*
• **sign, symbol, mark, expression, indication, proof, demonstration**

told
past tense see **tell**

tolerant *ADJECTIVE*
Do you think that people are more tolerant nowadays?
• **open-minded, broad-minded, easy-going, lenient, sympathetic, understanding, indulgent, forbearing**
OPPOSITE intolerant

tolerate *VERB*
❶ *I will not tolerate bad manners.*
• **accept, permit, allow, put up with**
❷ *Some species can tolerate extreme temperatures.*
• **bear, endure, stand, abide, suffer, stomach**

tomb *NOUN*
They discovered the tomb of an Egyptian pharaoh.
• **burial chamber, crypt, grave, mausoleum, sepulchre, vault**
– An underground passage containing several tombs is a **catacomb**.

tone *NOUN*
❶ *There was an angry tone to his voice.*
• **note, sound, quality, intonation**
❷ *The room is painted in dark earthy tones.*
• **colour, hue, shade, tint**
❸ *Eerie music sets the right tone for the film.*
• **feeling, mood, atmosphere, character, spirit**

took
past tense see **take**

a b c d e f g h i j k l m n o p q r s t u v w x y z

A B C D E F G H I J K L M N O P Q R S T U V W X Y Z

tool *NOUN*
The shed is full of gardening tools.
• **implement, utensil, device, gadget, instrument, appliance, contraption** (*informal*) **gizmo**

tooth *NOUN*

WORD WEB

Types of teeth:

➤ **canine (tooth)**
➤ **incisor**
➤ **molar**
➤ **premolar**
➤ **wisdom tooth**

- Upper canine teeth are sometimes known as **eye teeth.**
- A child's first set of teeth are its **milk teeth** or **baby teeth.**
- The canine teeth of a wild animal are its **fangs.**
- The long pointed teeth of an elephant or walrus are its **tusks.**

Common dental problems:

➤ **cavity**
➤ **plaque**
➤ **tartar**
➤ **tooth decay or caries**

SEE ALSO **dentist**

top *NOUN*
❶ *They climbed to the top of the hill.*
• **peak, summit, tip, crown, crest, head, height**
OPPOSITES bottom, base
❷ *The desk top was covered with papers.*
• **surface**
❸ *Remember to screw the top back on.*
• **lid, cap, cover, stopper**

top *ADJECTIVE*
❶ *Their office is on the top floor.*
• **highest, topmost, uppermost, upper**
OPPOSITES bottom, lowest
❷ *We set off at top speed.*
• **greatest, maximum, utmost**
OPPOSITES minimum, lowest
❸ *He is one of Europe's top chefs.*
• **leading, foremost, finest, best, principal, superior**
OPPOSITE minor

top *VERB*
❶ *The cake was topped with icing.*
• **cover, decorate, garnish, crown**
❷ *She is hoping to top her personal best.*
• **beat, better, exceed, outdo, surpass**

topic *NOUN*
What was the topic of the conversation?
• **subject, theme, issue, matter, question, talking point**

topical *ADJECTIVE*
Each week the programme discusses topical news items.
• **current, recent, contemporary, up to date, up to the minute**

topple *VERB*
❶ *His chair suddenly toppled backwards.*
• **fall, tumble, tip over, keel over, overbalance**
❷ *High winds toppled trees and brought down power lines.*
• **knock down, bring down, push over, overturn, upset, upend**
❸ *They plotted in secret to topple the president.*
• **overthrow, bring down, remove from office, oust, unseat**

tore
past tense see **tear**

torment *VERB*
❶ *He was tormented by bad dreams.*
• **afflict, torture, plague, haunt, distress, harrow, rack**
❷ *Stop tormenting the poor animal.*
• **tease, taunt, harass, pester, bully**
– To torment someone continually is to **persecute** or **victimize** them.

torrent *NOUN*
❶ *A torrent of water flowed down the hill.*
• **flood, gush, rush, stream, spate, cascade**
❷ *We were caught in a torrent of rain.*
• **downpour, deluge, cloudburst**
❸ *It all came out in a torrent of words.*
• **outpouring, outburst, stream, flood, tide, barrage**

torrential *ADJECTIVE*
The rain was torrential all day.
• **heavy, violent, severe, driving, lashing**

toss *VERB*
❶ *He tossed a pebble into the pond.*
• **throw, hurl, fling, cast, pitch, lob, sling**
(*informal*) **chuck**
❷ *We'll toss a coin to decide.*
• **flip, spin**
❸ *The little boat was tossing about in the waves.*
• **pitch, lurch, bob, roll, rock, heave**
❹ *She tossed and turned, unable to get to sleep.*
• **thrash about, flail, writhe**

total *ADJECTIVE*
❶ *What was your total score?*
• **complete, whole, full, entire, overall, combined**
OPPOSITE partial
❷ *The party was a total disaster.*
• **complete, utter, absolute, thorough, sheer, downright, out-and-out**

total *NOUN*
A total of 5 million viewers tuned in.
• **sum, whole, entirety**

total *VERB*
So far the donations total 2000 euros.
• **add up to, amount to, come to, make**

totally *ADVERB*
I totally agree with you.
• **completely, wholly, entirely, fully, utterly, absolutely, thoroughly**
OPPOSITE partly

totter *VERB*
The little girl tottered across the floor.
• **stagger, teeter, stumble, reel, wobble**

touch *VERB*
❶ *She gently touched him on the shoulder.*
• **feel, handle, stroke, fondle, caress, pat, pet**
❷ *The car just touched the gatepost.*
• **brush, graze, skim, contact**
❸ *Nothing in the room had been touched.*
• **move, disturb, interfere with, meddle with, tamper with**
❹ *Temperatures can touch 45 degrees in summer.*
• **reach, rise to, attain**
(*informal*) hit
❺ *I was deeply touched by her letter.*
• **affect, move, stir**
➤ **touch on something**
You touched on the subject of money.
• **refer to, mention, raise, broach**

touch *NOUN*
❶ *I felt a light touch on my arm.*
• **pat, stroke, tap, caress, contact**
❷ *There's a touch of frost in the air.*
• **hint, trace, suggestion, tinge**
❸ *She has added her own touch to the songs.*
• **style, feel, quality**
❹ *Are you still in touch with the family?*
• **contact, communication, correspondence**

touching *ADJECTIVE*
The film ends with a touching final scene.
• **moving, affecting, emotional, poignant, heart-warming, tear-jerking**

touchy *ADJECTIVE*
He's very touchy about his weight.
• **easily offended, sensitive, irritable**

tough *ADJECTIVE*
❶ *You'll need tough shoes for the climb.*
• **strong, sturdy, robust, durable, resilient, hard-wearing, stout, substantial**
OPPOSITE flimsy
❷ *She's tougher than she looks.*
• **strong, resilient, determined, robust, rugged, hardened**
OPPOSITE weak
❸ *The team struggled against tough opposition.*
• **strong, stiff, powerful, resistant, determined, stubborn**
OPPOSITES weak, feeble
❹ *Don't be too tough on her.*
• **firm, strict, severe, stern, hard-hitting**
OPPOSITES soft, lenient
❺ *The meat was overcooked and tough.*
• **chewy, leathery, rubbery**
OPPOSITE tender

A B C D E F G H I J K L M N O P Q R S T U V W X Y Z

❻ *The first part of the climb is the toughest.*
• **demanding, strenuous, arduous, laborious, gruelling, taxing, exhausting**
OPPOSITE easy
❼ *That's a tough question to answer.*
• **difficult, hard, tricky, puzzling, baffling, knotty, thorny**
OPPOSITES easy, straightforward

tour *NOUN*
We went on a sightseeing tour of the city.
• **trip, excursion, visit, journey, expedition, outing, jaunt**

tourist *NOUN*
The cathedral was full of tourists.
• **sightseer, holidaymaker, traveller, visitor**

tournament *NOUN*
We reached the finals of the basketball tournament.
• **championship, competition, contest, series**

tow *VERB*
Horses used to tow barges along the river.
• **pull, haul, tug, drag, draw**

tower *NOUN*
The abbey has a small tower.
– A small tower on a castle or other building is a **turret**.
– A church tower is a **steeple**.
– The pointed structure on a steeple is a **spire**.
– The part of a tower with a bell is a **belfry**.
– The tall tower of a mosque is a **minaret**.

tower *VERB*
➤ **tower above or over something**
The monument towers above the landscape.
• **rise above, stand above, dominate, loom over, overshadow**

town *NOUN*
They live in a seaside town near Melbourne.
– A town with its own local council is a **borough**.
– A large and important town is a **city**.
– Several towns that merge into each other are a **conurbation**.
– The people who live in a town are the **townspeople**.
– A word meaning 'to do with a town or city' is **urban**.

toxic *ADJECTIVE*
The flask contains a toxic gas.
• **poisonous, deadly, lethal, harmful**
OPPOSITE harmless

toy *NOUN*
He found a box full of old toys.
• **game, plaything**

trace *NOUN*
❶ *He vanished without a trace.*
• **evidence, sign, mark, indication, hint, clue, track, trail**
❷ *They found traces of blood on the carpet.*
• **vestige, remnant, spot, speck, drop, touch**

trace *VERB*
The police have been trying to trace her.
• **track down, discover, find, uncover, unearth**

track *NOUN*
❶ *They followed the bear's tracks for miles.*
• **footprint, footmark, trail, scent, spoor**
❷ *A rough track leads past the farm.*
• **path, pathway, footpath, trail**
❸ *The race is a single lap around the track.*
• **racetrack, circuit, course**
❹ *They are laying the track for the new tram system.*
• **line, rails**

track *VERB*
Astronomers are tracking the comet's path.
• **follow, trace, trail, pursue, shadow, stalk**

➤ **track someone down**
It took years to track everyone down.
• **find, discover, trace, hunt down, sniff out, run to ground**

tract *NOUN*
They had to cross a vast tract of desert.
• **area, expanse, stretch**

trade *NOUN*
❶ *The trade in antiques has been booming recently.*
• **business, dealing, buying and selling, commerce, market**
❷ *He took up the same trade as his father.*
• **occupation, profession, work, career, business, craft**

trade *VERB*
➤ **trade in something**
The company trades in second-hand computers.
• **deal in, do business in, buy and sell**

tradition *NOUN*
The Moon Festival is a Chinese tradition.
• **custom, convention, practice, habit, ritual, observance, institution**

traditional *ADJECTIVE*
❶ *The Maya have preserved their traditional way of life.*
• **long-established, time-honoured, age-old, customary, habitual, ritual**
OPPOSITE non-traditional
❷ *The dancers wore traditional costumes.*
• **folk, ethnic, national, regional, historical**
❸ *They chose to have a traditional wedding.*
• **conventional, orthodox, regular, standard, classic**
OPPOSITE unorthodox

tragedy *NOUN*
❶ *'Romeo and Juliet' is a tragedy by Shakespeare.*
OPPOSITE comedy
❷ *The accident at sea was a real tragedy.*
• **disaster, catastrophe, calamity, misfortune**

tragic *ADJECTIVE*
❶ *He died in a tragic accident.*
• **disastrous, catastrophic, calamitous, terrible, horrendous, appalling, dreadful, unfortunate, unlucky**
❷ *It is a tragic story of doomed love.*
• **sad, unhappy, sorrowful, mournful, pitiful, heart-rending, wretched, pathetic**
OPPOSITES light-hearted, comic

trail *NOUN*
❶ *Scientists have been following the trail left by the comet.*
• **track, stream, wake**
❷ *There is a bike trail through the woods.*
• **path, pathway, track, route**
➤ **on the trail of someone**
Police have been on the trail of the thieves.
• **on the track of, on the hunt for, in pursuit of, following the scent of**

trail *VERB*
❶ *Plain-clothes officers are trailing the suspect.*
• **follow, track, chase, pursue, shadow, stalk**
(*informal*) **tail**
❷ *She trailed her suitcase behind her.*
• **pull, tow, drag, draw, haul**
❸ *A few walkers trailed behind the others.*
• **fall behind, lag, straggle**
OPPOSITE lead
➤ **trail away or off**
Her voice began to trail away.
• **fade, grow faint, peter out, dwindle**

train *NOUN*
It was an unusual train of events.
• **sequence, series, string, chain, succession**

train *VERB*
❶ *All members of the crew had to be trained to scuba-dive.*
• **coach, instruct, teach, tutor, school, drill**

❷ *They are training hard for the Olympics.*
• **practise, exercise, get into shape** (*informal*) **work out**
❸ *He trained his gun on the bridge.*
• **aim, point, direct, target, focus, level**

trainer *NOUN*
She is a professional voice trainer.
• **coach, instructor, teacher, tutor**

tramp *NOUN*
❶ *I had to sleep rough like a tramp.*
• **homeless person, vagrant, down-and-out**
❷ *We went for a tramp through the woods.*
• **trek, walk, hike, ramble**
❸ *I could hear the tramp of marching feet.*
• **tread, stamp, march, plod**

tramp *VERB*
They tramped across the muddy field.
• **trudge, trek, traipse, stamp, march, plod**

trample *VERB*
Don't trample the flowers!
• **tread on, stamp on, walk over, crush, flatten, squash**

trance *NOUN*
The fortune-teller went into a trance.
• **daze, stupor, reverie, hypnotic state**

tranquil *ADJECTIVE*
❶ *They led a tranquil life in the country.*
• **calm, peaceful, quiet, restful, sedate, relaxing**
(*informal*) **laid-back**
OPPOSITES busy, hectic
❷ *Her face now wore a tranquil expression.*
• **still, calm, placid, serene, undisturbed, unruffled**

transfer *VERB*
Some paintings were transferred to the new gallery.
• **move, remove, shift, relocate, convey, hand over**

transform *VERB*
They transformed the attic into an office.
• **convert, turn, change, alter, adapt, modify, rework**

translate *VERB*
The book has been translated into 36 languages.
• **interpret, convert, put, render, reword**
– A person who translates a foreign language is a **translator**.
– A person who translates what someone is saying into another language is an **interpreter**.
– An expert in languages is a **linguist**.

transmit *VERB*
❶ *He was secretly transmitting messages in code.*
• **send, communicate, relay, convey, dispatch**
– To transmit a programme on radio or TV is to **broadcast** it.
OPPOSITE receive
❷ *Can the disease be transmitted to humans?*
• **pass on, spread, carry**

transparent *ADJECTIVE*
The insect's wings are almost transparent.
• **clear**
(*informal*) **see-through**
– Something which is not fully transparent, but allows light to shine through, is **translucent**.

transport *VERB*
Oil is transported in huge tanker ships.
• **carry, convey, transfer, ship, ferry, move, shift, take, bear**

transport *NOUN*
For types of transport see **aircraft, boat, vehicle**.

trap *NOUN*
❶ *The animal was caught in a trap.*
• **snare, net**
❷ *The last question might be a trap.*
• **trick, deception, ruse, ploy**

trap *VERB*
❶ *Sea creatures can get trapped in plastic bags.*
• **catch, snare, ensnare, capture, corner**
❷ *She was trapped into admitting she had lied.*
• **trick, dupe, deceive, fool**

trash (*informal*) *NOUN*
Sometimes I just feel like reading trash.
• **rubbish, drivel, nonsense**

travel *VERB*
I usually travel to school by bus.
• **go, journey, move along, proceed, progress**
– When birds travel from one country to another they **migrate**.
– When people travel to another country to live there they **emigrate**.

traveller *NOUN*
A busload of weary travellers arrived at the hotel.
• **passenger, commuter, tourist, holidaymaker, backpacker**
– A person who travels to a religious place is a **pilgrim**.
– A person who travels illegally on a ship or plane is a **stowaway**.
– A person who likes travelling round the world is a **globetrotter**.

treacherous *ADJECTIVE*
❶ *He was told about a treacherous plot to kill him.*
• **disloyal, traitorous, unfaithful, untrustworthy, double-crossing**
– A treacherous act is **treachery** or **betrayal**.
– A treacherous person is a **traitor**.
OPPOSITE loyal
❷ *The roads are often treacherous in winter.*
• **dangerous, hazardous, perilous, unsafe, risky**
OPPOSITE safe

tread *VERB*
Please tread carefully.
• **step, walk, proceed**

➤ **tread on**
Don't tread on the wet cement!
• **step on, walk on, stamp on, trample, crush, flatten, squash**

treasure *NOUN*
Divers are searching for sunken treasure.
• **riches, valuables, wealth, fortune**
– A store of treasure is a **cache** or **hoard**.

treasure *VERB*
I will always treasure the memory.
• **cherish, prize, value, hold dear, set store by**

treat *VERB*
❶ *They treated me as part of the family.*
• **behave towards, act towards**
❷ *We are treating the case as murder.*
• **regard, view, look on, consider**
❸ *This question is treated in more detail in the next chapter.*
• **deal with, discuss, explore, handle, tackle**
❹ *Two people are being treated for minor injuries.*
• **tend, nurse, attend to**
❺ *Let me treat you to lunch.*
• **pay for, stand, buy, offer**

treatment *NOUN*
❶ *The hospital is for the treatment of sick animals.*
• **care, nursing, healing**
❷ *This is a new treatment for asthma.*
• **remedy, therapy, medication**
– Emergency treatment at the scene of an accident is **first aid**.
❸ *Old documents need careful treatment.*
• **handling, care, management, use**

treaty *NOUN*
The two sides signed a peace treaty.
• **agreement, pact, contract, settlement**

A B C D E F G H I J K L M N O P Q R S T U V W X Y Z

tree *NOUN*

WORD WEB

Some varieties of tree:

➤ alder	➤ juniper
➤ almond	➤ larch
➤ apple	➤ lime
➤ ash	➤ maple or acer
➤ aspen	➤ monkey puzzle
➤ baobab	➤ oak
➤ banyan	➤ olive
➤ bay or laurel	➤ palm
➤ beech	➤ pear
➤ birch	➤ pine
➤ cedar	➤ plane
➤ cherry	➤ plum
➤ chestnut	➤ poplar
➤ cypress	➤ redwood
➤ elder	➤ rowan or mountain ash
➤ elm	➤ rubber tree
➤ eucalyptus	➤ silver birch
➤ fir	➤ spruce
➤ flame tree	➤ sycamore
➤ fruit tree	➤ tamarind
➤ hawthorn	➤ willow
➤ hazel	➤ yew
➤ holly	
➤ jujube	

- Trees which lose their leaves in winter are **deciduous.**
- Trees which have leaves all year round are **evergreen.**
- Trees which grow cones are **conifers.**
- A young tree is a **sapling.**
- An area covered with trees is a **wooded** area or **woodland.**
- A large area covered with trees and undergrowth is a **forest.**
- A small group of trees is a **copse** or **coppice.**
- An area planted with fruit trees is an **orchard.**

tremble *VERB*
The poor dog was trembling with cold.
• **shake, shiver, quake, quiver, shudder**

tremendous *ADJECTIVE*
❶ *There was a tremendous explosion.*
• **very great, huge, enormous, massive, immense, colossal, mighty**
(*informal*) **terrific**
❷ *Winning the cup would be a tremendous achievement.*
• **marvellous, magnificent, wonderful, superb, stupendous, extraordinary, outstanding**
(*informal*) **brilliant, fantastic, terrific**

tremor *NOUN*
There was a tremor in her voice.
• **trembling, shaking, quavering, quivering, vibration, wobble**

trend *NOUN*
❶ *There is a general trend towards healthier eating.*
• **tendency, movement, shift, leaning, inclination, drift**
❷ *Have you seen the latest trend in footwear?*
• **fashion, style, craze, fad, vogue**

trial *NOUN*
❶ *The film is about a murder trial.*
• **case, hearing, lawsuit**
– A military trial is a **court martial.**
❷ *Scientists are conducting trials on a new vaccine.*
• **test, experiment, check, evaluation**

tribe *NOUN*
Boudicca was queen of the Iceni tribe.
• **people, ethnic group, clan**

trick *NOUN*
❶ *Let's play a trick on her!*
• **joke, practical joke, prank**
❷ *It is a trick to get your log-in details.*
• **deception, ruse, fraud, hoax, ploy**
(*informal*) **con, scam**

trick *VERB*
He tricked them into believing he was a police officer.
• **deceive, dupe, fool, hoodwink, cheat, swindle**
(*informal*) **con**

trickle *VERB*
The sweat trickled down his nose.
• **dribble, drip, leak, seep, ooze**
OPPOSITE gush

trickle *NOUN*
The water flow had slowed to a trickle.
• **dribble, drip**
OPPOSITE gush

tricky *ADJECTIVE*
❶ *I found myself in a tricky situation.*
• **difficult, awkward, problematic, complicated, delicate, ticklish**
OPPOSITES simple, straightforward
❷ *I wouldn't trust her–she's tricky.*
• **crafty, cunning, sly, wily, devious**

trigger *VERB*
The smoke must have triggered her asthma attack.
• **set off, start, activate, cause, provoke, spark**

trim *ADJECTIVE*
He likes to keep his garden trim.
• **neat, orderly, tidy, well kept, smart, spruce**
OPPOSITE untidy

trim *VERB*
❶ *He was at the mirror trimming his beard.*
• **cut, clip, shorten, crop, prune, pare, neaten, tidy**
❷ *The gown was trimmed with fur.*
• **edge, fringe, decorate, adorn, embellish**

trip *VERB*
She tripped on the loose carpet.
• **catch your foot, stumble, fall, slip, stagger**

trip *NOUN*
We went on a trip to the seaside.
• **journey, visit, outing, excursion, expedition, jaunt, break**

triumph *NOUN*
The season ended in triumph for the team.
• **victory, success, win, conquest**

triumphant *ADJECTIVE*
❶ *He took a photo of the triumphant team.*
• **winning, victorious, conquering, successful**
OPPOSITE unsuccessful
❷ *A triumphant look spread across her face.*
• **elated, exultant, joyful, gleeful, jubilant**

trivial *ADJECTIVE*
Don't worry about trivial details.
• **unimportant, insignificant, minor, slight, trifling, negligible, petty, frivolous**
OPPOSITES important, significant

troop *NOUN*
A troop of tourists crossed the square.
• **group, band, party, body, company**

troop *VERB*
We all trooped into the main hall.
• **walk, march, proceed, stream, file**

troops *PLURAL NOUN*
see **army**

trophy *NOUN*
She has won several international tennis trophies.
• **cup, prize, award, medal**

trouble *NOUN*
❶ *He and his family may be in trouble.*
• **difficulty, hardship, suffering, unhappiness, distress, misfortune, pain, sadness, sorrow, worry**
❷ *There were reports of trouble outside the ground.*
• **disorder, unrest, disturbance, commotion, fighting, violence**
❸ *The trouble with this computer is that it's very slow.*
• **problem, difficulty, disadvantage, drawback**
❹ *Please don't go to any trouble.*
• **bother, inconvenience, effort, pains**

trouble *VERB*
❶ *Something must be troubling her.*
• **distress, upset, bother, worry, concern, pain, torment, perturb**
IDIOM **prey on your mind**
❷ *I don't want to trouble them at this hour.*
• **disturb, bother, inconvenience, impose on, put out**

troublesome *ADJECTIVE*
❶ *Do you find the heat troublesome?*
• **annoying, irritating, trying, tiresome, bothersome, inconvenient, nagging**
❷ *The boys have been troublesome all day.*
• **difficult, awkward, unruly, unmanageable, disobedient, uncooperative**

trousers *PLURAL NOUN*
see **clothes**

truce *NOUN*
The two sides agreed on a truce.
• **ceasefire, armistice, peace**

true *ADJECTIVE*
❶ *The film is based on a true story.*
• **real, factual, actual, historical**
OPPOSITES fictional, made-up
❷ *What if the rumours are true?*
• **accurate, correct, right, undeniable**
OPPOSITES untrue, false
❸ *The play aims to present a true picture of war.*
• **genuine, real, faithful, authentic, accurate, proper, exact**
OPPOSITES false, misleading
❹ *You've always been a true friend to me.*
• **faithful, loyal, constant, devoted, sincere, trustworthy, reliable, dependable**
OPPOSITE disloyal

trunk *NOUN*
❶ *He kept his things in an old travelling trunk.*
• **chest, case, box, crate, suitcase, coffer**
❷ *The trunk of a palm tree can bend in the wind.*
• **stem, stock**
❸ *Try to keep your trunk straight.*
• **torso, body, frame**

trust *VERB*
❶ *I've never really trusted her.*
• **be sure of, have confidence in, have faith in, believe in**
❷ *Can I trust you to keep a secret?*
• **rely on, depend on, count on, bank on**
❸ *I trust you are well.*
• **hope, assume, presume, take it**

trust *NOUN*
❶ *His supporters began to lose trust in him.*
• **belief, confidence, faith**
❷ *I'm putting the documents in your trust.*
• **responsibility, safe-keeping, hands**

trustworthy *ADJECTIVE*
She was the only trustworthy member of the crew.
• **reliable, dependable, loyal, true, honourable, responsible**
OPPOSITE untrustworthy

truth *NOUN*
❶ *They finally accepted the truth of his story.*
• **accuracy, correctness, truthfulness, reliability, validity, authenticity** (*formal*) **veracity**
OPPOSITES inaccuracy, falseness
❷ *The truth slowly began to dawn on him.*
• **facts, reality**
OPPOSITES lies, falsehood

truthful *ADJECTIVE*
❶ *I've not been entirely truthful with you.*
• **honest, frank, sincere, straight, straightforward**
OPPOSITE dishonest
❷ *Please give a truthful answer.*
• **accurate, correct, true, proper, faithful, genuine**
OPPOSITES untrue, false

try *VERB*

❶ *I'm trying to improve my technique.*
• **attempt, endeavour, make an effort, aim, strive**
❷ *Would you like to try a larger size?*
• **test, try out, sample, evaluate, experiment with**
(*informal*) **check out**

try *NOUN*

❶ *We may not succeed, but it's still worth a try.*
• **attempt, effort, go**
(*informal*) **shot, bash, crack, stab**
❷ *Have a try of this smoothie.*
• **test, trial, sample, taste**

trying *ADJECTIVE*

❶ *It's been a very trying day.*
• **difficult, demanding, stressful, frustrating, fraught**
OPPOSITE relaxing
❷ *My sister can be trying at times.*
• **annoying, irritating, tiresome, maddening, exasperating, infuriating**

tub *NOUN*

We shared a large tub of popcorn.
• **pot, drum, carton, jar, barrel, cask, vat**

tube *NOUN*

Roll the paper into a tube.
• **cylinder, pipe**
– A flexible tube for water is a **hose**.

tuck *VERB*

He tucked his shirt into his jeans.
• **push, insert, slip, stick, stuff**

tuft *NOUN*

The goat was munching on a few tufts of grass.
• **clump, bunch, wisp**

tug *VERB*

❶ *I tugged the rope to test it.*
• **pull, jerk, pluck, wrench**
(*informal*) **yank**
❷ *We tugged the sledge up the hill.*
• **drag, pull, tow, haul, lug, draw, heave**

tumble *VERB*

❶ *The whole bridge collapsed and tumbled into the river.*
• **topple, fall, drop, pitch, plummet, plunge, crash**
❷ *I tumbled into bed and fell straight asleep.*
• **dive, flop, sink, slump, stumble**
❸ *Her long hair tumbled down her back.*
• **flow, fall, cascade**

tumult *NOUN*

His voice could not be heard above the tumult.
• **uproar, clamour, commotion, din, racket, rumpus, hubbub**

tune *NOUN*

I am learning a new tune on the guitar.
• **melody, song, air, theme**

tunnel *NOUN*

The prisoners dug a tunnel under the wall.
– A tunnel dug by rabbits is a **burrow** and a system of burrows is a **warren**.
– A tunnel beneath a road is a **subway** or **underpass**.

tunnel *VERB*

Moles tunnel in search of earthworms.
• **burrow, dig, mine, bore, excavate**

turmoil *NOUN*

Her mind was in a state of turmoil.
• **chaos, upheaval, uproar, disorder, unrest, commotion, disturbance, mayhem**
OPPOSITES peace, order

turn *VERB*

❶ *The Earth turns on its axis once every 24 hours.*
• **go round, revolve, rotate, roll, spin, swivel, pivot, twirl, whirl**
❷ *Turn left at the end of the street.*
• **change direction, change course, wheel round**
– To turn unexpectedly is to **swerve** or **veer** off course.
– To turn and go back in the direction you came from is to **do a U-turn**.

❸ *He suddenly turned pale.*
• **become, go, grow**
❹ *They turned the attic into a spare room.*
• **convert, adapt, change, alter, modify, transform**
➤ **turn something down**
I turned down the offer of a lift.
• **decline, refuse, reject, spurn, rebuff**
➤ **turn something off**
Please turn off the computer when you leave.
• **switch off, put off, shut down, deactivate**
➤ **turn something on**
How do you turn on your phone?
• **switch on, put on, start up, activate**
➤ **turn out**
❶ *Everything turned out well in the end.*
• **end up, come out, work out, happen**
(*informal*) **pan out**
❷ *The photo turned out to be a fake.*
• **prove, be found**
➤ **turn up**
Some friends turned up unexpectedly.
• **arrive, appear, drop in**
(*informal*) **show up**
➤ **turn something up**
Can you turn up the volume?
• **increase, raise, amplify, intensify**

turn *NOUN*
❶ *Give the handle several turns.*
• **spin, rotation, revolution, twist, swivel**
❷ *We came to a turn in the road.*
• **bend, corner, curve, angle, junction, turning**
– A sharp turn in a road is a **hairpin bend**.
❸ *Whose turn is it to do the washing up?*
• **time, go, stint, slot, try, chance, opportunity**
(*informal*) **shot**
❹ *My sister and I are doing a comedy turn in the show.*
• **act, performance, scene, sketch**
❺ (*informal*) *You gave me quite a turn there!*
• **fright, scare, shock, start, surprise**

tutor *NOUN*
She is a professional singing tutor.
• **teacher, instructor, trainer, coach**

twig *NOUN*
They gathered twigs to make a fire.
• **stick, stalk, stem, shoot**

twin *NOUN*
❶ *Two of my cousins are twins.*
– Twins who look alike are **identical twins** and twins who do not look alike are **unidentical twins**.
❷ *Venus was once thought to be a twin of the Earth.*
• **double, duplicate, look-alike, match, clone**

twinkle *VERB*
The city lights twinkled in the distance.
• **sparkle, glitter, shine, glisten, glimmer, glint, gleam, flicker, wink**

twirl *VERB*
❶ *He paced up and down, twirling his umbrella.*
• **twiddle, twist**
❷ *A few skaters twirled on the ice rink.*
• **spin, turn, whirl, revolve, rotate, pirouette**

twist *VERB*
❶ *Twist the handle to open the door.*
• **turn, rotate, revolve, swivel**
– To twist off a lid or cap is to **unscrew** it.
❷ *The road twists through the hills.*
• **wind, weave, curve, zigzag**
❸ *He twisted and turned in his sleep.*
• **toss, writhe, wriggle**
❹ *Heat can twist metal out of shape.*
• **bend, buckle, warp, crumple, mangle, distort**
❺ *She twisted her hair into a knot.*
• **wind, loop, coil, curl, entwine**

twist *NOUN*
❶ *Give the handle a sharp twist.*
• **turn, spin, rotation, revolution, swivel**
❷ *The plot is full of unexpected twists.*
• **turning, surprise, revelation, upset**

twisted *ADJECTIVE*
The trunk of the tree was twisted with age.
• **gnarled, warped, buckled, misshapen, deformed**

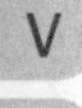

twitch *VERB*

One of the upstairs curtains twitched.

• **jerk, quiver, tremble, shudder, start**

two *NOUN*

The chairs come in a set of two.

- Two people or things which belong together are a **couple** or a **pair**.
- Two musicians playing or singing together are a **duo**.
- A piece of music for two players or singers is a **duet**.
- To multiply a number by two is to **double** it.

SEE ALSO **double, dual**

type *NOUN*

❶ *What type of music do you like to listen to?*

• **kind, sort, variety, category, class, genre, species**

❷ *The footnotes are printed in small type.*

• **print, typeface, font, lettering, letters, characters**

typical *ADJECTIVE*

❶ *It began as just a typical day.*

• **normal, usual, standard, ordinary, average, unremarkable, run-of-the-mill**

OPPOSITES unusual, remarkable

❷ *Special effects like this are a typical feature of action movies.*

• **characteristic, representative, classic**

OPPOSITE uncharacteristic

A B C D E F G H I J K L M N O P Q R S T U V W X Y Z

Uu

ugly *ADJECTIVE*
❶ *The view is ruined by an ugly tower block.*
• **unattractive, unsightly, hideous, ghastly, monstrous, grotesque, repulsive**
OPPOSITES beautiful, attractive
❷ *The crowd was in an ugly mood.*
• **unfriendly, hostile, menacing, threatening, angry, dangerous, unpleasant**
OPPOSITE friendly

ultimate *ADJECTIVE*
My ultimate goal is to be a writer.
• **eventual, final, concluding**
OPPOSITE initial

umpire *NOUN*
see **referee**

un- *PREFIX*
To find synonyms for words beginning with un- which are not listed below, try looking up the word to which un- has been added, then add un-, in- or not to its synonyms. For example, to find synonyms for unacceptable, look up acceptable and then work out the synonyms, unsatisfactory, inadequate, not good enough, etc.

unable *ADJECTIVE*
➤ **unable to**
I was tied down and unable to move.
• **incapable of, powerless to, unequipped to, unfit for**

unanimous *ADJECTIVE*
❶ *The judges came to a unanimous decision.*
• **united, undivided, joint, collective**
– *A decision where most but not all people agree is a* **majority** *decision.*
❷ *Critics have been unanimous in their praise.*
• **in agreement, united, in accord, of one mind**

unattractive *ADJECTIVE*
see **ugly**

unavoidable *ADJECTIVE*
The accident was unavoidable.
• **inevitable, bound to happen, certain, predictable**

unaware *ADJECTIVE*
➤ **unaware of**
They were unaware of the dangers that lay ahead.
• **ignorant of, oblivious to, unconscious of, uninformed about**
IDIOM in the dark about

unbearable *ADJECTIVE*
The stench in the cave was unbearable.
• **unendurable, intolerable, impossible to bear**

unbelievable *ADJECTIVE*
❶ *I found the plot frankly unbelievable.*
• **unconvincing, unlikely, far-fetched, improbable, incredible**
❷ *She scored an unbelievable goal.*
• **amazing, astonishing, extraordinary, remarkable, sensational, phenomenal, staggering, stunning**

unbroken *ADJECTIVE*
❶ *She sat in the one unbroken chair.*
• **undamaged, unscathed, intact, whole, sound**
OPPOSITES broken, damaged
❷ *There was a minute of unbroken silence.*
• **uninterrupted, continuous, non-stop**
OPPOSITE discontinuous
❸ *His Olympic record is still unbroken.*
• **unbeaten, undefeated, unsurpassed**

uncanny *ADJECTIVE*
❶ *Moonlight helped to create an uncanny atmosphere.*
• **eerie, weird, ghostly, unearthly, other-worldly, unreal, freakish**
(*informal*) **creepy, spooky**
❷ *He bears an uncanny resemblance to Elvis Presley.*
• **striking, remarkable, extraordinary, incredible**

uncertain *ADJECTIVE*

❶ *I was uncertain what to do next.*
• **unsure, doubtful, unclear, undecided, in two minds, in a quandary**
OPPOSITES certain, positive
❷ *The future of the festival is still uncertain.*
• **indefinite, unknown, undecided, debatable, unpredictable, insecure**
IDIOM **touch and go**
OPPOSITES definite, secure

unclean *ADJECTIVE*

see **dirty**

unclear *ADJECTIVE*

❶ *The instructions were unclear.*
• **vague, obscure, ambiguous, imprecise, opaque, cryptic**
❷ *I'm unclear about what you want me to do.*
• **uncertain, unsure, doubtful**

uncomfortable *ADJECTIVE*

❶ *The bed I had to sleep in was uncomfortable.*
• **hard, lumpy, stiff, cramped, restrictive**
OPPOSITE comfortable
❷ *She felt uncomfortable talking about herself.*
• **awkward, uneasy, embarrassed, nervous, tense**
OPPOSITES at ease, relaxed

uncommon *ADJECTIVE*

It's not uncommon to see dolphins here.
• **unusual, rare, strange, abnormal, atypical, exceptional, unfamiliar, unexpected**

unconscious *ADJECTIVE*

❶ *He was knocked unconscious by the fall.*
• **senseless, knocked out**
IDIOMS **out cold, out for the count**
– Someone who is unconscious for an operation is **anaesthetized**.
– Someone who is unconscious because of an accident or illness is **in a coma**.
OPPOSITE conscious
❷ *It was an unconscious slip of the tongue.*
• **accidental, unintended, unintentional**
OPPOSITES deliberate, intentional
➤ **unconscious of**
She was unconscious of causing any offence.
• **unaware of, ignorant of, oblivious to**
OPPOSITE aware of

uncover *VERB*

❶ *Archaeologists have uncovered a second tomb.*
• **unearth, dig up, excavate, expose, reveal, disclose, unveil, lay bare**
❷ *She finally uncovered the truth about her family's past.*
• **discover, detect, come across, stumble on, chance on**
OPPOSITES cover up, hide

undergo *VERB*

Guide dogs undergo rigorous training.
• **go through, submit to, be subjected to, experience, put up with, face, endure**

underground *ADJECTIVE*

❶ *He found himself in an underground cavern.*
• **subterranean, sunken, buried**
❷ *They were members of an underground resistance movement.*
• **secret, undercover, covert, clandestine**
IDIOM **cloak-and-dagger**

undermine *VERB*

Losing the race could undermine her confidence.
• **weaken, lessen, diminish, reduce, impair, damage, shake**
OPPOSITES support, boost

understand *VERB*

❶ *Can you understand what he's saying?*
• **comprehend, make sense of, grasp, follow, make out, take in, interpret, work out, fathom**
IDIOM **make head or tail of**
– To understand something in code is to **decode** or **decipher** it.

A B C D E F G H I J K L M N O P Q R S T U V W X Y Z

❷ *You don't understand how hard it is for me.*
• **realize, appreciate, recognize, be aware of, be conscious of**
❸ *I understand they're moving to Sydney.*
• **believe, gather, hear, take it**

understandable *ADJECTIVE*
❶ *The instructions are quite understandable.*
• **comprehensible, intelligible, straightforward, clear, plain, lucid**
❷ *It's understandable that you feel upset.*
• **natural, reasonable, justifiable, normal, not surprising, to be expected**

understanding *NOUN*
❶ *The robot has limited powers of understanding.*
• **intelligence, intellect, sense, judgement**
❷ *Coins can contribute to our understanding of the past.*
• **comprehension, knowledge, grasp, mastery, appreciation, awareness**
OPPOSITE ignorance
❸ *It is my understanding that the software is free.*
• **belief, view, perception, impression**
❹ *Sufferers need to be treated with understanding.*
• **sympathy, compassion, consideration, tolerance**
OPPOSITE indifference
❺ *The two sides reached an understanding.*
• **agreement, deal, settlement, arrangement, accord**

understanding *ADJECTIVE*
Thanks for being so understanding.
• **sympathetic, compassionate, caring, kind, thoughtful, helpful, tolerant, forgiving**

undertake *VERB*
❶ *He is asked to undertake a long and dangerous journey.*
• **take on, accept, be responsible for, embark on, set about, tackle, attempt**
❷ *They undertook to pay all the costs.*
• **agree, consent, promise, pledge, guarantee, commit yourself**

underwear *NOUN*
The drawer was full of underwear.
• **underclothes, underclothing, undergarments**
(*informal*) **undies**
– Women's underclothes are sometimes called **lingerie**.

undo *VERB*
❶ *She undid the laces on her boots.*
• **unfasten, untie, unbutton, unhook, unlace, loosen, release**
– To undo stitching is to **unpick** it.
❷ *I slowly undid the packaging.*
• **open, unwrap, unfold, unwind, unroll, unfurl**
❸ *They say nothing can undo the curse.*
• **reverse, negate, cancel, wipe out, annul**

undoubtedly *ADVERB*
She is undoubtedly our best player.
• **definitely, certainly, unquestionably, undeniably, indubitably, without a doubt, doubtless, clearly**

undress *VERB*
You can undress in the changing room.
• **get undressed, take off your clothes, strip**
OPPOSITES dress, get dressed

unearth *VERB*
❶ *We unearthed some Roman coins in our back garden.*
• **dig up, excavate, uncover, turn up**
❷ *She unearthed some old letters in a drawer.*
• **find, discover, come across, hit upon, track down**

uneasy *ADJECTIVE*
❶ *Something about her made me feel uneasy.*
• **anxious, nervous, worried, apprehensive, troubled, unsettled, tense, on edge**
OPPOSITE confident

❷ *There was an uneasy silence.*
• **uncomfortable, awkward, embarrassing, tense, strained**
OPPOSITE comfortable

unemployed *ADJECTIVE*
Since the factory closed, he has been unemployed.
• **out of work, jobless, redundant** (*informal*) **on the dole**
OPPOSITES employed, working, in work

uneven *ADJECTIVE*
❶ *The ground was very uneven in places.*
• **rough, bumpy, lumpy, rutted**
OPPOSITE smooth
❷ *Their performance has been uneven this season.*
• **erratic, inconsistent, irregular, variable, unpredictable, erratic, patchy**
OPPOSITE consistent
❸ *It was a very uneven contest.*
• **one-sided, unbalanced, unequal, unfair**
OPPOSITE balanced

unexpected *ADJECTIVE*
Her reaction was totally unexpected.
• **surprising, unforeseen, unpredictable, unplanned**
OPPOSITE expected

unfair *ADJECTIVE*
❶ *People protested that the tax was unfair.*
• **unjust, unreasonable, discriminatory, one-sided, biased**
OPPOSITES fair, just
❷ *I felt that her comments were unfair.*
• **undeserved, unmerited, uncalled-for, unjustified, out of order**
OPPOSITES fair, deserved

unfaithful *ADJECTIVE*
see **disloyal**

unfamiliar *ADJECTIVE*
We looked out on an unfamiliar landscape.
• **strange, unusual, curious, novel, alien**

➤ **unfamiliar with**
They were unfamiliar with the local customs.
• **unaccustomed to, unused to, unaware of**

unfit *ADJECTIVE*
❶ *He is too unfit to play tennis these days.*
• **out of condition, out of shape, unhealthy**
OPPOSITE fit
❷ *The water is unfit to drink.*
• **unsuitable, unsuited, unsatisfactory, inappropriate, ill-equipped**

unfortunate *ADJECTIVE*
❶ *The unfortunate couple had lost all their possessions.*
• **unlucky, poor, pitiful, wretched, unhappy, hapless, ill-fated**
OPPOSITES fortunate, lucky
❷ *The team got off to an unfortunate start.*
• **unwelcome, unfavourable, unpromising, inauspicious, dismal, bad**
OPPOSITES good, favourable
❸ *Sorry, that was an unfortunate choice of words.*
• **regrettable, unhappy, inappropriate, unsuitable, unwise**

unfortunately *ADVERB*
Unfortunately I cannot come to your party.
• **unluckily, unhappily, regrettably, sadly, alas**

unfriendly *ADJECTIVE*
He is likely to get an unfriendly reception.
• **unwelcoming, inhospitable, unsympathetic, impolite, uncivil, hostile, cold, cool, aloof, stand-offish, unsociable, unneighbourly**
OPPOSITES friendly, amiable

ungrateful *ADJECTIVE*
I don't want to seem ungrateful.
• **unappreciative, unthankful**
OPPOSITE grateful

A B C D E F G H I J K L M N O P Q R S T U V W X Y Z

unhappy *ADJECTIVE*
❶ *He was desperately unhappy away from home.*
• **sad, miserable, depressed, downhearted, despondent, gloomy, glum, downcast, forlorn, dejected, woeful, crestfallen**
IDIOMS (*informal*) **down in the dumps, down in the mouth**
OPPOSITES **happy, cheerful**
❷ *I'm still unhappy with my score.*
• **dissatisfied, displeased, discontented, disappointed**
OPPOSITES **satisfied, pleased**
❸ *It was just an unhappy coincidence.*
• **unfortunate, unlucky, ill-fated**
OPPOSITE **lucky**

unhealthy *ADJECTIVE*
❶ *He had been an unhealthy child.*
• **sickly, infirm, unwell, poorly, weak, delicate, feeble, frail**
OPPOSITES **healthy, strong**
❷ *She eats an unhealthy diet of junk food.*
• **unwholesome, harmful, unhygienic**
OPPOSITES **healthy, wholesome**

unhelpful *ADJECTIVE*
The receptionist was most unhelpful.
• **uncooperative, unfriendly, disobliging**
OPPOSITE **helpful**

unidentified *ADJECTIVE*
An unidentified aircraft was spotted at night.
• **unknown, unrecognized, unspecified, unnamed, nameless, anonymous**
OPPOSITE **named**

uniform *NOUN*
He changed into his police uniform.
• **costume, outfit, livery, regalia**
(*informal*) **get-up**

uniform *ADJECTIVE*
❶ *The air is kept at a uniform temperature.*
• **consistent, regular, even, stable, steady, unvarying, unchanging**
OPPOSITE **varying**
❷ *Pearls are rarely uniform in size.*
• **identical, equal, the same, matching, consistent**
OPPOSITE **different**

unify *VERB*
The new president promised to unify the country.
• **unite, bring together, integrate, combine, join, merge, amalgamate**
OPPOSITE **separate**

unimportant *ADJECTIVE*
Don't worry about unimportant details.
• **insignificant, minor, trivial, trifling, secondary, irrelevant, slight, small, negligible, petty**
OPPOSITES **important, major**

uninhabited *ADJECTIVE*
The island has been uninhabited for decades.
• **unoccupied, empty, deserted, abandoned**
OPPOSITES **inhabited, populated**

uninteresting *ADJECTIVE*
The journey home was fairly uninteresting.
• **dull, boring, unexciting, tedious, dreary, banal, humdrum**
OPPOSITES **interesting, exciting**

union *NOUN*
The city was formed by the union of two neighbouring towns.
• **uniting, joining, integration, merger, amalgamation, fusion, combination**
– A union of two rivers is a **confluence**.
– A union of two countries is their **unification**.

unique *ADJECTIVE*
Each person's fingerprints are unique.
• **distinctive, different, individual, special, peculiar**
(*informal*) **one-off**

unit *NOUN*
The shelves are built from separate units.
• **piece, part, bit, section, segment, element, component, module**

unite *VERB*
❶ *Their marriage united the two kingdoms.*
• **combine, join, bring together, merge, unify, integrate, amalgamate**
OPPOSITE separate
❷ *Local residents united to fight the plan.*
• **collaborate, cooperate, come together, join together, join forces**
– To unite to do something bad is to **conspire**.
OPPOSITE compete

universal *ADJECTIVE*
The idea met with universal agreement.
• **general, common, widespread, global, worldwide, international**

universe *NOUN*
Are we really alone in the universe?
• **cosmos, space, infinity**
SEE ALSO **space**

unjust *ADJECTIVE*
see **unfair**

unkind *ADJECTIVE*
What an unkind thing to say!
• **unpleasant, unfriendly, unsympathetic, inconsiderate, uncaring, hard-hearted, mean, harsh, cruel, thoughtless, heartless, unfeeling, callous, uncharitable, nasty**
OPPOSITES kind, sympathetic

unknown *ADJECTIVE*
❶ *The letter was in an unknown hand.*
• **unidentified, unrecognized**
OPPOSITE known
❷ *The author of the story is unknown.*
• **anonymous, nameless, unnamed, unspecified**
OPPOSITE named
❸ *We were now entering unknown territory.*
• **unfamiliar, alien, foreign, undiscovered, unexplored, uncharted**
OPPOSITE familiar
❹ *The main part is played by an unknown actor.*
• **little known, unheard of, obscure**
OPPOSITE famous

unlike *ADJECTIVE*
The landscape was unlike anything I had ever seen.
• **different from, distinct from, dissimilar to**
OPPOSITE similar to

unlikely *ADJECTIVE*
❶ *It is difficult to believe such an unlikely explanation.*
• **unbelievable, unconvincing, improbable, implausible, incredible, dubious, far-fetched**
OPPOSITE likely
❷ *It is unlikely that he will win.*
• **doubtful, improbable, dubious**
OPPOSITE likely

unlucky *ADJECTIVE*
❶ *Some people say that 13 is an unlucky number.*
• **unfavourable, inauspicious, ill-omened, ill-starred, jinxed**
❷ *She was unlucky not to get a medal.*
• **unfortunate, luckless, hapless**
OPPOSITE lucky

unmarried *ADJECTIVE*
He was the only unmarried man in the room.
• **single, unwed**
– If your marriage has been legally ended, you are **divorced**.
– An unmarried man is a **bachelor**.
– An old-fashioned word for an unmarried woman is a **spinster**.

unmistakable *ADJECTIVE*
There was an unmistakable smell of burning.
• **distinct, distinctive, clear, obvious, plain, telltale**

unnatural *ADJECTIVE*
❶ *An unnatural silence filled the room.*
• **unusual, abnormal, uncommon, exceptional, irregular, odd, strange, weird, bizarre**

A B C D E F G H I J K L M N O P Q R S T U V W X Y Z

❷ *Some of the acting was a bit unnatural.*
• **stiff, stilted, unrealistic, forced, affected, self-conscious**
❸ *His hair was an unnatural shade of yellow.*
• **artificial, synthetic, man-made, manufactured**
OPPOSITE natural

unnecessary *ADJECTIVE*
You can free up space by deleting unnecessary files.
• **inessential, non-essential, unwanted, excessive, superfluous, surplus, extra, redundant, uncalled for, expendable**
OPPOSITE necessary

unoccupied *ADJECTIVE*
❶ *The building itself was unoccupied.*
• **empty, uninhabited, deserted, unused, vacant**
OPPOSITES occupied, inhabited
❷ *The seat next to me was unoccupied.*
• **vacant, free, available**
OPPOSITES taken, occupied

unpleasant *ADJECTIVE*
❶ *He is a thoroughly unpleasant man.*
• **unlikeable, disagreeable, objectionable, obnoxious, unfriendly, unkind, bad-tempered, nasty, malicious, spiteful, mean**
❷ *The entire trip was an unpleasant experience.*
• **uncomfortable, disagreeable, upsetting, distressing, awful, dreadful, horrible**
❸ *What is that unpleasant smell?*
• **disgusting, foul, repulsive, revolting, repellent, offensive**
OPPOSITES pleasant, agreeable

unpopular *ADJECTIVE*
The new manager was unpopular at first.
• **disliked, unwelcome, unloved, friendless, out of favour**
OPPOSITE popular

unravel *VERB*
❶ *I unravelled the string and wound it into a ball.*
• **disentangle, untangle, undo, untwist, separate out**
❷ *No one has yet unravelled the mystery.*
• **solve, clear up, puzzle out, work out, figure out, explain, clarify**
IDIOM get to the bottom of

unreal *ADJECTIVE*
Everything seemed unreal, as if he was in a dream.
• **dream-like, imaginary, make-believe, fictitious, fanciful**
OPPOSITES real, realistic

unrest *NOUN*
A period of political unrest followed.
• **disturbance, disorder, trouble, turmoil, dissent, strife, agitation, protest**
OPPOSITES calm, order

unsafe *ADJECTIVE*
The coastal rocks are unsafe for climbing.
• **dangerous, hazardous, risky, insecure, unsound, treacherous, perilous**
OPPOSITE safe

unsatisfactory *ADJECTIVE*
The book comes to an unsatisfactory conclusion.
• **disappointing, displeasing, inadequate, poor, weak, unacceptable, insufficient**
OPPOSITE satisfactory

unscrupulous *ADJECTIVE*
The smugglers were cunning and unscrupulous.
• **dishonest, unprincipled, disreputable, immoral, unethical, shameless**

unseen *ADJECTIVE*
see **invisible**

unsettling *ADJECTIVE*
The silence was unsettling.
• **disturbing, unnerving, disquieting, disconcerting, perturbing, troubling**

unsightly *ADJECTIVE*
Litter makes the beach look unsightly.
• **unattractive, ugly, unprepossessing, unappealing, hideous, grotesque**

unsociable *ADJECTIVE*
Pandas are unsociable animals.
• **unfriendly, unapproachable, reserved, withdrawn, retiring**
OPPOSITES sociable, gregarious

unstable or **unsteady** *ADJECTIVE*
The table was a bit unsteady.
• **shaky, wobbly, insecure, unbalanced, rickety**
OPPOSITES stable, steady

unsuccessful *ADJECTIVE*
He led an unsuccessful expedition to the South Pole.
• **failed, abortive, futile, ineffective, fruitless, unproductive**
OPPOSITES successful, triumphant

unsuitable *ADJECTIVE*
The film is unsuitable for very young children.
• **inappropriate, unfitting, unacceptable, ill-suited, out of place, out of keeping**
OPPOSITES suitable, appropriate

unsure *ADJECTIVE*
She seemed unsure of what to say or do.
• **uncertain, unclear, undecided, doubtful, in two minds, in a quandary**
OPPOSITES certain, clear

untidy *ADJECTIVE*
❶ *The garden is looking a bit untidy.*
• **messy, disorderly, cluttered, jumbled, tangled, chaotic**
(*informal*) **higgledy-piggledy, topsy-turvy**
OPPOSITES tidy, orderly, well kept
❷ *His hair always looks untidy.*
• **dishevelled, bedraggled, rumpled, unkempt, scruffy, slovenly**
❸ *Her work was untidy and full of mistakes.*
• **careless, disorganized, slapdash**
(*informal*) **sloppy**

untrue *ADJECTIVE*
Almost every part of the story is untrue.
• **false, incorrect, inaccurate, erroneous, wrong**
OPPOSITES true, accurate

unusual *ADJECTIVE*
❶ *The weather is unusual for this time of year.*
• **abnormal, out of the ordinary, exceptional, remarkable, extraordinary, odd, peculiar, singular, strange, unexpected, irregular, unheard-of**
OPPOSITES normal, typical
❷ *Ebenezer is an unusual name.*
• **uncommon, rare, unfamiliar, unconventional, unorthodox**
OPPOSITE common

unwell *ADJECTIVE*
see **ill**

unwilling *ADJECTIVE*
He was unwilling to fight the old man.
• **reluctant, hesitant, disinclined, loath, resistant**
OPPOSITES willing, eager

unwise *ADJECTIVE*
It would be unwise to ignore the warning signs.
• **foolish, foolhardy, ill-advised, senseless, stupid, silly**
OPPOSITES wise, sensible

upheaval *NOUN*
I can't face the upheaval of moving house again.
• **disruption, disturbance, upset, disorder, commotion, turmoil**

uphill *ADJECTIVE*
❶ *The first half of the race is uphill.*
• **upward, ascending, rising, climbing**
OPPOSITE downhill
❷ *We are all facing an uphill struggle.*
• **hard, difficult, tough, strenuous, laborious, arduous, exhausting, gruelling, taxing**

A B C D E F G H I J K L M N O P Q R S T U V W X Y Z

upkeep *NOUN*
Which department is responsible for the upkeep of cycle paths?
• **care, maintenance, servicing, running**

upper *ADJECTIVE*
My bedroom is on the upper floor.
• **higher, upstairs, top**
OPPOSITE **lower**

upright *ADJECTIVE*
❶ *The car seat should be in an upright position.*
• **erect, perpendicular, vertical**
OPPOSITE **horizontal**
❷ *He is an upright member of the local community.*
• **honest, honourable, respectable, reputable, law-abiding, virtuous, upstanding, principled, worthy**
OPPOSITES **disreputable, dishonest**

uproar *NOUN*
The meeting ended in uproar.
• **chaos, disorder, commotion, confusion, turmoil, pandemonium, mayhem, rumpus, furore**

upset *VERB*
❶ *He must have said something to upset her.*
• **distress, trouble, disturb, unsettle, disconcert, displease, offend, dismay, perturb, fluster, bother**
❷ *Their arrival upset all our plans.*
• **disrupt, interfere with, interrupt, affect, throw out, mess up**
❸ *She upset a pot of soup.*
• **knock over, tip over, overturn, topple, spill**

upset *ADJECTIVE*
You sounded upset on the phone.
• **worried, troubled, bothered, disturbed, agitated, unhappy, disappointed**

upset *NOUN*
❶ *He is off school with a stomach upset.*
• **illness, ailment, disorder**
(*informal*) **bug**
❷ *There has been a major upset in the quarter-finals.*
• **shock, surprise, upheaval, setback**
IDIOM **turn-up for the books**

upside-down *ADJECTIVE*
❶ *A convex lens projects an image that is upside-down.*
• **inverted, upturned, wrong way up**
(*informal*) **topsy-turvy**
❷ (*informal*) *Suddenly her whole life was upside-down.*
• **in disarray, in disorder, in a muddle, chaotic, disorderly, jumbled up**
(*informal*) **higgledy-piggledy**
OPPOSITE **orderly**

up to date or **up-to-date** *ADJECTIVE*
❶ *Her clothes are always up to date.*
• **fashionable, stylish, contemporary, modern**
(*informal*) **trendy, hip**
OPPOSITE **old-fashioned**
❷ *The spacecraft uses the most up-to-date technology.*
• **new, recent, current, the latest, advanced, cutting-edge, state-of the art, up-to-the-minute**
OPPOSITES **out of date, out-of-date**
❸ *Keep up to date with all the celebrity gossip.*
• **informed, acquainted, in touch**
IDIOMS **in the picture, up to speed**
OPPOSITE **out of touch**
You write up-to-date (with hyphens) immediately before a noun: *The website provides up-to-date information.*

upward *ADJECTIVE*
It was a steep upward climb.
• **uphill, ascending, rising**
OPPOSITE **downward**

urban *ADJECTIVE*
Most of the population live in urban areas.
• **built-up, municipal, metropolitan**
OPPOSITE **rural**

urge *VERB*
She urged him to reconsider his decision.
• **advise, counsel, appeal to, beg, implore, plead with, press**
– To urge someone to do something is also to **advocate** or **recommend** it.
OPPOSITE **discourage**

➤ **urge someone on**
The home crowd urged their team on.
• **encourage, spur on, egg on**

urge *NOUN*
I had a sudden urge to burst into song.
• **impulse, compulsion, desire, wish, longing, yearning, craving, hankering, itch, yen**

urgent *ADJECTIVE*
❶ *I have an urgent matter to discuss.*
• **pressing, serious, critical, essential, important, top-priority**
OPPOSITE **unimportant**
❷ *The stranger spoke in an urgent whisper.*
• **anxious, insistent, earnest**

usable *ADJECTIVE*
❶ *The lift is not usable today.*
• **operating, working, functioning, functional**
OPPOSITE **unusable**
❷ *Is this voucher still usable?*
• **valid, acceptable**
OPPOSITE **invalid**

use *VERB*
❶ *You may use a calculator to help you.*
• **make use of, employ, utilize**
– To use your knowledge is to **apply** it.
– To use people or things selfishly is to **exploit** them.
❷ *Can you show me how to use the photocopier?*
• **operate, work, handle, manage**
– To hold and use a weapon or tool is to **wield** it.
❸ *Please don't use all the hot water.*
• **use up, go through, consume, exhaust, spend**

use *NOUN*
❶ *Would these books be any use to you?*
• **help, benefit, advantage, profit, value**
❷ *Can you find a use for this crate?*
• **function, purpose, point**
❸ *This is not an efficient use of your time.*
• **usage, application, employment, utilization**

used *ADJECTIVE*
They sell used computers.
• **second-hand, pre-owned, old, hand-me-down, cast-off**
OPPOSITES **new, unused**
➤ **used to**
She is used to getting her own way.
• **accustomed to, familiar with, experienced in, in the habit of, no stranger to**
OPPOSITE **unaccustomed to**

useful *ADJECTIVE*
❶ *A webcam is useful for chatting online.*
• **convenient, handy, practical, effective, efficient**
❷ *The leaflet offers some useful advice.*
• **good, helpful, valuable, worthwhile, constructive, productive, fruitful**
OPPOSITES **useless, unhelpful**

useless *ADJECTIVE*
❶ *Most of her advice was completely useless.*
• **worthless, unhelpful, pointless, futile, unprofitable, fruitless, impractical, unusable**
IDIOM **of no avail**
OPPOSITES **useful, helpful**
❷ (*informal*) *I've always been useless at maths.*
• **bad, poor, incompetent, incapable** (*informal*) **rubbish, hopeless**
OPPOSITE **good**

user-friendly *ADJECTIVE*
She has written a user-friendly guide to punctuation.
• **easy to use, straightforward, uncomplicated, understandable**

usher *VERB*
We were ushered into the dining hall.
• **escort, conduct, guide, lead, show, take**

usual *ADJECTIVE*
❶ *I'll meet you at the usual time.*
• **normal, customary, familiar, habitual, regular, standard**

❷ *It's usual to knock before entering.*
• **common, accepted, conventional, traditional**
OPPOSITE **unusual**

usually *ADVERB*
I don't usually get up this early.
• **normally, generally, ordinarily, customarily, habitually, as a rule**

utensil *NOUN*
A rack of cooking utensils hung on the wall.
• **tool, implement, device, gadget, instrument, appliance**
(*informal*) **gizmo**

utmost *ADJECTIVE*
This message is of the utmost importance.
• **highest, greatest, supreme, maximum, top, paramount**

utter *VERB*
The girl could scarcely utter her name.
• **say, speak, express, pronounce, articulate, voice, mouth, put into words**

utter *ADJECTIVE*
The three of us stared in utter amazement.
• **complete, total, absolute, thorough, sheer, downright, out-and-out**

vacancy *NOUN*
They have a vacancy for a trainee journalist.
• **opening, position, post, job, situation**

vacant *ADJECTIVE*
❶ *The house next door is still vacant.*
• **unoccupied, empty, uninhabited, deserted**
OPPOSITE occupied
❷ *The assistant gave me a vacant stare.*
• **blank, expressionless, emotionless, impassive, glazed, deadpan**
OPPOSITE expressive

vague *ADJECTIVE*
❶ *The directions she gave were rather vague.*
• **indefinite, imprecise, broad, general, ill-defined, unclear, woolly**
OPPOSITES exact, detailed
❷ *I have only a vague memory of that day.*
• **blurred, indistinct, obscure, dim, hazy, shadowy**
OPPOSITES definite, clear

vain *ADJECTIVE*
❶ *He is rather vain about his looks.*
• **arrogant, proud, conceited, haughty, self-satisfied, narcissistic**
OPPOSITE modest
❷ *I made a vain attempt to tidy my room.*
• **unsuccessful, ineffective, useless, pointless, futile, fruitless**
OPPOSITE successful

valid *ADJECTIVE*
❶ *The ticket is valid for three months.*
• **current, usable, legal, authorized, official, in effect**
❷ *The author makes several valid points.*
• **acceptable, reasonable, sound, legitimate, genuine, justifiable, cogent**
OPPOSITE invalid

valley *NOUN*
The village lies in a deep valley.
• **vale, dale, gorge, gully, pass, ravine, canyon**
(*Scottish*) **glen**

valuable *ADJECTIVE*
❶ *I believe the necklace is very valuable.*
• **expensive, costly, dear, high-priced, precious, priceless**
OPPOSITE valueless
❷ *He gave us some valuable advice.*
• **useful, helpful, good, beneficial, constructive, worthwhile, invaluable**
OPPOSITE worthless
The word invaluable is not the opposite of valuable: a piece of *invaluable advice* is one that is extremely valuable.

value *NOUN*
❶ *The house has doubled in value since they bought it.*
• **price, cost, worth**
❷ *He stressed the value of taking regular exercise.*
• **advantage, benefit, merit, use, usefulness, importance**

value *VERB*
❶ *I have always valued her opinion.*
• **esteem, respect, appreciate, have a good opinion of, think highly of**
IDIOM **set great store by**
– To value something highly is to **prize** or **treasure** it.
❷ *The painting was valued at 6 million dollars.*
• **price, cost, rate, evaluate, assess**

van *NOUN*
see **vehicle**

vanish *VERB*
His smile vanished in an instant.
• **disappear, go away, fade, dissolve, disperse**
OPPOSITE appear

vanity *NOUN*
Her rejection of him was a blow to his vanity.
• **arrogance, pride, conceit, self-esteem,**

self-importance
(*informal*) **big-headedness**

vapour *NOUN*
A thick vapour rose up from the beaker.
• **gas, fumes, steam, smoke**
– Vapour hanging in the air is **haze**, **fog**, **mist** or **smog**.
– When something turns to vapour it **vaporizes**.

variable *ADJECTIVE*
The weather is variable at this time of year.
• **changeable, fluctuating, erratic, inconsistent, unpredictable, fluid, fickle, unstable**
OPPOSITE **constant**

variation *NOUN*
❶ *There have been slight variations in temperature.*
• **difference, change, fluctuation, shift**
OPPOSITE **uniformity**
❷ *This recipe is a variation on a classic dish.*
• **alteration (of), modification (of), deviation (from)**

varied *ADJECTIVE*
She has varied interests.
• **diverse, assorted, mixed, miscellaneous, wide-ranging, disparate, motley**
OPPOSITE **uniform**

variety *NOUN*
❶ *The centre offers a variety of leisure activities.*
• **assortment, range, mixture, array, miscellany**
❷ *We stock over thirty varieties of pasta.*
• **kind, sort, type, category, form, make, model, brand**
❸ *Try to add more variety to your writing.*
• **variation, diversity, change, difference**

various *ADJECTIVE*
The shoes are available in various colours.
• **different, several, assorted, varying, differing, a variety of, diverse, sundry**

vary *VERB*
❶ *Try varying the volume on the speakers.*
• **change, modify, adjust, alter**
❷ *The length of daylight varies with the seasons.*
• **change, alter, differ, fluctuate**
❸ *Estimates vary widely.*
• **differ, be dissimilar, disagree, diverge**

vast *ADJECTIVE*
❶ *He has accumulated a vast fortune.*
• **huge, great, immense, enormous, massive, gigantic, colossal**
OPPOSITE **tiny**
❷ *A vast stretch of water lay between them and dry land.*
• **broad, wide, extensive, sweeping**

vault *VERB*
➤ **vault over something**
He vaulted over the fence and ran off.
• **jump over, leap over, bound over, spring over, clear, hurdle**

vault *NOUN*
The documents are stored in an underground vault at night.
• **strongroom, treasury**
– An underground part of a house is a **basement** or **cellar**.
– A room underneath a church is a **crypt**.

veer *VERB*
Suddenly, the car veered sharply to the left.
• **swerve, turn, swing, change direction, change course**

vegetable *NOUN*

WORD WEB

Leaf vegetables:

➤ Brussels sprout
➤ cabbage
➤ cauliflower
➤ Chinese cabbage or Chinese leaf
➤ endive
➤ globe artichoke
➤ kale
➤ lettuce
➤ mustard greens
➤ pak choi
➤ spinach
➤ Swiss chard
➤ watercress

Root vegetables:

- beetroot
- carrot
- celeriac
- daikon
- parsnip
- radish
- swede
- sweet potato
- turnip

Legumes or pulses:

- broad beans or fava beans
- butter beans or lima beans
- chickpeas
- French beans or green beans
- kidney beans
- lentils
- mangetout or sugarsnap peas
- mung beans
- peas
- runner beans
- snow peas
- soya beans

Other vegetables:

- asparagus
- aubergine
- butternut squash
- broccoli
- cauliflower
- celery
- courgette
- cucumber
- garlic
- Jerusalem artichoke
- kohlrabi
- leek
- marrow
- mushroom
- okra
- onion
- pepper
- potato
- pumpkin
- shallot
- spaghetti squash
- spring onions
- sweetcorn
- water chestnut
- yam

vegetarian *NOUN*

Many but not all Buddhists are vegetarians.

– A person who doesn't eat any animal products is a **vegan**.

– An animal that feeds only on plants is a **herbivore**.

OPPOSITES carnivore, meat-eater

vegetation *NOUN*

The rainforest is filled with lush vegetation.

• **foliage, greenery, growth, plants, undergrowth**

vehicle *NOUN*

WORD WEB

Some types of vehicle:

- ambulance
- bicycle
- bulldozer
- bus
- cab
- cable car
- car or (*old use*) motor car
- caravan
- coach
- double-decker
- fire engine
- forklift truck
- four-wheel drive
- hearse
- HGV or heavy goods vehicle
- horsebox
- jeep
- lorry
- minibus
- minicab
- motorbike or motorcycle
- people carrier
- pick-up truck
- police car
- rickshaw
- scooter
- skidoo
- sledge
- sleigh
- snowplough
- steamroller
- tank
- taxi
- tractor
- train
- tram
- tricycle
- trolleybus
- truck
- underground train
- van

Old horse-drawn vehicles:

- carriage
- cart
- chariot
- gig
- hansom cab
- stagecoach
- trap
- wagon

For transport by air and sea see **aircraft, boat**.

veil *VERB*

Her face was partly veiled by a scarf.

• **cover, conceal, hide, mask, shroud**

vein *NOUN*

❶ *Blood pumps through your veins.*

• **blood vessel**

– Major blood vessels which carry blood from your heart to other parts of your body are **arteries**.

– Delicate hair-like blood vessels are **capillaries**.

A B C D E F G H I J K L M N O P Q R S T U V W X Y Z

❷ *The story is told in a light-hearted vein.*
• **style, mood, manner, tone, character, spirit, humour**

velocity *NOUN*
The asteroid is travelling at high velocity through space.
• **speed, rate, rapidity, swiftness**

vengeance *NOUN*
The duke swore vengeance on his enemies.
• **revenge, retribution, retaliation**
OPPOSITE **forgiveness**

venomous *ADJECTIVE*
The adder is Britain's only venomous snake.
• **poisonous, toxic**

vent *NOUN*
Hot air escapes through vents in the roof.
• **outlet, opening, aperture, gap, hole, slit, duct**

vent *VERB*
The crowd vented their frustration by booing.
• **express, let out, give vent to, pour out, release, voice, air**

venture *NOUN*
His first business venture was a disaster.
• **enterprise, undertaking, project, scheme, operation, endeavour**

venture *VERB*
We ventured out into the snow.
• **set out, set forth, dare to go, emerge, journey**

verdict *NOUN*
We are waiting for the verdict of the jury.
• **decision, judgement, finding, conclusion, ruling**

verge *NOUN*
There is a grassy verge alongside the road.
• **side, edge, margin**
– A stone or concrete edging beside a road is a **kerb**.
– The flat strip of road beside a motorway is the **hard shoulder**.
➤ **on the verge of**
Some species are now on the verge of extinction.
• **on the edge of, on the point of, on the brink of, close to, approaching**

verify *VERB*
An eyewitness verified his statement.
• **confirm, prove, validate, support, back up, bear out, substantiate, corroborate**

versatile *ADJECTIVE*
❶ *He's an extremely versatile musician.*
• **resourceful, adaptable, flexible, multi-talented, all-round**
❷ *Cotton is a very versatile fabric.*
• **adaptable, multi-purpose, all-purpose**

verse *NOUN*
❶ *The entire play is written in verse.*
• **rhyme, poetry**
❷ *I have learnt the first two verses of the poem.*
• **stanza**

version *NOUN*
❶ *Write your own version of the story.*
• **account, description, report, statement**
❷ *She starred in a film version of 'Wuthering Heights'.*
• **adaptation, interpretation, rendering**
– A version of something which was originally in another language is a **translation**.
❸ *The new version of the game will be released in May.*
• **design, model, form, variation, edition**

vertical *ADJECTIVE*
Pull the lever back to its vertical position.
• **upright, perpendicular, standing, erect**
– A vertical drop is a **sheer** drop.
OPPOSITES **horizontal, flat**

very *ADVERB*
It was a very cold day.
• **extremely, highly, exceedingly, especially, particularly, truly, remarkably, unusually, exceptionally, singularly, decidedly, really, intensely, acutely** (*informal*) **terribly, awfully, seriously,**

ultra, mega
OPPOSITES slightly, rather

vessel *NOUN*
❶ *Small fishing vessels were bobbing about in the harbour.*
• **boat, ship, craft**
❷ *Archaeologists found clay vessels at the site.*
• **pot, dish, bowl, jar, jug, container, receptacle**
❸ For blood vessels see **vein**.

veto *VERB*
They vetoed the proposal for a skatepark.
• **reject, turn down, say no to, dismiss, disallow, ban, prohibit, forbid**
OPPOSITE approve

vex *VERB*
Her behaviour vexed him a good deal.
• **annoy, irritate, make you cross, anger, infuriate, exasperate**

vibrate *VERB*
Every time a train went past the walls vibrated.
• **shake, tremble, quiver, quake, shiver, shudder, judder, throb**

vicious *ADJECTIVE*
❶ *This was once the scene of a vicious murder.*
• **brutal, violent, savage, ferocious, bloodthirsty, cruel, callous, merciless, pitiless, ruthless, inhuman, barbaric, sadistic**
❷ *The dog looked extremely vicious.*
• **fierce, ferocious, violent, savage, wild**

victim *NOUN*
Ambulances took the victims to hospital.
• **casualty, sufferer**
– Victims of an accident are also **the injured** or **the wounded**.
– A person who dies in an accident is a **fatality**.

victor *NOUN*
A Canadian crew came away as the victors.
• **winner, champion, conqueror**

victorious *ADJECTIVE*
The trophy was presented to the victorious team.
• **winning, triumphant, successful, conquering, top**
OPPOSITES defeated, losing

victory *NOUN*
He led his team to an unlikely victory.
• **win, success, triumph, conquest**
OPPOSITES defeat, loss

view *NOUN*
❶ *There's a great view from the top floor.*
• **outlook, prospect, scene, scenery, vista, panorama**
❷ *She has strong views on the subject.*
• **opinion, thought, attitude, belief, conviction, sentiment, idea, notion**
➤ **in view of**
In view of the circumstances, they gave us a refund.
• **because of, as a result of, considering, taking account of**

view *VERB*
❶ *Both locals and tourists come to view the scenery.*
• **look at, see, observe, regard, gaze at, eye, scan, survey, inspect, examine, contemplate**
❷ *He viewed the newcomers with suspicion.*
• **think of, consider, regard, look on**

viewer *NOUN*
The programme invites viewers to tweet their comments.
– People who view a performance are the **audience** or **spectators**.
– People who view something as they happen to pass by are **bystanders** or **onlookers**.

vigilant *ADJECTIVE*
You must be vigilant when cycling in traffic.
• **alert, watchful, attentive, observant, wary, on the lookout, on your guard**
OPPOSITE inattentive

A B C D E F G H I J K L M N O P Q R S T U V W X Y Z

vigorous *ADJECTIVE*
❶ *She does an hour of vigorous exercise every week.*
• active, brisk, energetic, lively, strenuous, forceful, powerful
OPPOSITES light, gentle
❷ *He was a vigorous man in the prime of life.*
• robust, strong, sturdy, healthy, fit
OPPOSITES feeble, weak

vigour *NOUN*
When they sighted land, they began to row with renewed vigour.
• energy, spirit, vitality, liveliness, enthusiasm, passion, dynamism, verve, gusto, zeal, zest
(*informal*) oomph, get-up-and-go

vile *ADJECTIVE*
❶ *That medicine tastes vile.*
• disgusting, repulsive, revolting, foul, horrible, loathsome, offensive, repellent, sickening, nauseating
OPPOSITE pleasant
❷ *It was a vile act of cruelty.*
• dreadful, despicable, appalling, abominable, contemptible, wicked, evil

villain *NOUN*
He is an actor who enjoys playing villains.
• rogue, scoundrel, wrongdoer, criminal
(*informal*) baddy, crook
OPPOSITE hero

violate *VERB*
The court decided that the company had violated environmental laws.
• break, infringe, contravene, disobey, flout, disregard, ignore

violation *NOUN*
This is a serious violation of the rules.
• breach, breaking, infringement, contravention, flouting

violence *NOUN*
❶ *The film includes scenes of graphic violence.*
• fighting, physical force, aggression, brutality, savagery, barbarity
OPPOSITES non-violence, pacifism
❷ *The violence of the storm uprooted trees.*
• force, power, strength, might, severity, intensity, ferocity, vehemence, fury, rage
OPPOSITES gentleness, mildness

violent *ADJECTIVE*
❶ *There were violent protests in the streets.*
• aggressive, fierce, ferocious, rough, brutal, vicious, savage
❷ *The bridge was washed away in a violent storm.*
• severe, strong, powerful, forceful, intense, raging, turbulent, tempestuous, wild
OPPOSITES gentle, mild

virtually *ADVERB*
Plastics can be made into virtually any shape.
• almost, nearly, practically, effectively, in effect, more or less, just about, as good as

virtue *NOUN*
❶ *He led a life of virtue.*
• goodness, morality, honesty, decency, integrity, righteousness, rectitude
OPPOSITE vice
❷ *Your plan does have the virtue of simplicity.*
• merit, advantage, benefit, strength, asset, good point
OPPOSITE failing

virtuous *ADJECTIVE*
She always felt virtuous after doing some exercise.
• good, worthy, upright, honourable, moral, just, pure, righteous, law-abiding
OPPOSITES wicked, immoral

visible *ADJECTIVE*
The house was barely visible from the main road.
• noticeable, observable, viewable, detectable, discernible, evident, obvious, apparent, manifest
OPPOSITE invisible

vision *NOUN*

❶ *I began to have problems with my vision.*
• eyesight, sight, eyes
– Words that mean 'to do with vision or eyes' are **visual** and **optical**.
❷ *In the story she is haunted by nightmarish visions.*
• apparition, dream, hallucination, phantom, mirage
❸ *He was a science fiction writer of great vision.*
• imagination, inspiration, creativity, inventiveness, foresight

visit *VERB*

❶ *We're planning to visit friends in Toronto.*
• call on, go to see, drop in on, look in on, stay with
❷ *They'll be visiting eight European cities.*
• stay in, stop over in, travel to, tour, explore

visit *NOUN*

❶ *It was our first visit to Disneyland.*
• trip, outing, excursion, tour
❷ *Some friends are coming for a short visit.*
• stay, call, stopover

visitor *NOUN*

❶ *We've got visitors coming this weekend.*
• guest, caller, company
❷ *The city welcomes millions of visitors each year.*
• tourist, holidaymaker, sightseer, traveller

visualize *VERB*

I'm trying to visualize him with a beard.
• imagine, picture, envisage, see, conjure up

vital *ADJECTIVE*

It is vital that we all stay together.
• essential, crucial, imperative, critical, all-important, necessary, indispensable
OPPOSITE unimportant

vitality *NOUN*

She is bursting with vitality and new ideas.
• energy, life, liveliness, spirit, vigour, vivacity, zest, dynamism, exuberance (*informal*) get-up-and-go

vivid *ADJECTIVE*

❶ *He was an artist who loved to use vivid colours.*
• bright, colourful, strong, bold, intense, vibrant, rich, dazzling, brilliant, glowing
OPPOSITES dull, muted
❷ *She wrote a vivid account of her visit to China.*
• lively, clear, powerful, evocative, imaginative, dramatic, lifelike, realistic, graphic
OPPOSITES dull, lifeless

voice *NOUN*

❶ *Her voice broke with emotion.*
• speech, tone, way of speaking
❷ *He promised to listen to the voice of the people.*
• opinion, view, expression
For tips on describing voices see **sound.**

voice *VERB*

Local people voiced their objections to the plan.
• express, communicate, declare, state, articulate

volcano *NOUN*

WORD WEB

- Molten rock that builds up inside a volcano is called **magma**. When the molten rock reaches the surface it is called **lava**. Lava and ash pouring from a volcano is a **volcanic eruption**.
- A volcano that may erupt at any time is an **active** volcano. One that may not erupt for some time is a **dormant** volcano; and a volcano that can no longer erupt is an **extinct** volcano.
- The scientific study of volcanoes is **volcanology** or **vulcanology**.

volume *NOUN*
❶ *The volume of traffic over the bridge has increased.*
• **amount, quantity, bulk, mass**
❷ *How do you find the volume of the test tube?*
• **capacity, size, dimensions**
❸ *The novel was originally published in three volumes.*
• **book, tome, publication**

voluntary *ADJECTIVE*
❶ *Attendance on the course is purely voluntary.*
• **optional, discretionary, by choice**
OPPOSITE compulsory
❷ *She does voluntary work in a charity shop.*
• **unpaid**
OPPOSITE paid

volunteer *VERB*
I volunteered to do the washing-up.
• **offer, come forward, be willing**
OPPOSITE refuse

vomit *VERB*
Symptoms include fever and vomiting.
• **be sick, heave, retch, spew**
(*informal*) **throw up, puke**

vote *VERB*
Who did you vote for in the election?
• **cast your vote**
– To choose someone by voting is to **elect** them.

vote *NOUN*
❶ *The results of the vote will be known tomorrow.*
• **ballot, poll, election, referendum**
❷ *When did women finally get the vote?*
• **right to vote, suffrage, franchise**

voucher *NOUN*
You can exchange this voucher for a free drink.
• **coupon, ticket, token**

vow *NOUN*
They each took a solemn vow of secrecy.
• **pledge, promise, oath, bond, word**

vow *VERB*
He vowed never to reveal her identity.
• **pledge, promise, swear, give your word, take an oath**

voyage *NOUN*
The voyage lasted two weeks.
• **journey, crossing, passage, trip, expedition, cruise**

vulgar *ADJECTIVE*
❶ *The new colour scheme just looks vulgar to me.*
• **tasteless, cheap, tawdry, crass, unrefined**
(*informal*) **tacky**
OPPOSITE tasteful
❷ *The book sometimes uses vulgar language.*
• **indecent, rude, offensive, coarse, crude**
OPPOSITE decent

vulnerable *ADJECTIVE*
The cubs are vulnerable without their mother.
• **unprotected, unguarded, defenceless, exposed, open to attack, at risk, in danger**
OPPOSITES safe, protected
➤ **vulnerable to**
The town was vulnerable to attack from the north.
• **in danger of, at risk from, exposed to, open to, susceptible to**
OPPOSITES safe from, protected from

waddle *VERB*
A pair of geese came waddling towards us.
• **toddle, totter, shuffle, shamble, wobble**

wade *VERB*
❶ *The river is too deep to wade across.*
• **paddle, wallow, splash**
❷ *She has piles of paperwork to wade through.*
• **plough, labour, work, toil**

wag *VERB*
The dog was eagerly wagging its tail.
• **move to and fro, wave, shake, swing, swish, waggle, wiggle**

wage *NOUN*
How much is your weekly wage?
• **earnings, income, pay, pay packet**
– A fixed regular wage, usually for a year's work, is a **salary**.

wage *VERB*
The Greeks waged a long war against Troy.
• **carry on, conduct, pursue, engage in, fight**

wail *VERB*
All night long the wind wailed.
• **howl, moan, cry, bawl, whine**

wait *VERB*
I'll wait here until you get back.
• **stay, stay put, remain, rest, stop, pause, linger**
(*informal*) **hang about, hang around, stick around, hold on**

wait *NOUN*
There is a short wait between trains.
• **interval, interlude, pause, delay, hold-up, lull, gap**

wake or **waken** *VERB*
❶ *She woke from a deep sleep.*
• **awake, awaken, wake up, stir, rise, come to, come round**
❷ *The doorbell woke me at 7.30.*
• **rouse, arouse, awaken, disturb**

walk *VERB*
❶ *Would you rather walk or take the bus?*
• **go on foot, travel on foot**
❷ *I offered to walk her home after the party.*
• **escort, accompany, guide, show, lead, take**

OVERUSED WORD

❶ **To walk slowly, casually:**

➤ amble ➤ saunter ➤ stroll ➤ pace ➤ step ➤ tread

He **sauntered** *down the lane, humming a tune.*

❷ **To walk quietly:**

➤ creep ➤ pad ➤ slink ➤ prowl ➤ stalk ➤ steal ➤ tiptoe ➤ patter

I got up quietly and **padded** *downstairs in my slippers.*

❸ **To walk heavily, loudly:**

➤ stamp ➤ pound ➤ clump ➤ tramp ➤ trudge ➤ traipse ➤ plod ➤ wade

More police officers came **clumping** *through the house.*

❹ **To walk smartly, proudly:**

➤ march ➤ stride ➤ strut ➤ parade ➤ promenade ➤ swagger ➤ trot

She imagined herself **strutting** *down the catwalk in high heels.*

➤➤

❺ To walk unsteadily:

➤ stagger	➤ toddle
➤ stumble	➤ dodder
➤ shuffle	➤ lurch
➤ shamble	➤ limp
➤ totter	➤ waddle
➤ hobble	➤ lope

The creature **shuffled** *off into the night.*

❻ To walk a long distance:

➤ hike	➤ ramble
➤ trek	

They are planning to **trek** *across the Himalayas.*

❼ To walk in a group:

➤ file	➤ march
➤ troop	➤ stream

We all **trooped** *into the dining room for breakfast.*

walk *NOUN*

❶ *We went for a walk in the country.*
• **stroll, ramble, hike, trek, tramp, march, promenade**
❷ *He was a tall man with a shambling walk.*
• **gait, step, stride**
❸ *There is a pleasant tree-lined walk alongside the canal.*
• **path, trail, walkway, footpath, route**

walker *NOUN*

The path is used by walkers and climbers.
• **rambler, hiker**
– Someone who walks along a street is a **pedestrian**.

wall *NOUN*

This is part of an ancient Roman wall.
• **barricade, barrier, fortification, embankment**
– A wall to hold back water is a **dam** or **dyke**.
– A low wall along the edge of a roof is a **parapet**.
– A wall built on top of a mound of earth is a **rampart**.
– A wall or fence made of sticks is a **stockade**.

wallow *VERB*

❶ *Hippos like to wallow in mud.*
• **roll about, flounder, wade, lie, loll**
❷ *He is wallowing in all the attention.*
• **revel, take delight, bask, glory**

wander *VERB*

❶ *A few goats wandered down from the hills.*
• **roam, rove, range, ramble, meander, stroll**
❷ *We must have wandered off the path.*
• **stray, drift**
❸ *Try not to wander too far from the topic.*
• **digress, stray, drift, depart, deviate, get sidetracked**

wane *VERB*

❶ *The afternoon light began to wane.*
• **fade, fail, dim**
OPPOSITE **brighten**
❷ *My enthusiasm was starting to wane.*
• **decline, decrease, lessen, diminish, subside, weaken, dwindle**
OPPOSITE **strengthen**

want *VERB*

❶ *He desperately wants to win a medal.*
• **wish, desire, long, hope**
❷ *She had always wanted a room of her own.*
• **wish for, desire, fancy, crave, long for, yearn for, hanker after, pine for, hunger for, thirst for**
IDIOMS **set your heart on, be dying for**
❸ *Your hair wants cutting.*
• **need, require**

want *NOUN*

❶ *You soon come to understand the wants of your pet.*
• **demand, desire, wish, need, requirement**
❷ *Livestock died from want of food and water.*
• **lack, need, absence**
❸ *Many families are still living in want.*
• **poverty, hardship, need, deprivation, destitution**

war *NOUN*
❶ *The war between the two countries lasted many years.*
• **fighting, warfare, conflict, strife, hostilities**
❷ *This is a victory in the war against drugs.*
• **campaign, struggle, fight, effort**

ward *VERB*
➤ **ward something off**
❶ *Use sunblock to ward off the sun's rays.*
• **avert, block, check, deflect, turn aside, parry**
❷ *Garlic is said to ward off vampires.*
• **fend off, drive away, repel, keep away**

warehouse *NOUN*
The goods were stored in a large warehouse.
• **storeroom, depository, depot, store**

wares *PLURAL NOUN*
They make a living selling their wares to tourists.
• **goods, merchandise, produce, stock, commodities**

warfare *NOUN*
A carved panel depicted scenes of warfare.
• **fighting, combat, war, hostilities, conflict**

warlike *ADJECTIVE*
'The War of the Worlds' portrays Martians as warlike.
• **aggressive, violent, hostile, militant, belligerent**
– Someone who seeks to start a war is a **warmonger**.
OPPOSITES **peaceful, peace-loving**

warm *ADJECTIVE*
❶ *It was a warm summer evening.*
• **mild, balmy, sultry, summery**
– A climate that is neither extremely hot nor extremely cold is **temperate**.
OPPOSITES **cold, chilly**
❷ *Use warm, not boiling, water.*
• **tepid, lukewarm, hand-hot**
❸ *She put on a warm coat and went out.*
• **cosy, snug, thick, chunky, woolly, thermal**
OPPOSITES **thin, light**
❹ *Let's give our guests a warm welcome.*
• **friendly, welcoming, kind, hospitable, cordial, genial, amiable, sympathetic**
OPPOSITES **unfriendly, frosty**

warm *VERB*
Come in and warm yourself by the fire.
• **heat, make warmer, thaw out**
OPPOSITE **chill**

warn *VERB*
I warned you it was dangerous to come here.
• **advise, caution, counsel, alert, make someone aware**
– To warn people of danger is to **raise the alarm**.

warning *NOUN*
❶ *There was no warning of the earthquake.*
• **sign, signal, indication, advance notice** (*informal*) **tip-off**
❷ *Perhaps the dream was a warning.*
• **omen, portent, sign, premonition, foreboding**
❸ *The referee let him off with a warning.*
• **caution, reprimand**

warp *VERB*
Heat may cause the plastic to warp.
• **bend, buckle, twist, curl, bow, distort**
OPPOSITE **straighten**

warrior *NOUN*
He wore the armour of a samurai warrior.
• **fighter, soldier, combatant**

wary *ADJECTIVE*
❶ *She took a wary step towards the creature.*
• **cautious, careful, watchful, attentive, vigilant, on your guard**
OPPOSITE **reckless**
❷ *Foxes are extremely wary of humans.*
• **distrustful, suspicious, chary**
OPPOSITE **trusting**

wash *VERB*

1 *I washed quickly and went downstairs.*
• **bathe, bath, shower**
2 *How often do you wash your hair?*
• **clean, cleanse, shampoo**
– To wash clothes is to **launder** them.
– To wash something in clean water is to **rinse, sluice** or **swill** it.
3 *Wash the floor regularly with warm water.*
• **mop, wipe, scrub, sponge**
4 *Waves washed over the deck.*
• **flow, splash, lap, break, surge, roll**
5 *A huge wave washed him overboard.*
• **carry, sweep**

wash *NOUN*

1 *It's time to give the dog a wash.*
• **clean, bath**
2 *Put any used towels in the wash.*
• **laundry, washing**

waste *VERB*

Let's not waste any more time.
• **squander, misuse, throw away, fritter away**
OPPOSITE save

waste *NOUN*

A lot of household waste can be recycled.
• **rubbish, refuse, litter, junk, garbage, trash**
– Waste food is **leftovers**.
– Waste metal is **scrap**.

wasteful *ADJECTIVE*

We need to be less wasteful with our energy.
• **extravagant, uneconomical, profligate, prodigal, lavish, spendthrift**
OPPOSITES economical, thrifty

watch *VERB*

1 *I could sit and watch the sea for hours.*
• **look at, gaze at, stare at, peer at, view, eye, scan, scrutinize, contemplate**
2 *Watch how the goalkeeper reacts.*
• **observe, note, take notice of, keep your eyes on, pay attention to, attend to, heed**
3 *Could you watch my bag for a minute?*
• **keep an eye on, keep watch over, guard, mind, look after, safeguard, supervise, tend**
4 *I got the feeling we were being watched.*
• **spy on, monitor, track, tail, keep under surveillance**
(*informal*) **keep tabs on**
➤ **watch out**
Watch out! There's a wave coming!
• **be careful, pay attention, beware, take care, take heed**

watch *NOUN*

I was keeping a close watch on the horizon.
• **guard, lookout, eye, vigil**

watchful *ADJECTIVE*

She kept a watchful eye on the door.
• **alert, attentive, observant, vigilant, sharp-eyed, keen**
OPPOSITE inattentive

water *NOUN*

How much of the Earth's surface is covered by water?
– Animals and plants which live in water are **aquatic**.
For areas of water see **landscape**.

water *VERB*

Please remember to water the plants.
• **wet, irrigate, sprinkle, dampen, moisten, soak, drench**
➤ **water something down**
1 *Some paints need to be watered down.*
• **dilute, thin out**
2 *The story has been watered down for the film version.*
• **tone down, soften, tame, temper, moderate**

watery *ADJECTIVE*

1 *She gave me a bowl of watery, tasteless soup.*
• **weak, thin, runny, diluted, watered down**
2 *Chopping onions makes my eyes watery.*
• **tearful, wet, moist, damp**

wave *NOUN*

1 *We could hear the sound of waves breaking on the beach.*
• **breaker, roller, billow**

– A very small wave is a **ripple**.
– A huge wave caused by an earthquake is a **tidal wave** or **tsunami**.
– A number of white waves following each other is **surf**.
– The rise and fall of the sea is the **swell**.
– The top of a wave is the **crest** or **ridge**.
❷ *A wave of anger spread through the crowd.*
• **surge, outbreak, flood, stream, rush, spate**

wave *VERB*
❶ *The tall grass waved in the breeze.*
• **sway, swing, shake, undulate, move to and fro, flap, flutter, ripple**
❷ *He came in waving a newspaper in the air.*
• **shake, brandish, flourish, twirl, wag, waggle, wiggle**
❸ *She waved at us to go over.*
• **beckon, gesture, signal, motion, indicate**

waver *VERB*
❶ *For a second his voice wavered.*
• **quiver, tremble, quaver, flicker, shake**
❷ *Her new-found courage began to waver.*
• **falter, give way, weaken, crumble**
❸ *I wavered about whether to send the email.*
• **hesitate, dither, vacillate, be uncertain, think twice**
(*informal*) **shilly-shally**
IDIOM **hum and haw**

wavy *ADJECTIVE*
The quilt is stitched in a wavy pattern.
• **curly, curling, rippling, winding, zigzag**
OPPOSITE straight

way *NOUN*
❶ *He showed me the best way to make scrambled eggs.*
• **method, procedure, process, system, technique**
❷ *She is behaving in a very odd way.*
• **manner, fashion, style, mode**
❸ *Is this the right way to the castle?*
• **direction, route, road, path**
❹ *We've still got a long way to go.*
• **distance, journey, length, stretch**
❺ *In some ways, it's a good idea.*
• **respect, particular, feature, detail, aspect**
❻ *Things were in a bad way.*
• **state, condition**

weak *ADJECTIVE*
❶ *They were weak from hunger and thirst.*
• **feeble, frail, sickly, infirm, puny, weedy**
OPPOSITES strong, robust
❷ *He proved to be a weak leader.*
• **ineffective, powerless, timid, meek, soft, faint-hearted, spineless, indecisive**
OPPOSITE powerful
❸ *The footbridge was old and weak in places.*
• **fragile, flimsy, rickety, shaky, unsound, unstable**
OPPOSITES sound, sturdy
❹ *The story is spoiled by a weak ending.*
• **poor, feeble, unsatisfactory, inadequate, unconvincing, implausible, lame**
(*informal*) **wishy-washy**
❺ *The phone signal is weak here.*
• **faint, low, dim, muted, faded, diluted, indistinct**
OPPOSITES strong, clear

weaken *VERB*
❶ *Too much water will weaken the flavour.*
• **reduce, lessen, diminish, sap, undermine**
❷ *The storm had weakened overnight.*
• **decrease, decline, fade, dwindle, die down, peter out, wane, ebb**
OPPOSITE strengthen

weakness *NOUN*
❶ *Her illness left her with a feeling of weakness in her limbs.*
• **feebleness, frailty, fragility, infirmity, instability**
❷ *Our players have different strengths and weaknesses.*
• **fault, flaw, defect, imperfection, shortcoming, weak point**
OPPOSITE strength
❸ *I have a weakness for chocolate cake.*
• **liking, fondness, taste, partiality,**

penchant
(*informal*) soft spot

wealth *NOUN*
The family had acquired its wealth from oil.
• **fortune, money, riches, affluence, prosperity**
OPPOSITE poverty
➤ **a wealth of**
The website has a wealth of information on volcanoes.
• **lots of, plenty of, a mine of, an abundance of, a profusion of**
(*informal*) **loads of, tons of**

wealthy *ADJECTIVE*
He comes from a very wealthy family.
• **rich, affluent, prosperous, moneyed, well-off, well-to-do**
(*informal*) **flush, loaded, well-heeled**
OPPOSITES poor, impoverished

weapon *NOUN*

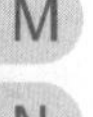
WORD WEB

Some types of weapon:

➤ bayonet	➤ machine gun
➤ blowpipe or blowgun	➤ missile
➤ bomb	➤ mortar
➤ club	➤ pistol
➤ cudgel	➤ revolver
➤ dagger	➤ rifle
➤ flick knife	➤ shell
➤ gun	➤ sword
➤ hand grenade	➤ taser
➤ harpoon	➤ torpedo
➤ machete	➤ truncheon

- Weapons in general are **weaponry** or **arms**.
- A collection or store of weapons is an **armoury** or **arsenal**.

Weapons used in the past:

➤ battering ram	➤ broadsword
➤ battleaxe	➤ cannon
➤ blunderbuss	➤ catapult
➤ bow and arrow	➤ crossbow
➤ cutlass	➤ sabre
➤ javelin	➤ scimitar
➤ lance	➤ spear
➤ longbow	➤ staff
➤ musket	➤ tomahawk
➤ pike	➤ trident

wear *VERB*
❶ *What are you wearing to the party?*
• **dress in, be dressed in, be clothed in, have on, sport**
❷ *She wore a frown all evening.*
• **have on, bear, exhibit, display, put on, assume**
❸ *The rug in the hallway is starting to wear.*
• **become worn, wear away, wear out, fray**
❹ *These boots have worn well.*
• **last, endure, survive**
➤ **wear off**
The effects of the potion are wearing off.
• **fade, lessen, diminish, ease, subside, die down, dwindle**
➤ **wear someone out**
All this talking has worn me out.
• **exhaust, tire out, fatigue, weary, drain**
(*informal*) **do in**

wear *NOUN*
❶ *Everyone was in formal evening wear.*
• **dress, clothes, attire**
(*informal*) **gear, get-up**
❷ *I've had a lot of wear out of this jacket.*
• **use, service**
(*informal*) **mileage**

weary *ADJECTIVE*
We all felt weary after a hard day.
• **tired, worn out, exhausted, fatigued, flagging, drained, spent**
(*informal*) **all in, bushed**
IDIOM **ready to drop**

weather *NOUN*
The weather should be fine tomorrow.
• **conditions, outlook, elements**
– The regular weather conditions of a particular area is the **climate**.
– The study of weather patterns in order to forecast the weather is **meteorology**.

WRITING TIPS

DESCRIBING THE WEATHER

Weather conditions:

- blizzard
- breeze
- cloudburst
- cyclone
- deluge
- downpour
- drizzle
- drought
- fog
- frost
- gale
- hail
- haze
- heatwave
- hurricane
- mist
- monsoon
- rainstorm
- shower
- sleet
- smog
- snowstorm
- squall
- storm
- sunshine
- thunderstorm
- tornado
- torrent
- tsunami
- typhoon

Cloudy:

- dull
- grey
- overcast
- sunless

Cold:

- arctic
- bitter
- chilly
- crisp
- freezing
- frosty
- icy
- (*informal*) nippy
- (*informal*) perishing
- raw
- snowy
- wintry

Hot:

- baking
- close
- humid
- muggy
- roasting
- sizzling
- sticky
- sultry
- sweltering
- torrid

Stormy:

- rough
- squally
- tempestuous
- thundery
- turbulent
- violent
- wild

Sunny:

- balmy
- bright
- cloudless
- dry
- fair
- fine
- mild
- summery
- sunshiny

Wet:

- damp
- drizzly
- lashing
- pouring
- rainy
- showery
- spitting
- teeming
- torrential

Windy:

- blowy
- blustery
- breezy
- gusty

Other:

- adverse
- changeable
- hostile
- inclement
- temperate
- foggy
- misty
- springlike
- autumnal

weather *VERB*

They had weathered many dangers together.

• survive, withstand, endure, come through, pull through

weave *VERB*

❶ *She has woven a thrilling tale.*

• construct, fabricate, put together, create, invent, spin

❷ *A cyclist weaved his way through the traffic.*

• wind, wend, thread, zigzag, dodge, twist and turn

web *NOUN*

A web of tunnels lay under the castle.

• network, labyrinth, complex, lattice, mesh

wedding *NOUN*

She was a bridesmaid at her aunt's wedding.

• marriage, union
(*formal*) nuptials

wedge *VERB*

❶ *The door was wedged open with a shoe.*
• **jam, stick**
❷ *A large man wedged himself into the seat next to me.*
• **force, shove, push, cram, ram, stuff**

weep *VERB*

She began to weep.
• **cry, sob, shed tears**
– To weep noisily is to **bawl** or **blubber**.
– To weep in an annoying way is to **snivel** or **whimper**.

weigh *VERB*

➤ **weigh someone down**
❶ *The streets were full of shoppers weighed down with bags.*
• **load, burden, lumber**
❷ *Many troubles were weighing him down.*
• **bother, worry, trouble, distress, burden, depress**
IDIOM **prey on your mind**
➤ **weigh something up**
She carefully weighed up the evidence.
• **consider, assess, evaluate, examine, study, ponder, mull over**

weight *NOUN*

❶ *We need to measure your height and weight.*
• **heaviness**
For weights and measures see **measure**.
❷ *Take care when lifting heavy weights.*
• **load, mass, burden**
❸ *His name still carries a lot of weight.*
• **influence, authority, power, pull, sway**
(*informal*) **clout**

weighty *ADJECTIVE*

❶ *The shelf was filled with weighty volumes.*
• **heavy, substantial, bulky, cumbersome**
OPPOSITES **light, slim**
❷ *They had weighty matters to discuss.*
• **important, serious, grave, significant**
OPPOSITES **unimportant, trivial**

weird *ADJECTIVE*

❶ *My sister has a weird taste in clothes.*
• **strange, odd, peculiar, bizarre, curious, quirky, eccentric, outlandish, unconventional, unorthodox, idiosyncratic**
(*informal*) **wacky, way-out**
OPPOSITE **conventional**
❷ *Weird noises have been heard in the tower at midnight.*
• **eerie, uncanny, unnatural, unearthly, other-worldly, mysterious, ghostly, surreal**
(*informal*) **spooky, creepy**
OPPOSITE **natural**

welcome *NOUN*

We were not expecting a warm welcome.
• **greeting, reception**

welcome *ADJECTIVE*

❶ *She makes a welcome addition to the cast.*
• **pleasing, agreeable, desirable, acceptable, favourable, gratifying**
OPPOSITE **unwelcome**
❷ *You're welcome to use my laptop.*
• **allowed, permitted, free**
OPPOSITE **forbidden**

welcome *VERB*

❶ *The elderly butler welcomed us at the door.*
• **greet, receive, meet, usher in**
❷ *I welcomed the chance to be alone for a while.*
• **appreciate, be glad of, be grateful for, embrace**

welfare *NOUN*

You are responsible for the welfare of your pet.
• **well-being, health, comfort, security, good, benefit, interests**

well *ADVERB*

❶ *The whole team played well on Saturday.*
• **ably, skilfully, competently, effectively, efficiently, admirably, excellently, marvellously, wonderfully**
OPPOSITE **badly**
❷ *Stir the mixture well and leave to cool.*
• **thoroughly, carefully, rigorously,**

properly, effectively, completely
❸ *Those colours go well together.*
• **agreeably, pleasantly, harmoniously, suitably, fittingly, happily, nicely**
❹ *I used to know her quite well.*
• **closely, intimately, personally**

well *ADJECTIVE*
❶ *She looks surprisingly well for her age.*
• **healthy, fit, strong, sound, robust, vigorous, lively, hearty**
OPPOSITES unwell, poorly
❷ *All was not well in the kitchen.*
• **right, fine, all right, in order, satisfactory, as it should be**
(*informal*) **OK or okay**

well-known *ADJECTIVE*
The new store will be opened by a well-known TV personality.
• **famous, celebrated, prominent, notable, renowned, distinguished, eminent**
OPPOSITES unknown, obscure

went
past tense see **go**

west *NOUN, ADJECTIVE & ADVERB*
Mumbai is in the west of India.
– The parts of a country or continent in the west are the **western** parts.
– To travel towards the west is to travel **westward** or **westwards**.
– A wind from the west is a **westerly** wind.

wet *ADJECTIVE*
❶ *All our clothes were wet and covered with mud.*
• **damp, soaked, soaking, drenched, dripping, sopping, wringing wet**
OPPOSITE dry
❷ *The pitch was too wet to play on.*
• **waterlogged, saturated, sodden, soggy, squelchy, muddy, boggy**
❸ *The paint was still wet.*
• **sticky, tacky, runny**
❹ *It was cold and wet all afternoon.*
• **rainy, showery, drizzly, dank, pouring, teeming**

wet *VERB*
Wet the paper with a damp sponge.
• **dampen, moisten, soak, water, douse**
– To wet something thoroughly is to **saturate** or **drench** it.
OPPOSITE dry

wheel *NOUN*
– A small wheel under a piece of furniture is a **caster**.
– The centre of a wheel is the **hub**.
– The outer edge of a wheel is the **rim**.

wheel *VERB*
❶ *A pair of seagulls wheeled overhead.*
• **circle, orbit**
❷ *Suddenly the whole herd wheeled to the right.*
• **swing round, turn, veer, swerve**

whereabouts *NOUN*
His whereabouts remain unknown.
• **location, position, site, situation**

whiff *NOUN*
I caught a whiff of perfume as she passed.
• **smell, scent, aroma**

while *NOUN*
You may need to wait a while for the next train.
• **time, period, interval, spell, stretch**

whimper *VERB & NOUN*
I heard a little whimper in the dark.
• **cry, moan, whine**

whine *VERB*
❶ *The dogs growled and whined all night long.*
• **cry, whimper, wail, howl**
❷ *What is he whining about now?*
• **complain, protest, grumble, grouse, carp**
(*informal*) **gripe, moan, whinge**

whip *VERB*
❶ *Slaves were whipped for minor offences.*
• **beat, flog, lash, thrash, scourge**
(*old use*) **scourge**
❷ *Whip the eggs in a separate bowl.*
• **whisk, beat**

③ *She whipped a piece of paper out of her pocket.*
• **pull, whisk, pluck, take**

whirl *VERB*
① *Dead leaves whirled in the autumn wind.*
• **turn, twirl, spin, circle, spiral, reel, revolve, rotate, pirouette**
② *Her mind whirled with new questions.*
• **spin, reel, swim**

whisk *VERB*
Whisk the oil and vinegar together.
• **beat, whip, mix, stir**

whisper *VERB*
What are you two whispering about?
• **murmur, mutter, mumble**
OPPOSITE shout

white *ADJECTIVE & NOUN*
① *I took out a sheet of plain white paper.*
• **snow-white, off-white, whitish, ivory, pearl**
– To make something white or pale is to **bleach** it.
– When someone turns white with fear they **blanch** or **turn pale**.
② *Her hair had turned white.*
• **hoary, silvery, snowy, platinum**

whole *ADJECTIVE*
① *Have you read the whole trilogy?*
• **complete, entire, full, total, unabbreviated, unabridged**
OPPOSITE incomplete
② *The skeleton appears to be whole.*
• **in one piece, intact, unbroken, undamaged, perfect**
OPPOSITES broken, in pieces

wholehearted *ADJECTIVE*
I would like to express my wholehearted support.
• **unconditional, unqualified, unreserved, full, complete, total**
OPPOSITE half-hearted

wholesome *ADJECTIVE*
We had a wholesome breakfast of porridge and fruit.
• **healthy, nutritious, nourishing**
OPPOSITE unhealthy

wholly *ADVERB*
I'm not wholly convinced by this story.
• **completely, totally, fully, entirely, utterly, thoroughly, absolutely, one hundred per cent**
OPPOSITE partly

wicked *ADJECTIVE*
① *In the story she meets a wicked witch.*
• **cruel, vicious, villainous, evil, detestable, mean, corrupt, immoral, sinful**
OPPOSITES good, virtuous
② *They hatched a wicked plan to take over the world.*
• **evil, fiendish, diabolical, malicious, malevolent, monstrous, nefarious, vile, base**
③ *He gave me a wicked grin.*
• **mischievous, playful, cheeky, impish, roguish**

wide *ADJECTIVE*
① *The hotel is by a wide stretch of sandy beach.*
• **broad, expansive, extensive, vast, spacious, spread out**
OPPOSITE narrow
② *She has a wide knowledge of classical music.*
• **comprehensive, extensive, vast, wide-ranging, encyclopedic**
OPPOSITE limited

widely *ADVERB*
The story of Robin Hood is widely known.
• **commonly, generally, far and wide**

widen *VERB*
The river widens as it nears the bay.
• **broaden, open out, spread out, expand, extend, enlarge**

widespread *ADJECTIVE*

❶ *Overnight storms have caused widespread flooding.*
• **extensive, wholesale**
OPPOSITE limited
❷ *The campaign has attracted widespread support.*
• **general, common, universal, global, worldwide, ubiquitous, prevalent**
OPPOSITE uncommon

width *NOUN*

What is the width of the left-hand margin?
• **breadth, thickness, span**
– The distance across a circle is its **diameter**.

wield *VERB*

❶ *A woman approached us wielding a clipboard.*
• **brandish, flourish, hold, wave**
❷ *He stills wields influence over his fans.*
• **exert, exercise, command, hold, maintain**

wife *NOUN*

Which goddess was the wife of Zeus?
• **spouse, partner, consort, bride**
IDIOMS **other half, better half**

wild *ADJECTIVE*

❶ *They came across a herd of wild horses.*
• **undomesticated, untamed, feral**
OPPOSITE tame
❷ *The hedgerow was full of wild flowers.*
• **natural, uncultivated**
OPPOSITE cultivated
❸ *To the west is a wild and mountainous region.*
• **rough, rugged, uncultivated, uninhabited, desolate**
OPPOSITE cultivated
❹ *It was a night of wild celebrations.*
• **riotous, rowdy, disorderly, unruly, boisterous, noisy, uncontrollable, hysterical**
OPPOSITES calm, restrained
❺ *The weather looks wild outside.*
• **stormy, windy, blustery, gusty, turbulent, tempestuous**
OPPOSITE calm
❻ *Take a wild guess.*
• **unplanned, random, haphazard, arbitrary**

wilful *ADJECTIVE*

❶ *She was wilful as a child.*
• **obstinate, stubborn, strong-willed, headstrong, pig-headed, uncooperative, recalcitrant**
OPPOSITE amenable
❷ *He was charged with wilful damage to property.*
• **deliberate, intentional, planned, conscious, premeditated**
OPPOSITE accidental

will *NOUN*

❶ *He had a strong will to succeed.*
• **determination, drive, resolve, willpower, tenacity, commitment**
❷ *She was forced to marry against her will.*
• **wish, desire, inclination, preference**

willing *ADJECTIVE*

❶ *Are you willing to help?*
• **ready, prepared, inclined, disposed, happy, glad, pleased**
OPPOSITE unwilling
❷ *I need a couple of willing volunteers.*
• **enthusiastic, helpful, cooperative, obliging**
OPPOSITES reluctant, grudging

wilt *VERB*

❶ *Without water the leaves will start to wilt.*
• **become limp, droop, flop, sag**
❷ *Both players seemed to wilt in the heat.*
• **flag, droop, become listless**
OPPOSITES revive, perk up

wily *ADJECTIVE*

Yet again he was outwitted by his wily opponent.
• **clever, crafty, cunning, shrewd, scheming, artful, sly, devious**

A B C D E F G H I J K L M N O P Q R S T U V W X Y Z

win *VERB*

❶ *Which team do you think will win?*
• **come first, be victorious, succeed, triumph, prevail, come out on top**
OPPOSITE lose

❷ *Last year we won first prize.*
• **get, receive, gain, obtain, achieve, secure**
(*informal*) **pick up, walk away with, land, bag**

win *NOUN*

This was a famous win over their old rivals.
• **victory, triumph, conquest**
OPPOSITE defeat

wind *NOUN*

The whole island was buffeted by strong winds.
– A gentle wind is a **breath, breeze** or **draught**.
– A violent wind is a **cyclone, gale, hurricane** or **tornado**.
– A sudden unexpected wind is a **blast, gust, puff** or **squall**.

wind *VERB*

❶ *A path winds up the hill.*
• **bend, curve, twist and turn, zigzag, weave, meander, snake**

❷ *She wound a bandage round her finger.*
• **wrap, roll, coil, curl, loop, twine**
OPPOSITE unwind

window *NOUN*

– The glass in a window is the **pane**.
– A semicircular window above a door is a **fanlight**.
– A window in a roof is a **skylight**.
– A decorative window with panels of coloured glass is a **stained-glass window**.
– A person whose job is to fit glass in windows is a **glazier**.

windy *ADJECTIVE*

❶ *It was a windy day in autumn.*
• **breezy, blowy, blustery, gusty, wild, squally**
OPPOSITES calm, still

❷ *We stood on a windy hilltop.*
• **windswept, exposed, draughty**
OPPOSITE sheltered

wink *VERB*

❶ *My friend winked at me and smiled.*
– To shut and open both eyes quickly is to **blink**.
– To flutter your eyelashes is to **bat** them.

❷ *The lights winked on and off.*
• **flicker, flash, sparkle, twinkle**

winner *NOUN*

The winner was presented with a silver cup.
• **victor, prizewinner, champion, conqueror**
(*informal*) **champ**
OPPOSITE loser

winning *ADJECTIVE*

❶ *For the second time he was on the winning team.*
• **victorious, triumphant, successful, conquering, top-scoring, champion**
OPPOSITE losing

❷ *She has a winning smile.*
• **engaging, charming, appealing, attractive, endearing, captivating, disarming**

wintry *ADJECTIVE*

I looked out on a wintry landscape.
• **snowy, frosty, icy, freezing, cold**

wipe *VERB*

I wiped the table with a damp cloth.
• **clean, rub, polish, mop, swab, sponge**

➤ **wipe something out**
The dinosaurs were wiped out 65 million years ago.
• **destroy, annihilate, exterminate, kill off, get rid of**

wire *NOUN*

Under the desk was a tangle of computer wires.
• **cable, lead, flex**
– A system of wires is **wiring**.

wisdom *NOUN*

She's a woman of great wisdom.
• **sense, judgement, understanding,**

intelligence, sagacity, common sense, insight, reason

wise *ADJECTIVE*
❶ *The soothsayer was very old and wise.*
• **intelligent, learned, knowledgeable, knowing, perceptive, rational, thoughtful, sensible, sagacious**
❷ *I think you made a wise decision.*
• **good, right, sound, sensible, astute, shrewd**
OPPOSITE foolish

wish *VERB*
You can make as many copies as you wish.
• **want, desire, please, choose, see fit**

wish *NOUN*
She had a lifelong wish to travel into space.
• **desire, want, longing, yearning, hankering, craving, urge, fancy, hope, ambition**
(*informal*) yen

wisp *NOUN*
She blew a wisp of hair away from her face.
• **shred, strand, lock**

wistful *ADJECTIVE*
She gave a wistful sigh as she read the letter.
• **sad, melancholy, thoughtful, pensive, nostalgic**

wit *NOUN*
❶ *No one had the wit to ask for help.*
• **intelligence, cleverness, sharpness, shrewdness, astuteness, brains, sense, judgement**
❷ *The film script sparkles with wit.*
• **humour, comedy, jokes, witticisms**
❸ *Uncle Charlie is a bit of a wit.*
• **joker, comedian, comic**
(*informal*) wag

witch *NOUN*
They say the family was cursed by a witch's spell.
• **sorceress, enchantress**
– A group of witches is a **coven**.

witchcraft *NOUN*
Thousands of women were accused of witchcraft.
• **sorcery, wizardry, enchantment, black magic, necromancy**

withdraw *VERB*
❶ *She withdrew a handkerchief from her pocket.*
• **remove, extract, take out, pull out**
OPPOSITE insert
❷ *They could still withdraw their offer.*
• **take back, cancel, retract**
OPPOSITES make, present
❸ *A number of riders withdrew from the race.*
• **pull out, back out, drop out**
OPPOSITE enter
❹ *The rebels withdrew to the hills.*
• **retreat, draw back, pull back, fall back, retire, adjourn**
OPPOSITE advance
❺ *Troops are being withdrawn from the city.*
• **call back, pull back, recall**
OPPOSITE send in

wither *VERB*
Crops were withering in the fields.
• **shrivel, dry up, shrink, wilt, droop, go limp, sag, flop**
OPPOSITE flourish

withhold *VERB*
He was accused of withholding vital information.
• **keep back, hold back, hold onto, retain, keep secret**
(*informal*) sit on
OPPOSITES release, make available

withstand *VERB*
The bridge is designed to withstand high winds.
• **endure, stand up to, tolerate, bear, cope with, survive, resist, brave, weather**

witness *NOUN*
Police have appealed for witnesses to the accident.
• **observer, onlooker, eyewitness, bystander, spectator, viewer**

witty *ADJECTIVE*
I tried to think of a witty reply.
• **humorous, amusing, comic, funny, entertaining, clever, droll**
OPPOSITE **dull**

wizard *NOUN*
❶ *The whole kingdom was under the wizard's spell.*
• **magician, sorcerer, enchanter, warlock**
❷ *I thought you were a wizard with computers.*
• **expert, genius, ace, master, maestro**
(*informal*) **whizz**

wobble *VERB*
❶ *The front wheel was wobbling all over the place.*
• **waver, sway, rock, totter, teeter, jiggle**
❷ *My voice wobbles when I'm nervous.*
• **shake, tremble, quake, quiver, waver, vibrate**

wobbly *ADJECTIVE*
❶ *The baby giraffe was a bit wobbly on its legs.*
• **shaky, tottering, unsteady**
OPPOSITE **steady**
❷ *My shopping trolley had a wobbly wheel.*
• **loose, rickety, rocky, unstable, unsteady**
(*informal*) **wonky**

woman *NOUN*
This event is for women only.
• **lady, female**
– A woman whose husband has died is a **widow**.
– An old-fashioned word for an unmarried woman is a **spinster**.
– Words used in the past for a young unmarried woman are **maid, maiden** and **damsel**.

won
past tense see **win**

wonder *NOUN*
❶ *We were speechless with wonder.*
• **admiration, awe, amazement, astonishment, reverence**
❷ *It is one of the wonders of modern science.*
• **marvel, miracle, phenomenon, sensation**

wonder *VERB*
I wonder why he left in such a hurry.
• **be curious about, ask yourself, ponder, think about**
➤ **wonder at**
You can only wonder at the skill of the craftsmen.
• **marvel at, admire, be amazed at, be astonished by**

wonderful *ADJECTIVE*
❶ *It's wonderful what smartphones can do now.*
• **amazing, astonishing, astounding, incredible, remarkable, extraordinary, marvellous, miraculous, phenomenal**
❷ *We had a wonderful evening.*
• **excellent, splendid, great, superb, delightful**
(*informal*) **brilliant, fantastic, terrific, fabulous, super**

wood *NOUN*
❶ *The little cabin was made from wood.*
• **timber, logs, planks**
❷ *We followed a nature trail through the wood.*
• **woodland, forest, trees, grove, copse, thicket**

wooden *ADJECTIVE*
❶ *We sat down on a wooden bench.*
• **wood, timber**
❷ *The acting was a bit wooden at times.*
• **stiff, stilted, unnatural, awkward, lifeless, unemotional, expressionless**
OPPOSITE **expressive**

woolly *ADJECTIVE*
❶ *He wore a woolly hat with ear flaps.*
• **wool, woollen**
– Clothes made of wool, such as hats and scarves, are **woollens**.
❷ *Seal pups are born with a woolly coat.*
• **thick, fleecy, shaggy, fuzzy, hairy**
❸ *This is not just a woolly idea.*
• **vague, confused, unclear, unfocused, hazy**

word *NOUN*
❶ *What's another word for 'chuckle'?*
• **expression, term**
– The words used in a particular subject or language are its **vocabulary**.
❷ *I'll have a word with her about it.*
• **talk, conversation, discussion, chat**
❸ *Do you have any words of advice?*
• **remark, comment, statement, observation**
❹ *You gave me your word.*
• **promise, assurance, guarantee, pledge, vow**
❺ *There has been no word since they left.*
• **news, message, information, report, communication**

word *VERB*
Be careful how you word the email.
• **express, phrase, put into words**

wording *NOUN*
I found the wording confusing at first.
• **phrasing, choice of words, expression, language, terminology**

wore
past tense see **wear**

work *NOUN*
❶ *It is hard work pedalling uphill.*
• **effort, labour, toil, exertion, slog** (*informal*) **graft, grind**
❷ *I've got a lot of work to do this weekend.*
• **tasks, assignments, duties, chores, jobs, homework, housework**
❸ *What kind of work does she do?*
• **occupation, job, employment, profession, business, trade, vocation**
For types of work see **occupation**.
❹ *Do you have a copy of the complete works of Shakespeare?*
• **writing, composition, piece, text**

work *VERB*
❶ *You've been working at the computer all day.*
• **labour, toil, exert yourself, slave, slog** (*informal*) **beaver away**
❷ *I used to work in a florist's on Saturdays.*
• **be employed, have a job, go to work**
❸ *My watch has stopped working.*
• **function, go, run, operate**
❹ *This camera is very easy to work.*
• **operate, use, control, handle, run**
➤ **work out**
❶ *He works out several times a week.*
• **exercise, train**
❷ *Things didn't quite work out as planned.*
• **turn out, happen, emerge, develop**
➤ **work something out**
See if you can work out the formula.
• **figure out, puzzle out, calculate, determine, solve, decipher, unravel**

worker *NOUN*
The factory employs around 200 workers.
• **employee**
– All the workers in a business are the **staff** or **workforce**.

world *NOUN*
❶ *Antarctica is a remote part of the world.*
• **earth, globe, planet**
❷ *He felt that the world was against him.*
• **everyone, humankind, mankind, humanity**
❸ *Scientists are searching for life on other worlds.*
• **planet**
❹ *She knows a lot about the world of sport.*
• **sphere, realm, domain, field, arena, society, circle**

worldwide *ADJECTIVE*
The award brought him worldwide celebrity.
• **global, international, universal**
OPPOSITE local

worried *ADJECTIVE*
She seemed worried about something.
• **anxious, troubled, apprehensive, uneasy, disturbed, concerned, bothered, tense, nervous, fretful, agitated, upset**
OPPOSITES unconcerned, carefree

worry *VERB*

❶ *Please tell me what's worrying you.*
• **trouble, bother, distress, concern, upset, unsettle, disturb, make you anxious**
IDIOM **prey on your mind**
❷ *There's no need to worry.*
• **be anxious, be troubled, be concerned, brood, fret, agonize, lose sleep (over)**

worry *NOUN*

❶ *She has a permanent look of worry on her face.*
• **anxiety, distress, uneasiness, apprehension, vexation, disquiet, agitation**
❷ *Money has always been a worry for them.*
• **trouble, concern, burden, care, problem, trial**
(*informal*) **headache, hassle**

worsen *VERB*

❶ *Anxiety can worsen an asthma attack.*
• **make worse, aggravate, intensify, exacerbate, add to**
OPPOSITES alleviate, relieve
❷ *Her condition worsened overnight.*
• **get worse, deteriorate, degenerate, decline**
IDIOM **go downhill**
OPPOSITES improve, get better

worship *VERB*

❶ *The Greeks worshipped many gods and goddesses.*
• **pray to, glorify, praise, venerate, pay homage to**
SEE ALSO **religion**
❷ *He used to worship his older brother.*
• **adore, be devoted to, look up to, love, revere, idolize, esteem**

worth *NOUN*

❶ *He had to sell the painting for a fraction of its true worth.*
• **value, price, cost**
❷ *How much worth do you place on friendship?*
• **importance, significance, value, merit**

worthless *ADJECTIVE*

It's nothing but a worthless piece of junk.
• **useless, unusable, valueless, of no value**
OPPOSITES valuable, useful

worthwhile *ADJECTIVE*

❶ *It may be worthwhile to get a second opinion.*
• **useful, valuable, beneficial, advantageous, rewarding, profitable, fruitful**
OPPOSITE pointless
❷ *They are raising money for a worthwhile cause.*
• **good, deserving, admirable, commendable, respectable, worthy**

worthy *ADJECTIVE*

The money we raise is going to a worthy cause.
• **good, deserving, praiseworthy, admirable, commendable, respectable**
OPPOSITE unworthy

wound *NOUN*

❶ *He is being treated in hospital for a head wound.*
• **injury, cut, gash, graze, scratch, laceration**
❷ *It was a serious wound to her pride.*
• **insult, blow, affront, slight, offence, injury, hurt**

wound *VERB*

❶ *Four people were wounded in the blast.*
• **injure, hurt, harm**
❷ *At first, he was wounded by her words.*
• **hurt, insult, affront, slight, offend, pain, grieve**

wrap *VERB*

❶ *I wrapped the presents in shiny gold paper.*
• **cover, pack, package, enclose, encase**
❷ *We wrapped ourselves in warm blankets.*
• **enfold, swathe, bundle**
– To wrap water pipes is to **insulate** or **lag** them.

❸ *Her death is still wrapped in mystery.*
• **cloak, envelop, shroud, surround**

wreathe *VERB*
❶ *The tree was wreathed in fairy lights.*
• **festoon, garland, drape, deck, ornament, adorn, decorate**
❷ *Mount Fuji is often wreathed in clouds.*
• **encircle, envelop, swathe, shroud, surround**

wreck *VERB*
❶ *His bike was wrecked in the crash.*
• **demolish, destroy, crush, smash, shatter, crumple**
(*informal*) **write off**
❷ *This could wreck my chances of seeing her again.*
• **ruin, spoil, put a stop to, shatter, dash, scotch**
(*informal*) **scupper, put paid to**

wreck *NOUN*
Divers discovered the wreck of an old Spanish galleon.
• **remains, ruins, wreckage**

wreckage *NOUN*
Wreckage from the aircraft was scattered for miles.
• **debris, fragments, pieces, remains**

wrench *VERB*
The wind wrenched the door off its hinges.
• **pull, tug, prise, jerk, twist, force**
(*informal*) **yank**

wrench *NOUN*
❶ *With a wrench he tore himself free.*
• **jerk, jolt, pull, tug, twist**
(*informal*) **yank**
❷ *It was a wrench leaving their old home.*
• **pain, pang, trauma**

wrestle *VERB*
❶ *They wrestled the suspect to the ground.*
• **grapple, tussle, fight, battle**
❷ *He'd been wrestling with the problem for weeks.*
• **struggle, grapple, agonize (over)**

wretched *ADJECTIVE*
❶ *She was left feeling wretched and alone.*
• **miserable, unhappy, desolate, depressed, dejected, downcast, forlorn, woeful**
❷ *They were forced to live in wretched conditions.*
• **squalid, sordid, pitiful, bleak, harsh, grim, miserable**
❸ *This wretched computer has frozen again!*
• **annoying, maddening, exasperating, useless**

wriggle *VERB*
She managed to wriggle through a gap in the fence.
• **squirm, writhe, wiggle, twist, worm your way**
➤ **wriggle out of something**
He tried to wriggle out of doing his fair share.
• **avoid, shirk, escape, dodge, duck**

wring *VERB*
❶ *She wrung the water out of her hair.*
• **press, squeeze, twist**
❷ *The actor paced up and down wringing his hands.*
• **clasp, grip, wrench, twist, squeeze**
➤ **wringing wet**
These towels are wringing wet.
• **soaked, drenched, soaking, dripping, sopping, saturated**

wrinkle *NOUN*
Her tiny hands were laced with wrinkles.
• **crease, fold, crinkle, pucker, furrow, line, groove, ridge**
– Wrinkles at the corners of a person's eyes are **crow's feet**.

wrinkle *VERB*
He wrinkled his nose in disgust.
• **pucker, crease, crinkle, gather, crumple, furrow, rumple, scrunch up**
OPPOSITE smooth

write *VERB*
❶ *He wrote the answer on a piece of paper.*
• **jot down, note, print, scrawl, scribble**

a b c d e f g h i j k l m n o p q r s t u v w x y z

– To write words or letters on a hard surface is to **inscribe** it.
– To write your signature on something is to **autograph** it.
❷ *She wrote a diary of her experiences.*
• **compile, compose, set down, draw up, pen**
– To write a rough version of a story is to **draft** it.
– To write something hurriedly is to **dash it off**.
❸ *I've been meaning to write to you.*
• **correspond (with)**
IDIOM (*informal*) **drop someone a line**

writer *NOUN*

WORD WEB

People who write:

➤ author
➤ biographer
➤ blogger
➤ composer
➤ correspondent
➤ dramatist or playwright
➤ journalist or reporter
➤ novelist
➤ poet
➤ scribe
➤ scriptwriter or screenwriter
➤ speech-writer

writhe *VERB*
The snake writhed and tried to escape.
• **thrash about, twist, squirm, wriggle**

writing *NOUN*
❶ *The writing is very difficult to read.*
• **handwriting, script, lettering, print**
– Writing that is engraved or carved is an **inscription**.
– Untidy writing is a **scrawl** or **scribble**.
– The art of beautiful handwriting is **calligraphy**.
❷ *I am reading an anthology of crime writing.*
• **literature, works, stories, publications, books**

wrong *ADJECTIVE*
❶ *These calculations are all wrong.*
• **incorrect, mistaken, inaccurate, erroneous**
(*informal*) **out**
OPPOSITES right, correct
❷ *Do you think it would be wrong to keep the money?*
• **bad, dishonest, irresponsible, immoral, unfair, unjust, corrupt, criminal, wicked, sinful**
OPPOSITE right
❸ *I must have said something wrong.*
• **inappropriate, unsuitable, improper, unwise, ill-advised, ill-considered**
OPPOSITES right, appropriate
❹ *There's something wrong with the TV.*
• **faulty, defective, amiss, awry, not right, out of order**
➤ **go wrong**
Everything started to go horribly wrong.
• **fail, backfire**
(*informal*) **flop, go pear-shaped**
OPPOSITES go right, succeed

wrong *ADVERB*
Have I spelled your name wrong?
• **incorrectly, inaccurately, mistakenly, erroneously**
OPPOSITES correctly, properly

wrong *NOUN*
❶ *I'm sure you know the difference between right and wrong.*
• **dishonesty, immorality, injustice, corruption, evil, wickedness, villainy**
❷ *It is important to admit the wrongs of the past.*
• **misdeed, injustice, offence, injury, crime, sin, transgression**

wrongly *ADVERB*
He was wrongly accused of stealing.
• **falsely, mistakenly, erroneously, incorrectly, inaccurately, in error**
OPPOSITES correctly, accurately

wrote
past tense see **write**

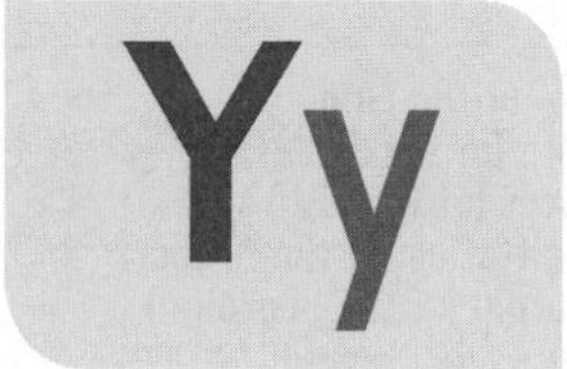

yank *(informal)* *VERB & NOUN*
Don't yank on the horse's reins.
• **tug, jerk, pull, wrench**

yard *NOUN*
A pony stood in the middle of the yard.
• **court, courtyard, enclosure**

yearly *ADJECTIVE*
The village holds a yearly festival in mid-July.
• **annual**

yearn *VERB*
➤ **yearn for something**
I yearned for some peace and quiet.
• **long for, crave, wish for, desire, hunger for, pine for, hanker after**
(informal) **be dying for**

yell *VERB*
He yelled at them to stop.
• **shout, call out, cry out, bawl, bellow, roar, howl**

yell *NOUN*
She let out a loud yell of surprise.
• **shout, cry, bawl, bellow, roar, howl**

yellow *ADJECTIVE & NOUN*

WORD WEB

Some shades of yellow:

➤ amber	➤ lemon
➤ buttery	➤ mustard
➤ cream	➤ straw
➤ gold	➤ tawny
➤ golden	➤ yellow ochre

- Yellow hair is **blonde** or **fair** hair.

For tips on describing colours see **colour**.

yelp *VERB & NOUN*
One of the guards let out a yelp of pain.
• **cry, howl, yowl**

yield *VERB*
❶ *The King stubbornly refused to yield.*
• **give in, give way, back down, surrender, admit defeat, concede, capitulate, submit**
(informal) **cave in**
❷ *These trees yield plenty of apples every year.*
• **bear, produce, grow, supply, generate**

yield *NOUN*
We had a poor yield of potatoes this year.
• **crop, harvest, produce, return**

young *ADJECTIVE*
❶ *The play is aimed at a young audience.*
• **youthful, juvenile**
OPPOSITES older, mature
❷ *This game is a bit young for teenagers.*
• **childish, babyish, immature, infantile**
OPPOSITES adult, grown-up

young *PLURAL NOUN*
All mammals feed their young on milk.
• **offspring, children, young ones, family, progeny**
– A group of young birds that hatch together is a **brood**.
– A group of young animals that are born together is a **litter**.

youth *NOUN*
❶ *She spent much of her youth abroad.*
• **childhood, boyhood or girlhood, adolescence, teens**
❷ *The fight was started by a group of youths.*
• **adolescent, youngster, juvenile, teenager, young adult**
❸ *My grandad says he does not understand the youth of today.*
• **young people, the younger generation**

youthful *ADJECTIVE*
She still has a youthful look about her.
• **young, youngish, vigorous, sprightly, young-looking**

Zz

zeal *NOUN*
She plays the leading role with zeal.
• **energy, vigour, enthusiasm, spirit, passion, verve, gusto**

zero *NOUN*
Four minus four makes zero.
• **nought, nothing**
– A score of zero in football is **nil**. In cricket it is a **duck** and in tennis it is **love**.

zest *NOUN*
After his recovery he had a renewed zest for life.
• **enthusiasm, eagerness, vitality, energy, vigour, passion**

zigzag *VERB*
The road zigzags along the coast.
• **wind, twist, weave, meander, snake**

zodiac *NOUN*

WORD WEB

Signs of the zodiac:

- Aquarius (or the Water-carrier)
- Aries (or the Ram)
- Cancer (or the Crab)
- Capricorn (or the Goat)
- Gemini (or the Twins)
- Leo (or the Lion)
- Libra (or the Scales)
- Pisces (or the Fish)
- Sagittarius (or the Archer)
- Scorpio (or the Scorpion)
- Taurus (or the Bull)
- Virgo (or the Virgin)

- An astrological forecast based on signs of the zodiac is a **horoscope**.
- Another word for a sign of the zodiac is a **star sign**.
- The study of the signs of the zodiac is **astrology**.

zone *NOUN*
The whole state was declared a disaster zone.
• **area, district, region, sector, locality, territory, vicinity, neighbourhood**

zoo *NOUN*
The zoo is enlarging its gorilla enclosure.
• **zoological gardens, wildlife reserve, safari park**
– A small zoo is a **menagerie**.

zoom *VERB*
❶ *A motorbike zoomed past us on the right.*
• **speed, race, tear, dash, streak, whizz, rush, hurtle, fly**
❷ *The camera zoomed in on a member of the audience.*
• **focus, close**
– A photograph taken at close range is a **close-up**.

Young Writer's Toolkit

Get started

Punctuation

Punctuation marks are used to make meaning clear. Even a slight change in punctuation can change the meaning of a sentence. Punctuation can also help you to create different effects in your writing.

full stop 

A **full stop** comes at the end of a sentence. The first word in a sentence starts with a capital letter.

Short sentences can make writing seem dramatic and add pace and longer sentences are often descriptive. Be careful not to use too many short simple sentences. It can make your writing seem childish.

- ➤ *The door slammed shut. We were trapped.*
- ➤ *The house looked as though it hadn't been lived in for years, with its peeling paint and broken windows.*

question mark 

A **question mark** is used at the end of a sentence to show that it is a question. If you are writing dialogue, remember the question mark goes inside the inverted commas.

- ➤ *Where are you?*
- ➤ *'Do you like football?' she asked.*

exclamation mark 

An **exclamation mark** is used to show that a sentence is about something urgent or surprising or to show a strong emotion such as delight or anger.

An exclamation mark can also show that a sentence is a **command** or **instruction.**

Even in informal writing, only one **exclamation mark** is needed.

- *What a lovely present!*
- *I can't believe you just said that!*
- *Run!*

comma 

A **comma** is used to separate items in a list:

- *Javed wanted to visit Spain, Italy, Greece and Portugal.*

A **comma** is often used before a **coordinating conjunction** such as ***or, and*** or ***but*** in a **multi-clause** sentence. It introduces a pause and helps clarify meaning.

- *We're just waiting for Cheri, and then we'll set off.*

Commas are used after a **subordinate clause** or **adverb** or **adverbial** at the start of a sentence:

- *When he realized how much money I had spent, my dad went mad!*
- *Suddenly, I saw how much trouble I was in.*

Commas make a difference to the meaning of a sentence.

In the examples below, the sentence with the commas means that all zombies attack people and all will be prosecuted. The sentence without commas means that only some zombies always attack people and only those will be prosecuted.

- *Zombies who always attack people will be prosecuted.*
- *Zombies, who always attack people, will be prosecuted.*

colon :

A **colon** can be used to introduce a list. A **colon** also introduces examples or explanations.

➤ *They came in four colours: red, blue, yellow and green.*
➤ *Athletes need to eat a lot of high-protein snacks: eggs and fish are popular choices.*

semicolon

A **semicolon** joins two sentences or main clauses which are of equal importance.

➤ *The film was brilliant; we had a great time.*

apostrophe

An **apostrophe** is used to show that letters are missing in words. These are called **contractions**. When writing formally, such as in exams, or for essays and letters, do not use contractions. However dialogue which shows the words that people say often uses contractions.

➤ *I can't = I cannot*
➤ *I don't = I do not*

An **apostrophe** also shows that something belongs to someone. If you are unsure of where to put the apostrophe, try to reword your sentence so that an apostrophe is not needed.

➤ *the murderer's fingerprints*
➤ *the children's shoes*
➤ *Where is Charles's coat?*

dash

A **dash** is often used in informal writing to show that sentences are linked or to introduce items in a list.

➤ *Jogging takes it out of you – especially if you aren't used to it.*
➤ *There are three of us – me, Sarah and Ali.*

brackets, commas or dashes

These can all be used to separate words or phrases that have been added as an explanation or afterthought.

➤ *I looked up (squinting because of the sun) and saw the birds flying.*
➤ *I looked up, squinting because of the sun, and saw the birds flying.*
➤ *I looked up – squinting because of the sun – and saw the birds flying.*

ellipsis

An **ellipsis** is three dots which show that a word has been missed out or that a sentence is not finished. It can add a feeling of suspense.

➤ *Suddenly, the door opened . . .*

An ellipsis can be used to show that words have been missed out of a long quote. This is useful in essays as it can save you a time.

➤ *From the lines, 'I picked him up . . . with just a toothbrush and the good earth for a bed' we learn that the hitchhiker is a drifter.*

hyphen

A **hyphen** joins words together and is important for making meaning clear.

They are useful if you create new words of your own.

➤ *my great-aunt*
➤ *a yellow-spotted, jelly-eating dinosaur*

inverted commas

When writing the exact words that someone has said, use **inverted commas** around the words. Be careful to always put the punctuation of the words that are spoken *inside* the inverted commas.

➤ *'Can I talk to you now, please?' she whispered.*

Sentences

A **sentence** may be a **single-clause** or a **multi-clause** sentence. You can often change a piece of writing by making a few changes to the structure of your sentences.

- Try to **vary the length** and type of sentences that you use. If you use too many of the same length and type, the reader can lose interest.
- Sometimes, **reordering** your sentence can give extra meaning and emphasis to a particular word or phrase.
  - ➤ *The noises began on the stroke of midnight.*
  - ➤ *On the stroke of midnight, the noises began.*
- Be careful not to join **two main clauses** with a **comma**. This creates a run-on sentence. You can fix it by making them into two sentences with a full stop and capital letter.
  - ➤ *Humans could not breathe on Mars, the atmosphere is too thin.*
  - ➤ *Humans could not breathe on Mars. The atmosphere is too thin.*

Paragraphs

A **paragraph** covers a single topic or idea. If you find you are starting a new point in your argument, or are moving on to a new scene in your story, it is time to start a new paragraph.

- In non-fiction writing, it helps to have a topic sentence which sums up the point of the paragraph.
- **Conjunctions** and **adverbs** can link ideas and paragraphs in your writing.
- You can use them to:

✔ sum up (***therefore***)

✔ add information (***in addition, also***)

✔ present points in order (***first, next, later, lastly***)

Formal language

Formal language is the language used in most of the writing you do at school.

- ✔ notes, letters or emails to a teacher
- ✔ exams
- ✔ official letters and emails
- ✔ essays or reports

When writing **formally**:

- ✔ write in complete sentences
- ✔ avoid contractions like ***don't*** and ***I'm*** (use ***do not*** and ***I am***)
- ✔ avoid informal words and phrases, such as ***thanks*** (use ***thank you*** instead)
- ✔ in a letter or email, begin with ***Dear*** and end with ***Yours sincerely***
- ✔ call the person you are writing to by their family name or title (if you do not know their name, call them ***Sir*** or ***Madam***).

Informal language

Informal language is the language we use in everyday situations.

- ✔ letters, emails and messages to family and friends
- ✔ notes
- ✔ shopping lists and to-do lists

Informal language in writing is likely to include:

- ✔ some words in capital letters for emphasis
- ✔ lots of exclamation marks for emphasis
- ✔ abbreviations such as **LOL**
- ✔ contractions such as ***didn't*** or ***wasn't***.

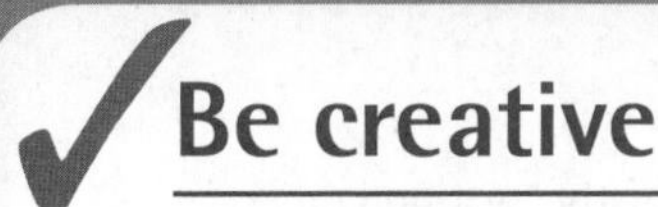

Be creative

Try using descriptive words

Have a look at the **WRITING TIPS** panels in this thesaurus. There are lots of ways to describe things in your writing and these will give you some inspiration.

For example, look up the word **light** to find words for describing light. Does the light ***glare***, or ***flicker*** or ***glow***? Is it ***muted***, ***luminous*** or ***bright***?

WRITING TIPS

DESCRIBING LIGHT
Effects of light:

- beam
- blaze
- burn
- dazzle
- flame
- flare
- flash
- flicker
- glare
- gleam
- glimmer
- glint
- glisten
- glitter
- glow
- lustre
- radiance
- ray
- reflection
- shaft
- shimmer
- shine
- sparkle
- twinkle
- wink

Adjectives:

- bright
- brilliant
- dappled
- diffused
- dim
- harsh

Avoid overused words

Words like ***bad***, ***big*** and ***nice*** are very useful but they become very boring and repetetive when used too often.

Using more specific words helps bring your writing to life in the mind of your reader.

You can look up the **OVERUSED WORD** panels in this thesaurus to help you. For example, look up the word **big**. Something might be ***mammoth*** or ***whopping***, a room might be ***roomy*** and a decision might be ***important*** or ***weighty*** or ***momentous***.

OVERUSED WORD

1 Big in size, scale:

- large
- huge
- great
- massive
- immense
- enormous
- gigantic
- giant
- colossal
- mammoth
- monstrous
- monumental
- titanic

(*informal*) **whopping, mega**

(*literary*) **gargantuan**

Our class made a **giant** *model of a human ear.*

OPPOSITES small, little, tiny

2 Big in area, distance:

- vast
- immense
- expansive
- considerable
- sweeping

Some day spaceships will be able to travel **vast** *distances.*

Try using accurate words

Using **accurate words** can make your writing factual and realistic. There are **WORD WEB** panels in this thesaurus which give you topic words and these will help you to be more precise.

For example, at **aircraft** you will find different types of aircraft such as ***biplane***, ***helicopter***, ***glider***, ***seaplane*** or ***spy plane***. You will also find names for the parts of an aircraft such as ***fuselage***, ***flight deck*** or ***rudder***.

WORD WEB

Some types of aircraft:

- aeroplane (*North American* airplane)
- airliner
- air ambulance
- airship
- biplane
- bomber
- delta wing
- fighter
- glider
- hang-glider
- helicopter
- hot-air balloon
- jet
- jumbo jet
- microlight
- monoplane
- seaplane
- spy plane
- (*historical*) Zeppelin

Parts of an aircraft:

- cabin
- cargo hold
- cockpit
- engine
- fin
- flap
- flight deck
- fuselage
- joystick
- passenger cabin
- propeller
- rotor
- rudder
- tail
- tailplane
- undercarriage
- wing

Use phrases and idioms

An **idiom** is a phrase that does not mean exactly the same as the words in it. For example, *to be in hot water* is an idiom which means to be in trouble (not to be in actual hot water).

Idioms can make your writing more lively and humorous, especially if you are writing in an informal style or if you are writing what characters say. But be careful not to use too many or the same ones repeatedly.

Look for the IDIOMS sign in this thesaurus!

blow your own trumpet	lose your rag
send you to sleep	think twice
prey on your mind	keep a lid on
dead to the world	give a hand to
over the moon	sweep under the carpet
full of beans	

Use metaphors and similes

Using metaphors and similes is a good way of putting pictures into your readers' imaginations and helping them to 'see' your characters and descriptions clearly.

A **metaphor** is where you describe something as if it *were* something.

➤ *The lawn was a carpet of daisies.*

A **simile** is where you describe something as being 'as' or 'like' something else. For example, someone might have *a face like a squashed pumpkin* or *skin as rough as the bark of a gum tree.*

similes using 'as'	
as blind as a bat	as graceful as a swan
as bright as day	as hard as nails
as clear as a bell	as light as a feather
as cunning as a fox	as nutty as a fruitcake
as deep as the ocean	as pretty as a picture
as dry as a bone	as quiet as a mouse
as fit as a fiddle	as strong as an ox
as good as gold	

similes using 'like'	
built like a tank	memory like an elephant's
chatter like a monkey	move like a snail
eat like a pig	run like a deer
eyes like a hawk	sing like a bird
fits like a glove	stand out like a sore thumb
fight like cat and dog	swim like a fish

Create new words

You can add to the words in your thesaurus by creating new words. Try building a new word starting with a word that you know, or one that you have found in this thesaurus, and adding one of these **suffixes** (endings) to it:

-ish	redd**ish**, tall**ish**, hairy**ish**
-less or *–free*	a tree**less** landscape, a chocolate-**free** zone
-like	crab**like** arms
-proof	a zombie-**proof** room

You can add different beginnings (**prefixes**) to a word to create a new one:

eco-	**eco-**friendly house
over-	**over-**plumaged bird
extra-	the **extra-**funny story prize
super-	**super**hero, **super**size

You can also build **compounds** by joining two words together.

-feeling	seasick-**feeling** face
-looking	wrinkly-**looking** skin
-smelling	liquorice-**smelling** plants
-smeared	blueberry-**smeared** cheeks
-faced	lizard-**faced** creature
-haired	purple-**haired** girl

Check your Writing

British and North American spelling

There are differences in the way that certain words are spelled in British and North American spelling.

The main differences are:

British English	North American English	example
-ence	*-ense*	defense
-ou-	*-o-*	mold
-our	*-or*	color
-s- or -z-	*-z-*	analyze, cozy

In British English, most verbs that end in *-ize* or *-ise* can be spelled either way e.g. ***recognize*** or ***recognise***. The ending *-ize* has been used in British English since the 16th century. It is also the spelling used in North America. It is a mistake to think that an *-ize* spelling is American.

There are some words that must always be spelled *-ise*.

words that are always spelled *-ise*		
advertise	devise	incise
comprise	enterprise	revise
compromise	exercise	supervise
despise	improvise	surprise

Here are some common words which have a different spelling in British and North American English.

British English	North American English
analyse	analyze
armour	armor
behaviour	behavior
catalogue	catalog
centre	center